THE UNKNOWN ORWELL

&

ORWELL:
THE TRANSFORMATION

THE UNKNOWN ORWELL

Peter Stansky and William Abrahams

ORWELL:
THE TRANSFORMATION

Stanford University Press
Stanford, California

Stanford University Press
Stanford, California

© 1972, 1979, 1994 Peter Stansky and William Abrahams
Orwell: The Transformation first published in the U.S.A. in 1979 by
　Afred A. Knopf, Inc.
　The Unknown Orwell first published in 1972 by Alfred A. Knopf, Inc.
Reprinted in 1994 in a combined edition by Stanford University Press
Printed in the United States of America
ISBN 0-8047-2342-7
LC 94-65009
This book is printed on acid-free paper.

The complete text, notes, and index of *The Unknown Orwell* is followed by the complete text, notes, and index of *Orwell: The Transformation*.

Stanford University Press publications are distributed exclusively by Stanford University Press within the United States, Canada, and Mexico; they are distributed exclusively by Cambridge University Press throughout the rest of the world.

BOOK ONE

THE UNKNOWN ORWELL

To Stan, Marina, and Fay
and also to Edward

> "The future work ferments in its future author."
>
> —*Paul Valéry*

CONTENTS

Foreword xv
Prologue xix

PART ONE From Bengal to St. Cyprian's 1
PART TWO Eton 81
PART THREE Burma 145
PART FOUR Becoming a Writer 213
PART FIVE Becoming Orwell 291

Notes 311
Index *follows page* 316

ILLUSTRATIONS

FOLLOWING PAGE 170

Mrs. Ida Mabel Blair with Eric, about 1903 *(courtesy of Avril Dunn)*

Roselawn, Shiplake, where the Blairs lived from 1912 to 1915 *(Peter Melleni, 1970)*

Eton, afternoon bathing at "Athens" *(courtesy of Denys King-Farlow)*

Eton, Field Day, Spring 1921 *(courtesy of Cyril Connolly)*

Eton, school photograph, 1921 *(Hills and Saunders)*

The Police Training School at Mandalay, Burma *(courtesy of Roger Beadon)*

FOREWORD

WE CANNOT EXAGGERATE OUR INDEBTEDNESS TO AVRIL Dunn, Eric Blair's sister, and to certain friends and acquaintances of his who knew him in the years before he became George Orwell. Much of what we have written is based upon their memories of him, and we are deeply grateful to them for their willingness to share their memories with us. Our book would not be what it is without their extraordinary generosity and cooperation—the extent of which will be evident in the pages that follow—and we trust that we have not misrepresented them. Of course, we take full responsibility for errors of fact and questions of interpretation.

When we began to work in the summer of 1962, our plan was to write a study of a number of young English writers of the 1930's, among them George Orwell, who had fought on the side of the Republic in the Spanish Civil War. But that first plan, as so often happens, proved unwieldy and uncongenial. We chose to limit ourselves to Julian Bell and John Cornford; our book about them, *Journey to the Frontier*, was published in 1966. The year before we had already returned to Orwell, intending to study his life and work in the 1930's, from the publication of *Down and Out in Paris and London* through his experience in the Spanish Civil War and his subsequent account of it in *Homage to Catalonia*.

As the reader will discover, that book is not the one we have written.

Where Orwell is concerned, the by now traditional formula that the man and his work are inseparable seems to us beyond dispute, yet it leads toward a succession of simplifications and reductions. The work is magnificently there; the man is elusive, simultaneously out of sight and in full view. We found it difficult to begin at the point where we intended to begin. Eric Blair was thirty years old when he published *Down and Out in Paris and London* and became George Orwell. Were the thirty years of Blair before Orwell to be dismissed as of no consequence? The question was raised and an answer provided by Sir Richard Rees, a friend of Orwell's since 1930 and an ambulance driver with Julian Bell in Spain, whose kindnesses to us extended back to the early stages of *Journey to the Frontier*.

In May 1967 we went to Rees's small house in Burnsall Street to talk about Orwell, as we had done many times before. At some point in that afternoon he remarked, in a characteristically offhand way, "But, of course, if you want to understand Orwell, you have to understand Blair"—his way of pronouncing the name was remarkable and can't be reproduced; he seemed to lengthen it by at least a syllable—"and to understand Blair—well, there's your book."

There, certainly, was a book, and we have attempted to make it ours: a study of Eric Blair becoming the writer George Orwell; and we have ended it where we had originally thought to begin, with the publication of *Down and Out in Paris and London*.

Richard Rees died in July 1970. We never had the opportunity to show him any portion of our manuscript, as we had done with *Journey to the Frontier*. We can only hope that he would not have been displeased with this book, which a casual remark of his helped to engender.

To Sir Richard Rees, then, and to Mrs. Avril Blair Dunn—

unceasing gratitude; and what a great pleasure it is to be able finally to acknowledge how much we owe to them—and to Cyril Connolly, the late Mrs. Vaughan Wilkes, Miss Ruth Pitter, Denys King-Farlow, Sir Steven Runciman, Roger Beadon, and Mrs. Mabel Fierz.

Also, A. L'e. Brownlow, R. M. Cazalet, Francis Cruso, the late Humphrey Dakin, A. Dunbar, James Gibson, A. S. F. Gow, Christopher Hollis, John Lehmann, W. C. A. Milligan, Sir Roger Mynors, the Hon. Michael Norton, C. B. Orr, Professor Richard Peters, R. Gordon B. Prescott, Lord Rathcreedan, Miss Brenda Salkeld, E. F. Seeley, George Wansbrough, Sir Maurice Whittome.

Our indebtedness does not end here with those who knew Blair before he became Orwell. There are many who knew him after 1933, whether as Blair or as Orwell, who were kind enough to talk about him with us, and whom we hope to have the pleasure of thanking in a later volume.

We are deeply grateful to Graham Bennett, Mrs. Valerie Eliot, Lord Harlech, Dr. Hamida Khuhro, Alec Livingston, Jeffrey Meyers, and the Master in College, Librarian, Captain of the School, and Keeper of the Wall, Eton College (1967).

The late John D. Gordan, a valued friend, was extremely generous in making the resources of the Berg Collection of the New York Public Library available to us.

We have had the benefit of editorial advice and encouragement from Benjamin Glazebrook, the Hon. John Jolliffe, and Andrew Mylett in London, and from Robert Gottlieb in New York.

Peter Stansky would also like to express his deep appreciation to the John Simon Guggenheim Memorial Foundation for granting him a Fellowship to work on this study.

PROLOGUE

THE MAKING OF A WRITER IS A COMPLEX PROCESS: AND who is to say with any assurance where it begins—with his first book, or his first day at school, the day of his birth, or generations back, lost in a tangle of genealogy? History of this kind is difficult to uncover and describe, for beginnings, apprenticeship, and the first stirrings of a talent that has yet to declare itself even to itself are not infrequently cast aside and forgotten, like a cocoon that has served its purpose, or else are lost sight of in the fame of what was afterwards achieved. Certainly this would seem to be the case with Eric Blair, who, in 1933, in his thirtieth year, upon the publication of his first book, *Down and Out in Paris and London*, became George Orwell.

At first Blair found in Orwell a nom de plume; then, later, virtually a second self, a means of realizing his potentialities as an artist and moralist to become one of the major English authors of this century. Orwell he became; but he was Blair before Orwell, and there was always in Orwell the residue of Eric Blair. He never changed his name legally. To those who knew him in his early years he remained "Eric" or "Blair"—Eric to women and members of his family. Friends of his later years called him "George" or "Orwell," and he often signed letters as George Orwell. The creation of George Orwell was an act of will by Eric Blair, and it was carried on at almost every level of his existence, affecting not only his prose style but also the style of his daily life. Becoming George Orwell was his way of making himself into a writer, at which he brilliantly succeeded, and of unmaking himself as a gentleman, of opting out of the genteel lower-upper-middle class into which he was born, at which he had only an equivocal success. But the significant result of the creation was that it allowed Eric Blair to come to terms with his world. Blair was the man to whom things happened; Orwell the man who wrote about them.

Much of his life before thirty was an attempt to escape from the system into which he had been born, and which inexorably provided him with an education, an accent, and a standard of judgment that might be turned against him. The system, he felt, had almost crushed him in his prep school days, and toward the end of his life he left a grim version of them in "Such, Such Were the Joys." Cyril Connolly, who was at school with him at St. Cyprian's, thought him a "true rebel" there, but in his own mind Blair was sure he was damned, and doomed to failure. Such, he felt, was the judgment of St. Cyprian's and by inference of the system. Even after he went to Eton, and from there to the Indian Imperial Police in Burma, he continued to believe that it was an unalterable judgment, and that your place in the world did not depend on your own efforts but on "what you were." This mood continued to afflict him until his return from Burma in 1927. It was only then, breaking with the system, that he began seriously to write—and so ultimately to disprove the judgment against himself in the breadth of his achievement; yet his novels early and late alike, down to *Animal Farm* and *1984*, accept the omnipotence of the system while his heroes are its victims.

As George Orwell, Blair made himself a happier man than he had ever dreamed of being, and a writer of extraordinary power. It was here that he was best served by his creation. Much as Orwell in conversation would pick and choose what he would reveal of himself—even to close friends, whom he tended to keep carefully separate, giving each his own quite different share of the truth—so Blair, through Orwell, could select, control, and put to use the elements of his rejected past.

Ironically, many of the qualities that contribute to the Orwell personality and style as we are familiar with them in his work are precisely the qualities Blair had thought despicable in his schooldays. Eric Blair saw himself as a smelly, impoverished member of the lower-upper-middle class who because of his being bright enough for a scholarship and coming from a suitable Anglo-Indian background had received an inappropriate gentleman's education. But George Orwell was an idiosyncratic Socialist, who, no matter how shabbily he dressed or austerely he lived, would never lose an air of authority—in his life as in his prose—that is sometimes thought to mark a Public School "Old Boy." Orwell could transform the values of the upper middle class that Blair resented, and infuse them with the egalitarianism he had witnessed among the miners in Wigan and experienced at first hand as a soldier among soldiers in Spain. Eric Blair looked back unforgivingly on the world before 1914—it was that world that had sent him to his prep school—while George Orwell could believe it was superior to what came after it, and looked back to it nostalgically in *Coming Up for Air*. And if Eric Blair came to disdain the platitudes and hypocrisies at a boys' school in England of the First World War, George Orwell was moved to a simple, intense patriotism during the Second World War when England was endangered.

There were moments when Blair and Orwell were at one: in the comradeship of the Spanish Civil War, and in the inspiriting early years of the blitz when it was possible to believe in a brave new England to come. They were moments of honor and decency, in which Blair and Orwell could participate and feel at ease. But such moments could not last: they would be undone by the Stalinists, as in Spain, or by the thought police, as in *1984*. Then the struggle would be resumed, between the patriot and the radical, the idealist and the skeptic, the sahib and the victim. Out of the tension came the many books that Orwell was to write between 1933 and his death in 1950.

In the churchyard in the village of Sutton Courtenay, where Orwell is buried, his grave is marked by a plain gray-brown stone on which has been inscribed

HERE LIES
ERIC ARTHUR BLAIR
BORN JUNE 25TH 1903
DIED JANUARY 21ST 1950

The inscription was specified by Orwell himself in the first part of the final sentence of his last will. The will was drawn up on January 18, 1950, three days before his death, in University College Hospital, London, where he had been a patient since the preceding September. Having chosen his epitaph, he went on to conclude the sentence with a request that no memorial service be held for him and no biography of him be written; and then he signed his name, Eric Blair. It was as though the creator were determined once and for all to separate himself from his creation—as though the two were not inextricably bound together. So long as Orwell exists, Blair exists too. Orwell he became. But he had been Blair first.

PART ONE

FROM BENGAL TO ST. CYPRIAN'S

ONE

THE COMPLEXITIES OF THE ENGLISH CLASS STRUCTURE are not to be unraveled in a single paragraph. It is nothing so simple as the conventional three categories: upper, middle, and lower; and one is only slightly nearer a resolution when the minimum number of categories is enlarged to five: aristocracy, upper, middle, lower, and working class. For it is in the middle classes where socially the nuances lie, and a gulf is fixed between upper middle and lower middle class. The most finicking discriminations are constantly being made. To what class does a bricklayer making five pounds a week belong? To what class does a clerk in a bookshop making three pounds a week, whose father is a clergyman, belong, as opposed to a clerk in a bookshop making three pounds a week, whose father is a bricklayer? Or in the latter case, suppose that it is not his father but his grandfather who has been the bricklayer and his father the clergyman; what then? Or to complicate it another way, think of a clerk in a bookshop whose grandfather was a clergyman but whose father is a bricklayer—a perfectly honest, respectable trade, after all—what class is he?

The question of class in all its ramifications and permutations has fascinated, irritated, reassured, and divided generations of Englishmen, and has provided English novelists, from Jane Austen to the present, with a seemingly inexhaustible subject. It is difficult to think of a single English novelist, even an overt fantasist like Lewis Carroll, who has not been affected by the question, or has failed to take it into account, directly or by implication, in his work. "Who is he?" tends to accompany "What is he?" and sometimes to precede it, and the consequences in life as in art are comic or tragic, or in the great gray wastes between.

Perhaps the luckiest are those at either end of the spectrum, the aristocrat and the working man. They are recognized and accepted without equivocation for what they are, not least by themselves, and so Who he is and What he is are of no concern to them. But for those in the middle of the spectrum, especially those on the lower edge, shading off downward from one class to another, the borderland of impoverished gentility, these questions are of the gravest import: the answers to them can decide or despoil a life. Orwell knew this at first hand, and as a young writer he was fascinated as well as embittered by the class question: it figures obsessively in much of what he wrote before 1936, in the novels *A Clergyman's Daughter* and *Keep the Aspidistra Flying,* and in the autobiographical portions of *The Road to Wigan Pier.* It is only in 1937 with *Homage to Catalonia,* his account of his experience in the Spanish Civil War, that he gets beyond it to what would be his principal concern thereafter—human freedom. (And yet at the end of his life he was still settling scores with the class discriminations of St. Cyprian's, from which he felt he had cruelly suffered.)

To what class, in fact, does a young writer belong whose books, articles, and reviews don't bring in even the austere minimum of money sufficient for survival; who therefore takes a series of lowly jobs, among them clerking in a bookshop; whose father is a retired colonial civil servant of the middle rank (and a younger son); whose grandfather was a clergyman, vicar of a country parish (and a younger son); and whose great-great-grandfather was a man of property married to the daughter of an Earl? The young writer, of course, was Eric Blair in the 1930's, when he was already writing as George Orwell, and Orwell's answer to the question of his class was a sardonic, finely shaded "lower-upper-middle." Toward the end of his life, when his spirit was no longer so exacerbated by questions of class and money, he wrote in the preface to the Ukrainian edition of *Animal Farm* that he came from an ordinary middle-class family of soldiers, clergymen, government officials, teachers, lawyers, doctors—in other words, the professional classes, a central group in English society in which money has always counted less than position and for whom it was more important to be of "some service" to the state than to make a fortune, although there was no objection to money should it appear in the process.

Family background and family history play a part in the making of any writer, however rigorously he himself may suppress overt references to them. In Orwell such references are not frequent, but one has a sense of continuity, of parallels and foreshadowings reaching back into an earlier age, of family styles and attitudes that presage the kind of writer he was to become. Or to put it another way, if Eric Blair as George Orwell is the most considerable of the Blairs, the culmination of a line, it is neither startling nor incongruous that it should be so. A glance at the history of the family will confirm this.

Charles Blair, his great-great-grandfather, who was born in 1743 and died in 1802, was a man of considerable wealth, the owner (we learn from his will) of "Estates, Plantations, Messuages, Lands, Tenements and Hereditaments . . . in the Island of Jamaica," as well as "Negro, Mulatto and other Slaves." It would appear that his fortune was increased when he married Lady Mary Fane, the second daughter of Thomas, eighth Earl of Westmorland, for there is a record of an exchange of deeds between his father-in-law and himself in 1765 in Jamaica. (Blairs, probably of the same family, had been prominent in Jamaica since the early eighteenth century; they might also have been associated with the abortive Scottish Darien scheme in Panama of 1698.)

Lady Mary, two years older than her husband, introduces an aristocratic aspect to the background, quite faded out by the time of the fifth, Eric Blair's, generation, yet there are strains in the history of the Westmorland family that are not without interest for the amalgam that made up both Eric Blair and George Orwell. Since the time the title was created in the Fane line in 1624, the Earls of Westmorland have served the state at the level expected of the aristocracy. Theirs too is a family in which there has been something more than the expected aristocratic patronage of the arts. There have been Fane poets, a Fane playwright, and a Fane composer. The second Earl was joint lord-lieutenant of Northamptonshire in 1660; he left poems in manuscript; his cousin and contemporary was Sir Francis Fane, the dramatist. The seventh Earl served under Marlborough, was installed as Chancellor of Oxford in 1759, and engaged the architect Colin Campbell to build him a country seat. The result was Mereworth Castle in Kent, one of the great Palladian villas in England, a copy of the Villa Rotonda at Vicenza, and only a few miles distant from the hop fields where Eric Blair was to work for a time as a hop picker in the 1930's—an irony that would be even more pointed if his kinsmen had still been in possession of the house. The tenth Earl, the cousin and godfather of Thomas Richard Arthur Blair, Orwell's grandfather, was a friend of Pitt's, a lord-lieutenant of Ireland, and Lord Privy Seal; he also helped replenish the family fortune by running away to Gretna Green with the heiress of Robert Child, the great banker and owner of Osterly Park. The eleventh Earl served in the Peninsular campaigns, had an active diplomatic career, and was also a composer. One of his sons, Julian Fane, was a diplomatist, translator, and poet. The twelfth Earl had a career in the military, and served in India. (So too, on a lower level, did Richard Walmesley Blair, Orwell's father.) But by then the connection, not to speak of communication, between the aristocratic Fanes and their distant relations, the worthy Blairs, was faint indeed.

To return to the generation when the connection was established: Charles Blair's properties were in Jamaica, but he was an absentee owner, in the style perhaps of Sir Thomas Bertram of *Mansfield Park,* and he and Lady Mary spent most of their married life at Winterbourne Whitechurch in Dorset. In 1793 they moved to nearby Blandford St. Mary, where they leased Down House. In the parish church of Winterbourne Whitechurch, whose chief claim to fame is that John Wesley, the grandfather of the great John Wesley, was its vicar from 1658 until he was ejected for his opinions in 1662, there is a plaque on the north aisle wall on which the vicissitudes of the family are recorded. Four of the children died young: Maria in infancy; Thomas at thirteen; Mary of consumption at sixteen; and Henry Charles Blair, at nineteen, in 1794, in the service of His Majesty at St. Domingo, as a Captain in the Twenty-third Regiment of Foot. (The family's affluence is evident in Henry's military career in the days of purchase: he entered the service at the age of fifteen or sixteen as a second lieutenant, was a lieutenant the next year, and a captain in 1793.)

Charles Blair's will, drawn up in 1801, the year before he died, is preserved in Somerset House. It is a document that might well inspire a novel—others like it already have, in abundance—dealing with matters of entail, primogeniture, and the plight of the younger son. The property was tied up in a trust for two hundred years, to be administered by two relatives of his wife (and their descendants), Francis Fane and Charles Michel from Lyndhurst near Southampton. The latter was a member of the Michel family of Dewlish, a village very near Winterbourne Whitechurch, and he was related to the Blairs through Lady Mary. The two trustees were to administer the estate in the interest of Charles Blair, junior, the oldest surviving son, who was assured an annual income of eight hundred pounds or more, at their discretion. Lady Mary was to receive three hundred pounds per year, the household goods, and "all her paraphernalia Jewels and Ornaments to and for her own proper use and benefit." There was a twenty-five-pound annual income for a faithful servant, and some provision was made for the wife and children of Charles Blair, junior, should he predecease his father. But he did not. The same year in which Charles Blair, senior, died—1802—Mrs. Charles Blair, junior, gave birth to Orwell's grandfather, Thomas Richard Arthur Blair. From this epoch of affluence very little appears to have remained in Orwell's family save for a portrait of Lady Mary Blair now in the possession of his sister Avril Dunn.

A step down was taken by Thomas Richard Arthur Blair. With apparently not many material advantages to speak of—revenues were in a general state of decline from Jamaica in the early nineteenth century—he was expected to fend for himself, choosing a career from among the handful of possibilities open to the younger son of a good family: Church, Army, the Colonies. True, he had the spiritual or social advantage of being the godson and cousin of the Earl of Westmorland. But the difference between his own and his cousin's situation was unmistakable, a gap that would have been closed only if he had married exceptionally well, which he did not. As it was, after a year at Pembroke College, Cambridge, where he enjoyed the distinguished rank for a student of a Fellow-Commoner, he went out to serve God and country in the Empire.

He was ordained Deacon in the Church of England by the Bishop of Calcutta in 1839, and Priest by the Bishop of Tasmania in 1843; in 1854 he returned permanently to England to become Vicar of Milborne St. Andrew in Dorset. Several years earlier, coming home from India on a visit, he had stopped at Cape Town, where he met and became engaged to a Miss Emily Hare, and then continued on his journey. On the return voyage, he stopped again at the Cape, intending to be married and bring his bride back with him to India, only to discover that she had married someone else in the interim. With great insouciance, he decided that since Emily was already married, he would marry the next Hare sister, Frances ("Fanny"), who was only fifteen at the time, and he promptly did. The marriage was a happy and fruitful one: there were ten children, the last two born after the return from the colonies.

Milborne St. Andrew as a parish has been in existence since 1067. The Pleydells were the great family at Milborne itself, with their hatchments adorning the church, but the parish is connected with the neighboring village of Dewlish, which has its own small church. The same vicar has ministered to both churches since at least the fourteenth century, and it was the family of Dewlish, the Michels, who had the gift of the living—an extremely good living of approximately a thousand pounds annual income. As we have seen, the Michels were connections of the Blairs through marriage. It was Lady Mary's niece's son, Sir John Michel—he too had had the experience of the colonies, having served as a Major General in India and Canada—who gave the living to his cousin in 1854.

In 1935, when Orwell's uncertainties and dissatisfactions were at their most acute, he wrote in a poem first published in the *Adelphi* and afterwards incorporated in his essay "Why I Write" that he would have been a happy vicar born two hundred years ago. One feels that the life of his grandfather, vicar of a quiet country parish remote from the tensions and disaffections of mid-Victorian industrial England, would also have fulfilled this ideal. (Of course it was an impossible ideal, as Orwell knew: that was the point of the poem, that we are living in "an evil time"—the phrase and the insight seem to have been in common use among poets of the 1930's, from Auden and Louis MacNiece down—and can't escape from it into a wish-dream of the past.) The Reverend Thomas Blair was not a diary-keeping clergyman like the Reverend Francis Kilvert, but the texture of daily life in Milborne St. Andrew finds its counterpart in the pages of Kilvert's *Diary*. There were the natural joys and sorrows, the pleasures of living in unspoiled countryside, visits back and forth between Dewlish House and the Vicarage. A son, Dawson, was born in 1855. Another son (Orwell's father), Richard Walmesley Blair, was born on January 7, 1857, and was baptized by his father in the church a month later. A daughter, Augusta Michel, died in 1862 at the age of twelve, and was buried in the Dewlish churchyard. So the round of days and years continued—in a sense it is recorded in the church register: births, marriages, and deaths. The last baptism Thomas Blair performed in his church was on July 28, 1867. A month later he died, at the age of sixty-five, having been Vicar of Milborne St. Andrew for thirteen years, and leaving a large family who thereafter must fend for themselves.

The second step down toward Orwell's "lower-upper-middle" was taken by Richard Walmesley Blair. Given his circumstances, this was inevitable. He was a child of late middle age; he was a younger son; like his father, he would go out to India to begin his career and unlike him, he would remain there. But he was starting out with even fewer material advantages than his father had had; and as for the social advantages of being well born and well connected, which in the end had proved of considerable value to his father, he was a further generation on—the great-grandson of the daughter of an Earl—and this rather tended to thin such advantages out: in fact, they were never to function on his behalf. But there he was, indisputably a younger son of good family, and so the traditional careers appropriate to such a young man had to be considered, and it was decided that he should go into colonial service. He hadn't money or education enough to go grandly. On August 4, 1875, at the age of eighteen, he joined the Opium Department of the government of India in the rank of Assistant Sub-Deputy Opium Agent, fifth grade.

The opium trade with China had been legalized after 1860, and was carried on under the supervision of the Opium Department. Blair, as a junior officer in the department, was posted to a variety of stations around India during his years of service—to Muzaffarpur; Gorakhpur; Sarsa, Allahabad; Salem; Rai Bareilly; Fuzabad; Shahjahanpur; Etah; Patna; Tehta; Motihari; and Monghyr. From the eleventh of August 1879 to the eleventh of January 1880, he was on deputation as Famine Relief Officer at Bellary. At the time of his retirement from the service in 1912, his rank was Sub-Deputy Opium Agent, first grade.

Blair married comparatively late—in 1896, at the age of thirty-nine—when he was stationed at Tehta in Bihar. His wife, several years younger than he, was Miss Ida Mabel Limouzin. The daughter of a French father and an English mother, she was born in Penge, Surrey, but from an early age had lived in Moulmein, Burma, where the Limouzins had conducted business enterprises almost from the time that port city had been ceded to the British in 1826. With the marriage two contrasting traditions were joined: the Blairs', English, genteel, dedicated to the idea of serving the state, and the Limouzins', French, bourgeois, dedicated to the idea of serving the family.

The Limouzins were people to reckon with in Moulmein: a street in the city is named after them. They were shipbuilders and teak merchants; and one member of the family ran a distillery. The founder of the business was G. E. Limouzin, who died in 1863. His son, Frank Limouzin, Orwell's maternal grandfather, was born in Limoges, but grew up in Burma, and in the natural course of events took over the business at his father's death. He appears to have been something of an inventor as well as a man of business, for he described himself in the *Maulmain Calendar,* a local periodical, as the "patentee of a life-boat, which is likely to prove invaluable to all commanders of vessels in case of mishap." He married twice. His first wife, by whom he had one child, died in 1865; his second wife, by whom he had nine children, one of them Ida, was an Englishwoman of impressive character. Over the years she became a power in the town, although toward the end of her life—she died in 1925, ten years after her husband—she was thought (by the British colony) to have gone "somewhat native"—that is, she chose to wear native dress (though she never learned the language), which gave rise to the rumor among acquaintances of Eric Blair's in the Imperial Police that he was himself part Burmese.

The first child of the marriage was a daughter, Marjorie, born in 1898 while they were stationed at Tehta. On February 5, 1903, Blair was transferred to a new post, at Motihari in Bengal, and it was there, on June 25, 1903, that the second child, a son, was born. His name was Eric Arthur Blair.

TWO

WE HAVE SAID THAT RICHARD WALMESLEY BLAIR (hereafter in these pages he will be simply Mr. Blair, and Ida Limouzin will be Mrs. Blair) took the second step down toward the fourth generation's "lower-upper-middle," but this would not become apparent until after his retirement from the Opium Department in 1912, when he was fifty-five, and had returned to England to live. Anglo-Indian life in the late Victorian and Edwardian period—when the Blairs were in India—has been described in countless memoirs, some fatuous, some estimable, but almost all forgotten, and set for all time by a writer of genius, Kipling, whose work is familiar to most English-speaking readers, and was greatly admired by Orwell himself. The vivid, exotic details are to be found there. It is enough here to note that while military pay and salaries in the civil service were not large, they were sufficient in the officer ranks and their equivalents to allow for marriage and the raising of a family, to provide for many-roomed bungalows and luxuriant gardens staffed by native servants—the inevitable ayahs, amahs, cooks, boys, bearers, chokahs (to pull the punkahs), gardeners, and their attendant relatives—and for a social life centered on the Club. It was a life based on ethnic and national distinctions—to be white and English; rather less, on class. However tenuous one's middle-class affiliation in England might be, however cockneyfied one's accent and gross one's manners, when in India, bearing the white man's burden and serving, building, enlarging, and defending the Empire, one was privileged, belonged to a privileged class and the Club. (It is all there in Kipling; and since much of the life he described was traditional and resistant to change through at least the first three decades of the century, it would also be in the work of later writers, in E. M. Forster's *A Passage to India* and Orwell's first novel, *Burmese Days*.)

Anglo-Indian privilege extended from the time of enlistment to the time of retirement. It didn't travel well: sahibdom dwindled away on the P. & O. steamer taking one back to England. There, forced more often than not to subsist on a small, barely adequate pension, one occupied an equivocal and difficult position, especially so when measured against the assurance and privilege of life in India. This was to be the experience of the Blairs.

Eric, their second child, was born in June in 1903 when they were stationed in Motihari, in Bengal. Nine months later, Mr. Blair, then a Sub-Deputy Opium Agent, fourth grade, was appointed to a new station, and the family moved on to Monghyr. On December 30, 1906, he was raised to second grade, and on May 21, 1907, after thirty-two years of service, to first grade. At the end of July 1907, he was granted a leave of three months and seven days, his first since 1902, and he took his family back to England, to an unpretentious small house, aptly named "Nutshell," in the Western Road in Henley-on-Thames. In November he returned to Monghyr; Mrs. Blair—by then expecting their third child, Avril—remained in Henley with Marjorie and Eric. Mr. Blair would not rejoin them until his retirement four years later.

The paragraph above contains all the ascertainable facts about Eric's first four years. Perhaps we should add one further fact, a family recollection of Mrs. Blair having recorded in her diary (either in India, or on board ship, or after their arrival in England) that Baby (Eric) called things "beastly." But because so little is known definitely of this period of his life, it does not follow that it is of no importance. Mrs. Blair's diary has disappeared; there is no reason to believe that her husband ever kept one; Eric Blair when he was becoming Orwell, and later as Orwell, wrote a considerable amount about Burma, based upon his experiences there as a young man, but about his earliest childhood in India he wrote nothing. Consciously he appears to have forgotten it all: his declared memories go back no farther than his fourth or fifth year, to a day when he dictated a poem about a tiger to his mother, by which time, of course, they were living in Henley, and the tiger, he felt, came from Blake, not Monghyr. Unconsciously though, the memory of that hot, sub-tropical, foreign country where he was born, with its spicy smells and pungent flavors, its flamboyant sights and exotic sounds, may well have survived within him: it might well account for the intensity of his response to Burma, about which he wrote in a highly charged, highly colored, sensuous prose that no other subject seemed to elicit from him. Years later, when he was firmly Orwell, he came to distrust such prose and shrugged it off as merely "purple." Yet, as Richard Rees has pointed out, "The descriptive writing in *Burmese Days* is the most elaborate and probably the best he ever did. Neither his evocation of Spain in *Homage to Catalonia* nor his many attempts to express his feeling for Southern England are so vivid and striking as his descriptions of the climate, landscape, trees, flowers, and smells of Upper Burma."

In any event, there was a dramatic change, a dramatic contrast in his life in 1907—it was then, very likely, that the sense of resentment and injustice had their beginnings, that he began to call things "beastly." In India the family had consisted of father, mother, older sister Marjorie, and himself the baby. In England, father was absent—Eric would not see him again until he was eight—and the family now consisted of mother, older sister Marjorie, himself, and the new baby, Avril. In India too there had been a houseful of servants, to free Mrs. Blair from time-consuming, worrying domestic responsibilities, and to cosset and beguile a small boy: for him the bungalow and its surrounding garden would have been a full, satisfying world. In England things were very different. There was a daily char to help in "Nutshell," but Mrs. Blair was busy with the new baby, and Marjorie, a nine-year-old schoolgirl, was away at school a good part of the day or playing with her friends. Eric, a shy child in a new and unfamiliar world, where one wore bulky clothes, clinging woolen stockings, and heavy shoes to protect one against rain and damp, the world of head colds and running noses and sore throats and wheezing chests, had difficulty in making friends and felt increasingly lonely. He adored his mother, but he was too shy ever to confide in her what he felt, and therefore felt himself neglected and misunderstood. Such feelings of loneliness, isolation, and resentment are classic symptoms in a literary history, and it is not surprising that Eric, by the time he was five or six, should have known that he would become a writer, that classic way of avenging oneself for an unhappy childhood.

He was shy and reticent as a child, and would continue to be so as an adult, even in his closest friendships. In this respect he resembled his middle-aged father. Neither Mr. nor Mrs. Blair was warmly demonstrative, or, rather, both had that reserve which some might say is natural to the English and which was not uncommon among those who spent much of their time in the East and had to keep up face in front of the "natives." But Mrs. Blair had her French side, along with her English decorum. She was lively, friendly, and sociable, very much a woman of her time and background, fond of playing golf and breeding poodles, who fitted in well in colonial society, and in the various places in

England where the Blairs were to live after their return from India. There is no question that life was more difficult financially, and grew progressively so, when they were living in England, but she was never obsessively worried about money: she had the knack—very French, some might say—of making the most of what there was. If she could not afford the more expensive sorts of food, then the inexpensive would have to do, but she served them with a dash and imagination not usual in the circumstances. Ruth Pitter, the poet, who was to be a neighbor of the Blairs after they moved from Henley to London, recalls Mrs. Blair, a handsome woman with her black hair in a bang and wearing long agate drop earrings, bringing to the dinner table cabbage *"en casserole,"* deliciously seasoned, very different from cabbage *"à l'anglaise,"* boiled and boiled to the point of tastelessness. She had a flair for managing things: she managed very competently while alone with the children at Henley, and afterwards, when Mr. Blair had returned. She is the more commanding figure of the two: by contrast he appears a bit pallid and at a loss, the inevitable fate, perhaps, of the retired Anglo-Indian civil servant. In her competent fashion she was devoted to her children, watched over them and cared for them, and was prepared to make considerable sacrifices for them. But Eric as a small boy craved for more than this, or else for something quite different, and he nourished a grievance.

This grievance and the unhappiness it gave rise to constitute a significant part, but by no means the whole, of his childhood, though it was the part Orwell chose to emphasize when writing directly about Eric Blair. Granting that most writers are likely to have had unhappy childhoods—to make a sweeping, unprovable, Orwellian sort of generalization—these things are relative: Blair was never to know anything even remotely like the cruelty and neglect that were the lot as children of two other Anglo-Indian writers transplanted early from India to England—Kipling and H. H. Munro ("Saki"). In fact, there was another, equally significant part of his childhood, and it was expressed by Orwell in the nostalgia he would always feel for the world as it was before 1914. This was the world he came to know as a boy in Henley-on-Thames, that most Edwardian of riverside towns, the scene of the great annual regatta, where the river wound its way through the tranquil surrounding countryside, and where life, viewed in retrospect, was an unending summer. Anger and nostalgia, the two emotions that animate so much of what Orwell was to write, had their beginnings here.

At five he was ready for school, and Mrs. Blair enrolled him at a day school nearby, Sunnylands, run by Anglican nuns, where Marjorie was already a pupil. It was an exciting and enjoyable experience for him. (Characteristically, therefore, he never wrote about it, much as he never went into detail about his time at Eton, which also he enjoyed. The compulsion to correct an injustice, to repair a grievance, was absent: the experience hadn't rankled enough.) He was a bright, intelligent, eager small boy who learned without difficulty whatever he was taught, a fact which Mrs. Blair took pride in (as any mother would) and which was at the center of the plans for his future she now began to make. Learning to read was the exhilarating discovery of these years. Inspired by the example of Marjorie, who was a great reader and passed on to him books she had outgrown or grown tired of, he began to read avidly, with the passionate indiscriminateness of a child for whom reading—books, magazines, newspapers, advertisements, *anything*—becomes an essential part of his existence. By the time he was eight, he had read, to single out only a few representative titles, *Tom Sawyer, Coral Island, Rebecca of Sunnybrook Farm* (no doubt a legacy from Marjorie), and *Gulliver's Travels*. His attachment over the years to his childhood reading and to authors whom he first read as a child was very strong. In the 1930's he raised the possibility of writing a biography of Mark Twain; the details of R. M. Ballantyne's *Coral Island* remained so clear in his mind that, writing of the book thirty years later, he could recall the telescope, six yards of whipcord, penknife, brass ring, and piece of hoop iron its three boy castaways had had to depend upon to survive on their desert island. He read *Gulliver's Travels* at least seven times at different stages in his life, the first time the night before his eighth birthday. It had been bought for him by his mother as a birthday present, but on the night before, Eric discovered the parcel, secretly opened it, and began to read at once. Thus began a literary attachment Orwell would celebrate in 1946 in one of his great essays, "Politics vs. Literature"; and two years before, *Gulliver's Travels* had provided a model or example for him when writing his own allegory, *Animal Farm*. Similarly, three other writers whom Blair would read for the first time before he was twelve— Dickens, Kipling, and P. G. Wodehouse—would be made the subjects of memorable essays by Orwell.

His taste was catholic: there was even pleasure to be got from reading advertisements. As a slightly older schoolboy he would pore over *Old Moore's Almanac,* and relish the advertisements promising ways to earn money, stop the drink habit, develop the bust, gain weight, or lose weight. He would amuse himself by writing to these altruistic agencies, asking for information and drawing them out, then simply stopping after they had sent him a flood of testimonials. At one point, as E. Blair, he carried on an extensive correspondence with Winifred Grace Hartland, who guaranteed a cure for obesity, and on the assumption that he was a she—in fact he was at this time a "fat little boy"— urged Miss Blair to come to see her before choosing her summer frocks, as her figure would change so. The correspondence went on for some time, while the proposed fee for advice shrank from two guineas to half a crown, until Miss

Blair finally terminated it by stating that she had been cured by a rival agency.

All this profuse, indiscriminate reading helped to educate him and to give him the air of a "wise child," older than his years and familiar with the ways of the world, although his knowledge was entirely theoretical. It also enriched his fantasy life. Shyness hampered him in making friends, and he tended to retreat into himself, conducting conversations with imaginary friends and telling stories in his head. A few years later Avril would be an eager and attentive listener to his stories, especially during the summer holidays, when Mrs. Blair would take the family to spend a few weeks in Cornwall, either in a house she rented or in the house of Anglo-Indian acquaintances who welcomed them as paying guests. But, for the most part, his was a childhood in which other children played no significant roles: there were no best friends, no confidants. At the convent school he fell passionately in love with a girl named Elsie, who was twice his age and in the last year of the school. It was very much a passion at a distance, never to be expressed, but it was a passion nonetheless, and he would not feel anything comparable to it again until, some twenty-five years later, he met the woman he was to marry. Elsie left the school at the end of the year, and Eric lost track of her—when he next saw her he was a sophisticated Etonian and she was a middle-aged woman of twenty-three, hopelessly past her prime, he felt. But he remembered her as his first love, and he chose her name for the first love of George Bowling in *Coming Up for Air*, the most sympathetic of his heroes.

At five he made some friends of his own age, the children of the plumber who lived nearby. With them he would go bird's-nesting; with them, too, he played games of a mildly erotic character, of a sort not uncommon among children. But these were children of the working class—their father was a plumber; their accents were vulgar—Mrs. Blair intervened and put an end to the friendship. Orwell, recounting the incident in 1936, has only sympathy for her position: as a middle-class parent she couldn't run the risk of her son growing up with an unsuitable accent. But what Eric Blair felt at the time we do not know. Nor do we know if Mrs. Blair learned of the erotic games, in which case, they, as much as the threat of class contamination, might have prompted her to act as she did. We do know that two years later Eric was noticeably prudish, offended by the casual obscenities of childhood, and anything that smacked of lavatories or sex. By then he was accepted on sufferance as the youngest member of a gang of middle-class Henley boys of whom the eldest and leader was a boy of fifteen named Humphrey Dakin. On one occasion he tagged along on an expedition up the Thames, where hooks and lines were brought out and he was introduced to the art of fishing, one of the great pleasures of his life, as it was also to be for George Bowling. For Orwell, that first experience proved unforgettable. He made an important place for it in *Coming Up for Air*, though there, re-created as fiction, there are some significant differences: George, like the other boys in the gang, comes from a lower-class family and he is given an older brother, Joe, hefty, virile, immoral, and illiterate, who runs away from home at eighteen and is never heard from again. Eric of course was the only boy in his family, but the heroes of his early childhood were young men of the working class: farm hands in Cornwall who let him ride along with them while they sowed turnips and who on memorable occasions would milk the ewes to give him a drink; and the workmen who built the house next door to the Blairs', from whom he first heard the word "bloody," a favorite word of Joe Bowling's. Then the taboos of the lower-upper-middle class were imposed upon him: there were to be no more heroes (except in books). The boys of the real gang had appropriate accents and backgrounds, and one of the boys would eventually become Eric's brother-in-law—Humphrey Dakin, who married Marjorie Blair in 1920. Orwell's estimate of himself as an unpopular child seems borne out by his brother-in-law's recollection of him as he was in 1910: "A rather nasty fat little boy with a constant grievance." And he adds, "It took him a long time to grow out of it."

At seven, the prudishness, which Dakin and the other boys in the gang did not share and disliked, had set in. He was acutely sensitive to dirt and smells; he was repelled by physical ugliness, the paunches, jowls, wrinkles, sagging breasts and stomachs, the flabby thighs and buttocks of adults; he was disgusted by dogs' messes on pavements and horse dung in the streets; his nostrils caught the whiff of sweat, bad breath, stale beer, and unwashed armpits; he was offended by mortality, the sense of decay made visible when he came upon the carcass of a frog being eaten by maggots. This was the hated aspect of childhood. Against this was the wonder of discovering each day something new in the world; the unfailing pleasures of reading; the love he felt for his mother (alone among adults); the tiny memorable satisfactions—visits to the sweet shop with a penny, street games, street songs, expeditions along the river . . . Disgust on one side; joy on the other. The tension between them was essential to him as an artist, and found a resolution in his work. But it was to take a long time.

THREE

When he was eight there was a new grievance, and it was the one to which Orwell would attach the greatest importance. In September 1911 he was sent away to school, the conventional fate of a boy of his age and class, in that time and place. The implication of the event was difficult in itself to cope with—that he was being thrust from the nest. But as it happened, in one of those ironic coincidences that are so pat as to seem contrived, it was at this time too that Mr. Blair came back permanently to his family, some months in advance of his official date of retirement. Thereafter, in that household of women, where Eric had been the only "man" for the past four years, there was Father, and there was "Father's room," overheated to a temperature as close as possible to India's, for he was uncomfortable in the chill airs of England.

Mr. Blair had been away too long, and came back too late, to play a decisive role in the life of his son, with whom he barely had time to become reacquainted before he went off to school, and whom he would see thereafter mainly in the holidays. There was little rapport between father and son. In later years there was a sharp divergence of interests—a taste for fishing was one of the few things they shared *—

---

* Even the taste for fishing was not a deep bond between them. As Avril Dunn comments, "Father was never really keen on fishing. He did it at Southwold because some of his cronies fished and it was simply a matter of

and always there was a shyness and a reticence on both sides that would have made intimacy difficult. Orwell's chief childhood memory of his father seems to be of an elderly gentleman whom he disliked saying, "Don't," in a gruff voice. Sons tend to deprecate their fathers, much as in their own fashion fathers tend to deprecate their sons, especially respectable fathers who discover that their sons intend to be writers—that alarming Bohemian possibility. Certainly this proved to be the case with Eric and his father, and it may account for the note of disparagement in Orwell's recollections. It is worth remarking, then, that others who knew Mr. Blair in England remember him as rather vague, gentle, and charming, but somewhat dry, fond of walking, around Henley and later in Southwold on the Suffolk coast (where the Blairs moved in 1921), passing the time of day in shops and on the sea front, watching cricket matches, chatting in pubs, striking up friendships, and when he had the luck to come upon an Anglo-Indian acquaintance, reminiscing about the good old days in the warm sub-continent.

During the four years of her husband's absence, Mrs. Blair had been the dominant figure in the household, and she continued in the role after his return, in part because he was quite content that she should do so. Where Eric was concerned, there was no disagreement between them: both wanted the best for him, and both had a clearly defined idea of what the best was. It may be argued that as much can be said for any parents who are concerned about the future of their children. But the year was 1911, the beginning of the reign of George V, and the Blairs were parents in England, the greatest, richest power on earth, on whose Empire the sun never set. Also, they belonged, however pre-

---

baiting a hook, slinging it into the sea and then balancing your rod on a rest, and waiting till the little bell rang, that was fixed to the top of the rod. No finesse, no skill needed. Eric was a dedicated fisherman with a genuine interest in various kinds of fish and their habitats."

cariously and minimally, to the upper middle class. From this conjunction of circumstances it followed naturally that they wanted their son to have a place for himself among the rulers of England, which is not to say that he should become a member of the Cabinet (although that would be possible) or a great landowner, but simply a member of the ruling caste, *one of those who counted,* whether in the legal or medical or political or ecclesiastical or learned professions, the jurists and civil servants and colonial servants, the company directors and bankers and publishers, the officers of the Foreign Service and the officers of the Army and Navy—in a word, the so-called Establishment as it existed in England before the First World War.

The usual passport to this Establishment was to have attended a Public School, preferably one of the "great" schools, best of all either Eton, Harrow, or Winchester. In 1911 the education to be had at an expensive Public School was likely to be superior to the education one got elsewhere, and its social advantages were undeniable. Fitted out with an accent and manner that were unmistakable and ineradicable—Blair, on the road, was never mistaken by his fellow tramps for one of themselves, but was accepted as an Etonian down on his luck—one was ready to enter an Establishment whose places went as if by right to Old Boys of Public Schools. It is understandable, then, that even those parents of the upper middle class who could ill afford the expense of such an education were prepared, as the Blairs were, to make considerable sacrifices to obtain it for their children and so secure their future. (In 1911, it was not only possible but usual to think of a secure future, a fixed society, a destined place in life.)

Whatever their advantages as a kind of social "forcing house," the Public Schools were primarily institutions of learning. Their standards for admission, particularly for a boy like Eric Blair, who wished to be awarded a scholarship, were high indeed. It was not a matter to be taken lightly: too much of a child's future depended on it, whether he would rise to a secure, respectable place in the world, or sink down, as Eric was warned would happen to him if he failed his exams, to the level of an ill-paid office boy or a clerk in a shop. Little boys of eight, fresh from their governess or Dame School or convent school in the village, who could hardly be expected to think in such fateful terms, had to be prepared, had to be taught Latin and Greek and otherwise educated for the Public Schools their parents hoped they might at fourteen be allowed to enter. In answer to this need, there grew up yet another unique English institution, the expensive private school where boys between the ages of eight and fourteen were taught, crammed, drilled, and beaten, up to the high standard the Public Schools expected of their prospective scholars. A handful of these prep schools were day schools, located mainly in London, and in Oxford and Cambridge, whose pupils escaped at the end of each day to the protection and solace of home and family; but the greater number were boarding schools, to which, from all over England, Scotland, Wales, and Ireland, came privileged little boys, there to be made miserable. It was to one such school, St. Cyprian's, at Eastbourne on the Sussex coast, that Eric Blair was sent in September 1911.

SINCE MR. BLAIR HAD NOT YET RETURNED FROM INDIA, IT was Eric's mother who took the lead in settling his education, although one has the impression that she would have done so in any case. It was she who chose St. Cyprian's, and made the arrangements for him to be enrolled there. Anglo-Indian acquaintances had recommended it to her: it was said to do very well in placing boys at the great Public Schools, where Mrs. Blair was determined Eric should some day go; but of more immediate importance, it made a practice of taking at reduced fees a few exceptionally bright, promising boys who might go on to win scholarships at the Public Schools, the sons of families of limited means in the Imperial Civil Service, or who were otherwise serving in the Outposts of Empire. That reduced fees would be essential if Eric was to attend a private school, just as he would need a scholarship for Public School later, was understood from the first by his parents: they knew the limitations that would be imposed on them by Mr. Blair's pension, down to the last shilling. But Mrs. Blair had no doubt that Eric was bright enough and promising enough to deserve reduced fees, so, in the spring of 1911, she went down to Eastbourne to present her case to the Headmaster-proprietor of St. Cyprian's and his wife, Mr. and Mrs. Vaughan Wilkes.

The school was situated on the outskirts of that much-frequented resort town, beyond the seaside promenade and the last of the grand hotels. At the point where the coast road begins its winding ascent to the top of Beachy Head, the immense chalk cliff overlooking the Channel, another road veers off to the right, down into a kind of sheltered bowl, and there, at the entrance to what is now a well-mannered suburban street, were the buildings and grounds of St. Cyprian's. They consisted principally of a playing field for cricket and football, and two large houses in the late Victorian styles that accommodated dormitories for the boys, classrooms, library, dining room, offices, living quarters for the seven masters and the matron, and on a grander scale, for the Headmaster and his wife and their growing family. From the upper stories of both houses one had an uninterrupted prospect of the Downs, which began virtually across the street from the school property and rose up steeply the quarter mile toward Beachy Head. For the boys it was a prospect of freedom: certainly Eric was happiest at St. Cyprian's when he could escape from its disciplined precincts and wander over the Downs as he pleased, alone or with the one close friend he made among his schoolmates, Cyril Connolly.

The Vaughan Wilkeses welcomed Mrs. Blair in the drawing room of The Lodge, the house nearest to the street, and conversation was conducted over tea.*

In 1911 St. Cyprian's was in its twelfth year, with an enrollment of approximately seventy boys; in contrast to a historic Public School such as Eton (founded in 1440 by Henry VI) it had barely begun to exist. But private schools, not being foundations, are private enterprises and sometimes do not continue beyond the life span of their proprietors, who are usually Headmasters, as was Mr. Vaughan Wilkes, and often responsible for much of the teaching—Mr. Vaughan Wilkes, for example, took the boys in "Classics." By 1911, in spite of its brief history, St. Cyprian's was already recognized as one of the better as well as one of the more snobbish and expensive of private schools. The larger number of its pupils were drawn from the affluent upper-upper-middle class, with a smaller number from the middle-upper-middle, and smallest of all, the group each year who were on reduced fees, the bright, promising products of the lower-upper-middle. Then, as exotics (and threatening to lower the high moral tone, for they tended to be sexually precocious) there were a few sons of South American mil-

---

* It was in the same room that the authors of the present work were received by Mrs. Vaughan Wilkes. She had then been a widow for some years, but continued to live with a companion in The Lodge, all that survived of St. Cyprian's. The school had ceased to exist during the Second World War, and the other house had been destroyed by fire. The drawing room was virtually a museum of school history: the walls, the mantel over the large fireplace, the tops of the glass-fronted mahogany bookcases, the numerous tables, all were covered with photographs, framed and many of them signed, of old St. Cyprianites. Sherry was offered; Mrs. Vaughan Wilkes's massive scrapbooks, crammed with fifty years of memorabilia, including Eric Blair's lost first published writings, were produced; and conversation began.

lionaires, and, as a source of particular pride to the Vaughan Wilkeses and proof that the school was coming on, a tiny aristocratic minority, boys whose fathers had a handle to their names—even, in Eric Blair's time, a boy or two who had a handle of his own, authentic lordlings. It would have been in keeping for Mrs. Vaughan Wilkes, over tea, to let fall such a name, giving full value to the handle.

Let us acknowledge, at the risk of some exaggeration, that snobbishness was rife at St. Cyprian's—for so it would appear in the memoirs of the school written by "Old Boys" who went on to become writers: E. H. W. Meyerstein, Cyril Connolly, George Orwell, Cecil Beaton, and Gavin Maxwell. In that respect, then, as in much else, St. Cyprian's was representative, or symptomatic, of the epoch. England in 1911, that halcyon period "before the war" that Orwell, in one mood, would look back on with so much nostalgia, was itself rife with snobbishness: it did not make even a pretense of egalitarianism, either social or political. It was a time when half the adult population was denied the vote, when a Duke was "better" than a baronet, just as a clerk at Harrods was "better" than a lorry driver, and so down, down to a coal miner in Wales, who was no "better" than anyone except, perhaps, a French or German coal miner. It was a time when the division between the classes seemed unbridgeable, and "Only connect," the motto of E. M. Forster's novel *Howards End,* published the preceding year, seemed an ideal impossible of fulfillment, always assuming that one would want, like the Schlegel sisters in that novel, to "connect" with someone in a class lower than one's own. By 1911 these assumptions had acquired the status of enduring natural laws, subscribed to by a majority of good, sound Englishmen from the lower middle classes up. (The Schlegel sisters were not sound; neither were the miners and railway men out on strike; neither were the suffragettes, whose behavior and aspirations were so unladylike.) But the age of almost undiluted privilege was without knowing it approaching its end: the terminal date was to be August 1914. And while privilege would be reconstituted in different forms after the war, it would never again be as pervasive or self-confident in its assumptions, nor as unbegrudgingly accepted, deferred to, or even tolerated by those not qualified to enjoy it.

Mrs. Blair was not a snob; certainly she did not adulate people who were better off or better placed than she, and rather tended to disparage them; but she would not have bristled when the Vaughan Wilkeses introduced the names of illustrious parents whose children were then at St. Cyprian's. It would have confirmed what she had already been told by her Anglo-Indian friends, that the school attracted the "right sort" of boy. Similarly she would have been reassured to hear that many "Old Boys" were now at Harrow—a favorite St. Cyprian destination—and also at Eton, Wellington, and others of the great schools. Clearly the Vaughan Wilkeses got results; they gave value in return for money received. For their part the Headmaster and his wife were impressed favorably by Mrs. Blair. She was obviously "one's sort" and it followed therefore that her son would be the right sort of boy for the school, especially since he had been doing well at his studies, was a bookish child, a great reader, from whom good things could be expected. This brought them to the question of fees.

Here again the Headmaster and his wife were impressed and sympathetic: the Anglo-Indian background, the thirty years of colonial service, the approaching retirement, the pension that, it went without saying, would not be generous—all this established the Blairs as a family of the sort to whom the Vaughan Wilkeses would feel obliged, would feel it right, to make a concession. It would be consistent with their own notions of service, which were as firmly ingrained in them as in other members of their class who had grown up in the heyday of Empire. Readers of Kipling who believed in him, they preached the ideal of service to their pupils, and instilled it in their own children, one of whom became a missionary, another the Headmaster of a Public School, and who distinguished themselves in uniform during the Second World War. So it was settled, as the interview drew to a close, that Eric would be accepted at half fees, and that he would enter the school the following September.

Orwell's account of his time at St. Cyprian's was written some thirty years later, but with an astonishing immediacy of detail, as though his experience there was an open wound he refused to allow to heal. He can see in the Vaughan Wilkeses' concession no trace of altruism, merely a plain piece of business speculation: that they were taking him at reduced fees because they expected him to win a scholarship at one of the great schools, which would redound to the credit of St. Cyprian's, which in turn would make the Vaughan Wilkeses richer, and their business a success. It is true that St. Cyprian's was owned by the Vaughan Wilkeses, that their livelihood depended on it, that a record of boys admitted to top Public Schools was essential to their continuing success. Yet their willingness to take boys at reduced fees was not inspired wholly by calculation. Ambitious though they might be, they believed at the same time in the ideal of service—it was a responsibility of privilege, an English version of *noblesse oblige*—that they instilled not only in their own children, but also in many of the boys who came to St. Cyprian's, even, perhaps, in Eric Blair. Cyril Connolly's account of the school, which he called "St. Wulfric's," was written eight years before Orwell's. In two brilliantly ironic paragraphs he suggests how easily—how inevitably—idealism and worldliness could coexist there without conflict:

> The school was typical of England before the last war; it was worldly and worshipped success, political and social;

though Spartan, the death-rate was low, for it was well run and based on that stoicism which characterized the English governing class and which has since been underestimated. "Character, character, character," was the message which emerged when we rattled the radiators or the fence round the playing fields and it reverberated from the rifles in the armoury, the bullets on the miniature range, the saw in the carpenter's shop and the hoofs of the ponies on their trot to the Downs.

> *Not once or twice in our rough island's story,*
> *The path of duty was the way to glory*

was the lesson we had to learn and there were other sacred messages from the poets of private schools: Kipling, or Newbolt.

Muscle-bound with character the alumni of St. Wulfric's would pass on to the best public schools, cleaning up all houses with a doubtful tone, reporting their best friends for homosexuality and seeing them expelled, winning athletic distinctions—for the house rather than themselves, for the school rather than the house, and prizes and scholarships and shooting competitions as well—and then find their vocation in India, Burma, Nigeria and the Sudan, administering with Roman justice those natives for whom the final profligate overflow of Wulfrician character was all the time predestined.

Mrs. Blair had reason to be pleased when she returned to Henley: the concession she had obtained at Eastbourne was large enough to permit Eric's going to private school; and to go from St. Cyprian's to a great Public School was a logical sequel—so that the respectable, gentlemanly, appropriate future she and Mr. Blair had envisioned for him seemed assured. Even so, it would not be managed without their making some quite stringent sacrifices. The Blairs would be paying ninety pounds a year at St. Cyprian's, a not inconsiderable part of their income. In addition, there was the expense of outfitting him properly. Cecil Beaton, a contemporary of Blair's at St. Cyprian's, noted some years later (1923) that "When preparing for this school, my mother was horrified at the length of the prescribed list: 12 pairs of socks, 6 pairs of pyjamas; school cap; blazers; 3 pairs of football shorts; 1 serviette ring and 1 Bible." And there were a good many other items, all of which Mrs. Blair faithfully assembled before Eric's departure in September: in this respect he would be indistinguishable from any other arriving St. Cyprianite. (His mother had not told him of the reduced fees when she brought home the news from Eastbourne; he was not to learn of his special status until his third year at the school, and then from the Headmaster.)

Whether or not Eric was pleased at the news, we cannot say: his own account of St. Cyprian's begins in the second week after his arrival. We do know that he was already an avid reader of P. G. Wodehouse's cheerful Public School novels, and he may innocently have imagined that life at boarding school would be as glamorous as it is made to appear there. In any event, September was still some distance away: by children's time, far enough in the future not to be immediately threatening. In June there was the excitement of his eighth birthday, made unforgettable by his mother's giving him *Gulliver's Travels;* later there was the return of his father from India; and the family holiday at Looe in Cornwall. But at last it was the day for him to leave. His parents took him up to London and saw him on to the specially reserved Pullman for St. Cyprianites. Inside, peering out, frightened, bewildered, already homesick small boys; outside, on the platform, parents smiling bravely, especially fathers (who have been through the whole experience themselves), mothers surreptitiously reaching for their handkerchiefs—a familiar, painful, classic scene, "The Departure for Boarding School," which figures inevitably in autobiography, biography, and fiction of growing up in the upper levels of English society. Then the train begins to move; he catches a last glimpse of Them. Thereafter he is alone.

What follows, just as inevitably, is Unhappiness, the common fate of boys at boarding school. We know that Somerset Maugham was unhappy at his school, and Winston Churchill at his, and Osbert Sitwell at his, but the catalogue of victims is interminable—an anthology of the miseries of life at prep school could be quickly assembled, and additions made to it seasonally, for the tradition is long-lived and production vigorous.

> The new school my parents chose for me was on the East Coast. At first I was miserable there and cried night after night.

This could come from any one of such memoirs. In fact, it is the opening of the chapter "White Samite" in Cyril Connolly's *Enemies of Promise,* and in the very next sentence the author's voice becomes unmistakably his:

> My mother cried too at sending me and I have often wondered if that incubator of persecution mania, the English private school, is worth the money that is spent on it or the tears its pupils shed. At an early age small boys are subjected to brutal partings and long separations which undermine their love for their parents before the natural period of conflict and are encouraged to look down on them without knowing why. To owners of private schools they are a business like any other, to masters a refuge for incompetence, in fact a private school has all the faults of a public school without any of its compensations, without tradition, freedom, historical beauty, good teaching or communication between pupil and teacher. It is one of the

few tortures confined to the ruling classes and from which the workers are still free. I have never met anybody yet who could say he had been happy there. It can only be that our parents are determined to get rid of us!

One might think that after such a trumpet blast, the walls of Jericho would have fallen at once; but, of course, nothing of the sort occurred, and one can discover an explanation for the continuing durability of the private school as an institution in Connolly's bland admission, in his next sentence, that St. Cyprian's, "where I now went was a well-run and vigorous example which did me a world of good." Orwell would have found little to take exception to in his old school friend's sardonic opening reflections, but the good-humored tolerance and sense of "fair play" implicit in the acknowledgment of their old school he would have found intolerable. At no time, early or late, would he believe that it had done him anything but a world of harm, and when he finally wrote of it, when he was already world famous as the author of *Animal Farm*, he did so with an unrelenting seriousness. The passage of more than a quarter century had not made him indulgent: in "Such, Such Were the Joys" nothing was to be recalled joyfully.*

The title came from a line in "The Echoing Green," one of Blake's "Songs of Innocence," which his mother had read aloud to him when they were first living in Henley. It is a poem of the mingling of the generations:

Such, such were the joys
When we all, girls and boys,

---

* The piece was written at Connolly's suggestion, and was originally intended for publication in his magazine *Horizon*, but Orwell decided it was probably too long for magazine publication and certainly too libelous, as he had written it, and put it aside. It was published for the first time, after his death, in *Partisan Review*, in 1952.

> *In our youth time were seen,*
> *On the Echoing Green*

Then, at nightfall, the gathering in:

> *The sun does descend,*
> *And our sports have an end.*
> *Round the laps of their mothers*
> *Many sisters and brothers,*
> *Like birds in their nest,*
> *Are ready for rest,*
> *And sport no more seen*
> *On the darkening Green.*

In its child-like cadences, it idealizes the cohesiveness and protectiveness of family life, which a boarding school by definition is meant to supplant. The contrast was painful. Fugitives from the nest, the little boys alighted at Eastbourne. Behind, the comfort and affection of home; ahead, the bare dormitory with its hard beds, the dining room with its meager portions of evil-tasting food, the lavatories smelling of drains. Children might well believe that their parents wanted to get rid of them—how else to explain their being there?—but it did not make them miss them any the less.

Homesickness, which was epidemic, expressed itself usually in tears. "During those first days at Eastbourne," Cecil Beaton recalls, "I blubbed at the most unsuitable times of day and night. I would suddenly be overcome by waves of homesickness and burst into tears in the middle of a sentence. . . . I got into the habit of waking early so that I could go to the lavatory and weep alone." Cyril Connolly, as we have seen, "cried night after night." Such boys, one feels, being able to express their unhappiness in uninhibited fashion, were luckier than Eric Blair, who was as unhappy as they but who could not weep, being too shy, too reticent, too proud. And it is curious that in "Such, Such Were the

FROM BENGAL TO ST. CYPRIAN'S 37

Joys," with its almost unremitting emphases on unhappiness, cruelty, snobbery, and disgust, and its numberless provocations for tears, Orwell should admit to having wept only once.

MRS. VAUGHAN WILKES, WHO WAS THEN A WOMAN IN HER mid-thirties and the mother of small children, made it a point that the boys should call her "Mum," and her attitude toward them was richly and complexly maternal, that is, it was not only benevolent, kindly, concerned, and doting, but also demanding, scolding, shaming, reproachful, capricious, and temperamental. Reading of her, one has the impression at times that the role of "Mum" was being played by Sarah Bernhardt as Queen Elizabeth. Her view of herself was as a mother to the boys, and a good number of them enjoyed the substitute relationship—or so the many photographs affectionately inscribed to "Mum" in the sitting room of The Lodge would suggest. Others did not enjoy it. Eric Blair did not. (And Orwell, in his memoir, will not even accept the use of "Mum" as a familiar form of "mother," but as a variant on "Ma'am," by which the wives of housemasters at posh Public Schools were addressed.)

Mrs. Vaughan Wilkes set to work briskly to cure homesickness—as the mother of small children she felt herself better qualified to do so than the staff of seven bachelor masters, and over the years had developed a number of techniques for coping with it. On the first day of the term she came upon Eric Blair, in his green jersey and corduroy shorts, standing apart, eyes dry but downcast, shoulders drooping, his whole expression woebegone: the familiar symptoms of homesickness. She knelt down, put her arms around him, and drew him close to her. What she expected was the familiar response—that he would rest his head on her bosom, or say "Oh, Mum," or merely weep, and so be over the worst of it and make the first step to recognizing that he was not "alone" at St. Cyprian's. But he did none of these things. She felt him stiffen, strain to get free of her. "He was not an affectionate little boy," she remembered. Undiscouraged by this first rebuff, the next day she had resorted to a favored technique, and took Eric and another of the new boys in need of encouragement along with one of her children closest to them in age, for a picnic on the Downs. The boys were allowed to wander about freely; they explored the winding chalky lanes; they picked wild blackberries; afterwards there was a feast of cake and sandwiches. But Mrs. Vaughan Wilkes got no further in bringing Blair out, in winning his confidence or affection, than she had the day before. "There was no warmth in him," she decided.*

He had such control over his emotions that he would not weep, or rage, or otherwise give outward expression to the unhappiness he felt. So it remained within him, unexpressed. Then one morning, after he had been at the school for about a week, he woke up to find that he had wet his bed during the night, something he had not done since being brought to England four years before. Such a reversion is not uncommon among children at a time of emotional crisis—which for Eric this assuredly was—and now, presumably even at a conservatively run boarding school, it would be dealt with psychologically. But we are writing of 1911, and of a school dedicated to "character, character, character": the remedy for such unmanly conduct was to exercise self-control and

---

* This account is based on the authors' interview with Mrs. Vaughan Wilkes. Orwell makes no mention of the picnic in "Such, Such Were the Joys." When Gavin Maxwell came to the school as a new boy in the mid-1920's, he was taken by Mrs. Vaughan Wilkes for a similar outing on the Downs. "It ought to have been a wonderful start," he writes, "and I don't see what more she could have done, but it didn't work because I was outside my environment and I behaved as an animal does in the same circumstances. I couldn't produce the right responses, and so I shrank."

stop it; otherwise, one would have to be soundly caned on the bottom again and again, each time one behaved like a messy baby, until finally, one stopped. Poor Eric. Waking up in the morning to sopping sheets and the smell of urine, he felt guilt, shame, fear, and disgust. At night, before going to sleep, he prayed fervently that it should not happen again. But it did. Prayers failed him; so did his own resolutions. By the third acrid morning, it was evident that he was lacking in "character": he would have to be punished.

He had been warned, in circumstances that, as Orwell records them in "Such, Such Were the Joys," mingled elements of the grotesque, the comic, and the plausible in the manner of a nightmare. Apparently it was the custom for the boys to be served tea under the supervision of Mrs. Vaughan Wilkes. On this occasion, she was entertaining a visitor, a woman of masculine appearance and threatening presence who wore—oddly, it might seem, for tea at a boys' school—a riding habit, or what Eric thought to be a riding habit. When the boys had finished their tea, they were allowed to leave the room, all but Eric, who was summoned up to the table where "Flip"—her nickname among the boys —formidable herself, sat chatting with the even more formidable stranger. No introduction was made, as he had naïvely expected. Instead, he was simply and humiliatingly described as the little boy who wet his bed every night. The stranger stared with an expression of disapproval and distaste. Furthermore, Flip continued, if he did it again, she would have him beaten by the Sixth Form. But Eric, too frightened or shamed to hear correctly, misunderstood her, and, with the plausibility of a nightmare where nothing is to be questioned, thought she had said "Mrs. Form" rather than "Sixth Form." And Mrs. Form, he thought, equally plausibly, must be the disapproving lady in the riding habit. It was she, then—his imagination raced ahead—who would have the pleasure of punishing him, and she would do it with a hunting whip. He stood there, a small boy "almost swooning with shame," incapable of saying a word, before those powerful, scornful women. The fear of punishment, the pain of being beaten, counted for less, much less, than the humiliation he suffered on that afternoon in September 1911, and would remember virtually until the end of his life and never forgive—that he had been exposed in his uncleanness, that another person (the more shaming that she was a woman) had been told of his disgusting sin.

It was an appalling experience, to undergo and to remember—emblematic for Orwell in its juxtaposition of humiliation and disgust—and its effects upon the boy Eric Blair and the man he became can hardly be overestimated: they are discernible at a number of crucial points in the narrative of his early life. The immediate effect, not surprisingly, was that he wet his bed that night and in the morning was beaten with a riding crop—not, however, by Mrs. Form, or the Sixth Form, but by the Headmaster in his study.

There was a ritual in these matters. First, Eric must "own up" to his offense, which he did—"owning up" being an important part of the code of behavior and training for a boy of his class; then the Headmaster must deliver the expected short homily on his misdeeds, which he did; and then the crop was applied, with only moderate severity. On both sides the forms of the ritual were being observed, and as such it was a characteristic encounter between a wielder of authority and one who was being brought up to wield authority in his turn.

(Often the forms themselves are carried on from schooldays into adult life. We are reminded by Harold Macmillan in his memoirs that the House of Commons is like a Public School writ large in its tendency to react favorably when a Member "owns up." He quotes a passage from Trollope in which one Member explains to another that if he "owned up" to the murder of his grandmother in a modest, apologetic way, the House would probably forgive him and might even quietly cheer. This sort of honesty—"I did it, and I am sorry, and I am willing to accept my punishment"—is indoctrinated early. One learns to deal with authority face to face, so to speak, as part of one's training to wield it. Rather than, as would likely be the case with a working-class child, to keep as far away from it as possible.)

There was always something equivocal in Blair's attitude toward established authority, something at once submissive and defiant, and so it proved in this first encounter of his with it. The proper form would have been for him to leave the Headmaster's study with a chastened and repentant air (however angry and unrepentant he might feel) as though to acknowledge the gravity of the offense and the justice of the punishment. But Eric emerged into the anteroom, grinning victoriously, and reported to the boys who happened to be gathered there that the beating hadn't hurt. It was not the sort of thing one said in the presence of Mrs. Vaughan Wilkes, whom he hadn't noticed in the anteroom, and she, indignant at this proof of an unchastened spirit, ordered him back into the study for a second beating. This time, as Orwell remembered, the Headmaster lost control and laid it on savagely—he was beaten for what seemed to him to be a period of five minutes, terminated only by the riding crop's snapping in half. The bone handle, he tells us, flew across the room. (It is a surprising detail—presumably the Headmaster would be grasping the handle, and the lower half of the crop would sail free.) For this mishap, too, the boy was blamed—apparently it had been an expensive crop.

He fell into a chair and wept. (It was the only time that a beating, whether at St. Cyprian's or Eton, would bring him to tears, and the only time in "Such, Such Were the Joys" that he describes himself as actually weeping.) That night, in spite of having been punished, and as though to prove to himself the impossibility of his being good, he wet his bed again, and the next morning he was beaten again. One might have expected (certainly Eric might have expected) that the cycle would go on indefinitely; instead, from that night forward the incontinent bladder recovered its controls—the bed-wetting immediately and permanently ceased. The traditional, no-nonsense application of corporal punishment to curb a defect of character had served its purpose.

The psychological cost, however, was considerable. When Eric had wept in the Headmaster's study, it was not because the pain was unendurable, for the second beating, in spite of its length and intensity, appears not to have hurt much more than the first. He wept in part out of a sense of obligation, a belated recognition that this was expected of him; in part out of repentance, for he never doubted that it was a sin to wet his bed; and in part, the greater part, out of a sense of abandonment and isolation, that he was alone in a system whose demands he could never possibly satisfy. He had sinned by wetting his bed: it was an action over which, so far as he could tell, he had no control, it happened in spite of him. But this did not excuse him from punishment: he was flawed, which was provocation enough. It followed therefore that punishment was one's lot in life; life made one a victim. So early, then, a crucial note was being sounded: the system makes its demands, which he is congenitally unable to meet; hence he is unworthy of its rewards. He is not at ease in the system, not the popular boy, the handsome boy, the favored one. He had already had some sense of this in Henley; the experience of his first weeks at St. Cyprian's confirmed him in his premature pessimism. As a sinner he felt the need of expiation, before he was aware of what he needed to expiate. In dealing with this bed-wetting episode, Orwell is finely aware of the difference it makes that he should be writing of it years later, when much of the ordinary life of his schooldays (the happier aspect, usually) has eluded his memory: but he would argue that what remains is what matters. After allowance is made for the expected distortions of the psyche, the Unconscious misremembering or altering as it must, it is evident here (as in all his work) how subtly Orwell captures the relation of the victim to authority—that one is to be blamed not only for the wrong one does, but also for whatever difficulties authority may have in enacting its role in the relationship. So Eric was unquestioningly ready to feel guilty rather than jubilant about the breaking of the Headmaster's riding crop with which he was being beaten. It was as though he were responsible for it; indeed, by a kind of perverse logic it could be made to seem so—if he had not wet his bed, he would not have had to be beaten; if he had not been beaten, the riding crop would not have snapped in half—therefore, the fault was his. It was this attitude, so early formed, that would allow him many years later to speak for the passive victims of society.

FOUR

ERIC WAS NOT THE SORT OF BOY TO TELL HIS PARENTS that he had wet his bed and been beaten for it, or that he was homesick and unhappy, or that the food was vile and the drains stank, or that he hated the Headmaster and his wife—so there are not even veiled allusions to these matters in the letters he wrote to his mother during his first four terms at St. Cyprian's, from September 1911 to December 1912. It is possible, of course, that these letters were written under the supervision of Mrs. Vaughan Wilkes or one of the Masters, inhibiting him from a frank outpouring of what he felt. But the number of uncorrected misspellings seems to argue against this having been a regular procedure. His own reticence, shyness, and pride explain more about what he left unsaid than possible intimidation. Quite simply, a frank outpouring would be as inconsistent with Eric Blair at eight or nine as it would be thirty years later with George Orwell. In any case, these letters—all that are known to survive from his schooldays—are of greater interest for what they include than for what they omit, for they help to fill in one of the conspicuous blanks in "Such, Such Were the Joys," the greater part of which deals with Eric's last three years at St. Cyprian's—from the time he entered the scholarship class and learned that he was at the school on reduced fees. Of his first two years there Orwell tells virtually nothing. After the traumatic bed-wetting episode, there seems to have been a relatively tranquil period; it is from the later period that he assembles most of the evidence for his indictment.*

If one had just the letters to judge from, Eric would strike one as an ordinary little boy—there is no evidence of literary precocity, no hint of the writer he was to become. It is the ordinariness of the schoolboy life described in so ordinary a fashion—with a full quota of jolly chaps and ripping games of footer—that enlightens us. At one level, at the level where art begins, Eric suffered a profound humiliation of the spirit and the flesh—never to forget the sight of the turd floating in the swimming bath—but at another level, he fulfilled the daily round at St. Cyprian's like any other little boy there, preoccupied with studies, games, and his stamp collection, and was not unhappy. The letters, in a handwriting that has not yet found itself but varies between the sloppy and the excessively neat, are addressed at first to Dear Mother, or My dear Mother, and upon his return from the Christmas holiday, thereafter to My darling Mother, and they are signed in a formal Victorian style, Eric Blair, or Eric A. Blair, or E. A. Blair, but always with love, or with much love, or from your loving son, and sometimes with a long row of kisses. Sometimes too they are illustrated with drawings—of boats or animals, and once of a pudding and once of an airplane. (Airplanes were a subject of great interest

---

* Orwell's letters to his mother from St. Cyprian's are now in the possession of his sister Avril (Mrs. William Dunn), who has very kindly made them available to us.

"Such, Such Were the Joys" is invaluable as Orwell's interpretation of Eric Blair's childhood, but it is less satisfactory as a biographical account. Written with admirable directness, those straightforward sentences create effortlessly an air of candor and intelligence, and lead one to believe that one is being told everything. In fact, Orwell has written a highly selective and purposive work of art, an "indictment" of the cruelty inflicted on children in the name of boarding-school education, and whatever will lessen the force of the argument has been omitted.

at the school that winter—some of the boys were building models for a competition, and in February there was an expedition to see a real one, but Eric and a lot of other chaps played footer instead. His own hobby was stamp collecting; in September he had written to his mother to send him his album, which she promptly did.)

His letters reflect the chief preoccupations of St. Cyprian's: studies and games. In his first year Eric had classes in Latin, French, History, English, and Arithmetic, and hardly a letter passes without a report on his standing: in each class he was at the top or near it. Mrs. Vaughan Wilkes would confirm this. As she said, "He was a very bright little boy," and she knew it at first hand, since she took the classes in History and French, and also taught Scripture. (The school was run on traditional Anglican lines: there was daily chapel, and the plunge each morning into the icy swimming bath.) At games he made up in enthusiasm what he lacked in skill. He played football vigorously—once, as goalkeeper, he fought off the opposing chaps who came at him, he told his mother, like mad dogs; he took part in swimming races, starting last and ending up third (but he was hampered by a bathing suit that was too tight); and he rejoiced in St. Cyprian's victories over its rivals, The Grange, St. Christopher's, and Kent House.

For the most part the daily round consisted of studies and games, and the spaces between were filled with the characteristic private interests of a small boy. We catch a glimpse of them in Eric's requests to his mother. At various times he asked for his stamp album; for newly issued penny stamps; for some of the duplicate stamps he had left at home to give to a boy named Moreno who was not English but wanted English stamps badly; for draughts; for dried peas to use as ammunition in a toy cannon belonging to one of the boys; and for cigarette cards. Occasionally there would be departures from the routine. These were events. On a hot, summer-like day in October the boys were taken to swim at the Devonshire Baths, a public pool where the water was pumped in directly from the sea, and Eric thought it "simply lovely." (Orwell would remember the pool as it was in midwinter, murky and cold, when swimming was an ordeal, not a pleasure.) On December 1, it was Mrs. Vaughan Wilkes's birthday, in celebration of which the boys were allowed to play games throughout the house; afterwards they walked in a crocodile across the Downs to Beachy Head. The next week, on Saturday evening, there was an end-of-term entertainment: some of the boys danced, others sang, and Eric recited a poem.

His mother had kept him in touch with happenings in Henley. The family pets were a source of interest and concern: the well-being of the cat Tojo; the possibility of acquiring a guinea pig—what color?; the bird Virey; and the reappearance in the house of a small family of white mice, suitably caged—Marjorie's. Eighteen days before the end of term (on December 2) he says he is sorry to hear that the smelly white mice are back, but that he won't mind them so much if they're *not* smelly. Actually seeing them over the Christmas holidays seems to have softened his feelings toward them: when he is back at school in February, he writes to ask if the mice have had babies—if they have, then his mother must see to it that Tojo doesn't eat them.

February was midwinter, season of snow, ice, head colds, and stuffy sickrooms. The playing field was frozen (so there could be no footer) and some of the boys went skating, but Eric was confined to the sickroom again with a head cold, his second that winter, along with a younger boy named Leslie Cohen. The reward of illness for a bookish boy like Eric was to have lots of time to read, but Leslie, who is earlier singled out in the correspondence as being especially naughty, gave him no peace; in the end Eric had to put his own book aside and read to him. A week later (February eleventh) he was out of the sickroom and back in classes, where he was second in everything, but it was not until the next week that he was judged well enough to play footer again.

February had its happier events. There was a "lovely" lecture on the moon by one of the masters, who gave a demonstration of an eclipse—a football topped with sugar served as a model. And there was also a "ripping" lecture on how things were made, the manufacture of steel, pen-knives, soap, and so much else Eric hadn't time to list them in his letter home.

On June 2, replying to a question from his mother, he wrote that he would like a gun-metal watch for his birthday. On June 25, his ninth birthday, he wrote to thank her for the various presents that had arrived from Henley, not only the ripping little watch that was her special present to him, but also a book from his father, and a knife, a box of toffee, and a cake that he had not yet tasted—presumably it would be shared at tea—but which he thought was a seed cake.

Only a few letters survive from the new term in 1912, the beginning of his second year at St. Cyprian's. It was a time when the family was making the first of the moves that were to be so characteristic of them in the next fifteen years, as though the pattern set in India, of moving from one post to the next, had to be unconsciously reenacted in England. This first move was to the nearby village of Shiplake, where the Blairs rented a house called Roselawn, in the Station Road. Roselawn, set in an acre of lawn and garden, was a larger and more spacious house than Nutshell; and Shiplake, though only a few miles from Henley, had a much more "country" feeling. Above the village was Binfield Heath, waiting to be explored during the holidays; and in the woods beyond Roselawn a pool in an abandoned quarry waiting to be fished, that Orwell (it seems fair to assume) would draw upon for *Coming Up for Air,* although 57 High Street, Lower Binfield, the Bowlings' house in the novel, is of a very different order from the Blairs' house in Shiplake.

The contents of these letters from his second year at the school (the last of them is dated December 8) are much as before, studies and games, but his handwriting has become larger, clearer, and more disciplined, and it won him a compliment from his mother.

The "events" of the term occurred on two successive evenings early in December. The first was a lecture illustrated with magic lantern slides. The second was the end-of-term entertainment, which the boys attended in fancy dress. Costumes ranged from the simple to the extravagant. There was a pirate, there were revolutionaries (shirt open at the throat, sash at the waist), there was a Puss 'n Boots, a frog, and a sunflower. Resplendent among them was Eric, who came as a footman in a red velvet coat, lace frill, white silk flowered waistcoat, red silk trousers, black stockings, and a powdered wig.

It is a last, lovingly detailed glimpse of him in the letters he wrote to his mother from the school—the correspondence doesn't survive beyond 1912—and, of course, it is very different from the picture of himself as a schoolboy that he chose to record in "Such, Such Were the Joys."

FIVE

In the autumn of 1913, at the beginning of his third year at St. Cyprian's, there would be a significant change: the reason for his having been sent there was brought into sharp focus.

He was ten years old, taller, wiser, and tougher than the sad-eyed, bewildered small boy with whose homesickness "Mum" had tried to cope. That was two years in the past. Since then he had survived homesickness in his own fashion, and the cold and damp, to which he was peculiarly vulnerable, suffering from head colds and chest colds, sneezing, coughing, and wheezing bronchially through the winter months. He had even survived the dreary institutional food, of which, no matter how unappetizing it might be, there was never quite enough to curb one's hunger, it still being an article of faith among Headmasters that a boy's mind was more easily crammed if his stomach was not.

The unhappiness Eric had felt as a new boy hardened into a stony resentment. Virtually to the end of his life resentment and anger would be at the base of his feelings for St. Cyprian's. While he was there, his experience provided him with a variety of reasons for disliking it, and he forgot none of them, and continued to dislike it, up to the day he left for good in December 1916, and beyond that to the day some thirty years later when he began to set down his recollections of it.

In his first two years Eric had done more than well enough to justify the expectations of his parents and the concessions of the Vaughan Wilkeses. Therefore, in the autumn term of 1913, he was placed in the scholarship class. He became one of the small group at St. Cyprian's, some from wealthy families, some not, who would be intensively prepared for three years to sit the Examination for "scholars" at one or other of the great Public Schools; the rest of the boys would be brought along more leniently toward the less exacting common entrance exams. (To win such a scholarship—to be made a King's Scholar in College at Eton, for example—was a distinction that bore no taint of charity. Financial need was not taken into account. The scholarship was a reward for braininess, as it showed to advantage in a set of formidably difficult exams. But it was also the one way for a brainy boy whose family had little money to get to a Public School and so begin a career in the Establishment.)

The boys of the scholarship class were worked hard. In term-time the pressure was unremitting; during holidays it was only a little less so—for then there were hundreds of lines in translation to be done at home, and, on at least one occasion as the exams drew near, the Vaughan Wilkeses arranged for Eric to stay at the school for an extra week to be tutored by one of the masters. The scholarship boys were taught in the approved, traditional manner that accomplished what it set out to do; their minds were crammed, drilled, force-fed—what feats of memorization were expected!—with a store of facts and received opinions that would allow them to show to best advantage on the exams. Like show dogs they would go through their paces. Everything was subordinate to the exams; and the fateful consequences of failure, especially for a boy like Eric, whose parents couldn't afford to send him to a Public School, were luridly evoked. If one failed, one disappointed one's parents, let down the school, and put oneself outside the pale, doomed to the gray world of clerks and drapers' assistants. In the circumstances, the possibility of finding pleasure or interest or significant meaning in one's studies was irrelevant: they were not meant to be enjoyed, but learned. History was reduced to names, dates, "events," sonorous phrases, and illustrative tableaux (The Princes in the Tower; the Field of the Cloth of Gold), all highlights and no relation. English literature was a pantheon of hallowed names, suitably tagged, from Chaucer to Shakespeare to Tennyson (by way of Keats) and forward from the Laureate to Sir Henry Newbolt. "Classics"—Latin and Greek—were lengthy, strategically chosen samplings from the approved authors, which one was made to read, parse, summarize, and memorize; such selections had turned up in exams in the past and were likely to turn up there again. Drill and memorization were basic techniques of this pedagogy, but at the root of it was fear—in Connolly's phrase, the boys learned "as fast as fear could teach us."

Fear was an orthodox, schoolmasterly method for counteracting sloth, inattention, and daydreaming, that classic trinity of schoolboy vices. The Exam itself, though constantly invoked and made fearful to contemplate, was yet too remote (until the last month or two) to be of much use in the day-to-day struggle waged at St. Cyprian's against lassitude and boredom. One had to be hectored, scolded, shamed, cajoled, and threatened. Besides this, there was a steady rat-a-tat of physical punishments and indignities. The Headmaster, who took the boys of the scholarship class in Classics, had a silver pencil (it grew in Orwell's memory to the size of a banana) which he would apply smartly to the skull of a boy who hadn't a correct answer ready to a question. Or he would kick a boy on the shins, jolting him awake, or tweak his ear, pinch him, pull his hair. As a last resort, after a repeated error in translation, perhaps, he would order a boy from the classroom into the study, there to be caned with a springy rattan cane—the successor to the split riding crop—after which Master and pupil would return to the classroom, and the lesson would be resumed.

Physical punishment was painful and therefore to be feared, but its psychological counterpart was perhaps even more effective, for Mr. and Mrs. Vaughan Wilkes were very skillful at stirring up feelings of guilt, shame, inadequacy, and unworthiness. Which brings us directly to Eric's situation as Orwell remembered it. It was not until his third year at the school that he understood the special circumstances of his being there: that he had been taken as a pupil at reduced fees. It appeared that his parents did not tell him of this concession made on his behalf, nor did the Vaughan Wilkeses when he came to the school. But from the time he entered the scholarship class, the Headmaster and his wife made use of the concession to intimidate him. It was the final psychological weapon (far more painful than the silver pencil or the rattan cane) to be resorted to when he was slack at his work, when his performance fell below the standard that was essential if he was to win a scholarship.

The Headmaster's way was direct: he bluntly reminded Eric of the shameful secret. (For it was thus, as a shameful secret, that Eric regarded it, and while one might cavil at shameful, a secret it undoubtedly was, and it was perfectly kept.) *

He would summon Eric to his study for a reprimand or punishment, depending on the gravity of the offense, and presently the boy would be reminded that he was there at his bounty—a no less humiliating way of saying that he was

---

* "Perfectly kept" is Cyril Connolly's phrase. Mrs. Vaughan Wilkes told us that a boy's being on reduced fees was a confidential matter between his parents and the Headmaster and his wife, and was never made public. Connolly, who of all the boys would have been the most likely to know and who was a member of the scholarship class, had no knowledge of Blair's special financial arrangement until he read about it in "Such, Such Were the Joys."

a charity boy. Was this how Eric chose to reward him for his kindness, by being inattentive and lazy, by not preparing his lessons etc. etc? Did he *want* to fail? Consider the alternative that loomed ahead: to fail the Exam, which meant to go down to the depths of degradation, to be cast out from the charmed circle and end up as a scruffy little office boy at forty pounds a year. There were times when it seemed, even to himself, that Eric was deliberately courting this fate and wanted nothing more than to go down and out—*not to go to a Public School*. Day after day he would be deliberately idle, as though asking to be punished, couldn't bring himself to work: this idleness too was a kind of torment. At such times Mrs. Vaughan Wilkes would add reproaches and exhortations of her own. Unlike her husband, she would not speak directly of the shameful secret. She merely alluded to it, a delicacy that proved even more guilt-inspiring. She would speak pityingly of Mrs. Blair, so proud of her son and making such sacrifices for him; was it decent, was it playing the game, was it straight of him, therefore, to be an idler, to throw his chances away? And as a final stroke: was it fair even to the Vaughan Wilkeses, who did so much for him— he knew how much, did he not? Oh yes, he knew. It wasn't necessary to spell it out: it was all there, to his guilty conscience, in the way she looked at him and in the way he could not meet her gaze straight on. The worst of it was that Eric felt that the indictment was deserved, or felt that that was what he ought to feel. So the guilt was compounded and the grievance deepened. The judgment of the adult world was unanswerable. Not even his parents would excuse him: he could not expect to win their approval by disappointing them. Here his intuition was sound, for however different their motives might be, the Blairs and the Vaughan Wilkeses were alike in wanting the same end for him: not down and out but up and in.

That winter, the winter of 1914, a new boy, Cyril Connolly, came to the school, and entered the scholarship class. This was a significant event in Eric Blair's history for Connolly was to become his first close friend—before then his only intimacy had been with his mother and sisters—as well as confidant, literary colleague, and fellow critic of the established order at St. Cyprian's. The two boys were of the same age, but each, in a different fashion, seemed older, precocious intellectually, quasi-adult in his way of looking at the world —Connolly remembered Blair as "one of those boys who seem born old." Cecil Beaton, who knew Blair only slightly but was another of Connolly's close friends at St. Cyprian's —it was characteristic of Connolly that he should have several close friends there, just as it was characteristic that Blair should not—summed up Cyril as "of all the boys . . . certainly the strangest, most fascinating character to me. He seemed so grown-up." Cyril was the more worldly, but also the more romantic; Eric was the more skeptical and unillusioned. Beaton writes of Connolly: "We admired one another, though I got a bit of a shock when I discovered how much he knew about life. A few of us vaguely realised that someone's parents were rich or titled, or had a large motor-car. But Cyril knew which of the masters had a financial interest in St. Cyprian's, and which were only there on sufferance. He said it helped you to know how to behave towards them." This worldly wisdom was of no use to Eric in smoothing his way at St. Cyprian's—Cyril was noticeably better at it—for then, as later, he was "incapable of courtship"; but it did allow him to objectify his dislike of the school. The favorites, the boys who were petted and made much of, who were allowed to go unpunished no matter how stupid or lazy, were now recognized to be those boys whose parents had pots of money or handles to their names or came down to visit them in expensive motor cars. Whereas boys like himself, whose parents were deficient in these crucial attributes, were subjected to punishments and deprivations, were not "in favor" with Mrs. Vaughan Wilkes, were not loved. The moral to be drawn reinforced him in his premature cynicism: you were no good unless you had a hundred thousand pounds; and as a corollary to this, which he felt his own experience of the school bore witness to day by day, those without money were those who had to work hardest. His sense of the unfairness of life deepened.

Of course he could not present this to Connolly except in the most generalized way, for to illustrate with the particulars of his own experience would have meant revealing the shameful secret, and this he was too proud (or too humiliated) to do. There was always a line drawn as to how much one would confide: this was true for both boys, though for different reasons. Eric was invincibly reticent; Cyril was a good deal more open, but he had his several friends, who played different roles in his life, and to each he distributed the confidences appropriate to the role. For Connolly, Blair represented "Intelligence" (Beaton, "Sensibility"), and "Intelligence" was an alternative to "Character," that shibboleth of St. Cyprian's and all the other expensive, snobbish, character-building schools like it in Edwardian England. Intelligence, of a precocious kind, made both boys alert to the pretensions of the school and dismissive of them: this set them apart, a club of two. It was not, however, the sort of intelligence likely to endear itself to the Vaughan Wilkeses. Both boys, properly curbed and held to a tight rein, might well go on to win scholarships—and so, as advertisements, justify the time and effort spent upon them—but neither would be likely to emulate Kipling and write that "Of all things in the world there is nothing, always excepting a good mother, so worthy of honour as a good school."

Connolly's family had more money than the Blairs; he was at the school as a regular paying pupil; he went home for the holidays to London, to a house in Brompton Square. The ambience of his childhood was much grander than Eric's.

His great-aunt, the Countess of Kingston, lived in Mitchelstown Castle in Cork, "an enormous eighteenth-century Gothic affair . . . with some thirty thousand acres," and his visit to her there, when he was five, "left a deep impression." His Aunt Mab, his mother's favorite sister, "had married a rich man." (Mrs. Blair's favorite sister had married a teacher of Esperanto.) "Aunt Mab was very beautiful but she also had special smells, smells of furs and Edwardian luxe . . . Wherever we went with Aunt Mab there were presents and large houses [she owned four] and the appeal her wealth made to an imaginative child was irresistible."

Yet there were interesting resemblances too. The Connollys were Anglo-Irish; the Blairs, Anglo-Indian. Eric's father had been in the colonial service, stationed in India; Cyril's father was an Army officer, who had been stationed in South Africa. Both boys had as background memories or impressions the exotic, foreign, un-English landscapes from which they had been sent back to England to be schooled, Edens in contrast. At seven, Cyril adored his mother, "but lived otherwise in a world of his own." Eric, at the same age, loved only his mother and was already making up stories. Each boy was an insatiable, passionate reader, and the passion for reading—good and indifferent books, and books that Mrs. Vaughan Wilkes would certainly have disapproved of—was one of the strongest bonds between them. Studies, games, and the noisy conditions of school life hardly allowed for time enough during official waking hours for them to read as much as they liked; so each would take a book to bed at night to have it ready to begin reading as soon as he woke up, especially in the bright summer mornings: it meant a satisfying hour or two before the dormitory was ordered up at seven and down to the icy swimming bath. Blair had a vivid recollection (which he omitted from "Such, Such Were the Joys") of stealing into the silent dormitory one summer morning at four a.m. and making off with the copy of H. G. Wells's *The Country of the Blind* that Connolly, still asleep, had put beside his bed.

Wells was a favorite author; so were Kipling, Wodehouse, Swift, Shaw, and Thackeray, all of whom they read while at St. Cyprian's. Orwell's loyalty to these writers was virtually unwavering throughout his life. When, during the Second World War, he wrote an attack on Wells as a liberal optimist, he admitted to feeling like a "parricide." What he valued in Wells was not the later polemicist, but the novelist whose evocation of certain aspects—the anti-St. Cyprian's aspect, one might say—of life in England before the First World War recalled to Orwell comparable experiences of his own. He and Connolly would leave the school grounds and set out across the Downs to Beachy Head, or far along the plunging leafy roads that led deep into the Sussex countryside, to villages that might have figured in a Wells novel: Eastdean and Westdean and Jevington. They would pause in each, and buy from the little old lady who kept the village shop penny candies and various fizzy drinks: lemonade, cherry-ade, and cherry fizz. They might have been a world away from St. Cyprian's. (Perhaps it is worth noting here that in an area full of prep schools, St. Cyprian's was one of the few that let its boys wander about on the Downs alone or take prodigious walks by themselves into the countryside.) This was the plain, decent bread-and-sunlit world that Orwell recalled so nostalgically the further it receded from him; but even the visionary works, such as *Country of the Blind*, which he and Cyril found enthralling, left their mark upon him. Eventually he would write Wellsian novels of both kinds, in *Coming Up for Air* (a re-creation of the past) and *1984* (a vision of the future).

Passionate readers, the two boys were also apprentice authors. As we know, Orwell felt very early—at five or six—that he would grow up to be a writer. At nine, before coming to St. Cyprian's, Connolly was already inventing sketches in the manner of Stephen Leacock. At the school, both boys wrote playlets, skits, stories, light verse and serious, none of it (except by hindsight) promising that these clever schoolboys would become two of the outstanding writers of their generation. It was a further bond between them: manuscripts were exchanged and commented upon, and sometimes, not without calculation, were shown to Mrs. Vaughan Wilkes. It was a way of securing her favor. Approving of what they wrote (or at least, of what they allowed her to see), she found a place for it in her voluminous scrapbooks, and even in her memory—fifty years later she recalled that Blair had written poems while at school and drew attention to them.

So, too, when Eric came home for the holidays that summer, Mrs. Blair was pleased with the poems he showed her and encouraged him to write more. No mother whose son would have to support himself would want him to grow up to be a writer—too risky an enterprise—and it is unlikely that the thought even occurred to Mrs. Blair; but she was proud of Eric, and saw his writing as another aspect of his cleverness, further proof that he deserved, as she believed him to be getting, the best possible education.

In August the family went as usual to Cornwall for their holiday. It was a happy time for Eric, who did his best to forget the lines of translation he was supposed to bring back to St. Cyprian's, bathing, rock-climbing, playing with his sister Avril (to whom he would sometimes tell stories) and the children of family friends, also on holiday. Nostalgia doesn't need to be added to the experience to make it seem idyllic—as anyone who has spent childhood summers at the seashore can testify—and Avril is speaking matter-of-factly when she says, "Really we used to have a lovely time down there." But, of course, this was not to be the usual summer: on the fourth of August came the thrilling news that England was at war with Germany. Even for a six-year-old girl the event—as it reached her from the grown-ups—was memorable, and her first conscious memory of Eric dates from "the day war broke out . . . He was sitting cross-legged on the floor of my mother's bedroom, talking to her about it in a very grown-up manner. I was knitting him a school scarf . . . and I think the school colours were either dark blue and green or dark green and blue. Anyway, it was one of those terrible garments that starts off very narrow and in some mysterious manner suddenly becomes terribly wide." It is a vignette for which one is grateful; and she concludes it on a very Blair-like note: "I don't suppose he ever wore it."

We do not know what Eric was saying in his "very grown-up manner" about the war to his mother on August 4, 1914; we do know what he was writing about it soon after. It must be borne in mind that in August 1914 the vast majority of Englishmen (and their wives and children) were intensely, unquestioningly patriotic, proud, excited, and confident. The mood would find its most memorable expression in the war sonnets of Rupert Brooke. Three years and eight hundred thousand deaths later would come the poetry of disillusionment, from Siegfried Sassoon and Wilfred Owen and Robert Graves. Skepticism only gradually made itself felt, as the war that was to have been won by Christmas went on year after year; it was very different from the pacifism that a minority had professed from the very beginning. We are speaking now of a progression of thought among adults, not schoolboys; but schoolboys, especially those who are precocious and questioning in spirit, will often parallel and sometimes anticipate a change in thought in the world outside, an attitude that runs counter to and will finally overturn orthodoxy. Eric's skepticism about the war —of which we will presently quote a famous example—was still some years in the future. In August 1914 he was very much the patriotic schoolboy.

Patriotism inspired him to verse. Before the month was

out he had written a call to arms in three quatrains which he entitled

Awake! Young Men of England

Oh! give me the strength of the lion,
The wisdom of Reynard the Fox,
And then I'll hurl troops at the Germans,
And give them the hardest of knocks.

Oh! think of the War lord's mailed fist,
That is striking at England today;
And think of the lives that our soldiers
Are fearlessly throwing away.

Awake! oh you young men of England,
For if, when your Country's in need,
You do not enlist by the thousand,
You truly are cowards indeed.

Debased Kipling or Newbolt, it has no claim to literary interest except as the first published work by a famous author. But it is not without documentary interest—in a general way for what it tells of the England of 1914 and of the training and education a schoolboy of the upper middle class would receive that would make him want to write a poem such as this and equip him to write it; and in a particular way for what it tells of Eric Blair. The intense and rather primitive patriotism—very different from jingoism—that inspired this poem written at the beginning of the First World War was to prove an essential and ineradicable strain in his character.

His parents were delighted with the poem—it echoed their sentiments perfectly—and when the family returned to Roselawn, Mrs. Blair sent it off to the local newspaper, the *Henley and South Oxfordshire Standard*. It was published there on October 2, 1914, with the author identified as Master Eric Blair, the eleven-year-old son of Mr. R. W. Blair. By then he was already back at St. Cyprian's. His mother sent him copies of the paper, and he had the exhilarating experience of seeing his work in print for the first time. Mrs. Vaughan Wilkes, to whom he presented a copy, was generous with her praise. For a few days, at least, he was among her favorites. She determined that he should read the poem aloud to the assembled school, and accorded it a place of honor in the scrapbook.

But Eric was incapable of being in favor for long. Being out of favor was the more usual state of his relations with Mrs. Vaughan Wilkes. It was a relationship unsatisfactory to them both—more to him than to her, for he, after all, was only one among the hundred boys under her charge, while she had the power, as one of the boys noted in his diary, to make life "not worth living"—and it would have a decisive effect upon him while he was at school and for many years afterward. Simplifying the relationship to its irreducible element, one can say that he wanted her approval and never got it, she wanted his affection and never got it. The pattern was set in Eric's first weeks at the school and it continued so to his last day there. Years later Mrs. Vaughan Wilkes's chief memory of him would be of a cold and unloving little boy who stiffened in her arms when she tried to console him; and Orwell remembered her as the woman who, on his last day at school, though she shook his hand and called him Eric rather than the customary Blair, made it clear by the expression on her face and the tone of her voice that she did not approve of him.

All the recollections of the school that old St. Cyprianites have written agree that Mrs. Vaughan Wilkes played the dominating role. We know from Cyril Connolly that it was she "around whom the school revolved"; from Cecil Beaton that "she had more influence than all the masters put together." Gavin Maxwell, who was there a decade after Connolly, Beaton, and Blair, has described the school as "a strictly matriarchal culture and the existence of an assertive male at the summit would have been unthinkable." At the summit was "Mum." ("They loved their 'Mum,'" she recalled fondly, as an old lady, and some of them evidently did, to judge from the inscribed photographs they sent her when they went on to success in the great world.) She was headmistress, task-mistress, teacher, business woman, hostess to parents, social arbiter, dispenser of rewards and punishments (which were carried out by her husband). She was also very much a woman, in temperament, and in physique (the boys were nervously, gigglingly aware of her full bosom, and it explained their nickname for her of "Flip"). As the only woman in a world of males she queened it over them: the school became a court in which the boys vied for her favor. Queenly smiles alternated with queenly displeasure. Connolly's witty summary is extravagant-sounding but accurate: "On all the boys who went through this Elizabeth and Essex relationship she had a remarkable effect, hotting them up like little Alfa-Romeos for the Brooklands of life." Gavin Maxwell quotes this with approval, adding that he himself appeared to be "unhottable" and "unpromising material for her particular techniques." Orwell too brings in Elizabeth—seemingly the inevitable comparison—along with Essex and Raleigh and Leicester, about whom he had read very early. In short, she was a queen to be taken seriously, to whom it was impossible to be indifferent, and whose favor one wanted and courted.

(These memoirs, of course, were written years later by men who had known Mrs. Vaughan Wilkes only when they were schoolboys. One wonders how she would have appeared to her contemporaries, this woman in her early thirties whose husband was Headmaster of a boarding school and who was herself the mother of young children.

As formidable as a queen? It seems unlikely. We know that Mrs. Blair was favorably impressed, and she was not a woman to suffer pretensions gladly.)

One wanted to be in favor. This was as true of Blair as of any other boy in the school. Favorites were boys notable for Character, or Prettiness, or Intellectual Prowess, or Charm, or an Affectionate Nature, or they were boys from aristocratic families or families that were very rich. One of these qualities in itself was not usually enough: a combination was desirable. The more of them one had to offer, the more secure one's favor. Connolly had Intellectual Prowess, but decided he lacked Prettiness and as a substitute would work on Charm, which he did, successfully. Gavin Maxwell had a strong plus in being a grandson of the Duke of Northumberland, but it was canceled out by the minus of his not having an Affectionate Nature. Whereas the only other boy of his time at the school "whose parents had what Flip called, with varying intonation, 'a handle to their names' ... chanced to be a boy of such stupefying good looks as to present Flip with the irresistible combination—like certain TV advertised detergents he was the best on the market because he was the only one to have *two* ingredients *never* combined before." Then there were special categories: for example, pretty Scottish boys who could be dressed up in kilts for the Sunday parade into Eastbourne for church were almost certain candidates for favor.*

In the long run, the indispensable quality was an Affectionate Nature, or the ability to simulate it. Eric had Intellectual Prowess, but not much else to assist him to favor—his face was too flabby to qualify for Prettiness; his grown-

---

* A detail that surely contributed to Orwell's long-standing dislike of Scotland, and of books about "the Highland, Celtic, or romantic side of Scottish life." Scotland was where the parents of rich boys at St. Cyprian's went to shoot in the holidays and play the laird. Toward the end of his life, however, he overcame his dislike and went to live on the island of Jura, off the coast of Argyll.

up, sardonic manner, the remarks he delivered in a "flat, ageless voice," would not be thought Charming; and he couldn't pretend to an Affection he didn't feel. There was an art to playing the courtier that he never mastered. Connolly did better. So too did Beaton: "Generally I remained her angel, for I knew how to suck up to her and curry favour. I pretended to read books that might impress her with my good literary taste. I even mowed the school lawn, and painted Christmas cards for her. In fact, I became such a positive favourite that she often took me down into the town of Eastbourne on her domestic shopping visits, and gave me a mid-morning coconut cake."

Eric was not above trying to suck up, but he could never achieve the blend of enthusiasm and deference that was desirable, only a servility he was thoroughly ashamed of even as he persisted in it. Still, he had his periods of favor. At such times he was given the run of Mrs. Vaughan Wilkes's own library—there, at eleven, he read *Vanity Fair* for the first time; and he was allowed to serve at table when Old Boys and parents came to Sunday night supper— a privilege much sought after, for one could claim the scraps; as Connolly observed, the waiters were "in a position to stuff their pockets with potato salad when they took it out." In each instance, favor followed upon some conspicuous evidence of Intellectual Prowess, as when he wrote "Awake! Young Men of England," or verses to order to mark a special occasion, or when he won the Harrow History Prize, for which the school competed each year, or the prize that Mrs. Vaughan Wilkes awarded for "the 'best list' of books taken out of the library during the term." (Connolly won both prizes too. Their library lists were top-heavy with impressive books, such as Carlyle's *The French Revolution,* but when they were caught out with Compton Mackenzie's novel of Oxford life, *Sinister Street,* which Blair had brought back after a holiday, they were banished from favor, for it was thought to be rather "fast" and certainly not the sort of book a boy with Character would read.)

Intellectual Prowess won Eric his periods of favor, but they were imbued with the feeling of a transaction, something earned; and rather than liberating him, they drew him back even more tightly to the Exam, to the pressure to work—he would work harder at St. Cyprian's than he ever would again—to the hateful awareness of his status as a charity boy. He was brought back to the shaming reminders from Mrs. Vaughan Wilkes that his family were making sacrifices for him, so he must not be extravagant with the spending money his mother sent him (but which the school took charge of and doled out to him more meagerly, he felt, than to other boys), that failure in the Exam meant he would not be able to go to a Public School. So that his being in favor never was a comfortable thing; it was too closely related to the anxiety attached to his special status. Meanwhile he saw with jealous, cynical, and deprecating eyes that other boys—boys of an invincible stupidity who were never made to work and who would nonetheless pass as smoothly as strawberry fondant into a Public School—were being petted and favored for reasons having nothing to do with Intelligence, and everything (as he felt) with Money: their families, unlike his, were rich. All this was in accord with the spirit of the age—Vanity Fair brought up to date in the heyday of Empire, and until recently presided over by jolly, fat King Tumtum. The sons of the plutocracy thrived at St. Cyprian's much as their fathers did in the great Edwardian world, of which it too was the product. There were occasions when the plutocrats would descend upon the school, on the way to or from a weekend in Brighton, to visit their heirs. Money was made visible then: in the Daimlers in which they drove up, in their uniformed chauffeurs, and their wives resplendent in velvet and furs and smelling of Parma violets. While Mrs. Vaughan Wilkes welcomed these visiting parents—and such a visit ensured a boy's being in favor—Eric felt the more apart, resentful and cynical, for his own parents had no automobile and couldn't motor down to see him. He arrived at an economic explanation of affection and of society. The loved were rich; the unloved were not. Being rich was something over which you had no control: you were born rich, or not, and if not, were doomed to be unloved. Again, it was something over which you had no control: to be unloved was like having a birthmark or wetting your bed. Of course, if one did well in the Exam, or wrote patriotic verses, one would be praised, called "Old chap," be smiled upon—even so, one would be doing no more than was expected of one, the maximum achievement turning out to be equal to the minimum requirement: working as hard as possible, being as clever as possible, never letting up pressure for a moment, in order simply to survive on the fringes of that world that the beautiful, the well born, and the rich—but especially the rich—took for granted as their own, and to which they gained entry without effort. They had the credentials: it was a matter of what they were, as much as or even more than what they did. And what they were, Eric early decided, he by definition was not: accordingly, he was damned.

This was the side of Edwardian life—the snobbish, opulent, mammonistic side—that Orwell despised, and it was irrevocably joined in his mind with St. Cyprian's. But there was another side—all simplicity, good-heartedness, and decency, a Wellsian side, so to speak—that he would always value, and associate with growing up in Henley. Orwell, when writing of his childhood, does tend to reduce it to overemphatic blacks and whites—as in a grim fairy tale— and his self-portrait as an ugly, smelly, friendless schoolboy is a feverish exaggeration. But fairy tales have a truth of their own, and the polarization he imposes on his childhood is a close approximation of what he felt: black for St. Cyprian's and white for Henley. Or to adopt the conventions of a fairy tale: at school he was a scullery boy; at home, Prince Charming. In fact, this was to be literally the case during the Christmas holiday of 1914.

The Blairs, habituated as they were to a "nomadic" life in the colonial service in India, had little difficulty in uprooting themselves from one place and putting down roots in another. Returning to England, they had quite soon established themselves in Henley and afterwards in Shiplake, and were on friendly terms with a number of local families. Among these were the Nortons of Bellehatch Park, a country house in nearby Harpsden, where Mr. Blair, an ardent golfer, was secretary of the local golf club. Mr. Norton, who shared memories of India with Mr. Blair, was at that time a Member of Parliament and assistant Postmaster General; in 1916 he would be created Lord Rathcreedan. When Eric came home for the Christmas holiday in 1914, he learned that Mrs. Norton had proposed a family pantomime be put on at Bellehatch Park, and plans for it were already under way. The piece chosen was *Cinderella* in the version by Lady Bell. Eric was cast as Prince Charming—with his schoolboy's awkwardness and flat high voice he was not altogether persuasive in the role; Marjorie Blair played the cruel stepmother, Avril a page, the Norton brothers the ugly sisters, and their sister, a schoolmate of Marjorie's, Cinderella. Bellehatch Park was not a fairy tale castle, but a handsome old house whose earliest portions dated back to the Tudor period, and whose front had been refaced in stone and sash windows inserted in the eighteenth century. At the end of the large drawing room a curtain was hung and a stage improvised, and there the first performance of *Cinderella* took place before an audience of some fifty people—family, friends, and servants. It went so well that a second performance was given "for the public" in Harpsden Village Hall, and a third in the Henley Town Hall, which had been converted into a hospital for wounded soldiers. The latter occasion was very much in the spirit of the times—St. Cyprian's too would devise entertainments for patients in an army hospital near Eastbourne.

Cinderella 1914 sheds a further light on the quality of the Blairs' life in Henley, which does not appear to have been unduly circumscribed: and as for Eric at home, one has a sense of good times, of an absence of pressures and duties, of affection freely given rather than as the reward in a transaction.* This was the polar opposite, of course, from his life at St. Cyprian's, where the inexorable daily question would be, What had he done? Had he done what was expected of him? On the whole, yes, but he saw himself as "scholarship fodder," a drudge rather than a favorite of fortune, and his cynicism deepened. Connolly writes, "I was a stage rebel, Orwell a true one." Orwell, however, writing his own memoir of the school almost a decade after Connolly's, wants to make it clear that he was a rebel only by "force of circumstances." In any event, at St. Cyprian's, and for a dozen years afterwards, his was an entirely inward

---

* Jacintha Buddicom, a few years younger than Blair, and her brother and sister Prosper and Guiniver saw a good deal of him in Henley during his holidays from Eton. In 1971 Miss Buddicom published a charming memoir, "The Young Eric," in the symposium *The World of George Orwell*, edited by Miriam Gross, in which she set down her impression of Blair as she knew him more than a half century before during the period of their friendship, from 1915 through 1921. "I knew plenty of boys to compare him with," she writes, "and in such a comparison Eric would rate a very high score. He may not have been quite so good-looking as the handsomest, or have achieved a place in a cricket XI or rowing crew; but among all the boys we knew, Eric was one of the most interesting, the best informed, the kindest, the *nicest*." The total effect of Miss Buddicom's memoir is to evoke in its own particulars the impression of an essentially happy life away from school, which Avril Dunn has certainly emphasized in her recollections of her brother.

rebellion. Outwardly Eric conformed to the codes of the school, worked hard, did well in his studies, won prizes, lived up to expectations; the appropriate conclusion to all this was that in the winter and spring of 1916 he took the scholarship examinations for two of the great Public Schools.

Eton was his prime objective—to be awarded a scholarship there, to be one of the King's Scholars living in College.* But it was also the objective for scores of other boys from prep schools all over England with whom he would be competing for the very small number of places available. It was a sensible precaution, the Vaughan Wilkeses felt, to have an alternative to fall back on. For Eric the alternative decided upon was Wellington College, and that winter he sat the scholarship exam there successfully. Cause for rejoicing: it meant he no longer need fear the possibility of becoming a scruffy little clerk at forty pounds a year. But although a scholarship at Wellington was a good thing, one at Eton would be even better: the difference between being at the top and the very top. In the late spring, therefore, he traveled to Eton (accompanied by Mr. Vaughan Wilkes) to submit to an elaborate series of exams that went on for two and a half days. They included Greek verse composition, a French oral exam, and on the last day, a *viva* conducted in the Headmaster's division room in which he was questioned by three or four senior figures, drawn from among the Provost, Vice-Provost, Headmaster, Master in

* To live in College at Eton College is not the tautology it may at first appear to be. Eton College belongs to the category defined as (in Britain and Canada) "a private secondary school." But when it is a question of College at Eton, the dictionary is unhelpful: one enters the zone of Etonian usage. King's Scholars are housed in the oldest buildings of the school (College), some of which go back almost to the time of the Foundation (1442)—hence it is literally the case that King's Scholars are "in College." The other boys at the school, paying its expensive fees, live *outside* College, in varying proximity to it in the town of Eton (and so are known as Oppidans, "men of the town") in dormitory-like houses presided over by Housemasters.

College, and Fellows. It was a formidable experience for a thirteen-year-old, but Eric carried it off very well, a tribute to him and to the training of St. Cyprian's. Precisely how well he had done, however, he would not know until the list was published early in June, so there was a period of some anxiety. (Yet even that was lessened by his having Wellington safely in reserve.)

Traditionally, the list of boys who have qualified to become scholars at Eton is arranged in order of merit. Usually it contains more names than there are places immediately available. There are never more than seventy King's Scholars in College. No more than ten to thirteen, comprising an Election, are admitted at a time, and the size of an Election depends on how many places among the seventy are vacant. Thus, the boys at the top of the list are certain of admission; those further down must wait for a vacancy. As (and if) it occurs, they are given the opportunity to enter.

The list was published in the *Times* on June 10, 1916. Blair's name was fourteenth, not quite high enough to include him in the Election that would be entering College in the autumn. On the other hand, there was good reason to expect that, if he were patient, there would be a place for him later. It was a very creditable performance, and Mrs. Vaughan Wilkes declared a whole holiday for the school to celebrate his having done so well. Such occasions were usually reserved to mark her birthdays, so Eric was truly a conquering hero. And the event was all the more remarkable because only a few days before, the school, like all of England, had been plunged into mourning for the death of Lord Kitchener.

It is one of the curious aspects of Orwell's memoir of the school that he should make no specific references to his having been there during the first two years of the war. Perhaps because he chose to present St. Cyprian's as it embodied the aspect of Edwardian life he hated, and because that era was swept away in 1914, the life he evoked and condemned is largely prewar. Yet the war was pervasive in England: a boys' boarding school, intended to train future proconsuls, would not be indifferent to it. War heightened the physical discomfort of daily life: the food appreciably worsened, although some of the things Orwell complained of, the bluish milk and the rancid margarine, were common beyond St. Cyprian's—Mrs. Vaughan Wilkes complained of them too—and shortages of coal meant that the radiators in winter gave off even less heat than before. Character and Patriotism were at a high pitch. One had to make sacrifices. The boys drilled on the playing field; pinpointed the famous battles on maps in the classrooms; visited army hospitals and gave out Woodbines; listened in chapel as new names were added to the Roll of Honour—in all, 155 old St. Cyprianites would serve in the First World War, an impressive total from a small school that had been in existence only a dozen years. It was in such circumstances that the secret guilt of a generation of survivors was implanted: the schoolboys who came of age too late to take part in the war in which a generation of older brothers was decimated.

"Your country needs YOU"—this was the message of the recruiting poster designed by Alfred Leete in 1914; above the message appeared a luxuriantly mustached, stern proconsular face, too famous to be identified: the face of Kitchener of Khartoum, one of the great heroes of the late Victorian epoch. In 1914, at the age of sixty-four, he was brought into the government, as a larger-than-life-size idol above the demands of petty politics, to become Secretary of War. His performance was woefully inadequate, and, as his biographer observes, "Kitchener's power to give unity to the Government vanished when his colleagues lost confidence in his judgement. But he continued to the last to give unity to the country, and to provide a façade behind which soldiers and politicians, Liberals and Conservatives, and the rival advocates of an eastern and of a western strategy conducted their disputes and intrigues." It was the façade, encrusted with fame, going back to the great days of Empire, that the vast majority of English knew and revered and presently were to mourn. On the fifth of June, 1916, Kitchener sailed on the cruiser *Hampshire*, bound for Archangel, and beyond that for the Russian Front, which he had been invited to visit by the Czar.

> At approximately 7:40 P.M., when about a mile and a half off Marwick Head, the *Hampshire* struck a mine which had been laid by the German submarine U.75 . . .
> It heeled over to starboard, settled down by the head, and sank within a quarter of an hour. Some dozen survivors only reached a wild and inhospitable coast with cliffs rising sheer out of the sea; and they gave no coherent account of Kitchener's movements during the few moments which elapsed between the explosion and the sinking of the cruiser. Kitchener, who was seen by one survivor in the gunroom flat immediately after the explosion, was extremely sensitive to cold; he probably kept on his heavy greatcoat and choked to death among the first in the angry waters. Fitzgerald's body [he was Personal Military Secretary to the War Lord] was washed ashore, but Kitchener's was devoured by the Atlantic.
> The news reached London on the morning of 6 June and was published at about midday. The journey to Russia had been a closely-guarded secret; and a sense of awed numbness gripped the land.

The event did not pass unnoticed at St. Cyprian's. Melancholy it might be, but how rich in those elements of Character and Patriotism that the school exalted, and Mrs.

Vaughan Wilkes made it a set topic, to be dealt with in prose or verse.

In July Connolly was writing to his mother: "I enclose a poem (?) I made up about Lord Kitchener a few nights ago. I got the chap who is considered the best poet to critisise (I know I've spelt that word wrong) it, which he did on the other side. He did a very good poem which he sent to a local paper where they took it . . . Think that there is only one more Sunday here!!"

The "best poet" was, of course, Blair. At the bottom of the page on which Connolly had written out his poem, he had added:

>Stern Criticism Please
>Dear Sir   I think your poem (?) is

Blair, ready to "critisise," turned the page over and ignored the parenthetical question mark. He thought the poem "dashed good." ("My dear Blair!!" Connolly interjected, "I am both surprised and shocked.") And while he took notice of some repetition and ambiguity, he found the scansion excellent, the epithets mostly well chosen, and the poem as a whole "neat, elegant, and polished."

It is unlikely that either of the thirteen-year-old poets was deeply moved by the death they were asked to commemorate, although Mrs. Vaughan Wilkes was very good at getting the boys "to mind" about Kitchener. But the poems they produced reveal some interesting contrasts. Connolly's is much the more romantic, musical, and melancholy. The particular circumstances of the event, death by drowning in the North Sea, struck a responsive chord that outweighed other considerations:

> *No honoured church's funeral hath he,*
> *The silent hero of a nation's fame*

No drone of muffled drums can greet his soul
No last post blown in sadness o'er the sea.
The time-worn rocks alone can mark his tomb,
His epitaph the roar of breaking waves.
No human mourner follows in his train
The wailing seagull chants his death song through.
None but the lonely curlews on the moor
Bewail a mighty empire's tearful loss.
   "Bury him not in an abbey shrine
   Midst tablets of stone and coffins of pine
   But let him be where no light can shine
   And the north sea waves rush on."

Perhaps what is most striking about this mournful exercise is the absence of even one perfunctory allusion to those qualities summed up in Character and Patriotism. It was as though, in writing his poem, Connolly had held himself aloof from the code of St. Cyprian's; it would be difficult to find an uplifting moral lesson here. By contrast, Blair's "Kitchener" is much more the official poem, as was his earlier "Awake! Young Men of England." The particular circumstances and setting of the death are not alluded to, only the unexceptionable public sentiments they have inspired:

No stone is set to mark his nation's loss,
No stately tomb enshrines his noble breast
Not e'en the tribute of a wooden cross
   Can mark this hero's rest.

He needs them not, his name ungarnished stands,
Remindful of the mighty deeds he worked,
Footprints of one, upon time's changeful sands,
   Who n'er his duty shirked.

Who follows in his steps no danger shuns,
Nor stoops to conquer by a shameful deed,

> *An honest and unselfish race he runs,*
> *From fear and malice freed.*

How many of the qualities that were valued at St. Cyprian's Blair has managed to include in his last five lines: never to shirk one's duty, to be brave and honorable, honest and unselfish, and free from cowardice and malice—for the second time within the month he had done the school proud. He himself was sufficiently proud of the poem to send it to the *Henley and South Oxfordshire Standard*, where it was published on Friday, July 21, 1916. For this second appearance in print he was no longer "Master Eric Blair" but simply E. A. Blair.

A copy of the published poem went as by right to Mrs. Vaughan Wilkes and so to her scrapbook. But there is no reason to think, therefore, that its sentiments represent an act of calculation. It is true that Connolly tells us that Blair rejected "the war, the Empire, Kipling, Sussex, and Character," and he quotes from a conversation in which Blair said to him, "Of course, you realise, Connolly, that, whoever wins this war, we shall emerge a second-rate nation." Originally, Connolly placed the conversation at St. Cyprian's; but he has since come to believe that he dated it too early, and that it belongs to a year or two later, when he and Blair were at Eton. This would be consistent with what is known of Blair as a fifteen-year-old—by then his cynicism, as it expressed itself in conversation, had become open and pronounced. It is also consistent with the progress, or lack of progress, of the war and its effect upon public opinion in England. In the early summer of 1916, when the boys of St. Cyprian's (and other schools) were writing their tributes to Kitchener, confidence had not yet been shaken: the campaign along the Somme was in its opening phase—surely it would lead to victory! In the autumn, when the campaign ended, victory was no nearer than before, and there had been four hundred thousand British casualties. The old assurances, confidences, and slogans began to be questioned. "Your country needs YOU" under the mustachioed face of Kitchener had been sufficient in 1914 to recruit an army; now it was deemed necessary to conscript one.

Having said this, it is not an injustice to Blair, at thirteen, to say that he would have had to be even more precocious than he was, more prescient and more concerned with world affairs, to have allowed the war to dominate his thoughts in the summer of 1916. In fact, and as one might expect, he was chiefly taken up with the problem of his own immediate future. His situation at St. Cyprian's had dramatically altered. No longer would there be lines of translation to take home for the holiday; no longer need he fear the banana-sized silver pencil, or humiliating reminders of his status, or any of the other devices the Vaughan Wilkeses had resorted to in urging him forward to his goal. The goal had been achieved. Whatever he had been before his success in the exams, he was now undeniably an object of value, proof positive that the school got results, and the Vaughan Wilkeses would have been content to have him remain there until a place became available for him at Eton. But he was already assured of a place at Wellington: should he not take it up immediately? It was a decision to be made by his parents, though his own wishes would not be ignored. For him it was simple: he wanted to be off to Public School at the earliest opportunity—therefore, Wellington. The Blairs recognized the greater prestige that would be conferred upon him as an Etonian; at the same time they had to take into account a practical consideration. The expense, even at reduced fees, of Eric's continuing at St. Cyprian's while waiting for Eton would not be negligible in a family budget already strained. (Wartime inflation was affecting Mr. Blair's fixed pension. In the latter part of 1915 the family had moved from Shiplake back to Henley, to a semi-detached house in St. Mark's Road. This new house, though comfortable, was noticeably smaller than Roselawn, and so may have appeared to Eric as "the sacrifice" that was being made on his behalf by his parents. He was twelve years old then—impressionable and surrounded by the sons of the top three percent; at such an age and in such circumstances the "step down" from Roselawn—say from the top five percent to the top seven percent—would have greater weight with him than the undoubted fact that in St. Mark's Road the Blairs were still living better than the majority of Englishmen.) In the end, the practical consideration prevailed. Mr. Blair wrote to Vaughan Wilkes to say that they had decided Eric should take up his scholarship at Wellington at the end of the year.

In December his last day at St. Cyprian's finally arrived—and it was truly his last day, for he would never, except in memory, return there again. Decked out in a new silk old school tie, he presented himself to Mrs. Vaughan Wilkes to say goodbye. She shook his hand, called him "Eric," congratulated him, wished him well. It ought to have been a happy moment, and yet . . . In her face and expression, Orwell tells us, he read a message of irony and condescension: that he had not been worthy of her, that he was not truly the right sort. As for Mrs. Vaughan Wilkes, she remembered that she had not been able to "reach him," and she was aware that he was glad to be leaving. Orwell concludes his account with what is virtually an aria to Failure, the word itself turning up five times in a twenty-one word sentence. He had failed in the past; he would fail in the future—that was the message he believed he took away with him from his prep school. In fact, he had succeeded. He had got from St. Cyprian's exactly what it was intended that he should get. The school had fulfilled its part of the bargain, and so had he. The explanation for the apparent discrepancy between what Orwell felt and Blair did is simple and paradoxical: that for Orwell, to succeed in the way that St. Cyprian's defined success was to fail. It was a discovery that Blair himself would make and act upon belatedly, more than a decade after he had said goodbye for the last time to "Mum."

PART TWO

ETON

NINETEEN-SEVENTEEN PROVED TO BE A YEAR OF DECIsive change not only for Eric but for all the Blairs. The war was in its third year, more pervasive and destructive in its effect than had seemed possible a year or two before, touching them all. That England might be defeated was unthinkable; but victory was still not in sight, and the prospect lengthened gloomily. In these trying circumstances the reaction of the elder Blairs was characteristic: they felt they must do what they could to help. The idea of service to the state was strong in the family, though not at all strident: simply, it was what one did in time of crisis, what one's forebears had done in the past, what one's children would do in the future. This same subdued but unwavering concept of patriotism was ingrained in Orwell himself, no matter how much he might wish to discount it, and it would emerge strongly in 1939.

His father, sixty years old in 1917, might permissibly have cheered from the sidelines as a civilian patriot. Instead, he decided to enlist, and it suggests something about England's circumstances in the third year of the war that he should have been accepted for duty. That September he was commissioned a second lieutenant and so became, according to family tradition, the oldest subaltern in the British army, looking after mules in a camp near Marseilles.*

---

* Or so Orwell later described his father's military career to Richard Rees,

However inglorious his job, the important point was that Mr. Blair in France was helping the war effort; and so, presently, was his wife. Before the end of the year Mrs. Blair moved the household from Henley to London, to a flat in Cromwell Crescent, Earl's Court, and she and Marjorie went to work for the duration of the war in the Ministry of Pensions, which had set up offices in the Tate Gallery. Avril, aged nine, was placed in a boarding school in Ealing; Eric by then was already in College at Eton.

Earlier in the year he had spent nine weeks, the Lent term, at Wellington College, where he was a Scholar of the school and lived in Blücher dormitory. He had come to Wellington with high expectations, envisaging a freer and more private life than he had known at St. Cyprian's—a cubicle of one's own where one could make cocoa at night, as in a Public School novel—but the reality, all austerity and restrictions, had disappointed him. The school, for its part, found Blair something of a disappointment too, for his performance as a Scholar was not of the high caliber that might have been expected. There were thirty-one boys in his Form, Upper III A, and he was placed a merely adequate thirteenth. But he had already embarked on a career at school of slacking off, doing as little work as was sufficient to get safely through, but no more: a reaction, Orwell later felt, to the unremitting pressure to which he had been subjected at St. Cyprian's.

That winter of 1917, the third winter of the war, was a time when an increasing number of older boys at Eton were leaving to enlist in the army. More places than usual came available in College. In March Blair was informed that he could now join the Election of 1916, if he so wished. He did not hesitate: Eton the unknown was preferable to

---

and very likely he drew upon it in *Coming Up for Air* for George Bowling's unheroic wartime duty—to guard a few cans of supplies in the south of England.

the Wellington he knew. Nor did his mother hesitate, even though it meant that for the second time in four months Eric would have to be outfitted, money would have to be found, sacrifices made.

Blair, K.S. (King's Scholar), entered College in May 1917, a month before his fourteenth birthday. His outfit included the famous cutaway Eton jacket, or "bumfreezer," prescribed for boys under five feet four inches; and the toga-like short black gown with interior pocket prescribed for Collegers. In appearance he was still very much the schoolboy. George Wansbrough, a member of his Election, speaks of his "extraordinarily plump cheeks," and Denys King-Farlow, who was also in the Election, of the "large, rather fat face, with big jowls, a bit like a hamster" and his "slightly protruding light china-blue eyes." His adolescent growing period, from which he would emerge conspicuously tall, was a year or so in the future. His voice, just beginning to change, was still uncertain. But there was only certainty in what he said and in his manner of saying it. King-Farlow, who had had an experience similar to Blair's —he too was a latecomer to the Election, entering College in May after two terms at Winchester—asked him at one of their first encounters what he felt about switching to Eton. Blair replied immediately, "Well, it can't be worse than Wellington. That really was perfectly bloody." Which was not the way a thirteen-year-old was expected to talk in 1917, and King-Farlow thought it "not quite right," although he found it tonic as well as slightly unsettling. To be outspoken and cynical became Blair's Etonian style. More than forty years later King-Farlow remembered that "He'd been the first person I had ever heard running down his own father and mother." This was not the done thing either: though it might be what one felt, one did not put it into such blunt words. But Blair continued to say what he pleased, undoubtedly aware of the effect that he was making, and what he had to say was often at odds with the pieties and received opinions of Eton and England in 1917.

The prevailing mood was still deeply patriotic, conformist, and attuned to gallantry. Not jingoistic precisely; still, it did not allow for a dissenting view. The year before, Edward Lyttelton, who had been Headmaster of Eton since 1905, was eased out of his position after saying he thought it monstrous automatically to depict the Germans as beasts. He even went so far as to declare "that the only ultimate object of sane policy must be to abolish war altogether." For this he was denounced in the popular press. To spare the school a continuing scandal he offered his resignation to the Governing Body, which rather cravenly accepted it, and in April 1916 he departed. He was not unhappy to go: "It is a huge relief," he remarked, "being quit of that dull nightmare organisation, in which I have come to believe less and less." Under the new regime—of C. A. Alington, who happened to be married to Edward Lyttelton's half sister—the news of Eton that figured in the press was of a more reassuring and conventional kind. Thus, when the traditional celebrations of the Fourth of June were curtailed in a spirit of saving money for the war effort, the *Times* reported that "Eton, like other parts of the country, practices economy, if only *pour encourager les autres*." But on a more serious, and admirable, level, tragically so, was the example Eton afforded of patriotism in action, as its young officers went up the line to death.

Since the mid-nineteenth century—that is, since the beginning of the great days of Empire—"Patriotism and the readiness to sacrifice one's life for one's country had been the quality to which Eton had paid especial—and what to its critics might appear exaggerated—honour." Christopher Hollis, a contemporary of Blair's in College from whose history of the school we are quoting, goes on to point out that while the late Victorian "code of patriotism" prescribed that "every English gentleman must at all times be prepared to die for his country, it was not expected that very many of them would in fact have to do so. In the Victorian security no one dreamed of even the possibility of catastrophes such as we have lived through in our days." 1914 changed all that, and as Hollis sums up, "Eton proved that her boasts of patriotism were not insincere. 5,687 Etonians served in the war. Of these, 1,160 were killed and 1,467 were wounded; 13 won the Victoria Cross, 548 won the Distinguished Service Order and 744 won the Military Cross."

It was against this wartime background that Blair was to spend his first two years at Eton. The patriotic theme was not new to him, of course: he had heard it at home; as an eight-year-old he had worn a sailor suit and been a member of the Navy League; at St. Cyprian's the theme had been sounded continuously. But there was a significant difference between being made to care about the death of Kitchener by Mrs. Vaughan Wilkes and being at a school where boys only a few years older than oneself whom one saw every day—heroes of the playing fields—were suddenly going off to fight for their country and perhaps to die for it. It was as though the fantasies of St. Cyprian's were being acted out at Eton. The impressions that these heroic departures and gallant sacrifices made upon the younger boys who were left behind were powerful at the time, perhaps even more so later in retrospect. Long after peace had come, a sense of having avoided but also missed a dangerous yet fulfilling experience would haunt many of those who were at school during the war. They heard the names of the dead read aloud in chapel; new and younger and more familiar names were added to the list each week, and were not forgotten and left a residue of quite irrational guilt. Years later Orwell said to Richard Rees that "his generation must be marked forever by the humiliation of not having taken part" in the First World War. Rees comments sensibly, "He had, of course, been too young to take part. But the fact that several million men, some of them not much older than himself, had been through an ordeal which he had not shared was apparently intolerable to him." It was not until 1937, by his heroic behavior during the Spanish Civil War, that Orwell erased this humiliation which had had its inception at Eton in 1917.

The background, then, can be defined by a particular moment in time—England at war. But the foreground, the run of everyday events, was peculiarly timeless—unchanging Eton, with its customs, traditions, and tribal rites, which have been described in so many novels and memoirs. Orwell himself wrote very little about Eton, perhaps because as a subject, unlike St. Cyprian's, it couldn't be made to serve his didactic intention: there is no full-scale, carefully wrought, deeply felt essay comparable to "Such, Such Were the Joys." Of the little he wrote on the subject, much was critical and depreciatory. But in a piece toward the end of his life, "Forever Eton," he singles out as the great virtue of the school its "tolerant and civilized atmosphere which gives each boy a fair chance of developing his individuality." The truth of this observation would seem confirmed by the noticeable variety among Etonians as they come of age: there is no prescribed or approved mold in which the schoolboy is cast to type. And yet, paradoxically, even as he is becoming an individual, he is also becoming, unmistakably and for the rest of his life, an Etonian. Our intention is to see how the process operated for Eric Blair, who, as Orwell, might be justly described, along with John Maynard Keynes and Harold Macmillan, as one of the three most famous members of College in this century.

In 1917, apart from the King's Scholars, there were approximately nine hundred other boys at the school. These latter were the Oppidans, who paid high fees and lived in one or another of the several Houses that were owned by the school but that were run, almost as private domains, by the housemasters. Oppidans, especially as they came fresh from prep schools, tended to feel superior to Collegers—or, as they called them, "Tugs"—whose families might or might not be in straitened circumstances, but almost certainly belonged to a class no lower than middle-middle-middle. It was just as certain that any boy who had had the sort of education that qualified him for a scholarship in College would have attended a prep school. (Truly uncommon would have been a working-class boy from a state school in College—where would he have got sufficient Latin and Greek to win a scholarship?) But Blair's case had its special Blairian aspect. Again, as at St. Cyprian's, he felt economically deprived and put upon. Collegers, regardless of financial background, were charged fees of some twenty-five pounds a year. Blair resented this: he told King-Farlow the fees were "exorbitant." He knew his family was having to make sacrifices to augment his scholarship. The full cost of a boy in College at the time was about a hundred pounds a year, which was much less than Oppidans would pay; nevertheless, it was a fair part of Mr. Blair's pension. There is little doubt that Eric was not as well off as most (though not all) of his contemporaries in College, that he had less pocket money and fewer luxuries, that he continued to wear trousers long after they were shiny and flapping above his ankles, and that at home money would sometimes be in short supply, literally so. (Once, when he had been home on a visit, Marjorie Blair had to borrow money from Ruth Pitter for Eric's ticket back to Eton from London. That was on a Sunday, and the next day, when the banks were open, the loan was repaid—but by then Eric was gone, and the need to have borrowed so small a sum of money must have left its impression upon a nature abnormally sensitive to such things.)

Looked at objectively, there was nothing in his parents' or his own situation to deprive him of the usual day-to-day life in College, and there is no evidence that he was deprived, especially since the fees the Blairs paid included "tuition, lodging, board and recreational facilities." *

Subjectively, it might be a different matter. Collegers had a kind of freemasonry or snobbery of their own as "intellectuals"—from which eminence they might look down on Oppidans. On the whole, they regarded one another as equals, paying little attention to the question of how much money one's people had. There is no reason to believe they condescended to Blair, nor did he ever say so. But against the pride he might feel in being a Colleger, there appears in his case to have been the shame (as he felt it) of being a "Tug," and it continued to rankle long after he left Eton. Richard Rees, who had been an Oppidan, tells how "One day in 1948, when I had known him for eighteen years, I incautiously used the word 'Tug,' and although he was too polite to say anything he winced as if I had trodden on his tenderest corn."

It was a question of temperament. There were boys in College—Cyril Connolly, for example, who came on from St. Cyprian's the next year—who had friends among the Oppidans. There were Oppidans every bit as "intellectual" as Collegers, sometimes more so—the very remarkable lit-

---

* Food, from a boy's point of view, tended to be meager, deliberate "underfeeding," Orwell later decided, and even more conspicuous at Eton than at St. Cyprian's. All the Collegers took breakfast and midday dinner together in the College Hall, and also supper at eight o'clock, except that for that meal the Sixth Form and Liberty (the form immediately junior) dined apart. The largest, the last solid, meal of the day, was at noon. There was a supper of soup or fried fish, or bread and cheese, with water to drink, at eight. Under the circumstances tea tended to be the grandest and most idiosyncratic meal. For this the boys would buy, were expected to buy, supplies of their own (eggs, sausages, sardines, buns, biscuits, cakes of varied hues and flavors) to add to the official bread and butter that was doled out to them, and they would often pool their resources.

erary magazine, *The Eton Candle,* was an entirely Oppidan enterprise. In the "tolerant and civilized atmosphere" of that ancient Public School much was possible. But venturing among Oppidans was a possibility—remote, indeed—that Blair chose not to explore. He felt safer among the members of his Election, and the story of his life at Eton virtually is the story of his life in College.

His Election, as the youngest, lived in Chamber, a hall in the oldest part of College. Then as now, wooden stalls, austere enough for a monastery, lined a wide uncarpeted passage. On one side a row of stalls was interrupted for a common room of sorts, open to the passage and furnished with some wooden chairs and a broad table in front of a fireplace; then the row resumed. Each boy was given a stall of his own—to that extent there was the illusion of privacy. But these stalls rose only to the height of a man and were open at the top; voices floated in from anywhere along the row; eyes peeped over the partitions; effectively one lived in public. Stretched out on one's folding bed, or sitting at one's desk—the whole furnishing of a stall—one could see, looking up, the massive carved beams high overhead; closer, one could read in the wood paneling countless initials incised by boys of all those preceding generations of Collegers. It was a historic and uncomfortable setting into which Blair fitted without difficulty; his joining the Election late made no significant difference.

On his first day there was a ceremonial beginning. In accordance with Etonian tradition he presented himself to the Provost to be gowned, and as he knelt, he was adjured to be good, docile, and truthful. This was the ideal. Later that same day he descended to the real: it provided the more vivid memory. Long afterwards he told his friend Mabel Fierz that he had had to bat at cricket, and, as he did badly, he was thrashed, and felt humiliated.

This would not have been an auspicious beginning, for

at Eton, as at any other school, to be good at games was an asset, but it did not usher in a season of humiliations such as he had suffered in his first weeks at St. Cyprian's. By now he had had long experience of being away at school—homesickness was not a problem, and he was poised and intelligent enough to hold his own nicely in the maze of Etonian traditions, customs, rules, regulations, codes, and disciplines. Inevitably he would be introduced to the punishments administered by Sixth Form, for pretexts were easily found, and "the Colleger had to expect to be beaten a number of times during his first two years." But this was traditional, the common fate of all members of the lowest Election, however rich they might be or whatever handles might attach to their names. If Blair was beaten, he had no reason to feel singled out or victimized. The same held true for "Chamber Singing," another tradition he was made to participate in soon after his arrival. For this, Collegers assembled in the common room in Chamber to listen to the new boys as one by one they sang solo, standing on the table in front of the fireplace. Blair's choice was an American song of the last century, "Riding Down to Bangor," and while his performance was not notably melodious, he was spared the indignity of having books thrown at him, which sometimes happened when the audience grew restive.

These details, trivial in themselves, point toward an important conclusion: Blair, joining the 1916 Election, would now have the experience of belonging to a community. The fourteen boys of the Election were a coherent society of their own, existing within a larger society, College, which in its turn was part of a still larger society, Eton. And beyond Eton was the world, of which Blair in these wartime years knew very little—hardly more than his mother's London flat and sometimes in holidays the golf club at Parkestone near Bournemouth where his uncle was secretary and with whom he and Avril would be sent to stay. ("There was really nothing to do except go to the local roller skating rink, where we both learnt to rollerskate incredibly badly. Neither of us were interested in it in the least," Avril remembers. "That was on wet days. On fine days we used to walk over the golf-course, which abounded in lizards, and try to catch them. The way of catching a lizard was to put your foot on it, so that the lizard was firmly held under your instep. Then it was possible to pick it up—rather gingerly, because they bit. Our chief nourishment out of doors was picking up pine-cones, of which there were any amount there, and knocking the seeds out and eating them. They tasted horribly of turpentine, but we quite liked them.")

In that world beyond Eton he felt essentially a stranger. For community, for the sense of belonging, he returned to the Election, sharing in its pleasures and difficulties, its grievances and rewards. The hierarchical structure of College—a ladder up which one moved in a group—helped to strengthen the communal bond. On the lowest rung were the boys in Chamber—as we have seen, Blair's Election, at the time he entered College. On the highest rung were Sixth Form, consisting of the top ten boys, and Liberty, the next six. The boys in Chamber had to do fagging, to which they were summoned by long, drawn-out cries of "Here," rather than "Boy," as in Oppidan Eton, where fagging was generally more rigorous. (The only excuse for not replying to a summons was that one was not dressed, or was getting dressed. Certain boys, figures of Eton mythology, are said to have kept themselves in a permanent state of semi-dress to avoid fagging.) Throughout the early years one had the terrors of "wantings," those fateful moments when a younger boy would be summoned by the Sixth Form, perhaps (if lucky) merely to be given instructions, information, or a verbal reprimand; or (if unlucky) to be beaten, sometimes for a specific offense, sometimes for his general good. Of course, as one went up the ladder and one's Election moved toward seniority, roles were reversed: the beaten became the beaters.

In this miniature world there were punishments and rewards; and for some the rewards were so alluring that the world beyond the school couldn't begin to compare. This latter group comprised the romantics and nostalgics for whom post-Etonian life was a long anti-climax. But Blair was an ironist: his commitment to the community was never to become a passion (least of all in retrospect); he was too cautious, or sensible, for that, and again it was a matter of temperament.

AN ETON COLLEGE ELECTION CONSTITUTES, BY DEFINITION, a kind of junior intellectual elite; and the 1916 Election is recognized to have been outstanding, there and afterwards, as its members dispersed into the world beyond Eton. Orwell apart, the other members of the Election went on to distinguish themselves variously as barristers, businessmen, civil servants, teachers, and scholars. Choosing examples only from the latter categories, we discern in Runciman, K.S., the present Sir Steven Runciman, the historian of Byzantium and the Crusades; Mynors, K.S., Sir Roger Mynors, the Professor of Latin at Oxford; and Longden, K.S., the late R. P. Longden, Headmaster of Wellington (where Blair had spent a single term), who was killed when a bomb dropped on the school during the Second World War.

Blair was on amicable terms with his Election as a whole and was more closely associated with its dominating members—he was not one himself—yet he gave the impression of being somewhat apart from them, of going his own way, not quite a heretic, but not an enthusiast either. In that promising company he was not one for whom great claims were made or from whom great things were expected. There were boys who were brighter than he, who were better at games, who were better-looking. Inwardly, in that highly competitive world, it may well have rankled.* Outwardly he maintained a judicious, sardonic calm, independent of the fads and fashions of the moment, and of those intimate friendships that are traditionally a part of schoolboy existence. Indeed, intimacy is precisely the note that will be absent in his relationships—at Eton and afterwards—until his marriage to Eileen O'Shaughnessy in 1936. What is difficult to say, of course, is whether he enjoyed this position, or whether he adopted it as a form of self-protection, or both.

Self-protection was linked closely to a dislike or fear of self-disclosure, as well as to a certain pleasure in secretiveness and mystification. Even to his friends he was something of an enigma: this was as true at Eton as later. One member of the 1916 Election writes, "I knew Eric Blair well at Eton for four and a half years." Then he adds the familiar, seemingly inevitable reservation: "I was not a close friend of his; I do not remember that any of us were. That

* On the "inward and invisible sense of being physically unattractive which worried Orwell throughout his life," Malcolm Muggeridge, a friend in his later years, makes the following comment: "In actual fact he was by no means ill-favoured, and possessed of great charm; women, perhaps even more than men, found him appealing, but nothing would cure him of the conviction that his body was ill-proportioned and graceless. The feeling may well have been due to his illness; without any doubt the tuberculosis from which he died was gnawing away at him long before he admitted to himself or others that he was sick. There is also the fact that, at a school like Eton with its strong homosexual climate, a boy who is considered unattractive from that point of view may well become morbidly conscious of lacking physical charm. I once asked Cyril Connolly, who was a contemporary of Orwell at his preparatory school and at Eton, about this, and he agreed that my supposition might be correct. Orwell, he said, was regarded as being decidedly not pretty."

does not mean he was unpopular, or that most of us did not like him; we did, but . . . he soon developed a kind of aloofness which left him on good terms with everyone without being the close friend of any." The note is sounded repeatedly by his contemporaries at Eton, even though, as one of them remarks, "We in the Election had the best chance of knowing him, as we were with him every day." But proximity did not make for intimacy: "Never an intimate friend or confidant"; "I knew Blair fairly well"; "I was never a close friend though I knew him quite well"; "We were all perfectly friendly and I don't think anyone disliked him. He and I were not close but had perfectly friendly relations."

George Wansbrough, a member of the Election who became Captain of the School (and in adult life, a Director of the Bank of England), remembers him as "obviously a very different type of boy. . . . The rest of us came from typical middle class professional homes with conventional outlooks. Eric was very reticent about his family background. He made no mention of his father, but he talked a lot about his Uncle [presumably this was his mother's brother, the manager of the golf club] who seemed to discuss matters with him in a very much more adult manner than the parents of the rest of us would have done." But in fact, Blair's background essentially was no different from that of other boys in the Election. His parents came from the same world of civil servants, rectors, barristers, and businessmen as did the parents of his schoolmates, though the Blairs' place in that world was admittedly dimmed by lack of notable success and money; they were at the circumference rather than the center. Blair's reticence, his sardonic enjoyment in keeping things in the dark—it seems extraordinary that he should not have mentioned his father's being in France—encouraged the notion that he was somehow different. At another school this might have made for difficulties; at Eton he got on very well.

AN EPISODE IN WHICH HE FIGURED WITHIN A MONTH OF HIS arrival in College extended his reputation beyond his own Election. Christopher Hollis, in the Election two years senior to Blair's, first heard of him as a successful practitioner of voodoo magic. As the "tale" was reported to Hollis at the time and recounted by him years later in *A Study of George Orwell*, Blair had taken a dislike to a boy in Hollis's Election for being noisy, especially at meals, and decided he must be punished. The boy, whom Hollis calls "Johnson major," was Leslie Runciman, the son of the Liberal politician and shipping magnate. He had no knowledge of Blair's existence—the "fags," who comprised the lowest Election, were generally an indistinguishable blur to the older boys. Runciman was not only noisy but also famous for having led a charmed life—during his first two years he had managed to avoid most of the beatings that were the lot of new boys in College. Blair, so Hollis heard, had decided to resort to a counter-charm. Lacking wax, he carved an image of Runciman in soap, which he stuck full of pins and placed under the mirror in his stall. It was only a matter of time before the magic would take effect. On Friday, Runciman's younger brother, Steven, who was also a member of the lowest Election and would become as close a friend as Blair would allow during his years at Eton, told his brother of the existence of the juju, and the curse it had set in motion. On Monday, and again on Tuesday, Runciman major, who had won for himself "something of a reputation of being magically protected by the gods," was summoned by the Sixth Form and beaten for various infractions.

Blair received the news with a "smile of wry triumph," so Hollis heard, and he concludes the tale, "That evening just before lights out . . . the soapen image slipped into a basin full of hot water and was dissolved. Blair did not re-erect it on its bracket. It was a symbol, we comforted the damaged elder brother, that the jealous gods were no longer athirst and the curse had been expiated."

The story as Hollis heard it and the power it reflects are somewhat misleading. The truth is not without its Byzantine aspect. For, according to Sir Steven Runciman, it was he who carved the juju from the soap, with his friend Blair acting as assistant mage, and their chosen victim was not Leslie Runciman—whose fall from grace was a fortuitous coincidence—but another boy to whom they had taken a dislike. The juju was carved, pins were stuck into it, spells were cast. Then the two magicians waited for results, which were not long in coming: the next day the chosen one fell and broke his arm. This proof of their magical powers so intimidated them that they decided to conduct no further experiments. But in a veiled (and perhaps threatening) way, the story was related by Steven to his older brother: would his turn be next? And indeed it was: the two successive beatings, coming so promptly, could be made to seem magically induced and apparently were. It was a feat neither magician had counted on, and Steven, as a younger brother, thought it prudent to yield to Blair a major share of the credit. Thereafter he enjoyed a certain cachet. As the incident filtered down to Hollis it convinced him that "Blair must be 'an odd fellow' and that it would be amusing to get to know him." He concludes:

> So the next time that we passed each other in the passage I said to him "Hullo, Blair"—which was an outrageous thing to say to a fag. He replied "Hullo" and smiled a little feebly.

There are limits to daring, and for the moment I could think of no more to say. So after stopping and staring at one another we both passed on without a further word. It was our first conversation, and it left on me the impression that here was a boy of peculiar humour—a saturnine perhaps and not wholly benevolent humour but above all a humorist. So he certainly was. It is as such that I primarily remember him—as a boy saying and doing funny things.

In spite of this promising beginning, Hollis and Blair never became close friends, partly because of the hierarchic nature of the Election system, partly because Blair was closer in temperament to such members of his own Election as King-Farlow, "a boisterous sceptic," or Steven Runciman, who Connolly remembers as dividing the world into "the stupid and the sillies." Such a world view would particularly appeal to Blair, and his meeting with Runciman was an act of recognition: one skeptic welcoming another into the brotherhood. Connolly himself, the first close friend, came up from St. Cyprian's the next year; and, as before, the two went for walks on Sundays, talking of Art and Life and other Subjects—it was now that Blair made his prescient remark that whoever won the war, England would emerge from it "a second-class nation." But the intimacy wasn't resumed on its old terms. Even without the Election barrier to surmount, they discovered that, as Connolly put it, "we belonged to two different civilizations. He was immersed in *The Way of All Flesh* and the aesthetic arguments of *Androcles and the Lion*, I in the Celtic Twilight and Lady Gregory's resurrected Gaelic legends." And there were differences of temperament too that in adolescence make for divergence—which is not to say that the friendship between them ended; rather, it shifted to another, less dominant key.

Blair was fortunate in his Election, and he was fortunate too in being at Eton when he was—a juxtaposition or combination of person, place, and time singularly favorable to him as "the young cynic," "the Election atheist," "a boy of peculiar humour." The school, like much of the country itself, was curiously ambivalent in mood as the war drew to a close. There was the belief, originating in nostalgia, that everything would go on as it had in the prewar past: a return to the time-honored certainties and pieties of English life. And there was the counter-belief, originating in disillusionment, that the aftermath of the war would see a repudiation of the past that had brought it into being, and change and uncertainty for English life in the future. The two contrasting attitudes had a first symbolic expression at Eton on November 11, 1918.

The celebration to mark the war's end was in the best tradition of schoolboy gaiety. One happy young Oppidan in his first year wrote to his mother:

On the Monday of the Armistice at 10:40 a.m. the Headmaster announced that it was to be a half holiday and a *non dies* (that is no work at all) on the morrow. Then a riot commenced, all the school rushed up and down the streets yelling and screaming, one person was beating a bathtub, another a tea tray, and you never *heard* such a noise, then for two or three days cheering and singing and fireworks continued and I nearly burnt the house down, then Mr. Booker gave a banquet, with fruit salad and chicken and pheasant and cider . . . and then we carried a maid up and down the house and sang songs until nearly 10 o'clock. Japanese lanterns were hung outside the houses, and the place is covered in flags. I have a Union Jack out of my window and a Belgian Flag inside the room. Oh, it was great fun . . .

But also on the day of the Armistice, a large group of Etonians marched upon the commander of the Officer Training Corps at the school and demanded his resignation now that peace had come.

College in the period immediately after the war gained the reputation of being rather "Bolshie." The new atmosphere—anarchic, questioning, and anti-authoritarian—was one in which Blair thrived: he became, as Hollis tells us, "a notable leader." Changes in what had hitherto seemed an inflexible structure were effected in College, and Blair played at least some part in bringing them about. Granted this was "revolution" on no more than a schoolboy scale, it seems a not inappropriate scale for schoolboys. To act on behalf of a principle in which one believes, even if it is only the injustice of excessive beatings by the Sixth Form, seems not wholly contemptible. Orwell, however, will have none of this—looking back fifteen years later, he is prepared to credit Blair at Eton chiefly with being an "odious little snob." Inevitably so. For Eton is the citadel of privilege, privilege breeds snobbery, snobbery is the vice of the privileged classes: this was the dogma Orwell the polemicist extracted from the experience of Blair the schoolboy.

Like most dogma it has its own degree of truth. There is no question that Blair was affected by, and profited from, that democratic elitism, or elitist egalitarianism, with which a supremely self-confident, privileged institution (such as Eton) is prepared to treat its members, and which is most noticeable at Eton in College. Orwell's complaint of snobbery has little to do with how Blair was regarded by his fellow Etonians, and much to do with how they, he among them, regarded all those others outside the pale. Simply by being there, inside, one was better, no matter how peculiar one's behavior might be, and more privileged than those outside. As a school at the very top Eton was self-confident enough to tolerate a wide spectrum of nonconformity, even the peculiarities of "Bolshies" and revolutionaries. Yet all the while it went about its appointed task of turning out Etonians, conformists and nonconformists alike, with their hardly being aware of the process, though its mark would be ineradicable.

By the end of the war, having been at the school for a year and a half, Blair already bore the stamp. In the spring of 1918 his mother had moved from Earl's Court to a flat in Mall Chambers, Notting Hill Gate, which would be home for the family for the next three years. Also living in Mall Chambers at that time was the young poet Ruth Pitter, who had been working as a Junior Clerk in the War Office, and became a good friend of the Blairs, especially Marjorie. When Eric was at home on holiday, Miss Pitter met him for the first time. He was five years younger than she, most memorable to her then for his pair of perfectly matched light blue eyes, and she thought him unmistakably the young Etonian, in his manner, dress, and way of speaking. (So, too, people later would claim that Orwell was recognizably an Etonian, though in his writing he would be making a determined effort to disentangle himself from it and to disavow its effects upon him.)

He was at the school for five years, the greater part of them in the period of anti-*blague*. For Blair it provided a kind of objective correlative: the cynicism and questioning spirit, so characteristic of the time and place, especially when his Election had control of things, corresponded to something already there in his own nature, something that had been there since childhood. But now the outward world, in its disillusionments and rejections, seemed to justify his way of feeling. When he and his fellow Etonians marched on the commander of the Officer Training Corps on Armistice Day, the episode announced a new tone for a new age: *postwar*.

It is a tone so much written about and experienced in the half-century since it was first heard that it requires no definition or documentation. But at Eton there had been premonitory murmurs even before the war's end. The shift in mood, with its repudiation of the past and espousal of the new, is foreshadowed in a mocking editorial in the *Eton College Chronicle* for 1918: "This school is not going to be much fun in a little while . . . look out for soft collars, they'll be the first sign. That in itself will mean a good many Masters sans starch, sans everything . . . Then of course you'll have rational dress by and by; flannel shirts, too, open at the neck; why not sandals? and no hat? Then schoolmistresses."

A year later the change in mood that had been predicted jokingly was accepted seriously. There was a tradition in College, inaugurated in 1878 by J. K. Stephen and faithfully observed since, that the Captain of the School should write a Retrospect for the College Annals—records of their time there, kept by the Collegers themselves. In his Retrospect for 1919 the Captain of the School felt obliged to write: "There are some who fear for the present restless state of College, and prophecy a dreadful end for her; but let such remember that, after all, there *has* been a War, and that peace has enabled many to stay on who had expected to serve; and that when unrest is universal, it is only natural that some trace should be found within our walls, and that it is inevitable that the general relief should have resulted in a certain amount of rowdyism."

Rowdyism, in the circumstances, seems an inappropriate word; the flight from tradition that was a characteristic of those first postwar years was sufficiently strong that *no* Retrospects, of any kind, were written for the College Annals in 1919–20 or 1920–1. And the Retrospect for Summer 1922 tells of the attempts within College to make it a more liberal institution—this would be the work of Blair's generation, the Election of 1916 arrived at the top. The Captain of the School recorded that they had managed to reduce enmity between Elections, and had eliminated what they thought to be the abuses by College Pop,* chiefly that group's having appropriated to itself exclusive use of the Reading Room, which had just been reconstructed as a Memorial to the sixty-seven members of College who had died in the war. The point at issue had to do with assumptions of unjustified privilege rather than with misuse of a Memorial of the War. (*That* had already become a subject for mockery, as is evident from this announcement in *College Days*, the humorous magazine of which King-Farlow and Blair were editor-publishers in 1920 and 1921: "It has been unanimously decided that the Eton War Memorial shall consist of a nunnery. The site chosen for its erection is the School Field.") Summing up, the Captain of the School (Denis Dannreuther, who was first on the list of the 1916 Election) could include as achievements of his Election that it had reduced the number of beatings to a minimum, and generally had substituted "a more harmonious system of government for the old methods of repression and spite."

The Master in College at this period was John Crace, a classicist, who did not take too enthusiastically to the new, reformist ideas put forth by his charges. Still, it was noted in the Annals that "he has cooperated with every Sixth Form and helped to carry out its ideas for the benefit of College." This would suggest some degree of tolerance on Crace's part. But Blair was a trial for him—one suspects he would have been too sardonic and irreverent for almost

---

* College Pop—a debating society within College that corresponded, but on a much less grand scale, to the Eton Society, or Pop, the most fashionable group in the entire school and predominantly Oppidan, although some of its members were Collegers. College Pop itself went into a decline in these years and did not start to hold debates again until 1923.

any schoolmaster to cope with, especially outside the classroom. Opinions of Crace vary: some remember him as "a kindly man," others as "a sex-obsessed prude"; but all are agreed that he was lacking in humor and, as such, easily teased. A story, well known at the time, relates an encounter between Crace and Blair over an allusion he believed Blair had made to him in a burlesque in *College Days*, though nothing in the magazine carried a signature. According to the story, whose source appears to have been Blair himself, the Master stormed into his room, waving a copy of the offending publication, and announced, "Blair, either you or I must go."

"Well, sir," Blair replied in what a contemporary describes as his "Woosterish" drawl, "then I think it better be you."

It fell to Crace also to prepare Blair for confirmation in the Church of England, an unenviable duty, since Blair was by then—inevitably, one might say—a confirmed skeptic, with little interest in religious or theological matters. He told his friends that at one of their discussions, when Crace had pointed out the power and helpfulness of the Holy Ghost, he remarked that he, Blair, had personally always considered "Old Man Ghost" rather a joke. But this sort of showy cynicism did not always go down well, and at least one member of the Election recalls "an address by the Reverend Neville Talbot in the school library, in the course of which he said something about 'the young cynic —and he is a real stinker, isn't he?' which we felt was a cap that fitted Eric."

He would never pretend to beliefs that he didn't have, and his skeptical attitude was not dented when he went up from Crace to Alington, the Headmaster, for further religious instruction. He had been reading with the greatest pleasure Shaw's preface to his recently published *Androcles and the Lion* in which an account of the gospels is set forth, very different in tone from what one would be likely to hear from an Anglican clergyman and one much more to Blair's taste.*

When he in his turn wrote a particularly irreverent, neo-Shavian essay and presented it to the Headmaster, Alington, more worldly than Crace and not without humor, declared that while he didn't mind impertinence to himself, he would not tolerate it to God, and gave Blair the standard hard punishment—"Take a *Georgic*"—that is, write out four to five hundred lines of Latin verse. (It should be noted that Alington let him off the punishment; nor did Crace ever take disciplinary action against him for his rudeness—which suggests that adults, at least, found Blair more tolerable than Orwell was willing to concede.)

In due time, along with the others of his Election, the young cynic was confirmed by Bishop Gore in the Eton Chapel. But the cricket field rather than the Chapel provides the setting for the most characteristic of the stories having to do with Blair and religion at Eton. Hollis tells how Noel Blakiston, newly arrived in College, was approached on the field by Blair with paper and pencil in hand. The following Shavian dialogue ensued:

Blair: I'm collecting the religion of the new boys. Are you Cyrenaic, Sceptic, Epicurean, Cynic, Neoplatonist, Confucian or Zoroastrian?

* E.g., ". . . the story of a prophet who, after expressing several very interesting opinions as to practical conduct, both personal and political, which now are of pressing importance, and instructing his disciples to carry them out in daily life, lost his head, believed himself to be a crude legendary form of god; and under that delusion courted and suffered a cruel execution in the belief that he would rise from the dead and come in glory to reign over a regenerated world. In this form, the political, economic and moral opinions of Jesus, as guides to conduct, are interesting and important: the rest is mere psychopathy and superstition."

Blakiston: I am a Christian.
Blair (gravely): Oh, we haven't had that before.

IN COLLEGE THE DAYS BEGAN EARLY. THERE WAS EARLY SCHOOL before breakfast, from 7:30 to 8:20; then, three hours of classes and an hour with one's tutor (in Etonian parlance, "m'tutor"). Lunch was at two. After it came organized games, then, on three afternoons each week, a further two hours of classes. Three days a week were half-holidays: those afternoons were also largely devoted to games, whose importance was crucial, not only as they related to *corpore sano* but also to one's popularity—to play noticeably hard on the field was to be admired; whereas to work noticeably hard in the classroom was to be a "sap."

M'tutor—the so-called classical tutor—was a significant figure, for it was his duty to act as academic and personal supervisor. Blair was particularly fortunate in this regard. He first was in the charge of A. S. F. Gow, then an Assistant Master and later to gain a distinguished reputation as a classicist at Cambridge. Gow—"Grannie" Gow, as he was known to the boys among themselves—recognized, under the shyness and surliness of Blair's manner, an authentic intelligence, and unlike Crace he was more amused than offended by his cynicism. For his part, Blair, privately, was fond of Gow, and over the years was to keep in touch with him. In public, however, he took the patronizing tone that would be expected from him—Gow's love of Homer was dismissed as "sentimentality," and of Italian painting as "affectation," and he wrote for the titillation of his friends a scabrous rhyming dialogue between Crace and Gow. It was the custom for four or five boys in the Election to gather in Gow's rooms on Sunday evenings, bringing with them to read aloud essays, poems, or stories of their own, something apart from the work they wrote for their English Master, Hugh Macnaghten. Blair enjoyed writing stories that pointed a moral, and Gow encouraged this—an act of kindness chiefly, one gathers. King-Farlow, a member of the group, found them irritating to listen to, in their self-conscious simplicity and banal point—e.g., "Honesty is the best policy." It should be emphasized that his unenthusiastic response to Blair's writing was not exceptional. James Gibson, who was with him in Macnaghten's English class in 1918–19, recalls that his essays were never singled out for praise there, which is suggestive because Macnaghten was "always very keen to commend any boy who wrote well or commanded telling phrases." In fact, none of Blair's contemporaries, or teachers, ever thought his writings at Eton remarkable—he was not one of those golden youths upon whose brow the laurel seemed destined to descend. Orwell himself looked back upon what he wrote then with a cold, dismissive eye.*

He wrote facilely and plentifully, but without the kind of distinction, those first stirrings of talent however awkward, that one might expect from a future writer. There

---

* Considering his ultimate development as a master of the plain style, it was probably just as well that he was not one of Machnaghten's boys, for Macnaghten was addicted to the "beautiful"; as an admirer of Pater, he would not have admitted Shaw to the canon. Connolly, in *Enemies of Promise*, writes of him: "Although a fine teacher, his learning possessed the faults or rather the literary vices of his time. He was an ogre for the purple patch, the jewel five words long, the allusion, the quotation, the moment of ecstasy. . . . He told us the most beautiful word in the English language was 'little,' he liquidated his 'r's' in reciting and intoned poetry in a special way . . .

> *and hear the bweeze*
> *Sobbing in ver little twees.*

Jolly good! he would exclaim, and to hear him chant 'Ah, poor Faun—ah, poor Faun' was a study in pity which made his severe and even harsh discipline appear the more surprising."

was nothing in his writing to set him apart. By definition, any boy in College is trained to write a clear, intelligent sentence: it is one of the marks of an Etonian. For his tutors and masters, over his four and a half years, he must have written a vast quantity of essays: all are lost and none are remembered. And he wrote verse and stories for the two periodicals with which he was associated in College.

The first of these was *The Election Times*—Editor, Mr. Mynors; Business Manager, Mr. Blair; Art Manager, Mr. King-Farlow—published from No. 32 Lower Passage. It was entirely the work of the 1916 Election, and it made five appearances, in March and June 1918, in November 1919, and in April and July 1920. There was only one copy of each issue, for the periodical was produced literally by hand—each author, under a pseudonym or anonymously, writing out his own contribution, with Mr. King-Farlow making the drawings directly on the page—and it was available for reading by other members of the Election at a charge of sixpence each.

Only one issue of *The Election Times* appears to have survived, No. 4, the issue for Monday, June 3, 1918.* Three of its unsigned contributions—a poem, "The Wounded Cricketer," a story, "The Slack-bob," and a parody of Sherlock Holmes, "The adventure of the lost meat-card"—are said to have been written by Blair. The story, the most considerable of these, very likely was one that he had read at Gow's Sunday evenings, and it is given here exactly as it appeared in *The Election Times*:

The Slack-bob

There was once a boy who was a slack bob. He used to walk about and say to his friends "what fools you are to go worrying about rowing & playing cricket. Look at

---

* It is the copy belonging to Mr. King-Farlow, who very kindly made it available to us.

me." And they used to look at him & go on their way. Then he went to the other slack bobs, & said to them, "We are the only sensible people, aren't we?" But they used to pretend that they were not slackbobs, so they laughed & went on their way. So then he decided that he was the only sensible boy in the school. But that year he went to Lords', being unable to avoid it, & there his mother introduced him to his cousins. He had never seen them before, & they were all big fat noisy girls with red hair, seven in number. "Why aren't you in the eleven?" asked Agatha, who was the eldest. "I expect he's in the second eleven," said Tabitha, the next. "Are you?" said the third, who was called Grace, (she turned her toes in & squinted.) "Eer, no. I'm afraid I'm not very fond of cricket," said the boy. "Perhaps he's a wetbob," squeaked Beryl, the fourth. "Yes," said the boy, glad of the chance, "I'm a wetbob." "I don't like rowing," said Mary, the youngest, who was considered the family beauty. "You're in the Eight, of course?" said all the other six together. "No, not quite," said He, "but," He went on desperately, "I'm not far off it; I've got my Lower boats, & I'll get my Upper boats next first of March." "That's not bad" said Eliza, the fifth sister. "I bet I'd be in the Eight if I was a boy," said Maudie, the sixth. By the end of the day He had told them that He was going to win junior sculling, & probably be in the Eight next year. But this made them so fond of him that he wished he had told them the truth. At last however he escaped, & thought that all was well.

A few weeks afterwards a postcard came saying "We are all coming to watch you. I hope you win," & signed by Agatha. "What's happening today?" he asked a friend. "Junior sculling," said the friend. The boy turned pale, but he went & met them. "If you win I'm going to give you a nice kiss," said Grace; "We all will" said Agatha. "I'm sorry, I can't row," said he, "I've hurt my arm."

"Never mind," said Tabitha. "I'm not allowed to, though," said he. "Don't mind that," said Grace. "But I can't," said he. "Coward!" said Mary. "You're letting us all down," said Eliza. "Never mind," said Agatha, "we'll all come & have tea in your room now, & next year we'll come & watch you in the Procession of Boats."

Moral. Honesty is the best policy.

The second of the publications with which Blair was associated was *College Days,* which he and King-Farlow inherited from the previous editor, George Binney, and which they published in 1920 and 1921. It was professionally printed, and, as King-Farlow has suggested, of interest to its editors as a money-making rather than a literary enterprise. And as such it did them very well: a net profit of 86 pounds in 1920, and 128 pounds in 1921. There was a wide circulation among Old Boys who returned for the Eton–Harrow match, when a number, priced at a shilling, was cannily brought out, and it carried several pages of paid advertisements—for Erasmic Shaving Stick ("Does not Dry on the Face"), for Pascall Versailles Chocolates, for Aertex Cellular Clothing, and along with Rolls-Royce and Sunbeam, for the Chalmers, America's Favourite Six ("Tell the 'Pater' about the Chalmers—you'll get him interested from the start. It's no end of a corking car, good to look at, topping to run, and you don't require a science degree to understand its works"). Read from the disadvantage point of fifty years on, its humorous contents aren't noticeably risible, though in its day they were thought to be "highly entertaining and scurrilous"—in fact, this was the publication that had so aroused the ire of the Master in College. But for the outsider, the drawings, all by King-Farlow, are much the liveliest aspect of it.

Orwell, in his famous essay of 1947, "Why I Write," tells us that the important writing he was doing at this time (and for several years more) was not on the page but in his head —a continuous fantasy in which he figured as someone to observe—and written, so to speak, in a style that altered as it reflected the writers he was reading and admiring. There is no question that he was a "late developer" as a writer. His first professional publication was literary journalism for a Paris weekly (on censorship in England) when he was twenty-five, and only hindsight of an exaggerated kind would detect there the future author of "Shooting an Elephant." Whereas Connolly's first professional publication, also literary journalism, was a piece on Sterne, written when he was twenty-three, and in its style and poise is a logical ancestor to *The Unquiet Grave*. Which is only to say that some writers are more precocious than others, and that a study of the making of a writer must take into consideration a good deal more than his juvenilia—the life as a whole, in which the juvenilia may be only an insignificant part.

There were two terms in 1919 when Blair switched his concentration from Classics to Science. During that period he left Gow and went successively to three tutors: first, George Lyttelton, who took him in Extra Studies in English Literature, and who formed a Literary Society in which Blair was a member; second, John Christie, newly returned as a Master to Eton from the battlefields of France, where he had won the Military Cross;* and third, M. D. Hill. With Hill he did Extra Studies in Biology, which yielded a memorable occasion when they dissected a jackdaw Blair had shot with his catapult. Nonetheless, in 1920 he returned to Classics, and Gow again became "m'tutor."

---

* Christie was at Eton until 1922. In that year he came into his inheritance, having satisfied the condition that he work for a while. There is no record of his having influenced the musical life of Eton (or Blair) as he was to influence the musical life of England generally by founding the annual festival of opera at his country house, Glyndebourne, in the 1930's.

His slow, undistinguished, but steady academic progress is recorded in the complexities of the *Eton College Calendar*, which is the basis for the summary that follows:

In 1917 he was a first-year specialist in Classics, ranking low in the class. In the first term of 1918 (Lent), he was more or less in the same position. (A typical week's program at this time would consist of one session of Divinity, seven of Latin, six of Greek, three of French, two of English, three of Mathematics, and three of Science.) In the Summer term of 1918 he moved into the First Remove of the Middle Division of the Fifth Form. (For non-Etonians, this is to say that he was moving upward, step by step.) But at this point he abandoned the notion, or was advised to abandon the notion, that he was one of those destined for great academic accomplishments, or to win prizes (he never did win any), and changed from a Classical specialist to the less demanding category of Classical General. In Mathematics he was not doing well at all; rather better in French. But in the next term, Michaelmas 1918, he made another change, this time to Science, perhaps in a vain attempt to find himself, academically speaking. He was now in the Third Remove of the Upper Division (B) of the Fifth Form.

Science seems never to have been a passion; in any case, it is hard to say how he could have succeeded in this category, when he was already in the lowest possible Mathematics group for his Form. On the other hand, he was still doing well in French (with Mr. Montmorency) and adequately in Classics (with Mr. McDowall). In the Lent term of 1919 he had moved into the Second Remove of the Upper Division of the Fifth Form. He was still doing Science —John Christie had become his tutor. He continued to do Classics (with Mr. Kindersley); he still lagged in Mathematics, in the VIIth group out of seven; in French he was in the IId group out of six. But most of his work this term was in Physics. Thanks to the College system of moving an

Election upward as a group, he moved upward, though most of his friends were in higher classes in the same division.

The next term, Summer 1919, he had moved up only one, still doing Science—Chemistry and Physics (Mr. Christie); Mathematics (Mr. Huson)—he had improved there, and was now in the VIth group out of nine; and French (Mr. Larsonnier) in the Ist group.

Then, in the Michaelmas term 1919, having given science a full year trial and proved that he was not meant to be a scientist, he made another change, and became a so-called General Division specialist. His subjects were Divinity, Geography, Ancient History, French, Shakespeare, and Latin; and he returned to where he had begun, with Mr. Gow. There was another move up, and he was now in the third group of the First Hundred of the Fifth Form, the group just below Sixth Form. In the next term, Lent 1920, he continued to pursue the same course; in the Summer term he had advanced to the Second Division. In July, when he did Trials, the end of term examinations, the results were as undistinguished as might have been predicted. Unlike a number of other boys in the 1916 Election—Denis Dannreuther, for example, or Roger Mynors, or Steven Runciman—he was not a brilliantly endowed scholar; he couldn't be expected to triumph on the exam by sheer bravura; nor had he descended to "sapdom" and chosen to work hard at his studies. That term the top grade recorded was 83.8. Blair's was 29.7—which placed him 117th on the list of 140. Only one of his Election had a lower grade.

In Michaelmas term 1920 he did mostly History and Classics in the General course, and he continued, alone of his Election, to pursue the same course in the Lent term of 1921. The next term, Summer 1921, he made a final change, from General Division to Classics. This brought him back with his Election, and he took some classes with the Headmaster—Divinity, of course, but also Homer and Lucretius. His last term at Eton, Michaelmas 1921, he was in the Sixth Form, the top of the school, although he had gotten there largely by seniority; and he continued with Classics, Euripides, Horace, as well as some other subjects. He was receiving the best education that Eton had to offer—and so by general consent the best education an English schoolboy at that time could hope to receive. But it cannot be said he responded to the opportunity with much enthusiasm: from first to last the performance was lackluster. Academically, he was a very ordinary schoolboy.

For his distinction at Eton—the degree to which he was *not* ordinary—one must look beyond the classrooms. Not, however, to the playing field, where the heroes of a school come into being. "He was not good at the ordinary run of our classical studies," a member of the Election comments, "his 'games' were no better." And another: "He was never very much good at games." And a third: "Organized games, with the regimentation, exhortation and dragooning which sometimes goes with them, depressed and annoyed him."

It was not that he was anti-sports. He would take up unorganized games enthusiastically. "Fives is a pleasant, not too strenuous game," Maurice Whittome, a member of the Election, recalls, "of which Blair and I were both very fond. It was played from January to March, and I used to be accosted two or three times each week by Blair asking 'Fives after twelve?' That was the only time of day at which one could be sure of finding a Fives court free. As at other games, Blair was not very good, but I was only a little better, and it did not matter who won; all one needed was four boys not too different in skill."

Of all sports he most enjoyed swimming—not competitively, but for its own sake; he was indifferent to "swimming fast or diving stylishly"—and this was a lifelong taste. At Eton he and his friends from the Election, sometimes joined by Connolly, would come to swim at a sharp bend in the Thames, where the river flows deep and fast, opposite the Windsor race course. This was "Athens," which Blair, with his sensitivity to smell, claimed to have "a subtly delicious exhalation of its own," and King-Farlow, who was an habitué of the bathing parties there catches their special quality: "Apart from swimming, it was idyllic simply lying about in the sweet hay at Athens, watching the river flow on, conversing about Life, memorizing from Theocritus and Gibbon."

In the jargon of the school, Blair was a "wet-bob," which meant that in summer his official athletic commitment was to the river rather than to the cricket field. But this did not save him at the time of interhouse competition from being forced to take a place in the Junior house cricket eleven. The experience is reflected in eighteen unsigned lines of free verse for *The Election Times*. Under the title "The Wounded Cricketer (Not by Walt Whitman)" the poet writes in the first person as a wet-bob who was trying to play cricket, "Not that I wanted to but because I had to," is hit in the eye by a ball, and then lies face down in the grass, counting grass blades and meditating—a fate preferable, apparently, to playing the game. He concludes, in a line unmistakably not by Walt Whitman, "I don't think I shall move. I feel nice and comfortable."

King-Farlow, given, like Blair, to a cynical view, observed that as his friend grew taller and heavier, his attitude toward games began to change. It will be recalled that when Blair first came to College in May 1917 he was not yet five feet four inches; King-Farlow, entering the same day, was already five feet eight inches, but over the next four and a half years he would grow barely another inch. Blair, however, seemed never to stop. In the summer of 1919 he had reached five feet seven inches, but still felt himself "undersized and puny." Two years later, over six feet in height and proportionately heavier, he was playing football enthusiastically, sometimes "sadistically," but never quite impressively enough to win his colors for it.

He also played in a game that is largely the specialty of College, and perhaps the most arcane of Etonian sports, the celebrated Wall Game. (Collegers celebrate it; outsiders wonder at it; a photograph of the game does little to clarify it.) It appears to be a kind of scrimmage or roughhouse played between two teams interlocked in deep mud alongside a brick wall, 110 yards in length; the actual playing area is 120 yards by 5—the object being to secure goals, at one end "throwing the ball against a garden door, at the other end against a mark on a tree." Since the rules of sportsmanship do not apply, nor do subtleties of technique, and since almost any defensive action is permissible, to score a goal is no mean feat—between 1945 and 1967, for example, it happened only once in the annual matches between College and the Oppidans.

As one would expect at Eton, the game has its history, going back in its present form to the early eighteenth century, when the Wall itself was built, although something like it had been played there long before. Over the years since it has acquired a terminology so esoteric as to be impenetrable: let "Good Calx" and "Bad Calx" stand as representative examples. The game, much of which takes place in and under mud that rapidly coats the players from head to foot, is not interesting to watch, but it is said to present the players with problems in the scientific use of force, and certainly it offers them the excitement of competition. (Although the Wall Game is primarily a College game, Oppidans play it too, and by tradition challenge the Collegers on St. Andrew's Day, the thirtieth of November—for this match, sentiment is at its fiercest, tears of joy and sadness flow among the mud.)

Blair was an active member of the Wall team his last

term in College, and a photograph of the team survives at Eton showing him with his arms crossed, cap down over his eyes, looking belligerent and powerful—with his great height and his weight of 170 pounds, his value was assured. But the Wall Book, a detailed record of each match kept by the Keeper of the Wall, was not lavish in his praise: "Erratic and not absolutely reliable, but is a long kick and has done some good things."

That winter was an arduous one, with two matches in September, seven in October, and two in November, leading up to the culminating event, the match on St. Andrew's Day against the Oppidans. On the fourteenth of October James Gibson, the Keeper of the Wall, recorded that "Blair made a fine kick more than half the length of the wall." On the twenty-ninth of October he was made a regular member of the team, and in that match he helped score the famous goal that Hollis has written about in his study of Orwell and that John Lehmann, too, mentions in his autobiography. (A new boy in College, Lehmann wrote a glowing account of the event to his father.) Goals, as we have said, may not be scored for years—in this memorable instance, Hollis, who was playing on the opposing side, recalls that Blair made an extremely difficult throw to Longden, who "passed it on to the door" and to immortality in the annals of the Wall Game. In the match of November fifth, the Keeper of the Wall felt he deserved special mention. On the twenty-seventh of November he received his colors, and Gibson, who presented them to him, remembers that Blair was "absolutely delighted"—they were his only athletic honor at Eton.

Finally, but anti-climactically, there was the great match itself on St. Andrew's Day. College was defeated, "1 shy to nothing." The Keeper, recording the score in the Wall Book, felt (not surprisingly) that it had been a disappointing game. But Blair had played well, and distinguished himself in the 10th "bully," which lasted ten seconds, during which he "kicked well out," saving the situation, and again in the 23rd "bully," when he "kicked soundly out of calx."

This account of his participation in sports at Eton is not intended, except incidentally, to point toward their possible influence upon him later, in his life and in his writing. (The numbers of sporting images, allusions, and scenes in the books; the attribution to hated characters—e.g., Verrall in *Burmese Days*—of excellence at games; the choice of sports and attitudes toward them as class indices.) Chiefly it is meant to reinforce what has already been suggested: the fullness of Blair's commitment to the Etonian way of life. However sardonic his tone, he was not moved to rebel against it or abstain from it. However aloof in spirit, he was willing enough to take part in what was, after all, a central preoccupation of most of the boys and many of the masters. With no notable gifts as an athlete, he did manage finally to win his colors. No matter that Orwell might later disapprove of Blair the Etonian; while there, he enjoyed himself—or perhaps it would be more accurate and truer to his temperament to say that he did not *not* enjoy himself—and conformed readily enough to tribal customs and costumes. So in 1921 we see him at the annual Eton–Harrow cricket match, at Lord's, wearing the approved formal morning clothes—with a certain untidiness, but looking quite grand and impressive, except for those outsize feet.

But sports did not dominate his life, any more than they did the lives of his friends. Collegers were not philistines: this was true certainly of the 1916 Election, and if Blair was not outstanding among them as a scholar, he was legitimately of their company, for he read voraciously, he wrote, he thought, he took positions, passed judgments, held attitudes: it is in the fusion of these aspects of his life—and they are inextricably bound up together—that we detect his individuality.

At fourteen, when he was first in College, he stood out as a precocious reader. George Wansbrough remembers that "he used to quote writers like Bernard Shaw, Chesterton, H. G. Wells and I think Samuel Butler, as if he had read them and absorbed their points of view; I doubt whether any others in our Election had read more than a very little of these authors by the time we arrived at Eton." There was that element of chance in his reading, so characteristic of the bookish adolescent who falls upon whatever comes his way, unhampered by preconceptions or academic obligations. It was in just this way, for example, that Elizabeth Bowen, who was at *her* school at this same time, happened to come upon a book of E. M. Forster's, *The Celestial Omnibus*, and the shock of recognition was all the greater for not having been introduced to it in the classroom. For Blair there was a comparable revelation when he walked into a master's study and, not finding him there, picked up a magazine from a table, leafed through it, and came upon a poem by which he was "completely overwhelmed." This was D. H. Lawrence's "Love on the Farm." Rather strangely, as Orwell later reported the occasion, he failed to notice the name of the author, and so the overwhelming moment did not have the sequel one might expect—that he would try to find more of Lawrence's poems. (Unlike Elizabeth Bowen, who, having read one book by Forster, was "ready to go any lengths, any expenditure of pocket money to get hold of more from the same pen.") It was not until five years later, when he was in Burma, that he read work of Lawrence's again—"The Prussian Officer" and others of his stories—and was deeply impressed. But perhaps at sixteen, in the range of his imagination and sympathies, he was not quite ready for Lawrence, for those highly charged, seismic relationships between men and women, so different, say, from the articulate, witty, and iconoclastic interchanges between the characters in Shaw that he then found so much to his taste.

As a reader he had been precocious only in the sense that he came very young to Shaw and Wells and Galsworthy; but these were staple reading for Englishmen of the time who were literate and progressive; and presently they were known in College. [*The Election Times*, No. 4, Mon. June 3, 1918, contains a lampoon, THE SHE-DEVIL, "by Rita Galsworthy (authoress of 'The Mountain of Tears,' 'Divorce,' 'The Sin of Laura Paton,' etc.)"—the work of Steven Runciman.] In succeeding years, though he continued to read avidly, he did not venture deep into the territory of the "new." (Not necessarily a fault, of course, but it must be kept in mind that he was at Eton when D. H. Lawrence and Virginia Woolf and T. S. Eliot and Wyndham Lewis were publishing their work, and were not wholly unknown to other Etonians.)

One writer he *was* ready for was A. E. Housman, a friend of Gow's who came down from Cambridge to lecture to the Literary Society. Housman was then at the zenith of his popularity, at Eton as elsewhere. So Blair was not unusual in his enthusiasm, only perhaps in the length to which he carried it, for at seventeen he knew by heart most of the sixty-three poems of *A Shropshire Lad*. Two of them— "With rue my heart is laden/ For golden friends I had," and "Into my heart an air that kills/ From yon far country blows"—he had to do into Latin verse, but even this did not diminish his affection for them. As Connolly acknowledged, in 1936, writing a re-evaluation of Housman shortly after his death, he is "a poet who appeals especially to adolescence and adolescence is a period when one's reaction to a writer is dictated by what one is looking for rather than what is there." Leaving aside the question of what is truly there, and making no attempt to argue for or against

Housman as a poet, one sees in Blair's case an immediate response to a cynicism agreeably akin to his own. Further, though *A Shropshire Lad* had been written in the last confident years of the Victorian epoch, it offered a cynicism unexpectedly suited to the immediate postwar mood.

A word Orwell was to apply to Housman, in *his* re-evaluation in 1938, and which he uses a number of times in regard to his own years at Eton, is "antinomian." In this view Housman comes to represent—how justly is not in question —the repudiation of the official beliefs and conventions of the age. This, in essence, was the attitude of Blair and his friends, who, as "Antinomians," claimed the right to set standards of their own. "Antinomian" seems to have been virtually a vogue word of the period, current in everyone's vocabulary. "College in Eric's time," a member of the Election writes, "was going through a rather antinomian phase," and he adds that Blair was "a strong supporter of the antinomian faction but could not have been called a leader of it."

The word is defined as "the theological doctrine that by faith and God's gift of grace through the gospel, a Christian is freed not only from the Old Testament of Moses and all forms of legalism, but also from all law including the generally accepted standards of morality prevailing in any given culture." In postwar usage, it was, of course, robbed of its religious or doctrinal connection, and any previously accepted code could be substituted for the "Law of Moses" —the discredited wisdom of the Old Men of Whitehall, for example, or the outmoded pieties of the Archbishop of Canterbury, or the tradition-bound disciplinary structure upheld by the Headmaster of Eton College.*

---

* In practice, finally, "antinomian" proved to be one of those high-flown words that can mean rather less than they are meant to mean. In 1936, reviewing Cyril Connolly's novel *The Rock Pool*, Orwell speaks of "the kind of sluttish antinomianism—lying in bed till four in the afternoon and drink-

Antinomianism, Skepticism, Disillusionment—they belong to the spirit of the age, and the spirit of the age originates in a historical fact: the cost for England of the war she had won—almost eight hundred thousand dead—a generation of young men decimated. The fact would seem sufficient to explain the "bad temper," as Orwell puts it, among those under forty. "The mood of bitterness that emerged from the First World War," a later scholar writes, "has no like in any other war that England has fought; no other British army felt itself so betrayed, or so scorned the causes for which it fought. In that mood the post-war generation rejected altogether the world-before-the-war, its propriety, its overstuffed luxury, its conceptions of society and manners, its confidence in England and in Progress."

It is not surprising that a group of highly intelligent boys, approaching maturity though still at school, should have been affected—admittedly at their own level and on their own terms—by the spirit of the age. Orwell, looking back in 1936, offers an example of the period's "queer revolutionary feeling"—in an English class at an unidentified Public School (he means Eton) fifteen out of sixteen boys included the name of Lenin on a list of the ten greatest men then alive. But there was an element of prankishness and teasing one's elders in this—as well as naïveté—that Orwell, making a polemical point, chose not to remember; and it did not follow from it (however "bolshie" it might appear to startled Old Boys) that the fifteen would march out of the classroom and enroll in the Communist party of Great Britain.

A peculiarity of Orwell's analysis of the mood of early postwar England is that it is based almost entirely upon Blair's experience of it at Eton—that was all that he knew

---

ing pernod—that Mr. Connolly seems to admire." (Which is perhaps more priggish of Orwell than antinomian of Connolly.)

at first-hand, for from 1922 to 1927 he was out of England—and from that Etonian sampling he extrapolates and generalizes a sweeping view of the adult world that would have gone down nicely at an officers' mess in Burma—an England with "bolshies" in fashion (but surely not in control?) and on every side "half-baked antinomian opinions," ranging from "humanitarianism" down to "free love, divorce-reform, atheism [and] birth-control." Orwell's implicit criticism has its point: that there was a good deal of revolutionary talk among the *bourgeoisie* and little else—much as a dedicated communist of the 1930's might legitimately complain of "parlor pinks" who were not prepared to go down into the streets and into the party.

But it is a criticism that is hardly fair, or, looked at with much realism, applicable to Blair and his antinomian friends in College. Political rhetoric is always easier than political action, even for schoolboys, and what is remarkable, one would think, is that they should have done as much as they did—*there*. Orwell, never prepared to be less than harsh to Blair, must of necessity cast a suspicious glance at the revolutionary atmosphere in College. A more generous (and persuasive) view comes from his friend Francis Cruso, two years below him in College, who writes: "Blair was naturally critical and impatient of nonsense, and that undoubtedly was the 'ethos' of College too in those days. The First World War was just over, and boys of eighteen were no longer leaving to be shipped out to France and slaughtered. There was an atmosphere of sudden relief and freedom, and a feeling among the young (naïve and absurd, no doubt, but very natural) that we had a real chance to clear away the cant and rubbish of the past and Make All Things New."

"Make All Things New" was a message that reached the school at many and sometimes unexpected levels. Things were in ferment. There was even a short-lived but intense period of avant-garde literary activity (precociously accomplished and the antithesis of Macnaghtenism) that was set off among a remarkable group of Oppidans: Brian Howard, Harold Acton and his brother William, Oliver Messel, Anthony Powell, and Henry Yorke (the novelist Henry Green); on their fringe were such Collegers as Cyril Connolly and Alan Clutton-Brock. They formed a Society of Arts, listening to music, looking at pictures, reading the "New" (not *Georgian Poetry* but *Wheels*), and to some degree led the life of aesthetic worldlings in the context of a Public School—no mean feat, the more so since they managed not to collapse completely into the dandyism of the 1890's. In March 1922 they published for the first and last time an elegant "little magazine," *The Eton Candle*, whose pages, bound in pink, offered small blocks of print surrounded by wide margins. Dedicated to an Etonian aesthete of an earlier age, Algernon Charles Swinburne, its fame spread far beyond Eton, and a greater contrast to the boyishness of *The Election Times* and *College Days* can hardly be imagined. There were poems and stories by the editor, Brian Howard (a protégé of Edith Sitwell), Harold Acton, William Acton, and Anthony Powell, along with contributions from Max Beerbohm and three recent Old Etonians, Osbert and Sacheverell Sitwell, and Aldous Huxley.*

Blair had no connection with this Oppidan group, although twenty years later, in 1941, he and Anthony Powell (who knew him as George Orwell) met and became friends. His sole contribution to aestheticism, it might be said, was to lend a copy of *The Picture of Dorian Gray* to Cyril Connolly. Too late, however—time had moved on, it was the

* From 1917 to 1919 Huxley was at Eton as a Temporary Assistant Master in English and French, as a replacement for one of the twenty masters at the Front. He drew upon his Eton experience to comic effect in the opening chapter of *Antic Hay*, but schoolmastering was an ordeal for him. He was ragged by the boys in his classes, who could do so with impunity because of his near-blindness—a cruel exploitation that Blair hated.

age of Lytton Strachey, and "I could not swallow it," Connolly wrote, "It was not necessary."

But these literary sorties into the New were marginal activities and had no noticeable effect on the traditional current of Etonian experience. The central "engagements," carried on under the banner of the New by the Antinomian or Liberal or Revolutionary faction, were aimed at changing a "life style" rather than a "prose style," and they did, visibly if temporarily, deflect the current: for a year or two tradition was subverted.

The center of the revolutionary movement was the 1916 Election, and the "moral leaders" of the Election—Connolly's phrase; we are drawing freely upon his account, which is admirably clear and detailed—were the so-called Caucus: Denis Dannreuther, Roger Mynors, Robert Longden, James Gibson, and R. M. Cazalet. They were "five scholar athletes, animated, unlike the rulers of college, by post-war opinions. They hated bullying, beating, fagging, the election system, militarism, and all infringements of liberty, and they believed in the ultimate victory of human reason." Blair, though on friendly terms with the Caucus, stood somewhat "aloof." While he shared all their dislikes, he was temperamentally incapable of believing in "the ultimate victory of human reason." In Connolly's words, he was "perpetually sneering at 'They'—a Marxist-Shavian concept which included Masters, Old Collegers, the Church and Senior reactionaries." At the same time, he held the belief, deeply and irretrievably, that in the "great scrum of life," "They" would be the winners, and he the loser. But cynicism did not immobilize him; and if he could not share the idealism of the Caucus, he did not hesitate to join their battle.

The symbol of militarism at Eton was the O.T.C., the Officer Training Corps. In the liberal view, "The Corps was a joke; it had no business to be compulsory and any tendency to increase militarism among a war-weary generation must be exposed and ridiculed." The O.T.C. was not a hallowed Eton institution, though developed from the earlier Eton Volunteers (or "dog potters"); it had been established only in 1908 as a part of Haldane's program of preparedness for the nation. During the war years its reason for being was self-evident, although its effectiveness might have been questioned. But as a postwar phenomenon it represented the outmoded, really detested thinking of the Old Men of Whitehall and their discredited associates, the Generals—the cast of characters in the poems of Siegfried Sassoon and the many yet-to-be-written anti-war novels and memoirs. On the very day of the Armistice, as seen, came the first Etonian demonstration against the O.T.C., and the Peace Celebrations of 1919, organized by the Corps as a kind of military triumph, provoked a riotous demonstration in the School Yard during which the boys invented mocking lyrics for the patriotic songs they had been expected to sing, and in general reduced the seriously intended proceedings to a level of low comedy. Ridicule thereafter became the accepted weapon to bring out the absurdity of its pretensions, and Blair, as might be expected, was very good at this. Francis Cruso, who for a time was a member of his section of the Corps, recalls "one sweating summer afternoon when we were on a Field Day somewhere in the Berkshire Downs, Blair sensibly decided that our uniforms were too hot and that we'd had enough of it; so he took us all off behind a distant haystack and we spent a pleasant 'shirt-sleeved' afternoon listening to him reading *Eric or Little by Little* [a famous, fatuous Public School novel] aloud. I can hear him too one day, as we marched along 'In Fours,' discussing Corporal Punishment with a friend and declaring, 'Of course the whole thing's completely disgusting and barbarous.'"

Since elderly bureaucrats are constitutionally unable to

hear the voices of young men who don't have the vote, the O.T.C. remained at Eton, but until the approach of the Second World War it was not on the whole taken seriously. Achieving the status of a tolerable nuisance and deprived of whatever military significance it may have aspired to, it continued to lend itself to ridicule:

> Signalling was delightful. One sat for hours beside a field telephone while little figures receded into the distance with the wire. "Can you hear me?" "No." "Can you hear me now?" "No." "Well, try this." "This" was the morse-code machine and nimbler fingers than mine would fill the air with a drowsy song. Iddy iddy umpty umpty iddy umpty iddy . . .

Student anti-militarism in the postwar years was a historical-universal as well as an Etonian phenomenon. But anti-Electionism, and the Election system against which it was directed, belong solely to the history of Eton College. Discipline in College—as it took physical form: beating, birching, caning, the Corporal Punishment that Blair called "disgusting and barbarous"—was in the hands of the boys of Sixth Form (*not* the Masters, who were not allowed to cane), and much would depend, then, on their intelligence, humaneness, fairness, and emotional balance.

Of beatings as a mode of discipline there are differing opinions.

Rayner Heppenstall, a friend of Orwell's from the mid-1930's, in his book *Four Absentees*, credits Christopher Hollis with "a good account of Orwell at Eton" in *A Study of George Orwell*, but complains that "he expects us all to take a sympathetic interest in the sort of caning that most of us have only read about." He continues:

> Nobody seems to have told him that caning upon the buttocks has long been assumed by some of the male

population to be a cause of homosexuality at public schools and among public school men in later life.

What strikes the outsider as particularly shocking, however, is that much of this ritual beating is (or was) done not by the masters but by sixth-form boys. As a reward, so to speak, for sticking it out, Etonians of eighteen were allowed to spend their last year at school bruising the hind parts of younger boys.

A different view is presented by J. D. R. McConnell, a House Master at Eton, in his book, *Eton—How It Works* (1967):

> The fact is that boys occasionally commit indiscretions which have to be sharply corrected. My view is that the alternative to corporal punishment may in the long run be more cruel to the offender. The salacious and picturesque stories of "savage floggings" related by certain Old Boys to fascinated audiences are quite outside my experience as a house master.
>
> Practically all boys accept beating as a natural and well-established feature of the give-and-take boy world. It is the adults who surround the question with such sinister implications. Boys who have been wicked generally prefer to suffer a penance which, though painful, is swift and salutary.

In a perfectly detached way it can be said that there is a difference between beating as a form of punishment and beating as a form of bullying. There seems to be general agreement that the Election immediately senior to Blair's were indiscriminate beaters, and along lines closer to Mr. Heppenstall's thinking than Mr. McConnell's. Painful experience only increased the idealistic fervor of the 1916 Election, some of whom, Blair among them, were still being subjected to mass floggings at the almost unprecedented age of eighteen. They believed that "Corporal punishment was a relic of barbarism . . . as bad for those who administered as for those who received it." But there was little, in a practical way, that they could do to put their beliefs into effect until, in the hierarchical order, they themselves had arrived at the top, in the autumn of 1921.

Meanwhile, that summer of 1921 "feeling ran so high against the Captain of the School . . . and the six other reactionaries in his election that they were cut to a man." Most of them, as it happened, were members of the Debating Society—College Pop. So too were Dannreuther, Longden, Mynors, King-Farlow, and Gibson, the Liberal faction. So too was Connolly, who felt it was his friendship with the rowing men that had got him in, for if he had been put up by the Liberals, he "would certainly have been blackballed." So too was Blair, who was elected on the twenty-seventh of July—it was the one society of which he was to be a member—even though four blackballs were cast against him. Debates had become increasingly acrimonious; one, on the "election system," and another, on "corporal punishment," had almost ended in blows. And, indeed, during Blair's remaining time in the society, no further debates were held, and in an effort to appease both factions the magazine subscription list was enlarged to include *The Workers' Dreadnought* as well as *Country Life*.

It was the custom to pass votes of thanks on those who were leaving from College Pop, but in 1921 the boys who were leaving were mainly the despised reactionaries of the senior election.

> For the first time in history [Connolly writes] these votes of thanks were blackballed. The genial ceremony collapsed: Cliffe the Captain of the School, Lea the Cadet officer of the Corps, Babington-Smith and the boys who

beat King-Farlow and Blair and Whittome on trumped-up charges for political reasons faced the unprecedented verdict. Name after name was read out, the vote of thanks proposed and seconded, the ballot box passed, the blackballs counted, and the transaction noted down in the annals.... The Master in College protested against the breach of tradition, the Old Tugs got to hear of it, the Vile Old Men [certain reactionary Masters] took it up, and there were whispers about Bolshevism which almost reached the newspapers.

It is pleasant to report that when the 1916 Election reached Sixth Form and so were responsible for the discipline of College, they were not corrupted by power. Idealism continued to flourish; hatred of beating, bullying, and the enforced segregation of Elections was as strong as ever, and many of the reforms the revolutionaries had advocated were put into practice.*

Denis Dannreuther, in his Retrospect for the College Annals, wrote:

When I was a fag it was considered a poor night for the senior if no one was beaten, and wantings occurred every night, whereas this last half it does not happen to have been necessary to use corporal punishment at all, scarcely a dozen to twenty wantings the whole half.... It is early yet to judge the success of these experiments, and the universal prediction of "the old men" *may* be verified, but I can at least honestly record that College has been

---

* Rayner Heppenstall remarks that neither Connolly nor Hollis "has told us whether Orwell himself in due course became an assiduous or an expert hand with the cane." The answer to the question would seem to be No. None of Blair's juniors with whom we have talked, or with whom we have been in correspondence, have any recollection of having been beaten by him.

in every way *happier* this year than at any time in the last six years.

Connolly, in his retrospect for *Enemies of Promise*, sums it up as "our short-lived and unpopular experiment in happiness," for, as Blair might cynically have predicted, the new order gave way to the old, and the bad old traditions were presently resumed. Blair himself chose not to write anything for the College Annals; there was nothing unusual about this; many others abstained from contributing "obituaries." After his name there is a large blank (where his accomplishments and reflections might have been written) and in another hand is inscribed "College Debating Society." The Retrospects in the various years in the Annals record the quite precipitous swings back and forth between Elections of the moods of College—but the Election of 1916, in part because it has been memorialized so effectively by Cyril Connolly, will be remembered as one that attempted to move College into the postwar era.

THE MOST FAMOUS DAY IN THE ETON CALENDAR IS THE FOURTH of June—the birthday of George III—that annual festival or ritual when parents and grandparents and Old Etonians (the latter very often being also the former) gather to see offspring and friends, and to feel pleasantly romantic about the old school. As the most recent explicator of Eton has summed it up, it is "an enormous family party."

The day is crowded with events, from Chapel in the morning to the Procession of Boats and Fireworks in the evening. But the most serious event is "Speeches," a series of declamations to a select portion of the assembled multitude by members of Sixth Form. For the Fourth of June celebrations in 1921, Blair was one of the boys chosen to deliver a speech.*

His participation, in the full fig of the ritual—knee breeches, silk stockings, buckle shoes, and the rest of court dress—was very effective and made a considerable, perhaps even a surprising, impression upon his contemporaries, for he was not the sort of boy who would enjoy putting himself forward in the limelight. He had had slight dramatic experience before this: he had played Prince Charming in the Christmas theatricals at Bellehatch Park in the first year of the war; at Eton, in 1920, when George Rylands was producing *Twelfth Night* (and playing Viola), he had mocked the enterprise but consented to fill the role of a nonspeaking officer; and the next year he allowed himself to be cast as a shepherd in *The Winter's Tale*. But Speeches was far more challenging. At it turned out, his flat voice, a liability in the theater, worked to his advantage in the selection he had chosen.

He had gone to an author he admired, Robert Louis Stevenson, and extracted a passage from "The Young Man With Cream Tarts," one of the three stories having to do with "The Suicide Club" in the *New Arabian Nights*. It comes at the point in the story when the members of the club have assembled to draw the two decisive cards, one to designate the member who will kill, the other his victim; and poor craven old Mr. Malthus, who was an honorary member (did Blair appreciate the irony of Malthus in the suicide club? very likely) and had never thought he would draw a fatal card, indeed does so—the card calling for his

---

* It is pleasing to learn that the program of Speeches for a Fourth of June in the 1960's included a selection from *The Lion and the Unicorn* by George Orwell. Among the other authors whose works were declaimed on that occasion were Goethe, Gladstone, Dante, Bertrand Russell, Aristophanes, Vanzetti, Dylan Thomas, and Osbert Lancaster.

murder. The episode, delivered in Blair's "passionless, detached dry tones," proved chillingly effective.

To participate in Speeches on the Fourth of June; to belong to College Pop; to win one's colors at the Wall Game —these are not contemptible items in an Eton dossier. They suggest that Blair was qualified to put himself forward more than he did, might have been more at the center of things . . . But he chose not to, fearful perhaps of becoming excessively involved and giving too much of himself. He preferred, no doubt with some private self-mockery, to be an attendant lord, one who would do to swell a progress, as T. S. Eliot had written a few years earlier.

Inevitably one asks Why? To find an answer—tentative, provisional, and conjectural though it must be—one starts by admitting that Blair-becoming-Orwell is unique, whereas Blair-being-Blair is not. The child who is solitary by nature or disposition is not uncommon; nor is the solitary child who is given to fantasizing. Such was Blair, when very young and as he grew older. To be solitary has nothing to do with the "realities" of one's situation: one can be alone in a room crowded with friends. Blair had his friends at Eton, yet it is striking how they are in agreement about his reserve, his aloofness, for all his "friendliness." Connolly describes Blair and King-Farlow as "bosom friends," but against that one must balance King-Farlow's own comment: "I was never sure that he really liked me." Orwell tells us that for the first twenty-five years of his life he was writing a story in his mind, in which he himself played a central role; but while he describes the technique of the story, he does not tell us what it was about.

Real life and fantasy life allow equally for imposture. In real life, for example, one can pretend to be brave and act bravely, all the while knowing that one is an impostor—this is to act out a fantasy. Alternately, one can in a fantasy dare to be a coward—as one would not dare to be in real life—and be punished for it. Bookish children take over characters from books they have read and assign them roles in their fantasies: there, often, they themselves become the characters, as Blair, at six or seven, thought of himself in his "story" as Robin Hood. Such children (and adults), given to the pleasures and guilts of imposture, are likely to question the validity of the roles they are playing in "real" life. They question their own authenticity—am I brave or a coward? Am I the child of my boring parents, or am I the illegitimate child of a duke abandoned on their doorstep, or, worse yet, am I the legitimate child of a duke, mysteriously exchanged in swaddling clothes with the child of a peasant? There is nothing unusual about this kind of thinking, of course; the whole of Gilbert and Sullivan seems to depend on imposture. So does much of Verdi. Or the comedies of Oscar Wilde. Or *Der Rosenkavalier.* Or *Twelfth Night.* Or the story of Jacob and Esau. Mark Twain's (or Samuel Clemens's) *The Prince and the Pauper* is a classic example for every well-born or low-born bookish boy to ponder on. Then there are Dr. Jekyll and Mr. Hyde: which is the more "real"? Not to speak of Dorian Gray, or the portrait of him hidden away in a room upstairs, becoming progressively more hideous? A boy of Blair's disposition might well be struck by the element of chance, or luck, or fate, as it determined one's life. As an Etonian one was the Prince; but twenty minutes away, on the road to Slough, one might as easily be the Pauper.

It can be argued that of all the books he discovered while at Eton, the one that was most to affect him was Jack London's *The People of the Abyss.* Years later it would have a direct influence on the writing of the first book he was to publish, *Down and Out in Paris and London.* As an Etonian, Blair read of the "abyss" and incorporated it into his fantasies and his life. Written in 1903, the book was (and still is) a vivid, powerful, and appalling first-hand account of poverty in the East End of London in the summer of 1902, during what were thought of as "good times" in England. (The beginning of "the Edwardian garden party.") Jack London, by his own choice, underwent the ordeal—for how else, he asked, could one truly know what poverty was? Having gone down into the "underworld" and lived there —not so many miles distant from Notting Hill Gate, but the difference in life was immeasurable—he could write in his preface with an authority denied to the sociologist, statistician, or clergyman: "The starvation and lack of shelter I encountered constituted a chronic condition of misery which is never wiped out, even in the periods of greatest prosperity."

It was an experience of one kind to read in the preface to *Major Barbara*, "The greatest of evils and the worst of crimes is poverty," and to go on from there to the dazzling pleasure of one of Shaw's most provocative and wittiest plays: a masterpiece of imposture, as any work of art must be. It was an experience of a different order to read the piling up of details—gruesome, sordid, and pitiful—in London's account, the more painful for being so unmistakably a transcription. One might be moved to pity and guilt, reading of all that suffering, so remote from one's own life. And yet, were these emotions truly authentic? (Questions of this sort were not uncommon during the years of the Edwardian garden party. They occur to the Schlegel sisters, thinking of the "abyss," in E. M. Forster's *Howards End*. They occur to Major Barbara herself.) Did one alter the current of one's life—go down the road to Slough—because of them? One had the fantasy of being guilty, of doing penance. Yet, even guilt, it seemed, could be a form of imposture. To have a true experience of guilt one must first know for oneself the evil that inspires it. To put it another way, one had somehow to get out of fantasy and into the real world.

In the summer of 1920, after the O.T.C. field exercise on Salisbury Plain (where he and King-Farlow had shared a tent), Blair went directly to Cornwall to join his parents on holiday rather than return first to the school.*

Wearing his cadet uniform, he boarded the train, along with a number of other Etonians. At Seaton Junction, where the train stopped briefly, he got out of his compartment, carrying all his gear, intending to join a boy in another carriage. But as he was walking along the platform, the train began to move. Burdened down with his kitbag and other paraphernalia, he was unable to get back on the train, and it pulled out of the station, leaving him behind. He seems not to have been alarmed or regretful: rather, one has the impression that he was enjoying himself—an adventure was about to begin. A thoughtful son, he first sent a telegram to his parents to say that he would be late. Then, after waiting for two and a half hours, he boarded the train for Plymouth, where he expected to change to the connecting train for Looe. But when he arrived in Plymouth, he learned that the train for Cornwall had already gone, and there would not be another until the next morning. Now the sense of "adventure" quickened. The post office was already closed and so it was impossible to telephone his parents. He was alone: no one he knew, family, friend, or housemaster, knew his whereabouts at that moment. Best of all, he had only a limited amount of pocket money— enough for his fare from Plymouth to Looe, and to choose between going without his evening meal or going without a bed—at the local YMCA where the charge for a bed for

---

* The preceding December Mr. Blair had been demobilized. Thereafter he was once again a retired gentleman, but less content in London than in Henley, where there had been cronies to talk with and the pleasures of a morning stroll along the river. A friend he had met while serving in France had recommended Southwold, the seaside town in Suffolk, as a place to live. There were no firm ties to hold the Blairs in London, and they moved to Southwold in December 1921.

the night was sixpence. He did not hesitate. He bought twelve buns, and spent the night sleeping in a field, under a large tree, in a clump of bushes. It grew very cold; the dogs in the neighborhood barked; and he slept fitfully. He got back to the station at Plymouth at about 5:20 in the morning, only to discover he had missed the first train, and had to wait until 7:45 a.m. for the next. When he finally arrived at Looe, there was a walk of four miles in the hot sun. All in all, it composed an adventure, as he wrote later to Steven Runciman, of which he was very proud. But he added, "I would not repeat it."

This boyish adventure—so far from the abyss and one that Orwell himself does not mention—offers a convenient example of the varieties of imposture. For Blair, in fantasy, he was an "amateur tramp." Passersby at twilight on the streets of Plymouth thought him a soldier not yet demobilized. In real life he was a schoolboy at Eton, wearing cadet uniform, who had missed a train. Least productive would be the imposture of a reader who would discern in this adventure an ironic prophecy of things to come—a prefiguration of *Down and Out in Paris and London*. For it is evident that Blair's emphasis in his adventure, quite normally and as one would expect, is centered on "I, myself" rather than on "I, feeling as another might feel." That extraordinary identification with "the others" that would find expression in the best of his writings was something yet to be learned.

Orwell, dashing off a witty sketch of himself as a seventeen-year-old snob and revolutionary, would have us believe that he divided his time between denunciations of the capitalist system and the rudeness of the working class. But this was no more than his metaphoric way of acknowledging how infinitely little he knew then about either the working class or the capitalist system. Before 1920 the official education of boys of what might be called the instructed class—for our purpose an inclusive category extending from lower-lower-middle up through the upper-upper-middle into the high reaches of the aristocracy—was remarkably circumscribed whether at a State or a Public School. Etonian education was the best a boy in England could hope for, and within its self-imposed limits was of exceptional quality. But how much it left out, how much it took for granted could be legitimately left out! Where, for example, would have been an appropriate place in Blair's schedule of instruction (Divinity, Geography, Ancient History, French, Shakespeare, and Latin Construe) for two works of great social importance which had appeared at the turn of the century, B. Seebohm Rowntree's *Poverty, A Study of Town Life* and Charles Booth's multi-volumed study, *Life and Labour of the People of London*? By the time Blair was at school, they had already had a positive effect on the thinking of the leaders of the Liberal party and so upon the political life of England. To anyone familiar with those books, *The People of the Abyss* was shocking but not surprising: it was one further document that proved the need for political action. This, of course, is as much a part of the mood of prewar England as "the Edwardian garden party"; and the war years (though one would never have guessed it at St. Cyprian's or Eton) were also years of aggressive social-political change. But of this Blair knew little or nothing; and fifteen years later, Orwell, sketching in the historical background to his time at school, feels the need to name only one political figure, that of the leader of the miners' union, Robert Smillie.*

The effect upon him of reading *The People of the Abyss*

---

* His statement that the Public Schoolboys he was meeting in 1936—how many?—were much more right-wing in their views than he and his friends at Eton had been seems the most questionable kind of Orwellian generalization. The career of John Cornford, to name a Public Schoolboy of the 1930's, is instructive in this regard.

was prolonged and subterranean and deferred; it would be years before the book would play an overt part in his life. Winston Churchill in 1911 might speak of "spreading a net over the abyss," thinking in terms of social measures to mitigate poverty—one of those "problems" for which objective political solutions had to be found. But for Blair it was as though he had heard a voice from the underground, addressed to him alone, to which he could not reply and which he could not forget.

By the summer of 1921 the time had come for him to make a decision as to his next step after Eton. According to the ladder theory the answer was simple: he should step up and on to university. This was the decision made for themselves by eleven members of the 1916 Election in College, who went on either to Oxford (Balliol and Trinity) or Cambridge (King's, Trinity, and Corpus Christi). Of the remaining three, two went into family businesses (newspaper publishing and banking) and so, in a manner of speaking, did Eric Blair.

Admirers of Orwell in these later years of the century, which have seen the university made as much a part of anyone's education as the nursery school or kindergarten, find it bewildering, even outrageous, that he should have been so deprived—as deprived, for example, as Dickens or Virginia Woolf or Ernest Hemingway—and have pursued a variety of explanations to account for it, helped rather than hindered by an absence of fact.

It can be taken as a general fact that in 1921 the "ladder theory" was not universally subscribed to at Eton. Many Etonians, who had gone through Fifth or Sixth Form, felt they had gone far enough, and preferred to go straight into the world. This would be especially true of Oppidans, a considerable number of whom did not go on to university. They had received an excellent education, and from a social point of view, Eton was far more important than Oxford or Cambridge. But Collegers were "intellectuals," and it was assumed that they would want to continue their education past Eton. Most of them did; but some did not—and what Blair's contemporaries found more surprising than his not going to university was the alternative he chose.

From the foregoing account of his career at Eton, it should be evident that Blair, while he might be called an "intellectual," was neither a scholar then nor did he give any signs of becoming one later. True, as Orwell tells us, he had made it a point not to work at his subjects, but then, not many Etonians, "saps" apart, ostentatiously do. It is possible that a hardworking Blair might have done better in Trials than he did. The fact is, academically, measured by the highest standard, he was undistinguished. But these are relative matters, and as a King's Scholar in College at Eton, he was qualified to go on to a university, always assuming that he wanted to and that he was able to pay the fees.

Both assumptions must be examined, the latter first. Money, certainly, was a complicating fact. Blair, all along, from St. Cyprian's through Eton, had been a scholarship student; even so, there had been fees for his parents to pay, which they had done gladly though not without difficulty. If he were to go on to a university without a very considerable scholarship, the fees the Blairs would be required to pay would be far beyond their means: this was one sacrifice more than they were willing or even in a position to make. Mr. Blair was in his mid-sixties; his pension, never munificent, was all that the family could count on in a time when life was growing more expensive (though some years later Mrs. Blair would come unexpectedly into a small inheritance). But the circumstances were very different from what they had been when it was a question of Eric's being at St. Cyprian's and Eton. Now he was eighteen; he had been educated at what many considered the best Public School in England; he was old enough and educated enough to make his way in the world. University would have been a luxury unless he was determined on one of the professions for which it was essential. In fact, none of them had even occurred to him. Therefore it was quite logical for Mr. Blair, concerned about his son's future, presently to suggest the Indian Civil Service. But it was offered at first as a suggestion, not an ultimatum, and his parents would do nothing to prevent Eric's going to Oxford or Cambridge if that was what he wanted. They made it clear, however, that if he were to go, it would have to be without any financial assistance from them; he must manage it on his own—that is, he would have to be awarded a scholarship.

The crucial fact, the true explanation for the decision he made, lies in his own diffidence. There is nothing in Orwell's writing later, or at the time in Blair's conversation with Etonian friends and members of his family, to suggest that he really wanted a university education or the experience of university life, that he did not all along think of Eton as a terminal point. His friends were not surprised that he had not gone to university for the sufficient reason that he had not given them any indication that he intended or wanted to go. In the light of his secretive nature this may not count as strong evidence; stronger is the fact that he did tell Steven Runciman he looked forward to being done with Eton and to going on to something new and different—an education in the world, an experience of life. And he took a rather patronizing view, as one might expect, of those contemporaries, Runciman among them, who had made the unadventurous choice of "more of the same." Admittedly there was a good deal of youthful romanticism in this, especially as it led him to choose a vocation for which he was "comically and tragically unsuited," but when he spoke of the future to Runciman, there was a clear recognition of his own limitations as a scholar and his distaste for life at the university as he imagined it to be. That was as early as the summer of 1920, and one has the impression of Blair thereafter doing what is expected of him in the circumstances—consulting with his parents, his tutor —while he had already reached a decision.

It is not uninteresting that it was only *after* the discussion with his parents, which effectively closed the question, that Blair should have broached it to his tutor, Mr. Gow. He himself was under no illusions as to his academic performance, and Gow certainly was not. As to his sitting for a scholarship, "there was not the faintest hope of his getting one," Gow later wrote, and he concluded, "He had shown so little taste or aptitude for academic subjects that I doubted whether in any case a University would be worth while." Given Blair's own feelings, this was hardly a blow, and he was free now to do as he pleased.

At the end of the Michaelmas half, in December 1921, he left Eton for good; but Eton, it might be said, did not leave him—its mark was upon him, in a certain authority and assurance of manner, as later in the authority and assurance of his prose. He had made a negative decision—that he would not go on to university; a positive decision, what his next step was to be, had yet to be made. That would be for the coming months in Southwold, where he rejoined his family.

It is pointless, with a writer of Orwell's stature, to wish a decision unmade. If Blair had gone on to Oxford or Cambridge, it is quite possible that afterwards, in the approved literary stereotype, he would have climbed aboard the literary express to London, have done his approved stint for the weeklies, have written—who can say?—something or other, the unwritten books of Eric Blair. But it is permissible to suggest that then there would not have been George Orwell. Not going to university was a decisive part in the making of the writer.

PART THREE

BURMA

In December 1921 the Blairs moved again, yet another of the transplantations that were so characteristic of them as a family. In Eric's own lifetime—he was now eighteen and a half—home had been first in India at Motihari and Monghyr. Then, when he was four, had come the return to England, and home thereafter was successively at Nutshell, Western Road, Henley-on-Thames (1907–12); Roselawn, Shiplake (1912–15); 36 St. Mark's Road, Henley-on-Thames (1915–17); 23 Cromwell Crescent, Earl's Court, London (1917); 23 Mall Chambers, Notting Hill Gate, London (1918–21); and now, 40 Stradbroke Road, Southwold. It was there—the eighth move for the Blairs in a span of eighteen years—that he joined his family at Christmas, a newly fledged Etonian Old Boy.

In Southwold for the next several months the resident family would consist of himself, his mother and father, and his younger sister Avril. (Marjorie, his elder sister, had been married since 1920 to Humphrey Dakin—the same Humphrey Dakin who had grudgingly allowed Eric to tag along on a fishing expedition years before in Henley—and they were now living in a flat of their own in Mall Chambers.) Southwold, on the Suffolk coast, was a typical, smallish, lower-upper-middle to middle-middle English seaside resort. If it had none of the pretensions to grandeur of Eastbourne, say, with its mammoth hotels along the front, or the elegance of Brighton, with its Regency terraces, neither was it Blackpool, with its gaudy pier and jovial fish-and-chips, working-class flavor. "Resort" may seem too sprightly a word for what Southwold actually was. Still, it had its promenade, its bathing huts, its bandstand for concerts on summer evenings, and souvenir shops where one could buy anything from Staffordshire figures to innocently obscene comic postcards of the kind Orwell would later write about with fondness in his essay "The Art of Donald McGill." And although the weather even in July and August was often treacherous, with chill winds and wet fogs blowing in from the North Sea, throughout the season stout-hearted Britons would be ranged in canvas chairs along the shingle, taking the sea air.

Crowded and bustling with the illusion of life in summer, quiet and relatively deserted in winter, Southwold was precisely the sort of place where an aging Anglo-Indian family might choose to retire. As things turned out, it served the elder Blairs very well. Southwold was where they would spend the rest of their lives (though they would move twice again, but within the town), where, soon enough, in a way that was characteristic of them, they had acquired a new set of friends to make up for the friends they had left behind them in London—or in Henley, or in the various stations in India—and with whom they would maintain thereafter only a tenuous connection. It was to be Blair's way, too, and easy for him in that his nature did not impel him to deep or passionate friendships. He got on well with the young people whom he met in Southwold—for example, Eleanor Jaques, the daughter of the family next door, and Dennis Collings, the son of the local doctor—just as he had got on well with friends at Eton. But he had felt no compulsion or even a mild curiosity to keep up the friendships and acquaintances he had made in College. When he boarded the train for the last time at Windsor

Station in December 1921, it was a symbolic as well as a literal departure. He had joined the Old Boys Association before leaving, but Eton was one phase in his life, definite and concluded, and he would never reappear there for celebrations on the Fourth of June. Southwold would be another phase in his life; Burma the next. Throughout his life, in each of its successive phases, there would be friends who belonged to a particular phase, though sometimes earlier friendships, after an interval of years, would be resumed—without embarrassment, explanation, or surprise on either side. That was Blair's way. Indeed, until his marriage in 1936, when for the first time in his life he entered into a deep and passionate bond, the only continuous relationship of any significance he maintained was with his mother.

Whatever the virtues of Southwold as a place for retirement, it was not the sort of place where a young man would choose to start a career. And the question of Eric's career was very much in the mind of the Blairs that Christmas. Since Eric himself had by this time decided firmly against sitting for a scholarship at either Oxford or Cambridge, Mr. Blair felt free to put forward again his suggestion of the colonial service.* But now it was less a suggestion than

* Orwell in the 1940's told a good friend of that phase that one of his reasons for not going to university was that he felt he had been too long associating mainly with boys who were much richer than he. But even in the early 1920's, and even at Oxford or Cambridge, it would have been possible to find students of his own economic level if he had wished, and students from the working class were not unknown there. As against this later reinterpretation of the past, there is Blair's contemporary feeling, recorded in the previous chapter, that academic things had ceased to interest him, and that he wanted the experience of something different. Such feelings were not uncommon: as Robert Graves has observed in *Good-bye to All That*, it is possible to become bored with the succession of academic ladders, reaching the top of one and then starting at the bottom of the next, which was one reason Graves welcomed the outbreak of the First World War—it enabled him to enlist, plausibly, in the Fusiliers, rather than, as would have been the ordinary course of events, going up the ladder from Charterhouse to Oxford.

paternal advice of a weighty kind—in which Mrs. Blair concurred—and the generalized notion of "colonial service" was narrowed down to the Indian Imperial Police.

Eric and his father had never been close. It had been Mrs. Blair alone, even after Mr. Blair had been demobilized, who would come to see Eric at Eton and take him and his friends out to tea, much to his satisfaction. Steven Runciman remembers her on such occasions as "a charming woman, a bit exotic and gypsy-looking with her bright-colored scarves and gold hoop earrings." And though, when she had gone back to London, Blair would adopt a supercilious tone about her to King-Farlow, deploring her lack of interest in books and serious things, it was evident to Runciman that he was actually deeply attached to her. In contrast, he spoke little of his father, and there were several boys in the 1916 Election who did not know that Mr. Blair was an officer in France, or even in the army. That a schoolboy during the fervid war years should have withheld information of this sort seems very odd: the family reticence carried to an extreme degree.

Eric's coming home to live, after being away at school for more than ten years, would make no appreciable difference in the way things went between himself and his father, except as it offered a day-to-day provocation and setting for disagreement. Given the nature of this particular father and son, and given the general proposition that eighteen, notoriously, is an age when sons know much more than their fathers, it may appear surprising that Eric should so readily have accepted his father's advice. But he had no reason to disagree with it, for it fitted in nicely with a wish of his own: that someday he might go out to the East, to India, to Burma.

Thus, with no argument at all, the Blairs and Eric arrived at the same conclusion, although for very different reasons. Mr. and Mrs. Blair, as one would expect of parents in their situation, put forth a variety of practical and sensible considerations. He was eighteen years old; he had finished his schooling; he had to support himself; he had expressed no interest in any of the learned professions, or in business. (At this time he would not admit, even to himself, that he wanted to become a writer, a denial that Orwell was later to describe as "outraging my true nature." But even if he had silently determined on such a career, had he broached it to his parents they would have been as appalled then as they would be later: was this how he proposed to earn his living? The precariousness of it, let alone its slightly Bohemian flavor, would make it unacceptable to them.) The important thing was to choose a career that was respectable and suitable, that would not require a good deal of costly training or other expense at the outset, that would provide a modest but sufficient yearly income, and that, entered upon early, allowed for early retirement—in his case at forty—after which he would receive an assured pension for the remainder of his life. The Indian Imperial Police answered all these particulars. (This, of course, was how a lower-upper-middle Anglo-Indian family like the Blairs might see it; from the point of view of Eton it would seem an unexpected choice, and it would be the odd Colleger indeed who would choose it.) There were other considerations. It was a career appropriate to family tradition—his grandfather Blair had gone out to India as a young man, his father had served there, his mother's people were teak merchants in Burma, her mother and a sister still lived in Moulmein—and it was suitable. To serve King and Country in an Outpost of Empire carried with it a certain distinction: one was placed, and not discreditably.

His parents' considerations, then, were mostly realistic and practical; his own were romantic and deeply colored by fantasy—a reminder to us that he was, after all, a very young and inexperienced Old Boy. He seems to have had no understanding or premonition of what it meant to become an officer in the Indian Imperial Police, what the job would demand of him. His entire interest was directed to going out, going back, to a dreamscape of India. He had been brought to England when he was four years old, but he had not forgotten his still earlier memories, or else they had been incorporated into his fantasies and gathered force there as they were transformed and intensified. He worshipped Kipling; *Kim* was one of the favorite books of his childhood. India, in his conversations with Runciman, stood for the furthest remove from Etonian life, and as such would figure in his fantasies of the future, although what precisely he was to do should he go there (be a journalist, like Kipling?) was never defined. That first, earliest childhood encounter with the hot, flamboyant, red and saffron landscape proved ineradicable—very different in its impact, for example, from Eton, to whose historic architecture and green fields (which have inspired so many other writers) he responded only diffidently. So that there was an almost uncanny congruence between the realistic wishes of his parents and his own romantic notion of going out to India, and it was decided in the early months of that winter of 1922 that he would put in for the examination for the Indian Imperial Police. Neither his parents nor Eric himself thought to ask the crucial question: whether in character and temperament he was suited to such an occupation. As it proved, by becoming a police officer in the service of Empire he was truly outraging his nature. And yet, paradoxically, by doing so he was suffering a wound that was essential to his development into the kind of writer he became.

ONCE THE DECISION HAD BEEN MADE, REALITIES BEGAN TO take precedence over romance. It meant, first of all, that he must re-enter the world of schooling and the competitive exam, which, upon leaving Eton, he thought he had left behind him forever. In January he enrolled in Mr. Hope's tutorial establishment in Southwold, which specialized in getting young men ready for the service examinations, and started to cram. The multi-part, comprehensive examination was not to be held until the end of June, by which time Blair would not only have been crammed, but would also have arrived at the minimum age allowable for a candidate—nineteen. (The maximum age was twenty-two.) The application, sent off to the India Office during the winter, required that Mr. Blair should give his consent to his son's applying to join the service and indicate his willingness to pay for the prescribed uniforms—Full Dress, Mess Dress, and Service Khaki. (Although the government gave a thirty-pound subsidy for this purpose, it didn't begin to cover the total cost, which came to 150 pounds. Once more, as at St. Cyprian's, at Wellington, and at Eton, the money was found.)

Two testimonials to Blair's character and scholarly attainments also had to be sent to the India Office. One of these was written by Mr. Hope; the other by the long-suffering Crace, the Master in College, who accompanied his with a cool little note which would suggest that the colonial constabulary was not often chosen as a career by Collegers: "I do not know at all what is required by the authorities for candidates for the India police. I send a formal certificate which is probably all that is necessary. If anything more is required, perhaps you will let me know."

The examination, identical in its many parts with that given to officer candidates for the army, navy, or air force, was administered over an eight-day period—in this particular instance from June 27 to July 4, 1922.

It began with English. In the first part Blair was asked to "Write a character sketch of an old gamekeeper, or a retired colonel, or an old farmer"; to "Write a letter to a relative about a visit to the theatre"; and to write a 250-word précis of a lengthy description of the battle of Sedgemoor. In the second part (one hour) he was to name and describe three members of the Cabinet, write something about mountaineering, and something about Burns, Wordsworth, Scott, or Dickens. With English taken care of he proceeded to the History paper. In that he had to deal with the chronology of historical events; speculate on such topics as "Who was the greatest Prime Minister since Pitt?" and "If Nelson had lost Trafalgar"; assess the contributions of three figures from a list including Adam Smith, Rhodes, Faraday, Hastings, Cook, and Burke; answer two out of eight questions in other areas of British history; and indicate on a map the main British possessions in 1763. After History came Mathematics, two two-hour papers; and then, at last, a choice—either a French or German paper. Blair naturally chose the former: two hours of translation—French into English and English into French—and one hour in which he was to write a two hundred-word story in French based on a series of pictures. For the remaining three papers he was allowed to choose from among German, Latin, Greek, Physics, Chemistry, General Science, Advanced Mathematics, and Freehand Drawing. He decided to exploit his years of having done Classics, and took the Latin and Greek papers, familiar, detested exercises in translation—*into* and *from*. For his final paper, since he was fond of drawing (and would continue to do a little all his life), he chose Freehand Drawing. Here he was asked within a two-hour period to *copy* a picture so that it would be of use to an officer, and *draw from memory* a chair at a certain angle, or a hut, or a bucket.

Blair, fresh from Eton and with the further advantage of having crammed at Mr. Hope's establishment, did relatively well on the examination. He was at his best, and for this Eton could take full credit, on the Latin and Greek papers, receiving 1,782 marks out of 2,000 in Latin and 1,702 marks out of 2,000 in Greek. On the other papers—in each of which there was again a 2,000 marks maximum—he received 1,372 marks in English, 1,256 in French, a rather-better-than-might-be-expected 1,158 in Mathematics (his weakest subject at Eton, so credit for this would go to Mr. Hope); and 1,019 in History. His drawing was apparently not of the sort that would be helpful—or recognizable—in battle, and he received only 174 marks out of 400.

The passing grade for the examination was 6,000 marks out of a possible 12,400. This did not mean, however, that all the numerous applicants who had received a passing grade would be accepted as candidates. From this particular group only the top twenty-six were; and Blair with a score of 8,463 was seventh on the list. In September he and the twenty-five other successful candidates were required to take a riding test, for which he prepared himself during the summer at a stable in or near Southwold, and was placed twenty-first on the list of twenty-three who passed.

Once having been accepted as a candidate, it was necessary for him to indicate where in India he wanted to be sent—with no assurance, however, that his request would be granted. He listed his choices in the following order: Burma, United Provinces, Bombay, Madras, Punjab. For the first choice he gave as his reason that he had relatives in Burma; for the second that his father had served in the United Provinces. Since he had done quite well on the examination, he probably could have gone to a more desirable post than Burma, which had the reputation of being the "Cinderella" province of India; but it was what he had asked for and what he was given. He was now committed to the service for a minimum period of three years, unless he was prepared to pay the expensive passage to and from the East himself (he was not), in which case he would be allowed to resign earlier, should he so wish.

Out of the list of twenty-six candidates, only three were posted to Burma. One of them, C. W. R. Beadon, had gone out earlier in the month; and on October 27, 1922, Blair and the other, A. J. Jones, sailed first class on the S. S. *Herefordshire*, from Birkenhead to Rangoon. He was on his voyage out to take up his appointment as a Probationary A.S.P., an Assistant Superintendent of Police on probation, under training in Burma, in the Indian Imperial Police.

"The voyage out" was in no way remarkable. By 1922, as a phrase and an experience, it was already a long-established cliché. Since the early years of the nineteenth century, intelligent, venturesome, educated young Englishmen had been going out to serve in the East, in the Outposts of Empire, whether as soldiers or police officers or civil servants. Still others went as clergymen, as teachers and missionaries, and some as planters, journalists, and merchants. Fifteen years before Blair, Leonard Woolf, for example, had made his voyage out—to Ceylon—to serve as a magistrate; fifteen years after Blair, Leonard Woolf's nephew, the poet Julian Bell, would make his voyage out, to China— to teach at Wuhan University. The accounts of their respective voyages are much alike; so, save for a few particulars here and there—the odd love affair, the squall at sea, the attack of dysentery—so are they all. But for the individual on the voyage out, it was not a cliché: it was his own, unique experience.

Blair was nineteen, and this was the first time in his life that he was free of the supervision of family or school. The experience for which he was bound was certain to be in the nature of a revelation. He was "on his own" in a more definitive way than those of his Etonian friends who were now in the transitional period of the University before entering the world of "telegrams and anger," and with more authority thrust upon him sooner than upon those of his friends who had gone straight into business. He was intelligent, impressionable, and well educated, yet there was something inchoate about him, ready to be formed; there had not yet been a challenge to put his undoubted abilities to proper use.

Until then he had lived the protected existence deemed appropriate to a boy of his class—not only at St. Cyprian's and Eton, but also at home. He moved within the limits of the upper middle class, from lower to upper; of the aristocracy he had only such firsthand knowledge as came from acquaintance with boys at school whose parents or grandparents, or who themselves, had handles to their names; of the working class he knew virtually nothing at all.*

As an omnivorous reader, he had acquired a not inconsiderable theoretical knowledge of the complexities of human existence, but it was a theoretical knowledge far removed from experience, and his cynical manner masked an ingenuousness that was less a personal than a class characteristic. Starting on the voyage out, he had a great deal to learn.

The *Herefordshire* was a small ship—very different in scale and style from the great transatlantic liners of the period, the *Mauretanias* and the *Leviathans*—but it was

* As a small boy, it will be remembered, he had played for a very brief period with the children of a working-class family, but that had been stopped by his mother; and his chief impression of the working class, as he grew older, was that they smelled. It was Orwell's claim, later, that he had been *taught* that they smelled, and that this was a lesson ingrained in all boys of his class from an early age on. (He would write some explicit and controversial pages on the subject in *The Road to Wigan Pier*.) But the whole question where Blair is concerned is a vexing one, for there is no doubt that his sense of smell was abnormally keen—and as such inspires epithets and metaphors in Orwell's prose that are worthy of Swift. If it is true (as Orwell claims) that Blair thought the working class smelled, he was equally convinced that as a boy he did too. In fact, none of his friends at Eton have any memory that he smelled: neither did Mrs. Vaughan Wilkes; nor Mr. Gow; nor his sister Avril; which is not to discount the psychological effect upon himself of thinking he did.

perfectly comfortable, and first class, in the eyes of a boy accustomed to the austerities of Eton and the economies practiced at home by his mother, would seem downright luxurious with its full breakfast, lunch, and dinner, broth and biscuits at eleven, tea and cakes at four, and a bowl of fruit in one's cabin at night. It also re-created at sea that milieu of "Superiority" of which he had been a part at school; but whereas at Eton the "others," the "outsiders," all those who were not Etonians, were far enough out of sight not to be worrisome, on the *Herefordshire* they were constantly, disturbingly in one's range of vision.

Orwell, with his gift for transforming the experiences of his life into moral and political examples, recalls of the voyage that he was "only twenty years old" (actually, nineteen) and, unlike the hard-working crew members, a parasite—that is, a "mere passenger." (Not merely on holiday, however; but *en route* to take up an arduous job.) His attention was particularly caught by one of the crew, a muscular, fairhaired quartermaster of perhaps forty, whom (Orwell tells us) he looked up to as a godlike being, rather as a new boy in College might look up to a Sixth Former. Then, one day after lunch, Blair saw him hurrying along the deck with something furtively concealed in his huge hands—a pie dish with the remains of a pudding (returned from the first class dining saloon) which had been smuggled to him by a steward. The quartermaster's air seemed guilty as he shot past, and Blair, like an outraged prefect, felt a "shock of astonishment." It is suggestive of his extreme inexperience at this time that he should have been so appalled. For this was not a question of hunger—clearly the muscular quartermaster was not suffering from malnutrition—but of sensual gratification; and life is neither the gentleman's code nor what is done or not done at Eton, which he must already have realized in a theoretical way but only now was beginning to learn from the particulars of experience encountered face to face. Orwell is quick to admit that he did not really understand the incident at the time; however, the moral he eventually drew from it seems questionable. Twenty-five years later he saw it as proving "the gap between function and reward" in a nonsocialist society—i.e., that a skillful quartermaster was so inadequately rewarded that he had to steal leftover food. But this conclusion is hardly confirmed by what Blair actually had seen—a strapping specimen of a man, ready to enjoy a pudding that had been given to him by a friend in the galley and not at all finicking because someone else's spoon had already been in the dish.

For the most part, though, the voyage was as noticeably lacking in event as such voyages usually are. That, after all, is a part of their charm: days melt into days, an undemanding routine of eating and sleeping, dozing on deck or playing deck games, or taking a brisk turn around the deck in the morning before the sun is too hot or in the evening as the sun is setting, reading in a desultory fashion, engaging in desultory conversation with fellow passengers. The degree that one enjoys this is largely a matter of one's own temperament—Roger Beadon, for example, making the voyage out two weeks before Blair, found it "a month of pleasure and interest and I was almost sorry to see it end."

But when the *Herefordshire* docked at Colombo, there was another incident that contributed to Blair's education, a first faint foretaste of the lesson he was ultimately to draw from his experience in Burma. Hardly had the ship weighed anchor than coolies swarmed aboard and, under the direction of a white sergeant and some native police, began to take ashore the luggage of those who were ending their voyage in Ceylon.

Blair, going on to Rangoon, and the other remaining first-class passengers watched the bustling scene from the upper deck. One of the coolies was carrying a long metal case in so clumsy a way that it might have struck people in the head as he passed by, and he was loudly cursed. This was enough to catch the attention of the white sergeant. Turning, he gave the coolie a "terrific kick in the bottom that sent him staggering." The response of the watching passengers, a number of women among them, was highly approving: that was how someone of *that sort* had to be treated.

Again Blair was shocked into a new awareness—and this time, as had not been the case with the quartermaster and the pie, there was no possibility of misunderstanding or misinterpreting what he had seen—shocked not only by the physical brutality to the coolie, so automatically applied, but also by the callous reaction of the white onlookers, in its own way as automatic, even from the women, as though the wretched creature were not even human enough to deserve a murmur of sympathy. (How appalled they would have been if the sergeant had kicked a dog!) For the first time the literary experience of *The People of the Abyss* was being translated into life—that people could be treated as though they were things.

But these unsettling incidents, whatever their momentary impact upon Blair, and though they were all of the voyage out that Orwell made specific literary use of many years later, were no more than that—incidents only, not crises or epiphanies that bring about a change of mind and heart, a change of life. Only the total Burma experience was to do that for him, the cumulative effect of five years in the service of imperialism. He watched the coolie being kicked, and turned away, and that evening, as the ship set sail again, he ate his dinner as usual in the first class dining saloon. Not long afterward, the *Herefordshire* was steaming up the wide, muddy Irrawaddy, and Blair was on deck, at the railing, watching the landscape glide by. As they approached Rangoon, monuments came into view—first the smokestacks of the Burmah Oil Company, and then the astonishing gold-spired Shwe Dagon pagoda, the ancient

Buddhist shrine, which dominates the surrounding countryside. It was the end of November, little more than a month since he had said goodbye to his parents in Southwold, and now he was coming down the gangplank in Rangoon, a coolie carrying his luggage, in Burma at last but not yet at his destination—the Burma Provincial Police Training School at Mandalay.

A fortnight earlier, Roger Beadon, the first of the Probationary A.S.P.'s to arrive, had spent two days in Rangoon paying "a hectic round of calls on His Excellency the Governor, the Inspector General of Police, and other officials of importance." Presumably Blair and Jones also paid the prescribed round of calls; in any event, late in the afternoon of November 28 they boarded the mail train for Mandalay. It was a sixteen-hour journey to the north; at eight a.m., the next morning, they arrived at the Mandalay station. Roger Beadon and two other young officers had come down to meet them, and Beadon has recorded his impression of the moment: "From the train stepped two young men. One, fresh-complexioned, of medium height and stocky build; the other, sallow-faced, tall, thin, and gangling, whose clothes, no matter how well cut, seemed to hang on him— Eric A. Blair." (And he adds, "George Orwell to be, could I have but foreseen the future!"—the surprised reaction, it must be said, of everyone who knew Blair at St. Cyprian's, Eton, and in Burma, and for a long time afterwards.)

The newcomers were taken off to the Police Mess, on the outskirts of the city and close to the school itself, where they were to live during the year of training. The Mess, regarded by its members as the finest among the several Regimental Messes in Mandalay, was approached by a semicircular drive through a compound blazing with acacia trees and cannas in full blossom. It was a long, low-lying brick building with six bedrooms on the upper floor, three for the Probationary A.S.P.'s and three for visiting officers; and on the lower floor was the Mess itself, an anteroom, and a billiards room. It was all carried out, as would be familiar to any reader of Kipling, with a certain amplitude of style, though not as amply in the inflationary years of the early 1920's as in 1914, when the Mess servants (paid for by the members) included a butler and second boy, a cook and his mate, a punkah puller, several gardeners, a billiard marker, and a lamp trimmer, and when, on the monthly guest night, the police band was in attendance and the Mess silver was on display.

R. G. B. Lawson, who was at the Police School in 1914 and who, later, as a District Superintendent of Police, would know Blair briefly, observes that "All this had to be done on a salary of 300 rupees (£20) a month. It was of course quite impossible and we all left the school heavily in debt. I do not know for certain," he continues, "but I believe that in Blair's time . . . the cost of living [had become] so high that the probationers no longer joined the Club and that they lived very frugally. Our pay was increased for the first time in over 20 years about 1924, but too late to have been of any assistance to Blair. Mandalay, to him, must have been a terrible hole to live in."

But 1914 would inevitably regard 1922 as "deprived," and 1922, not having known the good old days before the war, would see things differently. For one thing, there was the fascination of being where they were. Mandalay, for Blair, was Kipling country incarnate, a dream realized, and he delighted in exploring the city and countryside. This was a taste he shared with Beadon, with whom otherwise he had little in common. Although the two always got on well together, there was to be no real intimacy between them—the familiar Blair pattern—and at the end of training, after they had been assigned to their respective stations, they said goodbye and would see each other again only on one further occasion.

Mandalay in the early 1920's was still essentially two cities: the British fort and the native quarter. Fort Dufferin had originally been built as a palace-city by the Burmese king Mindon in 1856; it was captured by the British in 1885, at which time they dethroned Mindon's successor, Thibaw, and transferred the capital of the country to Rangoon. The Fort was a mile square, enclosed on all four sides by twenty-foot-high walls of rosy brick—in each side a great stone gateway guarded by a pair of stone dragons—and surrounding the walls a wide moat, dense with red and white lotus and shaded by a border of tamarind, acacia, and cinnamon trees. Within the enormous area of the Fort were various Regimental Messes and barracks, the Upper Burma Club—whose members included most of the Europeans living in Mandalay—the sometime royal palace surrounded by an inner moat of its own, bungalows for regimental officers and senior government officials, a polo field, a nine-hole golf links, tennis courts, and a chapel.

That was the Fort, an outpost of England. Beyond its rose-colored walls was the other city, with a pulsing life of its own; the unpaved roads leading out into the dense countryside and native villages; the hundreds of shrines, temples, and pagodas—the Yakaing-paya, with its colossal Buddha coated in gold leaf; the Kuthodaw, a sugarloaf-shaped pagoda surrounded by more than seven hundred smaller pagodas of identical design. "I suppose, though," Beadon writes, "that the great Bazaar was the most interesting part of the city with its colourful stalls—bolts of cloth, lacquer ware, gold, silver, jewelry and ivory jostling side by side with fruit, vegetables, fish, meat and spices—the whole a babel of mixed languages pervaded by flies and the assorted not always pleasant smells of the Silken East." And he concludes: "During the hot weather, which was never really unpleasant, everything looked dry and dusty, but in the monsoon and the so-called cold weather that followed it, everything took on a green fresh look, with the flowers and flowering trees and shrubs in full bloom. . . . I really believe that my most unforgettable memory of Burma will be a cold-weather evening in Mandalay, watching the glowing sunset colours, reflected in the moat, slowly fade, the purple-shadowed Maymyo hills merging into the twilight darkness, and the twinkling Mandalay Hill Pagoda lamps light up and vie with the star-studded sky."

If a young man of no literary pretensions whatever could have been moved to this degree by the town and its surrounding country, it is not surprising that Blair, storing up each day new sensuous impressions, would later call upon them for a novel of Burma in which the landscape would play a central role—*Burmese Days*—and which he would describe to Henry Miller in 1936 as the only one of his novels that he was pleased with.*

The reason for Blair's being there was not to immerse himself in the life of the town but to be trained to take up his duties as an Assistant Superintendent of Police, and the greater part of his time, from early December on, was spent in more humdrum settings: the Police School, the Police Mess, and the parade ground. The school was intended "primarily for training cadet sub-inspectors—well-educated high school boys, chiefly Burmese but occasionally Indian, Chinese, or from the minor races of Burma—Shans, Karens, and Arakanese. Instructors for these cadets were found from the ranks of serving police officers of the rank of Inspector or Deputy Superintendent." During the time that Blair was there, there were 120 such cadets in training. The three Probationary A.S.P.'s made up an entirely different category. To begin with, they were English; they had also passed the appropriate higher-level examination; they

---

* In the letter to Miller, he makes no literary claim for the novel other than to say that "the descriptions of scenery aren't bad."

were being trained to become officers—in due season the cadets then at the school would be serving under them as their juniors and assistants. With a separate set of instructors, the three were required to take courses in Burmese, colloquial Hindustani, Law, and Police Procedure. The only other requirement was that they attend, on Wednesday and Saturday mornings, a parade in full uniform of the cadets in training. The Wednesday morning parade was taken in turn by Blair, Beadon, and Jones. The Saturday morning parade was regularly taken by the Principal of the School, a senior District Superintendent of Police, who is described by Beadon in an affectionate sentence that fans out to suggest all too vividly why Blair, given the sort of man he was, would not find himself at home in the career he had so romantically chosen. "This officer," Beadon writes, "was a tall, powerfully built Scotsman with a large moustache, a non drinker and smoker, but on two glasses of lemonade on a Mess night, a holy terror if it came to a rough and tumble."

It was, as we have had occasion to remark before, a matter of temperament: Beadon took to the life and enjoyed it; Blair did not. Beadon, for example, reveled in the Christmas season in Mandalay, when (that year) the Governor and his staff came up from Rangoon to Government House, and there were polo and tennis tournaments, dances and dinners and a continuing round of festivities; Blair, by the time the last holly decorations had been taken down in Government House, had acquired the reputation of not being "a good mixer." He had only been in Mandalay a month, but already it was evident that he "cared little for games, and seemed to be bored with the social and Club life" that, normally, occupied much of off-duty time. He did his work in courses without difficulty, but even in this respect went his own way. While Beadon and Jones were struggling with the difficulties of learning Burmese and

Hindustani in successive hours, Blair, to whom the languages came easily, more often than not would not attend classes, preferring to stay in his room and read.

But though Beadon was "fond of going down to the Club and playing snooker and dancing and what have you" and Blair was not, friendship of a sort—the Blairian sort that asked for a minimum of commitment on either side—developed between them. In order to see more of the country outside the city, Blair decided to buy a motorcycle, about which he was entirely a novice, and Beadon, who had a new Hudson 2-stroke and was an experienced rider, agreed to teach him how to ride it. The lesson was to take place within the less crowded precincts of Fort Dufferin.

> He had an American machine of a make I had never seen before [Beadon writes] and have never seen since. It was very low with 4 cylinders running fore and aft, and the sight of Blair, over six feet tall, astride this midget was ludicrous, as his knees almost came up round his ears, or so it seemed.
>
> All went well until we came to one of the gates which, so we thought, would let us out of the Fort, and we were moving along splendidly when I realised it was not one of the exits, but a gate that was permanently shut. I shouted to Blair to stop, but he lost his head apparently and instead of slowing down, stood up, and the bike went on under his legs and hit the gate. Luckily we were not going fast, and no damage was done, but it was an amusing incident.

Beadon's anecdotes are all of this character, amiable in tone and slight in subject matter, and certainly not revelations; but they are of peculiar interest, for they deal with aspects of Blair's Burmese experience that Orwell found no place for when he came to write of it. Of course, his intention then was not to be autobiographical: he selected and shaped his material as it contributed to his chosen themes, and let the rest go. So it is good to be reminded that, whatever his psychological peculiarities and social awkwardnesses, Blair was still a young man capable of sometimes enjoying himself and was not always the anguished guilt-ridden protagonist in an anti-imperialist drama.

Another Beadon anecdote, of a would-be tiger shoot in which he and Blair participated, proves to be very different, both in its faintly comic circumstances and in its anticlimactic conclusion, from the successful tiger shoot that figures so decisively in *Burmese Days:*

> One night we decided we would go out after tiger, knowing I may say, nothing whatsoever of the method or dangers of so doing! Accordingly, he [Blair] borrowed the Principal's 12 bore shot-gun and ball cartridges and I had a Luger-Parabellum automatic pistol with a wooden stock. Armed with these, we set forth to our destination, the banks of a canal about 10 miles East of Mandalay.
>
> There, at a small village, we routed out an elderly villager, somehow explained our intentions, and asked him to get out his bullocks and bullock cart, which he did. Then, for several hours we sat in the back of the cart, guns cocked, eyes alert, waiting for some unsuspecting tiger to cross our path. To say that nothing happened is only the truth, and I imagine the wily old Burman had no intention of going anywhere near where such an animal may have been lurking.

But in spite of these agreeable, shared experiences, Beadon was never deceived that there was any real intimacy between Blair and himself. The next spring (1923), his father, a consulting mining engineer who was working in

Burma, came to spend some time in Maymyo, a hill station some three thousand feet above sea level, forty-two miles east of Mandalay. Beadon was given leave for a week to go and stay with him, and he took Blair along. They had a quiet, enjoyable time, playing golf and at the club in the evenings, in a landscape and atmosphere peculiarly evocative of England—as such, Orwell drew upon it for a point in *Homage to Catalonia*—but Beadon concludes, "I cannot honestly recall that anything out of the ordinary happened, except that I realized that he and I had very little in common, I presumably being an extrovert, he an introvert, living in a world of his own: a rather shy, retiring intellectual."

The curriculum at the Police Training School had been established before the First World War and continued without change in 1922, but one has the impression that it was less than adequate, insofar as it was meant to prepare the future A.S.P.'s for the duties ahead of them. Although their duties were to be of an extremely practical nature, some were ignored entirely and the rest were presented to them only on a theoretical level. Thus, during the year of training in Mandalay they never set foot in a police station. Again, though they could count on being posted all over Burma, sometimes to stations deep in the jungle, it was not thought necessary that they should be made familiar in advance with either the country, its customs, or the diversity of its people—at least not from first-hand observation. Their training, for Blair, Beadon, and Jones, was a matter of formal classes in Mandalay, except for a period of one month, when they were attached to the British regiment stationed in Maymyo, the South Staffords. "I have never discovered what use this was to us," Beadon writes, "apart from drill training, but it was a pleasant break in the normal routine and we thoroughly enjoyed it." *

---

* Blair apparently enjoyed the experience less; for Orwell, putting it to polemical use in *The Road to Wigan Pier*, describes the morning marches

The most curious omission from the curriculum—perhaps on the theory, demonstrably untrue, that politics and the administration of justice have nothing to do with each other—was any reference at all to the unsettled, changing political situation in Burma. And since Blair's interests at this time were not in "politics," he did little to repair the omission on his own.

A literary/classical English Public School education, such as he had had, helps to create a keen social observer, aware of the nuances of social distinctions and practices, and so (sometimes) helps to make a novelist. But it is a political education that helps to teach the *significance* of the ways in which people are separated, and so (sometimes) helps to make a moralist. Five years in the service of Empire would contribute to the making of Orwell as a novelist and a moralist, but his response to Burma was a very convincing demonstration that, for him, personal considerations (the particular experience) were more important than political considerations (the abstract experience) and that he had to move through the former to arrive at the latter. Orwell's single most memorable sentence, "All animals are equal, but some animals are more equal than others," may have had its beginnings in social observation—at St. Cyprian's, perhaps, as the boys competed for Mum's favor?—but it took final form and gained its international currency as a political statement and a moral judgment.

Blair in Burma, unlike Orwell in Spain, as far as any written record survives, seems to have been singularly uninter-

---

in the hot sun, so hot that presently the column of soldiers was steaming with sweat; and Blair, bringing up the rear with one of the junior officers, found the smell of their sweating bodies so offensive that it turned his stomach—an instance of class-inspired prejudice. But whatever its subjective aspects, his month with the South Staffords and his "service" with the O.T.C. at Eton comprised his military experience up to the time of the Spanish Civil War.

ested in the interesting political events that were taking place about him, except as they may be inferred in the background of *Burmese Days,* and in the two essays drawn from his police experience, "Shooting an Elephant" and "A Hanging." Yet, in an indirect but important way, the contemporary Burmese political situation had a considerable influence upon the creation of George Orwell. If Blair had arrived in Burma a few years earlier, he would have found a much more orderly, ordinary province, appearing to function in a smooth, untroubled way under a benevolent imperial administration. It is not inconceivable that the jarring, sometimes quite trivial events that stood out so painfully when he was there would have been less noticeable, less abrasive, less guilt-producing, if they had not taken place against a background of growing confusion and uncertainty for the once so self-confident British rulers in Burma. Paradoxically, it was the very attempts of the British government to liberalize its own administration and to allow the Burmese voice to be heard that made Orwell more conscious than he probably would have been otherwise of the Empire as a system in which he could not continue to participate and keep his self-respect.

Although Burma was an administrative part of India, it had had a very different history. The Burmese were a gentle people, much less caste-conscious than the Indians, and more accepting of their situation, which made them easier to govern. But they were beginning to resent the degree to which they were exploited commercially by the Indians and the Chinese, and by British and other European mercantile interests. Along with this went a growing restiveness at being under British rule.

British influence in Burma had been considerable since the middle of the nineteenth century; however, the country was not officially taken into the Empire until the 1880's. All went smoothly, even placidly, to the end of the First World

ERIC
BLAIR

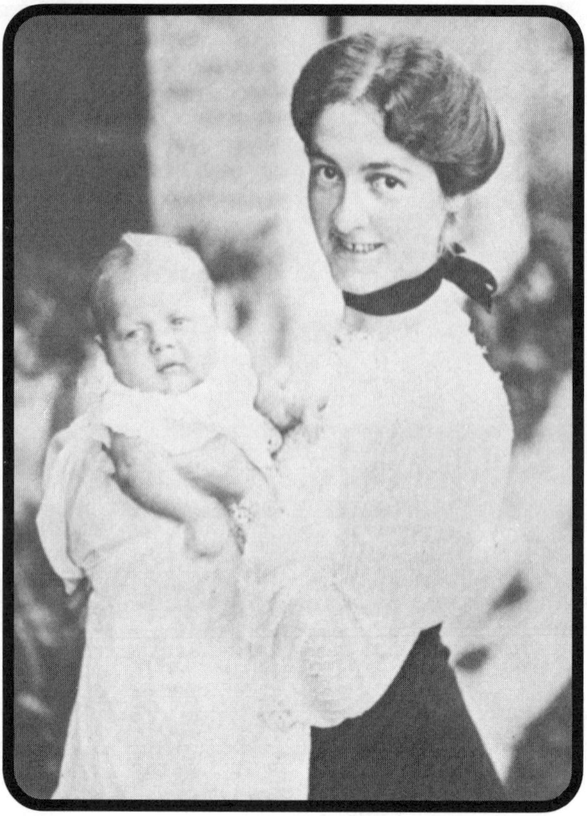

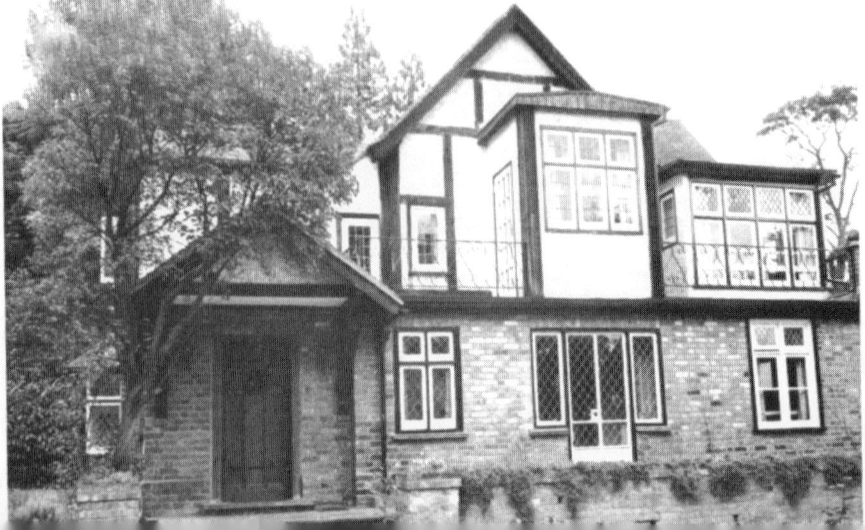

↖ MRS. IDA MABEL BLAIR WITH ERIC, ABOUT 1903
↙ ROSELAWN, SHIPLAKE, WHERE THE BLAIRS LIVED FROM 1912 TO 1915
↑ ETON, AFTERNOON BATHING AT "ATHENS." BLAIR IS ON THE RIGHT
↓ ETON, FIELD DAY, SPRING 1921. BLAIR IS THIRD FROM THE LEFT AND CYRIL CONNOLLY IS SECOND FROM THE RIGHT

↑ ETON, SCHOOL PHOTOGRAPH, 1921. BLAIR IS SITTING ON THE STEPS
IN THE CENTER, AGAINST THE LOW WALL
↓ THE POLICE TRAINING SCHOOL AT MANDALAY, BURMA. BLAIR IS
IN THE BACK ROW, THIRD FROM THE LEFT; ROGER BEADON IS THE
SHORT MAN TO BLAIR'S LEFT

War, and 1890 to 1920 is generally considered the "golden period" of imperial rule. The traditional English attitudes to the people over whom they ruled—benevolent, patronizing, and authoritarian—were evident in Burma, but perhaps in a less conspicuous way than elsewhere. There was a population of thirteen million, of whom some nine million were Buddhists. Since they were more "gentle" than many of the other "subject peoples," occasions for overt suppression or other extreme forms of discipline were infrequent. They were also "inefficient," or so it was alleged by the British— not disapprovingly, however, for did it not confirm the need for the British presence in the country to govern it efficiently?

But even during the "golden period" there had been faint stirrings of unrest. The Y.M.B.A., the Young Men's Buddhist Association, which had been founded in 1906 in a pro-British mood and with peaceful intentions similar to those of the Young Men's Christian Association, by the end of the war had become a center for the expression of Burmese nationalist sentiment. Such sentiment was fueled in 1919 when India, but not Burma, was granted, in accord with the Montagu–Chelmsford proposals, the system called Dyarchy, whereby the Indians were offered representation and a voice in the way in which they were governed, although important areas of activity were still reserved to the British administration. The inevitable resentment of the Burmese nationalists at being denied the privileges of Dyarchy couldn't be ignored, and in 1923, the system was also instituted in most of Burma. Thereafter, all Burmese men and women over the age of eighteen were eligible to participate in the election of three fourths of the membership of the national legislature. Ministers from the elected group were in charge of local government, education, health, agriculture, excise, and public works. There were also selected Ministers, British appointments, who were in charge of law and order, revenue, and finance. The advance toward self-government was considerable, but since the money that was essential to keep it all going was in the charge of a Minister appointed by the British, it meant (gracious rhetoric aside) that the British still had the ultimate power to decide what action should or should not be taken by the Burmese government.

The thought, or the hope, was that the granting of Dyarchy would satisfy nationalist aspirations, whatever they might be—the idea of "independence" had not yet been strongly brought forth except by a small militant Burmese minority, and it had scarcely entered into the calculations of the British. In any event, the hoped-for result was not achieved. As often happens when an imperial power grants some measure of political freedom to its subjects, the result was only to make it clearer to them that they were not truly and fully governing themselves: they were still a subject people. So there was, on the part of the Burmese, discontent, and a subterranean hostility that was moving closer to the surface: the impassive stare, or the titter, or the *sotto voce* sarcasm—any of the trivial gestures that in a period of strain can be magnified to major provocations. And on the part of the British government there was a continuing effort at improvement, liberalization, and reform. Indeed, it has been argued that, at the village level, their well-intentioned efforts to improve the traditional "headman" system were so drastic that in the end the system functioned worse than before. The British were caught in that classic dilemma of a ruling power not native to the country: to what extent should they interfere—where problems ranged from the introduction of Western economic enterprise to the modification of the Burmese passion for gambling?

The ideal of colonial administration found characteristic expression, to give only one example, in *Burma: A Handbook of Practical Information* by J. G. Scott, which was published in a third revised edition in 1921: "In Burma, as elsewhere in the British Empire the object of the ruling power has been to maintain the spirit of the native administration and interfere as little as possible with the native executive, legal and land systems, and with the customs and prejudices of the people." This was the ideal, but, of course, the British had notions as to how a country could best be governed, many of them eminently sensible, and it was next to impossible not to interfere and impose them, directly or indirectly, once they were there. The police—native at the bottom but English at the top—would be in the closest daily contact with the Burmese, in the swarming cities and the remotest villages, when it came to actually imposing and administering Western concepts of law and order, based on the straightforward "Anglo-Saxon" view that there was a right and a wrong way of doing things. Burmese ideas of justice were more flexible, the magistrate less a judge of the right or the wrong than an arbitrator who would attempt to achieve some sort of compromise, a Solomon-like figure presiding over civil disputes or litigation. Presumably there would be less flexibility where crimes were concerned, especially Violent or Important crimes—murder, dacoity,* or robbery—but even then, there were radical differences between Burmese and British ways of looking at things, which meant that the high ideal of not interfering with native customs and prejudices was difficult to achieve even when it was attempted. And at the constabulary level, where the British officers went about their daily job, often under adverse conditions and in trying circumstances, it was unlikely that much attention was paid to the ideal.

This was the level where Blair functioned, and it determined not only the peculiar angle of vision from which he

* Dacoity—in India and Burma, gang robbery, in which more than four men participate.

looked out at Burma, but also the outer figure he presented to the Burmese. They saw, and he knew himself to be (and later wrote of himself as), a representative of the institution to which he had voluntarily attached himself, the Indian Imperial Police. No matter how ill-fitting his uniform (in both the literal and metaphoric sense), such was his role, and it was as a policeman, not a journalist, or budding writer, or student of politics, that he had his experience of Burma. One profound lesson that he was later to draw from it was the great distance that exists between institutions and the life they are designed to maintain, but more often suppress or confine or destroy; that would be the lesson of Spain also; and the lesson of *1984*. But the immediate effect, in 1924 as he left the Police Training School and at his various postings thereafter, was to prevent him (even had he wished it) from entering into Burmese life except as it related to his institutional role. This in itself is sufficient to account for what he missed of the native experience, so little of which figures in his work; however, by the same token, it ensured him of a full exposure to the colonial experience, which he recorded with an unrelenting distaste in *Burmese Days*. The ferment of nationalist aspiration seems never to have caught his attention, except perhaps as a provocative nuisance, or enlisted his sympathy, or engaged his imagination. It is significant that in his Burmese novel the two principal native characters, the "good" Dr. Veraswami and the "evil" U Po Kyin, are alike in their aspirations: not to reclaim Burma from the English, but to be elected to membership in the English Club. Even the local "anti-English" riot that dramatically erupts toward the novel's end, and that the English respond to in the pukka sahib tradition, has no real political meaning: it simply has been whipped up by U Po Kyin to further his social ambition.

Of course, one does not turn to Orwell for a "history"

of the country during the period 1922–7. Our interest is in the history of Eric Blair, the experience of a young officer in the police in Burma, in its first version, not its exemplary recapitulation by Orwell, the anti-imperialist. Obviously, his experiences made him the anti-imperialist he became; the "becoming" extended over the whole of a five-year period during which, from first to last, he was in the service of imperialism, and outwardly at least exhibiting no qualms about it. That he happened, also, to be a writer-in-embryo adds to the peculiarity of his history.

EARLY IN 1924 [ROGER BEADON WRITES] WE SAT FOR AND passed our Lower Burmese and other exams and were confirmed in our appointment as A.S.P.'s, and so ended our spell at the School. I have always felt, however, that, though from the social angle Mandalay could not have been bettered, from the training point of view the method used at Toungoo, before the school was moved to Mandalay, was far and away more efficient, 'tho undoubtedly more drastic. At Toungoo, training was reduced to teaching the rudiments of languages and law, and then, after only a few months, I believe, trainees were posted to a remote Police Station where possibly only the Police Station Officer spoke English, and told them to get on with it or else!

And it worked and worked well, as not only did they have to learn to read, write and speak Burmese fluently, but also how to deal with the numerous crime and other registers at first hand. I, on the other hand, had never been inside a Police Station the whole time I was under training, which, on looking back, strikes me as most peculiar. Moreover, when I did pass both Lower and Higher Burmese, I took the laissez-faire attitude of so many, and expected everyone to speak English. As a result, my Burmese was never very good, though sufficient to get me along.

And so, in early 1924, came the parting of the ways, and we were posted to different districts to continue our training under district officers.

Beadon was going to Bassein, Blair to Myaungmya. They parted and wished each other luck, knowing that there was little likelihood of their meeting in the future, and with no suggestion that their friendship, such as it had been, ought to be continued by correspondence—though if their paths should cross, as fellow policemen meeting at a district headquarters or Club, fine. In short, it was a parting in the Blair manner. The next year, in circumstances to be described, they did have one further meeting, after which they never saw each other again, although Beadon notes that he "naturally heard of him from time to time and gathered he was looked upon as somewhat eccentric."

There was a dramatic, even intimidating contrast between the chiefly theoretical training Blair had received in Mandalay and the responsibilities that awaited him at Myaungmya; and it was reinforced in its impact upon him by the contrast between the two places themselves. The one was a fair-sized city, the capital of Upper Burma, equipped with at least some of the amenities of twentieth-century civilization one took for granted—electric light, for example. The other was a primitive, isolated outpost in the alluvial Irrawaddy Delta, where there was no electricity and one read at night (if one was eccentric enough to want to read) by oil lamp under mosquito netting. His colleagues agree that Blair was not "lucky" in this starting point for his career: there were other districts to be preferred to the Delta; and his superior officer, they suggest ever so tactfully, may have been a bit difficult. One has the impression from their impressions that his bad luck held through more than the first of his postings. One hears of less than enviable locales, and of other "difficult" superiors—of one who was a bully and gave him "a bad time," of another who was a melancholic and eventually a suicide, and of a third who took against Blair as an old Etonian.

In fact, his being an Etonian gave positive offense only to a few bigoted and mean-minded types of the sort he would later pillory in *Burmese Days*. "What struck most people as unusual," we are told by a man who was acquainted with him when he was stationed in Hanthawaddy District, "was that an Etonian should join the police services in Burma." (And he goes on to express the view generally held, then and perhaps even now, by non-Etonians: "Eton, as you know, is the school for the sons of aristocrats and plutocrats. Their sons can usually be found some lucrative employment at home and it was rare for them to serve in India except perhaps in the Indian Civil Service.") Although Orwell later may have enjoyed the incongruity of calling himself a "policeman," with its nicely homely, Gilbert and Sullivan, English overtones—and admittedly, anywhere, "a policeman's lot is not a happy one"—still, the "bobby on his beat" conjures up a very different picture from Blair on a tour of duty, going by motor launch or dugout canoe from one village to the next (for there were no roads or railways in the Delta)—not only enforcing law and order, as a policeman would do in the home country, but also playing a role in the administration of government.

Technically, the police officer was subordinate to the Deputy Commissioner, who was in charge of a District, but in many ways he was a parallel, independent authority, since he also took orders directly from his own Inspector General. The Indian Imperial Police had been formally organized in 1861 to cope with the growth of crime; or perhaps, rather, with the extent to which organized crime was interfering with the growth of English influence and power. In 1921, just before Blair arrived in Burma, there was a military garrison there of about ten thousand, a military police force of about fifteen thousand, and a civil police force of about thirteen thousand (mainly Burmese and Indian). It was to the last that Blair was attached. In his postings he would serve either as an Assistant District Superintendent in one of the thirty-six districts into which Burma was divided for administrative purposes, or as one of the fifty-nine Assistant Superintendents who were in charge of the more important sub-divisions. Over him was a hierarchy that culminated with the Inspector General and four Deputy Inspectors General, heading an organization independent of any form of popular control, even after the dyarchic reforms of 1923. Although from 1923 on there was a marked liberalization in recruiting, with Indians and Burmese being admitted to the officer ranks, centralization and bureaucratization intensified, which led, inevitably, to a curtailment of imaginative, individual action: the day of the gallant officer, on his own and out of touch with civilization, was virtually at an end. The telegraph, too, made its negative contribution in this regard: it stifled initiative, Orwell later thought, and because of it, thinking and action had been reduced to the "constipated" attitudes of those who were at their desks in Whitehall, the ultimate source of orders and power. Even so, the sense of adventure, of doing something uncommon, the challenge of responsibility and authority, were still inherent in the life he had chosen; and Blair, whatever his cynicism, evidently responded to them with some excitement. Putting on the uniform of the Indian Imperial Police, with its tight strapped trousers, was not a humiliation to the spirit. Many years later he remarked to his friend Anthony Powell, "Those straps under the boot give you a feeling like nothing else in life."

But, of course, there was a world of difference between

taking dress parade on a Wednesday morning in Mandalay, and finding himself Headquarters Assistant to the District Superintendent in Myaungmya. Once again, it might be said, he was "new boy," in a situation that reactivated the St. Cyprian's syndrome: friendless and inexperienced, not certain of what to expect and fearful of proving to be inadequate, a predictable failure. The post was regarded officially as a continuation of "training," but it was training of a wholly different order from what he had received at Mandalay. Without preliminaries he was thrust into the demanding responsibilities and, for a "new boy," highly confusing routines of a District Headquarters. He was expected to run the office; supervise the stores of clothing, equipment, and ammunition; take charge of the training school for locally recruited constables, as well as the headquarters police station with its strength of thirty to fifty men on active patrol duty and a contingent of escorts for hearings and trials in court. He would also check the night patrols in Myaungmya, and when his Superintendent was away, touring the sub-divisional headquarters within the District, he would assume general charge. For a young man not yet twenty-one, and fresh from the classrooms of the Police Training School, it was a daunting assignment, and there is reason to think that Blair did not manage it notably well. For he held the post an unusually short time, only two months, and it seems likely that his Superintendent requested (demanded) that he be moved on elsewhere. Granted that this particular Superintendent was more difficult than most, we are reminded by Lawson, speaking from first-hand knowledge, that no District Superintendent would welcome a junior officer as Headquarters Assistant where "the duties were highly onerous and calling for experience." It was part of Blair's bad luck in Burma that this should have been his first assignment.

His luck improved somewhat with his next posting,

farther east in the Delta, to Twante, a sub-division of Hanthawaddy District, where he was on duty from mid-May to mid-December 1924. As Sub-Divisional Police Officer he would be responsible to the District Superintendent, but he would not be performing his duties, as at Myaungmya, directly under his observation, and he would have a considerable degree of freedom in carrying them out. In charge of several police stations, he would spend most of his time on tour, inspecting them, checking the investigation of local crimes, holding inquiries into cases of police misconduct, and visiting as many villages as possible with a view to enlisting the cooperation of the village headmen and elders who had minor police powers and duties. He would also see that adequate surveillance was kept over the persistent criminals living in the area. This was the usual routine of his days and nights, but the arrival of a telegram advising him of the occurrence of murder or dacoity meant he must drop whatever he was doing and hasten to the scene of the crime and take charge of the investigation. A demanding life, certainly; perhaps a boring one; very likely a lonely one, for in a small town like Twante there would be no more than two or three Europeans about (though, given Blair's solitary nature, this might have proved less a hardship for him than for some).

Two possible views of the life he was leading in the Delta—that the same experiences could give rise to very different feelings—are suggested in letters written to the authors by two police officers who were in Burma at the same time as Blair, and who were kind enough to comment on it. One writes: "His work kept him busy on the move around a large area. He lived in his own government house—a roomy enough bungalow with stabling and quarters for servants. He travelled around his area with houseman, cook, orderly, etc., and put up in a Dak bungalow or any available shelter . . . Every journey from headquarters had its purpose & apart from that, despite some discomforts, yielded great delight & contained some essence of adventure."

The same writer adds, "He came by accident to a pleasant, warmhearted, tolerant Buddhist country which had no violent class distinction & found the older Europeans already enmeshed in Buddhist benevolence: loving the people of Burma & imposing no real imperialistic sway. Burma gave him time to think, cause to think, and much to think about." The first sentence may be taken as one point of view (very different of course from Orwell's); the second sentence is undoubtedly true. What is unclear is how much his thinking then had to do with Burma—he himself has left no contemporary record—for the reaction to what he experienced there would be slow in coming, and the revulsion he would ultimately express at having served in the cause of imperialism may well have been part of the greater guilt he came to feel in being a member of the upper middle classes. Or again, at the plainest, down-to-earth level, it might have been partly a reaction to the unpleasantness of the physical circumstances in which he found himself. That they could be, indeed were, unpleasant is evident in another letter describing the conditions under which he lived in Twante, in the "usual dismal teak box of a house with no sanitation, electricity, or piped water supply." As for the Delta itself, it was

> the most dismal and pestiferous tract in Burma . . . a vast featureless plain of alluvium extending for hundreds of square miles. A few trees exist near the villages and there are stunted nipa palms on the banks of the muddy creeks which intersect the land every few hundred yards. Near the coast there are many miles of mangrove swamps. The insect life, even in the dry season, is a penance to be borne. Mosquitoes both by night and day exist in their

millions. In the rain, the greenfly from the paddy fields invades the houses and makes it difficult to eat meals or drink without swallowing quantities of the insect. There is no water to be had other than that collected in small reservoirs. This is so stagnant that it is always opaque with red algae.

It is in this grim locale—of which, oddly, given his sensitivity to the degrading aspects of life, Orwell never wrote—that we catch some direct glimpses of him. R. G. B. Lawson at that time was District Superintendent of Police at Pyapon in the Irrawaddy Delta west of Hanthawaddy. It was there, on one occasion, and on a second occasion at Twante, that he met Blair, accompanying his own District Superintendent, at conferences to discuss matters of common concern—chiefly criminal—"the activities of robber gangs operating over a considerable area."

Writing of these two occasions some forty years later, Lawson remembers Blair as being "tall, good-looking, pleasant to talk to, easy of manner." Once again we are reminded that "He did not give the impression of being in any way remarkable; no one at that time would have imagined his later fame." Lawson found him reserved, but assumed that, "Naturally, as a very junior officer he would realise that it was better not to intrude his personality. On the other hand, it is possible that his air of reserve might disappear on closer acquaintance."

To Lawson, then, Blair was not noticeably different from the usual run of young officers, making due allowance for his being an Etonian. But one fact that he allowed to slip through the reticence barrier did give an impression of eccentricity:

He told me he was in the habit of attending the services in the little village churches of the Karens. The Karens, who inhabit the areas in the south and east of Burma, have been largely converted to Christianity by the American Baptist Mission. The average European official was, in any case, not noticeably religious and the idea of attending a religious service in a tongue—Karen—which he could not understand, was not likely to occur to him.

But Blair, it is clear now, was not "average," and even then, this particular eccentricity gained him a certain reputation. Beadon heard of it—"he was known to have spent a lot of time in Hpogyu-Kyaungs talking learnedly with the Hpyongis (priests) and intoning the Mantras"—and he was not surprised, for, as had been evident from the earliest days at the Police Training School, "the language came so very easily to him."

Another officer, A. L'estrange Brownlow, who knew Blair first at Twante, found him "a shy diffident young man . . . obviously odd man out with other Police Officers, but longing, I think, to be able to fit in." The two saw quite a bit of each other, for Blair's next post was at Syriam, and Brownlow by then had become Superintendent of River Police, Rangoon, only ten miles distant. But closer acquaintance did not bring them in any significant way closer. Blair asked Brownlow to take him out with him when he went snipe shooting (snipe were the only "game birds" in the Delta), and there were several such expeditions. But, as Brownlow recalls, "he had obviously little experience with a gun, and, if my memory serves me right, did not get a single snipe."

In mid-December 1924 he was posted to Syriam, the headquarters of the Hanthawaddy District. Two days after his arrival there, he received official notification that his probationary status was at an end, and he now held the rank of Assistant District Superintendent. His pay was appropriately raised, with various allowances coming to a total of 740 rupees per month; and this was to be his salary until he left Burma.*

Since Syriam was the site of the refinery of the Burmah Oil Company, it had a number of European residents and even what passed for a social life, but in its own way it was as desolate and dismal a place to be as Twante. The surrounding land was a barren waste, all vegetation killed off by the fumes of sulphur dioxide pouring out day and night from the stacks of the refinery. Eventually one got used to the ever-present noxious smell hanging in the air, but at first encounter it was suffocating in its effect, and a continuing irritation to the mucous membranes.

In Syriam Blair's job was a dreary one—looking after the security of the refinery. In the District—which was suffering from a rather high rate of crime, with more than three hundred murder cases each year—his duties were much as before, but now, responsible for a whole district rather than merely a sub-division, he would have to be on tour some twenty days each month. But whether in Syriam itself, making conversation with the Europeans who were associated with the Burmah Oil Company or with his notoriously difficult superior—no easy task for one as shy as Blair, and doubtfully rewarding in any case—or traveling from village to village, alone, isolated, weeks at a time, much of it during the rainy season, it was a life in which loneliness and depression would seem to have been almost inevitable. Lawson, who would end his career as City Commissioner of

---

* About £65 per month. By most standards, certainly by Orwell's, it would be an adequate sum in the early 1920's to live a comfortable life. It is worth noting in this connection that in 1948, when Orwell took part in a symposium on "The Cost of Letters" in Cyril Connolly's *Horizon*, to the question "How much do you think a writer needs to live on?" his reply was a minimum of £10 per week after taxes for a married man, and £6 for an unmarried man. The ideal figure he mentioned was a thousand pounds per year. Taking into account inflationary rises, that was pretty much what he had been earning in Burma.

Rangoon, speaks eloquently to the point: "The system of appointing boys fresh from school to the Indian Police, and then throwing them on their own resources in some foul climate with no one to talk to of their own race and kind, was a most pernicious one. The loneliness was too great and in consequence a number of suicides occurred, and at least two of my colleagues lost their reason. The other Services, the Indian Civil Service, the Forest Service, the Service of Engineers, the Education Service, the Medical Service, all recruited university graduates who began their career in India at the age of twenty-five years. Their maturity made life easier for them."

Blair was a novice police officer, just turned twenty-one. But he had always been remarkably self-contained, and so was better able to cope with the isolation than some of the jolly extroverts who tended to crack, away from the gregarious, ritualized life they enjoyed in the English clubs and compounds. It was a life Orwell would reproduce in *Burmese Days* with an unrelenting irony, an outpouring of resentment long deferred. That, after all, was years later; in Burma, isolation, whether physical or spiritual, was something to be endured—one has the sense of Blair being as lonely in the crowded Club as in the godforsaken dak bungalow with no one but his body servant to talk to. But the "resource" that got him through the ordeal was one that those who knew him in Burma had no reason to suspect. Although Orwell remembered these years as the time when he was trying to abandon the idea of becoming a writer, he was, in fact, consciously or not, already a writer-in-embryo: he could watch, observe, listen, and judge. Experience, his own or another's, was something he put to use; it became part of the nonstop "story" he was telling to his listening self. (And continued to tell until he was twenty-five, drawing from daily experience, Orwell reminds us, all through the non-writing years.) Even the most painful loneliness, the stupidity and racist cant one heard at the Club, the shame at one's role, the rancor of the natives became endurable as they were assimilated into the "story." If much of *Burmese Days*—and much of its hero or anti-hero, Flory —is subjectively drawn (and so, as those who are familiar with the milieu claim, at times overdrawn), much of it, including a good deal of Flory's personality and history, is simply an objective account of what Blair had known at first hand. (Objective, but not inclusive. The curious thing, as has been suggested earlier, is how much of what he had known in Burma he chose *not* to write about.)

For Blair the chief advantage of being at Syriam—and this would hold true also for his next post, Insein—was its proximity to Rangoon. A cosmopolitan seaport, Rangoon was the largest city in Burma, with a population of eight hundred thousand. That it was a mere ten miles' distance from a grim refinery town such as Syriam, or thirty miles from the dispiriting wastes of the Delta, made the difference from them only the more vivid and welcome.

W. Somerset Maugham, a writer whose work Blair greatly admired and whose influence upon Orwell's work is discernible, arriving there as a traveler in the mid-1920's, has caught something of the contrasts in which Rangoon abounded:

> . . . a cordial welcome; a drive in an American car through busy streets of business houses, concrete and iron like the streets, good heavens!, of Honolulu, Shanghai, Singapore or Alexandria, and then a spacious, shady house in a garden; an agreeable life, luncheon at this club or that, drives along trim, wide roads, bridge after dark at that club or this, gin *pahits*, a great many men in white drill or pongee silk, laughter, pleasant conversation; and then back through the night to dress for

dinner and out again to dine with this hospitable host or the other, cocktails, a substantial meal, dancing to a gramophone or a game of billiards, and then back once more to the large, cool silent house. It was very attractive, easy, comfortable, and gay; but was this Rangoon? Down by the harbour and along the river were narrow streets, a rabbit warren of intersecting alleys; and here, multitudinous, lived the Chinese, and there the Burmans: I looked with curious eyes as I passed in my motor car and wondered what strange things I should discover and what secrets they had to tell me if I could plunge into that enigmatic life and lose myself in it as a cup of water thrown overboard is lost in the Irrawaddy.

Admittedly these are the impressions of a world-famous author—Maugham at his most worldly and Maugham-like —and suggest, at the respectable end of the spectrum at least, a social life unlikely to be experienced by a junior police officer. Blair, not yet even an apprentice writer, settled for less, "the occasional festive weekend." He went into the city as often as he could manage: to browse in a bookshop (Smart & Mookerdum's) going over the new books (Maugham's among them) and periodicals arriving weeks late from England; to eat well-cooked food, imported beefsteak by choice, in a Western-style restaurant, a dramatic change from the ill-prepared chicken and rice served up to him night after night by his houseman in Syriam; to get away from the boring routine of police life and the company of fellow officers among whom he was "odd man out." Those were the rewards of Rangoon.

But his weekends had their disagreeable aspect too, for in the city he was brought face to face with the "new" Burmese—so different from the gentle villagers and their co-operative headmen—the students and Buddhist monks who "dared to dream of political freedom," whose faces expressed an infuriating contempt, and for whom Blair, as a police officer in uniform, would be imperialism personified. And there was nothing one could do, really—it was not illegal for a Burman to smile mockingly or snigger or brush past one on the railway platform—except to seem to ignore the provocation as best one could (or else to try to understand the "dream" that inspired it, a possibility that did not occur to him then). Dr. Maung Htin Aung, Vice-Chancellor of the University of Rangoon, has told of an episode at the end of 1924 that might have come from the pages of *Burmese Days*, in which a young officer whom he identifies as Blair figured. (Dr. Htin Aung at this time was a freshman at University College, Rangoon; Blair would have very recently arrived at Syriam.)

> One afternoon, at about 4 p.m., the suburban railway station of Pagoda Road was crowded with schoolboys and undergraduates, and Blair came down the stairs to take the train to the Mission Road Station, where the exclusive Gymkhana Club was situated. One of the boys, fooling about with his friends, accidentally bumped against the tall and gaunt Englishman, who fell heavily down the stairs. Blair was furious and raised the heavy cane that he was carrying, to hit the boy on the head, but checked himself, and struck him on the back instead. The boys protested and some undergraduates, including myself, surrounded the angry Englishman. . . . The train drew in and Blair boarded a first-class carriage. But in Burma, unlike India, first-class carriages were never taboo to natives, and some of us had first-class season tickets. The argument between Blair and the undergraduates continued. Fortunately, the train reached Mission Road Station without further incident, and Blair left the train.

Whether or not he went to the Gymkhana Club after leaving the train we do not know, though it would have been a logical inference to draw if he were the stereotype he might appear to a Burmese schoolboy, and given to doing what "one did." At times, as we will see, he overplayed the part of the imperial policeman; it is doubtful, however, that he "longed" to be like the others; he took a sardonic pleasure in being "unlike," and was drawn by temperament as well as by the curiosity of a writer-in-embryo, to the "odd case." In Mandalay, while at the Training School, he had become acquainted with one such—Captain H. F. Robinson, an Indian Army officer who had been seconded to the Burma military police, and after a scandal involving his native mistress, had been cashiered. He had chosen to remain on in Mandalay, becoming a Buddhist and an opium addict, and climaxed this phase of his life with a botched attempt at suicide. For a young officer, he would be a classic minatory example of the white man going to pieces in the East (as in a story by Maugham). But for Blair, the writer-in-embryo, meeting Robinson was a memorable experience, which he later drew upon for a number of biographical details when he was inventing the character of Flory—whose tone is undoubtedly autobiographical, but whose history is not.

In Rangoon he saw quite regularly an old Etonian who had come out to Burma as the representative of a British business firm. The two had first been acquainted in College, where Lawrence (as we will call him here) was in an Election some years senior to Blair's. In London very likely the acquaintance between them would not have been revived, given the ease with which Blair could go unencumbered by past friendships from one phase of his life to the next. But in Rangoon, Lawrence was a welcome "find," the more so as he was, in his own fashion, also "odd man out"—in this instance, with the English colony and especially its female members, having committed the unpardonable sin in their eyes of marrying an Indian woman. It was precisely the oddness of his behavior and the disapproving reaction to it that would have excited Blair's sympathy and interest. Privately, he confided to Christopher Hollis, who passed through Rangoon at this time, that he thought Lawrence's marrying the woman a mistake. No doubt he found Robinson's arrangement—a native mistress such as he would give to Flory—more sensible as well as more understandable: it fell so easily within the confines of fiction. But where Blair's contemporary attitudes toward marriage, women, and sex are concerned, and certainly when it is a question of his actual experiences, we enter into speculative or hearsay territory. Lawrence recalls him telling him—in what seems a most un-Blair-like burst of candor—that he frequented the waterfront brothels. Perhaps he did. Or perhaps he did not, and claimed that he did, out of pride and for effect, to impress a fellow Etonian whose experience in sexual matters was so much greater than his. Against these putative, man-of-the-worldly descents into the brothels, we must put Roger Beadon's forthright statement: "As for female company I don't think I ever saw him with one." It was the sort of thing Beadon would be likely to notice, for, as he says, "I had an eye for anything that was going." The next year, when he visited Blair at Insein, he detected no tell-tale hint of a female on the premises, no doll-like Ma Hla May, such as Flory had bought from her parents for three hundred rupees, to come to his bed upon demand.*

---

* Masculine pride, of which Orwell had his share, accounts for much, and almost certainly for the curious conversation between Orwell and Harold Acton in Paris in 1945 that Acton reports in his *More Memoirs of an Aesthete*: ". . . I prompted him to reminisce about his life in Burma, and his sad earnest eyes lit up with pleasure when he spoke of the sweetness of Burmese women . . . He was more enthusiastic about the beauties of Morocco, and this cadaverous ascetic whom one scarcely connected with

It was at Lawrence's house that Blair and Hollis had a brief reunion in the summer of 1925. Hollis, Malcolm MacDonald, and Christopher Woodruff had been on a world tour as debaters for the Oxford Union, and Woodruff and Hollis had come on to Rangoon from Australia and Indonesia. In the two years since Hollis had last seen Blair, they had not kept in touch. Although he "vaguely knew that Blair had gone 'out East,'" he was delighted to learn now that not only was he in Burma, but stationed so close to Rangoon that it would be possible for them to meet. They did have two dinners together, and the principal impression that Hollis carried away from their meetings was that Blair, the Etonian rebel and cynic, the friend of the "revolutionary" Caucus, had been transformed into the very model of a Kiplingesque empire builder, intolerant of any of the natives, the Buddhist monks in particular, who made nuisances of themselves, and so made the work of the

---

fleshy gratification admitted that he had seldom tasted such bliss as with certain Moroccan girls, whose complete naturalness and grace and candid sensuality he described in language so simple and direct that one could visualize their slender flanks and small pointed breasts and almost sniff the odour of spices that clung to their satiny skins. A description worthy of Gide, I mused, and equally sincere."

Orwell went to Morocco with his wife Eileen in September 1938, at the advice of his doctor that he spend six months in a warm climate. He had been in a sanitorium suffering from lung disease since March. The Orwells settled in Marrakech, where he began to write his novel *Coming Up for Air*. He worked at it steadily, and finished it in little more than three months, in January 1939. Then he and Eileen went for a week's holiday into the Atlas mountains. They returned to Marrakech on January 27; soon after, he fell ill and was bedridden for a period of three weeks. He and Eileen sailed from Casablanca to London on March 26. His letters from Morocco, and hers too, suggest that it was a time when they were extremely happy together. There is nothing in Orwell's published or unpublished writing of his having tasted "bliss . . . with certain Moroccan girls," although, in a letter to his friend Geoffrey Gorer he speaks of the native women as being "exquisitely beautiful." But what was most fascinating about them was that they were "so dirty . . . their necks almost invisible under dirt."

police more difficult. "In the side of him which he revealed to me . . . there was no trace of liberal opinions," Hollis writes. "He was at pains to be the imperial policeman, explaining that these theories of no punishment and no beating were all very well at public schools but that they did not work with the Burmese. . . . If I had never heard or read of Orwell after that evening, I should certainly have dismissed him as an example of that common type which has a phase of liberal opinion at school, when life is as yet untouched by reality, but relapses easily after into conventional reaction."

He was *at pains* to be the imperial policeman . . .

There was no mention of the loneliness, the boredom, the physical discomfort of life in the Delta, nothing to suggest disillusionment or dissatisfaction. Once more, as with his claim to experience of the brothels, it would seem to have been a matter of putting on a front, essential to his pride. Here was Hollis, who had gone on to University, as he, Blair, might also have done, and who would leave Rangoon in three days and return to London, to Oxford, to the literary-flavored life he, Blair, had romantically turned down; and here *he* was, committed to the Burma police for another three years! In the circumstances it is hardly surprising that he should have overplayed the role of the tough, no-nonsense imperialist. What one is "at pains to be" is not necessarily what one is. So the two friends went their separate ways, and they would not be in touch again until 1931.

Blair was at Syriam a little more than nine months; then, in September 1925, he was posted to Insein, ten miles north of Rangoon, as Assistant Superintendent at Headquarters. The advantage of Insein over his previous postings was its more agreeable climate—he had managed to survive two of the May to October rainy seasons, unpleasant in general, particularly so in Lower Burma—and now at last he was out of the Delta. The disadvantage of Insein proved to be his Superintendent, who, we are told, was something of a bully and "may well have played dirty tricks on him." But a Superintendent's duties kept him on tour through the District much of the time, and he would have been no more than an intermittently annoying presence. For a good part of each month Blair was in charge of Headquarters, caught up in a routine that by now he had pretty well mastered. Socially too he had, to all outward appearances, mastered the routine. Since Insein was a District Headquarters, life centered on the Club, where each night he made his obligatory appearance—there is no reason to think he enjoyed it—just as he had paid the obligatory formal calls and left cards on the married couples at the Station when he first arrived. He had also made his official calls on the senior civil officers—by tradition, these calls were made in full uniform, at noon, the hottest time of the day.

But if in public he conformed to what was expected of him at Headquarters and the Club, in private he could indulge his eccentricities. Beadon, who came out to see him one day when he was living at Insein, found his house a shambles, with "goats, geese, ducks and all sorts of things floating about downstairs." Beadon, who prided himself on his own neat house, was "rather shattered," and suggested to Blair that perhaps he might bear down on his houseman. The suggestion was shrugged aside: he quite liked the house as it was. Beadon changed the subject—was it true, as he had heard, that Blair was attending services in the native churches? Yes, it was true; it had nothing to do with "religion," of course, but he enjoyed conversing with the priests in "very high-flown Burmese" (Beadon's phrase); and he added in his sardonic (or leg-pulling) way that he found their conversation more interesting than that he was forced to listen to at the Club. Whereupon he took Beadon off for a farewell drink—at the Club!—before he set off for Rangoon. It was their final meeting.

Some years later, and after Blair had left Burma, Beadon heard that "it was the fact of being posted under a bullying D.S.P., who treated him and the men under him very unfairly, and was not the type of whom the police could have been proud, that turned him against Government Service." Another officer who knew Blair at the time, C. B. Orr, remarks, "I noticed that he did not seem happy but did not know what the trouble was," and he too advances the possibility that Blair had suffered from unfair treatment by his superior. But the trouble went deeper than this, and the outcome, it must be said, would have been the same no matter who had been over him or how he had been treated. He was the wrong man in the wrong place; the act of recognition began in Insein.

THERE WAS THE HEADQUARTERS WHERE HE WORKED, AND THE Club where, in a manner of speaking, he played, and the house where he ate and slept, undisturbed by the fowl and livestock "floating about downstairs," and where he read and reread the books he bought in Rangoon, their pages mildewed and their bindings buckling in the sodden air. There was also in Insein the prison, the second largest in Burma, with some two thousand inmates, which became the setting for "A Hanging," the first of the two Burmese pieces mixing reportage and reflection that Blair was to write after his return to England, drawing specifically and exclusively for their subject matter upon his police experience. (The second is "Shooting an Elephant," written in 1936. *Burmese Days*, the major literary production that grew out of what Orwell described as his "five boring years" in the Indian Imperial Police, though it contains an interrogation scene in a police station that is obviously based on the real thing, is for the most part centered on the colonial rather than the police experience, observed, heightened, and arranged for fiction.)

"A Hanging" by Eric A. Blair was published in the *Adelphi* in August 1931—some sixteen months before the name of George Orwell would appear for the first time on a title page. (The name itself is said to have made an earlier appearance, however, but would not have been seen by anyone but Blair, in a very early draft of *Burmese Days*. As he later told Richard Rees, he had originally given it to the character who was to become John Flory.) A brief, stylized essay of under three thousand words and one of Orwell's best-known works, "A Hanging" is as close to a contemporary document as we have from Blair himself for his Burma period. But a document composed five years after the event it describes, recollected in a mood of detachment, is contemporary only by courtesy and in a relative sense—that is, it is closer in time to its subject than are *Burmese Days* or "Shooting an Elephant" or the relevant autobiographical pages in *The Road to Wigan Pier,* or the many allusions and references to Burma and India scattered through Orwell's journalism and reviews. But it is very different in character from what a letter written a few hours after the event would have been, when the pain of confrontation with a particular reality would be at its freshest. Unfortunately, if he ever wrote such a letter, it hasn't survived, and for want of it, we will proceed here to treat "A Hanging" in an extra-literary way, as a document in Blair's life as a police officer.

In a number of respects, one must admit, it is not a satisfactory document. Too much is omitted for that; a complex of things left unsaid—those blotted-out surrounding details that set off in high relief the details that *are* presented, thus adding to the story's effectiveness as a work of art but detracting from its biographical utility. The story is very simple; it describes how on a morning during the rainy season, a condemned man is brought out of his cell, escorted across the jail yard to the gallows, and is there hanged. Who he is, what he has done in the past, what his offense has been that requires this punishment, whether he is innocent or guilty, we are not told. We know that he is a Hindu; that the six warders who are guarding him are Indians; that the head jailer, whose name is Francis (but whether this is his first or last name is uncertain) is a Dravidian. The superintendent of the jail—not to be confused with the bullying District Superintendent of Police—is a gruff army doctor, presumably English (though this is not stated). The narrator is "I," an eye—logically Eric Blair if this is not fiction, though about him we are given no information whatever. We do not know why, for example, or in what official capacity he is there. It would have been most unusual, though not impossible, Blair's colleagues in the police agree, for him to have been present at a hanging. As Headquarters A.S.P. his duties would not normally require his presence there; perhaps he was there out of "curiosity," as a future writer gathering "material," though almost certainly not consciously aware of doing so. On the evidence of the document, this was the first hanging he had attended, and he had been in Burma as a police officer for three years; so that one infers either that hangings were uncommon or that it was uncommon for an officer such as he to be in attendance at one.

The irony of the situation is beautifully and painfully communicated: the banal character of what is said and done—by everyone present, down to the condemned man himself—is projected in a succession of ordinary but closely, even microscopically observed details. It is out of one such detail that the crucial meaning of the experience was revealed to Blair. The prisoner, walking toward the gallows, at a certain point steps "slightly aside to avoid a puddle on the path"—quite as though it mattered to him, as though in another two minutes he will not be dead, swinging at the end of a rope. For Blair, following behind him on the path, the trivial, human gesture had the force of revelation. Five years later, recalling it, he wrote how until then he had never before understood what it meant "to destroy a healthy, conscious man. . . . I saw the mystery, the unspeakable wrongness of cutting a life short when it is in full tide." But the revelation did not lead to an immediate, decisive action; his life as a police officer continued unchanged.

Long afterward, when Eric Blair had become George Orwell, he could shrug off his time in Burma as "five boring years within the sound of bugles." But that was by no means the whole of the story, for he returned to England with a hatred of the imperialism he had served, the more intense for his having been in the police, where, as he put it, one saw "the dirty work of Empire at close quarters." Orwell, of course, was writing about something that had already happened; a position arrived at with difficulty and thereafter firmly held. Our attempt here is to describe the painful stages by which he arrived at the position.

If one considers first what Blair as Blair wrote on Burma and imperialism, and then what he wrote on the subject as Orwell, the progression is unmistakable. By the time he left Insein—in September 1926, when he was posted to the Town Sub-division of Moulmein—he had recognized, as indeed he must have done from the day of the hanging, his antipathy to the career he had voluntarily but so misguidedly chosen, his growing reluctance at having to do what his spirit rebelled against and loathed. Thanks to Orwell's later writings, one can read back into "A Hanging" (though not read on the page) all sorts of anti-imperialist significance. But if Blair had been a police officer in England, witnessing an execution in Wandsworth Prison, he might have produced a similar, equally moving, minute-by-minute account of the event. What was painful to him then was the power of life and death over others that was invested in him by his being an officer in the police, the power to treat people as though they were things. (Ideally, to do one's job properly, one could not afford to see the man who was to be hanged as other than a "thing"; to see him as human was to admit "the unspeakable wrongness" of taking his life.) Blair's dislike of being a policeman, growing more intense over the five-year period, leads to and reinforces his hatred of imperialism. Only then, in the fusion of the two deep negative feelings (and with a positive feeling involved also, as we shall see), does he leave Burma. Whereas in fact, he could have resigned and gone back to England, got free of the dirty work, at least a year before he actually did. By September 1926 he would have had enough money saved from his salary to pay for his passage home—as he would have had to do if he resigned from the police before having served a period of three years. Instead he went on to Moulmein.

Again he was Headquarters A.S.P., but now, for the first time since Mandalay, he was stationed in a city of considerable size, with a large European population. As a port and trading center dominated by the British since early in the nineteenth century, Moulmein offered a community where English customs were understood and practiced, and a way of life more agreeable than in such isolated stations as Myaungmya or Twante. More important for Blair, it had been the home of his mother's family for generations, and it was there that their teak interests, though diminished from what they had been at the turn of the century, were still centered. There were a number of Limouzin connections for him to meet, among them an aunt married to an official in the Forestry Service, and most impressively, his grandmother. A woman of intelligence and distinction, she made it a point—unlike the conventional memsahib—to wear the loose-fitting, colorful native costume, arguing sensibly that it was more comfortable and better suited to the hot, damp climate than European dress. In itself it was not an insignificant gesture. And given Blair's distaste for "Memsahibdom," which would find its ultimate expression in the character of Mrs. Lackersteen in *Burmese Days*, his grandmother's determination to do as she pleased would immediately have won his approval.

It is also possible that she won his confidence, for there is some reason to believe that he told her—or else she surmised—something of the anxiety and uncertainty about himself and his future that he was feeling at this time. A fellow officer, seven years older than he, who was to rise to great eminence in the service, has a recollection of meeting Blair at a sports competition when he was accompanied by two ladies, perhaps his aunt and his grandmother. "What has stuck in my mind," the officer writes, "is that I was asked for advice about Blair by the more elderly of the two ladies. I cannot claim to have given any advice but I did suggest that if Blair was certain that he would not be happy in a career in the Burma police he would be better to get out before he was too old to embark on another profession."

Whether he did or did not confide in his grandmother is a matter of conjecture—if he did, she respected his confidences and no news of his dissatisfaction was communicated from Moulmein to Southwold. But that he was unhappy in a career in the Burma police is fact, not conjecture. As his own hatred for the role he was forced to play grew, so he felt hatred growing around him and focusing upon him. "In Moulmein, in Lower Burma, I was hated by large numbers of people . . ." That, of course, is the opening of "Shooting an Elephant," a masterly essay—

one of the masterpieces of the genre in this century—that may well stand as Orwell's finest single achievement in prose. (As with "A Hanging," however, we will allude to it at this point only as a document, keeping in mind that it was written in England in the summer of 1936, when the incident that provides its subject and title came back to Orwell almost ten years after it had taken place in Moulmein.)

He hated his job by this time; and, as Orwell remembers it, he was also by this time equally convinced of the evils of imperialism. But though he knew he should, in the circumstances, get out (as his fellow officer had sensibly suggested at the sports competition), apparently he was not yet capable of the decisive act, had still to suffer through more of the (for him) ever more painful experience. Anxiety made him hypersensitive. He felt himself a prey to the rising anti-English feeling among the Burmans—singled out, as perhaps he was—subjectively, certainly; objectively, possibly—for insults and provocations everywhere. Orwell's citations are thought to be exaggerated by other English witnesses who were in Burma at the same time as he, but they brilliantly suggest his exacerbated state: European women going alone into the bazaars were said to be spat upon by betel-chewing natives; he himself had been deliberately tripped up on the football field by a Burman, and the Burman referee had deliberately ignored the offense, to the glee of the crowd; yellow-skinned faces, passing him on the streets, sneered at him; young Buddhist priests, in Moulmein by the thousands, stood on street corners and jeered at him. His anxiety was compounded by a characteristic ambivalence, for he was, in theory, on the side of the Burmese, the while he hated "their oppressors, the British." (That was how Orwell remembered it as being for Blair in 1926; he himself, writing in 1936, knew that the British had not been "oppressors" in Burma; the evil was in the nature of imperialism itself, simply their being there, as the ruling power in a country not their own.) But if, in theory, he was on the side of the Burmese, in practice he raged against them for making his job impossibly difficult, and he thought that "the greatest joy in the world would be to drive a bayonet into a Buddhist priest's guts." All this should be understood as "exaggeration for effect," a rhetorical strategy rather than a cool, clinical analysis of what Blair actually felt—this, after all, is the man who only a few months earlier had recognized the "unspeakable wrongness of cutting a life short when it is in full tide." And the generalization that Orwell drew from it in "Shooting an Elephant," that such extremes and divisions of feeling are to be expected from anyone in the service of imperialism, seems highly questionable. Certainly it is not borne out in the letters of his colleagues describing their individual experiences—let a single example suffice, from the officer of the sports competition: "I loved Burma and the Burman and have no regrets that I spent the best years of my life in the Burma police."

Blair's ambivalence grew out of resentment and sympathy, and his anxiety out of the belief that the two were inalterably opposed: sympathy for the oppressed, the underdog, the victim; resentment of the oppressor, the topdog, the victimizer. (From the advantage of ten years' perspective he could see, as he could not in Moulmein, how one might simultaneously resent and sympathize with the oppressed—and even the oppressor.) On the morning of the day described in Orwell's essay, the victim is the elephant, the victimizer is Blair, who feels himself victimized by the Burmese, and all of them together are the victims of imperialism. The situation of "Shooting an Elephant," in itself so "tiny," nevertheless proves large enough to establish the point Orwell wishes to make (he would never make it better elsewhere): the peculiar harm that imperialism as an institution does to all who enter its magnetic field, oppressed and oppressors alike. A tame elephant has gone amok, damaging property and killing a man. Blair, at Headquarters as the highest police authority in the town—presumably the Superintendent is "unavailable"—is summoned to the scene by a sub-inspector at one of the local police stations. By the time he arrives, the elephant has subsided in his fury and in due course is discovered standing in a field, calmly eating grass, apparently no longer a danger to anyone. It is now that the tyranny of the Institution—with its power to impose "roles"—begins to function. A kind of ritual ceremony is set in motion, which continues until the elephant has been killed and its carcass stripped. One feels that nothing can alter it: their roles have taken over the lives of the people who play them. The Burmese, virtually all the inhabitants of the quarter, will behave as the Institution expects them to behave; so, in his fashion, will Blair.

On that morning his resentments are directed as much against the Institution that has imposed the sahib role upon him as against the Burmese in their roles as "natives," who count on him (challenge him?) to shoot the elephant. No matter that, realistically considered, it is now harmless and itself a valuable property; no matter that he, privately, has no wish to shoot it. That he must do so is the Obligation of the Sahib; to do less, once the ceremony is in train, would be to lose face, to play the role badly, even to be laughed at by the "natives," and "that would never do."

His sympathies are as strong as his resentments, and they are all for the appointed victim of the ceremony, the elephant who must be sacrificed, and whose death Orwell invests with a dignity and pathos that are in painful contrast to the pettiness of the "natives" who have come to see the show, and of the police officer who is fearful of being laughed at. The death of the elephant, so magnificently and feelingly described, is the preordained conclusion of a ritual that satisfies the "natives," reaffirms Blair in his role as the servant (the victim) of imperialism, and adds to the burden of self-hatred and guilt he will take away from Burma.

There seemed to be no limit to how great the burden must be, how long it must be endured, in how many places. After Moulmein came Katha, a small town north of Mandalay, headquarters of the Katha District in Upper Burma, to which he was posted in April 1927 as Headquarters Assistant Superintendent. This time he could hardly have wanted a more temperate or pleasing climate (free of the extremes of the south, bearable even in the monsoon), or a more luxuriant or visually compelling landscape. (As against the alluvial wastes of the Delta, here there was a gorgeous profusion of color: blood-red of the gold mohur, cream ivory of the frangipani, purple of the bougainvillea, scarlet of the hibiscus, pink of the Chinese rose.) But his stay in Katha was to be as brief as he could arrange it—only three months. Even so, the place in its sensuous aspects made an unforgettable impression upon him: some years later he would reproduce it vividly as Kyauktada, the setting for *Burmese Days*. That was to be in the post-Kathan future: time, and a difficult apprenticeship, would be required before he could assimilate into fiction something (but not all) of what he had experienced, felt, and observed as a participant in the rite of imperialism. Yet if *Burmese Days* is a *roman à clef*, the key to its characters is not to be found in Katha, but in all the stations leading up to it, from Myaungmya to Moulmein, where Blair had stopped and suffered and, as it were, made notes *en route*. Katha, however beautiful, was no more than the culminating point of his five years in Burma, and Burma by then had become insupportable to him.

In November he would have completed five years of

service, which would automatically entitle him to a long leave. But soon after arriving in Katha he had been ill, and he chose the moment to apply for leave on a medical certificate rather than wait through the six months remaining before his regular leave would begin. At last the point of no return had been reached. In 1940 Orwell would say flatly that his health had been ruined by the climate of Burma. Of course, since early childhood in Henley, he had been susceptible to head colds, coughs, and bronchial congestion. He had wheezed through the damp, coastal winters at St. Cyprian's, and the damp Thames-side winters at Eton; and though he had passed the medical examination given to candidates for the police, the damp, steamy, tropical atmosphere of the Delta had had a debilitating effect upon him. Beadon, visiting him in Insein, had been struck by his pallor. And there is reason to believe that he was suffering from some sort of respiratory or chest ailment in the late stages of his time in Burma. In 1938, when he was hospitalized in Kent for several months, he wrote to Cyril Connolly of "an old T.B. lesion which has partly healed & which I must have had ten years or more"—in other words, since Moulmein or Katha. But this does not necessarily mean that his illness then had been *diagnosed* as incipient tuberculosis—although if it had, it might also account for his being sent, at that particular moment, from Moulmein to the more invigorating altitudes of Upper Burma.

His request for leave was granted promptly: a period of eight months to take effect on July 1, 1927. As soon as was feasible thereafter, he sailed from Rangoon. When he arrived in England in August, he appeared to be in good health, and he said nothing to his family of having been ill—but it would have been quite out of character for him to have done so—and nothing to suggest that this was not a usual period of leave, after which he would return to Burma. In fact, his Burmese years were at an end.

THE PRINCIPAL STORY OF THOSE YEARS BELONGS, ON THE surface where facts accumulate, to Blair the police officer. But there is a "shadow" story that accompanies it —under the surface and largely speculative—of Blair the writer-in-embryo. Orwell himself paid only perfunctory regard to it. As time went on, he progressively reduced the Burma period to no more than a dismissive sentence or two in the history of his literary development. In 1935, in the introduction to the French edition of *Down and Out in Paris and London,* he tells of having resigned from the police in Burma in the hope of being able to earn his living by writing, from which one infers that the thought of becoming a writer must have preceded the act of resignation, rather than vice versa. The inference would seem confirmed in the autobiographical note he supplied in 1940 to the editors of *Twentieth Century Authors.* There he states that he left Burma because, among other reasons, he had "the vague idea of writing books." But in 1946, in "Why I Write," he tells us that the years between the ages of seventeen and twenty-four were those when he "tried to abandon" the idea of becoming a writer. And in 1947, in the introduction to the Ukrainian edition of *Animal Farm,* he places the decision to become a writer as being arrived at in late 1927, *after* his return to England.

Strictly speaking, it can be argued that a writer becomes a writer at the point when he begins to write: "On such and such a day in such and such a month and year, X. wrote the first sentence of his first story . . ." But this is to oversimplify an exceedingly complex process: a writer may wake up one morning to find himself famous; but he does not wake up one morning, or sit down at the typewriter one afternoon, and then and there find he has become "a writer." There is a period of apprenticeship, whether brief or of several years' duration, itself no guarantee of a satisfying sequel. (The sad fate of how many failed writers is that they got thus far but no further.) And even before this, there will often have been—consciously, half-consciously, or, in Orwell's word, "vaguely"—a latent period, before the writer emerges.

Blair's apprenticeship belongs to the years after his return to England: it was then that he began in a practical and considered way to write. But he was a writer-in-embryo in Burma, and his trying to abandon the idea of becoming a writer during the time he was there is analogous to his being "at pains to be the imperial policeman." In each case the psychological need is understandable, and the responsive mechanism evident. As a policeman he had trapped himself in a career for which he was "totally unsuited" (Orwell's judgment in 1935), but before he could acknowledge this to himself, he had to exaggerate his commitment to it. Again, having tried to abandon the idea of becoming a writer—an ambition or certainty he had entertained since he was five years old—it was natural that he should overreact. He was at pains not to allow himself to "write"—even his letters home are remembered as being brief and infrequent. He was at pains also to emphasize his separation —as though a final choice had been made—from "writing" and the London literary life, affecting a Philistinism that would have gone down well at the Club in Kyauktada. At least he did so in retrospect, as when in the 1930's he told his friend Richard Rees, who was then an editor and part owner of the *Adelphi*, that he had read the magazine in Burma but thought it a "scurrilous rag" and used it for target practice. The story is perhaps more revealing than Blair may have meant it to be (and he may have meant it to be a joke, though, as Rees recalled, his manner of telling it was dour and unsmiling). For what he was shooting at from the veranda of his dak bungalow was a periodical of the sort in which his literary friends from Eton were just beginning to appear as they came down from Oxford and Cambridge, and in which, though he could not consciously admit it, he too would have liked to appear. (Later, the *Adelphi* would be a target at which he would aim for publication; and it is a nice irony that "the scurrilous rag" should have given him his greatest encouragement in the crucial early stages of his career. In its pages appeared poems, reviews, and essays, first by Eric Blair and afterwards by George Orwell.)

We have alluded earlier to the "non-writing" years, when Blair was transforming, or incorporating, the events of his life into a story he told to himself as they were happening. But what remains unwritten, no matter how precisely one imagines it to be phrased, is something very different from what is actually written, sentence by sentence, on the page. There is no doubt that Blair's apprenticeship was made appreciably more difficult for him by his not having *written* earlier. The fragments that survive of his earliest apprentice work—all of it unpublished—are proof enough of how far he had to go to arrive at a style. They suggest a writer whose native gift—at the level of language and composition—was remarkably small, considering his later development, or else, simply, remarkably undeveloped. If he had been psychologically prepared to *write* when he was in Burma, if he had allowed himself even to conduct a voluminous correspondence, buzzing with ideas and descriptions of his day to day experience—which is to say, if he had been very different from the young man that he was—he might have developed more easily and sooner, and solved some of the quite primitive difficulties that beset him when he made the decision—explicitly—to become a writer. But if he denied himself the chance to practice the rudiments of the craft he was eventually to master, he knew what the craft was. For he was an assiduous reader in Burma, and he read for the art and the craft as well as for the pleasure and escape that reading provided. What he read, though, depended on what was available in the bookshops in Rangoon, Mandalay, and Moulmein: this explains a great deal.

Blair was in the East at the very time when the "modern movement" was entering its decade of triumph, but its impact (and certainly its productions) seldom got beyond Suez. Joyce, Proust, Virginia Woolf, Aldous Huxley, Gide, Cocteau, Wyndham Lewis, the Sitwells, T. S. Eliot, Ezra Pound —such names did not figure in his reading in Burma, nor were they likely to turn up on the shelves at Smart & Mookerdum's. One is prepared to say "Just as well," for it saved him from ill-disguised, imitative neo-experimental writing (such as many of his contemporaries were doing under the spell of the great modernist inventors) for which he was suited neither by temperament nor talent. (This is not a speculative judgment; his readings of *Ulysses*, which he discovered after his return to England and greatly admired, prompted him to his one belated avant-garde gesture, the Joycean "night-town" chapter in *A Clergyman's Daughter*. He is ill at ease in the manner, though the matter is familiar to him and he presented it more convincingly elsewhere, in his own voice.)

He followed no program or curriculum, but simply read as he pleased—a heterogeneous and, on the whole, an orthodox selection. From nineteenth-century Russia, Tolstoi (but not Chekhov). From nineteenth-century America, Poe and Mark Twain (but not Henry James). There were authors with whom he was already familiar—Thackeray, Kipling, and Conrad—and authors newly encountered —Samuel Butler, D. H. Lawrence (the only "modern" whom he read in Burma), and W. Somerset Maugham. These latter three were to exert a powerful influence upon him, as much in the embryonic phase as in the years of apprenticeship. Influence, of course, takes many forms— whether in "the narrowly technical sense" as models of style or in the broader less easily definable sense, bearing upon subject matter, attitudes, and tone. In the *Note Books* of Samuel Butler, which he carried with him from station to station, he came upon a passage that might have served as a Guide to the Neophyte—if the neophyte was destined to become a writer like Orwell. (And the passage itself reads uncannily like Orwell at his most characteristic, offhand, and assured.)

> I never knew a writer yet [Butler declared] who took the smallest pains with his style and was at the same time readable. Plato's having had seventy shies at one sentence is quite enough to explain to me why I dislike him. A man may, and ought to, take a great deal of pains to write clearly, tersely and euphoniously: he will write many a sentence three or four times over—to do much more than this is worse than not rewriting at all: he will be at great pains to see that he does not repeat himself, to arrange his matter in the way that shall best enable the reader to master it, to cut out superfluous words and, even more, to eschew irrelevant matter: but in each case he will be thinking not of his own style but of his reader's convenience . . . I should like to put it on record that I never took the smallest pains with my style, have never thought about it, and do not know or want to know whether it is a style at all or whether it is not, as I believe and hope, just common, simple straightforwardness.

Maugham, with his conviction that the best style is the style that calls the least attention to itself, would have agreed that one must write "clearly, tersely and euphoniously," but he might have cast a sardonic glance at Butler's conclusion—in his own case, at least, he had taken great pains to achieve his undecorated, seemingly casual, highly readable style. So too would Orwell. (Of course, if one is meant to write in the transparent style—cf., Orwell's "Good prose is like a window pane"—once the technique has been mastered, brought to a high degree of ease and confidence, one writes fluently and plentifully thereafter. Some of Orwell's most characteristic examples in the style, where evidently there was no time for "working over" the prose even if he had wanted, are to be found in "As I Please," the column of comment on a variety of subjects that he wrote for *Tribune* from 1943 to 1947.) "I believe the modern writer who has influenced me most," Orwell acknowledged in 1940, "is Somerset Maugham, whom I admire immensely for his power of telling a story straightforwardly and without frills."

To produce writing that was clear, terse, euphonious, straightforward, and without frills—this was an objective to which he could legitimately aspire and ultimately achieve. But there was prose of another order, as he discovered and responded to in the stories of D. H. Lawrence, prose that was written with greater intensity than Butler or Maugham allowed for, expressing a greater intensity of vision and feeling than they were capable of—marvelous phrases and sentences that evoked a landscape, or the physical presence of a character, or the nuances of emotional response, a whole range of possibilities that the storyteller straightforwardly telling his story hadn't time or inclination for.

Maugham very shrewdly recognized the limits within which he must work as a writer: since he lacked the vision of the poet, to write "poetically" would have been to encumber the story with frills. He was above all interested in the behavior of his characters as they exemplified the ironies in which the human situation abounds. His notebooks are catalogues of such ironies, jotted down against the time he will transform them into stories. When he takes note of "local color" it is a view to the effective touch, the easy reference that lends verisimilitude to the tale. In his stories, no matter how exotic their locale, landscape is literally background against which the important action goes dramatically forward—a tale to be told.

Lawrence's Way led to the deeply felt descriptions of landscape in *Burmese Days*; Maugham's Way to the sardonic observation of the Kyauktada Club in action; Orwell's Way to the anti-imperialism that is a dominant theme of the novel and would find a more telling expression, released from the conventions of "plot" (for it turned out he was not at his best as a storyteller), in "Shooting an Elephant." This is to anticipate, however; the writing of *Burmese Days* belongs to the period of his life when he moved from apprenticeship to authorship. In Burma, as a police officer who was a writer-in-embryo, it was enough for Blair to have found in Maugham and Lawrence authors who revealed possible ways—to which, for all the differences between them, he was instinctively attuned—of imposing some sort of meaning and form upon the experience one lived: otherwise, how pointless it would have been. The determination to begin his career as a writer was the mirror image of his determination to end his career in the police. Leaving Burma in that summer of 1927, he was at last on his way.

PART FOUR

BECOMING A WRITER

ONE

He returned to England late in August, and went straight down to Southwold to join his family. There had been changes, of course. For one thing, the Blairs had made yet another move: from 40 Stradbroke Road to 3 Queen Street.* But the dramatic difference was in Eric himself, who had been last seen by the family as a tall, smooth-faced nineteen-year-old schoolboy, fresh from Eton, and who returned to them as a weathered veteran of five years in Burma in the Imperial Police. He had changed considerably in manner and appearance. Avril thought he now looked very much like their father, and "he'd grown a moustache. His hair had got much darker. I suppose being used to a lot of servants in India he'd become terribly—to our minds—untidy. Whenever he smoked a cigarette he threw the end down on the floor—and the match—and expected other people to sweep them up."

He said nothing to his parents of having been ill in Burma, and nothing to suggest that he would not be returning there when his leave was over. Lounging about, with nothing in particular to do that he was yet ready to admit, scattering cigarette ashes through the small rooms in the house in Queen Street, he soon grew restless and

---

* They were to move once more, for a last time as it turned out, to Montague House, a modest house in the High Street in Southwold, which Mrs. Blair bought in 1933, when she came into a small inheritance.

proposed that they all go down to Cornwall for a holiday as they had used to do. "We went down for the whole of September," Avril recalls, in a laconic sentence that contains a wealth of drama, "and it was during that time that he told my mother that he wasn't going back to Burma; that he'd resigned his commission."

It was as though he had wanted the reassurance of a familiar and happy childhood setting, as Cornwall had always been for him, and a return to the intimacy with his mother that had its beginnings in childhood, before he felt ready to make his sensational announcement. Sensational undoubtedly it was. In spite of the closeness between mother and son—naturally it would be she whom he would tell first— or perhaps because of it, his mother was "rather horrified," as Avril puts it, but that was as nothing compared to the reaction of his father, once Mrs. Blair communicated the news to him. Very likely it would have been simpler if Eric had slightly altered the facts of the case—if he had made much of his illness in Burma (borne out by his being on sick leave) and little or nothing of his wanting "to write." If he had told them that he was resigning his commission for reasons of health, his parents, although they would have been concerned, could hardly have complained. But he was careful to establish the reason for what he was doing, or rather, had already done; some time between his arrival in England and mid-September, he had sent in a letter of resignation to the India Office to take effect at the expiration of his period of leave, January 1, 1928. Why? Because, he told his family, he was "quite determined that what he wanted to do was to write." So the torrent of parental disapproval descended upon him, particularly from his father, as he must have known it would and perhaps wanted, for it would define the magnitude of the decision he had made. Throughout the glum remainder of their time in Cornwall and for the few weeks afterwards that he stayed in Southwold, he was not to be swayed by the objections that parents like the Blairs would summon up at such a moment—that he was throwing away a respectable, worthwhile career (very much like the one his father had followed) that assured his present and future well-being, for something that almost certainly would prove a will-o'-the-wisp, leading downward to poverty and failure. Then came the sensible, concerned, exasperating questions: How did he know he could write? What was the evidence to justify his attempting a career as a writer? What had be written? What had he published? There were no convincing answers available to him, not at that time of his life, and what was required instead was an act of faith, which *he* had, but which they, understandably, did not.

Life in the house in Queen Street after the family's return from Cornwall was not easy for any of them. It was one thing for Eric to be lounging about, doing nothing, scattering cigarette ash, when he was an officer home on leave; it quite another when he had resigned his commission and declared his intention of becoming a writer. He had also emphasized that he "was not going to be any kind of charge on the family"—which is to say that he had saved the greater part of his earnings in Burma and so had enough money of his own to live on while he began his new career. But when did he mean to begin it? Writers must always appear mysterious in their ways of working to non-writers, who imagine, innocently, that writing is the act of pushing pen across paper. A young man pacing from room to room flicking cigarette ash on the carpets may actually be working—thinking about what he is to write later—and for Blair starting out, these would be difficult thoughts—though to an indignant father or a well-meaning mother eager to chat, "since you're not busy, dear," he may appear to be simply wasting time. He was twenty-four, with no visible form of occupation, no clear plan of action that his parents could understand or share in, prospectively a ne'er-do-well. His presence in Queen Street was a source of daily concern and irritation. Eric and his father had never been close: now a kind of estrangement grew up between them, the coldness more pronounced, the difference of opinion more abrasive. While his mother quite soon came around to Eric's point of view—though it might be said that she believed in her son as much as she believed in the writer—his father did not, and would not, virtually until the end of his life.*

It is doubtful that Eric had ever thought of staying on in Southwold for an extended period, but the tensions in Queen Street hastened his departure, and early in the autumn of 1927 he moved to London; there he intended his literary career to begin. Before that, however, he had gone up to Cambridge to visit A. S. F. Gow, since 1925 a Fellow of Trinity. No doubt it was a traditional thing to do, for an Old Boy to call upon his old tutor, but it comes somewhat oddly from Blair, who had not written to Gow (or apparently to anyone else he had known at Eton, boy or master) during the five years he was in Burma.

The visit, in its essentials, bears a striking resemblance to that earlier meeting, in the autumn of 1921, when Blair had gone to "Granny" Gow ostensibly for advice as to his future, but in fact had already decided before seeing him what his future was to be. On that occasion Gow's advice and Blair's intention neatly coincided: perhaps it was the recollection of that that drew him to Cambridge now. Gow was too

* There was a reconciliation between father and son before Mr. Blair's death in 1939. Orwell told this to Richard Rees "with great satisfaction, adding that he himself had closed his father's eyes in the traditional way by placing pennies upon the eyelids. He further added," Rees writes in *George Orwell: Fugitive from the Camp of Victory*, "that after the funeral he had been embarrassed to know what to do with the pennies. 'In the end I walked down to the sea and threw them in. Do you think some people would have put them back in their pocket?' "

wise, too kindly (and perhaps too cynical) to try to undo a *fait accompli*. He was prepared to accept that Blair's going out to Burma in the Imperial Police had been a mistake, and the logic, therefore, of his resigning from the service. As to his determination "to write," Gow was carefully neutral: what could he do but appear to assent in a noncommittal way, when it was so evident that a decision had been made. True, he had rather liked the fables the boy had read aloud at those meetings on Sunday evenings in his rooms years before, but there was nothing in them to suggest a literary gift that was destined to prosper. Yet who was to say Not? He did feel called upon to point out the difficulties of the literary life, how little security it offered, and that talent and ambition were in themselves no guarantees of success. Again, though in a different key from the refrain that had already been sounded in Queen Street, the question was raised of how he was to support himself. But this, Blair suggested, would not be a problem: the Burmese savings were referred to. Drawn on frugally, they would give him a year in which to prove himself. A year, presumably, would be sufficient. (It seems clear that in 1927 there was a strong streak of optimism in Blair—strong enough to justify himself to himself in the course he was about to take—that Orwell later forgot: hence his statement in "Such, Such Were the Joys" that until he was thirty he was sure that he was "bound to fail.") Whatever Gow's reservations and misgivings at that moment, he kept them to himself, knowing that they would make no difference. Blair sensed them, however —years later he recalled having felt that he and Gow were no longer in the same orbit. Even so, the parting was amicable, and there would be a few exchanges of letters intermittently in the future. But they were not to meet again until twenty-three years later, a few days before Orwell's death, when Gow came to visit him at his bedside in University College Hospital.

From Cambridge Eric returned briefly to Southwold. There he wrote to Ruth Pitter, a friend of the family from the time when they had been neighbors in Mall Chambers, in Notting Hill Gate. In the years since then, Miss Pitter had published widely; she was now increasingly recognized as a lyric poet of rare quality. This did not mean, however, that she could live by what she wrote, and she supported herself by working in an arts and crafts studio in Notting Hill Gate. (In 1930, she and her friend the painter Kathleen O'Hara opened a studio of their own, not unlike the Omega Workshop, though on a very small scale, where they decorated tea trays, tables, chests, chairs, and other small objects with handpainted roses, flowers, birds, and butterflies. From this they earned a small but sufficient income.)

Eric, having begun by asking "Do you remember me?," rushed on to say that he was back from Burma and wondered if she might be able to help him find an inexpensive room somewhere in London. She replied that of course she remembered him—indeed, her first impression of him in Mall Chambers, a seventeen-year-old Etonian home on a visit, "a tall youth, with hair the colour of hay and a brown tweed suit standing at a table by the window, cleaning a sporting gun," has stayed with her through her lifetime—and that she had found a room for him in a house at 10 Portobello Road. So the matter was settled, and he announced his departure in Queen Street. Miss Pitter's association with the move would have lent it a reassuring respectability in Mrs. Blair's eyes; and though Mr. Blair remained stonily silent, the goodbyes were managed without drama—he was going to London, but it was only a departure from Southwold, not a break with it.

In London Miss Pitter was surprised to learn that he had resigned from the police; he hadn't explained this in his letter and she had thought he had wanted a room while he was on leave. Her next surprise, an even greater one, came when he told her of his ambition to become a writer, that this was why he had left the service. Privately she thought it a great mistake, but her response, like Gow's, was carefully noncommittal. Later, when he began to show her the stories and verses he was slaving over in his room in the Portobello Road—so pallid, jejune, and awkward—she couldn't believe his literary ambitions would come to anything. At the least there was a long, painful apprenticeship ahead of him; he was starting comparatively late; and though he lived very frugally, what would he do when his savings had run out? But she could not bring herself to say any of this to him: he was so manifestly happy in his new role, even though he was not well, and felt the winter keenly after Burma.

The room in Portobello Road was cheap, small, and austere—a good deal less spacious than his dak bungalow in Burma and almost as sparsely furnished as his stall in College—bed, wardrobe, chairs, a table on which to write. Still, it sufficed; and the house, in which he was the only lodger, reeked of respectability. His landlady, Mrs. Craig, at an earlier point in her life had been the maid to a lady of title—an unforgettable experience that left her, one might say, *plus royaliste que le roi*. From Mrs. Craig Blair had an early, absurd lesson in the lengths to which people in England would go to maintain their "class" position, the more precarious it actually was. On one occasion when the Craigs (there was indeed a Mr. Craig) and Blair were locked out of the house and it became evident that someone would have to climb in through an upper-story window, Blair suggested that they borrow a ladder from the neighbor next door. Mrs. Craig demurred. It would not do. In the fourteen years that they had owned the house in Portobello Road, the Craigs had never spoken to their neighbors, not knowing what *sort* they were (and in Notting Hill Gate one ran the risk that they might not be the *right* sort). To speak to them now, to ask a favor of them, might encourage them to become familiar. It was decided that the only safe thing to do was to borrow a ladder from a relative of the Craigs who lived almost a mile away; and the three of them trooped off to fetch it and carry it back to Portobello Road. Which they did "with great labour and discomfort." (When Orwell recounted the incident some seventeen years later, he ended it at that point, so one will never know whether or not the neighbors came to their windows to watch, peering out over the aspidistras, and if they did, how Mrs. Craig bore up under the *humiliation*.)

Alone in London, with a room of his own, his own life to be lived with no regard to the wishes, commands, or codes of others, he felt himself at last entirely free of the institutions that in their different ways had controlled him: first the family, then school, then the police. No longer were orders to come down from above. The glory of the writer's life—seen in its ideal, abstract form—is the freedom it allows. In his first few weeks in London Blair gloried in this freedom. Exhilarated by it, he was even prepared to renew Etonian friendships. He got in touch with Maurice Whittome, his old Fives partner. A dinner was arranged; some of the other members of the 1916 Election who were living in or about London joined them. It was a friendly and agreeable occasion but without a sequel, and during the next five years, from the spring of 1928 to 1933, he as effectively withdrew from his fellow Etonians as he had during the five years he was in Burma. The new exhilaration wilted in that reminiscent setting. A gathering of men around a dinner table inevitably has a clubbish air—perhaps this put him off. Or may have been merely his being among contemporaries who had followed a road so different from his own, down from Oxford or Cambridge, and who were now beginning their careers as barristers or dons or civil servants or businessmen, with a reasonable certainty that all would go well with them. From Blair's point of view, at this particular stage of his life, what could he say of himself? Disclosure had never been his style; he withdrew into the safety of the Etonian persona they all remembered—cynical, faintly aloof, reserved, rather man-of-the-worldly. After all, he had been out in the East, and they had not: if he had wanted he could have told exotic tales of Burma. But that evening the talk was of King-Farlow's experiences in exotic America, where he had been traveling and studying at what the Eton School Register was pleased to call Princetown University. Perhaps the oddest aspect of the occasion was that Blair said so little about himself in a specific way that Whittome came away with the impression that he had not even finally decided he would leave the police, and that even if he did so, he had no special idea of what he would do next.

HE HAD HIS ROOM IN THE HOUSE IN PORTOBELLO ROAD, JUST enough money to live on, and all his time free. He began to write. One can only speak tentatively of what he wrote during this first "London period"—from the autumn of 1927 to the spring of 1928, when he went to live in Paris. Almost nothing from the period has survived; there are only a few undated fragments that may be assigned to it, using the test of quality—i.e., the earlier in time, the poorer the writing. Orwell himself, in 1946, when he spoke of his early work in "Why I Write," was referring to *Burmese Days,* not to these unpublished first attempts.

As far as can be determined, the only person he was willing to show his manuscripts to at this time was Ruth Pitter. They would often meet for dinner over a bottle of cheap red wine, which Blair would insist upon paying for, although Miss Pitter, aware of his need to make his money last as long as possible, argued that she should at least be allowed to pay her share. They would go for long walks and talks along the Embankment. And sometimes he would show her what he was writing. Obviously he was more at ease with her than with his Etonian contemporaries; and it is suggestive of his state of mind at this period that he should have not got in touch with Cyril Connolly, who was also starting out on a literary career—but was much further along than Blair, having already published a number of reviews and essays in the literary weeklies. It is suggestive, too, that the friendship with Connolly should have been kept in abeyance until the early 1930's, by which time Blair was already a published author with two books to his credit, while Connolly, though a well-known critic, would not publish his first book (the novel *The Rock Pool*) until 1936. Miss Pitter was older than Blair, an established author, he did not feel in competition with her, and she had a sympathetic interest in what he was doing. She would be the first of the Egeria-like figures who were to play a part in starting him on his way as a writer.

His poems were neatly written, some in rhymed quatrains, some in unrhymed iambic pentameters. Their tone was cynical; their language, banal; their ironies, predictable. It was as though sub-Maugham subjects had been set to sub-Housman verse. One can sympathize with Miss Pitter: she had no wish to be harsh, but to have pretended that these exercises in verse had a quality they did not possess—the quality of poetry—and so encourage him to continue, would have been a cruel kindness. She contented herself with pointing out weaknesses in the versification—a misplaced accent here, a line deprived of a foot there. Then, tactfully, she suggested that perhaps prose was a medium in which he would be more at home. It is indicative of their relationship that he did not hesitate to take her advice. In the room in the house in Portobello Road he began to write short stories.

Presently he asked her to read them. None of these stories has survived. Apart from remembering how awkward and contrived they were, how patently made up, Miss Pitter herself has forgotten them. (She does recall, however, the amusement she felt at discovering that he couldn't spell the "rude words" he was fond of using.) The obvious tack to have taken at this point would have been to suggest in a kindly way that Blair should consider another vocation. But Miss Pitter had been increasingly impressed, not only by his determination but also by a sense of unfocused power stirring within him, a complex of intelligence and feeling that had yet to find a way of expression. So she made one further, simple, and, as it turned out, crucial suggestion: that he should try to write about what he knew.

A simple suggestion, however sensible, may be difficult to follow. This was to prove the case now.

There are two main themes that figure in Blair's life during the years between his return from Burma and January 1933: first, the struggle to become a writer; and second, the need to expiate the guilt he felt at having served in the Imperial Police. Eventually the two themes would be fused together, and from their fusion would result the only significant writing to be signed Eric Blair ("A Hanging") and the earliest significant writing to be signed George Orwell (*Down and Out in Paris and London*).

Orwell wrote virtually nothing about the first theme—his struggle to become a writer was a private matter, without moral or political application—and so it has gradually faded into invisibility. But he wrote very powerfully on the second theme—it belonged to a representative moral/political experience: the rejection of Imperialism—and it has a highly visible place now in his literary history. The result of this disproportionate treatment of the two themes is that the unwary reader dependent on Orwell's didactive and reductive version, might well decide that he had become a writer in order to describe the expiation of his guilt or, to put it as simplistically as possible, if there had been no guilt, there would have been no writer. In fact, the guilt of which he speaks certainly helped determine the kind of writer he became; it did not determine his becoming a writer.

In the purposefully selective autobiographical section of *The Road to Wigan Pier,* Orwell remarks that by the time he came back from Burma his hatred of the Imperialism he had served was so intense that he doubts (even nine years later) that he can make it clear. But, in fact, by 1936 he had become so accomplished a writer that he is able to do so brilliantly, in three dramatic, persuasive, and—in the famous "adulterous couple" episode—even lurid pages.*

In 1927, however, he had neither the technique nor perhaps even the insight to make it clear. When he came back to England it appears that he said nothing to his mother or father of the hatred he felt—it would be surprising if he had—or to Avril, or to Mr. Gow, or to his Etonian contemporaries. He told very little of his experiences in Burma to Ruth Pitter, though they were meeting often and talking about "everything." She does remember his once saying how "horrified" he was to have to watch a man being tried

* The episode is one in which Orwell describes an overnight train journey to Mandalay—presumably, judging from biographical evidence, it would have come at the end of his career in Burma, when he was being transferred from Moulmein to Katha. He shared a compartment with a stranger, an Englishman who was also in the service of Imperialism, and after a half hour of sounding each other out, they sat up all night, each in his own bunk, drinking beer and damning the Empire. It does them good to pour out their bitterness, but having done so, and having taken the precaution of not exchanging names with each other, they part "as guiltily as an adulterous couple." Old Burma hands tend to regard the details of the episode as perhaps "a bit exaggerated," but it shows an undeniable mastery of the dramatic epithet and detail. What, for example, can be more appropriate to the clandestine, adulterous nature of the meeting than that even the morning light, when the guilty pair arrive in Mandalay, should be "haggard"?

for murder in a language that he (the accused) didn't understand, and for a killing that was meritorious and perhaps even obligatory by the laws of his own people. But such glimpses into his experience were rare: more often when he talked to her of Burma, it was of its exotic birds and flowers and trees, its temples and gilded buddhas, its haunting landscape. Obviously Burma was what he knew best, and in an inchoate way felt about most deeply, and if he was to write about what he knew, then that was his subject. Yet he had not had time enough, as it turned out, to clarify, to define, to understand the experience. He would need months, years even, before he would be able to say what it was that he truly felt. If he was to make it clear to others (the writer's task), then he must first make it clear to himself.

Orwell has said of *Burmese Days* that it was written when he was thirty, but projected many years earlier. Conceivably its inception goes as far back as the first "London period." An undated manuscript fragment surviving from early drafts of *Burmese Days*, "'My Epitaph' by John Flory," has been posthumously published. It is conceivable that it was written in 1927–8; there has even been the suggestion that it was written when Blair was still in Burma. Our view is that it belongs to a slightly later time—early in 1930 perhaps—after Blair's return from Paris, where his literary apprenticeship had really got under way. The fluency in the writing suggests a considerable gain in technique. If his early attempts at putting to use his Burmese experience had been written in the house in the Portobello Road, it is hard to believe that he would not have shown them to Ruth Pitter, and she has no recollection of his having done so. We will be referring to them again; at this point we would emphasize only that they give no indication of that hatred of Imperialism that Orwell himself would later so eloquently describe.

London was a time of discovery. He had much to learn—in life as in art—beginning with the rudiments of the craft to which he meant to devote himself. As a would-be author, he found it was easier to write in lilting verse of a Burmese whore than to write a truthful, exact account of watching a man be hanged; more difficult still to describe as truthfully as possible one's own response to such an event; most difficult of all to describe the event in such a way that one's response to it would be implicit in the description. Obviously he was not yet ready, whether in terms of craft, self-knowledge, or a meaningful overview, to write of his experience in Burma—it was still too fresh, too raw, too much in need of sorting out. But this did not invalidate the advice Ruth Pitter had given him. If he could not write of the past he had known, perhaps he could write of the present he knew or, rather—to describe the process as it took place—certain aspects of the present that he set out to know and found himself able to write about almost contemporaneously.

In the winter months of 1928, after the cynical light verses and the cynical contrived short stories had come to nothing, he made his first approach to the abyss: he ventured into the East End of London, on the first of the occasional sorties he would make to discover for himself the world of abject poverty and the down-and-outers who inhabit it. Like Jack London earlier, he put on their rags and wandered among them, and suffered with them and for them, and reported back to the world above the abyss how it was down there. He had found a subject.

These sorties, explorations, expeditions, tours, samplings, or immersions were made intermittently over a period of five years. Some were only of a single night's duration, others extended to three or four weeks. They culminate with the publication of *Down and Out in Paris and London*, whereupon they cease.

How a writer comes to a subject and recognizes it, consciously or instinctively, as peculiarly suited to his art, must always be something of an enigma. And it will be so even to the writer himself, though he may write a persuasive-sounding explanation afterwards, when the subject is no longer alive for him—that is, when the subject is no longer material. All experiences are useful but some are more useful than others. It is the latter that provide a writer with his material—what he writes about best. Thus, the experience of Eton was of no use to Orwell as material; Burma was; so was poverty, degradation, going down and out.

He would not begin to convert the experience into material—a subject to write about—until after he had arrived in Paris; and we will postpone until then a consideration of the literary result. But what of the experience itself—at first, and as it continued? When, and how, and why?

Chronologically, it divides into three uneven segments. First, in London, a brief exploratory venture. Then Paris, where for a time circumstances make him one of the poor himself, a victim rather than an observer. Then London again, where the range widens—out of the East End, onto the road, and into the hop fields of Kent—and a new depth is brought to the experience, thanks to his ordeal in Paris. During the first London period, the only people he will tell of the experience are Ruth Pitter and Kathleen O'Hara. In Paris, as far as one can determine, there are no confidants at all. But in the second London period, their number has dramatically increased—Miss Pitter and Miss O'Hara again, Richard Rees, Jack Common, Brenda Salkeld, Dennis Collings, Eleanor Jaques, Mabel Fierz—an audience of friends who know of the experience when it has already become material and is undergoing a literary transformation. Toward the end of the five-year span there will be still another audience, any author's audience, that knows the material only as it has been transformed and is presented by the author; in Blair's case, the readers of the *Adelphi* and the *New Statesman and Nation*.

The question of "How"—the method he followed to obtain the experience—is easily answered: he was yet another recruit to a tradition that goes back at least to the *Arabian Nights*, when Caliph Haroun-al-Raschid put on the rags of a beggar and wandered freely and unrecognized among the lowliest of his subjects. Quite apart from the literary use of the tradition by many of the later Victorian and Edwardian storytellers whom Blair had admired since his schooldays—Robert Louis Stevenson, Oscar Wilde, Conan Doyle—it was not unknown for serious-minded students of the ills of society to disguise themselves as tramps for the purposes of investigation. R. C. K. Ensor, a Fabian and historian, had done so; so had Lionel Curtis, a Conservative political philosopher. But it is plain that Blair's principal guide to the underworld of the poor was *The People of the Abyss*. There are too many similarities of procedure in his account and Jack London's to shrug them off as mere coincidence—step by step, for example, when each writes of spending a night in a casual ward as an indigent, London in the chapter of his book he calls "The Spike" and Blair in his essay "The Spike," which later becomes two chapters in *Down and Out*. In 1928 the passage of years had not turned *The People of the Abyss* into an outmoded curiosity; it remained a useful and regrettably up-to-date guide. In spite of the political furor it had stirred up (as one of a spate of books and reports on poverty) when it was published in 1902, and in spite of the not inconsiderable advance in public welfare that had been made since then, the squalor and wretchedness that London had uncovered in his explorations had not disappeared. They were there, in the same streets and tenements, for Blair to see.

But why should he have wanted to see them?

Why in the winter of 1928 should Eric Blair have chosen

to go down into the abyss? Why should he have wished to expose himself to the taste, touch, feel, look, sound, and smell of poverty—to experience, as though it were his own, the ordeal of others?

Here Jack London provides a contrast, not a precedent, and the contrast emphasizes the strangeness of what Blair did.

Jack London, in 1902, was already a world-famous author. He had come to London from America during the Boer War as a foreign correspondent, intending to interview the British leaders. But his journalistic assignment was abruptly canceled, and as I. O. Evans tells us in his introduction to a recent edition of *The People of the Abyss,* it was

> a serious blow; he had spent his travelling allowance and was almost penniless and workless in a strange country. To Jack London [adventurous by temperament, and a convinced if idiosyncratic Socialist] this was a challenge and an opportunity he was not slow to seize . . . His sociological studies had told him that the East End of London was one of the most appalling of the western world's slum areas, and he could not forego the opportunity of investigating its conditions for himself.

London, in his preface from Piedmont, California, explains:

> The experiences related in this volume fell to me in the summer of 1902. I went down into the under-world of London with an attitude of mind which I may best liken to an explorer. I was open to be convinced by the evidence of my eyes, rather than by the teachings of those who had not seen, or by the words of those who had seen and gone before. Further, I took with me certain simple criteria with which to measure the life of the under-

world. That which made for more life, for physical and spiritual health, was good; that which made for less life, which hurt, and dwarfed, and distorted life, was bad.

After three months, his explorations—mostly in the East End, but also briefly in the hop fields of Kent—were concluded. As an experienced professional writer, who knew what he wanted to say about what he knew, he set briskly to work. Before the end of the year the result was in hand, a vivid, highly readable document whose value—to quote from Evans once more—"lies partly in its factual basis of first-hand observation, supplemented by an exhaustive study of the relevant literature, partly in its objective outlook. Only in a few places does Jack London give vent to his indignation that human beings should receive such treatment. For the most part he was content to record the facts and let them speak for themselves. . . . Nor does he suggest any remedy for the ills which he describes: he was writing not Socialism but reportage, and any suggestion of propaganda would have ruined the effect at which he aimed."

Here, then, is the example of an established author, with firmly held political and humanitarian positions, who takes advantage of an opportunity to explore at first hand a subject in which he has long been interested and which is congenial to him as a man and as a writer; who spends a summer on his researches, at the end of which time he has enough material to begin writing; who when he does, knows in advance that his reputation is so great that he need not explain who or what he is to the reader and simply prefaces his book with a brief, explicit statement of his intentions and expectations. The summer of 1902 and *The People of the Abyss* comprise a sympathetic episode in the history of Jack London; but if the episode had never happened, it would not significantly change one's view of his life and work.

With Blair it is altogether otherwise. He is twenty-four years old, a would-be author, unknown, untried, and unpublished, who at this time has written virtually nothing and is in no position to judge what is or is not, will or will not be, a congenial "subject." He has no politics; his humanitarian instinct is still dormant. By temperament he is fastidious "to the point of squeamishness"—offended by the sight of hairy bodies and the touch of unclean hands, by certain basic bodily functions (sweating, excreting), by the smell of decay, rancid food, soiled beds, grease in stale air—an obsessive catalogue of the foul and distasteful. So that the mere act of entering the abyss, where all that he is most repelled by is in the air he breathes, becomes a physical as well as a psychological ordeal.

Yet he subjects himself to it, voluntarily, again and again, intermittently over a period of years. Between times he is leading a different life, out of disguise, going on with his struggle to become a writer. When at the end of five years he publishes his first book, which is the culmination and termination of his experience of the abyss, there is no preface, no explanation of how the book came to be written or of what his intentions might have been, and he signs it with an invented name.

Nor does he give any clue as to why he should have chosen to go down and out in "The Spike" or in "Common Lodging Houses," the two most considerable pieces having to do with poverty that Blair published under his own name. Both are forms of reportage. "Common Lodging Houses" is a straightforward, impersonal, third-person account, a more generalized and factual rendering of much the same material that was presented as personal history in

"The Spike." But although the experience of "The Spike" is told in the first person singular, it is rigorously uninformative about "I." We know only that he is a "gentleman" down on his luck; and this single bit of biographical information is conveyed in an oddly oblique little recognition scene. The tramps, among whom is "I" the narrator, are ordered to strip and be searched in the disgusting bathroom of the Spike. As "I" goes in, he is approached by the man in charge, the so-called Tramp Major, who, after a hard look, recognizes that under his rags "I" is a gentleman. Asked if it is so, he reluctantly concedes that it is.*

Nor was Blair much more communicative about the subject with his friends. Some of them knew of his explorations, and that he was writing or planning to write about them. But in the past he had never confided his deepest feelings to anyone; it was unlikely that he would do so now. He explained, if pressed, that he wanted to find out what it was like to be a tramp, or a hop picker, or, as he told Brenda Salkeld, "what it was like not to have anything." His manner was friendly but reserved, his tone offhand, diffident, Etonian; and it comes as no surprise to find him writing to a friend in Southwold in the summer of 1931, just as he is about to go to pick hops in Kent, that he hadn't much of interest yet to report about "the Lower Classes," and reporting instead, in careful detail, his having seen a ghost in Walberswick churchyard.

In October 1934 Orwell wrote a brief preface for the forthcoming French edition of *Down and Out in Paris and London*. (It was published in Paris in May 1935 as *La Vache Enragée*.) His manner there was friendly but reserved, his tone offhand and diffident, as he provided a bare minimum of biographical background: first, the year of his birth; then a long blank until his arrival in Burma; a short

---

* When "The Spike," in altered form, was incorporated into *Down and Out in Paris and London*, this "recognition scene" was omitted.

sentence to dispose of his job as a policeman ("totally unsuited"); then 1928, resignation, the struggle to begin a career as a writer; and so to Paris, where in due course, finding himself "almost penniless," he is ready to take whatever job he can get. At that point—not before—the experience of poverty, which is the declared subject of the book, begins.

If one were to judge only by what Blair told his friends and Orwell his French readers, one might reasonably conclude that his going down and out was the result of economic necessity on the one hand (being penniless in Paris) and literary curiosity (wanting to know what it was like) on the other. At the level of the reasonable, such explanations are entirely convincing. But there are deeper levels than the merely reasonable, where much of human behavior in both its creative and destructive forms has its beginnings, levels that Blair was not willing to talk about, perhaps was not even wholly conscious of at the time. It was left to Orwell to approach them, eight years after his first descent into the abyss of East London, in *The Road to Wigan Pier*. The result was a vivid, highly selective, close-up account—so vivid that it has almost obliterated the more drab and inclusive reality—of his experience as he had come to interpret it in the summer of 1936, and as he could put it to exemplary use in the history of his political development from Imperialist to Socialist.

The difficulty with the Orwell version, it should be said at the outset, is that Orwell's genius is for the *reasonable*—one is made to hear in his prose the voice of a man who is eminently sensible, intelligent, and humane. It meant that when he came to write of the "irrational," inevitably he would have to explain it in a reasonable way; which, just as inevitably, meant that something had to be left out. One's own irrational acts can be made to seem rational, or understandable in a logical sequence, by tilting the mirror ever so slightly. And something like this does happen in the famous ninth chapter of *The Road to Wigan Pier*, in which Orwell looks into the mirror of the past to re-create the ordeal of Eric Blair.

More clearly and more dramatically than Blair or the friends who knew him in those early years, Orwell sees himself in 1927, coming back from Burma with a hatred of the imperialism he had served and determined to break with it. This he does (as we know) by the simple expedient of sending in his resignation. But to resign from the police is not sufficient to relieve him of a "bad conscience"; he must also be punished (and who better able to punish him than himself?) for having been one of the oppressors. "I was conscious of an immense weight of guilt that I had to expiate."

Elucidated in 1936, a kind of primitive political dialectic sets him in motion in 1928: the world is composed of the oppressors and the oppressed; in Burma, the oppressed were the Burmese, and the English their oppressors; in England it is the poor who are the oppressed; it is logical to transfer one's guilt from one group of the oppressed to another. If he were to go down among "the lowest of the low" in England, be accepted by them as one of themselves, be forgiven, so to speak, for his sins as an imperialist, then he would be cleansed of his guilt. Therefore, the descent into the abyss. In the Orwell version, what follows is a drama of expiation—the first act of a political pilgrim's progress. But "guilt" and "expiation" are theological (or psychoanalytical) rather than political concepts, and it can be argued that the deeper levels of human behavior are better approached through religion or psychoanalysis than through politics.

In 1936, writing an exemplary chronicle, Orwell passed over without a word—as though it had never been—his struggle to become a writer. The mirror reflected back only his struggle to cleanse himself of guilt. But in 1928, to judge from what he did—and the use he made of his experience—becoming a writer was his immediate and unremitting concern.

Early in that spring, like so many aspiring young writers before him, he went to Paris to live.

TWO

It was late in the day—historically speaking—for him to come to Paris. The halcyon time of the expatriate invasion was approaching an end that the poets, painters, novelists, and dilettantes who comprised it could not have foreseen: the great depression that began with the collapse of the stock market in October 1929. Thereafter the retreat was under way, and at the end of the year Blair returned to London. During the little more than eighteen months that he spent in Paris, however, he conformed not at all to the stereotype of the expatriate who turns up in the standard period memoir, talking of the books he will never write at a café table where the saucers are piled higher through the long lazy hours. Nor was it consistent with his character (or his extremely limited funds) to give way to a sluttish antinomianism, lying in bed until four in the afternoon drinking Pernod. In fact, he was an extremely hard-working as well as aspiring young writer, and the sheer amount of work he produced during this period testifies to the seriousness with which he dedicated himself to his career.

The official reason given for the move to Paris was that there he could live cheaply while going on with his writing. But he was paying very little for his room at the Craigs' in the Portobello Road, and it is hard to believe that there was much difference at that level between the cost of living in

London and in Paris. Evidently the six months in London had been a disappointment; he seemed at the end of them as far from his goal of becoming a writer as when he had started out, and meanwhile six months of his savings had been used up. He had written a few stories, a few poems, none of them publishable nor even of any discernible merit. Burma was still an unwieldy subject (how was he to get at it?) and while he had had the fascinating and disturbing first experience of the abyss, which he intended to write about, he had not yet been able to put it down on paper.

And so he crossed the Channel to Paris "to write," that traditional gesture of liberation since the days of George du Maurier, which meant traditionally "to live the Bohemian life and *then* to write." At first he went to stay with his Aunt Nellie and her husband. Nellie Limouzin Adam was his mother's favorite sister, a warm, vivacious woman whose experience of life had taken her some distance beyond the Portobello Road, where she had lived at the same time that the Blairs were living in Mall Chambers. From Notting Hill Gate she had gone on to the vaudeville stage and from there to Paris, where she had married a Frenchman who was a teacher of Esperanto. There was no question of Eric's not being welcome *chez* Adam—between aunt and nephew there was a genuine fondness—but to settle down in a French version of Queen Street was not why he had come to Paris, and he soon took up residence at 6 Rue du Pot de Fer, on the Left Bank, in the fifth *arrondissement*.

Rue du Pot de Fer was (and is) a narrow, shabby little street not far from the École Normale Supérieure, indistinguishable from numberless other little streets like it in the heart of Paris, lined with five- and six-story tenement-like hotels, the ground floors given over to shabby little bistros, garages, and the occasional frowsty shop or market. Nondescript and slummy, but unmistakably Parisian and local in flavor—you would never think you were in London, and Orwell's "leprous" when he came to describe it as the Rue du Coq d'Or seems too harsh, though Orwellian enough. It sheltered a heterogeneous population drawn from the working class, students, drifters, fringe types (from the middle class on the way down), White Russian exiles, the aged living on inadequate pensions, and the inevitable eccentrics and crazies—a not unpromising street for a young writer whose material came from the life about him; and for Blair in the end it proved to be exactly the subject he needed. It also had the virtue of being within walking distance of the Deux Magots, and naturally he would stroll there under the trees of Boulevard St. Germain —especially beautiful to him because their bark kept its natural color and hadn't been blackened by grime as in London—and on one occasion he was rewarded when he arrived by the sight of someone he took to be (and who may well have been) James Joyce.

There is little reason to doubt that Blair enjoyed the greater part of his time in Paris. Though Orwell himself said so only in a few oblique references—the pleasure he remembered in going to the Jardin des Plantes; his conviction that Paris was at its best for him when he was in his twenties and that on subsequent visits it seemed ghostly— one might safely make the deduction on the principle that enjoyable experience never ignited Orwell's moral or creative imagination. Of the eighteen months that he spent in Paris, he got usable material only from the weeks in February 1929 when he was hospitalized in a charity ward (the basis of his appalling essay "How the Poor Die," published in 1946) and from the last three months of 1929, when his money ran out and he underwent the ordeal he converted into the first part of *Down and Out in Paris and London.*

Most of the time he was writing—stories, novels, poems, articles, he was willing to try anything—and he wrote as though driven, not by what he had to put down in words but by the determination to prove that he was a writer. Time was precious, his savings were dwindling, the words came easily, and he wrote and wrote and wrote. During those fifteen months before he found himself almost penniless and had to take an exhausting, time-consuming job (which put a stop to writing), he produced a vast amount of work.

We know from his own account that he wrote two novels while in Paris and sent them off to publishers, from whom in due course they came back, in the summer of 1929 (and which he later destroyed). But as to what the novels themselves were, their subject matter, characters, settings, themes, and style (poetic-Lawrence or plain-Maugham), even their titles, we do not know. Still, if the minimum length of each was no more than fifty thousand words, they represented a formidable accomplishment in a short period. And they were only a part of what he was writing.

He also wrote several short stories, none of which was taken and which, like the novels, he later destroyed. Some of them he submitted to the McClure Newspaper Syndicate in Fleet Street, who in the person of a Mr. Bailey sent them back with the comment that "The Sea God" had too much sex and "The Petition Crown" too little action, and with the general observation that if he wrote stories that were a little less worldly, they would have a greater appeal. In spite of the advice of Ruth Pitter, he was still manufacturing fiction that had more to do with what he had read—one of these Paris stories bears the worldly title "The Man with Kid Gloves"—than with what he knew, and even more with what he hoped would sell. The excuse, of course, was that he needed money.

But novels and stories were not the end of his literary activity. He also wrote articles, and here his luck and his instinct were better. He was able to sell a number of them;

he had the satisfaction of seeing his name in print; and, although hardly a financial success, he had reason to hope that before too long he might be able to live by what he wrote and so vindicate himself in Southwold.

These articles make no claim to be more than journeyman journalism, written for the moment (and the small check) and with no thought of outlasting it. The notion had occurred to him that he might report, as a freelance, on Things French to the London weeklies, and on Things English to their Paris counterparts. The latter proved the more receptive. His first professional publication since the poem on the death of Kitchener in the *Henley and South Oxfordshire Standard* in 1916 was "La Censure en Angleterre," which appeared in *Monde* on October 6, 1928. It was something of a coup, and he would have more than ordinary reasons to be pleased, for *Monde* was a very highly regarded political/literary journal edited by Henri Barbusse and numbered some of the most famous contemporary European writers among its contributors. But the article itself—signed E. A. Blair, and "translated from the English by H. J. Salemson"—seems a bit pallid for its rather grand setting: it is the sort of piece on censorship in England that could be readily worked up by any competent journalist with a passing familiarity with the subject and neither the time nor inclination to go into it deeply. However, the article is undeniably competent, and that is what needs to be emphasized, for nothing he appears to have done in London would prepare one for it. There is a distinction made between the censorship of plays (*before* production; and he cites the obligatory examples, *Ghosts, Mrs. Warren's Profession, Damaged Goods*) and the censorship of novels (*after* publication—*Ulysses, The Well of Loneliness*). Then there is a brisk run through the puritanization of the English literary tradition—from Chaucer to Fielding to Dickens, with the Victorians substituting death for sex (a pornography of its own)—and, in conclusion, a disdainful, comic last judgment: that if censorship in England were ever to be abolished, in retrospect it would come to seem as fantastic as the marital customs of Central Africa.

Encouraged by this first success, he made time between the novels and stories that were his principal occupation for more reportage, and at the end of the year his articles were appearing on both sides of the Channel, in London in *G. K.'s Weekly* on December 29, 1928, and on the same date in Paris in *Progrès Civique*. The piece in *G. K.'s Weekly*—a paper edited by Chesterton—was "A Farthing Newspaper," and it is the only one of his articles published while he was living in Paris that did not suffer a sea change of translation. Perhaps because all of these articles were dashed off rather than worked over—it was the novels and stories that got the richly wrought prose, the similes and metaphors and purple patches that Orwell later deplored—one has a sense, at least in "A Farthing Newspaper," of a voice. That it is the voice of Eric Blair, rather as it had been heard by his Etonian contemporaries at dinner in London the year before—amused, detached, ironic, and skeptical—should come as no surprise. He is reporting on the recent establishment and rapid rise in popularity of a newspaper in Paris, the *Ami du Peuple,* which is sold at a remarkably low price and purports to be published in the interest of "the people." Actually, it is the creation of M. Coty, the millionaire industrialist, and it is being published to "sell" to the people the virtues of paternalistic capitalism. But the question that matters, Blair continues, is the effect that a low-priced paper such as this will have upon freedom of the press, since its success will crowd out some of its less affluent competitors and so cut down dissenting political opinion. But what can one do? In an appropriately ironic coda, it is suggested that English press lords might follow the example of *Ami du Peuple;* if their papers were priced at no more than a farthing, the public would at least be getting their money's worth.

We have referred to the sea change of translation. There are signs of it in Blair's piece in *Progrès Civique* that was appearing at the same moment as "A Farthing Newspaper." In London he began with a simple declarative sentence; in Paris, with a burst of rhetoric that might have been declaimed in the Chamber of Deputies: "England! Unemployment! One is not able to speak of the one without evoking the spectre of the other!" But after this initial concession to Parisian fervor—or perhaps it is not Blair's voice but that of his translator, Raoul Nicole—the prose cools down, and the rest is straightforward exposition.

The piece itself is one of three that appeared in successive weeks in *Progrès Civique* having to do with the miserable plight of the British worker. The first takes as its central topic unemployment, a continuing problem in Britain since shortly after the war—as Blair suggests ironically, it was the government's reward to its returning soldiers; the second, a day in the life of a tramp; and the third, the beggars of London. Although he begins with the basic problem of unemployment, the ordeal of those who want work but can't find it, and the dole, which is the government's attempt to cope with the result but not the cause, he is reporting mainly on life at the bottom (as he had glimpsed it in the winter of 1928), on the common lodging houses with thirty to forty beds crowded together in an airless dormitory, on the squalor, hunger, and interminable hardship, the life that is less than life of the lumpenproletariat.

Taken together the three articles foreshadow in a rudimentary and sketchy way many of Orwell's deepest concerns in the 1930's, particularly the question of poverty. In one or another of its destructive forms, poverty was to become his obsessive subject—at the heart of almost everything he wrote until *Homage to Catalonia*. His dealing with it expressed a genuine concern for others; it expressed too a way of coping with his own profound sense of financial inadequacy—to bring it down to its proper scale—for whatever inferiority he may have felt at St. Cyprian's or Eton for having less money than the others, it became a form of self-indulgence when his lot was compared to that of the truly destitute: the respectable working-class worker out of work; and far below, out of sight, the down-and-out who are the outcasts and unemployables of a capitalist society.

By mid-January 1929 he was able, for the first time, legitimately to call himself a writer: in the space of less than a month four articles by E. A. Blair had appeared in professional publications. He had even been paid for them: the rate of pay from *Progrès Civique* was seventy-five francs per page. But his prospects, bright at one moment, darkened at the next—there was no glowing sequel to his promising start. For the remainder of his time in Paris—another eleven months—he would sell only two more pieces, and his total earnings for almost two years of literary effort came to twenty pounds.

Meanwhile in February he had undergone a traumatic experience of illness and hospitalization whose effect upon him was to be decisive. It was a grim ordeal, so grim that Orwell could not bring himself to write about it until seventeen years later in "How the Poor Die"; and compared to the stark pages of that brief essay, with their even-voiced piling up of true and agonizing details, the horrific fantasies of *1984* seem suitable reading for schoolboys. In his unheated room in the Rue du Pot de Fer, in the Paris winter weather, he fell ill with pneumonia. After several days of high fever, he was taken to the Hôpital Cochin, a free hospital maintained for the teaching of medical students, providing them with an endless supply of the living and dying to practice upon, and for the care and treatment of the poor. He had, of course, no idea of what to expect. What he discovered was a version of hell, beginning with twenty minutes of questioning at the admission desk, continuing with a compulsory bath in five inches of warm water; then, in bathrobe and nightshirt but without slippers, being made to walk in the cold night two hundred yards across an open courtyard to the ward to which he had been assigned; searching for his own bed in the dim, sweetish, foul-smelling room jammed with three ranks of beds, each virtually head to foot; and then, having found it, after a few moments of rest being hoisted up by a doctor and student and forcibly cupped, which was only a beginning. For after the cupping (a succession of small glasses applied to the skin to draw out spoonfuls of blood), two slatternly nurses buckled him into a mustard poultice, the painfulness of which was unimaginable. It was the climax to a night of horror during which he slept not one minute.

There is no need to continue detail by detail with what Orwell has so ruthlessly engraved, like a modern Goya, for us to read. The significant point of these weeks in the Hôpital Cochin is that now he was among the poor, not as a visitor in tramp's clothing who after a night of self-abasement could return to his neat, austere digs and undergo the agony of writing his day's quota of words, but as one of them, one who suffered as they did, experienced the indignities, callousness, and stupidity which they endured as their lot. He watched, because he could not do otherwise, how the poor lived. He was the prisoner of his sick body and the victim of the temporary social position enforced upon him: for the time that he was in the Hôpital Cochin, he was one of the poor.

After several weeks, when he had regained his strength and could recover his clothes, but without waiting for a medical discharge, he fled back to the familiar world. He knew what he meant to write, and for the first time began to perceive how it might be done.

It was a year since he had made his first explorations in the East End, and he had drawn upon them in writing his pieces for *Progrès Civique*, but thus far the reality of the experience had eluded him. He had wanted to know what it was like. Now, thanks to his experience in Hôpital Cochin, he understood that there was a point of knowing that took one beyond *what it was like* to *what it was*. Reporting on poverty from the outside, no matter how skillfully, accurately, and sympathetically, you couldn't do more than describe what it was like. But to write about what it was, you couldn't be outside. The material he had accumulated until now had to be re-invented if he was to use it truthfully, which meant not a surface honesty but to get under the surface (any honest reporter could take care of the surface), to get down to the essence of it. He began to write in the first person, without intervention: simply, I was there.

But the "I" who was there was not Eric Blair, the St. Cyprianite, the Etonian, the man who had served five years in the Indian Imperial Police. "I" in the beginning had no biography at all. No previous history intervened. He was "I," one of a group. To be precise, and "I" was as precise about details as he could be possibly be, he was one of a group of forty-eight men and one woman waiting on a patch of lawn for a door to open. It was the door of a spike, a public workhouse, and when the door opened, they would be allowed in for a free meal and a free night's sleep.

He had known what it was like; now he knew what it was, and he began to write "The Spike." To be able to do so, he had to re-invent (or re-create) the experience, he had to invent a style, very different from the style of the novels he was writing at the time; and as the style took form, he began to become the person to whom the style belonged. The time was not far off when "I" would discover himself to be George Orwell.

"The Spike" was the first experiment in the new style. The plainness and directness that are its outstanding characteristics were not easily arrived at. His taste was still for the purple patch, the metaphor and the decorative phrase, all those encrustations that got between the experience and its literary reincarnation. Almost two years intervened between the writing of the early sketches of "The Spike" and its first appearance in print. What must have made the experiment of creating a new style more difficult for him was that he was still writing his novels and stories in the old style and still making brief excursions into literary and political journalism. But in early August, he thought (mistakenly) that "The Spike" was in its final form, and he sent it off to London to the *Adelphi*—the same "highbrow" *Adelphi* he used as a target for pistol practice in Burma. A month later, much too soon, he was writing to the editor the traditional letter of anxious and inexperienced authors, asking if a decision had been reached (it was his only copy, etc.). Soon afterwards the manuscript was back in his hands, presumably with a note of rejection that left the door open to submitting it again, for it was in the *Adelphi* that "The Spike" would ultimately appear.

But that was in the indefinite future. In the immediate present, September 1929, his situation was discouraging. Since he had come out of the hospital, things had been going from bad to worse for him. In March there had been a disconcerting experience with *Monde*. He had sold them a piece on John Galsworthy, and on the front page of the number for March 23, 1929, it was prominently listed. But inside the magazine, on the page where "John Galsworthy" by E. A. Blair was supposed to be, there was "J'execute les citoyens," translated from the Russian of Ph. Paneroff (and unlisted in the table of contents); while Blair's piece was nowhere to be found in the magazine, nor would it make a belated appearance in some future number. The episode began to take on the quality of an omen. During the summer his two novels were turned down; he hadn't been able to sell his stories; even his journalism, his one source of income from writing, petered out. In May he had published another piece in *Progrès Civique,* but they had taken nothing since. And the money he had saved to finance the first stage of his career was almost gone. A simple law of schoolboy banking had been in operation during the twenty-one months since he had left Southwold: if one takes out more than one puts in, the amount of money available to be taken out will diminish until there is none at all.

Orwell, in the autobiographical statements he wrote in 1934, 1940, and 1944, makes it clear that this is what happened. The day came when he was almost penniless. In *Down and Out in Paris and London,* the literary re-invention of his last four or five months in Paris, "I" tells us that the process had been hastened along when his and eleven other rooms in the hotel were burglarized by a young Italian with side-whiskers. All his money had been stolen except for forty-seven francs that had been overlooked in a pair of trousers.

A romantic variant of this circumstantial account (more circumstantial than anything in Orwell's three statements) came to light only in 1971. It was given by Blair to his friend Mabel Fierz in the early 1930's after his return to England. In Mrs. Fierz's retelling of the story, first heard on B.B.C. television and then reprinted in *The Listener,* Blair told her of "a little trollop he picked up in a café in Paris. She was beautiful, and had a figure like a boy, an Eton crop, and was in everyway desirable. Anyway, he had a relationship with this girl for some time. One day he came back to his room, and this paragon had decamped with everything he possessed. All his luggage and his money and everything." As Mrs. Fierz recalled, she went on to ask when Blair had told her the tale, " 'You would never have married this girl, would you?' And he said: 'Oh yes I would.'"

Whatever his explanation for his predicament—robbery by a young Italian with side-whiskers or robbery by a little trollop with an Eton crop, or the commonplace functioning of a law of economics—the fact was that by the middle of September 1929, after twenty-one months in which he had published five articles that brought him a total of twenty pounds, he was almost penniless and his career was at a standstill. The skepticism and foreboding that had been expressed in Southwold when he declared his intention of becoming a writer now appeared to be justified; the darkest fantasies of the St. Cyprian period—that one would end up "poor"—seemed on the verge of coming true.

Yet looked at objectively, there was really nothing unusual about where he found himself: the struggling young writer is the rule, not the exception; being penniless, he would have to do what most struggling young writers do— he would have to find a job. It was a quite ordinary predicament, and the ordinary solution would have been to return to London, to look for a job in publishing or teaching, tutoring or translating, on a paper or magazine, something suitable. The extraordinary thing—what makes him Orwell— is the solution he chose.

Nothing would have been simpler than to have borrowed money from his Aunt Nellie and gone home to England and Southwold. But there was to be no thought of borrowing, or going home in defeat. He would stay in Paris and look for work. His explanation in 1934 was that he hadn't wanted to go back to an England where there were already two and a half million unemployed and jobs were scarce. But it is hard to believe that after September 1929 there would be more jobs in Paris, especially for an inexperienced freelance journalist. Why he stayed is that he wanted the experience he had been taught since childhood to fear most. He had already repudiated the privilege of his class; now, with his money gone, there was nothing to protect him from it; the time had come to know life at the bottom, to be at ease there, home at last.

He adopted the same strategy while he was there as he would use afterwards, writing about it. Having *chosen* the experience, he had to go on as though it had chosen him. It meant that he had to stop being Eric Blair, for Eric Blair, penniless, was by definition in a different case from the man of the working class or below it without a sou in his pocket. He had to blot from his consciousness the invented or synthetic character of the experience—that he could terminate it at will, by the simple expedient of making a telephone call to his Aunt Nellie. Looking for a job, he had to close his mind to the suitable possibilities that might have been open and certainly would have occurred to Eric Blair, the Etonian beginning a career as a writer. At the bottom, where "I" had chosen to be, one took the bottom jobs.

The choice was made, the strategy adopted—and he held to it with an admirable courage and single-mindedness. On the surface at least, he obliterated Eric Blair. Not one document concerning him is known to survive from the autumn of 1929. There are no diaries or journals; no notes made on the spot to be worked up later; there are no letters by him, to him, or about him; there is no contemporary testimony at all. The document that one uses as a guide to Blair, Autumn 1929, is *Down and Out in Paris and London*, a literary re-invention, selected, rearranged, and written during 1930 and 1931, and published in an expanded and reworked version in January 1933. It is as though Blair had disappeared for three months and returned later in the guise of "I" to tell where he had been.

The composition and publication of *Down and Out* make a later chapter in his development: the conclusion to Blair's struggle to become a writer. Our intention here is very briefly to transmute the material back to its raw state, out of which the book grew. Doing so, one recognizes that much of it antedates autumn 1929. The life of the quarter, the local color, the raffish and picturesque types were all at hand from the first day he came to live in the Rue du Pot de Fer, and there is no reason to believe he began writing about them, or writing them up, early. Some of the types as he portrays them, especially in their Frenchified speech, are so typical as to be fictitious—Charlie, for example, the worn-out twenty-two-year-old amorist, whose tale of a night in a blood-red *bordel* might have been one of those lost, early stories for which Blair found no takers.

The crucial contemporary experience begins when his money runs out. He did then what a man of the newly poor would do who wanted to go on eating: he pawned all his clothes except what he was wearing, and used the token payment he got for them to live on while he looked for a job. Even at the bottom it was not easy to find one, and he reduced his chances drastically by looking for work only in the kitchens of restaurants and hotels—this on the advice of an unemployed waiter friend, Boris, whom he had got to know as a fellow patient in the Hôpital Cochin. Three weeks went by, used up in fruitless, picaresque misadventures and listening to Boris's colorful tirades against the Jews. Before the end of the third week he was penniless again, and with nothing left to pawn. For several days he had to live on hard bread; the last two days he starved. Then, at the moment of extreme desperation, tipped off by Boris, he went to one of the luxury hotels off the Rue de Rivoli and had the good luck to be taken on as a *plongeur*, a dishwasher. (What would have happened if his luck had not fallen out this way? Would Blair have emerged from behind the mask and telephoned his Aunt Nellie, as he was ultimately to do?)

The hours were long (from seven in the morning until nine at night with three hours off in the afternoon, six days a week); the work arduous and stupefying; the conditions dreadful, hellishly hot, underground, in filthy cellars and sub-cellars; the pay miserable. Still, it was an end to starving; and if he was a scullion, drudge, a beast of burden, there was a certain brute satisfaction in proving that he could survive, and in the rock-bottom, drunk-on-Saturday-night quality of the life itself. There was a certain justice, too, in this degrading role he had willingly taken upon himself—for if he had been at the top and was served by those at the bottom in Burma, now it was he who served: the sahib had become the victim.

The work proved more varied than his first grim experience of it promised. Presently he was sent up one day each week to act as assistant to a floor waiter. High above the infernal regions where he ordinarily sweated and slaved, he polished silver and crystal in a small pantry, helped prepare trays to be delivered to the elegantly fitted rooms, listened to stories of high life told by the cheerful, snobbish waiter, who at twenty-four looked eighteen and had the fresh face of an Eton boy. ("I" himself proved capable of a bit of snobbery: he was appalled that the guests of the hotel should know so little about good food—but, of course, most of them were Americans . . .)

He was at the hotel, as a *plongeur* in the *cafeterie*—in status as low as one could get—for about six weeks, and left it to work for a fortnight as a kitchen *plongeur* at a newly opened restaurant where his friend Boris had been hired as a headwaiter. In all he spent some two months as a dishwasher. Gradually, as he settled into the life, much as a soldier settles into the army, he grew used to it; for the time being he enjoyed the sensation of it, which he no longer even thought of as poverty. And so, although it was very different from his original intention, he had an experience of hotel and restaurant catering behind the scenes: harried and squalid in its operation; disgusting in the details concealed from customers (the cook spitting in the soup; the waiter, at one moment running his fingers through his brilliantined hair, at the next dipping them in the gravy); and fascinating in its social gradations and nuances.

From St. Cyprian's on he would always be acutely sensitive to the hierarchical structure of the organizations and institutions in which he found himself—as formal as government or as amorphous as the London "literary establishment"—and he soon recognized the pattern of rank, from top to bottom, at the hotel: *patron,* manager, assistant manager, chief cook, assistant cooks, headwaiter, waiters, and down at last (the list here is curtailed for convenience) to the *plongeurs.* Yet even they, at the bottom of the hierarchy, turned out to have a curious pride: an eagerness to be recognized as a *débrouillard,* a man who could do the impossible.

Was "I" himself a *débrouillard,* although he was too diffident in writing the account of his experience to say so? Diffidence, we know, was a characteristic of Blair's—he was no more likely at the hotel than at Eton to put himself forward. But there was also something characteristic, obsessive even, in the way he identified with life at the bottom, his need to abase himself as low as possible, to be the *plongeur* of *plongeurs,* so to speak. Merely by being what he appeared to be—one of them—was he not doing the almost impossible? And if every *plongeur,* as he tells us, wants to be a *débrouillard,* would he not, carrying the role to its logical conclusion, have wanted it also?

Among the *plongeurs* there was one, a German, whom Orwell singles out to exemplify the *débrouillard.* An English lord staying at the hotel had ordered a fresh peach to be sent up to his suite. The staff was in despair, for there were no peaches at all in the larder. At this point the German *plongeur* stepped forward: *he* would take care of it. As though determined to prove that nothing was impossible for him (a proletarian equivalent of the "Public School" spirit at its best), he set out into the streets, and before long returned in triumph. He had stolen four peaches from a nearby restaurant.

There is another version of this story, which appeared in print twenty-eight years later in an unexpected, not to say wildly unlikely, source—the memoirs of Loelia, Duchess of Westminster. But English life, especially in the higher reaches where everyone eventually knows everybody, seems to abound in just such coincidences as the Duchess here describes:

> We often stopped for a day or two in Paris—a town Benny [her husband, the Duke] much preferred to London. Looking back I think that Benny must have had a permanent suite in the Hotel Lotti, as we always had the same rooms. The staff bowed before him and hastened to gratify his slightest wish.
>
> Years later, at a party, I met a frail-looking man who said, "You won't remember me, but I have a very vivid recollection of you and your husband." He then told me that he had once worked at the Hotel Lotti. Late one night Benny had rung the bell for the floor waiter and asked for a peach. It turned out that there was not a peach in the hotel so my friend, who was an apprentice waiter, was sent out into the streets, and, under threat of instant dismissal, told not to return without at least one peach. Of course all the shops were shut, so he wandered forlornly about (I tell the story as he told it to me) until he saw a small green-grocer's with a basket of peaches in

the window. Desperately he rattled the door, pounded on it, but all in vain. He dared not go back empty-handed so, as the street was quite deserted, he picked up a cobble-stone from a heap where the road was being mended, smashed the window, seized a peach and dashed back to the Lotti, happy to think that he had kept his job. However, soon after that he gave up trying to be a waiter and became a writer. His name? George Orwell.

One has no wish to worry a charming coincidence into the ground by attaching too much importance to it; by saying, as one might, that it offers a neat example of the difference between life and art, and going on to speculate: in this case which is which? The significant point, anyway, is not in the discrepancies between Blair's version of the story when he wrote it and Orwell's when he told it to the Duchess—though if the latter version is the more "accurate," it suggests how ingrained the diffidence was: that Blair could not bring himself to admit that he had been a *débrouillard* but gave the honor to someone else.

What stands out, surely, is the "false element" in the story no matter how it was told: that Blair at the Hotel Lotti was acting a part in violation of his own nature and gifts—he was meant to become a writer, not a waiter. And as the Orwell version of the story suggests, he recognized this himself. To go on living at the bottom any longer would have been an absurdity, of no use to himself or to the submerged life he had chosen to know and now had to reinvent, to bring to life again on the page. The time had come to rise up to the level at which he could be the writer he wanted to be.

THREE

THERE IS THE RAW MATERIAL, AND THERE IS THE WORK of art that is made of it—as in *Down and Out in Paris and London*—and it is a convenient biographical fallacy when other evidence is lacking to assume that the two are identical. Especially this is so with the work of art that pretends *not* to be artful, where the strategy of the artist is to write as though he were giving us the material raw. It is a mark of Orwell's success in maintaining the strategy throughout the first of his books (and in much else that he was later to write) that over the years since its publication in 1933 the distinction has been so blurred that the "raw material" and the "work of art" have been treated as interchangeable and essentially the same. As to the occasional inconsistencies and obscurities that turn up in its lucid pages, there is a built-in rebuttal: since life is so often inconsistent and obscure, doesn't this add to the life-likeness of the story?—and so the strategy of "truth before art" has the further advantage of seeming to convert flaws into virtues.

To restore the difference neither reduces Orwell's literary stature nor impugns his honesty as an artist. It is simply to emphasize—as one must in a study of Eric Blair becoming the writer George Orwell—that a man's art and life are not indivisibly fused, although for a certain kind of writer (the quasi-autobiographer, drawing and enlarging upon his own experience) they may appear to be so. The story of

Blair, in Paris and coming back to Southwold, and the story of "I" as he wrote it in *Down and Out* during the two years after his return, are not indistinguishable, although they have grown so in legend. Our aim here is to consider them separately, and in turn: life first, then art.

EARLY IN 1930 HE WAS BACK IN SOUTHWOLD—DAMP, WINTRY, out-of-season—in his parents' house in Queen Street, and whatever his or their initial expectations may have been upon his return, he continued to live there off and on until the spring of 1932. It was more than a year and a half since he had come down to say goodbye before leaving for Paris, but nothing of any significance had changed in Southwold. The Blairs had been at home in the small, seaside town as long as anywhere before in the years of their marriage; they had put down roots, and were absorbed in a daily round that they thoroughly enjoyed. Mrs. Blair was an enthusiastic bridge player and golfer; Mr. Blair, out for a stroll in the High Street, armored against the English weather in one of the extra-thick tweed suits he had his tailor make up for him, was sure of meeting one or another of his cronies; and through Avril they were acquainted with younger people in the town.

Satisfying though this was, it hardly made for enlivening conversation: by the third cup of tea the last morsel of gossip would have been extracted. Whereas Eric had been in Paris, and presumably had tales to tell of his life there: these would make up for the uninformative letters he had sporadically thought to send home. In theory, of course, there was a great deal he might have told—the sum of eighteen months' experience. In fact, he told them very little, as little as he had disclosed in the past of his experience in Burma (no swapping anecdotes with his father) or at Eton or St. Cyprian's. The habit of reticence was by now second nature, and would never be overcome to the end of his life. Besides, it was not as though this particular homecoming was cause for celebration.

He had left Southwold for London in the autumn of 1927 intending to become a writer; he returned to Southwold from Paris in the winter of 1930 only imperceptibly closer to his goal and financially worse off than when he'd started. At twenty-six he was the author of six or seven magazine pieces which altogether had earned him some twenty pounds. It was not an achievement his parents would find reassuring, and while it didn't need to be said that he was to stay in Queen Street as long as he wanted, still, they couldn't help wondering among themselves, What would Eric do? How did he intend to support himself? As to the first question, the answer was evident in what he did almost from the day he came home: he intended to go on writing. Undeterred by his lack of success thus far—the two novels rejected and the stories that no editor wanted—he had made a total commitment to becoming a writer. It was the dominating passion of his life, which may account for the apparent thinness of his "personal relationships" in this period—no grand love affairs, no intense, time-consuming friendships, nothing to distract him from the chosen vocation. As to how he would support himself, the evidence was speculative and unsatisfactory—by whatever he might earn from his writing (and perhaps by the occasional odd job). In private Mr. Blair grumbled, and Mrs. Blair, also in private, gave Eric a little money—this, added to what he had got from his Aunt Nellie before leaving Paris (his passage and something over) and what she sent him on occasion thereafter, meant that he had enough to tide him along; not enough, however, for him to set up on his own.

One thing he did not intend to do, and gave no sign of doing, was to look for a "safe," respectable job, working on a regular schedule (for a regular salary) that would dominate his life, with such time as was left over to be given, if he had energy enough, to his writing. Immediately upon his return to England he had been in touch with the *Adelphi* to ask if there were anything he might do for them, and Max Plowman had sent him a book to review, Lewis Mumford's biography of Herman Melville. The review, signed E. A. Blair, appeared in the March–May number. Generally favorable, and written with quite as much assurance as though the reviewer had just come down from Oxbridge rather than back from the lower depths of Paris, it included in the next to last paragraph the observation that, though Melville's had been a "wretched life . . . at least he had an improvident youth behind him," when he had lived adventurously, ungenteelly, irresponsibly. The observation was not likely to be well received in Queen Street, where Mr. Blair, over the months, would interpret Eric's refusal to take a job, even to look for one, as proof of irresponsibility. Whereas he himself felt his responsibility to be a matter of literary obligation: to write, to make himself a writer. It is this sense of vocation that explains what must otherwise seem inexplicable: his willingness to stay on and on in his family's house (with interruptions, however) until the spring of 1932, to allow himself to become what he had vowed he would never be, a charge upon the family, while he wrote the successive versions of *Down and Out in Paris and London*.

During these two and a half years that make up "the Southwold period," the need to be writing outweighed all other considerations and appeared to domesticate him. But going down and out still had its adventurous, disrespectable appeal, as well as its sociological interest and its usefulness to him as a writer gathering material. Starting in the autumn of 1930, from time to time in the next two years, overnight or over a period of weeks, he would take off from

Southwold, when the pressure had built up and the need for the ungenteel experience was at its strongest, to go down and out.

His history in these years is marked by dualities and contrasts. There is Blair leading a respectable, outwardly eventless life at his parents' house in Southwold, writing (which of course is the crucial event), or in Bramley outside Leeds, where he went to stay for extended periods with his sister Marjorie and her husband, Humphrey Dakin, and went on writing; then, in contrast, there is Blair as Burton (the name he used in his down-and-out episodes) in search of experience in the kips and spikes, in the East End, on the road, and in the hop fields of Kent, at a punishing cost to his health and sensibilities. Contrasts as extreme as these are also to be found in his writings, his friendships, indeed in most aspects of his life between 1930 and 1933, so that "Blair/Orwell" seems only the final formulation of a division that had existed long before the mask was chosen and given a name.

PLEASED WITH BLAIR'S TREATMENT OF THE MUMFORD *MELVILLE*, Max Plowman sent him further books to review, the inevitable "mixed bag" that falls to the writer who can turn out a deft, authoritative-sounding thousand words or so on any book whatever. So in his first year of reviewing for the *Adelphi*, he is equally at home in the eighteenth century with Edith Sitwell's *Alexander Pope* and *The Course of English Classicism* by Sherard Vines; in the nineteenth century with the marriage of the Carlyles; in the twentieth century with contemporary fiction (J. B. Priestley's *Angel Pavement*); and he completed his first year's assignments with some brisk observations on French penological methods on Devil's Island. Blair proved surprisingly adept: he seems to have mastered from the start the technique of elegant reviewmanship as practiced in England. The prose flows along smoothly, aphoristically, and allusively; the manner is discriminating, unruffled, and faintly superior—but even as a schoolboy he had been at ease with the authoritative tone ("Of course you realize, Connolly, that whoever wins this war, we shall emerge a second-rate nation"). If there were only these *Adelphi* reviews to go on, one might have predicted the eventual emergence of Eric Blair as yet another useful, middle-range gentleman of letters, a kind of Desmond MacCarthy *manqué*. But the Blair who was writing about books for the *Adelphi* was very different from the Blair who was simultaneously writing about life for himself. The division between the two at this stage seems irreconcilable—in style, in subject matter, even (perhaps especially) in the contrasting persona each self adopted while writing, the one a "literary gent," the other a "down-and-outer."

When he was in Paris he had tried on the "down-and-outer" for the first time, writing his account of the night he had spent in a London spike in the winter of 1928. That piece had been rejected by the same *Adelphi* that now, in the winter of 1930, was accepting the productions of his gentlemanly other self. Nonetheless, it was the anti-Blair persona he assumed once again when the time came to deal with his Paris experience. The choice, here, was of the greatest significance in the emergence of George Orwell. For if he had been content to go on as a "literary gent," writing of Paris in the prose and pose of his first year's contributions to the *Adelphi*, we would have had, almost certainly, a variation on a familiar theme—the artist as a sensitive young man—as the first book by Eric Blair. But once he had decided on the "down-and-outer" persona, it meant that the greater part of his life in Paris was inconsistent with it and therefore not usable material: he had embarked upon a book whose subject matter would be far removed from the conventional unconventional Left Bank blend of Pernod and poetry.

In Southwold, early in the winter of 1930, he made his first attempts at writing a book about Paris. By March, when he went to stay with Marjorie and Humphrey Dakin in Bramley, he was already engrossed in it. The Dakins' house, standing between an elementary school and the local Liberal Club, had once been a vicarage. It was now in a sadly rundown state, but in those first hard years of the Depression, with Humphrey just beginning a new job as a civil servant, there wasn't money to spare to refurbish it. This wouldn't bother Eric: shabbiness would always appeal to him as a natural setting. Besides, there was the pleasure of his sister's company. Marjorie was in her early thirties, much warmer and more tolerant than Eric, as clever as he, but not astringently so, and a good listener. Her husband has described her as "the sort of human being who instinctively invites confidences." While Eric never confided to her what precisely it was that he was writing, he made it clear that writing was to be his life; and like her mother, she was sympathetic, and set about being helpful in a practical way. Money she couldn't give him, but she could provide him with a room of his own, a good place to work, for as long as he wanted. There he settled in for the next three months.

He wrote as though driven. The tap tap tap of the typewriter was heard all day and half the night. Long afterwards Dakin told Orwell's friend T. R. Fyvel, "I remember the impression he made on Marjorie and myself—that he was determined to be a writer, come what may. I must confess that I thought the chance of making a living from writing was hopeless . . . In common with most Philistines I used to tell him: 'For heaven's sake, get an income. Don't accept help from your mother or your aunt. You can always write in your spare time. Don't pursue an unprofitable career but get a job.'" But in Bramley, as in Southwold, Eric was not to be deflected from his chosen task: "All the time his typewriter would go tap tap tap in the upstairs room."

Dakin had always thought his brother-in-law something of a prig, dating back to their boyhood days in Henley, and nothing in his behavior now caused him to change his mind:

> I tried hard to get Eric to come to our pub round the corner in Bramley, the "Cardigan Arms." It was only a Yorkshire working-class local, but even in those years in the slump it was always bright, cosy, and warm, with a big fire going and quite a merry crowd in the evenings. From time to time I managed to persuade Eric to come along . . . but I could never make him join in any game or conversation. He used to sit in a corner by himself, looking like death, until it was with some relief that we'd hear him say: "I must go home." Through the window we'd see him walk past on the pavement, wearing a long muffler over a threadbare overcoat and no hat. The landlord used to say to me, "That bloody brother-in-law of yours gives me the willies!" I think he gave everybody there the willies. And half the night I'd hear his typewriter go tap tap tap.

In June he returned to Southwold, a much livelier place —with the coming of summer and holiday visitors—than when he'd left it, and there are some attractive, unexpectedly cheerful glimpses of him at this time. An Anglo-Indian family in the town, friends of the Blairs, were looking for a tutor-companion for their three schoolboy sons (Richard Peters, the eldest, was ten) who would be at home during the holidays; actually, what was wanted was a friendly and companionable young man who would keep the boys occupied and out of the way of the grown-ups for a few hours each day. Mrs. Blair suggested Eric for the job, Mrs. Peters welcomed the idea, and Eric himself, perhaps remembering his brother-in-law's strictures, or perhaps simply to please his mother (and knowing that he would still have most of his time free for writing), agreed to give it a try.

"Friendly" and "companionable" may not seem quite in keeping with the dour figure Blair cut at the Cardigan Arms; but as he is remembered by the Professor of Philosophy of Education in the University of London, Richard Peters, this "rather strange but very nice" young man proved to be an ideal holiday tutor. (The arrangement was so satisfactory to all concerned that it was resumed again the next summer.) From the first he was at ease with the three small boys, and they with him, perhaps because he never thought to treat them as "Children," never condescended or preached to them. He no doubt talked over their heads sometimes; when he held forth on the wickedness of politicians in his dry, analytical way, they had "a vague impression . . . that making money entered into it rather a lot." He would come round to the Peters's house on weekday mornings to collect the boys and off they would go: through the town, across the estuary to Walberswick, following the sea, or into the country, Blair leading the way, "swinging along with loose, effortless strides and a knobbly stick made of Scandinavian wood." And as he walked he talked entertainingly and informatively of anything that came to mind or into view. The conversation wound its random way from birds and animals—of the habits of the heron, of the redshanks and their nests, of the behavior of stoats—to the heroes of boys' magazines and the scientific fantasies of H. G. Wells. Chiefly one has the impression of a Blair who was natural and free with his small companions, as he was unable to be with his contemporaries and elders. He had no role to play or to live up to. Simply by being himself he won their admiration. Of course there was the glamour of his having been in Burma—he had seen the tiger and the elephant in their natural habitat. And they thought him very brave, very daring: once, going to Walberswick, he strode along the girder, about eighteen inches wide, from which the old disused railway bridge over the estuary was suspended, while they walked beneath him on the bridge itself. He took them bird's-nesting. He taught them how to make bombs—the same energy and detached interest went to making and firing a bomb as looking for a redshank's nest—and the boys, whose nickname for him was "Blairy-boy," took up the war cry of "Blairy-boy for Bolshie-bombs." In the millpond south of Walberswick he showed them how to catch roach with tiny hooks and pellets of bread. He talked about history: once he remarked that he would have sided with the Cavaliers against the Roundheads, because the Roundheads were "such depressing people." He brought the boys home with him to Queen Street for lunch, and impressed them by helping his mother to clean up afterwards—not for nothing had he been a *plongeur*. In the sand dunes outside the town he played war games with them, and they would stalk each other armed with small sandbags. "I suppose the nerve and quiet confidence with which he played . . . was the quality in him which we admired most," Professor Peters remarks, adding, "Perhaps he was really at home only with animals and children."

THE WRITING OF THE BOOK ABOUT PARIS WENT ON AT FULL speed throughout the summer. The pages of the manuscript were piling up, written with an exhilaration, vivacity, and naturalness that have their counterpart in his behavior with the Peters boys, and which explain better than its "sociological content" its continuing life into the present, why there are admirers of Orwell's work who have a special affection for it, and even some—Henry Miller, for example—who consider it his best book.

The material of *Down and Out* is sordid, but it is deployed with rare high spirits. The tone throughout is curiously boyish—not a defect, of course; so is the tone of *Huckleberry Finn*—and it is made more noticeable by the exclusion from the narrative of even one female character of any consequence to "I" who tells the story and is at the center of the action. Seldom can a book set in the lower depths of Paris have had so little to do with sexuality. Given its autobiographical nature, however, and given Blair's limited experience of women, it could hardly be otherwise. Before 1932 his closest relationships with women seem to have been with his mother and sisters, or with mother- and sister-surrogates. Possibly, as he had told Lawrence in Rangoon, he had frequented the brothels there; and possibly, as he was to tell Mabel Fierz, he had had a passionate *affaire du coeur* in Paris. But in each case the story was told to a single listener and to no one else, and in each case it is possible that he created the story, either to please or deceive the person to whom he confided it, with the end result that he would seem more experienced in such matters than he actually was.

It is enlightening to compare the Paris episodes of hunger, squalor, and bistro life among the lumpenproletariat in this earliest of his books with the account of his hospitalization written thirteen years later, the one so exhilarating to read, the other so truly painful, drawing upon material he was unable to use in *Down and Out*, although it might logically have fitted in. (There is only a glancing reference there to the narrator's having met his friend Boris when they were fellow patients in the hospital.) And it must be said that the description of starvation and squalor in the earlier work has none of the power and conviction, the terrible strength of the description of physical suffering and indignity in the later. It is as much a question of tone as of mastery: *Down and Out* is a young writer's book, the book of a young man who was in many respects still unformed and inexperienced.

Blair finished the book in October, and on the advice of Mabel Fierz, whom he had met earlier in the summer and who was knowledgeable in such matters, he sent the manuscript to the publishing house of Jonathan Cape. Mrs. Fierz, it should be said, had not been allowed to read the manuscript—nor had anyone else—but she did not allow this to stand in the way of her enthusiasm. She was convinced that he was a "true talent" and that the book would be splendid: that was how she was.

Mabel Fierz and her husband Francis, a London businessman, had been coming to Southwold in the summer for a number of years now, and were on friendly terms with the Blairs. Mrs. Fierz was a lively and enthusiastic woman in her late thirties; she kept up with the new books and plays and music and psychology and politics (socialist); she was artistic, and even wrote a bit herself; and she was always ready to sympathize, to draw one out, to listen to stories of difficulties, to give advice. It was natural, then, that she should have heard of the Blairs' brilliant son Eric, such a disappointment to them, who had been in College at Eton, and then had thrown up a promising career in the Indian Imperial Police to go off to Paris and write. In her eyes nothing could have been more splendid than to go off to Paris and live in a garret and have thrilling love affairs and write marvelous novels that nobody would publish . . . on the other hand, she certainly could understand and sympathize with dear old Mr. Blair, such a charming man, who had had such high hopes for his son—but such bourgeois notions of what would be sensible for him. And she did her best, especially after meeting Eric, to mediate between father and son, though with no conspicuous result.

Even so, Mrs. Fierz was to play an important role in the history of George Orwell. For along with her enthusiasm, she had her practical side, and it was on the practical side, between 1930 and 1933, that she proved extremely helpful to him. At first she had only his reviews in the *Adelphi* to be enthusiastic about, but she was unstinting in her praise and, by a happy coincidence, it turned out that she knew the *Adelphi* people. John Middleton Murry, who had founded the magazine in 1923 and continued as its editor until 1930, was an acquaintance. So too was Richard Rees, an associate of Murry's on the magazine, who in September 1930 became co-owner, restoring it to its status as a monthly (it had been coming out as a quarterly since 1927) and editing it jointly with Max Plowman. Most important, Plowman and his wife were particular friends of hers. Of course Eric must get in touch with Max—she would arrange it in the autumn when she was back in London. It would make a difference, for "knowing people" helped, she told him, and that was her practical side. Meanwhile they had long interesting conversations over tea, first in Southwold and later at the Fierzes' house in Golders Green. She was quick to sympathize with his literary ambitions, about which he spoke candidly, and curious as to what else he was writing, about which he was inexplicit . . . but she felt that he was confiding in her. Perhaps he was; or perhaps he was allowing her to have the impression that he was. Certainly he appears to have told her things he told no one else—from a literary point of view, the most sensational confidence was that his essay "A Hanging," which came out in the *Adelphi* the next winter, was not, as it purported to be, an eyewitness account but a work of the imagination, for (she remembers him telling her) he had never been present at a hanging.

There is not a great deal that can be said with absolute certainty about the first version of the book that in its second version became *Down and Out in Paris and London.* The manuscript, which Blair submitted to Jonathan Cape in the autumn of 1930 and which Cape in due course sent back to him, has not survived; neither has the reader's report on the manuscript, nor the letter from Cape to Blair turning it down. We know that this first version ran to about 35,000 words (the length of the Paris chapters in the published book) and that it was written in the first person in the form of a diary. Cape's letter, as Blair summarized it a year and a half later to the literary agent that Mabel Fierz had persuaded to represent him, was not an out-and-out rejection. It appears to have been a variant of the standard letter declining a manuscript—"We find this very (interesting) (remarkable) (unusual) and we wish that we could . . . BUT (insert reason) and so we can't"—that publishers send to promising young writers with whom they would like to keep in touch but not so strongly as to make any kind of formal commitment. ("A publisher will make mistakes. He will say no when he should say yes, and yes when he should say no . . . The common error is to say yes too often; no publisher ever went bankrupt because of MSS rejected." These cautionary thoughts appeared in Cape's house journal, *Now and Then,* in 1930.) According to Blair, Cape had liked the manuscript and wanted to publish it . . . BUT (it was too short and fragmented) and so. However, if he were to make it longer, "they might be disposed to take it." No hint of a contract, no suggestion that he come by to discuss the manuscript; in fact, it was a version of the formula. But there was no reason why an ingenuous and inexperienced young writer, as Blair evidently was, should know that it was a formula, nor any reason why he should not pore over the handful of sentences, reading into them subtleties and shadings that very likely were never intended, putting the brightest, most positive construction, as Blair evidently did, upon the formularized phrases of encouragement. And while it is true that the letter did not contain an offer of immediate publication or even an assurance of later publication contingent on his making such-and-such changes and additions, still, from Blair's point of view it represented a progression upward. For what the letter from Cape said, or seemed to say, as he read it, was very different from the outright terminal rejections he had suffered with his two novels in Paris.

Encouraged by this optimistic reading—and reinforced by it in his conviction that soon he would achieve the goal he had set for himself, and so was justified in staying on in Queen Street until he had—he began the revision. It was an arduous process that asked far more of him than literary expertise. Later, in his diffident fashion, he would minimize it as only a question of his making the book longer by putting in "some things" he had omitted and then sending it back to Cape. Actually, it was another year before he was ready to submit the manuscript again. No longer in the form of a diary, it had been recast as a continuous narrative, beginning with the adventures of "I" as a down-and-outer in Paris (chapters I through XXIII) and concluding with a major addition, his adventures as a down-and-outer in London (chapters XXIV through XXXVIII). Since it is impossible to compare the texts of the first and second versions, one must depend on circumstantial evidence; but that is sufficiently strong to justify the assumption that the London adventures were the things he put into the second version, and which he could not include in the first because many of them had not yet happened to him.

It will be recalled that he had made his first explorations of the abyss in the winter of 1928 before leaving for Paris; and in the summer of 1929 he had written the account of his stay in a casual ward which he offered unsuccessfully to the *Adelphi*. Early in the winter of 1930 he returned to Southwold. There he began to write the first version of *Down and Out*. He spent the spring in Bramley with the Dakins and continued to write. In the summer he was back in Southwold, tutoring the Peters boys and writing. The first version was finished and sent off to Cape early in October. Until that time, there is no evidence that he resumed the explorations of down-and-out life in England that he had begun almost four years before. It is hard to see how, writing as steadily as he did, he would have been able to fit them in.

In April 1931, his essay "The Spike," signed Eric Blair, was belatedly published in the *Adelphi*. Told in the first person, it is a graphically detailed account of his stay in an unidentified casual ward, from the moment its gates swing open at six in the evening to allow him into its reek and torpor until the moment two days later when the gates open again and let him out into the bright, sweet, windy air. Presently "The Spike" was to be cannibalized in the second version of *Down and Out*. There, rather curiously, the experience that had served for the original essay is apportioned out into two distinct chapters, one devoted to the spike in Romton, the other to the spike in Lower Binfield, with "I" out on the road for several days between them. That Blair should have dealt so thriftily with the material already available to him suggests the extent of the problem he faced once he had committed himself to bringing "I" from Paris to London (rather than simply adding "some things" to the Paris chapters) and describing his life in London as a down-and-outer. This new plan for the book seemed to offer an attractive symmetry in structure, along with an opportunity to contrast French and English life at the sub-poverty level. But it required not only obvious literary additions—some pretext would have to be invented to get "I" from Paris to London—but also additions of experience. The first literary result of his explorations in 1928 was "The Spike," and it had taken him as far as he could go: he still did not know enough about what he wanted to write about. At this point, from the autumn of 1930, an extraordinary, fluctuating pattern of down-and-out writing and living was inaugurated—comfortable Southwold for the manuscript, poverty-stricken London for the experience, the two interacting and alternating until the book had been lived and written. That would bring him to September 1931.

There were no schedules, no fixed periods decided upon in advance—so much time allotted for Southwold, so much for London—and he was more often and longer in Queen Street, writing, than he was in London going down and out. But when he wanted to go down and out, he did. The procedures for these episodes were simple. He would come up to London, stop off at Ruth Pitter's flat (or at the Fierzes' or at Richard Rees's) and put on his tramp outfit—he kept a suitcase of ancient clothes at Ruth Pitter's for the purpose—and disappear into the streets. A day or two later (sometimes longer) with a minimum of explanation as to where he had been and what he had seen and done, he would reappear, bathe, change clothes, become Eric Blair again. As Blair he would spend a bit more time in London, going out to dinner with Miss Pitter, dropping in for a cup of tea over the gas fire at the *Adelphi* office in Bloomsbury Street, staying overnight with the Fierzes, before returning to Southwold and continuing with his book.

Miss Pitter was struck by the change in his manner and appearance, and in his writing, since he had been in Paris. He was much more formidable-looking (wearing a broad-brimmed hat he'd brought back from the Left Bank), much more assured—his reviews in the *Adelphi*, surprisingly professional compared to the stories and verses he had showed to her in 1928, gave some substance to his literary ambitions. Even in the ragged clothes he put on to go down and out his height and bearing made for an un-tramp-like impression. One might apply to him the remark that Robert Graves made of himself in *Good-bye to All That*—that he feared that under the shabbiest of clothes he would always be recognizable as an English gentleman. As Miss Pitter has said in an observation confirmed by others of his friends in the period, "He didn't look in the least like a poor man. God knows he *was* poor but the formidable look didn't go with the rags."

Still, the rags were a kind of passport to the lower depths, and essential to the enterprise. If the poor wore rags and suffered in them, then he must too; hence even in winter he would go into the streets without overcoat, hat, gloves, or muffler. Miss Pitter was concerned about the effect on his health, which she knew was not good; as she later put it, "I felt he wouldn't make old bones." One day, "a perfectly horrible winter day with melting snow on the ground and icy wind," she ventured to protest. He listened politely but was not to be dissuaded: out he went. "I felt quite sure he was in what is called the pre-tubercular condition. And here he was, exposing himself in such weather in totally inadequate clothing. It wasn't just poverty. It was suicidal perversity." It was also a kind of heroism: a willingness to undergo whatever the experience of the abyss required from him. While he was down there, however briefly—the longest continuous time was the month when he went to pick hops in Kent—he wanted to be unconditionally there, not as a tourist or social worker.

He waited until 1936, in *The Road to Wigan Pier*, to describe the earliest of his experiences, but by then, as we have suggested, Orwell was interested in the exemplary, political character of what he had done, laying bare his secret motives and guilts as a "casebook" member of his class, and he made no reference at all to the quest for material that at the time and on the surface had been an animating force. At a friend's house he prepared his clothes, dirtied them, made them authentic-seeming (it is all a little too artful and self-conscious, and so differs radically from the involuntary first experiences that are thrust upon "I" when he arrives in London in *Down and Out*). Then, in his careful disguise he wandered through the East End, and came at last to a common lodging house in Limehouse. He was afraid to go inside, fearful of the working-class denizens of the place, so brutal and threatening as they must seem in the fantasies of any member of his class: what if they should recognize the Etonian under the rags and do violence to him? The image that occurs to him as he stands outside is of entering "a sewer full of rats." But eventually he screwed up his courage and went through the doorway and down the dark passage to the communal kitchen. There a drunken young stevedore was reeling about. He lurched toward Blair, who stiffened in his rags, readying himself for the violence he expected to come next. But instead, the stevedore offered him a cup of tea—that English communion—and called him "chum." He felt it was a baptism.

"Nearly all"—the words are Orwell's—nearly all of *Down and Out in Paris and London* is true: that is, nearly all of it is composed of incidents that Blair actually witnessed or participated in or heard about between the winter of 1928 and the summer of 1931. These incidents have been chosen and rearranged to take their place in the simple picaresque structure of the book, which covers a period of four consecutive months, the first three in Paris, the fourth in London. Blair was writing in a troublesome, suspect genre—the factual account, lightly (or not so lightly) fictionalized—which is something very different from the work of fiction based lightly (or not so lightly) on fact. Such an account, as *Down and Out* purports to be, succeeds to the degree that it persuades us that it is reporting things that actually happened. Whatever the author invents must blend invisibly with the rest. The best pages in *Down and Out* are those that have the most truthful sound; believing what we hear, we go with "I" from the Rue du Coq d'Or to the Hotel X to the Auberge de Jehan Cottard. The invented pages, by contrast, lack conviction: we hear the voice of "I," and under it, unmistakably, the machinery creaking. Most of the inventions are devices tailored to suit the plan of the story. Thus, in the second version Blair has to introduce "I" to down-and-out experience not once but twice, first in Paris, then in London. (Of course, if he had reversed the order, as in his own life, it would have been simpler; it would also have been autobiography, which *Down and Out* is not.) In Paris, it will be remembered, the precipitating cause is the theft of his money. He finds himself with barely a sou—explanation enough, in the context, for the events that follow, his introduction to and progressive intimacy with life at the bottom. In his third month down there, a moment comes when "I" can't go on any longer as a *plongeur* at the Auberge de Jehan Cottard, and being in a special case (one senses this from the first despite the deliberate absence of biographical information), unlike the ordinary *plongeur,* who has nowhere to turn, he writes to his hitherto unmentioned friend "B." in London, asking him to find a job for him, any job that will not require him to work seventeen hours a day. "B." replies promptly, like the deus ex machina or plot device that he so transparently is. He has found him a job, as a kind of companion or attendant to a congenital idiot, and he also encloses a five-pound note, enough for him to reclaim his clothes from the pawnshop and for third-class passage to England.

In London, "I" goes to "B." 's office, where his friend tells him—the creaking of the machinery is very noticeable here

—that the idiot's family have taken him abroad for a month, and the job won't begin until they return. He is so flabbergasted at the news that it is not until he is in the street that he realizes he had not even thought to borrow money from "B". To do so now would not be "decent," he feels—the creaking is louder still—and the situation on which the remainder of the book depends is that he is in London and in desperate straits. So it is down and out, as in Paris, all over again, a way of surviving for the month until his idiot returns; the thought that he might look for a temporary job never occurs to him.

Obviously, the exigencies of plot made it impossible for Blair to reproduce his own first experience of going down and out in London. If "I" were to go to the house of a friend and change into tramp clothes before venturing into the East End, it would have been necessary to explain at least something about him, to provide him with a few tags of biography and a motive for what he was doing, as well as an authentic-seeming costume. The plot required only the latter: he goes into a rag shop in Lambeth to trade the suit he is wearing (his second-best suit; his best one has been left with his luggage in the station cloakroom) for a tramp's coat, dungaree trousers, scarf and cloth cap, all superlatively filthy. He puts them on in a back room of the shop, then goes out into the street and into a new world.

Here invention ceases: the parallels to Blair's own experience are unmistakable. Like Jack London before him, he discovers that changing his clothes has changed everything:

> No sooner was I out on the streets than I was impressed by the difference in status effected by my clothes. All servility vanished from the demeanour of the common people with whom I came in contact. . . . I had become one of them. My frayed and out-at-elbows jacket was the badge and advertisement of my class, which was their

class. It made me of like kind, and in place of the fawning and too respectful attention I had hitherto received, I now shared with them a comradeship. The man in corduroy and dirty neckerchief no longer addressed me as "sir" or "governor." It was "mate" now—and a fine and hearty word, with a tingle to it, and a warmth and a gladness, which the other term does not possess.

So London wrote in *The People of the Abyss*, and Blair, in his turn, on his own first afternoon in the streets was to hear that "fine and hearty word" addressed to him. A hawker had upset a barrow, and when he went to help him pick it up, the man grinned and said "Thanks, mate." It was the first time: "No one had called me mate before in my life . . ." Moments such as this were of signal importance for Blair—the stevedore in the communal kitchen saying "'Ave a cup of tea, chum"; the hawker saying "Thanks, mate"—moments of comradeship and acceptance such as he had never felt at St. Cyprian's, or Eton, or Burma, which happened to him not as Eric Blair but as the man with an assumed name (Edward or P. S. Burton) who went down and out, and that culminate unforgettably in the Lenin Barracks in Barcelona during the Civil War in Orwell's brief exchange and handclasp with an Italian militiaman whom he was never to see again.

These epiphany-like moments were the psychological rewards of the down-and-out experience, making up for the physical discomfort and degradation inherent in it (although later he came to think of the bugs and squalor as a kind of reward also—an expiation). The literary reward would be in the book he was writing. Yet the experience itself, the role that he chose to play in the experience, had its evasive, inauthentic aspect: that he had the option to be free of it whenever he pleased. No matter how sincerely he participated in the experience at the time, or how convincingly he later presented it on the page, his friends and acquaintances in this period couldn't help noticing the element of pretense it entailed, the more so as they saw him only before or after the experience, and he was incapable of taking them into his confidence as to the details of what it had been.

The longer one had known Blair, or the more one knew of the actual circumstances of his comfortable lower-upper-middle life in Southwold, the more puzzling it became. An instance of this was in his relationship with Brenda Salkeld. They had met in the autumn of 1928 in Southwold, where she was the gym mistress at St. Felix School, and the friendship was resumed when he came back from Paris. They went for long walks, birdwatching and talking of writers Eric admired and felt she should read—Joyce, E. M. Forster, Swift—they went fishing and riding together, they dug in a Roman barrow, which yielded up only a bronze button. Although he wouldn't show her what he was writing, he talked of his literary ambitions and disappointments, so much written and so little published, the meagerness of the rewards. With a certain grim pleasure he told her that since coming back from Burma he had earned one hundred pounds by his writing, whereas in Burma, doing a job he loathed, he had earned two thousand pounds: obviously he had only to find a job he hated more than being a policeman and he would end up rich.

On the whole, judging from Miss Salkeld's recollections and those portions of Blair's letters to her she has allowed to be published, it was an agreeable companionship for them both, in Southwold and away from it. Once, for example, he took her to Eton for the day to show her his old school. On another occasion they had tea in London with an acquaintance of hers, the author of several books, the political theorist C. Delisle Burns, and the conversation was not about politics, in which Eric had no interest, but about the practical details of authorship—how to deal with agents, editors, and publishers—which were of absorbing concern to him.

Yet although he and Miss Salkeld got on well together, there were undercurrents of tension, perhaps because they were close in age to each other: it is evident in these years that Blair still was more comfortable with women who were older than he, with whom he fell easily into a kind of filial or fraternal or, as Richard Rees has suggested, a Candida–Marchbanks relationship. But Miss Salkeld was a forthright, intelligent, and independent-minded young woman. She was prepared to let Eric play a pedagogical role in literary matters, about which she agreed he knew much more than she; but she was not willing to yield her right to question and contradict the generalizations he was so fond of making (as he had been ever since he was at St. Cyprian's) on a minimum of evidence or none at all. She came to the conclusion that he really didn't understand people, women in particular, that he couldn't give himself . . . and while no doubt some of this grew out of their immediate circumstances, there clearly was a quality of "apartness" and abstraction about him that many had noticed before—a short-circuiting of the emotions, a failure to connect. And then there were these prejudices of his: he had not yet solved the problem of how to live with them. "He didn't really like women," was Miss Salkeld's verdict. "I used to bring up the women who I thought were good writers, and he would very occasionally praise their writing, but he used to say that it stuck in his throat to have to do it." Nor was he any more favorably disposed to people who liked music, whatever their sex . . . music and concerts were a waste of time (Miss Salkeld was very fond of them); and when she reasonably pointed out that his being tone deaf might disqualify him as a judge in the matter, he swept her objections aside. So it was not surprising that she should have regarded his tramping experience with considerable skepticism.

One morning he turned up at her house in Bedford, still in tramp's clothing, having spent the night in the local workhouse. After he had bathed, and before he set out on the road, aiming for the spike further along the way where he meant to sleep that night, they argued about what he was doing. He told her that he "was getting to know what it was like to be a tramp." But she was quite certain that "if you've put on tramp's clothes and walked, well, that didn't make you a tramp. It was the attitude of mind that was much more important; and how could you claim to have the attitude of a tramp, or know it and understand it, if you knew that you could always go back home." Of course, she had no way of knowing what it was that he felt, since he wouldn't tell her. But the only effective way the argument could have been resolved would have been for him to show her what he was writing about his down-and-out experience, and this he chose not to do.

It is understandable that Miss Salkeld and others who were familiar with his Southwoldian life should have found it difficult to reconcile the would-be writer and the would-be tramp. But even the new acquaintances and friends in London, to whom Southwold was unknown territory and his life there unimaginable, had some sense of the anomalies of his situation. (Though he told as little in a specific way as possible, and his disclosures were carefully selected.) Jack Common, a young working-class writer from Newcastle who had joined the staff of the *Adelphi* in 1930 when Rees and Plowman took over from Murry, has recorded the disappointment he felt at his first meeting with Blair. He had "heard of this interesting man who had been a tramp and who at the same time was capable of writing extremely good reviews for the magazine." But when Blair came into the office it was obvious that he was "a public school man, perfect manners, and had not known the desperation that makes the real tramp." It was a disappointing beginning—for here, it seemed, was just another struggling young writer, in that respect not so dissimilar from Common himself, and when it came to life among the proletariat (the Marxist term, like Marxism itself, was coming into vogue, even in the *Adelphi*), he felt he knew much more about it, having lived it, than Blair did. But they met again: "We had a cup of tea over the gas fire." So begins an anecdote by Common that catches the quixotic nature of Blair's enterprises at this time as they would appear from the outside. "It was just before Christmas . . . probably 1930. He outlined his plans for Christmas; he intended to spend the holiday in jail. His idea was to light a sort of bonfire in Trafalgar Square, and get run in. I counselled him against this. I always firmly held that if you were going to jail you might as well have something for it. My advice was 'Take to theft. A bonfire simply suggests something undergraduate-like.' He'd probably be let off. But Blair didn't take my advice . . . There was no jail. I don't know how he spent Christmas."

As time passed Common grew "very friendly" with him. There was no doubt that Blair was having "a hard time"—even though Common didn't accept his being a tramp out of necessity—and it was a mark in his favor that "he had to some extent dissociated himself from his class." Still, there were those embarrassing class signals that proved as ineradicable as a birthmark—the voice, the manner . . . Once on a summer afternoon Blair turned up at Max Plowman's house. Common was already there—he had been listening to Beethoven's music on Gramophone records—and now they went out into the garden to play badminton. "This put Orwell to shame. He had to remove his jacket." When he did so, he was discovered to be wearing braces, an invincibly upper-class thing to do, and it stayed in Common's memory.

The closest and most enduring of the friendships that Blair formed at this time was with Richard Rees. Theirs was a relationship that strengthened as it continued, and it lasted up to the day of Blair's death in 1950. But when they met in the winter of 1931, either a little before or after "The Spike" came out in the *Adelphi*, the prognosis could hardly have been favorable. Blair had his prejudices, and Rees, accordingly, had his liabilities. For one thing, he had, as Mrs. Vaughan Wilkes would have noticed with pleasure, a handle to his name, Sir Richard. (He didn't use the title, but it was *there*.) For another thing, he had money. (Not a great deal, but enough to subsidize a "literary mag" and to have a flat in Cheyne Walk, to buy books and pictures . . .) Then, at their first meeting—they were having tea in a shop in New Oxford Street not far from the *Adelphi*—Rees recalls "It came out that we had been at the same school, Eton, though the differences in our ages had prevented our knowing one another." But Blair had been in College, and Rees had been an Oppidan, a difference to which we have referred earlier, and to which, Rees felt, Blair attached excessive and unjustified importance. "I do not remember if it also came out that he had been there on a scholarship, but if it did he must certainly have been embarrassed, and I equally certainly was unaware of his embarrassment." Eighteen years later came that strange embarrassing moment, earlier referred to, when Rees "incautiously used the word 'Tug'" and Blair "winced as though [Rees] had trodden on his tenderest corn." Rees appends the observation: "That a famous middle-aged writer should have retained such a deep trace of boyhood sensitiveness and suffering seems remarkable."

But in spite of all these potential obstacles to their ever

being more than editor and writer in an amiable, quasi-professional acquaintance, the friendship between them took hold. Rees was so diffident about his "advantages"—the title and the assured income—as to neutralize their power to give offense; and in his attitudes he was at once reticent and sympathetic, a combination nicely attuned to Blair's suspicious temperament. His expectations on meeting Blair—and "expectations" is too high-pitched a word for the low-keyed curiosity he felt—were the reverse of Common's. He had published reviews by this interesting young writer who was also, for one reason or another, capable of living the life of a tramp—so that when Blair came into the *Adelphi* office, and they went nearby to the tea shop to talk, Rees was neither disappointed nor surprised: it would not have occurred to him that a tramp might have written those reviews. In the account he published of their first meeting, one sentence stands out: "He made a pleasant impression and I did not guess that he was having a struggle to live, though he struck me as rather lacking in vitality." But this was a first impression, and he soon recognized the intensity of Blair's commitment to writing, to which everything else was subordinate. He had a cynical disinterest in politics, and Rees, a socialist committed to social change, found it extraordinary that Blair should make no connection between the plight of the men he met on the road or in the spikes and the sickness of the society that could find no function for them. This, of course, was in 1931, when Blair, if pressed, would describe himself as a Tory Anarchist. Years later Rees said of him, "He was the most 'literary' man I've ever known—absorbed, obsessed with wanting to be a writer."

The book about his down-and-out experiences was only a part of his voluminous literary activity in the first eight months of 1931: the tap tap tap of the typewriter must have been incessant. In the March number of the *Adelphi* he had reviews of *The Two Carlyles* by Osbert Burdett and *The Horrors of Cayenne* by Karl Bartz; in the April number, his essay "The Spike," along with "Poverty—Plain and Coloured," a joint review of two novels, *Hunger and Love* by Lionel Britton and *Albert Grope* by F. O. Mann; in June, a review of Pearl Buck's novel about China, *The Good Earth* ("... can be added at once to the very small list of first-rate books about the East."). During this time too he had begun to write about Burma, his first serious attempts to deal in fiction with his experiences there, which took shape over the next three years as *Burmese Days*. But the immediate result was the essay "A Hanging," which was published in the *Adelphi* in August.

Literary activity, obsessive and unceasing, had the paramount place in his life. The extraordinary thing is that he found time and vitality also to go on with his down-and-out explorations. How many they were, and the duration of each, can't be precisely established. To judge by the relatively small number of incidents that make up the London chapters of *Down and Out*, they needn't have been very many to provide him with material enough for a manuscript of publishable length. But the search for material was only one of his motives; and that he should have continued his explorations, even after he had finished the second version of the book, suggests the extent of his involvement with them. Also his dissatisfaction with what he had made of them thus far. Arriving at the final page of the manuscript, he felt that he had not yet got beyond the "fringe of poverty"—someday he hoped to explore more deeply in the world of the down-and-out, to know its people "not from casual encounters, but intimately." That, however, would not happen. His class, his education, the complexity of his nature, the development of his still dormant political intelligence, his literary ambitions—all militated against it. These various strains would make themselves felt in *The*

Road to Wigan Pier, which vividly and sympathetically describes life in the depressed areas of the North in the winter of 1936. Yet the book is reportage, told by an outsider, that makes no claim to intimacy except perhaps in the second half, an account of Orwell's political progress to socialism, where he writes of himself with unshielded candor, as though in an intimate relationship with the reader.

He had been sustained since the previous autumn by the conviction that Cape would want to publish his book once he had suitably lengthened it. Now, in the summer of 1931, he grew impatient to be done. In July he was in Southwold, tutoring the Peters boys again, meeting with Brenda Salkeld and other friends. A month of agreeable diversions, but it meant that the amount of time free for writing was drastically reduced; and in August, when the Fierzes went back to London from their holiday in Southwold, he went with them. In their house in Oakwood Road, Golders Green, with Mrs. Fierz seeing to it that he should have ideal conditions for working, he wrote steadily, and before the end of the month he had written the last sentence, typed a title page, *Days in London and Paris* by Eric Blair, and sent off the manuscript to Jonathan Cape. It was all managed with such speed that there was not even the opportunity for Mrs. Fierz, who would have welcomed it, to read what he had written.

The haste and impatience of these weeks, the determination to have the book out of his hands no matter what, very likely account for a certain slackening, a haphazardness in the final portions. True, the plot, like an afterthought, enters once again at the very end: "I" will soon become caretaker for the wealthy idiot (rounding off the London month); and there is a reference to the Auberge de Jehan Cottard and to the word *plongeurs* to remind us of the episodes in Paris. But despite these rudimentary formalist devices, the effect is that of a book that simply stops (or runs down) rather than ends. Blair himself was aware of this: he does his best to disarm criticism by claiming to have written no more than a "fairly trivial story." Later, he would disown the book in a quite literal way, giving it a pseudonymous author, saying he was ashamed of it. Nonetheless, he sent it out, to be published or turned down. There is a time when an author can do no more with a manuscript than he has already done, even as he admits its flaws: that time had come for him now. A few days later, as though to prove he had not merely turned a phrase when he wrote that he wanted to explore the lower depths "more thoroughly," he went down and out again.

This was to be the most prolonged of his explorations, extending from the twenty-fifth of August to the eighth of October, and it is also the best documented, for he kept a diary covering the entire experience: three nights in London (one of which he spent sleeping out in Trafalgar Square), four days on the road, seventeen days picking hops on a farm in Kent; then back to London for two weeks in a common lodging house. The diary, fascinating as a record and admirably alive in the writing, was published for the first time twenty-nine years after it was written, under the title "Hop Picking," in *The Collected Essays, Journalism and Letters of George Orwell.* Reading it, one can only wish that Blair had not been quite so eager to have *Down and Out* off his hands—that he could have tolerated it for another two or three months—for the diary then might logically have been made an impressive part of the book, augmenting or supplanting the recast portion of "The Spike," which is the last of the down-and-out experiences that "I" chooses to describe. Four years later Orwell would draw upon the material of the diary for the hop-picking episodes and the "night scene in Trafalgar Square" in his novel *A Clergyman's Daughter.* And when he came to London from Kent, during the two weeks that he and his "mate"

Ginger were living in Bermondsey in a common lodging house (stinking kitchen and disgusting dormitory), he extracted passages from the diary for the article "Hop Picking" (by Eric Blair) that appeared in the *New Statesman and Nation* of October 17, 1931, nine days after the last entry in the diary. During the week that the article was current, it dispensed its quota of information capably enough—how hops are picked, and who picks them, and what the work pays—then sank from view, never to reappear—the common fate of most casual journalism—from which it was not rescued even by the Collected Edition.

What makes the diary exceptional among Blair's writings is the sense of happiness that pervades it. There are the squalid details as before, the bugs in the beds, the fecal stink, the vile food, the grime and poverty in London, the exhausting, ill-paid work in the hop fields, the sordid living conditions on the farm, the latrine too filthy to be used, etc. etc. . . . *and yet*. On the road (for example) he and Ginger are caught in a rainstorm and take shelter in a lych gate outside a church. Their clothes are drenched through; they have nothing to smoke; they had walked twelve miles that day—"yet I remember that we were quite happy and laughing all the time." One takes away the impression, as one does so seldom in Orwell, that this is the record of a joyful, not a miserable, experience. And when he draws upon it for that generally bleak, sad novel *A Clergyman's Daughter*, he allows Dorothy, his heroine, to reflect after an exhausting day in the hop fields: "Yet you were happy, with an unreasonable happiness."

It had been a kind of rough idyll, full of camaraderie and adventure and the smell of hops like a wind blowing from an ocean of cool beer. But like any idyll it couldn't be prolonged indefinitely. The nastiness of life in the kip when he and Ginger were back in London began to get on Blair's nerves. Mornings they would spend helping the porters in

Billingsgate; and in the afternoons, Eric (we learn from the diary that on this expedition he had been using his own Christian name) would go into the reading room of the public library in Bermondsey: there he wrote up the notes for his diary, and the article for the *New Statesman*. When he had been at the Fierzes, he had met a man who was starting a new paper, *Modern Youth*, who had asked him to send him some stories, and he felt that he should get to work on them. But he couldn't, not in those surroundings. He wrote to Southwold for money, which his mother sent him, enough so that he could take a room of his own in Windsor Street, Paddington. Then, on the eighth of October, the two friends parted, Ginger back to the road again, and Eric Blair back to the literary life.

It was in Windsor Street later in the month that he heard from Jonathan Cape. The letter hasn't survived; Blair's summary of it is laconic and to the point. The book was rejected.

PART FIVE

BECOMING ORWELL

THE FIRST LETTER FROM CAPE, UPON WHICH HE PLACED the most favorable construction possible, had inspired a period of optimistic activity during which he revised, lengthened, and completed the book they had now rejected. The effect upon him of the second letter was equally powerful: optimism, pitched too high before, gave way to an unwarranted pessimism, activity to a paralyzing diffidence. As far as the fate of his book was concerned, thereafter he resigned it to his friends, allowing it to become their concern, not his.

He had always been fearful of failure or rejection; indeed, the two were synonymous in his eyes. The next eight months, between November 1931 and June 1932, comprise a period so dispiriting, so negative, so unmitigated in its gloom, that in his memory he chose to let it infect all the years before he was Orwell. In 1946 he asserted that until he was thirty he had always expected that whatever he attempted would fail. Passing silently over the rebuffs and frustrations that marked his struggle to become a writer, he attributed the attitude to his experience at St. Cyprian's (as though he had actually failed there). The psychological mechanisms that determine his ways of dealing with failure and rejection are unmistakable in these eight defeated months: passivity, diffidence, and self-devaluation. The simplest, least humiliating course was to stand still: if one did not put oneself forward, offering one's manuscript, say, then one did not run the risk of rejection—not having tried, one couldn't be said to have failed. But if one had made the offer and it was rejected, the proper response was indifference, to behave as though it didn't matter. Or else, dangerously attractive to someone of his temperament, there was agreement, a devaluation of the self: to accept the fact that one (or one's manuscript) deserved to be rejected. It was as though he were to say, If I am not loved it is because I am unworthy, I smell, I am ugly, I don't have money or a handle to my name, I don't wear kilts to church on Sunday, I have written a fairly trivial book that doesn't begin to do justice to its subject, I am a failure.

Paradoxically, but not unusually, defeatism was paired to the will to succeed. In the end, it was the latter that triumphed: as Richard Rees would remark to Rayner Heppenstall in 1934, Blair was "doomed to success." Cape's rejection of *Down and Out* didn't swerve him from his determination to become a writer; the sense of vocation was as formidable as ever. If he were no more than the "defeatist" he represents himself as being at the time, surely he would have acknowledged that the career upon which he had embarked in 1927 had come to nothing, and turned to something else. Instead, within a few weeks he began writing *Burmese Days*.

But his faith in *Down and Out* had evaporated. He was all too ready, given his tendency to expect the worst, to accept Cape's verdict as the final word, and, unlike most beginning writers, he was unwilling to make the rounds with the manuscript. Having been once rejected, the work in which he had invested so much emotion, experience, and effort was to be written off as a failure. Here, fortunately, his friends intervened. Rees, when Blair some weeks later told him what had occurred, pointed out that it was not unusual for a book to be turned down by one publisher and accepted by another. Casually, for he did not want to seem to be patronizing him, he suggested that he might be able to help, and asked if he might see the manuscript. To this Blair agreed, but he added, as one would expect, that it was not much good really. Rees had already read "The Spike," and he had allowed Blair to use his flat when he changed into tramp's clothing, so to some extent the subject matter came as no surprise. Even so he was unprepared for the breadth and depth of experience that the book disclosed—neither then nor later was theirs a friendship that depended on intimate confidences. For Rees, the effect was disturbing, and difficult to reconcile with Blair as he knew him, though it added to the fascination of what he read. But summoning up as much detachment as he could, putting himself in the position of a reader who knew nothing about the author but what was revealed in his book, he felt certain that *Days in London and Paris* ought to be published, and with Blair's permission gave it to his friend T. S. Eliot, who was a reader for Faber & Faber (and later became a director of the firm).

Sometime earlier, Rees had already spoken to Eliot about Blair, as a young writer who was having a hard struggle, and who would welcome any sort of editorial odd job. On the strength of this, Blair wrote to him on October 30 to ask if Faber might be interested in his undertaking a translation of a recent French novel, *À La Belle de Nuit*, by Jacques Roberti. Realistic in style, operatic in situation, it tells of a prostitute's life and death—in love with a criminal, she is killed by the simple fisherman who loves her. Later Blair would describe it as "appallingly indecent." Eliot replied promptly and asked that he send Roberti's novel, which he did on the fourth of November. But the project came to nothing—unpublishable by reason of obscenity, Blair thought—and nothing came of his request that he be considered as a French translator if Faber might need one in the future. (As for À La Belle de Nuit, it was published without incident in 1933 by T. Werner Laurie as *Houses of the Lost* in a translation by Mary Ford.)

Everything seemed to be going wrong for him at this time. Even *Modern Youth*, the new publication for which he had concocted two short stories, went out of business for lack of funds before its first number could appear. He had money enough to live on, thanks to what his mother sent him from Southwold, but her checks, though essential, heightened his sense of guilt and failure; he asked for less and less, claiming to have something coming in from literary odd jobs, until he allowed himself to take only barely enough for survival. He was at a point in his life when he did not have to go very far down and out to know what poverty was like.

The down-and-out expeditions were still going on intermittently and would continue into the autumn of the next year. The last of them for which a record survives seems to have been made a short time before Christmas 1931. It began at Rees's flat, where Blair arrived and "asked if he might change his clothes. Having left his respectable suit in the bedroom, he went off again dressed more or less in rags." His aim was to be put in prison—to know what it was like to be a prisoner—but the provocation he decided upon, to be drunk and disorderly, was even less likely to produce the result he desired than to light a bonfire in Trafalgar Square. He did get drunk, having put down four or five pints of beer and finished off with a quarter of a bottle of whisky, and he did get picked up by the police—literally so, for he was falling down in the street. He was held at the Bethnal Green police station from Saturday to Monday morning, when he was taken before the magistrate and fined six shillings for drunkenness (which he refused to pay and so was returned to the jail for another few hours) but this was not the imprisonment he had hoped for. When he told the story to Rees he was prepared to alter the actual facts a bit (as he later recorded them in "Clink") to emphasize the absurdity of the outcome: "He had received a fatherly talk, spent the night in a cell and been let out next morning with a cup of tea and some good advice." Like so much else in his life in these months, even the attempt to go properly to prison—to be taken seriously at what he wanted to do—had ended in failure.

He made no effort to conceal his discouragement from Mabel Fierz, and she, quick to sympathize and eager to help, suggested that what he must do now was entrust his future to a literary agent—as all professional writers did—someone who would know to whom a particular manuscript should be offered, and how to obtain the best price for it. And of course it was very like her to know just the man, her friend Leonard Moore, of the firm of Christy & Moore. Late in the year, obedient to Mrs. Fierz's advice, Blair wrote to him, saying that he was sending him four stories (two new ones and the two survivors from the *Modern Youth* debacle), and mentioned as it were in passing the book that was then at Faber & Faber.

In January Moore replied to him at his parents' house in Southwold that he was doubtful that he could place two of the stories; about the others he would see; and he wondered if Blair had yet had any word of the book. No, came the answer, he had not; it was still at Faber—on the recommendation of a personal friend of Eliot's—they, he felt, were likely to be the only publisher who might do it. (It is unclear why he should have thought it was particularly *their* book; perhaps he was already so discouraged he wanted to close off the possibility of Moore offering it round.) He went on to ask that the story "The Idiot" be sent back to him, as he said that the *Adelphi* would take it. (Apparently the magazine must have changed its mind—Rees had no recollection of the story at all—for it never appeared there or elsewhere, nor did the other three stories fare any better.) Finally he asked if Moore might be able to get him some work as a translator, either in French, which he knew thoroughly, or Spanish, which he knew pretty well. A relationship, however tenuous, had been established between author and agent.

In February he was back in London, living in lodgings in Westminster Bridge Road. It was there at the end of the month that he finally heard from Faber & Faber. The letter, written by T. S. Eliot, was brief, courteous, and disheartening. It began with an apology for having kept the manuscript, went on to praise it, and then to reject it, and concluded with an expression of thanks for having been allowed to see it. In April Blair would tell Leonard Moore accurately enough that Faber had found the book interesting but too short. He passed over the perhaps more disquieting, because not wholly unjustified, of their objections: that the construction of the book was too loose, and the Paris and London episodes were only slightly connected. For Eliot the episodes in London evidently held the greater promise; and he suggested in a final sentence that Blair might be able to make a book of considerable interest if he were to limit himself to down-and-out life as he had known it in England. However well meant, it was a suggestion more easily made by a reader in a publishing house than accepted by a writer in a lodging house down to his last shilling.

The impact of this second rejection was decisive. Although he left no later record of what he felt at the time, his actions speak eloquently for him. It was as though all the illusions by which he had been living until then were stripped away, and he saw himself and his situation clearly for the first time.

He began by rejecting the book itself. When the manuscript was in his hands again, he carried it off to Golders Green, and left it with Mabel Fierz, telling her to read it or not as she pleased, and then to destroy it. "Burn it and keep the clips," he said.

Next he rejected the life dedicated to writing that he had pursued without interruption (save for the down-and-out expeditions that essentially were a part of it) since he had come back from Paris, and that he had allowed his mother, on however small a scale, to subsidize. If he meant to go on writing—and he did!—and to go down and out—about which he was less certain—then the cost henceforth would have to be borne by himself. What this meant, in the immediate practical sense, was that he would have to take a job. After five years he had arrived at the point where the greater number of young writers traditionally begin. From there his next step was traditional with young writers too, for he put on his respectable suit and went round to Truman & Knightly Associates to see if they might find him a place as a schoolmaster. They were not discouraging. Admittedly, his qualifications were not all they might be—he hadn't been at one of the ancient universities, which rather limited the possibilities, and he could hardly expect something of the first class. Still, he was an old Etonian who had been in College (which could be translated as good at Classics) and he had served in the Indian Imperial Police (good at games). Though it was an awkward time in the academic year to be starting out, a vacancy might unexpectedly come up; something might be found for him, and, in fact, in remarkably short order, something was. In April he was to begin teaching at Evelyn's School, a prep school for boys in Hayes, on the outskirts of London. With his fate thus decided, he went down to Southwold to wait for the beginning of term, to listen to the approving comments of his parents, to begin work on a long poem about a day in London that occupied him for the next few months (no trace of it survives), and to go for walks, separately, with his friends Eleanor Jaques and Brenda Salkeld.

Then came April, to a reader of *The Waste Land* inevitably "the cruellest month," and one ventures to think that the phrase would have occurred to Blair, for more than one reason, arriving at a waste land of his own: a dreary prep school in a dreary suburban town . . . so at least he found them on first acquaintance, and his view of them did not perceptibly brighten over the fifteen months that he was at Evelyn's. The school was like St. Cyprian's in its academic objective—to prepare boys for Public Schools—though a day school and less grand in its social pretensions, and much less secure in its financial aspect. (As business enterprises schools such as these had to make a profit or close down. The Depression was a perilous time for them, especially for those on the fringes, and in the end it did Evelyn's in. It collapsed after the academic year 1933-4, and Blair's first experience of schoolmastering was at an end. Unlike Evelyn Waugh, who had also been a prep-school master, he would never say, "It was very jolly and I enjoyed it very much." But he went on with hardly a pause to a much more solid and imaginative school, Frays College in Uxbridge, making the transition along with some of the physical effects of Evelyn's itself, which the principal of Frays had bought when the contents were put up for sale.)

After so many years to be back again in the ambience of St. Cyprian's darkened his view of everything: the school was "foul," the boys "brats," and Hayes "godforsaken." His only friend was the local curate. At night he would go home to the genteel dinginess of The Hawthorns, a house in the Station Road where he rented lodgings, and in his room he would try to work at his long poem or to evoke for his novel the flamboyant landscape of Upper Burma, while outside gray rain fell, and downstairs a woman banged hymn tunes on the piano . . . He had entered a world of gentility at the end of its tether that he had not known at first hand before, although he had read of it in Gissing and in some of Lawrence's stories (such as "Daughters of the Vicar"), and that in due course would be revealed to him as a subject for *A Clergyman's Daughter*. But that was still in the unforeseeable future, Orwell's future as a recognized, published author. In Hayes, at the beginning of April 1932, even the idea of Orwell did not yet exist; he was Eric Blair, stalled in an apprenticeship that had no successful end in sight, the unrecognized author of a twice-rejected and now abandoned manuscript.

Fortunately he had left the manuscript in good hands. This was the opportunity that Mrs. Fierz had been waiting for for more than a year, to read Eric's book, and once she had done so there was no question of her following his advice and burning it. True, it was not the book she had imagined him to be writing, for his reminiscences of Paris in their conversations tended to be more romantic than sordid; and it was hard to believe that the charming, attractive, sensitive young man who would go with her one night to an aesthetic drawing room in Chelsea to hear T. Sturge Moore read his poetic plays was the same young man who, perhaps a night later, would be sinking down into the squalor of a down-and-outer's life in the East End. But how remarkable a book it was, even so! Blair—diffident, passive, eager to believe the book a failure—had felt that the rejection by Faber & Faber settled its fate; Mrs. Fierz, blazing with enthusiasm, was determined that the book must be published. She now proceeded, in effect, to launch George Orwell. She took the manuscript herself to Leonard Moore, and over a cup of tea in his office, spoke enthusiastically of Blair and his work. Moore, who had had no success with any of Blair's stories, may well have identified the book as the one that had been offered to Faber & Faber with a personal recommendation to Eliot from a friend. He glanced at the manuscript—awkward length, difficult subject, unknown author—and said no. But Mrs. Fierz wasn't to be so easily put off. Here was a remarkable book—would she have brought it to him if it were not?—by a young author in whose future she believed, and so must he. She had a second cup of tea, and a third, and badgered him until, in order to get rid of her (as she later said), he agreed to keep the manuscript and give it a proper reading.

SUDDENLY, AND UNEXPECTEDLY, WE HAVE ARRIVED AT THE END of the unknown period of his life. Until April, there had been no reason to expect that the apprenticeship might extend itself interminably, not inconclusively: Blair one more failed writer with a closet stacked high with unpublished novels. Now, thanks to Mabel Fierz, and Leonard Moore, and presently Victor Gollancz, he was propelled forward toward a goal that had been continually receding as he approached it. Within eight months he was to be a published author, a name to be taken into account. Yet the writer who emerges at the end of the five years of apprenticeship is not to be Eric Blair, as one might logically have assumed, but George Orwell. That he should have decided to take a pseudonym is perhaps the most singular aspect of a literary history ("Becoming Orwell") that in contrast to the history of abrasive struggle preceding it ("Becoming a Writer") seems mysteriously negligent and noncommittal. Blair, sunk in depression in his first weeks at Evelyn's, had not been in touch with Mrs. Fierz since the afternoon he had left the manuscript with her, and so had no knowledge of her activities on his behalf. Toward the end of April he was surprised by a letter from Leonard Moore. It was the kind of letter that earlier would have stirred up a blaze of optimism such as had occurred with the first letter from Cape, for here was Moore saying that he had read *Days in London and Paris* and liked it and thought he might be able to place it, and asking for its history—had it been offered anywhere but at Faber? Blair was polite but depreciatory: the fires had been banked and he had no wish to be burned again. He supplied Moore with an account of the manuscript: first to Cape, then to Cape again, then to Faber, and so to Mrs. Fierz, who he had asked to destroy it, for it was not, in his opinion, "a good piece of work." Nor had his opinion of it changed. He was pleased of course that Moore should like it, and he was grateful that he should want to try to sell it, and of course he hoped that he would. But in the unlikely event of the book's being accepted, he would want to have it published pseudonymously as he was "not proud of it."

Here, in April 1932, five years after Eric Blair had embarked upon his literary career, is the first mention of a pseudonym, and it comes, significantly, at the first hopeful sign that his book—the most ambitious undertaking that he had attempted thus far—might finally be published. Until then, as we have seen, whatever he had written had appeared under his own name, even "Hop Picking" and "The Spike" (which had been incorporated into the book), whose subject matter he might have thought would reveal too much (to his parents) of his life away from Southwold, and cause them anxiety or embarrassment. Yet now he proposed to remove his name altogether from his work and replace it with an invention. Eliot's rejection, which really was not very damning, weighed upon him, and deepened his own conviction of the book's inadequacy, that it was not a good piece of work of which he could be proud. This is the sole explanation he resorted to. As a connoisseur of failure, he seemed to be preparing for the worst: if he was to fail in public, he preferred to do so under a nom de plume. It would not be inconsistent with his psychology, of course, but would this be sufficient cause for so dramatic a decision? Or was it (at first) perhaps no more than a gesture to prove to himself as well as to Moore how little he cared whether the book was accepted or not?

But the diffident role was difficult to sustain as the weeks passed and he heard nothing further from his agent. He taught; he reviewed *The Spirit of Catholicism* by Karl Adam for the *New English Weekly;* he worked at his poem; he planted marrow in a small square of garden behind the house; he went fishing. But he grew increasingly restive, and early in June, devising a pretext that would not suggest impatience, he wrote, not for news of the book, but to ask if Moore might be able to get him work as an "annotator" (Blair's word) from the Clarendon Press. An odd request, and Moore very likely recognized it for what it was, for when he did reply a fortnight later he made no reference to it: he had more important news. At the top of the letter Blair had sent him in April, Moore had scribbled in pencil the notation "Gollancz"; and it was there, astutely, with a successful agent's sense of matching house to manuscript, that he had sent *Days in London and Paris.* Now he could report to Blair that Victor Gollancz liked the book and wanted to publish it.

The question of a pseudonym became a practical rather than a theoretical concern. Blair met with Gollancz at the end of June to discuss minor alterations in the text (swear words to be taken out, and certain names changed for fear of libel), which were easily dealt with. And Gollancz asked for a new title. It would have seemed an appropriate time for Blair to mention to him that he would be using a pseudonym, but he did not. He waited another week until he wrote again to Moore. In that letter, even more diffidently than before, he remarks that he thinks, if no one objects, he would prefer to have the book come out pseudonymously. And he asked Moore to tell Gollancz this. The tone is oddly uncertain and self-effacing: after all, he has no reputation, and if this first book had any kind of success, the pseudonym would have some value, and he could use it for future books. But he gives no reason, and he had no particular name in mind, or none that he was ready to disclose. He found it easier to invent a new title (*The Lady Poverty*, a phrase from a poem of Alice Meynell's) than a new name. As far as publisher and agent were concerned, the book's author, with whom the contract was being made, was still Eric Blair. His tone at this time is such as to leave one uncertain as to how deeply the question mattered to him. It seems fair to say that if Gollancz had insisted upon the name of Eric Blair on the title page, he would have yielded.

At the end of July, he went down to Southwold for the summer holiday. His mother not long before had bought Montague House in High Street, but the family had not yet moved in. 3 Queen Street had been let to summer visitors, and Mr. and Mrs. Blair had gone to spend six weeks with the Dakins. Eric and Avril took possession of Montague House, where, in effect, they camped out for the month. The house "had very little furniture in it," Avril remembers, "because most of our furniture was in the other house. Eric was writing away hard all day, and I was out. I was at that time working in a tea-shop in the town and came back pretty late at night. For some unknown reason, we only had two electric-light bulbs. I don't know why we didn't buy more, but we each had one, and we used to take them round from room to room plugging them in wherever we wanted them."

At this time Eric told her that he thought he might have a book coming out soon, and that he had decided to publish it under a pen name because he was "ashamed" of it . . . He meant, he explained, that he thought their parents would be upset by it, it was all about his life in Paris . . . She felt that he must decide such things for himself; at the same time she was certain he exaggerated the effect the book might have on either Mr. or Mrs. Blair, who were a good deal more worldly than Eric seemed willing to admit, and not, as Avril says, "easily shockable, although my father was Victorian." But his mind was made up, except for one important detail: he did not know what the name was to be.

From Southwold he sent the signed contract to Moore to send on to Gollancz (who had not yet commented either on the change in title or the proposed use of a pseudonym) and he offered another title: *In Praise of Poverty.* The pseudonym was left up in the air. It was six months since he had first mentioned it to Moore, but he still had no definite suggestion to offer: the important thing, he emphasized, was a name that would be easy to remember. Even after he went back to Hayes to resume his dreary life as a schoolmaster he couldn't reach a decision. The book was being set in type, and its title page was still blank. In November, by which time it was already in proofs, Gollancz, growing impatient, proposed that it be called *Confessions of a Down and Outer,* and that the author's name be given simply as "X." Blair was not happy with either proposal. As a pseudonym for a young man passionately determined as Blair was on a literary career, and not merely the authorship of a single volume, "X" would not do at all. On the fifteenth of November he reminded Moore that the pen name must be one that he could use again, which "X" obviously was not. Yet even then, at virtually the last possible moment, he had not brought himself to the point of suggesting an alternative to either "X" or Eric Blair. Apparently he was willing to leave the matter to Moore and Gollancz to decide.

Four days later, he finally produced a list of possible pseudonyms. The first was his old tramping name, P. S. Burton. The second was Kenneth Miles. The third was George Orwell. The fourth was H. Lewis Allways. He himself admitted to a slight preference for George Orwell.*

For the title he now offered *Confessions of a Dishwasher*.

Moore hastily forwarded the suggestions. Time was running out, the book was scheduled for publication two months hence; there could be no further hesitations. Gollancz conflated the various suggestions he and Blair had put forward for a title, and he chose from among the four names Blair had offered him for a pseudonym.

Seldom can a man have shed one identity and taken another with less concern as to who he was finally to be. But it was not the name that mattered: it was the self, the essential second self, under the name, which had been set free.

DOWN AND OUT IN PARIS AND LONDON BY GEORGE ORWELL WAS PUB-lished by Gollancz on January 9, 1933. For a first book by an unknown author it did unusually well. The first edition

---

* As to the name itself, Anthony Powell, who became a friend of Orwell's in 1941, has written in a memoir of him: "The Orwell is a river in Suffolk, 'George,' the most characteristically English Christian name. I once asked him if he had ever thought of legally adopting his *nom de guerre*. 'Well, I have,' he said slowly, 'but then, of course, I'd have to *write* under another name if I did.'"

had been sold by the end of the month, and a second impression was ordered. Reviews were plentiful, prompt, and favorable. His career had been successfully launched.

"The family, of course, read it with great interest," Avril recalls. "It almost seemed as if it had been written by a different person."

A week or so after publication, returning from Southwold to Hayes, Blair met Mrs. Fierz in London. They paused outside a shop where a window was filled with copies of the book, his book, his name, George Orwell, again and again—a promise for the future.

NOTES

NOTES

NOTES

PART ONE

p.5, l.35   For Charles Blair's will, see Kenyon 522, Somerset House; for the exchange of deeds, see V. L. Oliver, *Caribbeana* (London, 1910).
p.9, l.10   Avril Dunn, "My Brother, George Orwell," *Twentieth Century* (March 1961); p. 255, and interviews.
p.10, l.22 For Dorset and the Blair family: Hutchins, *History and Antiquities of the County of Dorset* (London, 1863); The Assistant Archivist, County Record Office, Dorset, to authors; The Rev. J. L. Baillie, Milborne St. Andrew, to authors, and interview; *The Gentleman's Magazine* (1867), II, 542.
p.12, l.8   For R. W. Blair, see *History of Service, Opium Department*, India Office Records; for Limouzins, see R. R. Langhan Carter, *Old Moulmein* (Moulmein, 1947), copy courtesy of Mrs. M. Lecky-Thompson.
p.15, l.29 Richard Rees, "Afterword," Orwell, *Burmese Days* (Signet Classics edition, New York, 1963), p. 248.
p.17, l.16 Ruth Pitter, interview.
p.22, l.6   Humphrey Dakin to authors.
p.32, l.25 Cyril Connolly, *Enemies of Promise* (revised edition, New York, 1948), p. 160.
p.33, l.8   Cecil Beaton, *The Wandering Years* (Boston, 1961), p. 29.
p.35, l.4   Connolly, *Enemies of Promise*, pp. 146–7.
p.36, l.28 Beaton, *The Wandering Years*, p. 30.
p.38, l.36 Gavin Maxwell, *The House of Elrig* (New York, 1965), p. 83. See also E. H. W. Meyerstein, *Of My Early Life* (London, 1957).

p.55, l.16   Beaton, *The Wandering Years*, p. 31.
p.57, l.11   Connolly, *Enemies of Promise*, pp. 146–7.
p.58, l.2   *The Collected Essays, Journalism and Letters of George Orwell* (New York, 1968), I, 362–3; IV, 422.
p.60, l.11   Avril Dunn, "My Brother, George Orwell," pp. 255–6.
p.65, l.12   Beaton, *The Wandering Years*, p. 32.
p.71, l.1   Eton examination based on Philip Brownrigg, "College," in Bernard Fergusson, *Eton Portrait* (London, 1937), pp. 38–57.
p.73, l.30   Philip Magnus, *Kitchener: Portrait of an Imperialist* (London, 1958), p. 379.
p.75, l.12   Letter and poem, courtesy of Cyril Connolly.

PART TWO

p.84, l.22   About Wellington, Graham Stainforth to authors.
p.85, l.32   Quotations from Eton contemporaries here and throughout chapter come from Denys King-Farlow, interviews, and "College Days with George Orwell," unpublished manuscript; Cyril Connolly, interviews, and as cited; Christopher Hollis, interview, and as cited; George Wansbrough to authors; Sir Maurice Whittome to authors; Francis Cruso to authors; James Gibson to authors; R. M. Cazalet to authors; W. C. A. Milligan to authors; Sir Steven Runciman, interviews.
p.86, l.24   C. A. Alington, *Edward Lyttelton: An Appreciation* (London, 1943), p. 18. *Times*, June 5, 1916.
p.87, l.11   Christopher Hollis, *Eton* (London, 1960), pp. 297–8.
p.88, l.5   Richard Rees, *George Orwell: Fugitive from the Camp of Victory* (London, 1961), p. 154.
p.88, l.23   *The Observer*, August 1, 1948. The piece has not been reprinted. Two paragraphs are quoted in Christopher Hollis, *A Study of George Orwell* (London, 1956), pp. 18–19.
p.90, l.20   Rees, *Orwell*, p. 42.
p.92, l.11   Hollis, *Orwell*, p. 13.
p.93, l.14   Avril Dunn, "My Brother, George Orwell," p. 256.
p.94, l.9   See Cyril Connolly's "Theory of Permanent Adolescence," *Enemies of Promise*, p. 253, and Orwell's comment on it in "Inside the Whale," *Collected Essays* . . ., I, 517.

p.95, l.38	Malcolm Muggeridge, "Introduction," Orwell, *Burmese Days* (London, 1967), pp. viii–ix.
p.97, l.9	Hollis, *Orwell*, pp. 13–15, and interview. Sir Steven Runciman, interview.
p.99, l.30	Connolly, *Enemies of Promise*, p. 187.
p.100, l.33	Marie-Jacqueline Lancaster, *Brian Howard* (London, 1968), p. 21.
p.103, l.28	As quoted in Eric Parker, *College at Eton* (London, 1933), p. 216.
p.104, l.22	As quoted in Ibid., p. 239, p. 250.
p.107, l.2	Hollis, *Orwell*, p. 15.
p.108, l.38	Connolly, *Enemies of Promise*, pp. 215–17.
p.120, l.15	Elizabeth Bowen in Oliver Stallybrass, ed., *Aspects of E. M. Forster* (New York, 1969), p. 1.
p.121, l.33	Cyril Connolly, *The Condemned Playground* (London, 1945), p. 62.
p.123, l.14	Samuel Hynes, *The Edwardian Turn of Mind* (Princeton, 1968), p. 14.
p.126, l.21	Connolly, *Enemies of Promise*, p. 188.
p.128, l.13	Connolly, *The Condemned Playground*, pp. 140–1.
p.129, l.24	Rayner Heppenstall, *Four Absentees* (London, 1960), pp. 20–1. J. D. R. McConnell, *Eton—How It Works* (London, 1967), pp. 61–2.
p.131, l.10	Connolly, *Enemies of Promise*, pp. 204–5.
p.132, l.2	Ibid., p. 251.
p.133, l.34	McConnell, *Eton*, pp. 136–7.
p.136, l.13	Jack London, *The People of the Abyss* (London, 1962), p. 11.
p.143, l.19	A. S. F. Gow to Jeffrey Meyers, January 1, 1969, quoted in Jeffrey Meyers, "George Orwell, the Honorary Proletarian," *Philological Quarterly*, XLVIII (October 1969), p. 531.

PART THREE

p.149, l.25	T. R. Fyvel, "George Orwell and Eric Blair," *Encounter* (July 1959), p. 62.
p.150, l.10	Sir Steven Runciman, interviews.
p.151, l.7	*Collected Essays* . . ., I, 1.

p.151, l.31 As Orwell wrote in "My Country Right or Left," (1940), his early world was "tinged" with militarism, compounded by the five "boring" years he spent in Burma "within the sound of bugles." *Collected Essays*..., I, 540.

p.155, l.21 Information about Blair's application and examination from India Office Records: Judicial and Public Department file for 1922 (J & P 6079/22 vol. 1806).

p.159, l.7 *Collected Essays*..., IV, 266.

p.159, l.23 Roger Beadon, "Burma 1922–1927." We are very grateful to Mr. Beadon for this memoir (from which subsequent quotations are taken) and his assistance and advice in letters and interviews. See also "With Orwell in Burma—Roger Beadon Talks to Pamela Howe," *Listener* (May 29, 1969), p. 755.

p.160, l.15 Orwell, "Notes on the Way," *Time & Tide* (March 30, 1940).

p.162, l.22 The details of Blair's work in Burma are based on interviews with Roger Beadon and on letters from other contemporaries of his in Burma; R. G. B. Lawson to authors, also quoted on pp. 164, 177, 179, 182, 185.

p.164, l.34 Blair to Henry Miller, August 26, 1936, *Collected Essays*..., I, 229.

p.173, l.6 J. G. Scott, *Burma: A Handbook of Practical Information* (London, 3rd edition, 1921), p. 146. See also J. S. Furnivall, *Colonial Policy and Practice* (New York, 1956); H. Tinker, *The Foundations of Local Self-Government in India, Pakistan and Burma* (London, 1954); also the annual *Report on the Administration of Burma*.

p.178, l.26 For Orwell's later views, see *The Lion and the Unicorn* (London, 1941), p. 45.

p.178, l.34 Anthony Powell, "George Orwell," *The Atlantic Monthly* (October 1967), p. 63.

p.181, l.3 A. Dunbar to authors.

p.183, l.28 A. L'estrange Brownlow to authors.

p.184, l.36 *Horizon* (1948), IV, 201.

p.187, l.13 W. Somerset Maugham, *The Gentleman in the Parlour* (New York, 1930), pp. 7–8.

p.188, l.34 Maung Htin Aung, "George Orwell and Burma," *Asian Affairs* (February 1970), p. 23.

p.189, l.21 For Robinson, see George Orwell, "Portrait of an Ad-

NOTES 315

	dict," *Observer* (September 13, 1942), and also the book itself: Captain H. R. Robinson, *A Modern DeQuincey* (London, 1942).
p.190, l.5	"Lawrence" to authors, and interview; Hollis, *Orwell*, p. 27, and interview.
p.191, l.39	Harold Acton, *More Memoirs of an Aesthete* (London, 1970), pp. 152–3; Orwell to Gorer, *Collected Essays* . . ., I, 382.
p.194, l.13	C. B. Orr to authors.
p.199, l.25	R. Gordon B. Prescott to authors. Also quoted on p. 201.
p.204, l.22	Orwell to Connolly, *Collected Essays* . . ., I, 329.
p.206, l.29	Sir Richard Rees, interview.
p.208, l.30	For Orwell's reading, see *New Statesman* (January 25, 1941); also *Collected Essays* . . ., III, 105, 187–9; IV, 3–33.

PART FOUR

p.215, l.16	Avril Dunn, "My Brother, George Orwell," p. 257.
p.218, l.36	Rees, *Orwell*, p. 145.
p.219, l.34	A. S. F. Gow, interview; also, *Collected Essays* . . ., I, 225.
p.220, l.25	Ruth Pitter, broadcast and interview, also quoted from on pp. 223–5, 227, 274.
p.222, l.11	*Collected Essays* . . ., III, 155–6.
p.231, l.22	I. O. Evans, "Introduction," London, *The People of the Abyss*, pp. 9–11.
p.234, l.19	Brenda Salkeld, interview.
p.234, l.26	Orwell to Dennis Collings, *Collected Essays* . . ., I, 49.
p.235, l.5	*La Vache Enragée* (Paris, 1935), pp. 7–9.
p.241, l.26	Bailey to Blair, April 29, 1929, Berg Collection, New York Public Library.
p.243, l.13	"A Farthing Newspaper," *Collected Essays* . . ., I, 12–15.
p.244, l.16	*Progrès Civique* (December 28, 1928; January 4, January 11, 1929). For Blair's Paris publications we are indebted to the library of the Hoover Institution, Stanford University.
p.250, l.2	*The Listener* (February 4, 1971), p. 144.
p.256, l.7	Loelia, Duchess of Westminster, *Grace and Favour* (London, 1961), p. 225.

p.263, l.7   On the Dakins: Humphrey Dakin to authors; Fyvel, "George Orwell and Eric Blair," pp. 60–5.
p.266, l.25   Professor Richard Peters, interview, and broadcast.
p.269, l.33   Mabel Fierz, interview.
p.270, l.23   Michael S. Howard, *Jonathan Cape, Publisher* (London, 1971), p. 133.
p.278, l.7   London, *The People of the Abyss*, p. 23.
p.281, l.14   Brenda Salkeld, interview; and broadcast, November 2, 1960.
p.282, l.33   Jack Common, broadcast, July 6, 1958.
p.284, l.31   Rees, *Orwell*, p. 141, and interviews.

PART FIVE

p.294, l.17   Heppenstall, *Four Absentees*, p. 46.
p.295, l.30   *Collected Essays* . . ., I, 78.
p.298, l.6   Letters to Moore, in part unpublished, Berg Collection, New York Public Library. See also *Collected Essays* . . ., Vol. I.
p.298, l.27   We wish to express our gratitude to Mrs. Valerie Eliot for sending us a copy of this letter.
p.299, l.4   Mabel Fierz, interview.
p.300, l.22   Evelyn Waugh to Julian Jebb, *Writers at Work* (New York, 1967), p. 108.
p.305, l.30   Avril Dunn, "My Brother, George Orwell," pp. 257–8.
p.307, l.27   Powell, "George Orwell," p. 63.

INDEX

Acton, Harold, 125, 190–1 n.
Acton, William, 125
Adam, Karl, *The Spirit of Catholicism*, 304
Adam, Nellie Limouzin (Blair's aunt), 239, 250, 251, 253, 259
Adelphi, 9, 195, 206–7, 230, 248, 260–2, 269, 272, 273, 281–5, 298
À La Belle de Nuit (Roberti), 295–6
Albert Grope (Mann), 285
Alexander Pope (Sitwell), 261
Alington, C. A., 86, 105–6
Allways, H. Lewis (Blair's suggested pseudonym), 307
Ami du Peuple, 243
Androcles and the Lion (Shaw), 99, 105, 106 and n.
Angel Pavement (Priestley), 261
Animal Farm (Orwell), xviii, 5, 19, 35, 169, 205
antinomianism, 122–3 and n., 124, 126, 238
"Art of Donald McGill, The" (Orwell), 148
Auden, W. H., 10
Austen, Jane, 3, 7

authority, attitude toward, 41–3
"Awake! Young Men of England" (Blair), 61–2, 65

Bailey, Mr. (of McClure Newspaper Syndicate), 241
Ballantyne, R. M., *Coral Island*, 18–19
Barbusse, Henri, 242
Bartz, Karl, *The Horrors of Cayenne*, 285
Bassein, 176
Beachy Head, 27, 47, 58
Beadon, C. W. R. (Roger), 156, 159, 161–8, 175–6, 183, 190, 193–4, 204
Beaton, Cecil, 29, 33, 36, 55, 56, 62–3, 65
Beerbohm, Max, 125
Bell, Julian, xiii, xiv, 156
Bell, Lady, 68
Bellary, 11
Bellehatch Park, 68, 133
Bermondsey, 288, 289
Binfield Heath, 48
Binney, George, 111
Birkenhead, 156

Blair, Augusta Michael, 10
Blair, Avril, see Dunn, Avril Blair
Blair, Charles (E. Blair's great-great-grandfather), 5–8
Blair, Charles, Jr. (E. Blair's great-grandfather), 8
Blair, Mrs. Charles, Jr., 8
Blair, Dawson, 10
Blair, Eileen O'Shaughnessy (Mrs. Eric Blair), 95, 191 n.
Blair, Eric (after 1933 George Orwell):
anti-imperialism, 175, 197–8, 200–1, 211, 225–7, 236
appearance, 85, 95 n., 116–18, 161, 215, 220
birth, 12, 14
in Burma, xviii, 15, 160–211, 279; decision to go, 149–52, 155–6; examinations for Imperial Police, 153–6; leaves, 204, 211, 216; Mandalay Training School, 161–2, 164–5, 168–9, 175–6; police experience as theme, 225–7; salary, 184 and n.; voyage out, 156–61
characteristics: aloofness, 94–6, 126, 134, 280; bluntness, 85–6; cynicism, 85–6, 102, 104–6, 126; fantasies, stories told to himself, 134–5, 185–6; fear of failure, 293–4; grievances, 17–18, 22, 23, 50, 56, 89; nostalgia, 18, 58; patriotism, 61, 83, 87–8; prudery, 21–2; shyness, 16, 20; smell, sense of, 22, 157 n.; social class, consciousness of, xix, 4–5, 157 and n.

Blair, Eric (*continued*)
childhood: early, 14–22; at home, compared with school, 67–9, 69 n.
death, xx, 219
as dishwasher, 253–6
epitaph, xx
at Eton, xviii, 18, 41, 84–134, 139–44, 150, 152, 204, 245; adventure of missing trains, 137–8; Fourth of June speech, 133–4; leaves, 143, 148–9; periodicals edited, 104, 105, 109–11, 125; scholarship examinations, 70–1, 77; sports, 115–19; studies, 107–8, 112–15
as Etonian, 149, 177, 222–3, 299
family, 5–12
health, 204, 221, 274
as hop picker, 6, 229, 234, 261, 274, 287–8
in jail, 296–7
letters: to Connolly, 204; to Henry Miller, 164 and n.; to his mother, 44, 45 and n., 46–9
in London, 218, 220–37, 289, 298
marriage, 95, 149, 191 n.
as Orwell, see Orwell, George
in Paris, 229, 238–56
pneumonia in Paris hospital, 245–6
poverty, experiences of, 228–37, 245–7, 249–56, 261, 262, 271–3, 275–6, 278, 281–2, 285, 287–8, 296–7
poverty as theme, 244–7

INDEX 319

Blair, Eric (continued)
reading: in Burma, 207–9; in childhood, 18–19, 57–8, 65–6; at Eton, 120–2, 135–6, 139–40
religious opinions, 105–6 at St. Cyprian's school, xviii, 4, 23–79, 142, 169, 179, 204, 245, 250, 254, 293; bedwetting episode, 38–43; reduced fees, 30–1, 33, 53–4, 66; scholarship class, 51–4
sex experiences, 190, 190–1 n., 267
at Sunnylands day school, 18 as teacher, 299–300
tuberculosis, 95 n., 191 n., 204 as tutor, 264–6, 272, 286
university, decision on, 140–4, 149 and n.
at Wellington College, 70, 71, 84–5
women, relationships with, 20, 223–8, 241, 267–9, 279–81
as writer, 205-11, 223–307; apprenticeship, 206–7, 221, 223–5, 239–45; decision to write, 216–8; influence of other writers, 208–11; tries not to write, 151, 185, 205, 206
writings: for *Adelphi*, 9, 195, 207, 248, 260–2, 269, 272, 273, 283–5; on Burma, 169–70, 194–8, 201–3, 225–8, 285; diary of tramp experiences, 287–8; earliest published, 28 n., 61–2, 76; at Eton, 108–12, 116; first professional publication, 112,

Blair, Eric, writings (continued)
242–3; for *New Statesman and Nation*, 288, 289; in Paris, 240–9; for Paris journals, 112, 242–5, 248–9; poems, first, 59–62, 65, 75–6; poems, unpublished 221, 223–4, 299–300; stories, early unpublished, 224–5, 241; *see also* titles
Blair, Frances Hare, 9
Blair, Henry Charles, 7
Blair, Ida Limouzin (E. Blair's mother), 11–18, 20–1, 57, 77, 85, 99, 141, 147–8, 150–2, 157 n., 198, 215 n., 220, 258, 265, 266, 305–6; and Blair at St. Cyprian's, 24–8, 30, 54, 64; and Blair's first writings, 59, 61–2; character, 16–17; letters from Blair, 44, 45 and n., 46–9; relationship with Blair, 16, 57, 85, 149–50, 216–18, 226, 267, 289, 296, 299; in World War, First, 84
Blair, Maria, 7
Blair, Marjorie, *see* Dakin, Marjorie Blair
Blair, Mary, 7
Blair, Lady Mary Fane, 5–9
Blair, Richard Walmesley (E. Blair's father), 7, 10–11, 15–16, 23–7, 32, 54, 57, 61, 68, 77, 78, 89, 90, 96, 137 n., 141, 147–53, 215, 258, 259, 305–6; and Blair's service in Burma, 142, 149–51, 153, 216–17; character 16, 17, 24; death, 218 n.; in India, 11–14; relationship with Blair,

Blair, Richard Walmesley (cont.) 23–4 and n., 85, 150, 216–17, 218 and n., 220, 226, 260, 268; in World War, First, 83–4, 137 n.
Blair, Thomas, 7
Blair, Rev. Thomas Richard Arthur (E. Blair's grandfather), 6, 8–10, 151
Blake, William, 15; "The Echoing Green," 35–6
Blakiston, Noel, 106–7
Blandford St. Mary, 7
Booth, Charles, *Life and Labour of the People of London*, 139
Boris (waiter), 252, 253, 267
Bowen, Elizabeth, 120
Bramley, 261, 263, 264, 272
Britton, Lionel, *Hunger and Love*, 285
Brooke, Rupert, 60
Brownlow, A. L'estrange, 183
Buck, Pearl, *The Good Earth*, 285
Buddicom, Jacintha, 69 n.
Buddicom family, 69 n.
Burdett, Osbert, *The Two Carlyles*, 285
Burma, 151; Blair in, xviii, 15, 160–211, 279; Blair's writing about, 169–70, 194–8, 201–3, 225–8, 285; British rule of, 170–3
Burma: A Handbook of Practical Information (Scott), 172–3
Burmah Oil Company, 184
Burmese Days (Orwell), 14, 15, 119, 164 and n., 167, 170, 174, 177, 185–6, 188–90, 195, 199, 203, 211, 223, 227, 285, 294

Burns, C. Delisle, 279
Burton, P. S. (Blair's assumed name), 261, 307
Butler, Samuel, 120, 208–9; *The Way of All Flesh*, 99; *The Notebooks*, 208

Cambridge, 8, 140–3, 149 and n., 218, 222
Campbell, Colin, 6
Cape, Jonathan (publishing house), 268, 270–1, 286, 289, 294, 303
Cape Town, 9
Carlyle, Thomas, *The French Revolution*, 65
Carroll, Lewis, 4
Cazalet, R. M., 126
Celestial Omnibus, The (Forster), 120
"Censure en Angleterre, La" (Blair), 112, 242–3
Ceylon, 156, 159–60
Chesterton, G. K., 120, 243
Child, Robert, 6
Christie, John, 112 and n., 113–14
Christy & Moore, 297
Churchill, Winston, 34, 140
Cinderella (pantomime), 68–9
Clarendon Press, 304
Clergyman's Daughter, A (Orwell), 4, 208, 287, 288, 301
"Clink" (Orwell), 297
Clutton-Brock, Alan, 125
Cocteau, Jean, 208
Cohen, Leslie, 47
Collected Essays, Journalism and Letters of George Orwell, The, 287

College Days, edited by Blair, 104, 105, 111, 125
Collings, Dennis, 148, 229
Colombo, 159
Coming Up for Air (Orwell), xix, 20, 21, 48–9, 58, 191 n.
Common, Jack, 229, 281–4
"Common Lodging Houses" (Blair), 233–4
Confessions of a Dishwasher (Down and Out), 307
Confessions of a Down and Outer (Down and Out), 306
Connolly, Cyril, xviii, 29, 35 n., 52, 95 n., 131 n., 184 n., 262;
Enemies of Promise, 34–5, 108 n., 132; at Eton, 90, 99–100, 116, 125–6, 130–1, 134; family, 56–7; letter from Blair, 204; poem on Kitchener, 74–6; *The Rock Pool*, 224, review by Orwell, 122–3 n.; at St. Cyprian's, 28, 36, 53 n., 54–9, 62–5, 69, 76; on school life, 31–2, 34–5; *The Unquiet Grave*, 112; writings, 112, 224
Conrad, Joseph, 208
Coral Island (Ballantyne), 18–19
Cornford, John, xiii, 139 n.
Cornwall, 20, 21, 33, 59, 137, 216, 217
Coty, M., 243
Country Life, 130
Country of the Blind, The (Wells), 58
Course of English Classicism, The (Vines), 261
Crace, John, 104–7, 153
Craig, Mr. and Mrs., 221–2

Cruso, Francis, 124, 127
Curtis, Lionel, 230

Dakin, Humphrey, 21, 22, 147, 261, 272, 305; Blair described by, 263–4
Dakin, Marjorie Blair (E. Blair's sister), 12, 14–16, 18, 22, 47, 68, 84, 89, 102, 147, 261, 263, 272, 305
Dannreuther, Denis, 104, 114, 126, 130–2
Darien scheme, Scottish, 6
Days in London and Paris (Down and Out), 286, 295, 303, 304
Dewlish, 7, 9, 10
Dickens, Charles, 19, 140
Down and Out in Paris and London (Orwell), xiii, xiv, 135, 138, 205, 225, 228, 240, 301–7; French edition, *La Vache Enragée*, 234–5; material for, 228–37, 249–58, 261, 262, 271–3, 275–6, 285; pseudonym, 303–7; published, 304–7; rejected, 284, 293–4, 298–9; titles, 286, 295, 303, 304–7; writing of, 260, 262–3, 266–73, 275–7, 286–7
Doyle, Arthur Conan, 230
du Maurier, George, 239
Dunn, Avril Blair (E. Blair's sister), xiii, xiv, 8, 14, 16, 20, 23–4 n., 45 n., 68, 69 n., 84, 147, 157 n., 215, 216, 226, 258, 308; relationship with Blair, 59–60, 93, 305–6
Dyarchy, 191–2

Ealing, 84
Eastbourne, 26, 27, 69, 147
Eastdean, 58
"Echoing Green, The" (Blake), 35–6
Edwardian period, 66–7, 136
Election Times, The, 121, 125; Blair's writing in, 109–11, 116
Eliot, T. S., 121, 134, 208; Blair and, 295, 297, 298, 304; *The Waste Land*, 300
Elizabeth I, 63
Enemies of Promise (Connolly), 34, 108 n., 132
Ensor, R. C. K., 230
Eric, or Little by Little, 127
Essex, Robert Devereux, Earl of, 63
Eton, 25, 28, 30, 51, 151, 153, 157, 158, 161, 279, 283; Blair at, xviii, 18, 41, 84–134, 139–44, 150, 152, 204, 245; Blair in scholarship examinations, 70–1, 77; Chamber Singing, 92; College Annals, Retrospect in, 103–4, 131–2; College Pop, 104 and n., 130, 134; Collegers, 70 n., 89, 90 and n., 91–2, 117, 118, 141, 283; corporal punishment, protests against, 128–32; Elections, 71, 84, 91–7, 99, 100, 102, 104, 126, 128, 130–2, 140; Eton Society (Pop), 104 n.; Fourth of June celebration, 86, 132–4, 149; King's Scholars, 70, 71, 88, 141; literary group, 125; Officer Training Corps, 102, 126–8, 137, 169 n.; Oppidans, 70 n.,

Eton (*continued*)
88–91, 117, 118, 125, 140–1, 283; postwar period (antinomians, protest movements), 101–4, 122–4, 126–8; Sixth Form, 92–4, 97, 101, 115, 128–9, 131, 132; Wall Game, 117–18, 134; in World War, First, 84, 86–7
Eton Candle, The, 91, 125
Eton College Calendar, 113
Eton College Chronicle, 103
Eton–Harrow cricket match, 119
Eton—How It Works (McConnell), 129
Evans, I. O., 231, 232
Evelyn's School, 300, 302

Faber & Faber, 295, 296, 297, 298, 302–3
Fane, Francis, 7
Fane, Sir Francis, 6
Fane, Julian, 6
Fane family, 5–7
"Farthing Newspaper, A" (Blair), 243–4
Fierz, Francis, 268
Fierz, Mabel, 91, 229, 249–50, 267, 270, 273, 286, 289, 297; Blair's friendship with, 268–9; and *Down and Out*, 299, 301–3, 308
fishing, 23–4 n.
Fitzgerald (Kitchener's secretary), 73
Ford, Mary, 296
"Forever Eton" (Orwell), 88
Forster, E. M., 279; *The Celestial Omnibus*, 120; *Howards End*, 29, 136; *A Passage to India*, 14

Four Absentees (Heppenstall), 128–9, 131 n.
Frays College, 300
French Revolution, The (Carlyle), 65
Fyvel, T. R., 263

Galsworthy, John, 121, 248
George V, 24
Georgian Poetry, 125
Gibson, James, 108, 118, 126, 130
Gide, André, 208
Gilbert, W. S., 135
Ginger (tramp), 288–9
Gissing, George, 301
G. K.'s Weekly, 243
Glyndebourne music festival, 112 n.
Gollancz, Victor, 302, 304–7
Good-bye to All That (Graves), 149 n., 274
Good Earth, The (Buck), 285
Gore, Bishop, 106
Gorer, Geoffrey, 191 n.
Gow, A. S. F., 107–9, 112, 143, 157 n., 218–19, 226
Grange, The, school, 46
Graves, Robert, 60; *Good-bye to All That*, 149 n., 274
Green, Henry (Henry Yorke), 125
Gregory, Lady Augusta, 99
Gulliver's Travels (Swift), 19, 33

Haldane, Richard Burdon, Viscount, 127
Hampshire (cruiser), 73
"Hanging, A" (Blair), 170, 194–8, 200, 225, 269, 285

Hanthawaddy District, 177, 180, 183
Hare, Emily, 9
Harpsden, 68, 69
Harrow, 25, 30
Harrow History Prize, 65
Hartland, Winifred Grace, 19–20
Hayes, 299, 307
Hemingway, Ernest, 140
Henley and South Oxfordshire Standard, 61–2, 76, 242
Henley-on-Thames, 14–18, 21, 42, 67–9, 77–8, 84, 147, 148, 264
Henry VI, 28
Heppenstall, Rayner, 294; *Four Absentees*, 128–9, 131 n.
Herefordshire, S. S., 156–61
Hill, M. D., 112
Hollis, Christopher, 86–7, 97–8, 190–2; *A Study of George Orwell*, 97, 101, 106–7, 118, 128, 131 n.
Homage to Catalonia (Orwell), xiii, 4, 15, 168, 244
Hope, Mr. (tutor), 153–5
hop picking, Blair's experience, 6, 229, 234, 261, 274, 287–8
"Hop Picking" (Blair), 287–8, 303
Horizon, 35 n., 184 n.
Horrors of Cayenne, The (Bartz), 285
Housman, A. E., 224; *A Shropshire Lad*, 121–2
Howard, Brian, 125
Howards End (Forster), 29, 136
"How the Poor Die" (Orwell), 240, 245
Huckleberry Finn (Twain), 267

Hunger and Love (Britton), 285
Huson, Mr. (at Eton), 114
Huxley, Aldous, 125 and n., 208

"Idiot, The" (Blair), 298
India, 11–15, 147, 148, 151–2; Dyarchy, 171; Opium Department, 11, 13; *see also* Burma
Indian Civil Service, 142, 177
Indian Imperial Police, 150–2, 156, 173–4, 177–8, 299; examinations for, 153–6; Mandalay Training School, 161–2, 164–5, 168–9, 175–6; *see also* Burma
India Office, 153
In Praise of Poverty (Down and Out), 306
Insein, 186, 190, 192–4, 197, 204
Irrawaddy Delta, 181–2
Irrawaddy River, 160

Jamaica, 5–8
Jaques, Eleanor, 148, 229, 300
Jevington, 58
Jones, A. J., 156, 161, 165, 168
Journey to the Frontier (Stansky and Abrahams), xiii, xiv
Joyce, James, 208, 240, 279; *Ulysses*, 208

Karens (Burmese people), 182–3
Katha, 203–4
Keep the Aspidistra Flying (Orwell), 4
Kent House, school, 46

Keynes, John Maynard, 88
Kilvert, Rev. Francis, 10
Kim (Kipling), 152
Kindersley, Mr. (at Eton), 113
King-Farlow, Denys, 85, 89, 99, 104, 108, 109 and n., 111, 116, 130, 131, 134, 137, 150, 223
Kingston, Countess of, 57
Kipling, Rudyard, 13, 14, 18, 19, 30, 32, 56, 58, 61, 152, 162; *Kim*, 152
Kitchener, Horatio Herbert, Lord, 72–3; death, 71, 73, 87; poems on, by Connolly and Blair, 74–6
"Kitchener" (Blair), 75–6, 242

Lady Poverty, The (Down and Out), 305
Larsonnier, Mr. (at Eton), 114
Laurie, T. Werner, 296
Lawrence (in Burma), 189–91, 267
Lawrence, D. H., 120–1, 208, 210–11, 301
Lawson, R. G. B., 162, 179, 182–5
Leacock, Stephen, 59
Leete, Alfred, 72
Lehmann, John, 118
Leicester, Robert Dudley, Earl of, 63
Lenin, Nikolai, 123
Lewis, Wyndham, 121, 208
Life and Labour of the People of London (Booth), 139
Limouzin, Frank, 11–12
Limouzin, G. E., 11

Limouzin family, 11–12; in Burma, 198–9; in Paris, 239, 250, 251, 253, 259
Lion and the Unicorn, The (Orwell), 133 n.
Listener, The, 249
London, Jack, *The People of the Abyss,* 135–6, 139–40, 160, 230–2, 277–8
London: Blair family live in, 84, 102, 147; Blair lives in, 218, 220–37, 289, 298; Blair's experiences of poverty in, 228–37, 261, 262, 271–3, 287–8
Longden, R. P., 94, 118, 126, 130
Looe, 33, 137, 138
Lyttelton, Edward, 86
Lyttelton, George, 112

MacCarthy, Desmond, 262
Macdonald, Malcolm, 191
Mackenzie, Compton, *Sinister Street,* 65–6
Macmillan, Harold, 40, 88
Macnaghten, Hugh, 108 and n., 125
MacNiece, Louis, 10
McClure Newspaper Syndicate, 241
McConnell, J. D. R., *Eton—How It Works,* 129
McDowall, Mr. (at Eton), 113
Madras, 155
Major Barbara (Shaw), 136
Mandalay, 161–6, 189; Provincial Police Training School, 161–2, 164–5, 168–9, 175–6
Mann, F. O., *Albert Grope,* 285
Mansfield Park (Austen), 7

"Man with Kid Gloves, The" (Blair), 241
Marlborough, John Churchill, Duke of, 6
Marrakech, 191 n.
Marxism, 282
Maugham, W. Somerset, 34, 186–7, 189, 208–11, 224
Maulmain Calendar, 12
Maung Htin Aung, 188
Maxwell, Gavin, 29, 38 n., 63, 64
Maymyo, 168
Melville, Herman, Mumford's biography of, 260, 261
Mereworth Castle, 6
Messel, Oliver, 125
Meyerstein, E. H. W., 29
Meynell, Alice, 305
Michel, Charles, 7–8
Michel, Sir John, 9
Michel family, 9
Milborne St. Andrew, 8–10
Miles, Kenneth (Blair's suggested pseudonym), 307
Miller, Henry, 267; letter from Blair, 164 and n.
Mindon (Burmese king), 163
Mitchelstown Castle, 57
Modern Youth, 289, 296, 297
Monde, 242, 248
Monghyr, 11, 14, 15, 147
Montagu–Chelmsford proposals, 171
Montmorency, Mr. (at Eton), 113
Moore, Leonard, 297–8, 302–7
Moore, T. Sturge, 301
Morocco, 190–1 n.
Motihari, 11, 12, 14, 147
Moulmein, 11, 12, 151, 197–9, 203, 204

326 INDEX

Muggeridge, Malcolm, 95 n.
Mumford, Lewis, biography of Melville, 260, 261
Munro, H. H. (Saki), 18
Murry, John Middleton, 269
Myaungmya, 176–9, 203
Mynors, Sir Robert, 94, 109, 114, 126, 130

Nellie, Aunt, see Adam, Nellie Limouzin
Newbolt, Sir Henry John, 32, 52, 61
New English Weekly, 304
New Statesman and Nation, 230, 288, 289
Nicole, Raoul, 244
1984 (Orwell), xviii, xx, 58, 174, 245
Norton family, 68
Now and Then, 270

O'Hara, Kathleen, 220, 229
Old Moore's Almanac, 19
Orr, C. B., 194
Orwell, George (before 1933 Eric Blair), 4–5, 13, 17–19, 21, 64 n., 83 and n., 142, 151, 157 n., 158–60, 169, 182, 191 n., 204, 219, 222, 223, 236, 240, 269, 278, 287, 293; Blair becomes, xiv, xvii–xx, 15, 134, 144, 170, 175, 205–11, 257–8, 261, 301–8; on Blair's early writings, 108, 223; on Burma, 161, 166–7, 174–5, 177, 178, 185–6, 195, 197, 200–3, 211, see also

Orwell, George (continued)
Burmese Days; on cost of living, 184 n.; on Eton, 88, 101, 102, 106, 119, 122–4, 138, 139 and n., 141, 149 n.; literary style, 209–11; name, choice of, 195, 307 and n.; on school experiences, 29, 31, 35–7, 39–44, 45 n., 47, 50, 53, 71–2, 78–9; writings, see titles; for early writings, see Blair, Eric
O'Shaughnessy, Eileen, see Blair, Eileen
Osterley Park, 6
Owen, Wilfred, 60
Oxford, 140–3, 149 and n., 222

Paneroff, Ph., 248
Paris: Blair in, 229, 238–56; Blair writes about, 262–3, 266–8, 270–3, 276; Hôpital Cochin, Blair's experience in, 245–7, 267–8
Parkestone golf club, 92–3
Partisan Review, 35 n.
Passage to India, A (Forster), 14
Pembroke College, Cambridge, 8
Penge, 11
People of the Abyss, The (London), 135–6, 139–40, 160, 230–2, 277–8
Peters, Richard, 264–6
"Petition Crown, The" (Blair), 241
Picture of Dorian Gray, The (Wilde), 125–6
Pitt, William, the Younger, 6

Pitter, Ruth, 17, 89, 102, 220–1, 273–4; advice to Blair, 221, 223–8, 241
Pleydell family, 9
Plowman, Max, 260, 261, 269, 281, 282
Plymouth, 137, 138
Poe, Edgar Allan, 208
"Politics vs. Literature" (Orwell), 19
postwar period (after First World War), 101–4, 122–4
Pound, Ezra, 208
poverty, Blair's experiences of, see under Blair, Eric
Poverty, A Study of Town Life (Rowntree), 139
"Poverty—Plain and Coloured" (Blair), 285
Powell, Anthony, 125, 307 n.
Priestley, J. B., *Angel Pavement*, 261
Prince and the Pauper, The (Twain), 135
Progrès Civique, 243–5, 247, 249
Proust, Marcel, 208
Public Schools, 25–6, 51
Punjab, 155
Pyapon, 182

Raleigh, Sir Walter, 63
Rangoon, 156, 160–1, 163, 183, 186–91
Rathcreedan, Lord, 68
Rebecca of Sunnybrook Farm (Wiggin), 18
Rees, Sir Richard, xiv, 15, 83 n., 87–8, 90, 195, 206, 218 n., 229, 269, 273, 280, 281, 294,

Rees, Sir Richard (*continued*) 298; Blair's friendship with, 283–4; helps Blair, 294–7
Road to Wigan Pier, The (Orwell), 4, 157 n., 168–9 n., 195, 226 and n., 235–6, 274–5, 285–6
Roberti, Jacques, *À La Belle de Nuit*, 295–6
Robinson, Capt. H. F., 189, 190
Rock Pool, The (Connolly), 224; review by Orwell, 122–3 n.
Rosenkavalier, Der, 135
Rowntree, B. Seebohm, *Poverty, A Study of Town Life*, 139
Runciman, Leslie, 97–8
Runciman, Sir Steven, 94, 97–9, 114, 121, 138, 142–3, 150, 152
Rylands, George, 133

St. Christopher's school, 46
St. Cyprian's school, 84, 87–90, 92, 99, 139, 141, 153, 157, 161, 300; Blair at, xviii, 4, 23–79, 142, 169, 179, 204, 245, 250, 254, 293
St. Felix School, 279
Saki (H. H. Munro), 18
Salemson, H. J., 242
Salkeld, Brenda, 229, 234, 279–81, 286, 300
Sassoon, Siegfried, 60, 127
schools: private (boarding), 26, 33–4, 36; public, 25–6, 51
Scotland, Orwell dislikes, 64 n.
Scott, J. G., *Burma: A Handbook of Practical Information*, 172–3
"Sea God, The" (Blair), 241

Seaton Junction, 137
Shakespeare ,William, 133
Shaw, George Bernard, 58, 120, 121; *Androcles and the Lion*, 99, 105, 106 and *n*.; *Major Barbara*, 136
Shiplake, 48–9, 68, 77, 147
"Shooting an Elephant" (Orwell), 112, 170, 195, 199–203
Shropshire Lad, A (Housman), 121–2
Sinister Street (Mackenzie), 65–6
Sitwell, Edith, 125, 208; *Alexander Pope*, 261
Sitwell, Osbert, 125, 208
Sitwell, Sacheverell, 125, 208
"Slack-bob, The" (Blair), 109–11
Smart & Mookerdum's bookshop, Rangoon, 187, 208
Smillie, Robert, 139
snobbishness, 28–9, 101
social classes, xix, 3–5, 25, 29–30, 138–9, 157 and *n*.
Southwold, 23 *n*., 24, 137 *n*., 143, 147–9, 153, 155, 161, 215–18, 250, 258–61, 263, 264, 268, 269, 272, 273, 279, 281, 286, 289, 300, 305
Spanish Civil War, xiii, xiv, xix, xx, 169 and *n*., 174, 278
"Spike, The" (Blair), 230, 233, 234 and *n*., 247–8, 272–3, 283, 285, 287, 295, 303
Spirit of Catholicism, The (Adam), 304
Stephen, J. K., 103
Stevenson, Robert Louis, 230; "The Young Man with Cream Tarts," 133–4
Strachey, Lytton, 126

Study of George Orwell, A, see Hollis, Christopher
"Such, Such Were the Joys" (Orwell), xviii, 35 and *n*., 36–7, 38 *n*., 39, 41, 44, 45 *n*., 49, 53 *n*., 57, 88, 219
Sunnylands school, 18
Sutton Courtenay, xx
Swift, Jonathan, 58, 157 *n*., 279; *Gulliver's Travels*, 19, 33
Swinburne, Algernon Charles, 125
Syriam, 183–4, 186–8, 192

Talbot, Rev. Neville, 105
Tehta, 11, 12
Thackeray, William Makepeace, 58, 208; *Vanity Fair*, 65
Thames, 116
Thibaw (Burmese king), 163
Times, The, 86
Tolstoy, Leo, 208
Tom Sawyer (Twain), 18
Toungoo, 175
Trollope, Anthony, 40–1
Truman & Knightly Associates, 299
Twain, Mark, 19, 208; *Huckleberry Finn*, 267; *The Prince and the Pauper*, 135; *Tom Sawyer*, 18
Twante, 180–3
Twelfth Night (Shakespeare), 133, 135
Twentieth Century Authors, 205
Two Carlyles, The (Burdett), 285

Ulysses (Joyce), 208
unemployment, 244–5

United Provinces (India), 155
University College Hospital, London, xx, 219
Unquiet Grave, The (Connolly), 112
Uxbridge, 300

Vache Enragée, La (Down and Out, French edition), 234–5
Vanity Fair (Thackeray), 65
Vaughan Wilkes, Mr., 27–31, 51–4, 56, 63, 77, 78, 87, 157 *n.*
Vaughan Wilkes, Mrs. (Mum, Flip), 27, 28 and *n.*, 29–31, 38 and *n.*, 44, 47, 50, 51, 56, 57, 62–4, 70–4, 77, 169, 283; Blair's relationship with, 37–41, 46, 53 and *n.*, 54, 59, 62–7, 78–9
Verdi, Giuseppe, 135
Vines, Sherard, *The Course of English Classicism,* 261

Walberswick, 234, 265, 266
Wansbrough, George, 85, 96, 120
Waste Land, The (Eliot), 300
Waugh, Evelyn, 300
Way of All Flesh, The (Butler), 99
Wellington College, 30, 70, 71, 77–8, 84–5, 94, 153
Wells, H. G., 120, 121, 265; *The Country of the Blind,* 58
Wesley, John, 7
Westdean, 58
Westminster, Loelia, Duchess of, 255–6

Westmorland, Earls of, 5–6
Wheels, 125
Whittome, Maurice, 115, 131, 222–3
"Why I Write" (Orwell), 9, 111–12, 205, 223
Wigan, xix
Wilde, Oscar, 135, 230; *The Picture of Dorian Gray,* 125–6
Wilkes, *see* Vaughan Wilkes
Winchester school, 25
Winterbourne Whitechurch, 7
Winter's Tale, The (Shakespeare), 133
Wodehouse, P. G., 19, 33, 58
Woodruff, Christopher, 191
Woolf, Leonard, 156
Woolf, Virginia, 121, 140, 208
Workers' Dreadnought, The, 130
World of George Orwell, The (symposium), 69 *n.*
World War, First, xix, 30, 59–60, 71–3, 76–7, 83–4, 86–8, 149 *n.*; Blair predicts England will emerge as second-rate nation, 76, 99; end of, 100–2; guilt of survivors, 72, 87–8; postwar period, 101–4, 122–4
World War, Second, xix, 28 *n.*, 31, 58, 94
"Wounded Cricketer, The" (Blair), 109, 116
Wuhan University, 156

Yorke, Henry (Henry Green), 125
"Young Man with Cream Tarts, The" (Stevenson), 133–4
Young Men's Buddhist Association, 171

BOOK TWO

ORWELL: THE TRANSFORMATION

For Ruth
and in memory of Mark

CONTENTS

	Acknowledgments ix
PART ONE:	Beginning as Orwell 1
PART TWO:	Eileen 69
PART THREE:	The End of Eric Blair 147
PART FOUR:	An Education in Spain 233

Notes 289

Index 293

ILLUSTRATIONS

FOLLOWING
PAGE 114

George Orwell
   (*courtesy of Mabel Fierz*)
Frays College
   (*courtesy of H. S. K. Stapley*)
Eric Blair, Mabel Fierz, and the daughter of a neighbor
   (*courtesy of Adrian Fierz*)
Blair in the Fierzes' garden
   (*courtesy of Adrian Fierz*)
Blair and Eileen at the Aragon front
   (*courtesy of Harry Milton*)
Eileen
   (*courtesy of Jane Morgan*)
Sally
Kay

ACKNOWLEDGMENTS

THIS STUDY HAS BEEN BASED ON ORWELL'S PUBLICATIONS, manuscript collections, and interviews with those who knew him. We are intensely grateful to those who were kind enough to see us, most of whom are mentioned in the text. Without them, this book could not have been written.

We are extremely grateful for the use of Orwell material in the Berg Collection, the New York Public Library; the Humanities Research Center, the University of Texas; the Library, the University of California at Los Angeles; the British Library; as well as material in private hands.

William Allan of the Stanford University Library gave great help in acquiring needed material. And we would like to express our thanks to the Rockefeller Foundation for providing time at the Villa Serbelloni where we were looked after so well by Bill and Betsy Olson, and to Pasquale Vuilleumier of the Hotel Palumbo, Ravello. In Bellagio and Ravello, most of this study was written.

Following *Journey to the Frontier*, whose subject was John Cornford and Julian Bell, the publication of this book about George Orwell, along with its predecessor, *The Unknown Orwell*, completes our original purpose: a study of three British writers of the 1930's, and the reasons for their involvement in the Spanish Civil War.

P.S.
W.A.

PART ONE

Beginning as Orwell

ONE

On MONDAY, JANUARY 9, 1933, THE OFFICIAL PUBlication day of *Down and Out in Paris and London,* he entered literary history as George Orwell. Not that he, or any one else at the time, would have thought of the event in such grandiose terms, though as it now appears they do precisely sum up the case. Ordinarily, one would be the same person on the ninth of January that one had been on the eighth. What gave his situation its little peculiarity, set it apart from that of the general run of authors bringing out a first book, was that on the eighth he was Eric Blair, and on the ninth he was George Orwell—or so it stated on the title page of his book. And if, as we will see, the reviewers were much taken, relatively speaking, with this hitherto unknown writer George Orwell for the first week or two of his new existence (thereafter forgetting him until his next book would appear), his family and friends—those among them who had been told of the pseudonym—were not. To them, as to himself, he was still and only Eric Blair. So that on January 9, 1933, a day we now recognize as having some consequence in literary history, the difference between being Blair and being Orwell was as slight, as imperceptible, as the difference between Sunday the eighth and Monday the ninth of January: another day torn from the calendar.

After all, two months earlier the name itself hadn't existed. Blair had cautioned his agent, Leonard Moore, in April 1932 that if the book were accepted (which it was, by Victor Gollancz, in July), he would want it published pseudonymously, as he was "not proud of it." But in spite of repeated requests from agent and publisher, he did nothing to resolve the question of the pseudonym until November, the last possible moment, when the book was already in galleys with a title improvised by Gollancz, *Confessions of a Down and Outer,* and its authorship attributed simply to "X."

Even then there was a curious degree of equivocation. On the nineteenth of November he finally sent off to Gollancz (via Moore) not one but four possible pseudonyms, among them "George Orwell," which he admitted he "rather favoured." But the choice was left to Gollancz. Never once did Blair say "I *want* George Orwell," and there is reason to believe that if Gollancz had insisted on Eric Blair as the name for his author, Eric Blair it would have been: he would have resigned himself to it. Ever since his career as a schoolboy cynic, which had been launched at St. Cyprian's, his prep school, and had flourished when he was in College at Eton, he had come to accept as a matter of course—in *his* life anyway—life's ironies and disappointments: it would have been no more than the expected thing that the pseudonym he favored would not be the one to be chosen. In the event, however, his preference was followed: Gollancz made him Orwell.

Yet there is a further possible irony: that Blair may actually have preferred his own name to his chosen (or conferred) pseudonym. It seems worth pointing out in this connection that even after the publication of *Down and Out,* and in 1934 of his first and second novels, *Burmese*

Days and *A Clergyman's Daughter*, all three as by George Orwell, he was still making professional use of his own name. During 1934 he appeared several times in the *Adelphi*, as a poet and as a reviewer, and his contributions were always signed Eric Blair or E.A.B., never George Orwell. The question of the pseudonym and its possible significance must continue to run its way like a thread in a carpet through any biographical study of Orwell in the 1930's. Some years ago, Samuel Hynes in the *Times Literary Supplement* brought up the question of pseudonyms, their uses, and as it were their unintended revelations and self-disclosures. "When a writer chooses another name for his writing self, he is doing more than inventing a pseudonym: he is naming, and in a sense creating, his imaginative identity." Hynes's subject, Rebecca West, had been born Cicily Fairfield—"a name that in itself seems almost too good an example of English gentility"—and she chose for her pseudonym, with marvelous aptness as it turned out, the name of the rebellious young heroine of Ibsen's *Rosmersholm*. Then, as though to reinforce the point, Hynes brought up the case of Orwell, and what is in fact a story of considerable complexity was drastically simplified: "Hence, George Orwell—a commonplace Christian name and an English river—together name the plain-speaking Englishman that Eric Blair *chose to be* in his work." It is all phrased in so straightforward, plain-speaking a way, with such an absence of bothersome qualification, that one can only wish it were true: one of the more exemplary cases of name-changing and self-transformation in literary history. And indeed, if one follows the thread as we intend to do in the present volume, it seems inarguable that by 1938—after his return from Spain and the writing of *Homage to Catalonia*—the consonance between George

Orwell in his work and his life, the "creation of his imaginative identity," had been virtually completed. But it had not been achieved without struggle, nor was it a matter simply of a change of name. That in itself was a first step—by which "the essential second self was set free"—and what followed was a slow, arduous process of transformation.

TWO

THE PUBLICATION IN HIS THIRTIETH YEAR OF *Down and Out in Paris and London* marked not only the beginning of the literary career of George Orwell, but also the end of the literary apprenticeship of Eric Blair. When Blair, in the summer of 1927, returned to England from Burma and resigned his commission in the Indian Imperial Police, he was not prompted by some vague literary-romantic yearning. He knew, in the most ruthless and determined way, that he wanted to be a writer; in retrospect it seemed to him he had always wanted to be a writer, since his earliest childhood. He also knew that he had a lot to learn, and that he was starting out comparatively late, an unknown novice at an age when Cyril Connolly, his friend and contemporary at St. Cyprian's and at Eton, was already a conspicuous figure in the London literary scene. If he was a little envious and too proud to revive the friendship with Connolly during these years of obscurity, envy and pride helped to strengthen his determination. Wherever he happened to be living—in bed-sitters around London, in a shabby hotel in Paris, but most often in a room that was his by sufferance in his parents' house in Southwold—he wrote. Between 1927 and 1932 he would not take a regular job—he lived to write, a state made possible only by the generosity of his mother and his aunt Nellie Adam, who kept him in funds. It was an arduous apprenticeship, and his success in those five years was minimal. Still, it seems worth emphasizing—along with Blair's sense of literary vocation, which was fierce (however diffident he might seem) and unwavering—that he did enjoy some small degree of recognition. His was not an utterly hopeless cause, though at times it may have felt so to him and seemed so to his parents.

As Eric Blair he published a number of journalistic and literary pieces in the Paris weeklies during the year and some months he was living there. When he returned to England in 1931, he began to publish reviews, verse, and essays in the *Adelphi,* the *New Statesman and Nation,* and the *New English Weekly,* always in his own name. As Eric Blair he wrote and submitted to publishers two versions of the book we know as *Down and Out in Paris and London.* (Both were rejected by the firm of Jonathan Cape; the second and final version was also rejected by Faber & Faber upon the advice of their reader, T. S. Eliot.*)

For almost seven years he had been steadily writing and infrequently publishing as Eric Blair. It was only in April 1932, when Leonard Moore was ready to send off the manuscript of *Days in Paris and London* (the first title), that Blair raised the question of taking a new name as an author. His mention of a pseudonym in a letter to Moore (April 26) and in several further letters to him over the

---

* It was Eliot again, some years later, who advised Fabers against publishing *Animal Farm.* Orwell, not unmindful of these snubs, eventually got his own back with some adverse, not wholly unjustified or philistine, strictures on Eliot's poetry. Official relations between the two, however, were always cordial, and Eliot, at Orwell's request, would broadcast for the BBC Indian Service during the Second World War.

next seven months, culminating in the letter of November 19 when he finally and belatedly submitted a choice of four names for Gollancz—these constitute the only written contemporary evidence we know of a subject that has come to assume legendary, even mystical proportions in later commentaries. (The significance read into that plain Christian name, George—so working-class, to those who wish to think of it thus; so classless, to others; so rural or so royal— after all, six sovereigns have borne it; so *English*, from whatever stance. And then, that river, the Orwell—flowing through Suffolk out to the sea at Harwich—so plumbed by literary historians and critics for its symbolic yield.)

That summer of 1932, in Southwold, Blair told his sister Avril that he would be publishing his book under the pseudonym because he was afraid it would shock their parents. Avril replied with the directness characteristic of her that she felt he was overly concerned: their parents were more sophisticated than he seemed willing to admit, although their father, getting on in years, *was* something of the Victorian in his views on proper language. But of course, she concluded, with the diffidence that was very much a Blair characteristic, if Eric wanted to use a pen name for the book, that was his affair. His argument might have been more persuasive if he had not already published "The Spike" under his own name in the *Adelphi* (and would make it into two chapters of *Down and Out*); and "Hop Picking" and "Common Lodging Houses" in the *New Statesman and Nation* (also under his own name); and the three pieces together (which the elder Blairs seem to have taken in stride) gave a fair enough notion of what to expect in the book.

The one logical argument that he might have made, but which he did not make then or later, was that *Down and*

Out, presented as an autobiographic account of an author about whom nothing was known would carry much more weight, given its proletarian subject matter, than as the work of Eric Blair, an Old Etonian.

In any event, before the end of November, Victor Gollancz had decided that Eric Blair was to be George Orwell, and his book *Down and Out in Paris and London*. Then, with a celerity that must seem astonishing in the light of the difficulties that beset present-day publishing, the book was brought into being in a matter of weeks. Two days before Christmas, Blair, who was spending the holiday with his parents in Southwold, received a parcel from Leonard Moore: advance copies of the book, each bearing on the jacket the helpful, commercial phrase "A recommendation of the Book Society." So there it was at last, visible proof of his identity as an author, the book itself: to be weighed, examined, considered, approved, the size of it marveled at.

The advance copies could hardly have arrived at a more opportune moment: Christmas gifts for certain close friends of his in Southwold—Brenda Salkeld, who taught at St. Felix School on the edge of town, and Eleanor Jaques, who had been a pupil of Brenda's, and Dennis Collings, Eric's closest friend there, who was presently to marry Eleanor, although their engagement was not yet "official"— all of whom had been allowed to know that he was gathering material for a book about the lower depths. And copies too to the family, which meant there were none left over to send to such close friends in London as the Fierzes or Richard Rees.

Mabel Fierz had, of course, read the book in typescript, and it was she who brought it to Leonard Moore at a time when Eric himself had given up on it completely. She would now behave with the generosity that was typical of her: when the book was officially published three weeks later, she went to a bookshop and actually bought a copy—not all authors are so fortunate in their friends. Mabel's generosity went still further. At about this time she and her husband, Francis, went off for a weekend in Ostend. Knowing Eric's fondness for French books, she asked if there was anything she might buy for him there. "Yes," he said, "Joyce's *Ulysses*," for although he had already read a friend's copy, smuggled in from Paris—the novel still couldn't be published in England—he wanted one of his own. Mrs. Fierz, once again, was able to serve.

Avril and the elder Blairs seem to have read *Down and Out* with a good deal less shock or outrage than Eric had anticipated. Indeed, there is some question as to whether or not Mr. Blair ever did actually read it, though none at all that he heard about it at tiresome length from his Anglo-Indian cronies; the secret of the pseudonym was soon out in Southwold. Father and son continued to be estranged, as they had been ever since Eric had thrown up his commission to become a "writer." Now they were on a pretense of civil terms—after all, the son had been living, and intermittently would continue to live, under the father's roof—but their reconciliation, such as it was, was for the future. Mrs. Blair, like any mother, was distressed at the life Eric described himself as having lived in Paris—about which he had told her nothing—and so different from the accounts she had received from her sister Nellie: those reassuring, bourgeois evenings *chez* Adam, when Nellie and her husband, the professor of Esperanto, would entertain Eric at dinner. But, as any mother would, she rose above the mere subject matter of her son's book. After so many years of hearing him at the typewriter, the very existence of the book pleased her: did it not prove that Eric wasn't pursuing a will-o'-the-wisp? that he might do what he set out to do? Still, if the family were pleased with the book, for whatever reasons, they were not fervent in their enthusiasm: it would not have been their style to be so, any more than it was Eric's (or George's) style. Fervent enthusiasm he had already had from Mabel; if there was to be more of that, it would have to come from the reviewers.

THREE

At this time Eric was on holiday from his job as a schoolmaster at Evelyn's, a drab little private school in Hayes, outside London, where he had been teaching since the previous April. He disliked the job intensely—the first he had held since coming back from Burma—and looked forward to the day when he might be able to support himself as a full-time writer: would it happen with *Down and Out?* Meanwhile he took advantage of his holiday in Southwold to work away at his next book, a novel to be called *Burmese Days*, and he wrote to Moore that he "hoped to polish up a chunk" to show him when he was back in London. This was very much Orwell the professional writer, just as he had intended to be from the beginning, though he signed the letter Eric A. Blair: first book about to come out, and second already on the stocks.

It was all very well, even admirable, to write with such confidence of one's future plans. But the period between the arrival of advance copies and the official publication day of a book, especially for the author of a first book, is often a kind of limbo, wherein he alternates between euphoria and anxiety. For Blair it was a matter of eighteen days, which he filled with hours at the typewriter, long gossips with his mother, and much visiting to and fro between the Blairs' house, the Jaqueses' and the Collingses'. "It was a happy time," Dennis Collings would recall, long afterwards, "much freer, no standing on ceremony, everybody knew everybody else. Southwold was a nice place to be—I know that Eric enjoyed himself there."

A conviction of Orwell's—which at certain moments in his life was to rise to the level of paranoia—was that there was a literary racket in full-scale operation which determined the future of a book and its author. To be out of favor (a posture in which he had perennially liked to see himself ever since his time at St. Cyprian's) doomed one to failure. The members of the racket, *mafiosi* to a man, so to speak, were those "gilded young beasts," usually down from Cambridge, against whom he would rail in *Keep the Aspidistra Flying;* the literary editors of the weeklies (he was eventually to become one himself for some years at *Tribune*); Old Etonians; clubmen—a whole network of the charming, effete, unprincipled, and successful, who opened and closed the essential doors, making a Hell in Heaven's despite, or vice versa.

That this version of "the literary racket" had more to do with fantasy than with reality was to be proved by the widespread, highly favorable reception of *Down and Out,* though Orwell himself never drew the appropriate inference from it. In fact, he was eventually to have his experience with the racket, but it was the political not the literary racket—and even in the most celebrated instance, the rejection of *Animal Farm* by so many publishers in wartime England for what seemed to be valid political reasons, when it was finally brought out by the not unknown and perfectly respectable firm of Secker & Warburg, it proved to be a literary as well as a financial success: Orwell's most popular book.

We have no wish to explore here the racket as it actually is (very different, let it be said, from Orwell's fantasy of it), but one strategic point can't be overlooked: that a book from a publisher of established reputation, such as Gollancz, is more likely to be reviewed, though even that should not be considered an inflexible rule, than a book from a publisher who is unknown. The review itself may be highly unfavorable, but the book will at least have been noticed, and sent on its way to oblivion with a few cruel or patronizing epithets. To that degree, consciously or not, there is a literary racket: the book that is unnoticed might for all practical purposes never have been written. That was not to be Orwell's fate, at any point in his career, from his first book to his last.

Punctually on the first day of publication, and continuing generously thereafter, came the reviews of *Down and Out in Paris and London.* Gollancz had done its work efficiently, as one would expect, even to securing that recommendation from the Book Society. Of course, in England at the beginning of 1933, still deep in the Depression, a first-hand account of poverty and life among the unemployed would be almost certain to attract attention; and the fact that the author was unknown, might not even be a "writer" at all, would add to the "authenticity" of his book. Victor Gollancz himself, at the beginning of his relationship with Blair, seems not to have understood that he was dealing with a professional author. Hence his proposal that the book be signed "X." This Blair indignantly rejected—"X" would be of no use to him for all those books he intended to write in the future.

On the whole, the reviews were favorable and discriminating. Orwell was not one of those luckless writers who have to wait years for recognition and appreciation. Once published, after the ordeal of his two rejections, he was understood from the first, and the only serious particular in which past and present judgments differ is that no one in 1933 thought to describe his prose as Orwellian.

First came the daily papers, and the first of these was the *Manchester Guardian* on January 9. Its reviewer, M.H. (the initials of a woman named Muriel Harris), is deserving of a place in literary history, not only because she wrote the first review of George Orwell, but because she was also the first to recognize certain qualities that were to distinguish him as an author all through his career:

> Mr. George Orwell tells of things which to most people are horrible in a quiet, level tone which enables him also to use a vocabulary suited to his subject. No one . . . can fail to be deeply moved by the truth which is evident in every sentence. He has, in short, so much to say in that quiet, level voice of his that he has written a book which might work a revolution in the minds of those who are totally unable to look on down-and-outs as other than something entirely unlike themselves.

The next day came the *Morning Post*. The editor of the book page, E. B. Osborne, did the review himself, and it was something of a letdown. For the most part, his judgment was favorable, but Osborne (as Brenda Salkeld, Ruth Pitter, Jack Common, and others of Blair's friends had done at the time, and as many of Orwell's critics have done since) seized upon the problem that would dog him through all his down-and-out experiences: that he had put himself into a somewhat "false" or "inauthentic" predicament—he was not trapped in his situation as his fellow tramps were. "Because there was always a way out for him," Osborne wrote, "Mr. Orwell never felt the extreme misery of helpless, hopeless poverty." This was a severe if accurate observation; and the laudatory, even flowery sentence that followed it, however quotable from a publisher's point of view, must have been small consolation to a vulnerable young man not given to deceiving himself: "But his picturesque book touches several problems of the modern underworld with a finger of light."

Two days later, the big guns of middlebrow reviewing were heard from: J. B. Priestley in the *Evening Standard,* and Compton Mackenzie in the *Daily Mail.* It was perhaps just as well for Orwell that Priestley did not know him in his true identity, for Blair, as Blair, had earlier described him in the *Adelphi* as "blatantly second rate" and shrugged off his generally admired, best-selling *Angel Pavement* in standard reviewerese: ". . . excellent holiday novel . . . gay . . . pleasant . . . a good bulk of reading. . . ." For Priestley, *Down and Out* was "uncommonly good reading, and a social document of some value. It is, indeed, the best book of its kind that I have read in a long time." But Priestley was virtually mute in contrast to Compton Mackenzie, who let loose with a volley of praise. True, *Down and Out* came third in his column, after *A Passionate Prodigality* by Guy Chapman and *Pocahontas* by David Garnett. But when he finally arrived at Orwell's "immensely interesting book," Mackenzie summed it up as "a genuine human document, which at the same time is written with so much artistic force that, in spite of the squalor and degradation thus unfolded, the result is curiously beautiful with the beauty of an accomplished etching on copper. The account of a casual ward in this country horrifies like some scene of inexplicable misery in Dante."

It is not our intention here to supply either a history or

critique of book-reviewing in England, but it seems worthwhile—if only to correct the myth of a neglected Orwell and to suggest the amount of attention paid to him at the very start of his career—to note that yet another well-known writer of the period, H. E. Bates, reviewed *Down and Out* in the *New Clarion* and found it "fascinating but terrible reading." Even the *Tatler,* of all places, allowed room for a highly favorable review. That curious publication, then as now dedicated to recording the doings of society week after week, included an intelligent column on books by Richard King. (Some years later, the column would be taken over by Elizabeth Bowen.) King, rather adroitly, attuned his review to the magazine's preoccupations, quite as though Orwell were reporting on another "set" in society, albeit an unimportant one: "This terribly interesting but uncomfortable book will open up a new world—a world that has its customs, its prejudices, even its social sets, equally pronounced as in the world which passing it by and regarding its inhabitants is filled either with contempt, horror, or self-superiority, and occasionally pity."

Three other reviews deserve mention: those in the *New Statesman and Nation,* the *Adelphi,* and the *Times Literary Supplement.* Ordinarily, the review in the *New Statesman* of March 18 might be passed over in silence, for it has slight literary or political interest. But as a part of Orwell's checkered history with that publication, climaxing in an unhappy altercation during the Spanish Civil War, it has its place. The literary editor of the *Statesmen* at the time, David Garnett (author among many other works of *Pocahontas*) had had what he must have thought an inspired idea: to assign *Down and Out* for review to W. H. Davies, the poet and professional tramp. But Davies seemed to have a disdain for deadlines, and it was not until the middle of March that his review appeared. When it did, it proved to be just the sort of review that an author (quite understandably) dislikes most: a kindly sentence or two wherein, if he is lucky, the title of the book and his name are given (not always accurately), and the greater part of the precious space used for a potted essay in which the reviewer serves up notions of his own, or, more commonly still, serves up the author's notions as though they were *his*, with a knowing allusion to further work in the field already being done. (Further work, let it be said, is always being done: that is a basic law of literary life.) In the case of *Down and Out*, it was perfectly clear that its chief interest for Davies was the light it shed for him on his own experiences as a super-tramp.

With C. Day Lewis in the *Adelphi*, the situation was very different, in respect to both the review and the reviewer. W. H. Davies was in his sixty-third year, his reputation as a poet was in decline; most of his memorable lyrics had been written years before, as a pre-Georgian. In a representative anthology of modern British poetry, one finds him preceded by Charlotte Mew and Hilaire Belloc, and followed by J. M. Synge and Ralph Hodgson. Day Lewis, a year younger than Orwell, was already famous as a poet, and growing each day more famous as a member of the triumvirate of the young literary Left, whose other members were W. H. Auden and Stephen Spender. For many years Orwell would resent the triumvirate, and the writers associated with them, stigmatizing them as "the pansy Left" and singling out Auden as "a gutless Kipling." Eventually, certainly by the time of *Animal Farm*, fame had done its equalizing work, and Orwell, having met and grown to like some of them, Spender in particular, revised his contemptuous judgments. But it has to be said that the "quiet, level tone" we so value could at times rise virtually to a shriek and it is not a pleasant sound to hear.

Day Lewis was not only a poet, he was also a Marxist,

and, as was not uncommon among poets who were Marxists in 1933, he was also briefly a member of the Communist party—which is to say that he was politically committed in a way that would have been incomprehensible to Orwell *at that time*. One has no wish to patronize the author of *Down and Out* by saying that politics were above him, beneath him, or beyond him; it is closer to the truth to say that in January 1933 his political consciousness, insofar as it existed at all, was in a dormant state; and one of the themes of the present work is to trace the movements of its awakening. What this meant in practical terms is that while Day Lewis read *Down and Out* appreciatively, the thoughts it called to his mind had little to do with Dante or "the beauty of an accomplished etching on copper." He was taken with "the facts" that Orwell revealed; they "should shake the complacence of twentieth century civilisation if anything could; they are 'sensational' yet presented without sensationalism. He [the narrator] has no illusions about the extremely poor; he finds the effects of hunger and poverty upon himself and the rest compelling shame, lying, self-pity, bestial fatalism." But for Day Lewis, these facts, so unsensationally and convincingly presented, are not the stopping but the starting point. As a writer who is conscious of politics he goes on to ask, as Orwell himself never does, what the facts mean, and what inferences we are to draw from them. A curious and, considering its subject, an unexpected aspect of *Down and Out* is brought into focus: what a nondidactic and apolitical book it is. (Paradoxically, that may help to explain its continuing vitality and interest: tracts for the times seldom survive the times they were tracted for.) In part, of course, it is the effect and indeed the effectiveness of Orwell's quality (or trick, or technique) of understatement, but there does not even appear to be any crusading zest under the surface of the text; there is little feeling that the world that has excruciated these down-and-outers as its victims must somehow be remade. Life among the victims is terrible—a fact to be passively accepted and impassively recorded. The book is oddly static in its concept of the life it describes, as if nothing in it will ever significantly change, despite the patronizing and inadequate character of private charity, the boredom and ugliness of public assistance, all those devices that society invents to cover up its wounds, rather than to cure them.

Like Orwell, and unlike Day Lewis, the anonymous reviewer in the *Times Literary Supplement* refused to impose any social point on the narrative. "One lays down his book wondering why men living in such conditions do not commit suicide, but Mr. Orwell conveys the impression that they are too depressed and hopeless for such a final and definitive effort as self-inflicted death."

One would rather have liked a comment from Orwell himself on this chilling conclusion, but his attention was diverted by a letter to the *Times*, responding to the review, from one Humbert Possenti. Writing from the Hotel Splendide, London, Monsieur Possenti was moved to claim, "as a *restaurateur* and *hôtelier* of 40 years' experience," that the state of French hotel kitchens as described by Orwell and accepted by the reviewer in the *TLS* was "inconceivable," and added that in all good hotels customers can see over the kitchens at any time they wish.

Orwell, offended by the tone of the letter, decided to reply to it, and in doing so, made use of a well-known trick of schoolboy debaters. He was not referring to "Paris hotels in general," but to one in particular. Since Monsieur Possenti had no way of knowing which hotel the author had in mind, he had no way of verifying or contradicting his description of it. "So," Orwell concluded, ". . . in spite of his 40 years' experience, my evidence in this case is worth more than his."

Judged strictly in debating terms, there is no question that Orwell was the winner, but the habit of making generalizations, often outrageous and unprovable, was endemic with him throughout his lifetime, and they turn up even in *Down and Out*. It is difficult to imagine a reader, fresh from the pages of the book with its horrendous accounts of squalor in the scullery, who would not hesitate at least an hour or two before crossing the threshold of even a three-star establishment in Paris.

Meanwhile, like many such correspondences in the *Times*, this one led to a subsidiary point, with the book that had inspired it rather lost from sight. On February 17, Sir St. Clair Thomson wrote to suggest that there should be notices posted in restaurants inviting inspection by guests. A week later, Possenti, now transformed from Humbert to Umberto, announced that such a notice would indeed be posted at the Splendide. Orwell himself did not feel called upon to comment, and the correspondence languished.

FOUR

Blair had signed his letter to the *Times* "george Orwell," and those quotation marks around the name tell a story of their own. He was not yet at ease with the pseudonym. On the title page of his book, and in the reviews, he was George Orwell, but in the ordinary world where he lived he was still Eric Blair. The modest little fame that might have trailed in his wake as the author of a very well-received first book was denied to him, since he had made up his mind to deny his true identity. There were none of those congratulatory letters from absent or neglected or neglectful friends he might otherwise have counted on. In fact, it would be another two years before even such an Old Etonian friend as Cyril Connolly would learn that George Orwell was none other than Eric Blair. And by 1937, when new friends began to enter his life who had never heard of Eric Blair, the pseudonym no longer applied: to them he was George Orwell without quotation marks.

On January 17, the day before he was to return to his hated job at Evelyn's, he wrote to Leonard Moore. Diffident about his identity Blair might be, and diffident in his nature he certainly was, but he was also an author, and like any author he was anxious to know if the favorable reviews of the book were affecting its sales. More than that, he thought of himself as an author whose intention was to live by what he wrote: the sooner the royalties accumulated sufficiently for him to give up his job as a teacher, the better. But before raising the fateful question, he remarked that the notices were better than he'd expected, and that he was pleased no libel actions had been threatened. (This latter risk would be an obsessive concern of his, and with good reason, throughout his career.) Then, approaching the point that specially interested him, he noted that the *Sunday Express* had listed the book among the best sellers of the week, but he realized (and here the question was implicit) that it would be some time (would it not?) before Moore had the sales figures. To which the immediate answer was Yes.

But looking into the future, which was Blair's implicit concern at that moment, one can say that between a critical success, as *Down and Out* had undoubtedly been, and a popular success there is an enormous gap. Gollancz had ordered a first impression of 1500 copies, a second of 500 copies at the end of January, and later in the year an impression of 1000 copies. In the eyes of a novelist such as Hugh Walpole, to evoke one of Orwell's *bêtes noires* of the 1930's, a sale of 3000 copies might count for nothing, but it represented in less exalted company a promising launching of a literary career, and Gollancz, Moore, and Blair (perhaps in that order) had every reason to be pleased, the more so as the author was already at work on his second book, and was contemplating his third. What it did not mean was that he could give up his work as a schoolmaster.

The next day he went up to London from Southwold. He had spent his holiday profitably, for in his bag he was carrying the revised first hundred pages of his novel *Burmese Days*, which he meant to send on to Moore as soon as he had a chance to read them once more and judge their effect. In London there was a pleasant lunch with Mabel Fierz, which he insisted upon paying for on the strength of future royalties, and a pleasant pause with Mabel before a window of a shop in which his book was impressively displayed, and pleasant plans were made, as they were so often in those years, that he should count on spending the weekend with the Fierzes at their house in Golders Green. Then it was time to say goodbye, and off to the train at Paddington, and back to darkest Hayes.

His room in The Hawthorns, that genteel rooming house in Church Road, was just as he had left it in mid-December as Eric Blair, but returning to it as George Orwell, it must have seemed even damper, colder, and more dismal. His being Orwell was, of course, a secret not to be shared, certainly not with Mr. Evelyn, the headmaster and proprietor of the school, who had no notion that his staff now included the well-known young author of *Down and Out in Paris and London;* not even with the only friend Blair had made since coming to Hayes, an earnest young Church of England clergyman.

Fortunately for his novel in progress, schoolmastering demanded less of him now than it had in the autumn, when, in addition to his usual teaching he had taken on, or been given, the responsibility of writing, producing, and even making the costumes (suits of armor) for the end-of-term play. The costumes (cut from sheets of brown wrapping paper and glued together) were a particular nuisance from which, as he put it, he suffered "untold agonies." It was an experience he was presently to reproduce in exact, agonizing detail in his novel *A Clergyman's Daughter,* so from a literary point of view, it was not wholly wasted experience. Similarly, with his painting and gilding a cigarette box for the church bazaar, a task he had undertaken at the behest of his friend, the curate of St. Mary's, for whose sake also he felt he would ultimately have to take Holy Communion, something he hadn't done in years. Evidently in Hayes, Blair was a fairly regular churchgoer, more (it would seem) for social than religious reasons, and he feared that his curate friend would "think it funny if I always go to Church but never communicate." This, too, he would put to literary use, and it has to be said of Orwell that he was one of those writers who are remarkably thrifty with their experiences. Somehow, one way or another, they manage to get them into whatever they write; indeed, within a year, Blair would be in danger of cannibalizing his experience as it was taking place, or, to put it another way, having the experience for the sake of having something to write about.

But *Burmese Days*, which had been simmering in his mind for a long time, and upon which he resumed work immediately upon his return to Evelyn's, was meant to be a distillation of his five years in Burma. Beyond his routine schoolmastering, and the occasional church service for friendship's sake, there was nothing in Hayes to distract him from his purpose. The preceding September he had written to Brenda Salkeld that he'd spent a day reading through the rough draft of the novel and that it depressed him terribly. A month later the news to Eleanor Jaques was that he was making a little progress, but that he would have much to do when the rough draft was finished. In November he was writing to Moore to say that he preferred not to promise to have the book in final form by summer. In December, as we have seen, he planned to use the Christmas holiday in Southwold to "polish up a fair chunk."

A few days after returning to Hayes, he read over the hundred revised pages and was sufficiently pleased by them to send them to Moore. Then he tried patiently to wait for the verdict. Days passed, he heard nothing. Disconsolately he set out for Golders Green, where he was to spend the weekend with the Fierzes. Encouraged by Mabel—one got nowhere without *go*, of which Eric had deplorably little, she felt—he rang up Moore at his office. As it was a Saturday, Moore, not surprisingly, was not there. A partner in the considerable firm of Christy & Moore, he represented not only the newcomer George Orwell but a great many better-known clients whose manuscripts also had to be read—though not, usually, on weekends, which were consecrated to cricket—but no writer really ever understands this, and even if he does in theory, in practice he feels that his is the manuscript that should be read first.

The days of silence continued. On the thirty-first of January, with the publication of the indignant letter from Possenti, Blair had a legitimate pretext to write to Moore: he enclosed a copy of his letter of reply to the *Times*. The tone to his agent was diffident, as it usually was, even a little timid—in marked contrast to the assured manner of his letter to the *Times*—and as usual, the crucial questions, the real reasons for writing, were reserved for the last. (If one were attempting a psychoanalytic study, Moore would be an obvious candidate for a "father figure." Their correspondence, of which only a portion has been published, is of great interest in this and other respects.) What, came the belated, painful question, did Moore think of the first hundred pages? Characteristically, Blair was quick to admit they were "fearful from a literary point of view." But supposing various revisions were made, was this "the sort of thing people want to read about?" As though to provide Moore with the answer that he, Blair, was eager to hear (for he had no intention of being dissuaded from going on), he ventured to think that the fact of its being one of the very few novels about Burma might make up for its meager action and excessive description. (Later he would think of the description as the novel's sole redeeming feature.) Too proud to be assertive, Eric had written just the sort of letter that would make Mabel despair—obviously she hadn't been consulted on the writing of it: where was the *go?*—and even when he brought himself to admit that towards the end of the novel there would be a murder and a suicide, he felt constrained to add the dispiriting news that they would "play rather a subsidiary part."

To this bleak, wistful letter Moore replied in his own good time—the middle of the next month—with measured encouragement: he had read the hundred pages and liked them and looked forward to reading more. As to what people wanted, who could say? The vagaries of public taste are unpredictable; if they were not, all publishers would be rich, and the number of published authors drastically, sensibly curtailed. Clearly Moore had no intention of speculating in the future: his interest was in the present and there he had good news to report—he had made an arrangement with Harpers' for an American edition of *Down and Out*, a pleasant reminder to Blair, coughing and hacking in the damp gloom of The Hawthorns, that he was indeed the writer George Orwell.

His first reaction was simply pleasure; by mid-March, returning the signed contract, he was a little apprehensive because he could not remember if there was anything said in the book about Americans that they might find offensive and he should therefore cut out. (In fact, there is a contemptuous paragraph set at the unidentified luxury hotel —actually the Lotti—about the inability of Americans to know good food, but criticism of this sort coming from an

Englishman would only amuse Americans, and there are no textual differences between the two editions.) One has a sense at this time of some equivocation about the pseudonym: how stringently it was to be observed, how much to reveal, how much to conceal—he had heard of the way American publishers were supposed to misuse biographical details. It is not at all clear, though, what he had in mind, unless he feared that his being an Old Etonian and a former member of the Indian police (facts still unrevealed in England) might be exploited to his disadvantage. In any event, he had decided against sending a photograph: it would not be a good advertisement, he felt, perhaps too modestly.

It seems permissible at this point to jump forward in time a few months to conclude the brief, not especially happy history of the American publication of *Down and Out in Paris and London*. On June 30, 1933, the book was brought out by Harpers' in an edition of 1750 copies. Perhaps on Blair's assumption that nobody in America would know him anyway, and that since the book had been successful in England there was no need, after all, to be ashamed of it, perhaps feeling that the news of its true authorship ought to begin to be disseminated—whatever the reason, the copyright notice was in the name of Eric Blair, and the observant reader could make of that what he wished. (The English edition did not contain a copyright notice; such usage did not come into standard practice in Britain until after the Second World War.)

Reviews were slow in arriving—the first was in the *Herald Tribune Books* on July 30—and were relatively few and scattered thereafter. One of the last was by James T. Farrell in the *New Republic* five months after publication, who described it as "genuine, unexaggerated and intelligent."

Generally the reviews, such as they were, were favorable: the most enthusiastic being the first, by Fred T. Marsh; the most interesting by Herbert Gorman in the *New York Times Book Review*. Gorman, a well-thought-of novelist and critic, and an early biographer of James Joyce, was able to single out those qualities that explain as well as any why writers so dissimilar as Henry Miller and Mary McCarthy should have spoken of *Down and Out* as the book by Orwell they like best: "He possesses a keen eye for character and a rough-and-ready styleless style that plunges along and makes the reader see what the author wants him to see." Gorman regarded the author himself—that is, as he figures in the text—with a slightly jaundiced eye, and was perceptive about Orwell's tendency to arrange facts. In this first book the contrivance is apparent to any careful reader, and Gorman found the narrative not altogether unvarnished. It occurred to him that the author's imagination had "colored the facts a trifle," and although he does not specifically say so, one suspects that the "down there on a visit" element in Orwell's approach bothered him a little: "One reads on with a sort of horrid fascination happy in the suspicion (eventually verified) that this existence in the gutter is but the temporary condition of a man who rather enjoys being down and out." But it is the initial singling out of "the styleless style," which in fact is anything but artless, that distinguishes Gorman's review; and Orwell, along with Christopher Isherwood (and their common literary ancestor, Somerset Maugham), was to bring that antithesis of Mandarinism to its highest levels of achievement in the decade that followed.

Favorable though the American reviews had generally been, they were too few and sporadic to make any impact upon book-buying readers. By October, Moore was conveying the disappointing news to Blair that Harpers' hadn't been able to sell more than 1100 copies—not as lamentable a sale then as it would seem now, and Harpers' was sufficiently pleased and optimistic to take Orwell's next book when, in accordance with the option clause of the contract, it was offered to them, but it was a good deal less than was needed to liberate him from Evelyn's.

In February 1934, nine months after publication, the type was distributed, and 383 copies were remaindered. Upon which melancholy note, we return to the winter of 1933.

FIVE

"MELANCHOLY" MIGHT ALSO SERVE AS A WORD TO sum up the winter of 1933 itself: for Blair at Evelyn's, teaching; for Orwell in the evenings at The Hawthorns, writing his novel; and indeed (to make a ludicrous-seeming leap beyond the scale of our narrative thus far) for the Western world—it was on the thirtieth of January in that year that Adolf Hitler became Chancellor of Germany. But having made the leap, we draw back. We are not writing "history," using Orwell as an exemplary or typical figure (he was neither); nor do we intend to introduce snippets of history (clues and cues to great events in the world outside) in an effort to make a biographical study such as we are writing "historical," when all the evidence suggests that it could not be so. The truth is, in this winter of 1933, Blair had little interest in anything that did not directly concern himself— his teaching, the garden he had begun in a patch of ground behind The Hawthorns, letters to friends, a pubcrawl with Mabel Fierz through the East End one evening, in which, as she remembers, he was much less at ease in the public bars than he had led her to believe—and what would concern him most, through that melancholy winter and for several months beyond it, his novel *Burmese Days*.

Of all his books it was the one which he would think about longest—it can even be said that the period of gestation extended back to 1927—and the one on which he would work the hardest. In June, when he was two-thirds through the rough draft, he complained to Brenda Salkeld, to whom he had sent the manuscript, that he had to revise continually, and he added, "I wish I were one of those people who can . . . fling off a novel in about four days." Ironically, in the future he was to develop just that sort of facility, in and out of fiction, and some of his best, most characteristic pieces resulted from it, for journalism, which later came to occupy him increasingly, simply doesn't allow time for the sort of revisions that he was suffering through with *Burmese Days*, and it taught him to think and say what he had to say as soon as he sat down to write. Deadlines have a way of shortening the quest for *le mot juste*. Part of the difficulty now, however, came from the fact that this was his first novel; and since he was determined that it was to be very much a novelistic novel—not journalism tricked out as fiction—replete with all the traditional ingredients of the form (character, setting, theme, plot), it meant that he had to master, or at least to learn in a rudimentary way, a number of skills that he hadn't been called upon to exercise before. What he was attempting was something very different from the documentary reportage of *Down and Out*, the genre in which his gifts could most naturally develop and flourish.

To judge from the finished product, his aim seems to have been to write a well-made, dramatic, satiric, romantic, multicharactered novel in exotic settings that would have something of the narrative ingenuity and worldliness of Somerset Maugham, something of the ironic and sympathetic understanding of misunderstandings between East and West of E. M. Forster, something of the poetic descriptive power of D. H. Lawrence, something of his own, Eric Blair's, experience of Burma, and something of "the sort of thing people want to read about." A genius of pastiche might just conceivably have reconciled such disparate objectives; and the surprising thing is not that *Burmese Days* falls short of being the masterpiece one wishes it might have been, but that it should have turned out so good a novel as it is.

Perhaps he ought to have trusted more to his gift for writing about his own experience—what he had heard, seen, done, felt, and smelled—as in *Down and Out*. *Burmese Days* is far different from the autobiographical outpouring—from cradle to university—that is the expected first novel of a literary young man; almost a pity, in Orwell's case, that it should not have been, for the peculiarity of his passage from Eton to Burma was potentially so much more interesting than the passage from Eton to Oxbridge of the usual literary young man. And when he did come to write of it, in *The Road to Wigan Pier* in 1936, he was in the process of being politicized, and the material was exploited, albeit highly effectively, for its political, didactic value—how an Imperialist becomes a Socialist.

Much of the strength of *Burmese Days* does derive from its autobiographical detail—one knows that Orwell is writing from direct observation of a milieu he disliked intensely —but it is not autobiography in the guise of fiction and should not be read as such. If the eye is Orwell's throughout, the "I" is only seldom present, and not merely because the story is told in the third person—indeed, a great portion of his own Burmese experience has been excluded. Paradoxically, one is most aware of him—that is, of "I," the author—when he is most invisible, in the clear *de haut en bas* tone of the novel, which is not so much Maughamian as Etonian. Characters (in many instances drawn or caricatured from "real life") are scored off time and again for their commonness, their middle-classness, their vulgarity:

the ghastly Lackersteens and their husband-hunting niece Elizabeth, with her aversion to culture; the denizens of the Club, with their cartoon-like attitudes towards race and Empire; even Verrall, the polo-playing officer who is Flory's rival for the affections of Elizabeth—to both aunt and niece the blond young lieutenant is the epitome of upper-class *chic*—is revealed as having attended a *third-rate* public school. One does have the sense, especially in those portions of the novel revolving around the Club, of five years of accumulated grievances being paid off. At the same time, much that had happened to him during those five years (his own life, his own interior life, so different from the clichés of the novelist) he left untapped: the whole painful experience of his time in the Delta, for example. Perhaps the decision to write a "well-made" novel determined him to confine himself to Katha (the Kyauktada of the novel), even though he had been stationed there only during his final three months in Burma.

True, Katha was particularly vivid in his memory, with its hot pinks and flaming scarlets and smoldering purples —so different from the acid wastes of the Delta—and it is vivid in the novel, too. Kyauktada is a feat of evocation that may owe something to Orwell's having written it in the bleak, colorless setting of Hayes, that it was winter and he had a beastly cold, that smoke from the stacks of the H.M.V. Gramophone factory on the outskirts of the town had soured the fields and killed off the wildflowers that once had grown there.

Three years later, writing to Henry Miller, Orwell mentioned *Burmese Days* as the only one of his books he was pleased with—not as a novel, he hastened typically to say, but the descriptions of Burma weren't bad, he admitted, which is perhaps carrying diffidence too far.

SIX

Orwell was never very specific about his difficulties with the novel—it was prolix, too long, "broken backed" . . . beyond that he doesn't go. One suspects, though, that it was the fictional elements in *Burmese Days* that made the greatest trouble for him, beginning with the need to invent a biography for Flory that would put him at a remove from himself—for whom, at the same time, Flory serves as a spokesman: the man who sees clearly the awfulness of things as they are.

Very likely Flory, as a character, had his roots in Captain Robinson, the cashiered ex-officer whom Blair had met in Mandalay—with his opium-smoking and his native women, Robinson was already a stereotype waiting to enter somebody's novel. But his deepest roots are traceable to fiction, in a range from Conrad's Lord Jim through all those Englishmen gone to seed in the East that are one of Maugham's better-known specialties. Even the friendship of Flory with the Indian Dr. Veraswami, convincing though it is, has its stronger fictional counterpart in the friendship of Fielding with Dr. Aziz in Forster's *A Passage to India*. But the love story that Orwell invents for him with the ineffable Elizabeth is surely the weakest element in the novel, predictable in each of its turnings. However deeply felt, it comes out seeming false: in G. M. Young's phrase, "the gush of popular fiction." Perhaps Orwell thought this was "the sort of thing people wanted to read about." On the evidence here it was not the sort of thing he was able to write about best, and one reads *Burmese Days* for the accuracy of its reportage, its feeling for colonial and native life at several levels, its biting characterization, and the vividness of its settings.

Not that the "love story" as such is so badly done; it is written with sufficient skill to open an alarming prospect, that if Orwell had *really* wanted to be a popular novelist, in the middlebrow, best-selling sense of the term—as, until 1936, he intermittently thought he did—he might have brought it off, ending up as a kind of James Hilton *manqué*, with *1984* as his *Lost Horizon*.

Orwell himself would never again attempt so "romantic" and novelistic a plot as he had burdened himself with in *Burmese Days*, nor would the women characters in his future novels be quite so uniformly unpleasant. But then, "unpleasant" is a word that might be applied to almost all of the characters in *Burmese Days*, whatever their sex or nationality.

Misogynistic he was not. He was a late starter, but from the time of his return from Burma women would always be necessary to him. During these years he had a number of casual affairs, two quite considerably more than that. But he would be truly happy, and happily in love, for the first time in his life only after he married Eileen O'Shaughnessy in 1936. And yet, perhaps because he came to know women relatively late, he seems never to have been entirely at ease with them, or, as many of them thought, to understand them. The sentimental fantasy of his friendship with Eleanor Jaques, in which his feelings were deeply engaged and whose progress in letters—for he wrote to her more often than he saw her—can be traced in a telltale graph from Dear Eleanor to My Dearest Eleanor, foundered on a crucial misunderstanding: she was fond of Eric, but was in love with Dennis Collings, and intended to marry him, and did, in 1934.* "I don't think he really liked women," Brenda Salkeld says flatly. And another woman who knew him intimately at this period in his life offered as her considered opinion years later: "I don't believe he understood women, or had much interest in understanding them." She smiles in a reminiscent way; obviously she could tell more than she intends to tell. "They were ready to bed with him; therefore, what was there to understand? And of course they did—married women around Southwold—bed with him, I mean. He had quite a few little *affaires* that didn't count for anything. One or two that did. But all this talk of the ascetic Orwell! Not Eric! I do think he tended to be contemptuous of women—just a little. Until Eileen came along. That was a different story, of course."

* The eleven letters from Blair to Eleanor Jaques included in *The Collected Essays, Journalism and Letters* provide material enough for a novel on the scale of *Adolphe*. It is striking how many are concerned with suggestions for meetings that never occur. And how many more are recapitulations of the pitifully few meetings that actually did take place. Again, it is striking to notice that she did not respond when he asked where she would be at a particular time—his holiday in Southwold—and so, after a fortnight's interval, waiting vainly to hear, he wrote again, asking for the same information. Did she reply? It is the last of the published letters. None of which is surprising, considering, as we have said, that Eleanor was in love with Dennis Collings—a fact that Blair, in his loneliness, chose not to acknowledge, or at least not to admit into his fantasy.

SEVEN

Orwell's life in the early months of 1933, after the publication of *Down and Out* and his return to his job at Evelyn's School, provides a clearcut illustration of the difference between the quotidian and the creative existence of the writer. There was the tedium of his external, day-by-day routine: the teaching, the gardening—that pumpkin, would it or would it not survive?—the occasional letter received and in due course replied to (How nice to hear from . . . Forgive me for not . . .). There was, exacerbated no doubt by the tedium, an irruption of a slightly bogus-sounding world-weariness—"A few years ago I thought it rather fun to reflect that our civilization is doomed, but now it fills me above all else with boredom to think of the horrors that will be happening within ten years"—a remark that might have been made with perfect consistency by a character in *Point Counterpoint,* or some fifteen years earlier by the Young Cynic at Eton; but coming from Blair in 1933 it suggests the distance he would have to go before he truly became George Orwell.

The only excitement of these months was inward. He was a writer in full creative flow who happened to be "living and partly living" in Hayes, but his important life was being lived in recollections of Katha and restored to the page as Kyauktada.

Then the real world of 1933—of the Depression, Hunger Marches, and Unemployment, the stuff of headlines that counted for less than the look of a particular bird remembered from Katha—rudely intruded. In the spring, poor Mr. Evelyn had the disagreeable task of informing his staff that the school was collapsing. Despite its "very good reputation" as an independent preparatory boarding school, it simply wasn't attracting enough pupils for him to pay the bills, and this would be the final term. For Blair it meant that he would soon be joining the ranks of the unemployed.

The news of the approaching demise of Evelyn's School was relayed along the academic bush telegraph, and in May, Mr. John Bennett, the owner, founder, and headmaster of Frays College in nearby Uxbridge, a much larger and more affluent school, came over one afternoon to see what of its portable effects—desks, chairs, bookcases, etc.— he might buy. (The building that housed the school was presently to be taken over by Hillingdon Hospital for staff accommodation, and the name itself, with permission of the hapless Mr. Evelyn, was bestowed upon a county school which is now, some forty years later, a flourishing comprehensive mixed school, situated quite near the site of the original Evelyn's.)

On the afternoon of his visit, apart from acquiring some useful supplies at bargain prices, Mr. Bennett was introduced to Eric Blair, and acquired him as well. By a happy coincidence, there was a vacancy coming up on the staff of Frays that he seemed particularly qualified to fill. A certain Monsieur Souchard, who took the boys in French, had just been called up for military service in France, and would be leaving Frays in a few weeks. The only disadvantage from Blair's point of view was that Mr. Bennett would want him as a holiday tutor in mid-August to give private tutoring to the eight French boys who were living at the school. He had been looking forward to a long holiday in Southwold, in part because he could accelerate, perhaps even finish, the writing of *Burmese Days,* in part because he would have a chance to spend time with the friends he saw too seldom—Eleanor, Brenda, Dennis, not to mention his mother and his sister Avril; and the Fierzes, as was their custom, would be taking a house there for the month of August. But one did not quibble over details of jobs at a time when jobs were in short supply, and he speedily accepted it.

Freed from the worry of having to look for another post, which might have slowed him down intolerably, he hurried along with the novel. In May, three-quarters of it was in rough draft, and he sent off that much of the manuscript to Leonard Moore. In June he could report to Brenda Salkeld that Moore was quite "enthusiastic," though he added with that note of deprecation one comes to expect from him wherever this novel is concerned, "which is more than I am." Still, he was sufficiently pleased with it to send it to her to read, reassuring her that the final version would not be as misshapen as it might now seem. Early in July, while still at Evelyn's, he wrote to Eleanor Jaques to ask her holiday plans, and mentioned that he expected to have the novel finished by the end of the month. This good news he qualified (of course!) by saying that he disliked much of it and would spend months revising it. Two weeks later, writing to Eleanor again, he could announce that the novel was done. "But there are wads of it that I simply hate and am going to change." This was not so different in tone and strategy from what he'd written Brenda as long ago as the previous September, and from what he'd let fall in conversation with Mabel in the months ever since, that he'd been reading over what he had written and found it, each time, a depressing experience. The crucial difference now was that at last he had a *finished* novel, however much revision might still be needed, and in his letters to Moore that summer cheerfulness keeps breaking in. He could go off to his new job in a better frame of mind than when he had left his old one.

Frays College, where he took up his duties in August, had had its beginning in 1926, when John Bennett, unhappy about the education his children were receiving at their schools, decided to found his own—the Uxbridge High School—where he might put his more liberal teaching principles into practice. A short time later he changed its name to Frays College, after the Frays River, a rather narrow stream—too broad, however, for jumping—that flowed past the school property, and under that name it continued to thrive into the 1970's.

Uxbridge, like Hayes, is just outside London in Middlesex and, with its multileveled car park and other accouterments of the "outer city," has been thoroughly suburbanized. But in the 1930's it was still something of a country town. Frays, only a short walk from the center, had as its aim the preparation of students for the civil service, the universities, and the professions. It was coeducational and took children from the ages of five to fifteen or sixteen. At the time that Blair was there, from August through December 1933, there were about 180 students, some 30 of whom, 15 boys and 15 girls, were boarders. Blair had originally been taken on only as a "holiday tutor," but Mr. Bennett was soon satisfied that he was qualified to replace the departed Souchard, and engaged him formally to join the staff of 16. As an assistant master his chief responsibility was teaching French, but he was also expected to take classes in other subjects, English among them, and to supervise hockey and cricket. It was a full day of activity, and it meant, in practical terms, that work on the novel had to be put off until evenings, a repetition of his experience at Evelyn's, save that here he was spared the genteel dinginess and loneliness, as well as the expense, of The Hawthorns. The school occupied a large, rambling Edwardian villa, with a garden behind, extending in terraces down to the river. There was a series of small bedrooms, known familiarly as "the horse-boxes," assigned to members of the staff, and in one of these Blair lived and Orwell worked. At night, from behind his closed door, would be heard the sound of the typewriter: he was completing the revisions and typing the final draft of *Burmese Days*.

To judge from the recollections of those who knew him at Frays, he would seem to have been a successful master, popular with his students and on cordial terms with his colleagues, although he was still, as he had been in the past and would continue to be in the future, "somewhat aloof" —not unfriendly, but determined to go his own way and to use his time for himself. In the evenings he would not sit for long in the Masters' Common Room, but presently would slip away to his horse-box and his waiting typewriter. At meals, which the staff took at their own table apart from the students, he was always perfectly amiable, although he was more likely to respond to conversation than to initiate it. But he was not shy, and the other members of the staff were impressed by his courage, as a new master, in persisting in smoking at table (generally frowned upon), the more so as he made his cigarettes from very strong and odorous French tobacco. (It was thought to be quite a feat that he should roll his own, when it was extremely uncommon to do so, with one hand.) On one occasion, when a dance was held for the thirty boarders to the music of a wind-up Gramophone, he dutifully appeared, and even seemed to enjoy himself. Tall to the point of ungainliness, he made a memorable picture—memorable enough to be recalled forty years later—dancing with an older and extremely short mistress who rather terrified many of her colleagues.

There were two members of the staff with whom he was on relatively close terms: the Stapleys, a young couple, recently married, who had been given a larger suite of rooms in honor of their married state. With them in their sitting room, which Mrs. Stapley had done her best to de-institutionalize, he spent pleasant times, chatting and drinking cup after cup of strong coffee. To them—as to no one else at the school—he entrusted the secret of his second identity; he presented them with a copy of the American edition of *Down and Out;* he told them how much he had hated his time in Burma and allowed them to infer that that was to be the subject of his next book.

It was characteristic of him that his principal recreations at this time—as the Stapleys recall them—were solitary in nature: to fish; and to drive about the countryside on his newly acquired second-hand motorcycle, something he hadn't done since he and Roger Beadon, his fellow police officer, drove recklessly through the streets of Mandalay. Fishing, of course, was an abiding interest, which had had its beginnings in his boyhood in Henley-on-Thames, and he would spend a good deal of such free time as he had fishing in the river at the foot of the garden for trout, roach, and gudgeon. Mrs. Stapley has a clear memory of him one day coming in dripping from the river and handing her a mess of fish, which she rapidly transferred to the cook for dinner.

As these inconsequent but evocative details will suggest, the Stapleys—Mr. Stapley eventually became headmaster of Frays—have kept pleasant memories of him, and he gave them no indication during those months, when they were seeing him virtually every day, that he was unhappy at the school; on the other hand, he never pretended that teaching was anything but a stopgap career for him, to be given up at the first feasible moment. And like so many of his friends and acquaintances, once he had passed from their ken, they would never see or hear from him again.

There was one other person at Frays upon whom he made a strong impression, and that was Graham Bennett, the son of the headmaster, who was not at the school as a pupil but was living there with his parents. Blair, as an older man of wide and unusual experience, had great fascination for a boy in his late teens. Bennett found him likable, witty, quizzical, and unpatronizing; they would chatter away about "anything and everything"—although it seems worth pointing out that Blair never bothered to tell Bennett that he was in the process of writing a novel or that he had already published a book under another name. Even so, Bennett found him slightly "mysterious," which only added to his interest: he was "some sort of Socialist," in the sense, one gathers, that Sir William Harcourt's *bon mot* of the 1880's, "We are all socialists now," might have served as the motto for the 1930's. And of course his appearance was unforgettable, very different from the neatness and trimness that the schoolmaster of the day affected. Blair, in his thirty-first year, had the looks that he would keep for the rest of his life. He had lost the robustness and weight of the time when he was playing in the Wall Game at Eton, and the spruceness and firmness of the young officer in his first year in Burma. Those years in the Delta had taken their toll, as had ill health and the years of living on the cheap since his return. He was tall and weedy, and his style of dress, which was permanently decided upon by this time, helped to create an effect not easily forgotten. Graham Bennett still remembers a certain shabbiness: Blair in bags—trousers with wide cuffs—a frayed sports jacket, and checked shirt. He would be dressed much the same a year later when Rayner Heppenstall met him: "He wore baggy grey flannel trousers and a leather-elbowed sports coat, with a khaki or dark-green shirt, and a pale, hairy tie. He continued to favour this style of attire in the days of his prosperity." Years later, in the early 1940's, when T. R. Fyvel knew him, he still dressed like this, to Fyvel's mind a mixture of the seedy sahib and a French workman. Perhaps it would be simplest to say that in 1933 he had begun to dress as George Orwell: a transformative process that would work from the outside in.

Towards the end of November he wrote to Leonard Moore to say that the novel was finished, truly finished as far as he was concerned—"I am sick of the sight of it"—and he asked if he might bring it over to Moore's house in Gerrard's Cross the following Sunday, December 3. On the Sunday, with a characteristic disregard for the realities of the wintry weather, Blair went off on his motor bike, carrying the manuscript, and wearing his usual sports coat and flapping trousers, without even a scarf or pullover, despite the urgings of the Bennetts and the Stapleys. This was how he had dressed since coming back from Paris, how he would continue to dress, whether dashing about on the motor bike or walking through the streets of London or visiting his sister Marjorie in the North, not wearing a topcoat even on the coldest days of winter, as Ruth Pitter had begged him to do two years before in a vain attempt to make him take care of himself.

The result was predictable. In the middle of December, while out on his motor bike, he was caught in an icy rainstorm, got thoroughly drenched, and came down with a terrible chill—Graham Bennett remembers him being blue with cold. At first he was nursed at the school by Mrs. Bennett and the matron. But the chill developed into pneumonia; with his weak chest his condition worsened perceptibly; and at the advice of Dr. Bennet-Coles, whom the headmaster had called in, he was transferred to the Uxbridge Cottage Hospital, just up from the school on Harefield Road.

He was terribly ill; in fact, it was thought almost certain that he would die, and the Bennetts sent for Mrs. Blair from Southwold. Avril drove her down, but by the time they arrived in Uxbridge, the crisis had passed and the chances of his recovery had notably improved.

Avril remembers the nurse telling her that when Eric had been delirious, he had talked incessantly about money: one of the obsessions of his life emerging, as it were, from the unconscious and demanding to be heard. Now, as she and Mrs. Blair sat by his bedside, "We reassured him that everything was all right, and he needn't worry about money. But it turned out that it wasn't actually his situation in life as regards money that he was worrying about, it was actual cash—he felt that he wanted cash sort of under his pillow."

Dr. Bennet-Coles recommended that he must have at least six months' rest once he was discharged from the hospital, so there was no question of his continuing with his job at Frays. He took the doctor's recommendation one dramatic step further in a letter to Moore at the end of December: obviously he couldn't be back at the school at the beginning of term; therefore he had decided to chuck teaching, imprudent though that might be. Out of every misfortune a blessing, however; for now, without the distractions of having to teach, he would be free to work uninterruptedly at his next novel—that would be *A Clergyman's Daughter*—and with the enthusiasm of a prisoner on the point of liberation, felt he would have it finished within six months. Meanwhile, in the last sentence of his letter, where he usually tended to raise such questions, he ventured to hope that all would go well at Gollancz with *Burmese Days*.

That was on the twenty-eighth of December. A week later (January 4, 1934) he wrote to Moore that he was leaving the hospital and would spend a few days at a hotel in Ealing until he felt strong enough to travel, then go straight down to Southwold to his parents' house. There he would simultaneously convalesce and create. His career as a schoolmaster, which had never provided him with much satisfaction and which he would deal with in the future with more ferocity than accuracy, was at an end.

EIGHT

He RETURNED TO SOUTHWOLD IN A MOOD OF HIGH elation, to which his release from teaching, his escape from the threat of death, perhaps something of the flushed excitement symptomatic of TB, perhaps the child-like pleasure of being looked after by his mother and his sister Avril, all contributed. His mind was teeming with literary schemes and projects, enough to occupy him, if he wrote unceasingly, for the next several months. Surely, though, this was not the "complete rest" that Dr. Bennet-Coles had recommended?

He signified to Rees that he was ready to do reviews again for the *Adelphi*. He wrote to Moore about the possibility of his doing a translation from the French of Paul Gille's *Esquisse d'une philosophie de la dignité humaine*, which his Aunt Nellie's husband, under his professional name of R. Lanti, was busily translating into Esperanto in Paris (nothing came of this). In early February he proposed that he might undertake a short life of Mark Twain for a biographical series that was being published by Chatto & Windus (nothing came of this). And, of course, there was to be the new novel. That, indeed, did come into being at a much faster rate than its predecessor, which had proved such arduous work that, coupled with his schoolteaching, it may have contributed to his physical debilitation over the many months of its writing and revision.

Although the early news of *Burmese Days* was discouraging, Blair's mood remained high: he was confident that all would go well with it. By mid-January Gollancz had read the manuscript and admired it, but consulted his solicitor and then rejected it, fearful of its potentially libelous content, which seemed to be taken from Blair's own experience—a notion that Blair himself did nothing to discourage. Granting that a solicitor's advice to a publisher in such circumstances tends to be overly cautious, it was not unlikely that Gollancz might indeed be sued for libel if Blair had indeed drawn some of his characters, which again would not have been unlikely, directly from life. The most unexpected people have been known to read a novel as though it were a mirror; Roger Beadon remembers hearing that the Principal of the Police College in Mandalay, whom Blair thought an oaf, threatened to horsewhip the author when he read *Burmese Days*. So if someone had chosen to recognize himself in the text, publisher, author, and printer might well have been sued for damages.

Before the end of the month, Heinemann's, to whom Moore sent the manuscript next, had also rejected it, and for the same reason. It is possible that Orwell was the victim now of the reputation he had won with *Down and Out in Paris and London*. No one had questioned his veracity then as a faithful reporter of life as he had observed it, and it would be a logical assumption that his next book, though labeled a novel, would also draw in large part upon what he had experienced at first hand, faithfully described.

But even this news of a second rejection did not unduly depress him: he still had no doubt that the novel would be published. It helped to sustain his mood to learn from Moore that Eugene Saxton, the editor in chief of his American publishers, Harpers', who had an option for his next two books after *Down and Out,* happened to be in London at the very moment Heinemann's sent back the manuscript to Moore. Moore dispatched it immediately to Saxton at his hotel, and Saxton, in the fashion of American publishers in London on a "buying trip," read it in an evening, liked it, and was anxious to talk with the author about it. On Wednesday, the seventh of February, Orwell took the train from Southwold to meet with Saxton in London that afternoon. It proved to be an editorial rather than a legal conference: questions of libel didn't arise.

Rather surprisingly, considering that at the time he was writing *Burmese Days* he was very closely rereading Joyce's *Ulysses* (Mabel's gift from Ostend), and writing admiring didactic letters about it to Brenda, he was wholly uninfluenced (then) by that landmark of experimental fiction. He was thoroughly committed to straightforward, even old-fashioned, storytelling, and Saxton in a mild sort of way objected to the old-fashioned last chapter, after Flory's suicide, when the later careers and lives of the characters are taken beyond the proper confines of the story, much as in a fairy tale we are reassured that "they all lived happily ever after." Blair couldn't have disagreed more: "I hate a novel," he wrote to Moore the next day, "in which the principal characters are not disposed of at the end." Still, he would be willing to cut out the offending pages if he must—that is, if Saxton insisted; but he did not, and the tidying-up remains in the text. The chief result of this meeting between author and editor was that Orwell agreed to remove the offending phrase "It now remains to tell" from the beginning of the chapter, and it appeared that, so far as American publication was concerned, all problems had been resolved.

But in March the specter of libel again raised its head. The contract for the book was negotiated by Harpers' agent in London, Hamish Hamilton. Difficulties arose because it was known that two English publishers had already rejected *Burmese Days,* and it was surmised that they had been moved to do so out of fear of libel. A special clause was inserted in the contract, stating that Orwell would withdraw such material as Harpers' advisors might consider libelous; or if the publishers considered the material too libelous to be published, the book would be withdrawn and the contract annulled. The threat of libel sufficiently worried Orwell himself that he added a stipulation of his own: that a statement should be inserted in the book saying that all characters were fictitious, and this was done.

The contract was signed in March 1934. At the end of the month, Harpers' sent the manuscript to their lawyer in New York to be vetted for libel. A few days later he reported to them that he felt, despite the author's disclaimer, that quite a few characters were drawn from life, particularly Flory, and that the book did libel several people, although it was unlikely they would bother to sue. Still, there was some risk. Harpers' decided to take the matter further. In April their lawyer wrote to a solicitor in London to inquire if Harpers' as an American firm could be sued in England. Apparently the reply was equivocal enough to be reassuring; Harpers' decided to go ahead and publish, and in the autumn sent the agreed-to advance, payable on publication, of fifty pounds.

Once again for the sake of clarity we ignore chronology and leap forward to deal with the history of *Burmese Days,* first in America, correctly as Orwell's first novel, and then, in England, where it was published as his second novel, having been preceded there by some months by *A Clergyman's Daughter*. Harpers' brought out *Burmese Days* on October 25, 1934, in an edition of two thousand copies, far more, as it turned out, than would ever be needed. Again, although the book was by George Orwell, it was copyright by Eric Blair. This time, however, a certain amount of publicity material was forthcoming—enough, it was hoped, to tantalize prospective readers: that the book itself couldn't be published in England for fear of libel; and that the author had served in the Indian Imperial Police in Burma, resigning, in the words of the reviewer for the *New York Times Book Review*, because "he disliked putting people in prison for doing the same thing which he should have done in their circumstances." The most conspicuous of the American reviews, and the only one that Blair himself saw, was in the *New York Herald Tribune Books*. It had been given pride of place, first among the fiction of the week and prominently headlined, but it was quite unfavorable. The reviewer, Margaret Carson Hubbard, found that all of Orwell's sympathies were with the natives, which does not suggest a very careful reading of the text, and that "as a result, the only characters that seem real are U Po Kyin and the native doctor Veraswami. The trouble with this novel is that the ax Mr. Orwell is grinding is so vastly important to him that it has chopped to pieces all interest in the very situation he most wants to expose. The ghastly vulgarity of the third-rate characters who endure the heat and talk and nausea of the glorious days of the British Raj, when fifteen lashes settled any native insolence, is such that they kill all interest in their doings." Not, as a publisher might say, "a selling review," though Blair consoled himself, in a note to Moore, with the thought that it had been given big headlines, "which I suppose is what counts."

The reviewer for the *New York Times Book Review* was the same Fred T. Marsh who had written so favorably of *Down and Out* the year before in the *Herald Tribune*, and he was a good deal more discriminating than Mrs. Carson Hubbard. But the most discerning American review appeared in December, in the high-toned and gentlemanly *Boston Evening Transcript*, a newspaper long since defunct that survives, so to speak, as the subject and title of a minor poem by T. S. Eliot. The anonymous reviewer for the *Transcript*, noticing that the book had been refused publication in England, admitted to some bafflement on the point, for it was hardly a book which painted the English as all black—*pace* Mrs. Carson Hubbard—and the natives as all white: Burmese, Indians, Eurasians, and English are made equally to appear silly and mean. If Orwell disliked the English more than the others, it was simply that they happened to be the most powerful: "Virulent as at times are Mr. Orwell's strictures, he visualizes as candidly those native—well, racial—idiosyncrasies against whose passive resistance all the power of Western Empire repeatedly proves unavailing." The central figure was thought to be "analyzed with rare insight and unprejudiced if inexorable justice," and the entire book was praised as full of "realities faithfully and unflinchingly realized." But kind words in Boston were not enough to save a hopeless situation, and before long, Harpers' gave up on the book entirely: in February 1935, just four months after publication, the type was distributed, and 976 copies were remaindered.

Blair himself, though dissatisfied with the book, was not at all ashamed of it, and there was no reason that he should have been. But he was sufficiently concerned that a complete record be kept of his literary output that in December 1934, he personally presented, and inscribed as George Orwell, a copy of the American edition of *Burmese Days* to the British Museum, which had not automatically received the book, as it would have done if it were an English publication.

But in fact, perhaps because no libel actions had ensued from the American edition, English publishers picked up courage. In September 1934 Jonathan Cape expressed interest in the book. Blair's first reaction was skeptical. He told Moore he thought there was little point in showing it to them, as Cape had the same libel lawyer as Gollancz—which has the sound of an improvised reason; quite possibly he just did not want the book to go to Cape, for they were the publishers, it will be remembered (Blair certainly hadn't forgotten), who had twice rejected *Down and Out*. But then he had a second thought. After all, they had *asked* to see it; perhaps they would be the ones brave enough to accept it. In October he reminded Moore that Cape had published *The Best Poems of 1934*, in which a poem by Blair as Blair had been included, and perhaps this should be called to Cape's attention when he was shown *Burmese Days*—a rather naïve misunderstanding of the realities of publishing. But his third and final thought was realistic enough—that Cape would not want the book; and when they were sent the manuscript, that proved to be the case.

Then, in February 1935, Victor Gollancz, who would be publishing *A Clergyman's Daughter* in March, decided to reconsider *Burmese Days*. This time his response was enthusiastic. Whether Gollancz himself hadn't done more than glance at the manuscript the first time around, or whether the political overtones and implications of the novel, its caustic picture of the Raj in action, now made a special appeal to him, one can't say for certain. But he did want to publish it; and although Blair would tell Henry Miller in 1936 the fanciful story that his publisher had been afraid the India Office would try to suppress the book, all that actually stood in the way was the libel problem— still existing, of course, but for which a solution would somehow be found. Towards that end, even while the same lawyers who had originally recommended against publication were giving the book another microscopic reading, it was arranged that Blair should come to the Gollancz office to discuss the problem with Norman Collins, deputy chairman of the firm. Their meeting, certainly as recalled by Collins long afterwards, had its elements of comedy; perhaps only Orwell's friend of his later years, Anthony Powell, could do justice to its more subtle ramifications.

Collins, four years younger than Orwell, had become a director of Gollancz in 1934. From 1929 to 1931 he had been assistant literary editor of the *News Chronicle*. Then in 1932 he had begun his own career as a writer with *The Facts of English Fiction*, and in 1934 had followed it with a novel, *Penang Appointment*. (A decade later he was to have an immense international success with his novel *England Belongs to Me.*) He was a trim, elegant figure who personified, inadvertently as it were, the rewards and privileges of the literary life that for Blair were equivalent to the shades of the prison house. This has to be kept in mind to savor the comedy that followed.

Collins hadn't met Blair before, but he had read his books, and *Down and Out* had prepared him for a writer out of the usual run. Even so, he was taken aback at the entrance of a tall, painfully thin figure, shabbily dressed, wearing a jacket whose sleeves were much too short for him, with a ravaged face that looked, Collins thought, as though it belonged to an El Greco saint.

There was an attempt at social conversation before getting down to the serious business of the day. Tea, always a useful tactic for getting over initial awkwardness, was sent for. Blair spoke. Collins had no difficulty in recognizing that Etonian accent, which doubtless became more noticeable as the interview progressed, and which explained the shabbiness as a form of eccentricity.

Collins arrived at the problem of libel itself. In a general way he made it clear—he was really being very helpful—what sort of answers were required from Blair; once given, they would simplify everything for everyone. But Blair, despite his El Greco face, was in a puckish rather than a saintly mood, and was not yet ready to cooperate.

"How much of *Burmese Days* is actually based on fact?" asked Collins.

"All of it," said Blair.

"All of it?"

"All of it."

Pause.

"Now then, about the characters. Would you say they are drawn from life?"

"Yes."

"Well, one or two, or how many?"

"All of them."

"All?"

"All."

Pause.

Collins had never had an experience with an author quite like this one before. "But surely you've changed their names for the novel?"

"Oh no."

"You mean that you've used their actual names?"
"Oh yes."
"How many?"
"All of them."

It was Blair in a mood and style that would not have been unfamiliar to friends, acquaintances, and masters who had known him at Eton.

Eventually, however—if not that afternoon—he accepted the seriousness of the problem as it was put to him. He did, after all, want his novel published in England, and Gollancz agreed to publish it if certain changes were made.

In the light of Blair's sweeping claims to Collins, it comes as something of an anticlimax to discover that the changes were only three in number, a matter of new names for certain characters: most importantly, the evil Burmese magistrate U Po Kyin became U Po Sing, and Dr. Veraswami became Dr. Murkhaswami.*

* In later editions of *Burmese Days*, beginning with the Penguin edition of 1944, the names of the characters were restored, and the American and English editions have since that time been identical.

NINE

A Clergyman's Daughter WAS PUBLISHED IN MARCH 1935, but to give it its proper place in Orwell's history, one must go backwards in time to its inception. It will be remembered that at the end of December 1933, even before Blair had left the hospital in Uxbridge, he was writing to Leonard Moore that one advantage of his giving up teaching was that he would be able to write his next novel in six months.

In January he was in Southwold, convalescing in his parents' house, and already at work. In April he was able to report to Moore that the novel was not going badly, and that he had made even more progress on it than he had anticipated, though it was still in very rough form. By now Blair really saw himself as a professional man of letters: one or two novels a year . . . reviews, essays . . . a typewriter never silent. *Down and Out* had been published in England and America, and contracts for French and Czechoslovakian editions were being drawn up. Arrangements had been completed for the American publication of *Burmese Days;* there was no reason to doubt that eventually it would find an English publisher.

The difficulty that faced him, although he was still unable to recognize it—the significant difficulty any author of Orwell's bent would find himself having to face—was that his literary capital was drying up; some of the experience that went into the new novels was not sufficiently digested; and his power of imagination was deficient—whole areas of life eluded him, especially where women were concerned. For his best, most persuasive work he had to draw upon what he had himself experienced. Burma had had a long time to ripen and formulate in his mind, and the same would be true of *Animal Farm* and *1984*. *Coming Up for Air* in 1939, written after a break from fiction of four years, drew upon the milieu and recollections of his childhood in Henley-on-Thames. But *A Clergyman's Daughter* in 1935 and *Keep the Aspidistra Flying* in 1936, the novels he wrote in immediate succession to *Burmese Days,* industriously and with hardly a pause to think or invent between them, are generally thought to be his weakest. So Orwell himself came to feel: he gave instructions that they were not to be reprinted, and during his lifetime they were not.

The lessons to be learned from the writing of *Down and Out* and *Burmese Days* Blair was as yet unable to accept: that his gift was for reportage rather than the invention of plot, that his depictions of women were drawn less from life than from the stereotypes of fiction. Although his books were best when they were truest, he was determined to prove himself an authentic novelist of a traditional kind, capable of a full-dress, traditional, imaginative characterization. How better to prove it than to write from the point of view of a central character who would bear no relation to himself—not even tangentially, or as a spokesman, as with Flory—and what better way to prove *that* than to make his central character a woman? Hence: Dorothy Hare, the luckless heroine of *A Clergyman's Daughter,* whose last name is borrowed from Blair's paternal grandmother, and whose pathetic adventures are meant to be fictional but all too soon and too recognizably are drawn from Blair's own. It is a classic case of an author misjudging his talent and his material.

Orwell himself never explained why he should have chosen to write about this particular character or the crisis in her life—her loss of faith as a believing communicant of the Church of England—that provides the novel with its thematic spine. In 1934 it couldn't be claimed that the plight of the genteel spinster daughter hadn't already been explored in some depth by earlier writers, perhaps less often in the novel than the story, a genre to which it seems peculiarly suited: by Katherine Mansfield, for instance, in "The Daughters of the Late Colonel"; and by D. H. Lawrence in "The Daughters of the Vicar." As for the loss of faith, that hallmark of the postwar age, it had been a "resource" all through the 1920's, along a spectrum in time and quality that would range from Joyce's *Ulysses* in 1922 to Noel Coward's "Twentieth Century Blues" ("they're getting me down") in 1931. The best justification for Blair's entering such well-mapped territory—apart from his wish and his need "to write a novel"—would have been if he had felt deeply enough for Dorothy to bring her to life on the page: not as life observed, but as life lived. Orwell, in Herbert Read's phrase "the last great English journalist in the line that begins with Defoe," would acknowledge in a piece in *Tribune* in 1945 that a major difference between himself and Lawrence (and in fact what made the latter a genius) was that Lawrence was able to know imaginatively what he could not know by observation. The particular work of Lawrence's to which he refers in this piece is "The Daughters of the Vicar," a long story whose theme of the genteel spinster he doubts Lawrence could have dealt with successfully in a full-length novel. Perhaps this was Orwell's own way of admitting that he hadn't been up to the task either.

And yet, he had begun very well, and one can understand his cheerful tone when he wrote to Moore in April. The opening portions of *A Clergyman's Daughter* are in the best traditions of English social fiction. Its setting, the village of Knype Hill, is precisely evoked, with a shrewd eye for its awful and all too credible social discriminations —not for nothing had Eric been strolling the streets of Southwold, or dropping in at the tea shop that Avril and a friend were managing at this time off the High Street, or engaging in long conversations and gossips with his mother at home. Dorothy herself is much more sympathetically rendered than Elizabeth in *Burmese Days*. Poor thing, she is instantly recognizable as one of life's victims, and her victimship is compounded by her particular circumstance: as the only and devoted daughter of an altogether selfish man, the vicar of St. Margaret's (C. of E.), in whom are united snobbish intellect, un-Christian spirit, and insufficient income, and to whom Dorothy ministers in the multiple role of daughter, quasi-wife—the actual spouse, Dorothy's mother, having wisely deceased years before— and housekeeper and bookkeeper. The last is a particular source of anguish to her, for the Hares are the embodiment of gentility at the end of its tether, piling up bills with the local tradesmen which they can never entirely pay.

Dorothy's long day's journey into night provides the substance for the long, excellent first chapter. It begins with her enduring, for the good of her spirit, an ice-cold bath; and then in lonely attendance, for the good of her spirit also, at early morning service, over which her father presides with weary disdain. Thriftily, Blair could make use of all that he had observed at St. Mary's in Hayes, and his friendship with the curate there now paid handsome dividends. Once or twice the tone does go slightly off, when certain Orwellian obsessions with what is physically noisome and disgusting are foisted upon Dorothy: as she takes the communion cup from a slobbering old lady, she forces herself to drink from the cup precisely where the slimy mouthprint still lingers. But on the whole, the air of truth envelops it all, whether at the vicarage or in the streets of Knype Hill: Dorothy dutifully calling upon aged and infirm parishioners; her humiliation at the butcher shop as she attempts to stretch credit past the breaking point; even her visit that evening with the slightly louche but not unamiable Mr. Warburton. He is the one man she knows who offers her a possible escape from the limitless tedium and bleakness that extend before her, but it is an escape she cannot take, since, in addition to being one of life's victims, she is also one of its pathological virgins. At an attempted pass from Mr. Warburton, she flees down the road from his house, back to the vicarage, the tyranny of her father, and her joyless, self-lacerating faith in God.

It is at this point that Blair's difficulties with the novel began. By July his early optimism had given way to despair. "I am so miserable," he confessed to Brenda Salkeld, "struggling in the entrails of that dreadful book . . . loathing the sight of what I have done." This was neither diffidence nor panache, but a true cry from the heart.

Sometimes an author will know, as it were by instinct, when he has plumbed his material to its proper depth, when he has discovered the formal structure that will show it to its best advantage; this would happen only once in Orwell's career, with *Animal Farm*.

In *A Clergyman's Daughter,* having written at length and

with copious persuasive detail of a day and a night in the life of Dorothy Hare, Blair discovered that he had told all that there was genuinely to tell about her, the character he had *imagined*. The end, which in the novel comes after another two hundred pages, was already suggested at the very beginning of the first chapter, and might have been left for the perceptive reader to conclude for himself at the chapter's end, as Dorothy disappears down the road from Mr. Warburton's house, on her way back to the vicarage: one of those pathetic figures who lose their faith and yet, if they are to survive at all, must go on with the forms of the faith in which they no longer believe.

Blair had written what he failed to recognize: a long story of considerable power, firmly rooted in the realistic tradition. But he had intended to write, and was still determined to write, a full-length novel. In practical terms this meant that he somehow, some way, had to find a further narrative for her; and he found it, as one might expect, by returning to his own experience. Ostensibly Dorothy continues as the heroine of the novel, but his true subject, his inevitable model, was himself in disguise. The result, artistically, must count among his failures, as he himself recognized; but for a biographical study such as this, it has its peculiar interest.

His powers of imagination seem to have deserted him completely. What will happen next? is the primitive, essential question any novelist must ask of himself. In the case of Dorothy Hare, considered as a character in her own right, the question would have been complicated for Blair by the very skill with which he suggested the likelihood that hers was a life in which *nothing* would happen next: that was the whole sad scarifying point of her story. But once he was determined to go on with it, and make a novel of Dorothy's story, certain suppositions of a novelistic kind might have been considered—supposing *this* were to happen, *then* she might in turn do thus and so—suppositions not wholly inconsistent with her character as it had been so clearly, so convincingly drawn in that opening chapter. To the question What will happen to her next? Blair answered that this clergyman's daughter would go down and out, even as he had done at various moments in the years before he became "George Orwell."

There is a significant difference, of course, between the situations of Eric Blair and Dorothy Hare. Blair chose voluntarily to go down and out as a writer in search of material and experience: the last such descent into the lower depths he had made three years earlier in August to October 1931, when he went to pick hops in Kent as soon as he had finished the final version of *Down and Out*. For Dorothy there was no logical, or underlying psychological, motive for this particular experience, nor was she to have the choice (as he had had) of returning from the depths to ordinary normal life whenever it pleased her to do so. Like a ballet dancer performing the choreography of someone else's invention, she is simply to undergo a number of the experiences that were Blair's own—many, one discovers, are taken quite unchanged, even as to phrases, turns of speech, and emotional responses, from his hop-picking diary. The crucial difference—one is tempted to say, the fatal difference—from the point of view of fiction, is that what had happened to him is now to happen to her.

All that had to be invented was a fictitious device for getting her there—down into the lower depths. By no stretch of the imagination can we persuade ourselves that a girl like Dorothy would ever have voluntarily chosen such a fate—as unlikely, almost, as her emerging naked from a pie at a church bazaar. Therefore the fate must be imposed upon her, and Blair's device is a massive, prolonged attack of amnesia, brought on (we are left to conclude, for it is left unexplained) by the traumatic effect of Mr. Warburton's pass—in any event, this is the last night that she will be in Knype Hill for months to come. There is a period of five days and nights that are never accounted for, long enough for her to get to London, and to have had experiences of some sort that are never to be described. Then she reemerges, her memory and her wardrobe totally gone. When we next see her—it is indeed Dorothy—she is wearing a scruffy version of a tart's costume, soiled satin dress and black mesh stockings. Remarkably, her virginity appears to have remained intact, and continues so to the end of the novel: the transforming, apocalyptic sexual experience a Lawrence might have had in mind for her, Orwell will have none of.

What he had in mind for Dorothy was that she should reexperience, while still in her amnesiac state, something of his own experience as a hop-picker in Kent—and he had his hop-picking diary, kept faithfully from August 25 to October 8, 1931, to draw upon for that. Then, having recovered her memory, she shall reexperience something of the poverty he had known in his down-and-out explorations of London, descending to ever more disgusting and filthy lodgings, until she is literally penniless and homeless, and must spend a night in Trafalgar Square, one among the many shivering derelicts huddled together for warmth—and for that he could draw upon his memories, as well as *Down and Out* itself, where they had already figured. Finally, she will reexperience a kind of grotesque, luridly exaggerated version of his own experience as a teacher in a private school: he could draw equally upon his memories of Evelyn's and his nightmares of St. Cyprian's for that.

From even this cursory summary it will be evident how rapidly Blair was using up his literary capital. After all, he had chucked teaching only a few months before, and here, in however distorted a form, was the material already being used: no matter that the teacher in question was Miss Hare rather than Mr. Blair. Given his difficulty in inventing a plausible or engrossing plot, and given his determination at the same time to write a novel a year, he really had no choice but to draw upon his own continuing experience, touching it up here, smoothing it down there—mere grist for the fictionist's mill. But at the rate he was going—Burma done, London and Paris underworld done, schoolteaching done, even the gentilities and gossip of Southwold done— he really had no choice but to start acquiring a new set of experiences. He was sitting at his desk writing a novel: that was virtually the sum of his winter and spring activity in Southwold now. As usable capital, to be drawn upon in the future, it was alarmingly meager: was he next to write a novel about a novelist writing a novel in a seaside town out of season? No wonder he was eager to be finished with Dorothy Hare and the awkwardly connected chapters of sordid experience he had imposed upon her, and to be on his way to London. He had set October as the deadline.

His comments as he was writing *A Clergyman's Daughter* grow bleaker the further he gets into it: it was dreadful, it was loathesome, it was awful; reading over the manuscript made him want to vomit. Even as one makes allowances for the conventional exaggeration and discontent of an author in midbook, one senses a malaise here that goes deeper. For him there was really nothing and no one of significance (except his mother) in Southwold any longer. There were only the trivialities of everyday life, as enervating to the spirit as the round that Dorothy Hare was being made to experience in Knype Hill: a hedgehog, small as an orange, turns up in the bathroom; the daily stroll with his mother and the poodle down the High Street to the lighthouse, the landmark of the town, with perhaps a pause, on the walk back, at Avril's tea room; he goes to a film, which his father already has seen and spoils for him (as fathers will) by insisting on telling him the plot beforehand. The significant thing was the departure of Eleanor and Dennis Collings for Singapore—a marriage and a departure that had deprived him of "two friends at a single stroke," as he complained to Brenda, and even she, his other close friend in Southwold, had given up her job at St. Felix and gone to teach at another school, not as far away as Singapore, but no longer as readily available as she had been.

His sense of isolation was almost total. Still, with no significant happenings to engage his emotions or distract him from the daily stint at the typewriter, there was nothing to do but write, which he did—his novel, his reviews for the *Adelphi;* and on the third of October, precisely on schedule, he informed Leonard Moore that he was sending him the completed manuscript of *A Clergyman's Daughter.*

PART TWO

EILEEN

TEN

During his nine months (January to October) of convalescence, creativity, and boredom in Southwold, he had kept in touch with his friends at the *Adelphi*, in particular its editor-proprietor Richard Rees, who came from London for a weekend visit in the summer and found the family house in the High Street perfectly comfortable; Avril and Mrs. Blair, whom he was now meeting for the first time, excellent company; and the elderly father more benevolent and less intransigent than the son had allowed him to believe. Throughout these nine months of exile, Eric, while writing his next novel as George Orwell, had continued to be a frequent contributor to Rees's magazine, always, it will be remembered, in his own person—that is, as Eric Blair. Now that the time was finally at hand—health recovered and novel finished—for his next move, the *Adelphi* connection led directly to a job and a place to live.

There had never been a question of his remaining in Southwold. At this period in his life London was where he wanted to be. "Coming to London" was a strategic move for a young writer whose career was in its early postapprentice phase—so, for example, Rayner Heppenstall from Yorkshire and Dylan Thomas from Wales, both of whom Blair was soon to meet under Rees's auspices, were arriving in London and writing for the *Adelphi* at almost the same time as he. But the fact that he was still making professional use of both his pen name and his own name suggests some uncertainty in his mind as to the nature of the career he meant to pursue: a writer, yes; but beyond that, a realistic novelist? or a poet and man of letters, at ease with French Romanticism and medieval Catholicism (on both of which he wrote for the *Adelphi*) or whatever else an editor, usually Rees, sent his way? (In fact, for George Orwell—if not for Eric Blair, whose signed work terminates at the end of 1934—a literary career could and did include a wide variety of genres, far more than he must have contemplated, starting out. In his own fashion he was to prove almost as versatile a writer, if not as prolific, as his sometime master of French at Eton, Aldous Huxley. And in Orwell's career, as in Huxley's, the poet and realistic novelist ultimately would give way to the fabulist and polemicist.)

In August, still in Southwold, Eric was informing Brenda Salkeld that it would choke him to live in Bayswater, where a friend had offered him a lease of part of a flat, and which must have figured for him as a London version of Knype Hill (or Southwold). His preference, he told her, was for "somewhere in the slums." When she took this to mean a return to the common lodging houses and squalor of three years back, he hastily explained that his intention was nothing so drastic: simply, he wanted to avoid a respectable quarter. At that moment, Islington seemed a likely possibility.

But once he came up to London, he was to live from mid-October 1934 until August 1935 in Hampstead, where respectability and the Bohemian life are blended in an altogether congenial and very English way: he was anywhere but in the slums.

At that time in Hampstead, at No. 1 South End Road, there was a secondhand bookshop with the Knype-Hillish name of Booklovers' Corner. Its owner, Francis G. Westrope, a Welsh pacifist and friend of the *Adelphi* people, mentioned to Rees's co-editor, Max Plowman, that he was looking for an assistant to work in the shop afternoons. For mornings he already had a young man named Jon Kimche. (Kimche would later become well known as a writer on Jewish and Middle Eastern affairs, and editor of the *Jewish Observer and Middle East Review*.) Plowman mentioned the job to Rees, who thought immediately of Blair, just up from Southwold and staying with the Fierzes until he found some way to support himself. Here, surely, was a lucky find for a writer in need of money, whose chief aim was to have as much free time as possible for his writing—which had not been the result when he was a schoolmaster—especially since, in addition to a small salary, Westrope would include, rent-free, a furnished room in the family flat, directly round the corner from the shop. Rees promptly mentioned the job and its attractive perquisite to Blair. It did appear to solve both his working and living problems simultaneously, and he went round to be interviewed by Westrope, who hired him on the spot.

Two days later Eric moved from the Fierzes' house in Golders Green to the small block of flats in Pond Street that bore the rather too grandiose name of Warwick Mansions. Mabel came along with him to help him settle in, and to inspect the dim furnished room with its view of the backs of the row of shops in South End Road. Privately she thought it a bit dingy, which of course would not disqualify it in Eric's eyes, but she kept her counsel; at the least it promised a fair amount of independence and privacy. And the neighborhood itself was agreeably villagey, with large trees all along the rising slope of Pond Street, an attractive terrace of perhaps-Georgian houses adjoining Warwick Mansions, and directly in front of Booklovers' Corner, a small triangle with benches where passersby might contemplate the fountain and horse trough a civic-minded Miss Crump had caused to be erected in 1880.

As for the job itself, it seemed to Mrs. Fierz, as it had to Rees and even to Blair, pleasant in prospect, making small demands and ideally suited to someone of bookish temperament. Alas for optimism and fine beginnings! Although he was at Booklovers' Corner some fifteen months, he grew to loathe it, and in the novel he would be writing at this time, *Keep the Aspidistra Flying*, he described it, or revenged himself upon it, with acerbity and wit and spleen—also, according to Kimche, with a good deal of exaggeration.

Since Kimche's hours to clerk were between nine-thirty and two, and Blair's between two and six-thirty, they were, in a manner of speaking, ships passing in midocean, with barely time to semaphore a message of sympathy and good will before disappearing over the horizon. But Blair had the key to the shop, and would come down after making his breakfast to open the door and wait for Kimche's arrival, and they would talk a bit then before he went back to his room to begin his morning's writing. When he returned after lunch, for his own stint in the shop, he and Kimche would talk a bit again.

Gradually a kind of friendship—the Blairian kind, affable but reserved—developed between the two young clerks with literary ambitions, though in this respect Blair was much ahead, for he had already published two books (the second, admittedly, only in America thus far), he had just finished a third, and was starting work on his fourth. Sometimes he would invite Kimche to come round to his room in

Warwick Mansions (and to the bed-sitter to which he would presently move), where he held a sort of court. His circle of acquaintances had begun to widen, drawn from Sunday afternoons at the Fierzes', Wednesday evenings at the Sturge Moores', casual visits to Rees's flat in Cheyne Walk (which was now also being used as the *Adelphi* office), and the occasional evening in Soho with Rees—it was in those circumstances, early in 1935, when they were having dinner in Bertorelli's in Charlotte Street, that Rees would introduce him to Heppenstall and Dylan Thomas. Evidently his social life was a good deal less circumscribed and more enjoyable than the life he permitted to Gordon Comstock, the angry young man and anti-hero of *Keep the Aspidistra Flying*, who is sometimes thought, erroneously, to be a portrait from life of the author himself. But whether in a group or with an audience of one, Blair tended to hold forth on subjects on which he held firm views, a favorite in the autumn of 1934 being the baleful influence of the Roman Catholic Church. And for all his affability, he did tend to address one, so Kimche remembers, as if one were a student in a lecture room, or a recruit on the inspection line at a Burma Police parade.

In November 1936, several months after he had given up his job at Booklovers' Corner and only a month before he was to leave for Spain, Orwell published in the *Fortnightly* his brief and generally even-tempered "Bookshop Memories." Here, as in the much more caustic first chapter of *Keep the Aspidistra Flying*, which Gollancz had published in April of that year, he describes the haphazard visitors, intruders, browsers, time-wasters, would-be shoplifters, and occasional customers he had had to put up with in the shop. They ranged along a spectrum from the rare person who knew and cared about books to the "not quite certifiable lunatics," of whom, as he remarks, there are always "plenty . . . walking the streets, and they tend to gravitate towards bookshops." But from this heterogeneous, even lurid, catalogue of bookshop types there is a significant omission in the light of his own experience: namely, the women a male clerk such as himself was in a position to become acquainted with, first as a clerk, then as a friend, moving from the dusty precincts of the shop to the world outside, and with whom, if circumstances were favorable, he might eventually embark upon a "relationship" of considerable intensity. This, for Orwell the author and Blair the man, was the chief reward of working at Booklovers' Corner.

As we have already suggested, his experience of women thus far in his life—he had celebrated his thirty-first birthday in June—seems to have been meager and belated, and it was reflected in those stumbling attempts at female portraiture in his first two novels: in *Burmese Days,* the stereotyped Elizabeth Lackersteen (blond, cold, English, and snobbish) whom Flory loved in vain, and the stereotyped Ma Hla May (dark, spicy, Burman, and vicious) whom he took to his bed; and in *A Clergyman's Daughter,* the hapless Dorothy Hare, implausibly pressed into service as the author's surrogate. Now, thanks to two women he met at Booklovers' Corner—one succeeding the other as object to be pursued, though there was some overlap for a time and he continued seeing them both—his experience was considerably enlarged, broadened, and deepened. (Love itself he had still to experience, for though they were fond of him, neither of these two women was in love with him, nor he with them.) Meanwhile the literary consequence of these new "relationships" made itself evident in the novel he was writing precisely while they were in progress. Rosemary, the heroine of *Keep the Aspidistra Flying,* drawn from his experiences rather than his fantasies of women, is an achievement he had never managed before: a credible female portrait.

The first of the two women—each of whom recognizes aspects of herself in Rosemary, and both of whom were kind enough to see the authors of the present work and share their memories of Eric Blair as they knew him in 1934/1935—was Sally; the second was Kay.

The daughter of an American mother and a South African father of European descent, Sally had been brought up in the south of England in conventional, traditional middle-class circumstances—"boarding school and all that"—and although she felt that she and Eric were, temperamentally, both "odd people out," she was essentially a girl of her class. The point is worth emphasizing, for it holds true of all Orwell's women, then and later: they all came from the middle class—say, from middle-middle to middle-upper-middle, to borrow Orwell's own gradations, with Orwell himself in the lower-upper-middle. Whatever compulsions drove him to explore the lower depths, to go down and out, they stopped short of urging him towards women of the working class or below: there was no hint of *nostalgie de la boue* in that particular, nor of a missionary impulse such as inspired George Gissing, a novelist Orwell especially admired, and made Gissing's life, unlike Orwell's, a misery. Orwell's ladies, one and all, were ladies who might have been introduced without embarrassment to Mrs. Vaughan Wilkes, the headmistress of St. Cyprian's.

A commercial artist and illustrator, Sally was twenty-seven ("But holding on to her girlishness," as she puts it) when she first met Eric. This would have been towards the end of 1934. At the time, she was working for an advertising agency (see Rosemary in *Keep the Aspidistra*), but in retrospect she makes no claim to having supplied Eric with the details about advertising or agency routine that are scattered through the novel—"Hardly necessary, do you think? Anyone who looks at a newspaper or magazine could invent that sort of thing, the slogans and the rest of it." She lived in Hampstead, in the vicinity of Booklovers' Corner, and came into the shop late one afternoon in search of a copy of *The Decameron*—there was a possibility, which never materialized, of her doing an illustrated edition. She returned to the shop for further books, and after the second or third time, she and Eric were on chatting terms, friendly enough for him to ask her name and where she lived.

Discovering that they were neighbors made it easy for him to suggest that they have dinner together, which they did, and soon they were seeing each other quite frequently and continued to do so, in spite of a basic disagreement that was never resolved, for more than a year. He would have her come to his "evenings"; he brought her round to the Fierzes' (as he would presently also do with Kay); they went on an excursion to Brighton; they had dinner fairly often at local restaurants, where he kept up a constant complaint about having no money, but was adamant (as he had been with Ruth Pitter) in not allowing her to share the bill (and as Gordon Comstock would be with Rosemary). At their dinners they drank lots of chianti, which she thought fine and he thought sordid. That they couldn't afford a better wine—having lived in Paris, he was something of a wine snob—was simply one more proof, like his being obliged to work in a bookshop, that the world was awful. In his conversation he was very much the ambitious, nonstop, hardworking professional writer (which indeed he was, unlike Gordon Comstock with his single slender published volume of verse, *Mice*, and the long poem he worked at fitfully but never finished). Politics, after 1936 a ruling passion in his life, figured in his conversation then almost not at all, except for an occasional disparaging reference to William Morris and Socialism—no matter that he was *pro forma* a Socialist himself. But at this time, early in 1935, his view of the world was more solipsistic than Socialistic; his concerns were chiefly with himself and his deprivations: the wine he wanted and couldn't have; the literary success he wanted and didn't have—would it come with his next novel, or with the serial he was thinking of writing?—and, most vexingly, so far as the immediate moment was concerned, the woman he wanted, Sally herself, and was not to have. That, of course, was the basic disagreement between them.

The difficulty was that Sally knew what *she* wanted, not marriage especially, for she thought of herself as a woman of advanced ideas, but a Grand Romantic Passion, and early on she recognized that Eric was not that. She felt that he regarded her, and women in general, as "a plate of greens," which she had no intention of being or of serving up to him. So while she was prepared to go back with him to his room—no ogre barred the door as in the Gordon/Rosemary story—and was prepared to indulge in playful kisses and caresses, a line was drawn and adhered to, prompting a good deal of quarreling, and from him the ultimate period epithet, that she was a "Victorian." Nevertheless, they continued to see each other for more than a year, even after he had met and was frequently seeing another woman, Kay, who was more amenable than Sally, and even after he'd met a third woman, Eileen, with whom he fell instantly in love, though that epochal encounter did not deter him for some months further from continuing to see both Sally and Kay, all three separate relationships being maintained simultaneously. One does have an impression of Blair on a carousel in this almost Schnitzlerian season of his early thirties, making up enthusiastically and adroitly for time lost in his early twenties.

However pleasurable, vexing, tantalizing, satisfying, and educational the pursuit of women might be, he was concerned even more with the literary pursuit: his determination to become a writer—what Richard Rees described to us in conversation as "Blair's obsession." So it followed naturally that in those first months in London in the autumn of 1934 he would be preoccupied above all with the fate of the novel he had just completed, *A Clergyman's Daughter*, and the future of the as-yet-untitled novel he had just begun. His experiences with *Down and Out* and with *Burmese Days*—the latter still to be taken by a publisher in England—would make him wary of optimism in any case. He knew now, as he had not known two years earlier, that between sending a novel to a publisher and a publisher's accepting the novel, much could intervene, usually of a frustrating nature. But in the case of *A Clergyman's Daughter*, he was especially uneasy because he believed that what he had written fell short of being a truly successful novel: "It was a good idea, but I am afraid I have made a muck of it."

Moore, as an efficient agent with a manuscript to place by an author of proven talent, was not put off by his client's regrets and self-depreciatory judgments—they were as much a part of his "style" as another author's exuberant egotism. After all, only two years before, Blair had made an impressive start as George Orwell with *Down and Out in Paris and London*. That book had sold well enough for him to be remembered by booksellers, and certainly he would not be overlooked by reviewers such as Compton Mackenzie, who had so conspicuously "invested" in him. Although Gollancz, on the advice of lawyers, had rejected *Burmese Days*, and in so doing had forfeited official option rights to the author's future work, it occurred to Moore that he might be strongly attracted to the "down-and-out" aspects of this new, and so far as English readers were concerned, this "first" novel by George Orwell. Accordingly he sent the manuscript to Gollancz, from whom in early November came a qualified acceptance. There were the inevitable complaints that portions of the book were libelous, and there were passages marred by obscenity—all of which would have to be attended to. But other, more serious objections were raised, chief among them that Dorothy's grim-to-grotesque experiences as a teacher at Mrs. Creevey's School were thought to be incredible. However—and this was the crucial point— Gollancz wanted to publish the novel, and would do so if the author was amenable to making changes.

From Warwick Mansions, having received the essentially good but peripherally irritating news, Blair wrote to Moore in mid-November. His mood was at once despondent and docile. He had feared all along that there might be difficulties with the publication of the book, which he himself seemed to value for a few of its parts rather than as a whole. But it was precisely for those few parts that he was anxious that it be published, and therefore he was prepared to revise. The libel and the obscenity (swear-words) presented no problems at all. Still, he did need to know specifically what was wanted done before setting to work, and with that in mind he asked that Moore arrange an interview for him with Gollancz—an hour, he thought, should be sufficient to decide upon the revisions.

About the adverse reactions to the school scenes he was both amused and bruised. When first sending the manuscript to Moore, he had emphasized that the school was imaginary, and this was not merely a precautionary declaration. Indeed, he admitted that a fault in the novel was that it was "rather unreal." Much of what is described as happening at Mrs. Creevey's School belongs to the world of caricature and nightmare, though when Dorothy makes suits of armor for the school play, struggling with wrapping paper and glue, she suffers precisely the same agonies that Blair had suffered in precisely the same situation at Evelyn's. But whether or not the particular school in the novel was invented or faithfully described, he was sure that there were still beastly abuses in the private schools in general— he had suffered them himself only twenty years before at his own school, St. Cyprian's, even though it was so much grander and more respectable than Mrs. Creevey's, at the very top of that particular heap—and to say, as Gollancz's incredulous readers had done, that such abuses had been ended thirty or forty years ago, was simply an easy way of dismissing them from one's mind and conscience. Still, though he claimed to be willing to tone down the details a little, and presumably did so, the picture of Mrs. Creevey's School as it appears in the published novel is, at the least, "rather unreal," and it is hard to think what it must have been like before revisions. One has only to compare the fictional Mrs. Creevey's with the actual Frays College to realize how ill-judged it is to read this portion of the novel as though it were a factual account.

Which is not to claim that Blair did not hate teaching, which so interfered with his writing; hated it at the deeper levels of his being, while outwardly he appeared to be enjoying himself at Frays, just as he was soon to hate being a clerk in a bookshop. If, as we have seen, he drew upon details of his own experience as a schoolmaster to produce an air of verisimilitude, it was hatred, festering within and bubbling to the surface, that compelled him to exaggerate and undermined his credibility. Hatred, rancor, and unforgiving responsiveness to pain in whatever form (the social wound and the battlefield wound)—all these can be animating forces for the writer, and were to be so for Orwell throughout his career. In the novels before 1936, especially in *A Clergyman's Daughter* and *Keep the Aspidistra Flying*, such forces tend to turn inward. The result is a subjective response to private experience: the nightmare that mistakes itself for a true account of life as it is. But once these forces that were so much a part of his nature could be turned outward, and he could concern himself with the plight of *others*, identify with the existence of others, objectify the angers that stirred him and transmute them into a concern for others, which he began to do in 1936 in *The Road to Wigan Pier* and in "Shooting an Elephant," his identity as a writer would come into sharp focus: he would be truly Orwell.

But on the fourteenth of November 1934, writing to Leonard Moore, he was still "yours sincerely, Eric A. Blair," and what concerned him was a flaw in the structure of *A Clergyman's Daughter* that he did not think could be corrected. In his letter to Moore, he fails to identify the flaw; but whatever it might be, it had not bothered him until now because he hadn't meant the novel to be read as a realistic account (as the people at Gollancz were reading it), nor to be judged on that basis. This would seem to contradict his position of a month before when he acknowledged as a fault of the book its being "rather unreal"; yet he could hardly pretend to himself that much of his subject matter was not drawn from his own experience, faithfully recorded, in the hop-picking episode literally so. True, the novel does contain a slightly *expressionist* interlude, the night scene in Trafalgar Square, told entirely in dialogue, which most critics have accepted as written under the influence of *Ulysses*, as it strives for the intensity one associates with poetry rather than prose—and with Joyce rather than Orwell. But most of *A Clergyman's Daughter* has the specificness of detail that is characteristic of the English novel even when it is crossing the border of nightmare and fantasy. If his novel was being read as a kind of document of experience—as his generally straightforward style invites one to do—Blair may have decided that the flaw was his failure to provide any details of the missing five days in Dorothy's life, not even a shadowy explanation of how she got from Knype Hill to London and what happened to her on the way. This is a conspicuous omission, certainly; and assuming that it is the "flaw," one wonders why he should have thought it could not be corrected—unless his imagination simply did not take in and respond to the intimate details of female existence, of female degradation.

He met with Gollancz later that week. Everything went smoothly enough between them so that he could tell Moore that a month's time would be sufficient for the revisions and changes wanted. A month later, on Christmas eve, he sent off to Gollancz the novel in its final form, and was through with it. Once again he began to suffer something like the despondency he felt after he had given the twice-rejected manuscript of *Down and Out* to Mabel Fierz and told her to "Read it, burn it, and keep the clips." For he announced to Moore that if Gollancz decided not to publish this revised version, he would extract from the manuscript the one chapter that he liked—presumably the night scene in Trafalgar Square—and try to have it published separately in a magazine. As for the rest of it, the implication was clear: he would simply throw it away. But such drastic action was not necessary. Less than a month later Gollancz had decided that he would definitely publish *A Clergyman's Daughter,* and his terms were so good as to elicit from Blair the rueful comment, "I am afraid he is going to lose money this time, all right."

That was in mid-January. Immediately the wheels began to turn, at a rate that reminds us again how much simpler and more efficient publishing was in the old-fashioned 1930's than at present, after four decades of technological advance. Proof copies existed and were sent out for comments to the famous before the end of February;* bound copies of the finished book were in hand the first week in March; and the official publication day was March 11, 1935.

Pleased Orwell undoubtedly was to have the book published, and pleased at the terms Moore had secured for it. He was also pleased when Gollancz in mid-February reopened the question of publishing *Burmese Days* and soon had agreed to do so. But he could not persuade or deceive

* Sending advance copies of a book for flattering comment is a tradition of the trade that continues unabated in the 1970's, even though the proportion of replies is discouragingly low. One famous writer to whom the publicity people at Gollancz sent *A Clergyman's Daughter,* along with the traditional polite letter hoping for a laudatory sentence or two, was Sean O'Casey. He declined to comment at the time, but the request seems to have lingered in his mind, and he finally did make a comment in 1954, in his autobiography, *Sunset and Evening Star.* "They were sure the scene in Trafalgar Square was one of the most imaginative pieces of writing they had ever read—equal to Joyce at his best," he recalls. Then, with evident relish: "Orwell had as much chance of reaching the stature of Joyce as a tit has of reaching an eagle." O'Casey was convinced that his refusal to comment favorably on *A Clergyman's Daughter* was the reason for Orwell's unfavorable review of his own book, *Drums under the Window,* in the *Observer* many years later—a fine example of authorial paranoia, a state of mind from which Orwell himself was known occasionally to suffer.

himself, then or later, that he was pleased with *A Clergyman's Daughter*. Sending a copy to Brenda Salkeld four days before publication, he assured her, "It is tripe, except for chap. 3, part 1 [the night scene in Trafalgar Square], which I am pleased with, but don't know whether you will like it." Did she like it? Years later she spoke of *A Clergyman's Daughter* without enthusiasm—it had never been one of her favorites among his works, she said.

Gollancz published the novel in an edition of 2000 copies, and it was widely noticed in a gamut extending from the *Sunday Times* to the nonconformist *British Weekly*. Compton Mackenzie predictably led the van in the *Daily Mail*. As enthusiastic as when he had reviewed *Down and Out* just two years before, he had recourse yet again to the Dantean allusion, warning that "the book should be avoided by all readers who lack the courage to descend to the innermost circle of the social inferno. . . . [It] chastens without revolting, horrifies without disgust. . . . By telling the story through the medium of a woman Mr. Orwell has secured a perfect objectivity, and thereby avoiding conveying an impression that he is once more exploiting his own experiences in the guise of fiction . . . definitely a novel, and a very fine novel at that."

Other reviewers were more restrained. Bonamy Dobrée, in the *Morning Post*, while he thought "The description of a night in Trafalgar Square . . . unforgettable," extracted a social moral from the text that one suspects was not present in the author's mind when he wrote it: "A patchy book, at times brilliant, which raises the question of the position of the clergy in outlying districts."

The young V. S. Pritchett, in what must be the first of many perceptive attentions he was to pay Orwell over the years, gave the book second place in the fiction column in the *Spectator*. He was rather taken with Dorothy, enough to think her quite badly treated by her creator. The satire, Pritchett felt, was essentially "a whip for the vicarages," and in the circumstances it was not surprising that the "plain, obstinate, stoical and delightful Dorothy at last breaks down," though he was constrained to add that "one does not believe that she would not have put up a more intelligent fight." About the episode in Trafalgar Square, unlike Dobrée, he had his reservations: "This scene shows an immense knowledge of low life, its miseries, humours and talk, but unfortunately has been written in 'stunt' Joyce fashion that utterly ruins the effect."

In the *New Statesman and Nation,* the novel was one of eight reviewed together by Peter Quennell, who found it ambitious and unsuccessful. He, too, raised objections to the Trafalgar Square episode ("would be more impressive if it were less reminiscent of the celebrated Nighttown scenes at the end of *Ulysses*") and his final judgment was that "We have no feeling that [Dorothy's] flight from her home and her return to the rectory have any valid connection with the young woman herself."

There was a rather patronizing review from L. P. Hartley in the *Sketch,* who complained that the book was "hardly constructed at all," and then paid Orwell a double-edged compliment: "It is not a work of art, but it is worth reading for its vivid, if overcolored pictures of certain unfamiliar aspects of social life."

So it went: a characteristic English reception for a not especially notable novel, with here and there the usable quotation—"A brilliantly clever, brilliantly disagreeable book" (Sylvia Lynd, *Harper's Bazaar*); "Interesting and exciting reading" (*Times Literary Supplement*)—along with a fair amount of caviling.

Reviewers, especially of fiction, have only so much space and time at their disposal: novels arrive in alarming quantities from publishers each week. Even writers as gifted as Pritchett and Quennell, faced with the impossible problem of the omnibus review, must be done before they have hardly begun, to make room for the next novel awaiting its turn. It could be argued that Orwell was fortunate to be paid as much attention as he was, the more so as it became apparent that he was going over ground that in many respects he had already covered in his first book. (From this point of view it is regrettable that *Burmese Days* hadn't followed directly upon *Down and Out* in England, showing a broader range for Orwell as a writer and defusing the argument that he could only do "down and out.") But having made all allowances for the difficulties imposed upon the London book reviewer practicing his trade, it must also be added that the most pertinent and valuable review would not appear until the novel was published in America more than a year later, with a slight change of title as *The Clergyman's Daughter*.

Only the streak of quixotry that makes publishing so odd a business can explain the American publication at all. Harpers', in spite of having failed twice with Orwell, decided to try once more, though there was nothing in the English reviews to suggest they would fare any better this time than before—unless, perhaps, the notion of a novel of a *woman* going down and out might titillate readers who had hitherto been obstinately indifferent. But having been twice burnt, Harpers' in the matter of *A Clergyman's Daughter* behaved cautiously as well as quixotically, and at a very stately pace. It was not until December 1935 that they decided they would import 500 sewn sets of sheets (that is, unbound books) from Gollancz—rather than go through the more expensive process of printing it in America—for which they would pay a royalty of 1/10½d a copy, and Gollancz accepted the offer. Publication was scheduled for August 1936. In July, when there appeared to be a shade more interest in the bookshops than Harpers' had anticipated, they asked for another 500 copies from Gollancz, but it was too late. By then, some fifteen months after the novel had been published, the first printing of 2000 copies had been sold; no second printing had been called for; and the type had been distributed. Harpers' solved the problem by acquiring a further 500 copies by photographic process, and for these they agreed to pay a royalty of fifteen cents a copy, terms Moore readily accepted. This meant 1000 copies were available in America; more than were needed, as it turned out, for 256 copies ultimately were remaindered. A *Clergyman's Daughter* was the last book by George Orwell to be published in an American edition until *Animal Farm* in 1946.

Such facts and figures, while dismal to contemplate, have little relation either to the quality of the book itself, or to its critical reception, which, generally speaking, was enthusiastic or reserved in a way comparable to its reception the preceding year in England. But the review by the young poet and novelist Vincent McHugh, which appeared in the *New York Herald Tribune Books*, deserves to be singled out, for it must be the first in which Orwell's affinities with George Gissing, the late-nineteenth-century writer he so greatly admired, are recognized and declared.

"The motto for this novel," McHugh began, "might have been taken from George Gissing's reflection on 'the life which is not lived for living's sake as all life should be, but under the goad of fear.'" Poor Dorothy Hare, with "her faith and her almost gallant drudgery," living a life that in all its turnings has fear as its base, is the heroine of "a minor novel in Gissing's tradition, a shade more lively as to tone, rendered in a quiet, fluent texture which has a way of making detail count, and garnished with modest incidental ironies."

McHugh had a fine awareness of Orwell's difficulties with characterization and structure—"Dorothy's peregrinations have been arranged more to bring the author's various materials into play than to set up an internal pattern for her life. Perhaps for this reason she remains a little indistinct. . . ."—and an equally fine awareness of the skill with which he evokes the village of Knype Hill, "so minutely and with such honest grimy detail that it becomes almost a new picture. . . ." No small feat, since McHugh felt constrained to add that by this time "The English village has been chronicled almost to extinction."

But his aim was not simply to award a reviewer's pluses and minuses, but to place the novel in a particular tradition, that of Dickens and Gissing:

Mr. Orwell too writes of a world crawling with poverty, a horrible dun flat terrain in which the abuses marked out by those earlier writers have been for the most part only deepened and consolidated. In all his characters . . . there is the present equivalent of that sense we have been accustomed to think of as Victorian: the subjectively unquestionable, even remotely comforting conviction of the eternity of English social forms. It was this belief which lay at the root of what has been called Gissing's "pessimism"—the rigid round of custom, the loneliness, the causeless ennui. And it is precisely this almost unrecognized social compulsion by instilled pattern which determines Dorothy Hare's final decision that it would be best to take up once more the service of a church she no longer believes in.

McHugh was at his most prescient in his final paragraph, especially if one remembers that the year was 1936—decades before Orwell was to become a subject for critical explication—and that he knew nothing of the author beyond the two books of his that he had read (the other was *Down and Out*) and what he inferred from them:

> It may be that the theme of *The Clergyman's Daughter* has the extra value of an ironic symbol unnoted by its author. The stages of Dorothy's plight—the coming to herself in the London street, the sense of being cut off from friends and the familiar, the destitution and the cold—enact an almost perfect dream-logic for the secret nightmare of that lower middle-class she had come from: the nightmare in which one may be dropped out of respectable life, no matter how debt-laden or forlorn, into the unthinkable pit of the beggar's hunger and the hopelessly declassed.

Whether or not Orwell noted the ironic symbolism of which McHugh speaks one can't answer with certainty—there are no contemporary diaries or journals to call upon, and his comments on the novel are brief, disparaging, and uncommunicative—but there is no doubt that the nightmare itself was one with which he had been made familiar from the time that he was a schoolboy at reduced fees at St. Cyprian's, threatened with the consequence of failure on the scholarship exam for Eton: "to go down to the depths of degradation, to be cast out from the charmed circle." That was the logic not only of a dream, but also of life itself, as it had been set forth for him in his childhood.

ELEVEN

Considering that Orwell was a man who yearned to put down roots, there is a special poignancy in the way he was virtually always on the move, never quite coming to rest or at home anywhere for an extended, uninterrupted period, at any time throughout his life. Of all the many addresses that were to be his in his forty-seven years, beginning with Motihari in Bengal, where he was born, and ending with University College Hospital, London, where he died, it seems fair to say that none was to lead to greater happiness for him than 77 Parliament Hill Road in Hampstead, where he lived from March to August in 1935.

On the sixteenth of February, in the course of a letter to Brenda Salkeld, he remarked that he would have to give up his room in Warwick Mansions within a few weeks. "Isn't it sickening," he began, but that was merely a way of speaking, and it would seem that Eric might have given a more circumstantial account had he been so minded. There was no suggestion that he might have some alternative available; when he next wrote, on the seventh of March, replying to a letter of hers, he was already at his new address, 77 Parliament Hill Road, NW 3, with no hint as to how he had happened upon it.

There had been a growing strain with Westrope, not in

the shop, where his work was entirely satisfactory, but in the flat in Warwick Mansions, where his life was not. The proprietor, anticipating a solitary lodger of whose existence one would hardly be aware, was irritated by the considerable and no doubt audible social life being lived in the back bedroom, and the situation was not improved when Mrs. Westrope fell ill. Presently it was agreed that Blair would move elsewhere, though continuing to work in the shop, and his wages would be adjusted upward to take this into account. He was relieved, actually. Except for its proximity to Booklovers' Corner, he hadn't been especially happy with the room, and Mabel, who had disliked it from the first, had a solution to the problem of his finding another place to live as soon as he came to discuss it with her.

Her friend, Rosalind Henschel Obermeyer, whom he would have met at the Fierzes'—a pleasant woman in her early forties, a niece of Sir George Henschel, the conductor and composer, and herself pursuing an advanced course in psychology at University College, London—lived at the top of Parliament Hill, on the very edge of Hampstead Heath. There, Mabel felt, was where Eric should live too: so much healthier, especially considering his weak chest, the next best thing to living in the country itself, and so much nicer than the small back room in Warwick Mansions. Rosalind and her husband were separated; he was traveling in America for an indefinite period, lecturing on philosophy; her flat, very comfortable, light, and airy, was too large for her alone. She might be willing to let out a spare room. Mrs. Fierz remembers saying that she would ring up Rosalind there and then to make sure it was all right, and she did, and it was—in fact, Rosalind had already let a room to a female medical student. But there was one further room that should do nicely, nor would the rent for it be beyond his means, for what Rosalind wanted primarily was to have someone there, someone of the right sort, and Eric, as a rising young author and friend of the Fierzes', obviously qualified.

By the end of February he was comfortably installed in his bed-sitter in Mrs. Obermeyer's first-floor flat. It was a ten-minute walk uphill from Booklovers' Corner, and he had indeed moved upward in every sense, from Warwick Mansions. No. 77, the last house of all in Parliament Hill Road, is a smallish but solid brick structure—it then contained only three flats, one to a floor—built in the later years of the nineteenth century, and overlooking at the back a small garden of its own. It was the sort of house, typical of its style and period, that was meant to suggest a certain degree of affluence and stability, and continues to do so to this day. What made it remarkable was that one stepped from the front door and almost immediately was on the Heath, had only to ascend a knoll and there before one were great grassy stretches of field; clumps of woodland; birds and insects and plants to observe, the life of nature that Orwell would always value; and far in the hazy distance, the panorama of London, unfolding as far as the eye could see. It was a very different country from the land of the aspidistra to which he consigned poor Gordon Comstock.

The flat, arranged in a square around the central staircase, three bedrooms, living room, kitchen, and bath, was large enough and so arranged as to offer privacy as well as comfort. Mrs. Obermeyer, Blair, and Janet Gimson, who was studying medicine at University College, were all occupied with their respective careers—the two women were away weekdays from morning to evening—and there was no attempt to create a bogus family of three. Nor, contrariwise, was there that anonymous, dispiriting atmosphere of the usual respectable furnished flat segmented into rooms to let. Mrs. Obermeyer was anything but the nosy, emotionally impoverished landlady for whom a place has been made in so many realistic novels since Balzac—a monstrous specimen of the stereotype, Mrs. Wisbeach, is exhibited in *Keep the Aspidistra Flying*. From the start she and Blair got on well together: within the month they had progressed from Mrs. Obermeyer and Mr. Blair to a more cordial, even amiable, Rosalind and Eric. But she never failed to recognize that his room was his domain, and the sound of the typewriter behind his closed door meant that he was not to be interrupted.

Similarly, Janet Gimson, living in the room adjoining his and so particularly aware of him at work—out of sight but within earshot—respected his privacy. Indeed it might be more accurate to say (as she herself has said, some forty years on) that this straightforward young woman—who had been Head Girl at Bedales, one of the most progressive Public Schools of the period, and who had just turned twenty-one—was perhaps more indifferent than respectful in her attitude towards Blair. To her he seemed so old— he was past thirty—and looked ill and cadaverous besides, and so (as she thought) almost as much out of things as "Obie"—her nickname for Mrs. Obermeyer—who was over forty! Older than that she couldn't imagine, then. Now, older than that herself by some twenty years and a distinguished physician, she recalls having seen Eric continually, a part of everyday life in the flat, as they would pass through the doors of kitchen and bathroom, and to that degree she was "conscious" of him. But she had no "feeling" about him, one way or another. As she remembers, she was neither in a state nor had the time to pay much attention to Eric, except in a perfunctory way. She had failed her medical exam, the consequence of a romantic attachment that distracted her from her studies and now was ending badly, and she had to work particularly hard to catch up. Even so, there was some social life of a pleasant, low-pressure sort among Eric, herself, and "Obie." They led their separate lives, and the motto of the flat might have been "Do What You Will," but on those occasions when one or another of them would have people in for wine or coffee parties, the others were frequently asked to join in. Characteristically, Mrs. Obermeyer would change for these parties into a flowered tea gown, while Eric came as he was, looking weathered and a bit scruffy, like a perpetual research student who would never take his degree.

As a former Head Girl, Janet tended to be censorious where cleanliness and neatness were concerned: in those respects Eric's room simply would not pass. She thought it then and remembers it still as "filthy." He seems to have been a firm believer in the principle of "sweep it under the carpet" or "move it out of sight." The result of the latter was that forgotten, half-finished boxes of biscuits grew old at the back of his cupboard and were taken over by mice —at night Janet could hear them rustling about; and after Eric moved from Parliament Hill the next summer, she and Obie discovered a family of mice nesting in an extra blanket he had tossed out of sight on the floor of the closet.

The difference between their rooms must have been remarkable to anyone who would notice such things, and not merely because she was neat and he was not. Janet had agreed to take her room unfurnished—an advantage from her point of view—and proceeded over the three and a half years that she lived in "Obie's" flat to fill it sparely but beautifully with furniture of remarkable quality, much of it the work of her great-uncle, Ernest Gimson, perhaps the most famous and gifted maker of furniture in England in this century. Eric's room, by contrast, had been furnished rather higgledy-piggledy with Rosalind's "discards," serviceable still but hardly beautiful—not that it would have mattered to him if they were, for he tended to be loftily or gloomily indifferent to such details in his surroundings. The important thing was that the room was large, and filled with light from the window that looked down on the shrubs in the back garden. Unlike Janet and Rosalind, he had no "view" from his room, though if he opened the window and crawled out on the roof of the adjoining garden shed, he could catch a glimpse of the Heath. The absence of a "Heath view" was not a disadvantage; indeed, if it had been there to look at, gaze at, daydream over, it might have distracted him from the manuscript on his table and the blank sheet of paper in the typewriter. The flat was quiet, and his room excellent to work in. Religiously he did three hours of writing each morning, determined, as he wrote Brenda Salkeld, that this new novel, unlike *A Clergyman's Daughter*, was to be truly a work of art. And in the evenings, when he was not otherwise occupied, he would write again.

Rosalind had arranged the room as a bed-sitter, so that he could and soon would entertain there: no restrictions were placed upon him, he was free (as he hadn't felt himself to be in Warwick Mansions) to do as he pleased, which meant that many evenings were occupied otherwise than with writing. In an alcove curtained off with India-print fabric, he had a gas cooker, the "Bachelor Griller," upon which he cooked deftly, for himself and sometimes for others. Rayner Heppenstall and his friend Michael Sayers, also an aspiring young writer, who shared "two rooms on a top floor in Kilburn at a combined rent of ten shillings a week," were asked to dinner in Parliament Hill. Heppenstall, describing the occasion in his memoir *Four Absentees*, recalls that "Blair cooked for us himself. He gave us a very good steak, and we drank beer out of tree-pattern mugs, which he was collecting."

Evidently these aesthetic appurtenances made a greater impression upon Heppenstall than upon Janet Gimson, who would have been less likely than he to be impressed by a collection of tree-pattern mugs and has no memory of them; indeed, there were many other niceties of Blair's style of living that struck Heppenstall as unusual, not to say unforgettable, yet that to another eye might have seemed commonplace. He remembers (again in *Four Absentees*) that when they would meet in restaurants, Eric "would order red wine, feeling the bottle and then sending it away to have the chill taken off, a proceeding by which I was greatly impressed. I had never seen it done in France, but then," Heppenstall adds, "my French experience, like most of my English experience, had been provincial, while Eric had worked as a *plongeur*, long after he had learned how to order up a bottle of *vin ordinaire*." But, as we shall presently see, there were between Blair and Heppenstall significant little failures to connect, such as Eric's believing that red wine was better drunk "unchilled," the differences of age, of background, of experience, and of attitudes towards life, art, drink, and each other, which would affect the course of their friendship as it moved through 1935 and into the future.

A more frequent guest in the bed-sitter than Heppenstall or Sayers was Eric's new girl, Kay, who had not so much replaced as been given a place alongside or perhaps to the front of Sally on the carousel. Typically, and in this instance quite sensibly, he was at pains not to introduce the one to the other. As Kay wrote to the present authors, "he compartmentalized his women friends so much that one only met one's predecessors or successors by accident, mostly elsewhere than with him."

Like Sally, Kay had wandered into Booklovers' Corner —she too lived nearby—and there the friendship had its beginning, progressing fairly rapidly from bookshop to tea room to restaurant to theater to Parliament Hill. Unlike Sally, she had no fantasy to come between them of a "Grand Romantic Passion," certainly not with Eric, about whom she entertained no illusions or expectations. She was another who felt he did not understand women very well and was afraid of being committed to anyone. Since her own wish was to be independent, this posed no problem, and a fondness developed between them, a kind of intimacy without depth. They agreed, however, that if either of them found "someone else," they would not hesitate to say so; and in the summer of 1935 he did tell her of his feelings for Eileen. Thereafter she saw him less and less frequently, like Sally gradually fading out of the picture, and they met for a last time several months before he and Eileen were married. It was an amicable but complete severance, although she wrote to him after the publication of *The Road to Wigan Pier* to object to the more extravagant generalizations and assertions of its second part, wherein he set forth his own idiosyncratic views of Socialism, past, present, and future—a not uncommon reaction among readers, beginning with Victor Gollancz, who published the book.

This is virtually to end the story before it got under way.

They happened to meet in Booklovers' Corner, but they might as easily have met first in Richard Rees's flat in Cheyne Walk, for Kay, who had literary aspirations, in the fashion of the time had struck out on her own, and supported herself by running a small typing and secretarial service which did a good deal of work for the *Adelphi*. Hence her acquaintance with Rees, whom she saw quite often (sometimes in company with Eric) and whom she thought exceptionally nice.

"Nice," let it be said, was not the first word that would have come to Kay's mind to describe Eric when she knew him, nor did it occur to her, first or last, when she sat down to talk about him some forty years later. He was too prickly to be nice, too cynical, too perverse, too contradictory, too paradoxical, a strange mix of shyness and assertiveness, endowed with a fundamental honesty and common sense that she never questioned, along with small-minded envies and prejudices that she did not hesitate to call into question. (With no noticeable effect, it must be added; perhaps she took him too seriously, or allowed herself to be baited by his rather malicious sense of humor. Eileen's was evidently the more effective technique: not to rise to the bait and argue, but to smile and ever so gently to lead him on, question by question, until he would have to acknowledge the silliness of his more extreme impromptu pontifications.) What was one to say, for example, to a man who declared that the best proof of Conrad's genius was that women disliked him? Or who saw "conspiracies" everywhere? In the Roman Catholic Church; in the highbrow literary world, where, as he put it in *Wigan Pier*, you succeeded only by "kissing the bums of verminous little lions." Even PEN—that rather innocuous and well-intentioned international organization of writers, of which Kay was a member, and which, at her mild suggestion that he do so, he indignantly refused to join—was not an organization to be trusted. Then there was his dislike of the Scottish—his hatred of them, really—which he justified to her by his aversion to the whisky-drinking Scottish planters he had met in Burma. (Cyril Connolly thought this particular prejudice could be traced back to St. Cyprian's, where the pretty little Scottish boys of good family wore kilts on Sundays and were much in favor with Mrs. Vaughan Wilkes.) So that when Kay proposed taking him to meet her friends Edwin Muir, the distinguished poet, and his wife Willa (together they were the translators of Kafka) at one of their informal "literary evenings," he refused outright, because Muir was Scottish and hence beyond the pale. No matter that, as she reasonably pointed out, Muir was the gentlest of men, no one less like a whisky-spewing planter was to be imagined, and a native of Orkney besides, with a dislike of his own of mainland Scotland. That argument got her nowhere: Eric went on to proclaim a detestation of literary salons, which might have carried more weight had he not been himself a frequenter of Sturge Moore's evenings in Well Walk, an "aesthetical salon" if ever there was one—on two occasions he asked Kay to come with him there, forgetting his earlier declaration. For that matter, his own little evenings of seven or eight people in Parliament Hill were, whatever he might choose to call them, salons of a sort, where the discussion was predominantly literary, with only the briefest of excursions into politics.

In short, he was too inconsistent to be nice. But niceness is not all. Niceness is not necessarily stimulating or exciting, and what drew her to him was his powerful intelligence, his articulateness, his integrity, his sense of literary vocation from which he would not be swerved.

He was at this time, she felt, heart and soul a writer, and his writing took precedence over everything else in his life, including, of course, their own quasi-romantic attachment. What puzzled her then was the envy and resentment that seemed inseparable from the vocation, the more puzzling because in her eyes, as an aspiring writer herself, he was so clearly on the way to being recognized: his poems, essays, and reviews were regularly in print in the best magazines; his books were not merely being published but were conspicuously and favorably noticed. True, he was not yet making much money from them; but did he not claim to despise money? And the writers for whom he had an abiding contempt were the Priestleys and the Walpoles in all their lordly affluence. So that as a grievance it hardly held up. Yet the grievance was there. It was as though he enjoyed thinking himself ignored and a failure—unloved, so to speak.

About his writing itself he was, as one would expect, close-mouthed: intimacy did not bring about a rush of disclosure. He did tell her that, after finishing *A Clergyman's Daughter,* he had begun work on what he intended as a kind of contemporary version of *The Canterbury Tales,* in which the characters would embody the various political views of the day; but he had had to abandon the project because, as he candidly admitted, he did not know enough about politics to write it. Instead, he was now writing a new novel, which he slaved at each morning before starting down the hill to Booklovers' Corner. What he did not tell her was that he was using her, along with Sally, as a model for the character of Rosemary in the novel, and that certain of their experiences were being virtually transcribed in its pages: a painfully embarrassing lunch at a Thames-side restaurant in Maidenhead, when for all his Etonian assurance he was intimidated by the waiter into ordering a much grander meal than either of them wanted or he could afford; a dinner with Richard Rees at the Café Royal, which Eric had insisted upon paying for, during the course of which he got blind drunk, though not, as in the novel, arrested.

Between fiction and reportage the line was becoming increasingly blurred as he had to draw upon more and more recent experience; this at a time when he was determined to write "a work of art." Even so, his powers of imagination are more in evidence in *Keep the Aspidistra Flying* than might have been expected, particularly in the creation of Gordon Comstock, the failed, nonwriting poet who is best understood as the anti-self of George Orwell, the failure he feared he might be but gave no evidence of becoming. Not surprisingly, it was at this time that Rees said of him that he was "doomed to success"—the conjunction of doom and success having their special Orwellian irony.

One does have the sense of his beginning to emerge at this period, if not into the limelight, then out of total obscurity. Before, when he had lived in London or its fringes, and despite a few early literary friendships—with Ruth Pitter reading his first faltering attempts; with Richard Rees opening the doors and pages of the *Adelphi;* with Mabel Fierz introducing him to a variety of types in and around the arts—he had led a sort of isolated, subfusc existence. Certainly he had not figured in the literary life of the capital: from that point of view he had been nobody. Now—let us arbitrarily choose as a date the end of March 1935, a few weeks after the publication in London of *A Clergyman's Daughter*, a few months before the publication there of *Burmese Days*—even though he himself might not think so, he was becoming a small somebody; his pen name, which he was affixing by this time to his articles, poems, and reviews, as well as to his novels, would not be unfamiliar in the literary world. He began to meet more people, began to contribute to more journals, began to enjoy himself more. By the end of the year he would be in a position to live entirely, if frugally, by what he earned as a writer. It was not an altogether unpleasant existence—writing in the morning, clerking in a bookshop in the afternoon, going out in the evening to a cinema or pub or music hall or theater or dinner party or giving an occasional small dinner party of his own—though no trace of its pleasant aspect found its way into the novel he was busily, angrily writing then as a work of art.

One of the very first of his dinner parties in 77 Parliament Hill—and it suggests the widening spectrum of his acquaintance—was for the elderly, white-bearded, skull-capped poet T. Sturge Moore and his daughter Risette, to whose house in Hampstead, 40 Well Walk, he had been introduced some time previously by Mabel Fierz. Mabel herself completed the party that evening. Though the same tree-pattern mugs might make their appearance, and the menu be modest (for there are limits to what one can do on the "Bachelor Griller"), the tone of this dinner would have been a good deal more "serious" than that with Heppenstall and Sayers. To judge from his own account, Heppenstall was then living the life of a rowdy young writer in and out of Bohemian Soho, often in the company of a writer even younger and rowdier than himself, the cherubic-looking Dylan Thomas, recently arrived in London from Wales. T. Sturge Moore was a very different case, a survivor from the aesthetic eighteen-nineties of irreproachable character who still kept in the nineteen-thirties, at least in certain quarters, a most impressive reputation. The

American critic Yvor Winters, for example, writing in *Hound and Horn,* declared: "In my opinion, Mr. Moore is a greater poet than Mr. Yeats." It would be rather like having an Institution to dine.

Frederick L. Gwynn in his study of the poet, significantly titled *Sturge Moore and the Life of Art,* tells us that "in the mid-1930's, 40 Well Walk became a kind of minor Garsington Manor."

Moore and his wife [Gwynn continues] instituted the custom of Friday Evenings at Home, to which writers and artists like George Rostrever Hamilton, John Gawsworth, Christopher Hassall, Owen Lewis, Ruth Pitter, Edward Garrick (Gordon Craig Jr.), and nearer contemporaries like Mona Wilson and John Copely came to read and discuss traditional and experimental art. The house was also a haven for literary men of other lands, and one might meet the Indian Ranjee Shahani or the Chinese Seyuan Shu appreciatively absorbing the host's discourse and hospitality. . . .

Wilfred Gibson's recollection of this period vividly describes the poet

              with snowy beard
And dreaming eyes declaiming a new work
To a hushed circle in his house at Hampstead,
A visionary mosaic of coloured words
That, with a craft, half poet's and half painter's,
Aural and visual, to the inner eye
Revealed in rhythm the old heroic world. . . .

It may be difficult to credit the presence of the author of *The Road to Wigan Pier* at this aesthetical salon in Hampstead. (Even Gwynn's qualifying "minor" hardly seems to cover the realities of Well Walk: there was no pride of lions there comparable to Lady Ottoline Morrell's at Garsington, no D. H. Lawrences, no Virginia Woolfs, no Aldous Huxleys or Lytton Stracheys.) Perhaps Blair was present chiefly as an onlooker and listener to the discussions of "traditional and experimental art," but Adrian Fierz, the son of Mabel and Francis Fierz, recalls attending one such evening in Well Walk with his mother and Eric, where Eric read aloud a sonnet to the company, either Keats's "When I Have Fears That I May Cease to Be" or Milton's "On His Blindness." The important fact is that Eric was there, in Well Walk, fairly frequently—once he even brought his mother, visiting from Southwold, but the event bored her and she slept through most of it—and on sufficiently close terms with the aging poet to lure him out of those aesthetical precincts to come to dinner in Parliament Hill. But that was in the years *before 1936*, when Blair's ambition was still to write a novel that would be a work of art, a decade before Orwell's declaration that nothing he had written since 1936 hadn't been at least implicitly political—in opposition to totalitarianism of the Left or the Right; when he had not yet turned in revulsion against the Life of Art, that is, against his own life as a novelist before 1936, in which politics had played so negligible a part. Orwell as a writer would always need something to stir up his anger, something to be in revolt against: it was the spur that drove him, paradoxically, to his most enduring achievements. If we are to understand the emotional and intellectual impact upon him of the events of 1936 and 1937 in which he participated, we must accept him also as he was in the years preceding them—poetical salon, tree-pattern mugs, and all—however disharmonious with the realities and legends of the later Orwell.

TWELVE

Sometime that spring Eric suggested to Rosalind Obermeyer that they give a party together. An evening was decided upon, each was to invite a group of friends—but when it came to the point, it turned out that Eric had only one friend whom he wished to ask, and that was Richard Rees. Jointly he and Rosalind invited Janet Gimson. The rest of the guests were friends and acquaintances of Rosalind's, the greater number being fellow students of psychology at University College, London. One of these was Elizaveta Fen, a Russian emigrée in her early thirties, who had been living in England for more than ten years, had been married to a scientist at Cambridge, and was later to have a distinguished career as a psychiatrist, translator, and author of memoirs. Another was an attractive young woman whom Rosalind did not know especially well although they often sat next to each other at lectures: her name was Eileen O'Shaughnessy.

Of the party itself, a major event (as it seems to us now) in the life of George Orwell, only a few recollected details survive. This is hardly surprising, for with only one exception those who were present would have had no reason to think it unusual, and Orwell, who knew from the moment of Eileen O'Shaughnessy's arrival that it was, never wrote a word about the occasion, which again is hardly surprising, given his instinctive reticence in personal matters and the highly selective and polemical character of his autobiographical writing.

Mrs. Obermeyer, years after this first meeting of Eric Blair and his future wife, could recall with preciseness a particular detail from the party itself: Eric and Richard Rees standing in front of the fireplace, both of them tall, thin, and ungainly, talking together, glancing at guests as they entered the room and going on with their conversation. Elizaveta Fen, who came to the party with Eileen—they had first met in 1933 and were very close friends—also remembered the two men "draped" at the fireplace, looking, she thought, "moth-eaten and prematurely aged."

Nevertheless, at the first glimpse of Eileen's face across the room, Blair was sufficiently stirred to detach himself from the fireplace to go to be introduced to her. Once, years afterward, attempting to describe the effect upon him of certain phrases in Yeats's poetry—inside the political Orwell there was an aesthete always struggling to get free—he remarked that they "suddenly overwhelm one," and then, as the most powerful comparison he could find, added, "like a woman's face seen across a room." Accepting the remark as one of those "impressions" that have more to tell us about Orwell than Yeats, it would seem to provide a clue to his feelings that spring evening in 1935 at the party in 77 Parliament Hill. Especially in the light of the immediate sequel, it is a reasonable conjecture that Blair was himself overwhelmed then, for when the last guests had departed and he and Rosalind were cleaning and straightening things in the living room, he turned to her—it is the only other detail of that far-off occasion that Mrs. Obermeyer still vividly, exactly remembers—and said, "Eileen O'Shaughnessy is the girl I want to marry."

The next day at University College Eileen sought out Rosalind to thank her for the party: she had enjoyed herself very much. And what, Mrs. Obermeyer recalls asking her, had she thought of Eric Blair? Oh, a very interesting man, full of the most curious and decided opinions, Eileen replied, one of the most interesting men she had met in a long time, and it would be nice to see him again; but whether she did or not, she intended to read his books. This was hardly comparable to Eric's flat-out declaration, but there was a warmth in her tone that was sufficient to kindle Rosalind's matchmaking proclivities. She suggested that Eileen might come to the flat for dinner one evening soon, all very informal: it was understood that Eric would be there too. That dinner, when it took place, was a success. It reinforced him in his conviction that she was the woman he wanted to marry, and her in her conviction of his oddness, his remarkableness—and also his fascination. Walking her to the Hampstead tube station for her long journey home to Greenwich, he suggested they meet again, and she readily agreed. He also, she afterward reported in an offhand way to Elizaveta Fen, "as good as proposed to her."

"What! already?" [Miss Fen] exclaimed. "What *did* he say?"
"He said he wasn't really eligible but . . ."
"And what did you reply?"
"Nothing . . . I just let him talk on."
"What are you going to do about it?"
"I don't know . . . You see, I told myself that when I was thirty, I would accept the first man who asked me to marry him. Well . . . I shall be thirty next year . . ."

"That remark," Miss Fen tells us, "was typical of Eileen. One could never be certain whether she was being serious or facetious." But perhaps in this instance facetiousness was a way of concealing from herself, as well as from her closest friend, the seriousness of what she was already beginning to feel for this very interesting man.

ONE CANNOT EMPHASIZE TOO STRONGLY THE IMPORTANCE OF Eileen O'Shaughnessy in the life of Eric Blair, and hence of George Orwell—indeed, her entrance into his life would hasten the transformation. It was as though, in choosing her that night at Rosalind Obermeyer's, though they did not actually marry until June 1936, he was obeying an injunction of Rilke's that became famous in the 1930's: "You must change your life."

Eileen did not actually *change* him—at thirty-three he was much too set in his manners and habits for her to do anything but accommodate herself to them, which she did quite willingly and with a certain affectionate asperity—but her *influence* upon him was profound, in his life and his work. That being so, it seems both ironic and sad that in the years since her death in 1945 so little attention has been paid her. An unexpected consequence of Orwell's request in his will that no biography of him be written is that his wife should have gradually faded, been obscured, in the perspective of time. Humbling though it may be for a biographer to admit it, a writer will live in his work whether or not a biography of him ever be written, and no matter how much at variance his work may be from the facts of his life. A writer's wife, however—unless by chance she is a writer herself, as capable as he of sustaining her "image"—grows dim and shadowy when there is no biography, inevitably so; she becomes no more in the end than that useful, enigmatic, unilluminating phrase "his wife."

Fortunately we have had the opportunity to talk with a number of Eileen's friends and acquaintances, some of whom knew her as Eileen O'Shaughnessy, others, in the early years of her marriage as Eileen Blair, still others, coming later upon the scene (the wartime years) as Eileen Orwell. From their testimony, generously given, some of it surprisingly vivid—considering how long ago they last saw her—we have materials for at least a partial portrait, and taken together, they are persuasive enough to justify the claim for her importance we are making in these pages.

ORWELL, WHO WAS ENDOWED WITH A SENSE OF SOCIAL PLACE-ment worthy of Proust or Henry James, a quivering enraged responsiveness to who and what and where one was in the English class system, from which he could never quite get free, described himself as coming from the lower-upper-middle class. On a calibrated scale of such distinctions, upper-middle is conspicuously further up, and even lower-upper-middle ranks higher, than mere middle. In lower-upper-middle, who-you-are counted for more than what-you-had, which counted for a great deal in middle— hence the seeming paradox of a prosperous burgher locked firmly into the socially inferior middle class, while an impoverished civil servant or clergyman, making do on an inadequate pension, could cling, however precariously, to his superior social position, in the lower-upper-middle. Within that subtle subclassification, Orwell explained, a fairly wide spread of income was permitted: from two thousand down to three hundred pounds a year. But what happened to the luckless born gentleman who fell below the three-hundred-pound mark? Or the rare eccentric who chose to opt out of his class, and fell down, down to the nether regions below? Where did one land, then, in that decisive tumble? Obviously not in the middle class, for he didn't begin to have enough money to qualify. But not, dropping a notch lower, in the working class either, from which he was debarred by certain ineradicable indicators of class that betrayed him: his accent, for one; a certain authority of manner, for another. It seemed that one was doomed to one's class, as Orwell discovered in his down-and-out explorations: disguised in rags and tatters, he opened his mouth and was recognized at once as a gentleman down on his luck. And, as we shall see, when he journeyed among the coal miners in the North, he had only to speak in that Etonian way of his for them to know him for what he was: not one of them.

The upper-middle class—without lingering any further here over Orwellian subdivisions—included civil and colonial servants, members of the professions and clergy, officers of the army and navy—the respectable center of the nation, above whom (as by right) were the upper class, above whom were the aristocracy. So much for social calibrations! Their usefulness, simply, is that they locate the class background out of which Eric Blair had come, and out of which came Eileen Maud O'Shaughnessy, born in 1905, the daughter of a civil servant (Eric's father had been a colonial servant). Adjusting the calibrator more precisely, one could say that the O'Shaughnessys (Anglo-Irish) were a shade more securely placed than the Blairs (Anglo-Indian) because they were a shade better off.

All this might seem like worrying a trivial matter more than it deserves, were it not for the legends that accrete to Orwell like barnacles to a boat and are as difficult to dislodge. Elizaveta Fen, in the vivid memoir of Eileen she published in the *Twentieth Century* in 1960, begins on a note of understandable indignation:

> Years ago I happened to overhear a youthful admirer of George Orwell telling another young enthusiast with a splutter of excitement: "Here's a man for you—he practices what he preaches: He's married to a woman of the people, and leads the life of a labourer."
> A woman of the people [Miss Fen bursts out]: No two words could be less appropriate in describing Eileen O'Shaughnessy....

Born in South Shields and raised in the North—ultimately the family would settle in London—she was educated at the excellent Sunderland High School. In the autumn of 1924, she entered St. Hugh's College, one of the women's colleges at Oxford. Like most undergraduates—and unlike her adored older brother, Laurence junior, who was a dedicated medical scientist from the beginning—she seems to have been somewhat uncertain as to her particular aim. Perhaps she would teach, and being of a literary bent, possessing a marked gift for storytelling (her friends confirm this) and a lively prose style (her letters reveal this), she decided to read English. In 1927 she received a very good Second, and in the Michaelmas term she took her B.A. Missing her First, however, she gave up all thought of an academic career: either the standards she set herself were unyieldingly high, or, as is probably more likely, the notion of teaching was no more than that—certainly not a dedication comparable to Laurence's—and so could be put aside without regret.

Still, it left a question: what was she to do with herself? In prewar days the question would hardly have arisen. Pretty, and pert, and intelligent, and charming, she would simply have stayed at home and chosen among the suitors who would in due course present themselves. But that was not at all the kind of action, or inaction, that appealed to Eileen—any more than it had to Sally or Kay, the girls she was to supplant in Eric's life—and there was no reason why a bright young woman, just down from Oxford in 1927, shouldn't think of having a career (1927 was also the year when Eric Blair returned from Burma and resigned his commission in the Indian Imperial Police, determined to have a career as a writer). The difficulty—not only for Eileen but for so many young women, and for that matter, for so many young men, down from the ancient universities—was to find a career that would engage her deeply, in which she could put her undoubted gifts to their best use. And that did not happen all at once. Indeed, one has the sense of her floundering in search of a solution for some years.

By choice she was in and out of a succession of jobs, of no special consequence and with no connection from one to the next, which she held briefly (though sometimes as long as a year), which amused her and provided her with a fund of entertaining, sometimes fantastic, stories to draw upon afterwards, and, in much less impressive quantity, with funds to live on—fortunately, like so many young women of her class, she was never wholly dependent on her earnings. (Like so many young men of her class, too—it will be remembered that Eric, during the most arduous years of his long apprenticeship, when his savings from

GEORGE ORWELL

ERIC BLAIR, MABEL FIERZ, AND THE DAUGHTER OF A NEIGHBOR
PICTURE TAKEN BY ELEVEN-YEAR-OLD ADRIAN FIERZ

FRAYS COLLEGE, UXBRIDGE

BLAIR IN THE FIERZES' GARDEN, NURSING A PET RABBIT

AT THE ARAGON FRONT. BLAIR IS STANDING, EILEEN IS SITTING AT HIS LEFT

EILEEN

SALLY **KAY**

Burma were used up, received just enough financial help from his mother and his aunt so as not to have to take a job.)

Eileen began as an assistant mistress at Silchester House in Taplow, in the Thames valley, a girls' boarding school, comfortably housed and set in pleasant grounds that included a playing field and a large swimming pool: evidently a very different sort of establishment from the nightmarish Mrs. Creevey's School that Orwell invented for *A Clergyman's Daughter*. She seems to have enjoyed herself there, "making a humorous study of the species of female who own and staff such schools," but not to the point of staying beyond one term. Her next job, we learn from Elizaveta Fen, was "secretary to a formidable business woman who revelled in reducing all her female staff to tears. Eileen led a successful 'revolt of the oppressed' against her before she walked out in triumph." After this industrial imbroglio, a period of quiet: she became a reader for the elderly Dame Elizabeth Cadbury, a member of the well-known Quaker and chocolate-manufacturing family. Her next job was with the Archbishop's Advisory Board of Prevention and Rescue work—which has a fine Gladstonian ring—presumably, social work among prostitutes. That didn't suit, however, and in 1931 she became the proprietor of an office in Victoria Street, London, for typing and secretarial work, experience that would prove useful to her later when she was helping her brother, and later still her husband, with their manuscripts. But the early years of the Depression were not an ideal time for such a venture (as Kay also discovered), and after a year she closed it down, in favor of free-lance journalism, selling an occasional feature piece to the *Evening News*. However, the work she most enjoyed was helping her brother Laurence, "a brilliant chest and heart surgeon, by typing, proof-reading and editing his scientific papers and books."

At that time Eileen and her mother were sharing a flat and having their differences in Greenwich, while Laurence and his wife, Gwen, also a doctor, were living in Blackheath. But early in 1935 the Laurence O'Shaughnessys moved to Greenwich, to 24 Crooms Hill. It was a large, handsome house, directly across from the park, with more than ample room for Laurence's mother and sister, and thereafter that was where they all harmoniously lived—a tribute to Gwen O'Shaughnessy in particular; from all one can learn, a most intelligent, warmhearted, and understanding lady. Laurence senior had died sometime earlier, with no discernible major effect—with the O'Shaughnessys, as with the Blairs, the father was a subordinate figure. Laurence continued to be his mother's favorite child; and for Eileen, certainly, he was the dominant figure: someone to worship. Perhaps it was merely the example he set of a dedicated, unselfish life, or perhaps he may even have confronted her with the purposelessness of her existence, but by 1934 she could no longer avoid the palpable truth—that her years since leaving Oxford had been largely wasted: the time had come for something better than another inconsequential job.

So it came about that in the autumn of 1934 she enrolled at University College, London, in a two-year graduate program in Educational Psychology that would have led, in the ordinary run of events—preliminary course, thesis, advanced course—to her M.A. degree. It was an atmosphere in which she thrived; her fellow students were anything but dilettantes. Dedicated to their work, they were aiming for careers of one sort or another in psychology. From the first Eileen threw herself into her studies with interest and enthusiasm, urged on by Professor Cyril Burt, who recognized in her a more than ordinary aptitude. She was particularly attracted to intelligence testing in children, and quite early decided upon that as the subject for the thesis she would presently be writing.

Elizaveta Fen—a fellow student who went on, as Eileen did not, to become a professional psychiatrist—met her then for the first time, and has recorded a vivid impression of her:

> She was then 28 years old and looked several years younger. She was tall and slender, her shoulders rather broad and high, giving an impression of a slight stoop. She had blue eyes and dark brown, naturally wavy hair. George once said that she had "a cat's face"—and one could see that this was true in a most attractive sense— it was rather short, soft in outline, the nose slightly up-tilted, the eyes large and round with a look of disarming innocence. Those eyes could dance with amusement, like a kitten's watching a dangling object. Her skin had a milky whiteness, and without makeup her pallor could look unhealthy. She was, in fact, far from strong, but she somehow succeeded in doing more work than many strong women I know.

Elizaveta Fen became one of Eileen's closest friends and continued so until her death. By contrast, John Cohen, now the professor of psychology at the University of Manchester, knew her only as a fellow student. He and Eileen acted as partners in psychological experiments, which are usually conducted by pairs of students, and although he was to lose touch with her after the University College years, he still keeps a vivid recollection of how she looked, and a diagnostic impression of her as "bright, rather tough, could be argumentative and 'provocative.'" Rosalind Obermeyer was yet another fellow student and friend of Eileen's who made a postgraduate career in psychology. It was Rosalind who was responsible, as we have seen, for Eileen's meeting with Eric Blair, and so, albeit unwittingly, for her abandoning the career as a child psychologist in which Elizaveta Fen continues to believe she would have had a notable success. Perhaps so. Certainly there was reason to assume in the early part of her time at University College that Eileen, at last and however belatedly, had found in her study of psychology something to which she could dedicate herself. It is an irony of some importance to literary history, that, having done so, only a few months later she would meet the man to whom she dedicated her life.

Eric's dedication, his obsession, had been declared long before his meeting Eileen: to be a writer, first, always, and last. And so he was: only in *kind* was there a progression— from an "art" writer to a political writer. Falling in love with Eileen, wanting her for his wife—this for him was an additional dedication, not, as in her case where Eric was concerned, an alternative.

The year of their meeting, 1935, the year also of the publication in London of *A Clergyman's Daughter* (March) and *Burmese Days* (June), was the beginning of the most important period in Blair's life, continuing through his return from Spain in 1937. During that time he transformed himself from a self-absorbed, minor novelist with little or no interest in politics to an important writer of fiction and essays who had a view and a vision and a mission. *Keep the Aspidistra Flying*, the novel he was writing in the mornings in 1935—in the afternoons he was still a clerk at Booklovers' Corner—would be the last of the "art" novels. Intending it to be "a work of art," Orwell himself judged it a failure. He may have been too harsh in his judgment: the novel, restored to the canon after his death, has won its admirers, notably Lionel Trilling, who found it "a *summa* of all the criticisms of a commercial civilization that have ever been made." But whether accepted at Trilling's or Orwell's evaluation, *Keep the Aspidistra Flying* has too often come to be read as autobiography in the form of a novel, with wee Gordon a calculatedly shrunken version of the very tall Orwell (Gordon is a mere five feet seven inches) and Rosemary, his girl friend, so a recent reference book would have us believe, "a portrait of Orwell's wife, Eileen." Part of the misapprehension must be blamed on Orwell himself: his habit of drawing upon experiences of his own, while they were still fresh in mind, and reproducing them in the novels virtually unchanged. And often Orwell's later nonfiction seems to corroborate what he has written earlier as fiction. His *Fortnightly* essay "Bookshop Memories" runs over the same ground, rather more amiably, that he covers with such ferocity in the first chapter of *Keep the Aspidistra Flying*. In the nonfiction version, the account of working in a bookstore is told in the first person; in the fictional version in the third—but the *voice* in both is unmistakably Orwell's. *Ergo*, the innocent reader of the two accounts will conclude, same setting, same voice, change the names and it's the same life: the novel is *really* autobiography.

In general, it seems fair to say that the further Orwell was away from an experience, the more likely he was to write of it objectively and without exaggeration. He had three goes at Booklovers' Corner, and the third time, in an autobiographical note in 1940 for an American reference work, he wrote that working in the shop had been interesting, and that his chief resentment was that it forced him to live in London, which he hated. Yet in spite of its disagreeable aspects—chiefly the people who came in to browse, and the dust-laden air of the underheated shop—the work cannot have been excessively demanding; in October 1935 he contemplated taking three weeks off in the country and coming up once a week to tend the shop, and although the plan didn't materialize, the idea of it raised no objections from Mr. Westrope.

But if the picture of life at Booklovers' Corner, as drawn in *Keep the Aspidistra Flying*, is grimmer than the reality warranted, it points to a curious paradox, involving the novel itself and the circumstances of its composition.

Nineteen thirty-five was by any standard a happy year for Eric. He was living comfortably in Parliament Hill; his career as a writer was perceptibly advancing; his social life was richer and more varied; he had girls aplenty, and one girl in particular with whom he had fallen in love—something altogether new to him. As the months passed, his love for Eileen deepened; and she, having first found him "very interesting," gradually responded to him, grew to love him, fell in love with him, and by the autumn of that year agreed to marry him the following June when she had completed her courses. It was now customary for him to have dinner in Crooms Hill, usually on Sunday evenings, after an afternoon in the country with Eileen, or sometimes at the Westminster Skating Club, with Elizaveta, Eileen, and Laurence and Gwen O'Shaughnessy—no matter that he was the clumsiest of them on skates, the sheer pleasure of being together with people who were fond of him was invigorating. Toward Laurence O'Shaughnessy—who was known in the family by his second name of "Eric," which made for a certain amount of amusing confusion—he entertained a slightly cautious attitude at first; perhaps at first there was the slightest tinge of jealousy, knowing as he did how Eileen worshipped her brother. (And here it seems reasonable to interject that if Eileen had not met and fallen in love with Eric Blair, she might well have ended as Dr. E. O'Shaughnessy, and the beloved Aunt Eileen of Laurence and Gwen O'Shaughnessy's children.) But once Eric felt assured of Eileen's love, he was able to recognize his prospective brother-in-law's remarkable qualities. He listened carefully when Laurence talked of politics—which were less doctrinaire Socialist than those adhered to by Rees and other Adelphians—and especially to his account of the rise of Hitler, which Laurence had seen at first hand, during a period of research in Germany. It was he who introduced Eric to the idea, which seems not to have occurred to him until then, that Hitler intended to carry out the program of *Mein Kampf*, and if allowed to go on unchecked, would bring down catastrophe upon the world. However foreboding these conversations might be in themselves, the occasions on which they occurred were convivial and affectionate, creating an atmosphere of civilized discourse and good feelings—within a family—such as Eric had seldom experienced before. As against his inveterate pessimism, here was the possibility that one could, after all, be happy.

And then, after those pleasant Sundays in Greenwich, he would go back to Parliament Hill, or, later in the year, to the flat in Lawford Road he shared with Rayner Heppenstall and Michael Sayers, and continue writing what proved to be the grimmest, bleakest, and most obsessive of any novel he was to write until *1984* thirteen years later. The mood of splenetic despair that hangs like a pall over most of *Keep the Aspidistra Flying* owes nothing to Orwell's situation in 1935 and everything to those months in the winter and spring of 1932, when Jonathan Cape and Faber & Faber rejected his first book, and Blair had given up on it and left the manuscript with Mabel Fierz to do with as she pleased. As we know she turned it over to Leonard Moore, who sent it to Victor Gollancz, who decided to publish it. But the depression he had felt during those intervening months, the conviction of failure, had been almost overwhelming, and the memory of it stayed with him vividly, oppressively, like a nightmare that had to be exorcised. It would be written out in *Keep the Aspidistra Flying*, and to that extent the novel is undeniably autobiographical, but to that extent only. No matter that Orwell drew upon his later experiences to fill out the narrative, or that his *obiter dicta* and extravagant generalizations are strewn through its pages, or that the poem Gordon Comstock is writing during much of the novel appeared, virtually unchanged, in the *Adelphi* that November as "St. Andrew's Day, 1935" under the name of George Orwell—no matter how many such resemblances, coincidences, and parallels turn up (and they are inherent in Orwell's method of writing naturalistic fiction), Gordon Comstock is *not* a disguised self-portrait of the author, nor even a consistent spokesman for him. He has his own fictional reality.

Keep the Aspidistra Flying is a very peculiar book: there are many passages and episodes of great power and interest, but they tend to be vitiated by the incessant harping on money, money, money that goes on and on and on through the novel—as though it were not only the root, but also the trunk, the branches, and the fruit of all evil. Surely the view presented here is too constricted to sustain the weight of generalizations about life and the contemporary world that are drawn from them. When we first meet Gordon he is a clerk in the bookshop, loathing it and the people who frequent it, earning just enough for a miserable existence, barely above the poverty level, returning at night to his bleak bed-sitter, and there, as Gordon Comstock, author of a promising first book of poems, writing fitfully and despondently at what is meant to be its successor. And all the while he rages against the injustice of life—for he has no money, and without money, how can he write, how can he be accepted in the literary world, how can he have friends, how can he have women, how can he be loved, how can he have cigarettes enough to last him through the week until the next installment of his meager earnings? It is only toward the end of the third chapter that we discover that Gordon's grim situation has been self-imposed: that he has quit his job as a copywriter for an advertising firm and chosen near-poverty as a gesture to himself—his private war against the money-god who rules over modern life. As Orwell puts it in a sentence whose echo of D. H. Lawrence is too clear to have been unintentional: "One's got to get right out of it, out of the money-stink."

It is one thing to choose poverty, as a Franciscan does, to live among the poor and alleviate their suffering; it is another to do so for one's own salvation, to cleanse one's nostrils of the money-stink. There is nothing selfless in Gordon's defiance of the money-god. It is one of the peculiarities of this novel set in 1935 that its rebellious poet hero should be only fitfully aware of the hundreds of thousands of unemployed in England, living through no fault of their own below the poverty level, looking for work and unable to find it. And he is equally indifferent to any sort of political solution to the evils of the money world from which he is in flight. The Socialism espoused by his friend Ravelston, the editor of *Antichrist* (a character based in outline, but not in detail, on Orwell's friend Richard Rees, and a magazine suggested by the *Adelphi*), elicits from Gordon a profound boredom, a cynical No to everything Socialism claims to stand for: indeed, for Gordon there are no political solutions; the world must fend for itself. Cleansed of the money-stink, he will have his integrity, be free to bring his promise to fulfillment. The view is resolutely blinkered and solipsistic, as befits a poet to whom poetry is the beginning and end of existence. But does Gordon answer to this description? Orwell's attitude toward the question is ambiguous, perhaps because he recognized only when he was fairly deep into the novel that the struggle to be a poet and the struggle against the money-god are not synonymous. In any event he was committed to a poet hero, and he gives us as the one example of Gordon's poetry, line by by line as it is being written, a poem of his own, which he must have thought well of, for, as we have noted, he offered it to Rees for the *Adelphi*.*

It seems fair to conclude, then, that Gordon's flaw, in Orwell's view, is not in the quality of his verse but in his dedication to writing. Orwell himself had never wavered in this respect: he had continued to write under the most adverse conditions and in circumstances that would have discouraged anyone less determined than he. Life was difficult, yes; but if one wanted to be a writer, one wrote—otherwise one was not a writer. This was a basic conviction of Orwell's. His work came before anything and anyone else—it was as simple and ruthless as that, and he knew it, and so did Eileen. But Gordon was irresolute; he did not

---

* In all he would publish seven poems there; three—not, however, "St. Andrew's Day, 1935"—have been included in *The Collected Essays, Journalism and Letters*.

seriously write—oh, there were reasons enough to explain (to himself) why he did not; and many of the reasons were valid—up to a point—but the dedicated writer got past that point, and wrote, as Orwell had done and would continue to do until his final illness, no matter what.

Better than Orwell may have suspected, he had learned the lesson Mrs. Vaughan Wilkes had taught the boys of St. Cyprian's—character, character, character—and it is a defect of character in Gordon, his failure to work, which his creator held against him, and for which he is "punished." He will lose his war against the money-god; he will drop the manuscript of his unfinished book-length poem *London Pleasures* down the drain and never be a poet again; he will marry Rosemary, whom he has accidentally impregnated; he will return to the New Albion advertising agency and spend his life writing slogans; he will even have an aspidistra, that symbol of lower-middle-class respectability, in the front window of their flat—and that is the ending that Orwell devised for Gordon Comstock, failed poet and failed rebel.

However one chooses to interpret its ending—as the justified defeat of an unjustified ideal (immature, unworthy Gordon); or the victory of the age-old life force over the modern death-wish (symbolized for Orwell in the use of contraceptives, the French Letter being for him truly a *bête noire*); or a simple coming to terms with reality (mature, sensible Gordon)—the novel as a whole reeks of bitterness, grievance, and festering discontent. From its pages can be garnered a wealth of evidence to support the generalization Isaac Rosenfeld was later to make about Orwell in an article in *Commentary:* "Under the bland, fair, mild, empirical and fair-minded manner which he perfected in the essays, I feel he was full of self-hatred, rage, spite and contempt.

... He condoned his own failure to be a gentleman or—it came to the same thing—managed to forgive himself for being one." Any fair-minded admirer of Orwell will recognize a degree of truth in this; but it is our contention that in the writing of *Keep the Aspidistra Flying*, he was exorcising a ghostly, malignant companion, the man he feared he might have become—Mrs. Vaughan Wilkes's "failure"—and in doing so, liberated himself as a man and a writer. That he should have done so at a time of great personal happiness is a paradox, but not, as any student of psychology will verify, an impossibility.

THIRTEEN

June 1935: A MONTH OF LANDMARKS IN THE LIVES OF Eileen O'Shaughnessy and George Orwell.

Eileen, at University College, successfully passed her qualifying examination for the M.A. In one more year she would have the degree, she and Eric would marry, and then . . . But "and then" brought them into a region of potential disagreement that neither of them—in June 1935 —was willing to explore. Eric had his old-fashioned lower-upper-middle-class notions and was no more likely to approve a wife pursuing her career than he would allow a woman he'd invited to dinner to pay the bill or even her share of it. And Eileen, as an independent-minded woman whose sister-in-law was a successful M.D. in her own right, was not likely to believe that a wife must subordinate her life to her husband's. But "and then" remained a region neither need explore for a while longer. Sensibly, they chose to see the landmark as a midpoint; they were halfway on the way to being permanently together.

For Orwell, June was the month of the belated English publication of *Burmese Days*, bringing his work into the bookshops for the second time in four months. Familiarity was not a deterrent: *Burmese Days* sold better than either of his previous books. A first printing of 2500 copies was soon exhausted, and Gollancz ordered a second impression of 500—this proved sufficient for the demand. So far as sales were concerned, Orwell was still a decade away from the success to which he was doomed. Nor were the reviews much consolation. *Burmese Days* was less extensively noticed than its predecessors—very likely it suffered in this regard from having come so soon after *A Clergyman's Daughter*—and most of the reviews it did receive were tepid and condescending. The anonymous reviewer in the *Times Literary Supplement* was prepared to admit that "The book has traces of power and it is written with a pen steeped in gall. That gall is merited for these people exist, but a little less would have carried more conviction." What especially bothered the reviewer, and others of similar mind, was the sweeping character of Orwell's attack on the British establishment in Burma. He (or she) pointed out, snobbishly but perhaps with some justification, that when Orwell says that few of the Burmese magistrates' English superiors "work as hard or as intelligently as the postmaster in a provincial town, he shows he can hardly have mixed with the men who really run the country." In the *Spectator*, Sean O'Faolain, not likely to be troubled by an anti-imperialist point of view, nonetheless found the novel rather heavy-handed. "Poor Flory," he lamented, "hasn't a dog's chance against his author"—a remark that might equally be applied to poor Dorothy in *A Clergyman's Daughter*, and to poor Gordon in *Keep the Aspidistra Flying*. All was not disapproval, however; from Compton Mackenzie came the by now customary, but even more fervent, tribute in the *Daily Mail*,* and in the *New Statesman and*

---

* "It can hardly be much more than a year ago that there apppeared a remarkable volume of personal experience called *Down and Out in Paris*

Nation there was a highly favorable brief notice by Cyril Connolly, which, in a biographical study of Orwell, deserves to be treated separately.

Although Connolly and Blair had been close friends at St. Cyprian's and quite close friends at Eton, there was no communication between them thereafter, through the five years that Blair was in Burma, and even after his return to England. This was not unusual: virtually none of Blair's Etonian friends were allowed to keep in touch with him, and those who persisted and made the effort found themselves politely but firmly discouraged. As Connolly recalled the sequence of events for us, he knew that Blair had returned from Burma and had been in touch with Maurice Whittome, who arranged a reunion dinner with several other Old Etonians that Connolly had been unable to attend. Then Blair dropped from sight again. He chose to go underground, and evidently did not intend to surface until he had firmly established himself as a writer. But the Etonian network is pervasive and enduring and more powerful than the whim of a sometime member to drop out. Early in 1935 Connolly heard from a mutual Etonian friend that Blair had become the writer George Orwell. So when *Burmese Days* appeared he asked for an advance copy, read it, admired it, and determined to review it for the *New Statesman and Nation*.

---

and London. It is not six months ago that there appeared an even more remarkable novel called A *Clergyman's Daughter*. Last week there was published by the same author a more remarkable book than either of its predecessors, and after reading *Burmese Days* by George Orwell I have no hesitation in asserting that 'no realistic writer' during the last five years has produced three volumes which can compare in directness, vigour, courage and vitality with these three volumes from the pen of Mr. George Orwell."

The difficulty was that Connolly's column there, "New Novels," was expected to cover the week's crop of fiction, and in the week of July 6, 1935, he had eight novels to deal with. The luck of the game depended on the company you kept; even so, it is rather disconcerting, forty-odd years later, to discover one of the enduring novels of the century in the company of seven others that must be gathering dust on the top shelf of a Booklovers' Corner somewhere, earning the contempt of some latter-day version of Gordon Comstock. But Connolly was not the man to be daunted by a situation with which he was all too familiar—viz., his vastly entertaining "Ninety Years of Book Reviewing"—and he very deftly sandwiched *Burmese Days* between *She Fell Among Thieves,* an adventure story, and *Star Against Star,* a novel of "a normal young girl toppling into the well of loneliness." He begins briskly and quotably, in a way that must have gladdened the heart of Gollancz: "*Burmese Days* is an admirable novel. It is a crisp, fierce, and almost boisterous attack on the Anglo Indian." And he has a very winning way of balancing criticism with praise: "His novel might have been better if he had toned down the ferocious partiality of the Lawrence-Aldington school, but personally I liked it and recommend it to anyone who enjoys a spate of efficient indignation, graphic description, excellent narrative, excitement, and irony tempered with vitriol."

Conceivably this burst of enthusiasm played a part in furthering Orwell's career; what is not in doubt is that it revived the friendship between Blair and Connolly. Blair wrote to thank Connolly for the review; Connolly replied; soon they were meeting frequently, the old bond was restored, and the friendship continued without interruption until Orwell's death in 1950, and thereafter, in an impressively loyal and generous fashion, until Connolly's death in 1974.*

He was not the only friend of Orwell's to write admiringly of his work at this time. Michael Sayers reviewed *A Clergyman's Daughter* and *Burmese Days* together in the *Adelphi* for August 1936, more than a year after their publication. He managed the difficult feat of being both praising and perceptive. "George Orwell is a popular novelist sensitive to values that most other novelists are popular for ignoring," he began. "At present Mr. Orwell appears to be most concerned with presenting his material in the clearest and honestest way. . . . The lucidity—so to speak, the *transparence*—of his prose is a necessary quality of the realistic novel, which aims at exhibiting action rather than significant language. . . . Neither pity, nor bitterness, nor cynicism, nor contempt, is permitted to obscure the insidious degradations of Imperialism acting on white and col-

---

* The conversation with Connolly referred to above, the last we were privileged to have with him, occurred on July 29, 1973. In the course of it he corrected an error, concerning himself and Blair, in our *The Unknown Orwell*. The portion of the sentence there that begins "It is suggestive, too, that the friendship with Connolly should have been kept in abeyance until the *early* 1930's, by which time Blair was already a published author with two books to his credit," should be revised to read, "It is suggestive, too, that the friendship with Connolly should have been kept in abeyance until the mid-1930's, by which time Blair was already a published author with three books to his credit," and continue unchanged, "while Connolly, though a well-known critic, would not publish his first book (the novel *The Rock Pool*) until 1936."

In this same conversation, Connolly said he was puzzled by the remark of Orwell's quoted by Denys King-Farlow and repeated in *The Collected Essays, Journalism and Letters*: "Without Connolly's help I don't think I would have got started as a writer when I got back from Burma." Connolly felt Orwell may have made some oblique reference to the review of *Burmese Days* as having helped him in his career, which King-Farlow must have misheard or misinterpreted.

oured alike . . . the consciousness of being an interloper and a despoiler, or a victim. . . . All this is shown rather than stated by Mr. Orwell." And he concluded prophetically, accurately, "Mr. Orwell's career has only begun." Granted that there was some ambiguousness in his use of "popular novelist," which Orwell all too evidently was not, and granted that the word "popular" itself was not a word of high praise in the vocabulary of Sayers and Rayner Heppenstall, who fancied themselves as unpopular highbrows, the review paid Orwell the compliment of treating him with the utmost seriousness, as though his as yet entirely theoretical popularity needn't debar him from serious consideration. Sayers's review would contribute to Orwell's growing reputation in literary circles, but it had no practical effect. Even if the *Adelphi* had had a considerably larger readership than it did, and even if all its readers had rushed off to the bookshops in search of the novels, it would have made no difference, for by that time (a year and a few months after publication) both *A Clergyman's Daughter* and *Burmese Days* were out of print, and their type had been distributed.

WITH EILEEN HALFWAY TO HER DEGREE AND HALFWAY TO marrying him, and with *Burmese Days* at last published in England and selling sufficiently to ensure him at least a little more money than he usually had, Eric allowed his dissatisfaction with his living arrangements, which he had hitherto felt but not expressed, to come to the surface. There was much to be said for Parliament Hill, but as his social life broadened in general, and his relationship with Eileen deepened in particular, the disadvantages of Rosalind's flat began to outweigh whatever might be said for it; it remained *her* flat that he had a room in. The theoretical "room of one's own" that Virginia Woolf had written of with such fervor as all a writer needed no longer would satisfy him: however tactful Rosalind might be, she was there, on the other side of the door, and he was never more conscious of this than when Eileen was with him—her being Rosalind's friend and fellow student added to the vexing aspect of the situation, for one couldn't pretend Rosalind didn't exist and simply close the door in her face. "Liberty Hall, Liberty Hall" was the cry, but he felt himself increasingly imprisoned. Still, he had no wish to hurt Rosalind's feelings, there was a certain delicacy in his situation, and he turned for advice, as he so often did in the years before he married Eileen, to Mabel Fierz.

Eric's position in the Fierz household, which he frequented from 1932 on whenever he lived in London, is difficult to sum up precisely—"visitor" is too distant, "guest" too formal—perhaps one does better merely to approximate the reality and say that he was welcomed as a friend, a quasi-son-and-older-brother, and as a sage. "Eric says . . . ," "Eric says . . ." was a phrase much heard in the household, Adrian Fierz recalls, and what Eric said, as readers familiar with his work might expect, was often a wildly exaggerated generalization—"Eric says all scoutmasters are homosexuals," for example—and while Eileen, at such a pronouncement, might have smiled and said quietly, "*All,* Eric?" Mabel was quite prepared to accept it as true because Eric said it, although part of her knew very well that he was going too far. Exaggeration never bothered Mabel: she liked enthusiasm, living boldly, being in touch with what was new, what was going on, what was exciting, in the arts, in politics, in philosophy, in psychology. If she had been a painter—rather surprisingly, she was not, for she was ready to try anything—she would have painted in vivid colors, in a free self-expressionist manner. Eric was her candidate in the literary sweepstakes, which was astute of her, before anyone else had heard of him, even, one is tempted to say, before he had heard of himself. Francis, her husband, a businessman associated with the Baldwin Steel firm, took a skeptical view of most of her protégés, who were forever overrunning the house and often, it must be said, taking advantage of Mabel's generous nature—there is a fictionalized, not especially accurate sketch of her in Rayner Heppenstall's memoirs that bears this out—and of them all, Francis really liked and approved of only three: Eric was one; another was the arts-and-craftsman Richard Middleton Murry, a brother of John Middleton Murry; and the third was the composer Ralph Vaughn Williams. As for the Fierz children, Adrian and Fay, they were always pleased to see Eric, for they knew he would always have time for them. Adrian's recollections of him are preeminently happy: Eric coming out in the garden to play cricket; Eric talking about books—Sherlock Holmes, P. G. Wodehouse—and giving him a copy of Marlowe's *Doctor Faustus;* taking him to the British Museum, and a few years later to see Maurice Evans in *Hamlet* at the Old Vic. His last memory is of Eric and Eileen coming to his, Adrian's, wedding in 1941—a very simple occasion in wartime, with no more than ten people present, but it was understood that the Blairs would be there, though it must have been difficult for them to arrange. (About Eileen, Adrian is equally enthusiastic: "She couldn't have been nicer and sweeter, and much better looking than the run of his girls—he was very lucky to get her.")

Mabel was always good at giving advice, and one of the

reasons she was good at it was that she never nagged at one with objections that put one off from what one had already decided. She recognized over the first cup of tea that Eric was determined to move from Parliament Hill into a flat of his own. Therefore she agreed that he should. The only questions were How was it to be managed? and How was Rosalind to be tactfully told? This was the sort of situation on which Mabel thrived. Before Eric had downed his second cup, she had the answers to both questions. By a lucky coincidence, Rayner Heppenstall and Michael Sayers, whom he already knew and liked, of course—that was Mabel's "Of course," though Eric did know them, and did rather like them—were just at the point of being evicted from their grimy little rooms in Kilburn. Why, she proposed, shouldn't the three of them share a flat? It would be much more sensible, *financially,* for Eric, since Michael, the drama critic of the *New English Weekly* and a promising short-story writer, would be able to contribute at least a third of the rent. True, Rayner was having a hard time of it at the moment—with a little here from the occasional poem sold, and a little there from the occasional review, and a small advance (already mostly spent) from a publisher for a book about the dance. But he would contribute what he could when he could. Three congenial chaps, she reasoned, wouldn't get in each other's way; essentially it would be Eric's flat, only he wouldn't be paying as much for it as he would if he were trying to swing it alone. Furthermore, this particular solution would please Rosalind: when she heard that Eric was leaving for the sake of Michael and Rayner, as an act of kindness and charity to them, she would not be offended by his departure. Even Eric, for all his eagerness to leave Parliament Hill, must have realized that Mabel's logic was highly questionable, but at such moments she was rather like a force of nature, and he fell in with her plan. So too, when she consulted them, did Heppenstall and Sayers, who had a great deal less to lose by it than Blair. Sayers was interested in a flat, any flat, only as a kind of *maison de passe*, a place to bring his girls, of whom he had a number; at other times he intended to go on living at his parents' very comfortable house in Golders Green. As for Heppenstall, he was in no position to quibble—he wanted a roof over his head—and though it did occur to him to wonder why Blair would want to share with him, Mabel (he tells us), in an enthusiastic flurry of invention revealed a surprising secret; that Eric had a suppressed homosexual passion for him, or so she deduced from his having mentioned that he admired Rayner's hair. Whatever the particulars, and it is not unlikely that time has distorted them, in August of 1935 Blair left his pleasant room on Parliament Hill to share a flat with Heppenstall, and at times Sayers, at 50 Lawford Road in Kentish Town.

The area was rather slummish and grubby, which would not distress him, and a relatively short distance from the pleasant airs and graces of Hampstead—one of those contrasts in which London abounds—which meant that he was still able to walk in the afternoon to his job at Booklovers' Corner. The flat itself was in a small house in a row of semi-detached villas, but with some land between each pair of houses. It contained three rooms, the largest going to Blair, and the smallest, hardly more than a cell, to Heppenstall, with the middling room serving Sayers as his occasional love nest. In this characterless flat Blair would live until the end of January 1936, when he set out on the road to Wigan Pier, and for the greater part of the time he was there it was his exclusively: the ménage of Blair, Heppenstall, and Sayers was doomed, one is tempted to say, virtually from the moment it came into being in the mind of Mabel Fierz. It was not one of her happiest inspirations, for she had failed to take into account differences in age, temperament, education, experience, and class, all of which (to judge from Heppenstall's memoir, *Four Absentees*, the only document of the ménage) were brought into sharp relief as soon as the three men began to share the flat. Until then, after all, their relationship had involved little more than occasional meetings in a pub or a restaurant. They had been friends of a pleasant, uninvolved sort—"intimacy" is not the word that springs to mind—and once they were free of the flat, they would be friends of that sort again, Heppenstall and Blair particularly: one has only to read Blair's letters to him over the years to recognize it. But in the confinement of the flat, Michael and Rayner, though ten years younger than Eric and far less established as writers than he, tended to patronize him. Heppenstall—and it cannot be emphasized too strongly that this account is based entirely on his —found him in many ways naïve and foolish. In his attachment to little bits of Old England, "country parsonages, comic postcards, *The Magnet* and *The Gem*, anecdotes about Queen Victoria and bishops," he was "quite inaccessible" to them. As young *littérateurs* only recently in London from their provincial universities, and keenly responsive to "the New" in literary fashion, they could not share his admiration for Samuel Butler (old hat) or Henry Miller (not yet really being worn, although stocked by Eliot & Co.). They also rather patronized Eric's writing, finding it too "commercial" for their taste: good enough novels in their way, but very traditional, and with no attempt to absorb the crucial modernist influences. As for the poems he was writing and that Richard Rees, the mutual friend of all three, was publishing, they were no further along, with their carefully metered, neatly rhymed quatrains, than the late Georgians, whereas Rayner's experiments in verse that appeared in the *Adelphi* had the look and feel of the 1935 avant-garde—not likely to appeal to an anthologist such as Thomas Moult, who had chosen one of Eric's for *The Best Poems of 1934*.

But in spite of literary differences, Rayner and Eric would have quite a jolly time together, chatting away about this and that, when Rayner would emerge late in the morning from his room after a rowdy night in Soho and Eric was finishing his three-hour stint at the novel. Some subjects, books apart, were less satisfactory than others. Rayner felt he was not providing the sort of information about the working class (from which he was rising) that Eric expected of him. As he puts it in *Four Absentees*, "Orwell was already contemplating a guide to working-class life. With my information on this subject he was dissatisfied. He wanted leaky ceilings and ten in a room, with scrabblings on slag-heaps if possible. Himself he hankered after the simple life. He compared the process of writing, unfavourably, with that of making something *real* like a chair, on which you could then sit down. I thought him a wonderfully nice man, but confused."

Eric ran the household, the flat was rented in his name, and he did most of the cooking. Meals were served in his room, at the large plain table that at other times he used as a desk. He was also the one who tried to keep the place straight; he felt about Rayner much as Janet Gimson had felt about Eric himself in Parliament Hill, that he was very messy. (And very likely he was—a young man attuned to the ways of Soho would not worry if his few possessions were scattered about his tiny room, or the mattress that served him as a bed was in perpetual disarray.)

In due course the inevitable occurred: there was a parting of the ways, over the now notorious shooting-stick incident. It was first brought to light by Heppenstall in the reminiscences of Orwell that he published in the *Twentieth Century* in 1955 and went on to incorporate (with some revisions) in *Four Absentees*. His motive in writing of the man he knew as Eric Blair, he explained in a second volume of memoirs, *The Intellectual Part,* was that "There was growing up a whole Orwell mythology, which seemed to me to bear no relation to the man I had known." Heppenstall's less than reverential tone, as evidenced in the mildly ironic passage quoted above, "nice, but confused," was not likely to please the uncritical admirers of Orwell, and it drove his hagiographers up the wall. The man in the shooting-stick episode was impossible to reconcile with the secular saint they were then in the process of canonizing. Perhaps Heppenstall would have been on safer ground if he had limited himself to a bald recital of facts, but he drew upon a wide range of literary devices—as Orwell himself was wont to do—to enrich his account: heightening for effect, introducing offhanded generalizations that don't bear too close inspection, a tone of ironic condescension that at times is indistinguishable from malice. In short, as one might say of Orwell writing of St. Cyprian's, Heppenstall was carried away by the occasion, and he too had some old scores to settle. Orwell had drawn an unflattering vignette of him, which he recognized, in *The Road to Wigan Pier,* and it is not inconceivable that he caught more than a glimpse of himself in Gordon Comstock. The ironic result, however, so clear after the passage of two decades, is that the official portrait hasn't been redrawn; the saint remains, but poor Heppenstall has been incorporated into the mythology as a kind of devil figure. Scandal gave to the shooting-stick episode an importance that, as we shall now see, it scarcely deserved.

A shooting stick is a cane-shaped, cane-sized object that has the virtue of opening at the top to form a small seat or perch: one goes out into a field, opens one's shooting stick, perches upon it, and looks in an approving, upper-class way at the surrounding landscape. Yes, class has to be brought in, even here, for as Heppenstall makes clear, a shooting stick is not a traditional appurtenance of the well-equipped working-class home. Eric, however, owned a shooting stick. So, too, we learn from Heppenstall, did Eileen, in spite of which he liked her very much, thinking her much the nicest, prettiest, and most intelligent of Eric's girls. Eric and Eileen would take their shooting sticks with them on their Sunday excursions into the country, and when they had walked to a picturesque point, they would open them, and perch, side by side, admiring the view in the best upper-class manner, which was theirs by right.

Most of this, it has to be said, is pure supposition by Heppenstall: he did not accompany Eric and Eileen on their Sunday excursions, and hence did not see them perched; he did not know for certain that Eileen even *had* a shooting stick, and it is highly improbable that if she had, she would have brought it round with her when she visited the flat in Lawford Road. Conceivably Eric told him that she had one, though it seems an odd bit of information to impart. Out of all this prefatory business, the one sure fact that emerges, and all, really, that matters to the episode, is that Eric had a shooting stick.

One evening Rayner had come home to the flat very drunk, and according to his account, Eric had made very upper-class noises at him; it wouldn't do, it was not the sort of thing one did, and so forth and so forth. Rayner, a good deal shorter than Eric, drew himself up and said he would hit him if he didn't go away, and when he tried, Eric punched him on the nose, knocking him down and briefly out. Rayner than dragged himself as far as Michael Sayers's unoccupied room, where a bed was more or less made up, and lay down, bloodied nose and all, to try to sleep. A moment later he heard the key turning in the door: Eric, he realized, had locked him in. This had the effect of waking him entirely. In a fury he began shouting and tried to crash through the door. At which point Eric opened it and stood there, holding aloft his shooting stick, and when Rayner lunged forward, he struck him with it, his face alight "with a curious blend of fear and sadistic exaltation." By this time the people downstairs, aroused by the noise, came up and separated them. The next morning, in his best district commissioner's way, Eric told Rayner he would have to go.

This is the story as Heppenstall told it, and no doubt it has the elements of exaggeration: after all, it is the work of a gifted novelist. There would be no reason to take the episode seriously—or any more seriously than Orwell and Heppenstall themselves did, for it did not, as one might expect, put an end to their friendship; apart, they were on better terms than ever before—except that, in certain quarters, it has been taken too seriously. Heppenstall's lurid phrase "a curious blend of fear and sadistic exaltation" has had the unfortunate effect of calling into being a stereotype of "Orwell the sadist" that is as exaggerated as that counter-stereotype, "Orwell the virtuous man." Undoubtedly there were elements of sadism—more properly, brutality—in Orwell; he has emphasized them in his exemplary accounts of his experience as an Imperialist, and there are pages in 1984 that are shocking in their cruelty. Certainly from the time of his return from Burma, and through the remainder of his life, his "sadism" was principally turned against himself. Perhaps in making this statement, we seem to be falling back upon the third stereotype, "Orwell the masochist." But it is our belief, reinforced by what we have learned of him from admirers and detractors alike, that he had to suffer himself, to experience suffering in his own person, before he could understand the suffering of others and so re-create it on the page for his readers.

THE IMMEDIATE EFFECT OF RAYNER'S DEPARTURE—HE went off to stay with the Middleton Murrys in Essex—was that Eric at last had a flat of his own, as he had wanted from the beginning. (Sayers, who had never been deeply involved in the Lawford Road scheme, withdrew from it even before the shooting-stick debacle, having made other arrangements.) The advantage of Eric's being in sole possession was that now he and Eileen could be together as often and as long as they pleased, and without having to converse in whispers behind the closed door of his room. The disadvantage was that a flat of his own, no matter how thriftily and frugally he lived, used up his money at an alarming rate. At this time, autumn 1935, he was living on his small wages from Booklovers' Corner, the remains of his small advance from Gollancz for *Keep the Aspidistra Flying*, and the small trickle of royalties from *A Clergyman's Daughter* and *Burmese Days*. In all it came to just barely enough, and he cast about for ways to augment his income. For a brief time he put aside the novel, deluding himself that he could turn out commercial formula fiction to order—a serial story for a newspaper—and like many another gifted writer who turns to hackwork of the sort that makes hacks rich, he found it more difficult than he'd anticipated. After four tormented days he'd written just two pages of manuscript, and although, ultimately, he was able to produce a synopsis and a first chapter, it was a hopeless enterprise. To discover that he was not born to be a serial writer, he had wasted three weeks of time that might have been spent on the novel, and it was with a sense of relief that he got back to it.

In the light of Orwell's full-blown emergence as a Socialist in 1936, it may be hard to credit that he should have been so unremittingly nonpolitical as late as 1935. And yet only by a feat of verbal acrobatics can *Keep the Aspidistra Flying*, his principal literary preoccupation in that year, be made to seem a *political* novel, and then only by implication. Gordon's hatred and all-out condemnation of the money-world are too infuriated and subjective to permit a calm "analysis of the situation," but indirectly he might be thought to be arguing that the evils of the money-world must be wiped out—not however, by a political solution, but in an apocalyptic catastrophe. Hence those fleets of bombers, pouring down death on London, that recur so excitingly in his fantasies. (Of course, by a still more agile feat of acrobatics one can read those fantasies as no more than a realistic political prophecy—a prefiguring of the Luftwaffe in action during the Second World War.) But if Orwell held any firm political ideas in 1935, one might logically expect a more straightforward, less symbolic expression of them to find its way into his journalistic writing. Not so, however. That year, as it happened, most of his time was devoted to the novel, except for a handful of reviews in the *Adelphi* and the *New English Weekly*, the two journals with which he was most closely associated at this period. Neither was free of a certain crankiness in the principles and the politics it espoused: the *Adelphi*, under Middleton Murry and Rees, a mix of Marxian Socialism, Tolstoyan Christianity, and Pacifism; the *New English Weekly*, under A. R. Orage and Philip Mairet, a mix of Major Douglas's Social Credit as elucidated by Ezra Pound, Christianity as practiced by T. S. Eliot, and Tolstoyan Agrarianism. For all their differences, the two journals were alike in being firmly political in their point of view, and each had its literary side. Orwell, with his sweeping generalizations, his sometimes odd but always strong opinions on so many subjects, was not without his own elements of crankiness, and he found the atmosphere of the two magazines congenial. Richard Rees, who had succeeded Middleton Murry as the editor of the *Adelphi*, was perhaps his closest friend; and he got on very well with Philip Mairet, who had succeeded to the editorship of the *New English Weekly* upon the death of Orage. Still nonpolitical in 1935, Orwell made his contributions only to the literary side of each magazine, and Rees and Mairet were resigned that it should be so.

For the *Adelphi* that year he wrote a very favorable review of the autobiography of a working man, *Caliban Shrieks*, by Jack Hilton, which had, he felt, the rare and invaluable quality of giving one, "instead of a catalogue of facts about poverty, a vivid notion of what it *feels* like to be poor"; an unfavorable review of a biography of Henry Crabb Robinson; and a scathing review of Amy Cruse's *The Victorians and Their Books*, in which he "dipped his pen in gall" and held forth on the difficulty of dislodging the Victorians from their pedestals. (This was in 1935, seventeen years since Lytton Strachey had done that particular job so efficiently that it would take another two generations before the despised Victorians would be restored to something like their original eminence.) In a fit of bad temper he excoriated Mrs. Cruse for her affection for those "slimy Low Church scoutmasters," Charles Kingsley and Thomas Hughes. But not even the fact that Kingsley and Hughes had been Christian Socialists imparts a political color to his anger; one comes away from this forgotten review—it has never been resurrected—with an impression of Gordon Comstock in possession of George Orwell: an angry young man still uncertain of what to be angry about.

The two pieces that he wrote for the *New English Weekly* are as untouched by politics as the three for the *Adelphi*, but one of them is of enduring interest: his early, appreciative review of Henry Miller's *Tropic of Cancer*, where anger gives way to discernment and a generosity of spirit that are wonderfully invigorating. It is something of those qualities that would illuminate the best of his political writing. But politics were still for the future: the surprising thing is that they proved to be much closer than Eric must have anticipated late in the autumn of 1935 in Lawford Road, finishing *Keep the Aspidistra Flying*, adding to the manuscript twiddly bits of verbal decoration, and contemplating an Epilogue he never bothered to write. As Richard Rees wryly observed, long after Orwell's death, "I spent more than three years trying to convert him to Socialism, and he remained unconvinced, and not really interested. Then he went North. When he came back in the Spring of 1936, the conversion had already taken place."

PART THREE

THE END OF ERIC BLAIR

FOURTEEN

EARLY IN DECEMBER THE LAST OF THE TWIDDLY BITS HAD been applied to *Keep the Aspidistra Flying* and Blair delivered the manuscript to Leonard Moore, who sent it on to Gollancz, who accepted it as a matter of course. By now Orwell was an established author on his list, perhaps so well established that it was thought unnecessary to read him with very close attention; he was in danger of becoming predictable: ". . . another scathing . . . poverty . . . depression England . . . worthy to stand beside the same author's . . ." Hence everything got under way with the usual startling speed. The novel was scheduled for publication at the beginning of March 1936. Proofs were in hand in January. And then, belatedly, someone at Gollancz seems to have subjected the text to the closest scrutiny, for all at once a crisis over the possibility of libel erupted: the name of the advertising firm where Gordon and Rosemary worked bore some faint resemblance to an actual firm. Once again Orwell found himself in conference with Norman Collins, to whom he had taken a firm dislike—the aftermath, no doubt, of that earlier, similar conference over *Burmese Days* —discussing the potentially actionable points that would have to be altered. As before, Orwell yielded to reason— what could one do? But the anger he had suppressed in the Gollancz offices he vented in letters: to Richard Rees, on

February 29, he reported that the required alterations had spoiled an entire chapter; by the time he wrote to Jack Common a fortnight later he felt that they had utterly ruined his novel. (Remembering his despair over the changes he had had to make in *Burmese Days*—a matter of a few names—one is prepared to recognize here some slight Orwellian exaggeration.) There is no record of his having prepared an unamended, pristine text for American publication, perhaps because it was not needed. Harpers' decided against *Keep the Aspidistra Flying* as "too English."

With the novel written and in the hands of his publisher, a crisis of a different but equally familiar sort confronted him, which he had had to face with each book since *Burmese Days:* what was he to write next? He was a dedicated professional writer, whose life, as we have said earlier, was his literary capital. He had drawn upon it continually for the events and substance of the four books he had written during the past four years. Even in his novels, where he was free to invent, the reality of his own experience sustained what he invented, imparting to it a convincingness and a conviction it would not otherwise have had. What would he write next? The question had a particular urgency now, for it seemed he had used up his capital: he had come to a point where he would have to live more before he could write more.

Here, providentially, Victor Gollancz enters the picture.

Gollancz was not only a successful publisher but also a dedicated social reformer. Sometimes he confused his two roles: but for a brief period, from 1936 to 1939, as founder, owner, and chief spirit of the Left Book Club, he united them with historic consequences.* In 1935 he had already

---

* These years were the heyday of the Club; it would continue until 1948.

published within a space of months two novels by Orwell; the arrival of a third in December, which he admired and marked for publication in early spring, provoked a belated act of recognition: that here was an author who responded as deeply as Gollancz himself to the "abomination" of poverty and who was able, indeed was compelled, to describe it in all its cruel, degrading, and abominable reality. As a social reformer, a Socialist, and an idealist, Gollancz had an unquestioning, perhaps overly optimistic faith in education: if only people could be made to know the nature of poverty, he thought, if they could be educated as to what it was, then, surely, they would want to eradicate it, remove from power the government that tolerated it, and transform the economic system that brought it into being. As a successful publisher, however, he was realistic enough to know that if a book about poverty in England in 1936 (not, on the face of it, a subject of broad appeal) was to reach the large audience he wanted for it, it must be something more than a well-intentioned, carefully researched collection of facts, statistics, graphs, and hortatory conclusions. It must, instead, be a sympathetic report from outside—the account of an eyewitness rather than a victim (so that the middle-class readers whom Gollancz intended to be moved could identify with the reporter as one of themselves), written by someone with experience enough to know what to look for, and with the ability to describe what he saw so vividly as to make it unforgettable. Who better to undertake the task than George Orwell?

The proposal—that Orwell should travel through the depressed areas of the North, observing the effects of unemployment among the coal miners, and write about what he had seen—was made by Gollancz through Moore. He offered a larger advance for whatever book might result from the journey than he had ever paid Orwell before; and, as a further inducement, the likelihood that the book would be made a selection of the Left Book Club, which was already germinating in Gollancz's mind, would be announced at the end of February, and come into existence in May, with himself, John Strachey, and Harold Laski as selectors, choosing from amongst books to be published and often commissioned by Victor Gollancz Ltd.

When Moore put the proposal to Orwell, he accepted it immediately. It resolved in a challenging and very stimulating way the crisis of what he was to write next. And the prospect of earning more money as the time approached when he and Eileen would marry was agreeable to contemplate, though in no sense crucial. The sheer elation that went with being in love with her persuaded him that they would somehow manage: things would arrange themselves, as he told Rayner Heppenstall. (Besides, neither of them cared that much about money.) Perhaps inspired by just having married off Gordon to Rosemary, Eric did suggest to Eileen that they might marry earlier than June. But he deferred to her sensible objection: immersed as she was in her course, she hadn't time to earn anything herself and so would be a drag on him; whereas after she had finished and taken her degree, almost certainly she would have a job and would be able to make her contribution. Things would arrange themselves.

The chief attraction of Gollancz's proposal was that it offered Orwell a way out of the enclosed world of the realistic novel, where the characters a novelist invents are in a leech-like relation to him, preempting his experiences or fantasies of life. Even the notion of the journey exerted a powerful attraction: he would be going towards new experience. Secure at last in his own life, thanks to Eileen, he could allow himself to be responsive to the lives of others, become absorbed in a world outside himself—and in so doing, replenish his literary capital. He started without preconceptions, literary or political. He had no idea, beginning the journey, of what the book he would ultimately write about it would be, and when the journey was over and he was settling down to write, he was only certain that it would not be a novel. He had no clearly defined politics to prejudice him or to assist him in evaluating what he saw. Gollancz, noting the affinity between his own response to the "abomination" of poverty and Orwell's, may have assumed that, like himself, Orwell was a dedicated Socialist. He would not have been the first to make that sort of assumption, depending upon instinct rather than concrete evidence. The present authors were told by Philip Mairet, of the *New English Weekly*, that when he first met Blair in the early 1930's, he took it for granted from his manner and general style of conversation that he was a man of the Left —though they never actually talked much about politics— and so, in 1936, when Orwell publicly declared himself a Socialist, Mairet wasn't surprised, but felt—again depending on instinct—that he would not make a very good "party man." On the whole, Mairet seems to have been sounder in his instincts than Gollancz, who got in *The Road to Wigan Pier* a very different book from the one he'd anticipated. In 1945, in the introduction to the Ukrainian edition of *Animal Farm*, Orwell would make the rather surprising claim that he had been a Socialist since 1930; still more surprisingly, he would state that for many years he had made a systematic study of the life and labor of the miners of the North. Perhaps he felt that for Ukrainian readers he needed to give his credentials a more impressive sound. But what is truly impressive is how fast and perceptively he traveled

—in a more than literal sense—along the road to Wigan, even though he never succeeded in finding the pier. (He thought, mistakenly, that it had been destroyed.)

A WRITER MUST WRITE, AND IN JANUARY HE DASHED OFF BOTH a memorial tribute to Kipling and an omnibus review of ten novels for the same issue of the *New English Weekly*. Then he gave up his detested job at Booklovers' Corner and the flat in Lawford Road—he would not live in London again until 1940—and on the last day of the month set out on his journey. It was winter, cold and rainy, and in the North there would be snow. Rather unusually for him, he was prepared to concede something to the hostile weather: he wore a raincoat and scarf. In his haversack he carried a minimum of personal belongings, and the proofs of *Keep the Aspidistra Flying*, which he intended to read, correct, and alter (as agreed with Norman Collins) while he traveled.

There was a loosely improvised quality about the expedition that was very much in accord with Gollancz's proposal, which left him on his own, free to write as he pleased within the expandable/contractable boundaries of the subject. He made no plans in advance, beyond consulting with Rees, who promised to send him the names of people in the North connected, one way or another, with the *Adelphi* or the Adelphi summer school, who might be helpful to him. And they were—it is difficult to imagine how the first part of *The Road to Wigan Pier* could have been written without their interventions. At the least, it would have been a more impressionistic, less documented and explicit account than it turned out to be.

But if he had chosen to travel without plans—simply to go and see, letting each day lead to the next—he had one principle to which he held firmly during the next two months, following a jagged crescent route from Birmingham to Manchester to Leeds, and when he sat down in April to write about what he had seen. Orwell would not be writing "from the inside" as Jack Hilton had done in his autobiography, but he was determined to get as close to the inside of working-class poverty as he could, and to convey the *feeling* of it—precisely the sort of thing that tended to be lost in an objective book by an author who had not known, or was not prepared to know, the experience of living on two pounds a week. He had abandoned the elements of masquerade and disguise of his earlier adventures, on the bum among down-and-outers. He was content to be what he was, but he knew that if he was to write honestly and sympathetically of the lives of working-class men and women, he must live as they did. Hence the stringencies he imposed on himself.

The first days and nights of the journey are illuminating in this respect: they set a pattern of extreme thrift and a willingness to endure discomfort and hardship, not out of guilt and a need for expiation, but simply to make the experience as near to unexceptional as possible, and hence, closer to the inside. Arriving in Coventry late in the afternoon of the thirty-first, he has one pound in his pocket: in theory, enough for the first half of the week. That night he stays in a "bed-and-breakfast" rooming house; the next day he walks in the occasional rain twelve miles towards Birmingham, then takes a bus into the city, where he has lunch. Afterwards, a bus again, this time to Stourbridge, then another four- or five-mile walk to a Youth Hostel for the night. The next day, returning on foot to Stourbridge, he takes a bus to Wolverhampton. Lunch there; afterwards a ten-mile walk to Penkridge in the rain, a warm cup of tea, and a further two miles on foot, at which point he manages to catch the bus to Stafford. That night he stays in a Temperance Hotel that hasn't even the virtue of being cheap. The next day he travels by bus from Stafford to Hanley; thence on foot to Eldon, where he has lunch in a pub; continuing on foot to Rudyard Lake, and another mile to a Youth Hostel for the night. End of four nights and three days: he had walked forty-four miles, and spent some two shillings less than the pound he had started out with; another pound would see him through the week.

Most of the details in the paragraph above are culled from the diary Orwell kept from the thirty-first of January through the twenty-fifth of March, which records, virtually day by day, the unretouched material that he would in due course develop into the first part of *The Road to Wigan Pier.* The diary, a work of unusual interest, was found among Orwell's papers after his death, and published for the first time in 1968 in the *Collected Essays, Journalism and Letters.* One hopes that it may eventually be published together with the book it inspired in a single volume, as has been done with *The Counterfeiters* of André Gide and his *Journal of the Counterfeiters.* The relation between Orwell's unretouched diary and the artfully rearranged and highlighted final version of the material it contains is a fascinating example of what a creative writer brings to nonfiction, as a reading of the two together in sequence will immediately make apparent.

The self-portrait of Orwell that emerges un-self-consciously from the diary is, we would argue, far more sympathetic and credible than the highly stylized, self-conscious *portrait moralisé* he painted of himself in the second part of *The Road to Wigan Pier*. It is not difficult to account for the difference: in the diary (and in the first part of the book) he is *learning;* in the second part of the book he is *lecturing,* never Orwell's most impressive or convincing literary posture. (Compare, for a definitive example, the indictment of Imperialism made by implication in "Shooting An Elephant" with the attack on it by direct statement and overstatement in the second part of *The Road,* the two works written within a few months of each other after his return from the North.)

The Orwell of the diary is earnest, serious, a little naïve— that is, uncynical about, and given at moments to sentimentalizing, what he sees—but also eager to learn, unpretentious, making no claims to expertise, grateful for kindnesses shown to him, which he is quick to notice though sometimes too shy to acknowledge, liking many of the people whom he meets and hopeful that they will like him in return, above all admiring the virtues of the working class, as he learns to recognize them, even under conditions of extreme adversity. And following as it does immediately upon the all-inclusive angers and phobias of Gordon Comstock in *Keep the Aspidistra Flying,* the diary is even more impressive for its freedom from "self-hatred, rage, spite and contempt." In its unretouched pages, perhaps more clearly here than in any other single work, we have the sense of Orwell *changing:* of his accessibility to new experience.

At first, new experience was not forthcoming. There was a possibility that he might penetrate no further than the bleak edge of poverty, sampling the marginal existence, nasty enough in itself, of a solitary man on the move from the slummy areas of one town to the next, a dismal roster of "bed-and-breakfasts," of quirky encounters and conversations with commercial travelers, lodging-house keepers, and odd types in buses, pubs, and teashops, along with some townscapes and landscapes meticulously observed. Then, on the fifth day of the journey, he arrived in Manchester, and found a letter waiting for him there from Rees, with a list of people in the North whom he should see. One of them, Frank Meade, lived in Manchester—a Trade Union official and the business manager of *Labour's Northern Voice*, who also had in charge the printing of the *Adelphi*. Orwell went to see him two days later, having spent the day before in a common lodging house (shades of *Down and Out*), and Meade couldn't have been more welcoming. He insisted that Comrade Orwell must stay with the Meades in their house at 49 Brynton Road until he got launched in his investigations, and he was with them there from the sixth to the tenth of February. Brynton Road turned out to be in one of the new building estates, and the house itself, with bathroom and electricity, set a standard for comfort that Orwell would only rarely encounter during the rest of the journey, most notably when he spent a few days with his sister Marjorie and her husband, Humphrey Dakin, in their house outside Leeds, and with John and Mary Deiner —she had been Middleton Murry's secretary at the Adelphi summer school—at their house in a suburb of Liverpool. But Meade, Orwell decided, had suffered the inevitable, ironic fate of the working man who becomes a Trade Union official (or a Labour party politician). Earning perhaps four pounds a week, he adopts the ideology appropriate to his class—despite which, both Meade and his wife persisted in the habit of calling Orwell "Comrade," discomfiting him. Still, he was careful to note that they had been very decent to him; and Meade, bourgeoisified or not, would direct him towards the new experience he must have if he were to write a book of the sort Gollancz had proposed, rather than

—the risk inherent in the proposal—"Down and Out Revisited." For once Orwell had made it clear what it was that he wanted—to be among working men, and to live as they did—Meade sent him on to Wigan to meet his friend Joe Kennan. Kennan, an electrician and a militant Socialist, like Meade had a "decent Corporation house" but he struck Orwell as "more definitely a working man." He was "very anxious to help" and gave him a letter to Paddy Grady, an unemployed miner and secretary of the local branch of the National Unemployed Workers Movement. He, too, was "very anxious to help." Indeed, all the men at the NUWM shelter were friendly and helpful: when they heard that Orwell was a writer gathering material about working-class conditions, they were anxious to supply him with information. At this point in the diary he notes with a quite winning naïveté, "I cannot get them to treat me precisely as an equal, however. They call me either 'Sir' or 'Comrade.'"

To live in a decent Corporation house was an impossible ideal for the majority of working-class men and their families in 1936, and Orwell, reasonably enough, chose to do without the comforts of Parliament Hill or even the basic amenities of Lawford Road in favor of getting closer to the "inside." Guided by Paddy Grady, he found lodgings in Warrington Lane, in the house of the H.'s—five rooms, outside lavatory, for Mr. H., unemployed miner, Mrs. H., their fifteen-year-old son, working night shift in the pit, a cousin also on the night shift, and two lodgers, both unemployed. Orwell would share a room with one of the lodgers, be supplied all meals (in the kitchen) and would wash (no hot water) in the scullery sink—for twenty-five shillings a week.

He began in Warrington Lane, planning to fan out through Lancashire and Yorkshire, and almost immediately he realized that the two months he had allowed himself for the task wouldn't be sufficient; he liked the miners, they were nice and warmhearted and took him for granted, he would have liked to spend a year among them. But that was impossible: first, and crucially, it would have kept him away from Eileen far too long; besides, in a couple of months he would have to get back to work, by which he meant his writing. (Oddly, he seems never to have thought of his day-to-day life among workingmen in the North as "work.") Considering that he was in Wigan for only three weeks (the longest single stop he would make), and that he was not a professional journalist dropping in for a "crash course" in poverty before hurrying off to another, different assignment, it was no small feat that he should have gathered enough material, and responded to it deeply enough, to present a vivid picture of life in a mining town where a large proportion of the miners were unemployed, and where employment itself was no guarantee of living above the poverty level.

Wigan, of course, was not the only stop on his itinerary, but as it was the longest, it seems worthwhile to let his time there represent the scope and method of his activities in Lancashire, and the next month in Yorkshire. In Warrington Lane, he took carefully detailed notes, on the conditions of the house itself and on the existence of the H.'s, what they ate, and earned, and how their meager earnings were spent. He walked up and down the streets of Wigan, bleak vistas of the terrible houses of the poor, and along the industrial canal—"one-time site of Wigan Pier," he notes in the diary—towards the mountainous slagheaps in the distance. He attended a political talk in the Co-op Hall by a Communist speaker, Wal Hannington, head of the NUWM, that in spite of being padded with Socialist clichés ("Socialist" and "Communist" seem to be used interchangeably) excited the audience. And he notes in the diary: "surprised by the amount of Communist feeling here." But perhaps he ought not to have been, for, as he also noted, the members of the audience were "all obviously unemployed."

He went out with the NUWM collectors on their rounds, wanting to see for himself the terrible housing conditions Mrs. H. had already described to him (by comparison, the H.'s were well housed)—a harrowing visit among the crowded, primitive caravans. From that day he took away an impression that, as he recorded it in the diary, is one of the most moving passages he would ever write. Coming up an alley, he saw a woman "kneeling by the gutter outside a house and poking a stick up the leaden waste-pipe, which was blocked. I thought how dreadful a destiny it was to be kneeling in a gutter in a back alley in Wigan, in the bitter cold, prodding a stick up a clogged drain. At that moment she looked up and caught my eye, and her expression was as desolate as I have ever seen; it struck me that she was thinking the same thing as I was." He would reproduce this in *The Road,* as a glimpse caught from a train, and while more details are added—for a sense of exactness—and it is skilfully finished, it is no more *moving* than in the hastily noted first state.

He moved to squalid lodgings over a tripe shop in Darlington Road, the setting he would choose for the opening chapter of the book. He attended an NUWM "social" to raise money for the defense fund for Ernst Thaelmann, the German Communist leader, imprisoned and awaiting trial by the Nazis since 1933—some two hundred people were present, the greater number women, dispirited and sheeplike *en masse,* but he supposed them to be the more revolutionary Wiganers. Which prompted him to add in the diary a significant "If so, God help us."

He witnessed one of the most exotic but characteristic

experiences available to a "foreigner" visiting Wigan in the 1930's and eager to describe its life as it was. With Paddy Grady he went out to watch the unemployed miners at their dangerous and illegal "coal-picking." Waiting by the railroad tracks, they would leap onto the fast-moving train bringing carloads of dirt and shale from the mine to be dumped on an ever-growing heap at Fir Tree Siding. As the loaded cars were uncoupled, and before they could be dumped, the men began shoveling the stuff to their women and children below, who would scrabble through it for pieces of coal to put in sacks, boxes, carts, anything that could be used to carry away the "loot," useless to the companies but precious to the scrabblers as fuel.

And he witnessed, too, the most central experience in Wigan life, upon which all else—even, as he would presently argue, life in England—virtually depended. He made his first descent into a coal mine ("Crippen's"). He went down with Joe Kennan and a number of other men, in the charge of an engineer who worked in the pit, crowded into a cage that very swiftly went down nine hundred feet. From there, he proceeded painfully, torturously—such it was for Orwell anyway; for he was in a bent-over position throughout, too tall ever to stand upright—almost a mile to the coal face.

All these "events," summarized here, are described in sharp, flashing notes in the diary: the immediate impressions he intended to draw upon and develop for the book. But there was a significant portion of his time in Wigan that is not accounted for in the diary: certain tasks that went with his being a writer that couldn't be put aside entirely while he was on the journey, and that couldn't be done in his crowded lodgings in Warrington Lane and Darlington Road. He had the proofs of *Keep the Aspidistra Fly-*

ing to correct and send back to Gollancz, and he had research to do. Although he had no intention of writing a dry-as-dust handbook, he knew that he wanted his book, however amorphous it still might be in his mind, to carry more weight than a mere collection of impressions—he would need facts and figures to reinforce them (on unemployment, and housing, and conditions in the mines, the sort of thing one got from *The Colliery Year Book* and the *Coal Trades Directory*, from government documents and from a close reading of the local newspapers). Correcting proofs; looking things up—these were the nonwriting parts of his work as a writer; they couldn't be postponed, and he found time to do them, day after day, in the library at Wigan, among all the unemployed who drowsed and browsed and used the library as a place to keep warm.

Carlton Melling, who was then in charge of the reference library in Wigan, still remembers Orwell. In 1974 he offered an entertaining glimpse of him in the library to the novelist John Farrimond, which Farrimond has generously shared with the present authors: "Very soft-spoken, with a handsome, intelligent face. He never spoke except on the subject in hand. I spent two weeks 'looking after him' at the library. He signed the visitors' book as Eric Blair, and an excited assistant came upstairs to tell me, 'Do you know who that is, Carlton? *George Orwell!*'"

He went down Crippen's mine on Monday the twenty-fourth of February, and the next day was too done in by the experience to move from his bed. But time was running short, March was already allotted to Yorkshire: on Wednesday he persuaded himself that he was well enough to spend the day in Liverpool, where he still had to look up the Deiners and George Garrett, who were all on Rees's list. But by the time he arrived there he was feeling "unwell." When he presented himself at the Deiners' door, Mary Deiner realized he was in no state to collect facts about housing or anything else, nor was he up to even the restorative cup of tea and biscuit. Almost at once, he was "ignominiously sick," and Mrs. Deiner put him to bed in the spare room. There was no question of his going back to Wigan that night: indeed, she thought he ought to stay two or three days more at least. But that was not Orwell's way. The next morning he insisted he felt appreciably better and must get on with his work. From Mary Deiner he now learned—with some surprise, for Rees had neglected to mention it—that George Garrett, under the pseudonym of Matt Low, was a writer of stories for the *Adelphi*. Orwell knew the stories, thought them impressive, and the man himself, when they met late that morning, equally so. A Communist absorbed in party politics, a seaman, a docker, as well as an occasional writer, Garrett was more often than not unemployed: he had had about nine months' work in the past six years, being "blacklisted everywhere as a Communist." His checkered history, which included a period of bootlegging in the U.S.A. in the prohibition era, was fascinating to listen to. Orwell, already impressed by his literary gift, suggested that Garrett should write an autobiography. But the plain facts of his situation —on the dole, married and with kids, the family crowded into two rooms—made it impossible for him to attempt any extended piece of writing. They also made a striking contrast to the situation of poor Gordon Comstock, dreadful no doubt when seen from a middle-middle- or upper-middle-class vantage point, but how would his situation look from a working-class point of view—quite so dreadful, or perhaps a little self-indulgent? Indeed, the more Orwell would see of the working class on this journey—their poverty and, so often, their courage, their endurance—the more he must have begun to have qualms about *Keep the Aspidistra Flying.* Obviously he couldn't deny having written it, but it becomes understandable that he should claim in his letter to Jack Common—himself a writer from the working class—that the alterations he had been forced to make in the text had ruined it. As the years went on, he wouldn't seek even this sort of excuse: poor Gordon's keening displeased him to the point of disavowing the novel entirely.

Garrett—evidently *not* the sort ever to be thought of as "poor George"—proved to be yet one more of the working-class men Orwell met in these two months who were eager to be helpful. He took him around to the docks, and to see the new housing estates and the great slum-clearance projects. It was a full afternoon of learning; even so, between lessons, he'd found time to indulge himself by browsing in an antique shop near the docks. When he got back to the Deiners', he showed Mary Deiner a pair of brass candlesticks and a ship in a bottle he'd bought there, and told her that he was thinking of opening an antique shop of his own. That evening, the Deiners drove him back to Wigan, and he took the candlesticks away with him, but the ship in the bottle was too fragile to be carried around Yorkshire in his haversack. He left it temporarily with the Deiners. He would write, he said, as soon as he was settled, telling them where to send it on. But he never did. Very likely he had intended from the first that they should have it: this was his diffident, Orwell-like way of thanking them for their kindness to him. And the ship in the bottle remains with them to this day.

March was for Yorkshire, and he began in Sheffield. By this time he had established a network of contacts through the NUWM, and it led him, in Sheffield, to the Searles' house—two up, two down, outside WC—in Wallace Road.

They were a very likable couple, with a five-year-old child, living on the dole—Mr. Searle unemployed, Mrs. Searle working as a char at sixpence an hour. Orwell noted in the diary: "I have seldom met people with more natural decency." They were kind and helpful, and so too was William Brown (on Rees's list), unemployed, a sometime contributor to the *Adelphi*, who played a Garrett-like role and took him at a nonstop pace all over Sheffield, showing him slums, housing estates, and factories—supplying him with facts and more facts, grim and unavoidable, to add to those he had already collected in Lancashire. Once more the familiar note—of kindness that asks nothing in return, as he encountered from first to last in his travels—was made: "very anxious to help." But in the privacy of the diary Orwell felt constrained to add that B. was "tiresome . . . to be with," being "too conscious of his Communist convictions." Immediately he had pigeonholed Orwell as a bourgeois, remarking on his "public school twang." But in spite of this initial difficulty, they got on well together, inspiring a famous phrase in the diary—that Brown (Orwell felt) was disposed to treat him as "a sort of honorary proletarian." Too much has been made of the phrase by later admirers of Orwell, who fail to recognize that he himself was not deceived by it (as he might have been four years before, as a part-time down-and-outer), however much it may have pleased him. One of the lessons he was already learning from his two months of collecting facts was that between the working class and the middle class was a gulf that could not be bridged. He could admire, sympathize, support, fight for, and some would say sentimentalize the working class; he could and henceforth always would be *with* them; he could never be *of* them.

After Sheffield, he spent a week with the Dakins outside

Leeds, a reminder, if one were needed, of the gulf—not that Marjorie and Humphrey lived grandly. In fact, they lived very simply, in their house in Headingley, and in their cottage on the edge of the moors. But oh, the differences: theirs was another world. And he left to return to the working-class world, across the gulf, to a house in Barnsley—lodgings with a miner and his family—arranged by Wilde, the "kind and helpful" secretary of the South Yorkshire Branch, Working Men's Club and Institute Union. Again, there was the collecting of facts: by now he knew what his principal themes would be: the appalling housing to which the working class, employed and unemployed, were fated; the appalling conditions under which they worked, when they were lucky enough to have work; and the appalling poverty that befell them—the humiliations of the Means Test and the inadequacies of the dole—when there was no work for them and they became that abstraction, "the unemployed." But Barnsley, from which he doubted he would learn much that would be of interest, nonetheless was close to the mines: and he arranged to go down a "day hole" pit on Thursday, and on the Saturday down the Grimethorpe pit, which was very up-to-date, and promised to be less physically taxing. These two further "descents" would give him an authority, when he came to write about the mines, that he would not otherwise have had. But the impact of the first time, the descent in Wigan, was "devastating"—physically, and (more important) psychologically and intellectually. From the physical aftermath of those three hours underground in Crippen's, he would recover (as Joe Kennan remembered) after a couple of days in bed. But the psychological and intellectual consequence—the chief legacy of the journey North—stayed with him through his life, shaping his politics and his vision: here was a world underground, which he had not been aware of before, a world in the dark where men—not in the abstract, but men whom he'd met and liked and admired and who had been decent and kind to him—were spending the greater part of their lives. Theirs was an existence—and thousands of men like them shared it—that would have been unimaginable to him if he had not seen it, if he had not experienced it himself, however briefly and incompletely. He came away from the mines and the North in a state of guilt, anger, and compassion, and with a new, untested belief in the necessity of a political resolution.

FIFTEEN

WHEN ORWELL GAVE UP THE FLAT IN LAWFORD ROAD at the end of January and started on his journey to the industrial North, he had no intention of returning to London to live. He wanted, in a modest sort of way, to be a countryman, with a bit of land, enough for a vegetable garden and flowers, some animals to tend, with great trees, birds to observe and recognize, and a nearby stream to fish. As though to make certain that he would not backslide from his intention, he went ahead in February, while he was still in Lancashire, to rent sight unseen (through friends) a very small house at a very small rent (7/6 weekly) in the very small rural village of Wallington in Hertfordshire, midway between London and Cambridge. The nearest town was Baldock, three miles distant along the narrow, winding road that twice each week was the route for the bus between Baldock and Wallington. There was, along with other amenities in Baldock, a railroad station, and it was there, after more or less an hour train ride from London, that Orwell alighted on the second of April. As it was not a bus day, he walked across the fields to his new home, The Stores, Wallington—his sixth address since the publication of *Down and Out in Paris and London*. Although he would be away from it for considerable periods—most dramatically when he went off to fight in Spain—it would be his for a longer time than any other house (or flat) in his adult life; and when Eileen came to live with him he would be happier there than anywhere else.

The village was small, unspoiled, dull, remote in feeling if not in actual distance from London, and free of the dangerous quaintness that might attract tourists or stockbrokers. It had a population of less than a hundred, mostly aging—the school had been closed and converted into a lending library, and the dozen or so children were taken by bus to school in Baldock. The landmark was predictable: the twelfth-century parish church of St. Mary's. At the point where Kit's Lane and The Street came together, stood the village pub, The Plough (the other landmark), and next to it a low, two-storied, very small, very narrow—it was only eleven feet wide—three-hundred-year-old house of lath and plaster: this was The Stores. There was what passed for a little garden in front, and a somewhat larger one in the back, both, when Orwell took possession, in a state of ruination. Entering the house, you came directly into the main room—also very small—with low ceiling and heavy oak beams, which the previous tenant had fitted out with counter and shelves to serve as the village store, and which Orwell intended to revive. Adjoining it was a slightly smaller room, a sitting-dining room, whose connecting door had a row of peepholes cut out along the top so that one could look through to see if there were customers in the shop, and a minute kitchen with a sink and little oil stove. Upstairs were two small bedrooms and a bathroom (there was only a cold-water tap, and in the winter the toilet frequently froze over). Of course there was no electricity; heat was provided by Calor gas, and a fireplace that smoked and was unmanageable. But these defects, such as they were, hardly were defects in Orwell's eyes; the house answered to his practical and imaginative needs—his own place, in the country, with a little shop that would bring in (perhaps) money enough to cover the cost of the rent, and a garden that would in time produce a harvest of vegetables for the table, etc., etc., a good and quiet place to write, a spare room to put up friends who might come for a weekend; and if living was admittedly a bit primitive, he would eventually (say in a year or two) put in the conveniences. Fortunately, Eileen, when he brought her to see it the next week, shared his enthusiasm for it as well as his indifference to its defects: they were neither of them "mod-con" addicts. She was as drawn as he to the notion of reviving the store, undaunted at the prospect of reclaiming the garden, and delighted at the idea of their keeping animals—hens, of course, in a yard of their own, which would supply eggs; and goats, which would supply milk and be stabled in the shed behind the house, but put to graze in the common land, a fairly large area of rough grass and bushes and brambles, some distance from the cottage. Very likely the tininess of The Stores, its being little more than an oversized "playhouse," appealed to her fantasy side. For if Eileen was ironic, witty, practical, and immensely rational—always ready to bring Eric down to earth from one of his wilder flights—she was also deeply imaginative, and enjoyed "inventing" another world, populated with farmyard animals, whose traits of personality she developed with the skill of a psychologist or a novelist, bestowing names upon them—Kate and Mabel were the goats at The Stores—and creating for them an ever more complex, interminable series of adventures. For a time she thought of incorporating them into a children's story that would be set in a farmyard, whose animal characters, in that ancient tradition going back to

Aesop, would reproduce the traits of their human prototypes. But when the war came the project was gradually abandoned (like The Stores itself), and it survived only in the conversations she and Eric would have in bed at night, amusing themselves as the bombs fell over London, and they invented new adventures: foibles and follies for the animals of their imaginary farm.

But there was one significant flaw in The Stores—evident immediately to Eileen's closest friends and to her brother Laurence—that she either did not or chose not to recognize. It was an ideal place for a dedicated writer eager to get on with his writing, and to be at a safe distance from the encroachments of the London literary and political world. But for a child psychologist about to embark on a career, living there would have insuperable disadvantages. The awkwardness of reaching London from Wallington virtually ruled it out; and Cambridge, the other logical alternative for a starting point, was equally difficult to reach. But when Eric brought her to the village and showed her the house with such unbounded enthusiasm, it did not occur to her to raise objections. She seemed to fall into wholehearted agreement with his plans, quite as though she had no plans of her own.

THAT SPRING WAS DEDICATED TO SETTLING IN, WITH MRS. Anderson, a neighbor, coming in to "do" for him—rarely was an English gentleman so poverty-stricken that he could not afford a char—and the shop gradually being stocked with a heterogeneity of things—penny candy, biscuits, tea, string, rice, flour—that the villagers might possibly want, and the struggle with the garden under way (he told Rees that he expected within a year to make it "really nice") and a certain amount of planting around the house: rambler roses (from Woolworth's), three polyantha roses, two bush roses, six fruit trees, two gooseberry bushes, and he had hopes of planting walnut, quince, and mulberry trees. (According to a later occupant of the house, which is now known as Monk's Fitchett, the survival rate was not high, and there is nothing left to show of Orwell's tenancy but a few of the roses in front of the house.)

But he enjoyed it all—it was the country life that he had not so much idealized as yearned for—and he enjoyed playing the role of a storekeeper, though in the end, as a venture, it had far less staying power than the rambler roses from Woolworth's. Cyril Connolly, when he saw the shop, was immediately reminded, in a rather haunting, Proustian way, of Blair and himself at St. Cyprian's, and the long, long walks they had taken over the Downs,stopping at the little shops of Eastdean, Westdean, and Jevington for penny sweets. It was that sort of long-ago shop Blair had opened in Wallington, and Connolly had the impression that he saw himself as a kind of Edwardian shopkeeper out of a novel by H. G. Wells. Such a shop might have just done in 1910, but it was 1936, and what Eric and Eileen had failed to take properly into account was that the people of the village enjoyed their twice-weekly shopping expeditions into Baldock, which they combined with a visit to the cinema there. So that the most assiduous customers of The Stores were the village children, coming in to buy sweets. Eileen, either to amuse herself or to teach the children arithmetic, had priced the sweets thus: four for a ha'penny, seven for a penny. Obviously one did better coming by the shop twice and buying a ha'penny's worth each time, so that there was rather more bustle in the shop than the day's receipts reflected.

A COUNTRYMAN'S LIFE IS NOT IDYLLIC, AND CERTAINLY NOT the idyll a city man daydreaming of living in the country imagines it to be. Even at best it is demanding. Eric soon realized that if he were to take care of the animals, and the garden, and the shop, and the absolutely essential things that would restore the house to a modestly livable condition, he would have no time at all for what still came first: the work he had neglected while on the journey North, his writing. Accordingly, much of what had to be done was left undone, or postponed until after his marriage to Eileen, when she could share those time-consuming daily chores that are an unavoidable part of living in the country.

He set up his typewriter on the table in the sitting-dining room, and began to write. For the *New English Weekly*, a review of Cyril Connolly's novel, *The Rock Pool*. To friends, letters acquainting them with his changed circumstances. Most importantly there was the new book, on which, as he told Geoffrey Gorer, he'd made "a fairly good start."

Meanwhile, on April 20, Gollancz had published *Keep the Aspidistra Flying*. Its reception suggested that Orwell had arrived at a paradoxical point in his career. This was his fourth book, and by now he had his ready-made reputation, his niche where harried reviewers (and booksellers) could conveniently place him: "The more depressing his theme, the more effectively is his skill displayed" (*Times Literary Supplement*). There is a point at which praise becomes praise-by-rote. He had gone in four books from being unknown to being predictable: something new would have to be said of him to make him an interesting as well as a respected writer; or perhaps he had to write something new, not simply another version of what he had made familiar, to become interesting.

The man in the *Daily Mail*—this time, unluckily, not the faithfully enthusiastic Compton Mackenzie but one Douglas West—having paid the predictable tribute, "No realistic writer of today has produced books of greater vigour and reality," went on to add the ominous *but*. "But among the aspidistra Mr. Orwell seems to lose touch with reality. He gives us, it is true, a measured portrait of an ineffectual young man, and drives home the moral that all he needs to restore his self-respect is the sort of job he could have had for the asking. There is some searching talk, and one or two ideas are given an airing which, though not strictly fresh, will pass as original. A novel, however, needs something more than this."

On the other hand—and once an author has his reputation, there is always a reviewer to play "the other hand"—the poet Richard Church, in *John o' London's Weekly*, rose to the lyrical in his praise: "Mr. Orwell writes (and I hope he will pardon my trite phrase) in his heart's blood. The result is painful, but it is also convincing, human, and beautiful."

Keep the Aspidistra Flying was the third novel by George Orwell to be published in thirteen months, and Gollancz, trusting that by now there was an audience who would recognize his name and be eager to read whatever he wrote, ordered the largest first printing he had yet had: 3000 copies. But the reviewers were not sufficiently enthusiastic, or when enthusiastic were not sufficiently enticing to arouse anyone but a dedicated Orwellian. Three thousand copies turned out to be far more than were wanted; no American publisher had been found to take the place of the disillusioned Harpers' and import sheets; within a month the type was being distributed.

PARADOXICALLY, THE GRAY FATE OF THE NOVEL, HASTENING into semi-oblivion, hastened him towards the happiest period of his life. There was nothing to be gained by postponing any longer his marriage to Eileen, hoping for some dramatic improvement in his financial position that would make things easier for them. Once again the rewards of fiction had been meager. He had given up his earlier notion —never very seriously adhered to—of someday writing a best seller. His experience told him there was little likelihood that he would grow rich from the novels he intended to write in the future—and at this time, it should be emphasized, he still thought of himself primarily as a novelist, the sort who would write thirty novels by the time he was sixty. He appears to have been relieved that this was his situation —to be liberated even from the fantasy of a worldly success so at odds with the kind of life that both he and Eileen valued most. Indeed, his existence exactly as it was then, in the late-arriving spring of 1936, simple, austere, rural, seemingly timeless—living at The Stores, at work already on another book—only needed Eileen as his wife to fulfill an ideal of settled happiness he had never before allowed himself. (And it was an ideal that would be borne out by the reality. As his friend Geoffrey Gorer was later to say, "I think the only year that I ever knew him really happy was that first year with Eileen.")

It had been understood between them for some time that eventually they would be married. The sensible September argument had been that they should wait until Eileen had finished her course and found a job. It was doubtful whether on his own earnings he could afford to support them both. But in the spring, when he returned from the North and moved into The Stores, these scruples evaporated on both sides. They agreed they might be able to eke out an existence with the vegetables, livestock, sale of eggs from the hens, the shillings and pence the shop might bring them, and Eric's chancy literary income. (In fact it was rather larger than usual at the moment, thanks to the advance for the book on the North, of which he'd used up very little.)

For Eric the decision to marry Eileen was so logical and inevitable that it was more in the nature of a culmination than a decision. For Eileen, however, the decision involved a very conscious choice: either to marry Eric or to go on with her course, take her degree, and embark upon a career as a clinical psychologist. The two alternatives were irreconcilable, no doubt had been so from the beginning, and became so unquestionably from the time he settled on The Stores as the place where they would live. But as against the possibility of a career in which she might have done as well as her friends expected (or might not), there was the reality of marriage, and that is what she chose. To be Eric's wife was what she wanted. As for the course, she never bothered to finish it. Ahead of her was a marriage that would occupy her life fully, excitingly, necessitously, and in the years of the Second World War exhaustingly, until her death in 1945.

They decided to marry in the traditional month of June, but with a minimum of traditional fuss. Orwell, though a nonpracticing member of the Church of England, was sufficiently a traditionalist to wish to be married in it—besides, St. Mary's in Wallington was more convenient than the registry office in Baldock. On the morning of the appointed day, June 9, he found time to dash off a letter to Denys King-Farlow, his old friend from Eton, whom he had not seen since then, and who had written out of the blue to reestablish the friendship and to invite him to a birthday party. He had to decline the invitation, but he proposed that King-Farlow should drop in whenever he was anywhere near, and added the news that he was getting married that very day, and reading the Prayer Book to brace himself against what he considered the "obscenities" of the wedding service. Geoffrey Gorer, a more recent friend, also was told the news in a letter, and to him Orwell confided the melodramatic prospect that the Blairs and the O'Shaughnessys might join forces to prevent the wedding, though there is no evidence on either side to support the notion.

Mr. and Mrs. Blair and Avril, bearing some of the family silver as a wedding gift for the young Blairs, drove over from Southwold, and Laurence and Gwen and Mrs. O'Shaughnessy came up from London to attend the service in the church, which was performed by the vicar of nearby Galston, with Eric's father and Eileen's mother acting as witnesses. They had a little party in The Stores afterwards —more than enough with the eight of them to crowd the tiny house—and at some point Avril and her mother took Eileen upstairs, as she later told her friend the novelist Lettice Cooper, to warn her of the burden she was taking on. (What must Eric have thought? But perhaps the private little chat occurred when he, his father, and the O'Shaughnessys had already stepped next door to The Plough for a celebratory drink.)

Actually, what Eileen was taking on was not so much a burden as a burdensome role: the writer's wife. She proved to be very good at it, because she was intelligent, sympathetic, humorous, and appreciative of what Eric wrote; and because she recognized and did not struggle against the quite special way his being a writer would shape the course of their lives together.

SIXTEEN

Orwell belonged to the category of writers who write. For him a day without writing was not a good one. There were, effectively, no pauses in the process: if not a novel, then a review, or an essay, a letter, a diary, a shopping list. For such a writer, as Eileen once said, not reprovingly, "his work comes before anybody"—even his wife!—and alas for the wife who cannot accept this. Indeed, Orwell's relation to writing was oddly like a marriage: in sickness and in health, for richer or for poorer, till death do them part, it would go on.

In May he was writing the first chapter of *The Road to Wigan Pier.*

On the afternoon of June 9, he was married. That morning, as we have seen, he found time at least to write a letter.

On the morning of June 10 he was back at the typewriter as usual. Work on *The Road* had to wait while he put the finishing touches to "Shooting an Elephant," which proved to be one of his best, and subsequently one of his most famous, essays.

The circumstances of his writing "shooting an elephant" cast an interesting light on Orwell's tangential relation to the dominant literary movement of the 1930's in England, that group of gifted young poets and novelists who became celebrated during the decade and would enter literary history as "Auden & Co.": W. H. Auden, Stephen Spender, C. Day Lewis, Louis MacNeice, Christopher Isherwood, John Lehmann, Rex Warner, and Edward Upward. Orwell's name would properly be omitted from such a list, no doubt to his satisfaction, by anyone familiar with the politics and *placement* of literary London in the 1930's: he was not in the "movement." But in 1939, in the autobiographical portion of his *Enemies of Promise,* Cyril Connolly had written of Orwell as Eric Blair, his friend at St. Cyprian's and Eton, and in the critical-historical portion he had written of him as the novelist George Orwell, bracketing him with a leading member of Auden & Co.: "In England the ablest exponents of the colloquial style among the younger writers are Christopher Isherwood and George Orwell, both leftwing and both, at the present level of current English, superlatively readable." This would lead to misconceptions. To a critic such as Q. D. Leavis, writing in *Scrutiny* in 1940, it was sufficient evidence to place Orwell in the suspect, charmed circle. In her review of *Inside the Whale,* a collection of three of his essays brought out by Gollancz in 1939, she writes: "Mr. Orwell . . . belongs by birth and education to 'the right Left people', the nucleus of the literary world who christian-name each other and are honour bound to advance each other's literary career; he figures indeed in Connolly's autobiography as a schoolfellow. This is probably why he has received indulgent treatment in the literary press. He differs from them in having grown up . . . by the force of a remarkable character."

But not only did he differ from them, he was not *of* them. In the title essay of the book under review, he had written scathingly of the Auden group, in its literary, social, and political aspects. And this was only the most recent of his attacks upon what he was fond of describing as "the pansy left." In particular he was offended by their politics, which did not seem to him justly earned—"a kind of playing with fire by people who do not even know that the fire is hot." He himself came to politics much later than they—not until 1936—but he stayed longer. From the time of his experience in Spain until his death in 1950, politics would be a center for his life in a way that it never was for the writers we more readily associate with the political 1930's.

Principle prompted his attacks, but especially in the early years of the decade, when he was so obsessively concerned with a literary career of his own, elements of spite and animosity played a part too, as he later acknowledged. Whether they intended to or not, Auden & Co. did rather hog the limelight, and there would have been a sense of revenge on Orwell's part in sneering at Auden as "a gutless Kipling." But from 1936 on, really from the time of his marriage to Eileen, as he became more at ease with himself, more confident and more recognized, he began gradually to renew old acquaintanceships with Etonian contemporaries, and even to allow himself to become acquainted with members of the "movement," some of whom he liked a good deal—notably Stephen Spender, to whom he was introduced by Cyril Connolly.

Nonetheless, old prejudices lingered on, and when, in the spring of 1936, he received a letter from John Lehmann, asking him to contribute to a journal of which he was editor, he was immediately on guard.

Lehmann did have just the sort of credentials that Orwell distrusted. Like Orwell himself he had been in College at Eton. Unlike Orwell he had gone on from there to Trinity College, Cambridge. He was a poet whose books of verse had been published by Leonard and Virginia Woolf at the Hogarth Press. His work had been included in those seminal anthologies, *New Signatures* and *New Country*, at the beginning of the decade that announced the arrival of "the movement," and not only was he one of the right Left people, he also knew and was a friend of the right people who wrote. That spring (1936) he brought out the first number of what was to become one of the most influential and admired publications of the 1930's and 1940's. He called it *New Writing*—evidently everything in the 1930's had to be *new*—and he intended to issue it as a book twice yearly, dedicated to writing of superior quality and to anti-Fascism. These aims were generalized enough to allow him to consider as a prospective contributor virtually anyone who was not an avowed hack or an avowed Fascist. As an editor with a highly developed sense of who was writing what and what was worth publishing, it was highly logical that he should write to Orwell to ask if he had anything he might be willing to send to *New Writing*.

Orwell's reply on the twenty-seventh of May was guarded: he would like to write "a sketch . . . describing the shooting of an elephant. It all came back to me very vividly the other day . . . but it may be that it is quite out of your line. I mean it might be too lowbrow for your paper and I doubt whether there is anything anti-Fascist in the shooting of an elephant." Then, having protected his flank, so to speak—a more diffident reply can hardly be imagined, or a more depreciatory or less enticing "brief description" of what would be one of the great essays of this century—he got to the crucial point: Would, or would not, such a sketch be in Lehmann's line? "If not, then I won't write it; if you think it might interest you I'll do it and send it along for you to consider."

Could Orwell have been serious? Supposing Lehmann

had said "No?" Would we really, then, not have had "Shooting an Elephant"? Such speculations are trivial-sounding, no doubt, but of such, sometimes, is literary history.

It is literary-historical fact, however, not speculation, that Lehmann replied promptly to say that he would very much like to read the piece (knowing that a sketch of shooting an elephant by the author of *Burmese Days*, which he greatly admired, would never be confused with the reminiscences of a big-game hunter), that Orwell sat down promptly to write it, and sent it off to Lehmann on June 12, three days after the wedding, that Lehmann read it, admired it, bought it, and published it in the second number of *New Writing* in the autumn of 1936. His editorial acumen or "instinct," for which he would become famous in the next two decades, had led him straight to a masterpiece.

"Shooting an Elephant" marks the beginning of the major phase of Orwell's career, and it is not just coincidence that the time of its writing should coincide with the beginning of his marriage. There is an uncramped expression of feeling, a generosity and humaneness, an acknowledgment of the complexity of seemingly simple experience that had been absent from his earlier writing, and that would be present in his work thereafter, which can be attributed at least in part to the influence of Eileen. (It is noteworthy that the vehement bitterness and rancor, so evident in much of his early work, reassert themselves only after her death, and reach a kind of culminating, nightmarish intensity in *1984*.)

"Shooting an Elephant" is the third of his efforts to draw upon his Burmese experience. As early as 1931, when he was still writing as Eric A. Blair, he had made a first attempt with his essay (or "story") "A Hanging"; then in 1934 there had been *Burmese Days;* and now, this sketch of the shooting of an elephant. It had come back to him vividly, how, as a young police officer in Burma, he had been called upon to shoot a tame elephant that had gone on a rampage. He had no wish to perform what he recognized would be an act of unnecessary murder, for the maddened elephant had subsided and was no longer a danger to anyone; but the Burmese, two thousand of them, gathering to watch their imperialist oppressor in his predestined role, *wanted* him (as he suddenly realized) to play out the role to its bloody end—*to kill*—and in the end he did so, simply not to lose face. But not so simply, of course. In this single episode—exotic to the Western imagination, but a fairly routine part of the life of the police officer in Burma—Orwell found a way, as he had not been able to do before, of suggesting the evil, the dilemma, and the pathos of imperialism: his sympathy for the victims that the system called into being, the ruled and the rulers alike, which made his recognition of its "impossibility" all the more impressive.

THE PROSE IN "SHOOTING AN ELEPHANT" IS SUPPLE AND UN-forced, deceptively simple in its intelligent, conversational tone—one hears a voice that is by now recognizably Orwell's. He had arrived at a level of assurance that augured well for the book of the journey North that he had begun a few weeks earlier, and that was to be his principal literary occupation for the next several months. He would have a rough first draft done by October, and he would send off the final version to Moore in December.

A book written in six months suggests a book written easily. In fact, *The Road to Wigan Pier* presented a number of problems that he never solved to his satisfaction, and although it was the book that was to make him famous (and in some quarters, infamous), it is a curiously uneven achievement. He had come back from the North full of impressions and information: it was all vivid and fresh in his mind (and in his diary), and in theory it should have been less difficult to transcribe on the page than an experience in Burma from many years back. But shooting an elephant had been *his* experience, he had been at the center of it. Now he was to write of the experience of *others* as he had observed it—the intent of the Gollancz commission was clear enough—and paradoxically, it made for an odd degree of literary self-consciousness in the early stages of the writing.

He had great difficulty, at first, in finding the right tone. In a book of this kind, art that calls attention to itself is "too much art," and the artist too conspicuous. In retrospect, the answer to the problem seems clear enough: the right note was available all along in the un-self-conscious, unexaggerated, un-"literary" pages of his diary. But he began by thinking of the diary as no more than "raw material" to be reworked, as though he had embarked on a Zolaesque or Dickensian novel of life in the lower depths, rather than what *The Road*, in its first part, became: a sympathetic, honest, and angry report of life in the industrial North, still suffering the effects of a Depression that neither the Tory government nor the capitalist system seemed able to relieve.

Unlike the day-by-day, chronological form of the diary, the book begins—and we are writing here of the book as published; no manuscript either of the "rough draft" or the "revision" is known to have survived—in the middle of the journey. (Indeed, the sense of a journey, of the author being on "assignment," has been artfully suppressed.) In the first chapter we are simply there—in an unnamed industrial town in the North—with "I" the narrator, who is staying in squalid lodgings over a squalid tripe shop owned by a squalid couple, the Brookers. This first chapter is a detailed, leisurely introduction to the elder Brookers, to the other members of the family, to their ill-used lodgers, and the literally disgusting circumstances in which they live. On the first page alone there is such a wealth of unpredictable particulars that one assumes Orwell must have jotted them down on the spot for future reference. But that is not the case. From the diary we learn only that he shared a room with three other lodgers, that one of the other beds jammed across the foot of his, making it impossible for him to stretch out his legs without hitting its occupant in the small of the back. An eloquent detail in itself, but the book adds others even more remarkable. The bedroom, we learn, was formerly a drawing room, into which "four squalid beds" had been crowded alongside a good deal of furniture surviving from drawing-room days: "gilt chairs with burst seats," a horsehair armchair, "something between a sideboard and a hall-stand," and—perhaps most astonishing of all—we are told of "a heavy glass chandelier on which the dust was so thick that it was like fur." It is Orwell in his best "down-and-out" vein, and it goes on for pages, culminating in "a full chamber pot under the breakfast table"—the detail that decides him to leave—but one may wonder if it is the best vein in which to introduce the people of Wigan, most of whom (among those he met) he came to know and admire, with whose lives and struggles he so deeply sympathized, and who would play so significant a role in his conversion to Socialism.

The responses of two very different, differently qualified readers to this first chapter of *The Road to Wigan Pier* are instructive. The poet Edith Sitwell, qualified by breadth of sympathy and highly refined literary sensibility, wrote to the mother of Geoffrey Gorer: "The horror of the beginning . . . is unsurpassable. He seems to be doing for the modern world what Engels did for the world of 1840–50. But with this difference, that Orwell is a born writer, whereas Engels, fiery and splendid spirit though he was, simply wasn't a writer. One had to reconstruct the world from his pages for oneself." John Farrimond, qualified by experience—a Wiganer and a sometime miner, the author of *Dust in My Throat* and *Pick and Run*, who began his career as a novelist at the age of fifty—has written to the present authors: "In all my years around Wigan—I was a lad of eighteen about the time that Orwell was going his rounds researching—I have never met, nor heard of anybody as filthy as the Brookers. Dirt there was in plenty, but *filth* was something different. Unemptied chamber pots? All those I ever saw in those days were spotless. You had only to look over somebody's back yard, and they'd be lying there by the waste grid, emptied and washed."

One might fairly conclude from these so different responses that the poet, unfamiliar with the world Orwell was describing, recognized the truth which transcends particular details, and that the novelist—as a native more familiar with that world than Orwell the short-term visitor—recognized the exaggerations and errors while taking the larger truth for granted. (And viewing the chapters on Wigan altogether, Farrimond felt that they presented "a fairly accurate picture.")

Consulting the diary one discovers that Orwell was in Darlington Road, Wigan, in lodgings over a tripe shop, with people named F—— (who became the Brookers of *The Road*) from the fifteenth till the twenty-fifth of February 1936. Evidently the house, though larger than most in which he stayed, was squalid, smelly, and overcrowded. On the twenty-first of February he noted that it was getting on his nerves. Also that there was an unemptied chamber pot under the breakfast table that particular morning. (Which may, though he doesn't say so, have been emptied and washed out an hour later.) Nowhere else in the diary, except this page at the F——'s, is there a reference to chamber pots, unemptied or otherwise; nor, for that matter, does the diary tell us that at any of the other of the several working-class houses in which he stayed during the journey did he encounter a squalor even remotely comparable to the F——'s. That, clearly, was the appalling exception, and one can only wonder at his willingness to put up with it, as he did, for more than a week—surely his friends in the NUWM could have made a tactful arrangement for him to lodge elsewhere. Comfort apart, to have done so would have served his purposes better: the more he had seen and experienced for himself of housing in Wigan, the more impressive, authoritative (and influential) the total picture might have been. The Brookers, we learn from the diary, were not "so badly off." As a model, then, for the awful housing conditions in Wigan, their lodging house and tripe shop was perhaps too picturesquely awful to be typical. That fur-bearing chandelier, the filthiness of the Brookers themselves, with Mrs. B. wiping her mouth with strips of newspaper and littering the floor with "crumpled-up balls of slimy paper," make the situation seem too special. Or perhaps Orwell, in his eagerness to start out memorably, has worked it up with a shade too much art. There is more than one way to write a purple passage. In June, he would demonstrate in "Shooting an Elephant" the crucial balance between truth unadorned by art and truth heightened by artifice. Getting the new book under way at the end of April, he had yet to strike that balance.

Two further quotations seem in order. On the twenty-fourth of February, after his first descent into a coal mine, Orwell notes in the diary that he "went home [to Darlington Road] and had dinner and soaked myself for a very long time in a hot bath." From which we realize that the F——'s house, squalid though it might be, still had what the houses of most miners didn't have: "A proper bathtub" and "hot water laid on."

Finally, John Farrimond, in the same letter in which he points out exaggerations and omissions in *The Road*, concludes handsomely, "You certainly won't go far wrong in using Orwell as a Guide to Wigan in the thirties."

HE HAD FINISHED "SHOOTING AN ELEPHANT" AND THOUGHT IT good, a rare occurrence with him—for once there seems to have been none of that putting-down of his own work (botched! dreadful! loathe the sight of it!) one comes to expect from him in the thirties. Now he returned to the book for Victor Gollancz. In May he thought he had made a "fairly good start." Then came the Lehmann interruption. The interval away from the Wigan manuscript—so carefully wrought as far as he had gone, so ambitiously more than mere journalism—and the time spent sketching "Shooting an Elephant" had both been salutary. Letting the book simmer allowed him time to reconsider what Gollancz had proposed and what he himself wanted: a report on the North as he had observed it. And the writing of the "sketch" suggested a way to go on more easily and naturally with the book. Writing without exaggeration for literary effect, trusting in the material he had gathered, for its own sake as well as his responses to it, remembering the people he had met, places seen, certain crucial experiences—in *their* coal mines, *their* shelters, *their* houses—allowed him to record the lives and sufferings of others. The tone of the first chapter of *The Road,* those vivid, artfully rendered, and heightened scenes of life in the depths *chez* Brooker—that tone, in itself and certainly by contrast to what comes afterward, seems more appropriate to a novel than to reportage. (It is enlightening to compare the first sentences of Hemingway's novel *To Have and Have Not*—Havana in the early morning—with the first sentences of *The Road*—Wigan in the early morning—and discover their similarities of rhythm and phrasing. In both cases one is aware of the presence of a highly developed and self-conscious literary sensibility.*) This is not to discount the effectiveness of the first chapter—think of its impact upon Edith Sitwell—but simply to agree with Orwell's own decision in mid-June that it was not a productive direction in which to continue. Thereafter, from the second through the seventh chapter, Part I of the book, he was essentially a guide to Wigan, a reporter one comes quickly to trust.

Even so adverse a critic of Orwell as Harry Pollitt, who would trounce the book in the pages of the *Daily Worker,* was forced to concede some merit to its first part, and readers less biased will find in those seven chapters a portrait of poverty and its consequences that catches at the imagination and awakens sympathy and anger even now,

---

* In *Enemies of Promise* Cyril Connolly called attention to the Hemingway/Orwell stylistic resemblance. In a very ingenious way he fused together sentences from *To Have and Have Not, The Road to Wigan Pier,* and Isherwood's "Sally Bowles" into a composite paragraph that illustrated the qualities of "the colloquial style."

some forty years later, when the appalling conditions it describes have long since been ameliorated—perhaps, in some slight degree, a consequence of the book itself. Without consciously aspiring to do so, Orwell had written a work of reportage that endures as a work of art.

SEVENTEEN

PART I, AS WE HAVE SEEN, OPENS WITH A WORKING-CLASS "interior" at its most squalid, and it concludes (in the seventh chapter) with a working-class "interior" at its most idealized, where "you breathe a warm, decent, deeply human atmosphere," not likely to be found elsewhere. The progression from negative to positive in these two dramatically contrasting "interiors" represents the other journey that Orwell made when he went North, the subtext of Part I that becomes explicit in Part II: his own road to Socialism. The journey transformed him, as Rees observed, from a *je m'en foutiste* to a militant Socialist, but he was so much a Socialist of his own sort that perhaps it would have made it easier for those who attempt to write about him if he hadn't bothered to label himself.

The heart of his creed was simplicity itself: a belief that "economic injustice will stop when we want it to stop . . . the method adopted hardly matters." Appalled by the oppressed and neglected lives of the unemployed as he had seen them close up, he felt that something drastic would have to be done to change a social and economic situation that was no longer tolerable—something beyond the makeshifts of private philanthropy or the humiliating, inadequate government dole, something along the lines envisioned by Socialism. What precisely those lines might be, however, he never bothered to say, perhaps because he didn't know, or because, in the first fervor of conversion, he thought it unnecessary to worry over details: it was enough simply to declare oneself a Socialist.

To judge by what he wrote, or what he said to friends such as Rees, it is evident that he did not come to Socialism through ideological commitment. Socialist doctrine, as it argued for state ownership of the means of production and for a planned society, did not excite his imagination or awaken his deepest sympathies. He was much too idiosyncratic to be doctrinaire, and too independent by nature to take happily to the idea of plans (or, to adopt a post-Orwellian version of Newspeak, "social engineering"), even when, as in questions of public housing and slum clearance, the need was inarguable, the advantage undeniable.

What he wanted was a Socialism without planning—surely a contradiction in terms?—founded upon ideals of honor and decency: "Economic injustice will stop when we want it to stop." As he would presently discover, such ideals have only a tenuous connection to the world of practical politics, and honor and decency are not unique to adherents of a given party line, even if the party happened to be his own. The least one can say beginning or concluding a discussion of Orwell's politics in general, and his Socialism in particular, is that a man who believes that "the method . . . hardly matters" will prove to be an unorthodox Socialist.

Unorthodoxy is written all over Part II of *The Road to Wigan Pier*, not simply in its exposition (or invocation) of Socialism as Orwell understood it, but also in the metamorphosis of the book itself. For what had been begun as a work of reportage was transformed at midpoint, and with questionable logic, into a mix of politics, polemics, and selective autobiography. Part I had been, as Gollancz proposed, a report of the working class in the North, *their* lives, their work—and want of it—their struggles, all recorded with candor and sympathy, and as such a prime document of the 1930's. Part II became, as Orwell decided it must, *his* life, his ideas and speculations, his critique of Socialism, drawing upon illustrative moments of theoretical or actual experience, exhilarating in the writing and sometimes infuriating (at least to its early readers), and as such a prime source of confusion in sorting out truth from legend in the story of George Orwell.

The explanation he devises for the shift in the book is simple, and perhaps a shade disingenuous. He had gone— on his own, as it were; there is no mention of the commission—to the North, where unemployment was the worst in Britain, to see it in its true nature, and to be as close as possible to the working class, who were its victims. This self-imposed mission symbolized his two-pronged approach to Socialism. First, you must decide that things are intolerable. Second, you must adopt "a definite attitude on the terribly difficult issue of class," those attitudes, habits, customs, and prejudices that define the classes and come between them. "Terribly difficult"—or, as he put it more pungently in a letter to Jack Common, "Class-breaking is a bugger."

What he had seen in the North, the substance of Part I of *The Road,* proved beyond doubt the intolerability of things. The class question, as exemplified by the history of his own attitudes towards it, and the attitudes of all those others like him who were across the gulf from the working class, is dealt with implacably (and sometimes comically, as in a discussion of table manners and eating habits that foreshadows Nancy Mitford's U and non-U) in Part II, though whether the question is satisfactorily answered therein is hard to say. The facts of unemployment, in all their reams and charts, are something one can report on objectively. Class "attitudes" and prejudices, and the hostilities they give rise to—the belief, for example, that the working class smells, one of Orwell's most notorious animadversions in *The Road*—tend to be subjective and not susceptible to objective proof. (It was Orwell's bad luck or peculiarity to be hypersensitive to smells, especially unpleasant ones, which induced in him both a physical and a psychological reaction. He tells us that as a young man, before he had rid himself of the prejudiced class attitudes he had been taught, he found the smell of sweat exuded by working-class bodies, even when out of doors in the sunlight, so offensive that it turned his stomach. Doubtless his was an extreme reaction, but it does not invalidate his claim that he was representative or symptomatic of his class in accepting as true the notion that the working class did smell.)

At this point a crucial distinction has to be made if one is to understand Orwell's strategy in *The Road*. Although it was written primarily *about* the working class, and on their behalf, the book was not written *for* them. (When the Wiganers whom he had observed finally got to read what he had written about them, they were not entirely pleased.) Evidently the readers whom Orwell envisioned, at whom the book was aimed like a weapon, were more or less of his own class—lower-upper-middle—and so he could put himself forward to them as a "symptomatic figure." His experience (in his own mind) would stand for theirs—he thought the working class smelled and so must they; his progress, beginning in prejudice and ending in enlightenment, might prove exemplary. His tone is that of the man who has been through it all and knows whereof he speaks. Having freed himself from the divisive class attitudes he so deplores (and that make the achievement of a true Socialism impossible), he is determined that they shall do likewise. He brings before them as an object of contempt your typical middle-class Socialist—who would almost certainly turn out to be the typical reader of a book such as *The Road*— and observes disapprovingly that a Socialist of that sort is more likely to associate with someone from the middle rather than the working class. What price Socialism? Such a figure may be Socialist in his politics—meaning that he votes Labour and reads the *New Statesman*—but he is still invincibly bourgeois in his tastes, in food and wine and books and ballet. "Most significant, he invariably marries into his own class."

This damning indictment, drawn up by Orwell within weeks of his making precisely such a marriage himself, sounds odd indeed, the more so as one knows that it was written in a state of unmitigated domestic happiness. But the tone of the sentence on the page carries all before it: it is hard to believe that the man who wrote it would not himself be liberated from so bourgeois a fate. In the circumstances, one can understand why those early readers who knew no more of Orwell than what Orwell chose to tell them in his forthright-sounding prose might leap to the conclusion that had so irritated Elizaveta Fen: "He's married to a woman of the people, and leads the life of a labourer."

Very likely, in the abstract, it would have pleased him to get free of his class altogether—although he seems never even to have entertained the notion of marrying a woman of the working class. His attempts to declass himself were more fantasied than real, and his successes equivocal: at best, as in Sheffield, when he was forgiven his Public School accent and treated for the day as an "honorary proletarian". (Being called "Comrade," a not unusual custom among working-class Socialists and Communists, made him ill at ease then, as we have seen. At the end of the year, however, arriving in Barcelona, he was thrilled to discover that honorary class titles such as "Don" and "Señor" had been abandoned, and everyone was called "Comrade.") He did affect certain habits and attitudes towards food and drink that he considered to be "working class"—especially when with friends and acquaintances who belonged, like himself, to the lower-upper-middle or above—but he was quite aware that they *were* affectations, a form of irony or teasing. (Sometimes, though, it was a case of his left hand not knowing what his right was doing. Life at The Stores was determinedly simple, as both Eric and Eileen preferred it—still, there was the family silver; the portrait of an ancestress, Lady Mary Blair; wine with dinner; vegetables and herbs brought in from the garden; old brass candlesticks; the poodle, Marx. Their life was simple, even austere, in many respects uncomfortable, and they were hard-pressed for money; but by no stretch of the imagination would one say the Blairs were living in a working-class interior.)

No doubt it is unfair to hold a polemicist, whose principal interest is in scoring points, to accuracy in matters of fact, when it's the general impressions, not the minute or exact particulars, that count; nor to expect restraint from him when exaggeration will better serve his purpose. The portrait with which Orwell inaugurates Part II—a portrait of Eric Blair on the way to becoming George Orwell—is as harsh, as biased, and in some respects as misleading, as any that follow of delinquent or deficient fellow Socialists, but it does make up in conviction for what it lacks in precision. We witness the transformation of a snobbish, class-ridden servant of Imperialism (Blair) into a veritable Jeremiah among Socialists (Orwell). With that passion for generalizations so characteristic of him, and with the fervor of a new convert, he launched a splendidly unmoderated attack upon Socialists of the middle class, virtually all of whom are judged and found wanting. There are, in a category of their own, the horror types of the crank fringe—beardless eunuchs and bearded sandal-wearers, fleshy middle-aged scoutmasters in shorts drawn tight across their obscenely bulging buttocks, and vegetarians (a pet hate of Orwell's), immediately recognizable by their peculiar vegetarian smell (whatever that may be). Then, in another category, are those aforementioned bourgeois party members with their gentlemanly waistcoats (bottom button undone) and their insincere table manners (won't drink tea out of saucers). And as a third category, in a chapter or pillory of their own, the latter-day admirers of H. G. Wells (such as Eric Blair had been years before at St. Cyprian's), who share Wells's out-of-date faith in progress and a scientifically perfected future.

If these three categories provide a fair sampling of Socialists—cranks, snobs, and optimistic simpletons—is it any wonder the plain, straightforward, no-nonsense English workingman is put off Socialism? How can he make common cause with these unsavory specimens? Orwell is at pains to insist that he is writing as a convinced Socialist himself, and it is only as a true believer that he takes on the painful role of devil's advocate. Pointing out faults and faults and faults, he does so very much in the spirit of a headmaster (Mr. Vaughan Wilkes, say) administering a caning to an erring schoolboy (Blair, say)—not because he enjoys doing it, but for the good of the boy. What Orwell does, he reminds the reader who may misunderstand, he does for the good of the cause, to bring about the day (still in the future) when Socialism will triumph, as it must, in England's blighted and undernourished land. But as he sweeps along from chapter to chapter, unflagging in his sometimes outrageous, sometimes justified critique, the sheer zest with which he makes the devil's case against Socialism knocks the proportions of the second half of the book askew. The case *for* Socialism is late in coming, and when it does, in the brief final chapter, it proves to be thin and disappointingly generalized. All very well to say Orwell knew he was preaching to the converted—and so needn't resort to argumentation that would already be familiar to them—but here was yet one more paradoxical instance of the devil getting off with the best lines.

Of course there is no reason to believe that he intended this to happen. There is an air of improvisation about Part II that suggests that Orwell started out with a number of notions he meant to pursue, paramount among them the iniquity of class differences, and trusted to luck, instinct, and high spirits to bring him safely to the end. It is indicative that while he had no difficulty in raising the problem of class—he would always be very good at raising a problem—he did not allow himself anything like a rigorous attempt to come up with a solution to it. Apparently, as with economic injustice, he felt that a change of heart was the essential answer; the method adopted hardly matters. Perhaps if he had had more time to reflect before writing, if he had not been writing in so euphoric a state—which makes even his outbursts of extravagant indignation so exhilarating to read—he might have infused his new Orwellian idealism with a saving drop of his old Blairian cynicism. For in the long run, a change of accent might prove more effective as a leveler than a change of heart, though more difficult to achieve. But he was enjoying himself too much, firing off his salvos in rapid succession—taking aim in every possible direction—to allow himself to be deflected by complicating questions. Never before had he written with such zest and pleasure, no book of his had been turned out in so short a time and with such freedom from self-doubt. If, moving towards the end of the second draft, he felt it perhaps did not quite hang together as neatly as it should, he was not unduly concerned. Certainly he was not troubled by the ever-widening gap between the reality of his own experience and the angry fantasies that enliven his polemic.

ONE EXAMPLE PERHAPS WILL SUFFICE. IN PART II OF *The Road* there is a curious passage on working-class intellectuals, whom he divides into two categories: those who remain working-class (admirable), and those who climb into the middle class (less admirable). The latter have no choice, if they wish to succeed, but to come to terms with the corruption of the London literary world. In that world, Orwell assures us in the accents of bitter experience, you don't get ahead by virtue of ability, but by frequenting literary cocktail parties and by "kissing the bums of verminous little lions." A vivid summary, worthy of a latter-day Jeremiah (or a Juvenal), but does it square with reality? Well, at the very moment that these scathing observations on how to get published in the most influential places were being written into Chapter 10 of *The Road,* the second number of *New Writing* was being made available in the shops. It confirmed the impression of its predecessor: here was one of the most distinguished and influential literary periodicals that London had to offer (then or later). To appear in its pages was a mark of genuine distinction. Orwell himself led off the list of contributors with "Shooting an Elephant"—and be it remembered that John Lehmann had read and admired his work, especially *Burmese Days*, and it was Lehmann who had written out of the blue to ask for a contribution, not the reverse. There, too, along with Orwell, was V. S. Pritchett, in no sense of the term an "establishment" man, with "Sense of Humour," which has since won an enduring place for itself in the history of the English short story. And in this second number of *New Writing* there was notable work by Ralph Bates, Ignazio Silone, W. H. Auden, André Chamson, Rex Warner, and Ralph Fox. Most remarkably, however, in the light of Orwell's vigorous assertion that bum-kissing and partygoing counted for more than talent in getting on and getting into print, in the same number there was also a story by George Garrett, whom Orwell had met in Liverpool in February. (Garrett seems to have been one of the two working-class writers Orwell actually knew at this time—the other was Jack Common.) His presence in *New Writing*, far more than Orwell's own, would seem to call into question the polemical point being made, for Garrett, as we know, was an unemployed docker, blacklisted as a Communist, living on the dole, an even less likely habitué of cocktail parties than Orwell himself; plainly he had been included in Lehmann's periodical on his merits alone. One would think that this inconvenient fact might possibly have stirred up second thoughts—mightn't the Jeremiad properly be reconsidered, the language moderated? Nothing of the sort happened. The phrase was too memorable to be sacrificed, the point seemed worth the making, and in a polemic it's the most vividly expressed thoughts (however questionable or superficial) that are the best remembered. With what relish, what zest those working-class climbers were fed to those verminous lions!—and so, ultimately, to the folklore of London literary life in the 1930's.

ONE UNDENIABLE ADVANTAGE OF WRITING WITHOUT PAUSING for second thoughts is that a book gets written fast: by the end of September, a mere five months since he'd started, the first draft was finished; he estimated that he would have completed the necessary revision by December. To Jack Common he admitted that he felt he'd made "rather a muck of parts of it," by which, it seems reasonable to assume, he meant parts of Part II. Since no manuscripts of *The Road to Wigan Pier* are known to survive, one can only speculate as to how and what he revised. But the close correspondences between the Diary and Part I constitute evidence of a sort—revision in Part I almost certainly must have been *stylistic*. Whereas a passage in Part II that couldn't have been written at the earliest before the end of October (it refers to the Fascist bombardment of Madrid) is proof of revision by *adding to the text*. But before carrying such speculations further, and saying more about the revised and completed manuscript that would be given to Gollancz in December, we prefer to look back to that marvelous summer during which the first draft was being written.

In any study of Orwell's life, the summer of 1936 must occupy a unique place. His health was good, his spirits high; he was able to work as he wished; he had the pleasure of living in the country, which he had long wanted to do; above all, the pleasure of being married to Eileen, of being with her, week after week, untroubled by illness or absence, or the strains they were later to experience, working, surviving, physically worn down, in wartime London. Indeed, only in that summer of 1936 would there be such a combination of elements and circumstances as to fulfill an ideal of happiness for him. (Thereafter, one element or another would always be lacking, one or another circumstance would interfere, and after Eileen's death during minor surgery in 1945, even the ideal itself was abandoned: the happiness of that long-ago summer would never be recaptured.)

The friends who visited them at The Stores—Elizaveta Fen, Geoffrey Gorer, Patricia Donohue, Cyril Connolly, Denys King-Farlow—testify to the quality of the life there, the sense of a deep attachment between the Blairs, the mix of affection and irony (of which Eileen was as capable as Eric), of mutual appreciation and understanding: they were, beyond doubt, a couple. (Or, in Elizaveta Fen's words, "a partnership . . . in which Orwell's needs came first," an unspoken understanding that Eileen willingly assented to, even though it had meant, in practical terms, closing off the possibility of a career of her own.)

Miss Fen, from whose memoir we have quoted earlier, is the only one of their friends to have written of them at this period in this setting, and since her 1960 memoir has never been reprinted, we quote from it again at some length. (We have also followed her usage in conversation with us, and substituted Eric for George whenever the name occurs in the printed text.)

> However much I enjoyed Eileen and Eric's company, the weekends at the cottage were, in a sense, a test of endurance. Like all Russians, I cannot bear being cold

indoors, and the spare bedroom upstairs was as cold as an ice-box, even on June nights. Birds built their nests between the ceiling and the room, and although their singing was delightful in the morning, at night they would sometimes stamp and struggle overhead like an army of demons. "People think they are *rats*," Eric told me with the characteristic smile he had whenever he indulged in being mildly sadistic, and expected you to be frightened and shocked.

Whatever people might think, or Eric might say in that way of his, Eileen knew that in addition to birds in the eaves, the cottage was full of mice—not that this bothered her any more than it did Eric. Patricia Donohue (who had met the Blairs through Elizaveta Fen, and visited them at The Stores from time to time, and continued to see them afterwards in London during the war until Eileen's death) remembers Eileen once telling her that "battalions of mice were standing by at night, shoulder to shoulder on the shelves and pushing the china off."

Visitors unused to that sort of thing might look askance, but birds in the eaves and mice on the shelves were among the amenities, not the vexations, of country life, and Eileen and Eric thrived on it. Eileen, about whose good looks all who knew her are agreed, had never looked fresher or more attractive. "I remember," Patricia Donohue writes (in a letter to the authors), "Eileen as she stood once in the living room of the cottage at Wallington. She was wearing a tweed suit which suited her, and I noted how good-looking she was, with a good figure. At that time she was looking well and cheerful." Later, Miss Donohue goes on to say, "sometimes in London I thought she seemed very tired. [In fact, her physical state was a good deal more precarious than

Eileen or Eric ever realized, or were prepared to admit.] But of course that was a time of air raids and blackout and she was doing a good deal—housekeeping and cooking—and also a fulltime job at the Ministry of Food."

(These latter remarks go a good way to explain Anthony Powell's impression of Eileen, whom he met for the first time during the war years and "never knew very well," as someone "not usually given to making light of things, always appearing a little overwhelmed by the strain of keeping the household going, which could not have been easy." Here too one should add Elizaveta Fen's observation that after Eileen's beloved brother Laurence was killed by a bomb during the evacuation from Dunkirk, "her grip on life, which had never been very firm, loosened considerably.")

But the grief of 1940, the fatigue and depression that were to be a kind of background to the Blairs' London life during the war, while they went on living as though there weren't time to be upset or unnerved by such minor difficulties as being bombed out of their flat—in short, the future that awaited them—all those complexities of wartime life were at a still unguessable distance from the rural simplicities of Wallington in the summer of 1936. Very early, and without difficulty, they settled into the pattern of working writer and devoted wife. At 6:30 a.m. the alarm clock pealed through the house, and George got up to feed the chickens. By the time he was done, Eileen had come downstairs to the kitchen and was preparing breakfast: eggs (from their hens), bread (which she would have baked the day before), bacon (bought from neighbors who kept pigs), a pot of steaming coffee with chicory in the mix—a blend in the French manner Eric had grown fond of in Paris. Then they went their separate ways: he to the typewriter or to work in the garden; she, to wash up the dishes, take care of household chores, think about the next meal. (She once told Patricia Donohue, in a half-joking way, that "she reckoned there were only 25 minutes between the clearing up of one meal and the start of preparations for another.") But she enjoyed cooking and was very good at it—her apple meringue pie was delicious and memorable. Inez Holden, the author and journalist who introduced George and Eileen Orwell to Anthony and Lady Violet Powell one evening in the Café Royal in 1941, continued to remember that delicious pie, and evoked it for the present authors years after Eileen and Eric were dead, along with a host of other evocative, affectionate, and poignant details. Her summing-up of Eileen—"so intelligent, so nice"—might stand as a universal verdict. (From the many people to whom we talked about her, we never heard an adverse opinion. The only differences had to do with her complexion. Men tended to speak of her "high Irish coloring"—the phrase comes from Bob Edwards, a member of the House of Commons, who had known her in Spain and liked her immensely; women tended to speak of her very white skin. When we pointed out the contradiction to a woman friend of hers, she explained it thus: Eileen wore rouge, but applied it so lightly men wouldn't recognize it.)

There was, it seems, more than enough for each of them to do to fill their days at The Stores. Eric was racing ahead with *The Road*, or reading books sent to him for review by the *New English Weekly*, *Time and Tide*, and the *Fortnightly*. Eileen tended the shop, whenever it needed tending, which was not very often. As we have already said, the most assiduous customers were the village children in search of penny candy. (Earnings from the shop generally came to half a crown a week. Balanced against expenses, it was not a munificent return, although there was the advantage, they argued not very convincingly, of getting supplies at wholesale.) Late in the afternoon, smoking furiously, Eileen would walk Mabel and Kate, the goats, along the verges of the common. (One wonders if it was Eileen, with her sense of mischief, who named those goats—Mabel, as in Mabel Fierz, Eric's Egeria; or Mabel, as in Ida Mabel Blair, Eric's mother? One feels certain, in any case, that it must have been Eric who picked out "Marx" for their dirty white poodle, for Eileen's imagination did not tend to run along political lines.) Then there were the hens to be taken care of; she gathered the warm eggs to sell in the shop or for their own use; or to exchange with neighbors for bacon and sausage, or for fruits and vegetables they weren't growing themselves. She was especially fond of hens; for a time, when there were spare hours to fill, she thought that she might even write a children's book with a cast of hens in the leading roles, but, as it turned out, there wasn't time. How much there was to do in a day! Even though, when a friend like Elizaveta Fen, busy with her career, came to visit and one tried to describe to her what one did in Wallington, it seemed that one did nothing—nothing of importance. And yet the day was full. Before one knew where the hours had gone, it was time to prepare dinner. And after dinner, a stroll in the summer night; then homeward across the fields to bed. The logical end of such a life, to which both Eric and Eileen looked forward with a passion, ought to have been children. But Eileen did not become pregnant, and eventually they were to learn—though not for another two years; nothing was to flaw that summer of 1936—that Eric was sterile, as he told Rayner Heppenstall, and as Eileen confided in Elizaveta Fen.

Perhaps the most rewarding visit that summer—from a literary point of view, and at that, inadvertently—was paid to them by Denys King-Farlow, who came out to renew a friendship that had been long in abeyance. We have mentioned how a letter from him, forwarded to Blair by Cyril Connolly, arrived at The Stores on the morning of June 9, an hour or two before Eric and Eileen were to be married. Putting aside the prayer book in which he'd been studying the "obscenities" of the marriage service, he found time to dash off a friendly reply, urging King-Farlow to drop in if he should be passing anywhere near. "I should love to see you again."

They had been in the same Election in College at Eton, and together had been editors, first of the one-copy handwritten paper *Election Times*, and then of the printed "humorous" magazine *College Days*, a considerably more sophisticated and profitable venture—it included a good deal of paid advertising. The two young men had enjoyed a quasi-affectionate, rather peppery relationship; and in an oddly similar style the relationship was picked up in 1936 where it had been left off in Eton in 1922. They had parted then, each to go his own way, Blair to Burma, King-Farlow to Cambridge and then to Princeton and to work for Royal Dutch Shell. They had not been in touch in the intervening fourteen years. As though to emphasize the difference between them now—Eton, their common bond, was something in the distant past!—Blair in his letter of invitation ("I should love to see you") made it a point to say that he'd heard that King-Farlow was "very rich and flourishing," whereas *he* had had "a bloody life . . . but in some ways an interesting one." All in all, a quasi-affectionate but provocative greeting to which King-Farlow responded in kind when he dropped in at The Stores the next month.

Old school friendships only rarely are sustained, and continue to grow, as one grows older oneself. Most such friendships are "living and partly living" in the limbo of a past one has outgrown, however one may choose to remember it—fondly, indifferently, or with active loathing. The meeting of Blair and King-Farlow at The Stores—he dropped in in time for lunch and to be charmed by Eileen and to conclude that in that regard Blair had done very well for himself—did not inaugurate a new, richer, or different friendship on either side. It was all very much as it had been in College.

As King-Farlow has recalled the visit: "He came out and croaked a warm welcome in that curious voice of his . . . rather bored and slightly apologetic. . . . He was burnt a deep brown and looked terribly weedy, with his loose shabby corduroys and a grey shirt. . . . We had some cold lunch and some very good pickles that Blair and his wife were very proud of."

All most amiable; but the reunion had its peppery moments, too. Orwell wrongly presumed that his past experiences and present existence would impress his long-lost friend, offering him glimpses of a world that he, in his rich and flourishing life, would never have known: "He said quite kindly that he supposed a lot of what he was saying must be quite incomprehensible to [King-Farlow] who probably never had to work outside a comfortable office and never had to do a job of any sort with [his] hands."

King-Farlow was not prepared to be patronized: "I asked him whether he'd ever had to do any work with his hands apart from washing a few dishes in French restaurants." And to make the point even sharper, he added that he "didn't regard traipsing about England as a tramp as manual labour."

The game of one-upmanship continued. Blair said, Well, he had done quite a number of odd jobs with his hands from time to time, and he was, of course, now running this store and raising chickens. Unimpressed, King-Farlow said, "I've raised chickens since I was a boy and I never regarded that much as manual labour." Then, as he puts it, "I went on with some pleasure to tell him that when I first went to Texas, I had worked for two years in the oilfields as an oil roustabout, doing every sort of odd job as a tool dresser, then as a driller's help, then as a truck driver."

This was just the sort of give-and-take that Blair had enjoyed at Eton with King-Farlow, and he enjoyed it now; the remainder of the visit went pleasantly, and when it was time for King-Farlow to leave, they agreed that they must keep in touch and see each other often in the future. (In fact, they did not.)

But it would seem that King-Farlow's visit, however fortuitous, couldn't have occurred at a more fortunate moment for Orwell. He had made up his mind by this time that he would write about aspects of his own life—to point a moral —in Part II of *The Road*. In particular he wanted to evoke Eton (though he could not bring himself to name it in the text) as he had known the school in the first years of the postwar period, the time of "anti-*blague*," when he was himself that not-unfamiliar combination of schoolboy snob and revolutionary. Meeting after all these years with King-Farlow almost certainly helped him to recover that mood of mockery and irreverence, and especially the sort of details they had expressed with such youthful glee in *College Days:* "It has been unanimously decided that the Eton War Memorial shall consist of a nunnery. The site for its erection is the School Field."

What had it all come to? Schoolboy revolutionaries they

had been, but what had they ever known of the working class? Nothing—except to rail at their bad manners or to recoil at their smell. And how easily they had shed their revolutionary convictions, leaving Eton! He himself had gone off by choice to Burma to serve in the Imperial Police; and King-Farlow, though he had worked with his hands in the Texas oilfields, had done so, not as a member of the working class, but as someone from the upper-middle having his adventure, and as a first step toward his goal (which he seemed to have achieved) of making a lot of money.

Hardly had this long-lost, newly found friend driven off into the blue whence he came than Eric was back at the typewriter putting the two of them (and all the others like them) in their inglorious place. Eileen, downstairs, cleared away the luncheon plates and began to think about dinner. The even tenor of their ways resumed. Goats to be walked; chickens to be fed; vegetables to be picked; children turning up in the shop for penny candy; the tap tap tap of the typewriter.

It was very quiet in the late afternoons in Wallington: one heard the buzzing of the bees, the sound of the cuckoo. On such a day it must have seemed that their life could go on just as it was, for as long as they wanted. History—not in Wallington but in the world—would put an end to it all.

EIGHTEEN

Still, for a week or two, even a few months longer—until work on the book was nearly done—the world and its events hardly impinged upon Eric and Eileen in Wallington. For the time being, history was elsewhere. Yet if their life at The Stores had its idyllic aspect, it was very much an idyll in the tradition of the writer at work and his wife attending to his wants. For both of them, in their different ways, the book came first. Even the Spanish Civil War—which broke out in mid-July and which before another year was over would have such transformative and traumatic effect upon him, as a man, a writer, and a Socialist—could not distract him from the road to Wigan he had followed that winter and was traveling again, as best he knew how, on the typewriter that summer.

Only once did he allow a brief pause—two days—in the task he had imposed upon himself, and that was in early August, when he agreed to give a talk at the Summer School of the Adelphi Centre. The School was the most conspicuous and successful offshoot of the spiritual *communitas* and Socialist *universitas* that Middleton Murry had brought into being three years before. The Centre, though less influential, was as much a phenomenon of the 1930's as the Left Book Club, but its pedigree, mixing utopian and messianic strains, extended back as far as Coleridge and his Pantisocracy, and reflected too the yearnings of D. H. Lawrence, Murry's sometime idol, for a colony of kindred spirits (or disciples) with himself as Master (or leader).

In the Centre's three-year history, inseparable from Murry's own restless history and his continually evolving position vis-à-vis the world and himself—variously Communist, Socialist, Christian, and Pacifist—it had already been twice uprooted, as Murry would uproot himself and his household from one setting to the next, as Lawrence himself had done, always in search of his right place. The Centre was now situated where Murry, with his third wife and her child, and his two children by his second wife, had come temporarily to rest: in The Oaks, a large house in Langham, Essex, near Colchester. (The house had once belonged to a successful Edwardian courtesan in her years of opulent retirement. After the Murrys moved on, as inevitably they did, it became a temporary home for Basque children, orphaned victims of the Spanish Civil War.)

In the summer of 1936, the Centre was a meeting and holiday place for several hundred believers in self-education and -improvement, readers and contributors of the *Adelphi*, ardent Socialists, doctrinaire Communists, passionate Pacifists, along with such diversified celebrities (who came to speak) as the Marxist popularizer John Strachey and the theologian Reinhold Niebuhr. The greater number of those in attendance were Comrades of the middle class, but there was a smattering of the genuine working class—usually male and unmarried—and if a male Comrade of the working class found himself in due course in the arms of a female Comrade of the middle class, that was one of the unadvertised but undoubted rewards of attending the Centre's Summer School.

It was all very high-minded and yearnfully "matey," Bohemia looking Leftward in a way that Orwell thought contemptible, but a target ready-made for his use just then. He came, he observed, and he went home to vilify. Meanwhile, as against the displeasure of seeing and listening to Murry, whom he thought a "creeping Jesus," as master of his self-created *communitas*—and if ever a man was born not to be anyone's disciple it was Orwell—there was the pleasure of meeting with Rees for the first time since his return from the North. Also, unexpectedly, and more enjoyably than either might have anticipated, there was a reunion with Rayner Heppenstall, whose quest for money to live on while writing his book on the ballet—he had used up a meager advance from a publisher—had led him to Langham. Murry, with a certain logic, engaged him as his secretary, and with no logic whatever, as cook for the Centre. (It will be remembered that in Lawford Road all the cooking had been done by Orwell.) Neither job proved of long duration, and the most lasting consequence for Heppenstall of his stay at The Oaks was that it was there that he met the young woman he would presently marry.

Murry (who in his relation with Lawrence had cast himself in the role of Judas) decided that Heppenstall should be in the chair at Orwell's talk, a decision that cannot have been entirely free of malice and that must have made for a certain tension: this, after all, was the first time the two would have seen each other since the breakup of the ménage in Lawford Road. All went smoothly, however. Orwell spoke on poverty in the North, impromptu with a dry assurance, reinforcing his firsthand impressions with a formidable battery of statistics, and (especially surprising to Rees, who was in the audience) introducing, as though it were second nature to him, the occasional appropriate Marxist allusion. In effect, he was making a public declaration of his newfound Socialism, but since everybody there, more or less, had already found it before him, the impact (except upon Rees) was negligible. Indeed, Heppenstall, in his memoir of the event, didn't even feel the subject of the talk worth mentioning, but resumed his account with its sequel, when he and Orwell adjourned for an hour of amiable conversation in a nearby pub. Neither of them mentioned the shooting-stick debacle, and it is fair to say that their friendship, in its truest sense, began that evening at the Shepherd and Dog in Langham, and would continue thereafter, unmarred, until the end of Orwell's life.

In retrospect, it seemed odd to Heppenstall, or at least noteworthy, that Orwell should have said nothing to him during their conversation about the Spanish Civil War, in which, by the end of the year, he would be so deeply engaged. But it was not all that odd: it was early in August, and the Civil War had yet to reveal itself beyond Spain as the great anti-Fascist cause it was presently to become. A dedicated young English Communist like John Cornford, going off in August to fight for the Republic (one of the first English volunteers), was truly an exceptional figure. The only evidence to suggest that Orwell was more than mildly interested in the war from its very beginning, and immediately responsive to its significance, is to be found in the "autobiographical" Introduction he provided for the Ukrainian edition of *Animal Farm* in 1945. It was there he revealed to his Ukrainian readers that he got married "in the same week almost" that the Civil War "broke out in Spain. Both I and my wife expressed the wish to go to Spain and fight on the side of the Spanish government. We were ready within half a year. . . ." No doubt such an Introduction was not the proper place for the finer shadings and discriminations: even so, if one did not know the piece was Orwell's, one might reasonably assign it to some hard-pressed hack in a Ministry of Misinformation. (The actual manuscript, as written by Orwell, has disappeared. Translated into Ukrainian, it was retranslated back into English, in which form it appears in the *Collected Essays, Journalism and Letters*. In the movement from version to version, it may well have lost something, not least a style that is recognizably Orwell's.)

All the *contemporary* evidence would seem to agree that at the time of his visit to the Adelphi Summer School, and well into the autumn of 1936, Orwell's principal concern was his book. Even had it not been, the Summer School would not have served as an ideal testing ground for the question of Spain. Murry had undergone one of his deeply felt conversions, this time to Pacifism—presently he would make the facilities of the school available to the Peace Pledge Union—and Pacifism, as orchestrated by Murry, was the dominant theme, stirring up a good deal of unease among the Adelphians gathered there. Especially was this true for those among them—Rees, for example, who would soon break with the magazine altogether—who recognized the anomalous position history was forcing upon them. Until the summer of 1936, it was possible as a dedicated young man or woman of the Left to declare oneself a Socialist, an anti-Fascist, and a Pacifist, and not be troubled by a sense of inconsistency in any of these particulars. But Spain changed things. Suddenly reality caught up with one's idealism: it became possible (perhaps necessary) to bear arms against Fascism. And by so doing, did not one bring that much closer the nightmare of war that had haunted the European imagination since 1918, and shaped the generation in England that only three years earlier had sworn never to bear arms for King and Country?

In the September *Adelphi*, Murry made his commitment to Pacifism public; in the February 1937 number his co-editor, Max Plowman, a Pacifist of long standing, sought to grapple more specifically with the troublesome question history had thrust upon them. "Go Not to Spain," he argued, pointing out that there were "more ways of winning a fight than by rushing upon the enemy's bayonets." In March, however, Murry allowed a reply to Plowman by N. A. Holdaway, a Marxian theorist and a director of the Centre, which he entitled "Go Not to Pacifism." But for Orwell, and for thousands of other young men like him, such questions had become academic. By the time the February *Adelphi* appeared with its adjuration "Go Not to Spain," he had already taken the road to Barcelona and beyond, and was fighting on the Aragon front.

HE RETURNED FROM HIS HOLIDAY AT THE SUMMER SCHOOL eager to hurry the book to its conclusion. Early in October he had his first draft done, and immediately began work on the revision. He had set a timetable for himself: the final version to be in Gollancz's hands by mid-December.

As to what the first draft actually was, we can only speculate. He himself described it to Jack Common as "a sort of book of essays," which says rather less than it suggests: certainly, after the revision was done, no one would ever resort to so diffident or reductive a description of *The Road to Wigan Pier*. The two-part form he had chosen ought to have served him well, with the first part setting forth the problem, and the second its solution. The problem, of course, was poverty; the solution, Socialism. But the neatness of the formal design was undone by the encroachments of history. The problem of poverty, looming so large in the first part of the book (as he intended), begins to recede in the second—displaced, so to speak, by a further problem, whose urgency, whose emotional claim upon him, he could not have anticipated: "the onslaught of Fascism" in Spain. In the eleventh chapter (only two from the end), events at the very moment they are happening in the world enter the book like bulletins of disaster: "As I write this, the Spanish Fascist forces are bombarding Madrid. . . ." We know this could not have been written before the end of October, for, as Hugh Thomas writes in *The Spanish Civil War,* "A heavy bombing campaign against Madrid was mounted from 29 October onwards, partly to satisfy the German advisers who were curious to see the civilian reaction."

It seems fair to say that from this time forward, Orwell was increasingly preoccupied with events in Spain and determined to go there to see them for himself as soon as he had finished his book. Uncertainty added a special urgency to the task: "It is quite likely that before the book is printed we shall have another Fascist country to add to the list. . . ."

The problem of poverty—which had called the book into being—is subordinated in these final chapters to the problem of Fascism, though the answer to both remains, as he intended, the same: the Socialism to which he had been converted after his journey North only six months before, and for which, only a few months in the future, he would be willing to risk his life—not simply in the rhetorical but even in the literal sense.

"Everyone who knows the meaning of poverty"—as he did—"everyone who has a genuine hatred of tyranny and war"—as he did—"is on the Socialist side"—as he was. "Socialism is the only real enemy that Fascism has to face," he wrote as he hurried to the end of his book and the beginning of his next journey. But such a formulation can be exactly reversed: *Fascism is the only real enemy.* . . .

Until now, until the book was done, this could not be other than what it was: the rhetoric of "the struggle," bravely phrased; the time was almost at hand, however, to close the book, to get beyond rhetoric, to discover its reality.

NINETEEN

Outwardly, at least, the decision to go to Spain —which he had reached by mid-November and presented to Eileen, not for her advice nor conditional upon her approval but as a *fait accompli*—was free of rhetorical flourishes. How, one wonders, Orwell being Orwell, could it have been otherwise? The "struggle"—that word of the decade that sounds with such resonance, like a bell tolling in Auden's "Spain" ("Today the struggle") and in countless other poems, fiction, and varieties of agitprop—hardly entered into it. Sensible, practical, realistic—and from his point of view the decision was all of these—it could be made to seem (and quite possibly it was) as much an act of literary professionalism as of political idealism. One book was by now virtually finished, another would have to be started: that was how he lived. A novel, perhaps? But he had no compelling idea or experience that lent itself to fictionalization; besides, he had found he was much more at ease with the reportage of *Wigan Pier* than with the invention and role-playing demanded of him in the two novels that preceded it. It was more congenial, certainly, to write about what one saw and felt and knew in one's own person, whether as observer or participant, than transmuted, say, through a clergyman's spinster daughter, or a self-pitying mini-poet at war with the Money God. Spain and its Civil War offered a great and logical subject for a writer such as himself, eager to see and know what was going on. And it coincided with his simple, straightforward, bourgeoning anti-Fascism: it was a subject to which he felt himself already deeply committed.

Then, too, it had the special virtue of answering Eileen's misgivings before she could even express them: how could she object if her husband carried out in practice the anti-Fascism her beloved brother had introduced to him, and to which Laurence was firmly, fatalistically dedicated? There might be some slight risk involved, Eric acknowledged in his offhand way—and her friends were quick to point the danger out to Eileen and to each other a good deal more emphatically, for they disapproved of Eric's going, thought it selfish of him to set out for Spain as though he had only himself to consider, and leave her isolated in Wallington, a mere six months after they were married, with the responsibility of The Stores and so little money—how would she manage? (Evidently the possibility of her going back to live with the O'Shaughnessys in Greenwich while he was away was never considered.) But the risks and dangers would be appreciably lessened, since he had decided to go as a journalist, a writer gathering materials for a few articles on the war, or perhaps with luck a new book. After all, he was not going as a soldier. That, at least, was what he told her, and what she told her friends when they expressed their concern; and it was very like her, whatever she might have felt, to pretend to believe him: it would make the parting that much easier. Yet she must have suspected, even as he himself must have understood at the back of his mind, that once he was there, he would do precisely what he did do two days after his arrival in Barcelona—volunteer to serve in the militia. His own subsequent explanation was a marvelous example of deflationary rhetoric in action: "It seemed the only conceivable thing to do."

At the end of November the writing was finished and Eileen had set to work, as she had used to do for Laurence, to type the final manuscript. On the eleventh of December, Orwell acquainted Leonard Moore with the no doubt welcome news that the book was finished—exactly on schedule —and the no doubt surprising news that he would be going to Spain at the earliest moment: while he was there, his wife would be empowered to act on his behalf. We can only conjecture as to what Moore made of this double announcement. No doubt as a sensible man of business, accustomed to the peculiarities of his authors, he glided over the Spanish venture and fixed upon the book—his legitimate concern—raising the possibility that Gollancz would make it a selection of the Left Book Club. Orwell was not so sanguine, however. On the fifteenth of December, when he sent off the manuscript, he was doubtful that it would be chosen for the Club: "Too fragmentary and, on the surface, not very left-wing." In any event, he hoped it would be possible for Gollancz to look at the book as early as possible, since he would be leaving for Spain within a week.

Sheila Hodges, in *Gollancz: The Story of a Publishing House 1928–1978*, tells us that "Victor read the manuscript in a couple of days, and afterwards he and Orwell had one of their rare meetings to discuss it." But what author and publisher said to each other at this rare meeting—which must have occurred sometime shortly before Christmas— she cannot tell us. Working back from what ultimately was to happen—*The Road* would become the Left Book Club selection for March 1937, and the special club edition in its standard limp orange binding would include a foreword by Victor Gollancz—one is free to speculate as to what might have been said. Gollancz, predictably, and like many readers of the book to this day, was divided in his reactions: impressed by Part I and distressed by Part II. But on balance, whatever its defects, he felt they were far outweighed by its virtues: "It is a long time since I have read so *living* a book, or one so full of a burning indignation against poverty and oppression." Very likely he had already made up his mind that he would urge the book, defects and all, upon his fellow selectors, John Strachey and Harold Laski, confident that they would share his enthusiasm (and no doubt also, his reservations). Very likely, too, he mentioned the possibility of its being chosen for the Club, and stipulated that he would, in that case, want to write a foreword, replying to certain debatable points in Part II. Orwell agreed. One has the impression that, in his haste to be off to Spain, he would have agreed to any condition, short of rewriting a single sentence, or allowing a single sentence to be tampered with. In fact there was no rewriting and no tampering. Author and publisher parted amicably. (Theirs would always be an amicable if not especially warm or confiding relationship, with more than a little skepticism on both sides. When Orwell finally saw Gollancz's foreword—in May 1937 in Barcelona—he wrote to thank him, saying that it was "the kind of discussion . . . that one always wants and never seems to get from the professional reviewers." This may, of course, have been no more than an instance of Orwell's inbred courtesy—a tribute equally to his mother and to Mrs. Vaughan Wilkes— or it may have represented irony of the most subtle sort. In which case it seems worth noticing that when Orwell decided to sever all ties with Victor Gollancz Ltd. in 1945 and to move for good to Martin Secker and Warburg, who had already published *Homage to Catalonia* and *Animal Farm*, he wrote to Moore about Gollancz: "I have no quarrel with him personally, he has treated me generously and published my work when no one else would but it is obviously unsatisfactory to be tied to a publisher who accepts or refuses books partly on political grounds [as Gollancz had done with *Homage*, refusing it before a word was written, and with *Animal Farm*] and whose political views were constantly changing . . .")

So Orwell set out for Spain, and Gollancz set out to launch what Franklin D. Roosevelt might have called his "hot potato," and what Frederic Warburg later described as a "lemon in an orange jacket."

The publication of *The Road* would make Orwell famous, it would win him more readers than he had ever had before—close to 50,000—and an equal measure of praise and abuse, and all this (it seems fair to say) was a consequence of the book's being made a selection of the Left Book Club. It is a part of Orwell's myth, though not of his history, that the book had been commissioned by the Club; in fact, the Club did not even exist in January of 1936 when he received his commission for the book from Gollancz. The first public announcement of the formation of the Club appeared as a two-page advertisement in the *New Statesman and Nation* for February 29, 1936. Its first selection appeared in May of that year. But because Gollancz was Orwell's publisher, and also the progenitor and leading spirit of the Club, it is understandable that some confusion should have arisen as to which came first. The truth, not the legend, is that *The Road* would have been written by Orwell and been published by Gollancz whether or not there had been a Left Book Club. It was the Club, however, that made the book a success (of a sort Orwell would not have again until *Animal Farm*) and among a number of its members a *succès de scandale*.

By March 1937, when *The Road* was sent out to its more than 40,000 members, the Club was already a resounding success—yet another coup for Gollancz, who had refused previously, in his style of advertising and in other ways, to conform to the taboos which were inherent in the "profession for gentlemen" which English publishing considered itself. But quite apart from its value as a way of distributing large quantities of Gollancz books, the Club fitted into his increasingly intense political interests, which moved ever more to the Left: a mix of Socialism, anti-Fascism, and Popular-Frontism. A shrewd publisher who was also something of a guru figure, Gollancz can be seen as a very accurate reflector of fellow-traveling trends in Britain in the 1930's. Shocked by the Nazi-Soviet pact—which seemed to him the embodiment of evil—he turned against Russia. Nonetheless, when the decisive *volte-face* occurred and the Soviets transformed themselves into Britain's gallant ally, he would not hesitate in his support of the alliance or allow anything to jeopardize it—hence, like so many other wartime publishers in Britain, he refused *Animal Farm*, fearing it might cause offense: politically unwise.

There is little question that in its early years the Club was at no great remove from the Communist "line." Strachey, though not officially a party member, was notably subservient or contributory to it, and both Laski and Gollancz tended to be cooperative: to the degree that one was committed to the cause of militant Socialism and anti-Fascism, cooperation with the party that shared those objectives had its logic. But too much can be made of this. The thinking of the three selectors was not as monolithic and undeviating as has sometimes been suggested. *The Road to Wigan Pier* was not designed to give aid and comfort to the party; and in due course it received a vitriolic review in the *Daily Worker* from Harry Pollitt, the general secretary of the party. That was to be expected, perhaps was even welcomed as showing that the Club was an independent agent. The "hot potato" aspect of sending out *The Road* as a Club selection was not the inevitable negative reception by Harry Pollitt, but its effect upon the majority of Club members who might imagine, not without cause, that they were pilloried in the second part of the book. It is very much to the credit of Gollancz, Strachey, and Laski that they decided to go ahead anyhow, and the choice was announced in the February issue of the *Left News*.

The book would be distributed to Club members, as usual, through bookstores and news agents at the ordinary members' price of 2/6 (the price for nonmembers was 10/6), and 43,690 copies were printed. Both the Club and trade editions contained thirty-two photographic illustrations and the Foreword by Victor Gollancz. The latter, however, was "addressed to members of the Left Book Club . . . and to them alone; members of the general public are asked to ignore it. But for technical considerations, it would have been deleted from the ordinary edition."

Gollancz's Foreword, interesting as a response to Orwell, is of equal interest as a "period" document. Why, he asks, should the selectors have thought a Foreword desirable? "Because," he answers

> we find that many members . . . have the idea that in some sort of way a Left Book Club choice, first, represents the view of the three selectors, and secondly, in-

corporates the Left Book Club "policy." A moment's thought should show that the first suggestion could be true only in the worst kind of Fascist state, and that the second is a contradiction in terms. . . . The Left Book Club has no "policy": or rather it has no policy other than that of equipping people to fight against war and Fascism. . . . it would not even be true to say that the People's Front is the "policy" of the Left Book Club, though all three selectors are enthusiastically in favour of it. What we rather feel is that by giving a wide distribution to books which represent many shades of Left opinion . . . we are creating a mass basis without which a genuine People's Front is impossible. In other words the People's Front is not the policy of the Left Book Club but the very existence of the Left Book Club tends towards a People's Front.

All this was by way of prelude, and suggests a certain uneasiness in approaching the subject: "We feel that a Foreword to *The Road to Wigan Pier* . . . is desirable . . . because we believe that the value of the book, for some members, can be greatly increased if just a hint is given of certain vital considerations that arise from a reading of it. The value can be *increased:* as to the positive value itself, no one of us has the smallest doubt."

Gollancz's Foreword runs to fourteen pages; of those, less than one page is given to Part I—"a terrible record of evil conditions, foul housing, wretched pay, hopeless unemployment and the villainies of the Means Test: it is also a tribute to courage and patience—patience far too great. We cannot imagine anything more likely to rouse the 'unconverted' from their apathy than a reading of this part of the book. . . . These chapters really are the kind of things that make converts."

But most of the Foreword is concerned with that troublesome Part II, with its crank speaking crankily, and its embarrassing admission that "in the opinion of the middle class in general, the working class smells," and its outspokenness and wrongheadedness at so many points that Gollancz "marked well over a hundred passages about which I thought I should like to argue with Mr. Orwell. . . ." But that would have diverted him from his serious purpose: to point out the elements of anti-intellectualism in a man who is an intellectual in spite of himself, his romanticism, his refusal to accept industrialism, his dislike of Russia (most unusual in a Left Book Club book), and his failure to explain what he meant by those thrilling abstractions, Socialism, Justice, and Liberty. The last point is the most telling, and it catches the chief failing of Orwell's positive thought. He was a brilliant "against figure," and he could puncture pretensions and cant, but he could not envision an alternative society that one would want to live in other than to define it as decent and honorable. (He was of course a master at describing an alternative society in which one would rather die—or be dehumanized—and gave us a classic example of that sort in *1984*.) Gollancz's point is made decently and honorably:

> It is indeed significant that so far as I can remember (he must forgive me if I am mistaken), Mr. Orwell does not once define what he means by Socialism; nor does he explain how the oppressors oppress, nor even what he understands by "liberty" and "justice." . . . What is indeed essential, once that first appeal has been made to "liberty" and "justice," is a careful and patient study of how the thing works: of *why* capitalism inevitably means oppression and injustice and the horrible class society which Mr. Orwell so brilliantly depicts; of the means

of transition to a Socialist society in which there will be neither oppressor nor oppressed. In other words, *emotional* Socialism must become scientific Socialism. . . .

"A careful and patient study." The phrase sums up as well as any precisely what Part II was not, nor would Orwell have claimed it to be. And Harold Laski, who reported on the book in the March issue of *Left News*, would ask for something similar: there was more to be learned, to be studied, to be understood. Laski's review was favorable and sympathetic. He compared the first part of the book with *Hard Times*, as well as to Zola and Balzac. But when he arrived at the second part, doubts rose to the surface. "Having, very ably, depicted a disease, Mr. Orwell does what so many well-meaning people do: needing a remedy (he knows it is Socialism) he offers an incantation instead." Much in the manner of a teacher ticking off inadequacies on the part of a bright but insufficiently prepared pupil, Laski complained that Orwell's conception of Socialism "ignores all that is implied in the urgent reality of class antagonism. It refuses to confront the grave problem of the State. It has no sense of the historic movement of the economic process. At bottom, in fact, it is an emotional plea for Socialism addressed to comfortable people." Of course, as Laski probably realized, most of the members of the Left Book Club were "comfortable people," and probably Orwell's appeal to them—to be Socialists—perverse though it might be in some particulars, was one to which they could respond in an emotional if not a scientific way.

While the press, generally, received *The Road* with a good deal more enthusiasm (despite some strictures) than had been the case with *A Clergyman's Daughter* or *Keep the Aspidistra Flying*, there seems to have been an almost missionary response on the part of the Club membership. In the April number of the *Left News*, Gollancz reported that the book had produced

> both more, and more interesting, letters than any other Club Choice. The book has done, perhaps in a greater degree than any previous book, what the Club is meant to do—it has provoked thought and discussion of the keenest kind. While members with a training in scientific socialism have been surprised at the naïveté of the second part, they have for this very reason found it valuable, as showing how much education they still have to do before the mass of vague humanitarianism can be turned into truly constructive channels: and middle class members have been so profoundly shocked by the conditions revealed in the first part of the book—a revelation which they have been all the more ready to accept precisely because Orwell's attitude in the second part is largely their own—that they have written to us, not one or two, by the hundreds, saying "Tell us, please, what can we do."

Indeed, so powerful was the response that Gollancz decided to issue the first part separately, along with its illustrations, for a shilling. Announcing it in the *Left News*, he felt that it would "prove one of the best weapons in rousing the public conscience about the ghastly conditions of so many people in England today."

Essential to the whole notion of the Left Book Club was a belief in education: careful and patient study leading no doubt to a better world. But Gollancz and Laski, believing in a scientific rather than an emotional Socialism, believing (in 1937) that it was still possible to equip people to fight against war and Fascism, were caught in a time warp: history was leaving them behind. Orwell in Spain was continuing his education—in a real war against Fascism—and it was very different from anything envisioned by the selectors of the Left Book Club. What he was learning had less to do with scientific Socialism than with the morality of politics, and it would change his life.

PART FOUR

An Education in Spain

TWENTY

His six months in Spain proved the most decisive experience of his life, and released within him the energy and insight—the transformation—to accomplish the work by which he is best remembered: the two most significant (and popular) of his novels, *Animal Farm* and *1984*; the greater number of his literary and political essays; and of course, his memoir-analysis of his war experience and the war itself, *Homage to Catalonia*.

Once having made up his mind to go, he recognized that he would need official auspices of some sort or other to get into Spain—he didn't much care which, so long as they served his immediate purpose. As one logically would in the circumstances, he turned to the Communist party, who were well known as intermediaries. More specifically, he turned first to the Old Etonian network, and asked his friend Richard Rees to arrange for him to meet *his* friend John Strachey, who had been at Eton with him—so, for that matter, had Orwell, but he and Strachey had never met. Rees took care of things with a telephone call, and Strachey brought Orwell round to headquarters in King Street to talk to Harry Pollitt, the general secretary of the party. Pollitt had his virtues, but tact was not among them, and he had a way of dealing with writers that some of them tended to find grating. Stephen Spender, for example, during his brief membership in the party, was taken aback when Pollitt suggested that he go out to Spain and get himself killed—"The Lord Byron of the Spanish Civil War!" —that would be a distinction; but Spender demurred. Pollitt's meeting with Orwell was less dramatic, but equally unproductive. Pollitt quizzed him, and Orwell's answers weren't satisfactory. He admitted to a sympathy for the Anarchists, who were already in the party's black books, so to speak, and when Pollitt asked if he would agree to join the International Brigade, he replied that he would make no agreement until he had seen what was going on. So that was that, as far as Pollitt was concerned, although he recommended that if Orwell was determined to go that he should get a safe-conduct at the Spanish Embassy in Paris.

With King Street behind him, he turned to another left-wing political group, the Independent Labour Party, whose Summer Institute at Letchworth he had briefly attended, and with whose weekly paper, the *New Leader,* he was not unfamiliar. It was typical of Orwell's luck (or fate) that he should have turned to a group that was in a state of declining influence and membership, and that would also, thanks to its special connections, determine the unpremeditated but formative course his experiences in Spain would take. The ILP had once been an important force in English politics—among the leading progenitors of the Labour party—but in the 1920's it had become increasingly sectarian and had disaffiliated from the Labour party in 1932. Fairly or not, it was regarded as the "crankiest" of the Labour groups, and it is a nice irony that Orwell, the anti-crank crank, should have become associated with it, even if for no other reason than to facilitate his trip to Spain. The party was more ideological than the newly politicized, independent-minded Socialist Orwell would have liked—it was more militantly Marxist and much more willing to cooperate with the Communists than with the Labour party. Its policies had cost it members, and it now had only slightly more than 4,000. But the party was willing to accredit Orwell as a correspondent for the *New Leader* and thus provided the means for him to go legitimately to Spain.

He was further equipped with a letter of introduction to John McNair, the ILP representative in Barcelona, from H. N. Brailsford, a well-known author, figure on the Left, and political journalist, who had edited the *New Leader* from 1922 to 1926. Orwell himself did not actually become a member of the ILP until June 1938, a year after he returned from Spain, and remained in the party only briefly —there is no indication that he paid more than one annual subscription. But in 1936, with his useful political introduction, his political press card, and a nonpolitical reading knowledge of Spanish, he departed for the war after Christmas, in order to report and perhaps to fight on the side of the Republic.

En route, he stopped off in Paris, and after collecting his safe-conduct pass at the Spanish Embassy, paid a visit to Henry Miller. Orwell, one of the earliest admirers of Miller's work at a time when it was banned from England and the United States, had, as we have seen, written an admiring and discerning review of *Tropic of Cancer* in the *New English Weekly* in 1935. The two men had corresponded, and Miller managed to get hold of a copy of *Down and Out,* long since out of print; later he would say it was the book of Orwell's he liked best. Their meeting, in the sort of bistro-Paris each knew and enjoyed to the dregs, went very well. Miller, completely apolitical and predictably outspoken, did not hesitate to tell Blair he thought him a fool to be going to Spain for any reason other than curiosity—certainly not any sense of political commitment. Nevertheless, he gave him a corduroy jacket of his own to help him keep warm, and Orwell was off, arriving in Barcelona on December 30.

In a somewhat belated, convoluted way, Orwell was beginning to achieve that identification with and recognition by the proletariat he had earlier yearned for. Perhaps in a foreign country, in the midst of a civil war, it might be possible, even for an Englishman of the lower-upper-middle, to declass himself. In Paris, on his way to Miller's in a taxi, he had had an argument with the driver and come away angry. The memory of that altercation rankled. But now, on the journey to Spain with his fellow recruits—and what a mixed bag they were, proletarians and honorary proletarians all jumbled together—he noticed as the train passed on its way through the countryside the peasants coming to attention and giving the Communist "raised-fist" salute: a "guard of honor." Retrospectively, he felt himself in sympathy with that Parisian taxi driver, who naturally would have regarded him as a rich Englishman rather than as a potential comrade. It is indicative of Orwell's excited state that he should have seen himself, the pugnacious taxi driver, the brave recruits on the train, and the cheering peasants in the fields as all united in the struggle against Fascism. He was prepared to be overwhelmed by his experience in Spain.

ON HIS ARRIVAL, BARCELONA SEEMED TO HIM TO BE A SOcialist paradise. He could not have known that such a world was not to be found elsewhere in Spain, except perhaps in certain other Catalan towns and parts of Aragon. Barcelona appeared to his dazzled eyes as a city where the workers were triumphant—hats and ties had vanished, rents had been reduced by half, churches, convents, and monasteries had either been burned or taken over for use of the army, hotels had been commandeered by the people, tipping abolished, shops and cafes collectivized, not to mention 70 percent of all industry. It would strike a sympathetic newcomer from gray, class-ridden Britain that here equality and freedom had triumphed.

In fact there was already developing a power struggle between the great Anarcho-Syndicalist organization, the CNT, which was dominant in Catalonia, and the party of the Socialists, the PSUC, supported by the Communists. But Orwell, in the first flush of enthusiasm, was unaware of such tensions. Here was a world that he felt he had no choice but to fight for. It was the moment which T. R. Fyvel, his close friend and professional associate after 1940, labeled as "the starting-point for the ideas of a new humanist English left movement which he [Orwell] tried later to express." Certainly it was the moment that Orwell's particular dream of democratic Socialism began to take its mature form. The mood—not the maneuvering of the various factions and counter-factions within the government—was what counted, and propelled him forward.

In fact, although Orwell had too recently arrived and was too briefly on the scene to know, the "revolutionary" period was just about over, and the participation in the government of the Anarcho-Syndicalists and even the splinter Marxist party, the POUM, meant that the halcyon stage of the revolution—the tail-end of which Orwell had arrived to experience and which so fascinated him—had virtually run its course. But the hope and possibility it represented still lingered on to be responded to, especially by the unsuspecting and untutored observer who did not detect what lay beneath the surface. Starting in October 1936, with Russia's decision to send the Republic arms, the only one of the great powers to do so, the balance of power in the government had begun to shift, and the preconditions that would be so important in forming Orwell's later thought were taking shape. In the exhilarated mood that transformed him from an observer to a participant, Orwell wished to fight for common decency and against Fascism—objectives no civilized soul could take objection to. He had no desire to be involved with, and at that time certainly hadn't the knowledge to understand, the complicated and "tiresome" details of Spanish political life. In some senses he did not mind depicting himself in the role of the political naïf and would consciously do so in *Homage to Catalonia*. But even if he had been preternaturally wise in the intricacies of the situation as it was, it is unlikely that it would have modified his exhilaration and commitment to the cause. (Still, it is ironic to contrast the "devil's advocate" tone he adopted in the second part of *The Road*, putting down an English Socialism still in its theoretical, larval stage, with his "born-again" tone in the early chapters of *Homage*, seeing, as it were, the Socialist Light of a newborn society.)

Shortly after his arrival in Barcelona, he presented his introduction from Brailsford to John McNair. McNair, a Newcastle man in his late forties, a self-taught workingman and dedicated Socialist, had spent twenty-five years in the leather trade in France. He came back to England in 1936, and attended the ILP Summer Conference at Letchworth. There, James Maxton, leader of the party, and Fenner Brockway, then the party secretary, had asked him to go to Spain as the party's representative. Quite apart from his dedication as a Socialist, his fluency in French and Spanish would be of inestimable value. Early in December he was in Barcelona and had established an ILP office on the Ramblas, one of the great avenues of the city, bustling with activity and famous for its central promenade. There, on a morning in January, Orwell came to see McNair in his office, and, according to McNair, that first meeting was not a success: he was put off by what he took to be Orwell's Etonian manner, and apart from this initial social chill, which the *pro forma* "Salud" on both sides did little to dispel, there was a misunderstanding of intent. McNair, understandably, thought that Orwell had come out as a journalist, and his mind leapt forward thinking of useful introductions to political leaders, possible interviews with ILP volunteers from England—that sort of thing. But no, Orwell, it turned out, rather thought he wanted to join one of the militias—he had had, which was more than could be said of most of the volunteers, actual military experience—and he wanted to go up to the front and fight. McNair had only some hazy familiarity with Orwell's literary reputation, such as it was: it was not as though an André Malraux or an Ernest Hemingway had appeared in the office. (Recollecting these events many years later, he thought it more than likely that he would not yet have read anything Orwell had written.) But he was also blessed with a mix of good-humored cynicism and common sense: Barcelona was swarming with writers from abroad who were sympathetic to the cause of the Republic; one writer more or less hardly made a significant difference. Whereas a man with military experience was not to be valued lightly. If this tall Englishman with his rasping, rather high-pitched voice and his diffident yet confident manner wanted to join the militia as a fighting man, McNair would do what he could to assist him; and it was settled that Orwell would come back to the office the next day.

The ILP's sister party in Spain was the POUM, the self-styled Party of Marxist Unification, though its very existence suggested the extent of disunity among Spanish Marxists. At the risk of offending or confusing readers with a plethora of all those initials that are endemic to a discussion, even a simple discussion, of Spanish Civil War politics, we must say that the POUM, that Marxist splinter party, was somewhat within the orbit of the CNT, the principal Anarcho-Syndicalist party, which was opposed by the PSUC, the Socialist party, which was increasingly influenced by its Communist members.

Now, it was the particular fate, one might say the fatality, of the POUM that it should have been caught up in the ever more bitter struggle, and in the end the bloody struggle to the death, between the CNT and the PSUC. And as a further aspect of its ultimately fatal history, that the POUM should have incurred the particular hostility of the Communists because of its alleged Trotskyist affiliations.

From the beginning of the Civil War in the previous July, virtually each of the many political parties had established a militia of its own, ranging along a broad spectrum of ideological "positions," and these "independent fighting units," taken together, comprised in the loosest sort of way the Army of the Republic. If this was not the most professional, or even the most sensible, method of waging a war, it was undoubtedly casual (which made joining up essentially a matter of choice or chance) and very much in the spirit of what has been called "the Bohemian period" of the Revolution. But the chief objection, which was already coming clear in the early winter of 1937, was that it did not seem to be leading to the defeat of Fascism.

Keeping in mind the situation as it was in December 1936, John McNair's advice and conduct is entirely understandable. As we have said, the ILP's sister party was the POUM, and ILP members coming out from England to fight in Spain automatically enlisted in the POUM militia. As arranged with McNair, Orwell came round to the ILP office in the Ramblas the day after their first meeting, and McNair conducted him to the Lenin Barracks. There were the headquarters of the POUM militia, and there Comrade Blair joined up. It could hardly have been more casually done, and very much in the spirit of the time; but it was a crucial step for Orwell himself, determining the shape of his Spanish experience, and of his commitment then and thereafter to the cause of human freedom.

2

HE RECEIVED VERY LITTLE TRAINING IN THE LENIN BARRACKS, but of course he had his considerable experience as a Burmese policeman and in the officer training corps at Eton to stand him in good stead as a soldier. Approximately a week after joining the militia, he set out with a contingent of very young and inexperienced volunteers for the front. They went by train from Barcelona to Barbastro, midway between Lérida and Huesca, then by truck to Siétamo, and then on to Alcubierre, on the Saragossa section of the Aragon front. The brigade was positioned a half-mile from the enemy. Orwell, eager for action, volunteered for patrols, and was soon promoted to corporal. But of action he saw little: Aragon, now, was "a quiet front." Danger, hardship, the risks of death, the chance of meeting in any significant way with the enemy—these were elsewhere. The reader of *Homage to Catalonia,* coming upon it for the first time and knowing its reputation as a classic of the

Spanish Civil War, may be surprised at how little intense, sustained, or large-scale military engagement it commemorates. But of course this is true of any number of other classics of war: genius (unfair though it should be so) can endow with equal intensity the long dull hours and days and nights when nothing important ever happens, and that incandescent moment of excitement and crisis when life itself seems to explode and is burnt out forever.

I T SEEMS USEFUL TO SAY SOMETHING FURTHER HERE ABOUT *Homage to Catalonia*. It has become, deservedly so, inseparable from the Spanish Civil War, as much a part of its literature as *Man's Hope* or *For Whom the Bell Tolls*. And yet, paradoxically, in its very permanence as something we all know and value and take for granted, it stands in the way of our seeing the transformation of Orwell as it happened, simple though it is to recognize the transformation after it occurred.

Part of the difficulty is inherent in the nature of the book itself: its sense of the present is so strong that one tends to forget that it was lived before it was written, and thought about after the events it describes. Then there is its peculiar formal organization: those contrasting sections of personal experience and of political-historical analysis— they are made to exist side by side in the text, as though happening together, or at the least as filtering through the same sensibility and in the same evocative process. But there is a difference that has to be kept in mind between writing that is lived and writing that has been worked up. As we will presently show, the actual composition of the book had its unusual aspect—it certainly was not written in its entirety in the traditional chronological fashion—and this too may account for the difficulty. We have no wish here to devalue *Homage to Catalonia,* but if we seem to circumvent it, or to lay less than conventional emphasis upon it as a literary achievement or a compendium of celebrated quotations, it is simply that we think it more useful—for who has not yet read *Homage to Catalonia,* or will not someday read it?—to look behind the book for its author.

TOWARDS THE END OF JANUARY HE WAS TRANSFERRED FROM his largely Spanish group to join several English volunteers who had come out from the ILP under the leadership of Bob Edwards—members of the International Militia, as distinct from the International Brigade, by then predominantly under Communist control and fighting heroically on the crucial and very bloody Madrid front. This group of ILP volunteers, twenty-five strong, was assigned to the 3rd Regiment, Division Lenin, POUM, on the Aragon front at Alcubierre. For Orwell, and for Bob Williams, another English volunteer who had gone up with him earlier in the month to join the 3rd Regiment, it was essentially a matter of carrying one's rifle from one trench to another. Life became more interesting, not because the war showed any sign of hotting up—it was still very much a quiet front—but because, being among English-speaking comrades, one could talk a lot, and talk among soldiers tends to be engrossing, at least while it is going on, though elusive in memory.

The 3rd Regiment included some more than ordinarily interesting figures: the Comandante was Georges Kopp, a

Belgian who had been engaged in smuggling war matériel from France into Spain, until, on the verge of discovery, he simply crossed the border into Spain to take part in the fighting. He and Orwell became close friends—one of the few of Orwell's friendships from Spain that continued into the Second World War; in 1944, after an adventurous wartime history, Kopp made a second marriage: to a sister of Gwen O'Shaughnessy. Then there was Stafford Cottman, only seventeen, who looked up to Orwell, almost twice his age, as a model of wisdom and experience—he describes the English contingent as divided into Intellectuals, ready to argue issues, with whom he associated Orwell; Fundamentalists, who had a direct, uncomplicated commitment to winning the war; and Prolis (pronounced "proleys"), the ordinary "blokes," who complained, enjoyed themselves, and did what had to be done. Perhaps the best-known of the group was Bob Smillie—son of Bob Smillie, the Scottish Labour leader, one-time M.P., and a leading figure in the ILP—who would later die in prison in Valencia, possibly murdered by the Communists and certainly ill-treated by them.

Then, too, there was Bob Edwards, who still keeps a vivid memory of Orwell in battle dress: "corduroy riding breeches, khaki puttees and huge boots caked with mud, a yellow pigskin jerkin, a chocolate-colored balaclava helmet with a knitted khaki scarf of immeasurable length wrapped round and round his neck and face up to his ears." (Sybil Wingate, a nurse in Spain at the time, remembers Kopp telling her that Orwell was so tall "that one needed to climb up and talk to him.")

Adding up their glimpses and recollections—and there are others we shall be giving in due course—one comes away with an impression of an Orwell who was cheerful, agreeable, companionable, decent, interesting, uncomplaining—yes, even happy, and very different from the caustic, sardonic, dour figure one has encountered at most of the earlier stages in his life. Indeed, the Orwell evoked by those who knew him in Spain bears a strong likeness to Orwell in Wallington, with Eileen, tending to The Stores, the garden, the goats. So striking is the likeness that it does not seem unduly sentimental to suggest that the happiness that had its inception then, continued into Spain, sustaining itself under the most adverse and trying conditions.

Regrettably, the correspondence between Eileen and Eric has not survived. (A number of her letters to Jack Common, written from Morocco, are in the Berg Collection in New York, and they make for delightful reading.) But John McNair, who acted as postman for the ILP volunteers at the front, remembered a steady flow of letters between the two; beyond this, we have the quite extraordinary evidence of what happened.

Once Eileen heard from Eric that he had volunteered to serve in the POUM militia, she decided that she would go out to Spain too, not for political reasons (though her sympathies were entirely with the Republic) but simply because she wanted to be near him, and because she felt that there must be something useful she could do. What she proposed was not easy: the number of wives of foreign volunteers who got into Spain must have been few indeed. But Eileen was determined. Following the precedent set by Eric himself, she turned to the ILP for assistance. When she learned that John McNair needed a secretary who could type and deal with correspondence in English, she volunteered for the post, was accepted, and with a supply of Indian tea and Havana cigars in her suitcase was soon on her way. By mid-February she was at her desk in the office in the Ramblas.

Her arrival in Barcelona did not signal an immediate reunion. We know that she was at the front for two days early in March; conceivably Eric went into Barcelona to be with her before that. But, in the phrase that would become popular in the next war against Fascism, "there was a war on," Orwell was a soldier who took his duties seriously, and with his unwavering belief in "fairness," it is hard to think he would have requested a leave to which he was not entitled. In any event, the correspondence between them continued more regularly than before, and with a significant difference. Letters sent abroad from Spain were opened by the censors, and one put things in and left things out accordingly. But letters carried by hand and delivered at either end of the route by John McNair were a different matter.

From this time on, Eric wrote a kind of journal-letter for Eileen, reporting the day's events as they happened. Hastily scrawled in pencil on scraps of paper, crammed with abbreviations, jottings, initials, and fragmentary phrases, they would certainly prove useful as "raw material" for the book about Spain that he intended eventually to write. But the letters themselves were in a fragile state—even unfolding a page for the first time one ran the risk of tearing it—and Eileen, who had had the experience of typing the manuscript of *The Road* and her brother Laurence's book on chest surgery, decided to prepare a continuing typescript of these journal-letters as they arrived. McNair, who helped her to decipher them, long afterwards described them as "first drafts" for *Homage to Catalonia*, but this would seem to be so only in the loosest and most optimistic manner of speaking. "Raw material," as we have suggested, better describes the typescript that Eric and Eileen brought away with them in their hasty departure from Spain in June 1937, and a lot of writing would have to be done before the raw was cooked. On the thirty-first of July, back home in Wallington, he wrote to Rayner Heppenstall, "I have started my book but of course my fingers are all thumbs at present."

3

His experience at his second posting was as uneventful as his first: he went out on patrols; he tried to keep warm; the trenches stank of shit; he talked knowingly about politics, about which he knew less than he claimed, improvising from point to point, and prompting Bob Edwards to scoff at him as "a bloody scribbler." Most important, of course, he stored up for future use the "incidents" of military life at the front: a battle by megaphone, where each side tried to convert the other—which he regarded as improper—and a small engagement in February, when the Fascists were celebrating the victory of their army at Málaga, and he came under fire seriously for the first time— he was at pains to record how scared he was.

One incident that he failed to record—rather surprisingly, given its latent political implication—is included in Bob Edwards's introduction to a deluxe edition of *Homage to Catalonia* published in 1970. A friend of Orwell's was wounded, and he and Edwards strapped him to a donkey to take him to a first-aid post in the darkness. "We were new to this territory but mutually agreed that if we followed the valley immediately behind our lines we were bound to arrive at the small village in which the first-aid post was situated. Leading the donkey, we groped our way through the darkness and reached the village as dawn was breaking. We were both wearing at this time huge all-covering

Spanish cloaks, and as we trooped up the only road in the village we were saluted at frequent intervals by small groups of patrolling soldiers. As we reached the village square, however, the gold and red flag of the Fascists was flying from a large building, and both Orwell and I instantly realized that we had entered a Fascist-held village. We retraced our steps as quickly as we dared. . . ."

This incident may have been one origin of an accusation made by Frank Frankfort the following September in the *Daily Worker*. Frankfort, who had been one of the English volunteers in the 3rd Regiment, now accused the POUM of having been Fascist spies. He claimed, among other things, that a cart carrying food had crossed each night from the POUM lines to the Fascists—he himself had heard the rattle of the cartwheels; that a mysterious light (presumably a signal?) had been seen between the lines; and that Georges Kopp had been observed visiting the enemy. In the September 24 *New Leader*, Orwell wrote a rebuttal to these charges, and had it signed by as many members of his group as he could find on short notice—fourteen in all.

Frankfort's letter, of no consequence in itself, was symptomatic of the campaign to blacken the POUM after the May events in Barcelona, and a good deal of Orwell's time when he returned to England was used up in attempting to refute such charges. It was the price exacted by his "political education."

He came an extraordinary distance in an extraordinarily short time—but, of course, the circumstances were extraordinary. The original impetus that led Orwell to fight with the POUM militia—and if his meeting with Harry Pollitt at Communist party headquarters in King Street had been less grating, he would just as certainly have fought with the International Brigade—was a fundamental innocence that was easy to ridicule and difficult not to honor. He believed simply that it was a matter of fighting against Fascism and for common decency. Measured by Stafford Cottman's standard, Orwell began as a Fundamentalist and became an Intellectual. Bob Edwards, more experienced in such things, was startled by his political naïveté. So too was Harry Milton, a young American dissident of the far Left, a union organizer and a Trotskyite who came to Spain to fight against Fascism, and gravitated to the POUM militia (a logical place for someone of his political disposition), ending up beside Orwell in the 3rd Regiment. After only an hour of conversation with the very tall Englishman, the very short New Yorker felt that Orwell's political education would have to begin at "square one."

Orwell's attitude, in the abstract and divorced from events, was utterly logical and sensible, and if it had been more widely held (especially by Spaniards) and if it had prevailed, the end of the war might possibly have been different: since all of the various political parties under the Republican government umbrella were in the war together, and since all of them had everything to lose in a Fascist victory, it followed that they should cooperate and work to ensure the defeat of Fascism. This did not happen; that it did not happen is a matter of history. Logic and common sense, those virtues beloved of the English, measured in the scale, do not weigh much against passion, and irrationalism, and hatred, and envy, and greed, and all those other toxins that poison the human spirit. A major reason Orwell became so disillusioned about the war—which brought out the best and the worst in many of the people who were involved in it—was that his expectations were so high. His previous actual experience with the dirty deals of politics—as opposed, say, to what he had read of them in the *New Statesman*—had been nonexistent. It was easier to be the young cynic at a fashionable English Public School, or sampling life at the bottom in Paris and London, than to be in Spain in the winter of 1937, believing in the cause of the Spanish Republic, at a time when Nazi Germany and Fascist Italy were blatantly intervening on behalf of the insurrectionary government of General Franco, when the United States, Great Britain, and France were cravenly non-intervening on anyone's behalf, and only Soviet Russia and Mexico were intervening on behalf of the Republic. Spain revealed to him the heights and depths of human experience; ultimately, Spain transformed him.

But he was, or so it would appear, a political innocent. It seems hard to grasp to what extent this was so, although he testifies to it himself in *Homage to Catalonia,* and it is in this context that one should read Bob Edwards's account of his part in Orwell's political education: "I found it very difficult to convince Orwell that the civil war in Spain was essentially a political conflict—a conflict of ideas—and that without the willing support of the overwhelming majority of the Spanish people the war could not be won against Franco, and this involved social changes based on social equality and a democratic structure of Government." From Harry Milton he would have heard a more sophisticated line of argument, emphasizing and sorting out the divagations among the parties of the Left. But it is permissible to wonder how much influence either of these would-be educators had upon him at this time. Orwell's contradictory and argumentative nature was such that while he enjoyed (and may even have profited from) a good political discussion, he equally enjoyed a good disagreement with prevailing orthodoxy—in this case, the POUM/ILP line, which put winning the revolution ahead of winning the war, for only the right sort of revolutionary government would ensure the right sort of victory. And there can be no doubt that, at this stage of things—in the spring of 1937—such a line did not deeply appeal to him. It was a case of actions speaking louder than dialectic.

Orwell was too much the experienced police officer and old public schoolboy not to be appalled at the inefficiency of the POUM's military activities. In spite of being rebuffed by Harry Pollitt, he was still drawn to the International Brigade and the drama of the active fighting in defense of Madrid. Early in April he had mentioned the possibility to John McNair, when he came up to the front, and in a letter to Eileen at this time he suggested that she too might say something to McNair "abt my wanting to go to Madrid etc." When he came on leave to Barcelona less than a month later—that is, immediately prior to the May "events"—he had every intention of resigning from the POUM and signing up with the International Brigade. A German whom he met upon his arrival in Barcelona remembers that they "argued quite vociferously about political matters. At the time he [Orwell] was serving in the militia of the POUM, but he sharply criticized the politics of the party and demonstrated great sympathy for the politics of the Communists and for the popular front." Orwell himself recorded this preference in the pages of *Homage to Catalonia*. There seems no question but that the "winning of the war" was more important to him than the "winning of the revolution." In the circumstances, joining the International Brigade would have been a logical next step.

But history arranged things differently.

Whatever his dissatisfactions—and they were, as we have seen, essentially on a pragmatic level, the urgency of a man determined to get on with it and get things done—Orwell was increasingly aware of the ways in which the POUM was being misrepresented as a counterrevolutionary party of the Fascists in disguise. The Stalinists, and those who supported them, were intensifying their campaign, as part of the purges going on in the Soviet Union, against all those who called themselves Marxists but were unwilling to follow the line from Moscow.

Ironically, POUM had the reputation of being the most unrelentingly doctrinaire of the Spanish Marxist parties. Formed in September 1935, it argued that the workers and not the bourgeoisie must lead the coming revolution. Andrés Nin, formerly Trotsky's secretary (but now broken with him), was its present leader. Although believing that the great Anarchist party, the CNT, was weak on doctrine (however full of revolutionary ardor), the POUM had no choice but to become an ally of the CNT if it wished to have any influence at all.

It is not inconceivable that (as its enemies claimed) there were some spies and agents provocateurs in the POUM, as it was perhaps the easiest party to join at a time when it was dangerous not to belong to a political party. But why secret supporters of the Right would want to join a small party increasingly under attack by other parties on the Left and clearly in some state of disarray is not at all obvious. It hardly offered much in the way of cover.

POUM had only seven to eight thousand men at the Aragon front. It had little trade-union support. Nin had for a time been Minister of Justice in the Catalan government, but had been eased out in December at the insistence of the PSUC. Franz Borkenau, whose book *The Spanish Cockpit* Orwell greatly admired, there describes the December crisis, a foretelling of the far more traumatic interparty struggle still five months in the future:

It is difficult to say whether [the POUM] was more hateful to the PSUC on account of its anti-Stalinism in Russian affairs or its extreme Leftist tendencies in Spanish questions. . . . As a matter of fact the POUM was liked by nobody, being overbearing and claiming with its small forces leadership over the old established mass organizations, both anarchist and socialist. All through the time of their supremacy the anarchists had handled the POUM rather rudely, but this time they felt they were themselves concerned in the attack. The PSUC claimed the exclusion of the POUM from the Catalan Government on the ground of their alleged "counterrevolutionary activities," meaning by that the pretended collaboration of Trotsky with the Gestapo. The anarchists resisted, and a ministerial crisis of four days ensued. But the Russians withheld important arms they had promised, and finally the anarchists had to give in.

This December crisis had, of course, occurred before Orwell's arrival in Barcelona, and very likely McNair would have thought it too complicated to explain it to him at their first meeting: the departure of Nin, the one POUM man in the government, would hardly suggest the party as wielding much power. But the war of words between POUM and other parties of the Left continued unabated. POUM attacked the Communists as "the Mensheviks of the Revolution"; the Communists counterattacked: the POUM were "demagogic Bukharinites." Such slanging might stir the passions in Barcelona, but even assuming that Orwell caught the reference (and Harry Milton's recollections suggest that he didn't), their potency would be appreciably diminished in the trenches of Alcubierre. There is nothing like a whiff of gunpowder to clear the mind of questions of doctrinal purity.

In mid-April, when the subterranean tensions in Barcelona were moving closer to the surface, Orwell had a night of military action of the sort for which he yearned and too seldom got. At 1:45 a.m. he led out a party of fifteen men in a surprise raid. The result was a gain of several thousand yards, which forced the enemy to retreat from its advance position. Orwell's account, familiar to all readers of *Homage*, is in the clear, exact style we now think of as Orwellian. Kopp's account, immediately after the raid, is in the manner of a front-line dispatch during the First World War: "We have had a complete success, which is largely due to the courage of the English comrades who were in charge of assaulting the principal of the enemy's parapets. Among them I feel it is my duty to give a particular mention of the splendid action of Eric Blair, Bob Smillie and Paddy Donovan." And the account of the raid in the *New Leader* for April 30 is in a style pleasantly reminiscent of all those adventure stories for boys that used to be written under the influence of G. A. Henty: " 'Charge' shouted Blair. . . . In front of the parapet was Eric Blair's tall figure, coolly strolling forward through the storm of fire. He leapt at the parapet, then stumbled. Hell, had they got him? No, he was over, closely followed by Gross, of Hammersmith, Frankfort, of Hackney, and Bob Smillie, with the others right after them."

Whether as a consequence of this rare taste of military action, or the coming of spring and the end of the cold from which he particularly suffered, or, more likely his approaching leave and reunion with Eileen—"what a rest we will have, and go fishing too if it is in any way possible"— Orwell's spirits noticeably lifted in these last weeks on the quiet front. One of Stafford Cottman's recollections of this time is of Orwell asking him to whistle the "Eton Boating Song" for him.

He had spent some hundred and fifteen days at the front. They represented an accumulation of boredom and impatience and the sort of physical hardship and discomfort that went with being in the trenches, of long days of inaction, of patrols at night with nothing to show for them . . . earthbound, commonplace. Yet he valued this period, when it was happening and afterwards when he came to write about it. It was imbued for him with a sense of comradeship, freely and generously given, and which had been prefigured on his first day at the Lenin Barracks when he had met and clasped hands, exchanging hardly five words (in Italian and Spanish) with an Italian volunteer like himself. Better than any political slogan, it explained and justified his being there.

On April 25 the group was relieved and went down the line quickly to Barcelona. His impressions of the city, in the first weeks in January, had made it seem paradisal; now, in the first weeks of May, he was to experience his expulsion from Paradise.

4

THE POLITICAL SITUATION IN REPUBLICAN SPAIN HAD changed in the early months of 1937, had become more complex in its aims, more openly disharmonious in its notions of how to achieve them, and more fatally polarized between Anarchists on the Left and Communists on the Right. Orwell, acutely responsive to the situation in which he found himself on the Aragon front, had only the vaguest notion of what was happening away from it. He seems to have had no inkling—and indeed, why should he have had? —of the Communists' determination that Largo Caballero, the Premier of the Republic—too independent-minded, and a Socialist whom they thought to be too favorably disposed to the Anarchists—must be ousted from office. This was the prime motive in a complex of motives that would set off the events of May.

The mood of Barcelona to which Orwell returned late in April was very different from what it had been when he arrived there at the end of 1936. Month by month it was becoming steadily less expressive of a revolutionary workers' state (which Orwell had found so attractive), dominated from the Left of the spectrum by the Anarchists of the CNT. Instead, it showed more overtly the influence of the progressive/democratic/bourgeois government of the Republic, in which, odd as it might seem, the Socialists and their Communist allies were on the Right. The hope, of course, was that the Republic, in its evolution rightward, might prove itself so respectable a member of the Popular Front, and so unrevolutionary under the moderating influence of the Soviet Union, that it would win the approval and support of the middle classes without whom it could not survive.

Underlying the immediate disagreements of the various parties as they wrangled for control of the government (and hence the direction of the war) were two crucial questions that had yet to be resolved. In the words of Raymond Carr, in his *Spain 1808–1939*, "Was the Civil War part of a social revolution, set off prematurely by a generals' revolt . . . ? Or was it a war to defend an advanced form of democracy, a war whose successful prosecution was incompatible with radical social revolution which would alienate support abroad and drive out of the Republic those very classes whose skills and loyalty could best organize victory?"

Through the winter and early spring of 1937 there was a succession of provocative incidents: the relations between the two great parties of the state, the Anarchists and the Socialists (and within the latter, between the Socialists and the Communists), became potentially explosive—all that was needed was a final provocation.

Towards the end of April the pace quickened.

On the twenty-fifth, the day before Orwell's return to Barcelona, the Anarchist paper *Solidaridad Obrera* attacked the Communist commissar for public order in Madrid, José Carzorla, who had shut down an Anarchist paper in the capital which charged the Communists with maintaining a secret prison for their enemies.

Also on the twenty-fifth, the Socialist premier, Largo Caballero, dissolved the defense committee in Madrid, which was dominated by Communists.

Also on the twenty-fifth, in the border town of Puigcerdá in Catalonia, there was an armed clash between government carabineros and Anarchists who had taken over the operation of the frontier post there. Also on the twenty-fifth, the body of Roldán Cortada, a leading Communist in Barcelona, was found shot—it was assumed he had been slain by Anarchists.

On April 26, the day Orwell arrived in Barcelona, Cortada's funeral was made the excuse for a huge Socialist demonstration.

Also on the twenty-sixth, the police chief of Barcelona authorized a punitive expedition to the suburb where Cortada's body had been found, and a number of Anarchists were rounded up and arrested.

Also on the twenty-sixth, the mayor of Puigcerdá, an Anarchist, was shot when the Anarchists tried to regain command of the frontier post from which they had been driven the day before.

The various headquarters of the parties in Barcelona—

CNT, PSUC, and POUM—began to prepare for the next and fatal stage in the power struggle: the point at which slogans would give way to bullets.

It was against this extraordinarily explosive background that Orwell returned from the front, and in the joy of his reunion with Eileen, in his rediscovery of those small-scale pleasures that loom so large in the mind of a returning soldier—a hot bath, clean clothes, dinner in a restaurant, a night between sheets—he was able to defuse the situation of its urgency. For a few days longer, even another week, it was possible to pretend that life was going on as usual, that at the end of his second week of leave he would be returning to the front.

In fact, if life *had* gone on as usual, when his leave was up he would have served on a very different front. He had come back to Barcelona firmly decided to withdraw from the POUM. He would have preferred to join the troops of the Anarchists, with whom he was politically and temperamentally in sympathy, but this would not have resulted in the difference he wanted: above all, he was anxious to get to Madrid, the heart of the struggle, and for that the practical, positive answer was to serve with the International Brigade.

Shortly after his arrival in Barcelona, he got in touch with a friend in Spanish Medical Aid who was able to make arrangements for him to go to Albacete, where the Brigade had its headquarters, and enlist—the first stop, as it were, on the road to Madrid.

His friend, an English.Communist, urged him to move promptly, the sooner the better, and to bring along with him, if he wanted, any other members of the ILP contingent who might welcome, as he would, the opportunity to be where the fire was hot—to take part in military action on a significant, even a decisive scale, and by so doing, play a more valuable role in the struggle against Fascism. Restless as he was, after three months of inactivity on the Aragon front, and dissatisfied as he was with the rather slipshod way things were done in the POUM, he might well have accepted the offer, gone to Albacete, joined the International Brigade, been assigned to the Madrid front. Had he done so, his history would have been very different. But he was determined to wait in Barcelona a bit longer: he was entitled to a second week of leave, not something a soldier would give up lightly, and he meant to enjoy it to the full—perhaps he and Eileen would go to the seaside for a few days. More than that, he had ordered a pair of boots that were in the process of being made for him—his feet were large, and the boots he had been issued in the Lenin Barracks were too small, and he had come to doubt that any boots in the Spanish army would be big enough for him— therefore he couldn't think of leaving until he had his new, specially fitted boots, that was understood, and it was unlikely they would be ready for him (to judge from the experience of soldiers from here to eternity) until the last or next-to-last day of his leave.

Staying on in Barcelona, he missed the opportunity to participate significantly in the actual fighting against the Fascist forces; instead, he witnessed and participated in the war within the war within the Republic—the struggle on the Left—in that first week of May 1937, as the contending parties and splinter parties warred among themselves to take control of the government, and so determine the course of the "revolution" and the conduct of the war against Franco and his German and Italian allies.

Orwell, coming straight from the front, was unprepared for the changed atmosphere of Barcelona. The idealism of

December, to which he had responded with such excitement, was virtually dissipated; the working class was no longer the one class in a classless society; the bourgeoisie were reemerging. As against the earlier promise of a "revolution" that would fulfill the dream of Socialism, now there was the disillusioning prospect of sectarian wrangling, Socialism betrayed, and the emergence of a capitalist Republic. Before the year was out, Orwell would be looking back nostalgically to that time when people believed in the "revolution": for him it had been a strange and moving experience, and the memory of it would prove ineffaceable.

That, of course, was the retrospective view. In May, one saw a city where the hateful signs of class differences were in evidence again. One felt a great rise in tension. At the headquarters of the three parties, preparations went forward, fatalistically and combatively, for the explosion everyone felt was bound to occur. (The PSUC launched a prophetic slogan—"Before we capture Saragossa, we have to take Barcelona"—which would be fulfilled only in the latter condition: Saragossa, to the end of the war, remained in Nationalist control.)

Determined though Orwell was to enjoy his leave, he couldn't help being aware of the "situation," which he saw, perhaps too simply, as the struggle between those who wanted the "revolution" to go forward (CNT and POUM) and those who did not (PSUC). Despite his educative political discussions at the front, starting at "square one," there were nuances of the situation in Barcelona he failed to recognize, complexities he oversimplified. Perhaps, in some sense, he still saw the war, and the war within the war, too firmly in terms of black and white, even though not the black and white he had originally expected. If, on the government side, there was a power struggle coming to a climax in Barcelona, he may have recognized it without recognizing sufficiently that the question of "revolution" in Spain (which had such considerable implications for Russian foreign policy, which in turn had such effect upon Spanish domestic policy) was precisely the issue upon which the fate of the Republic depended. And this may explain, better than totting up a list of omissions, errors of fact, and misinterpretations, why the historian Hugh Thomas should conclude that *Homage to Catalonia,* "marvellously written though it is, is a better book about war itself than about the Spanish War."

The troubles, the May Days, had their beginning—and a comic beginning it was for events that were to have so tragic an ending—on the second of May in the Telephone Exchange Building on the Plaza de Cataluña, the huge square at the top of the Ramblas, and a center for demonstrations. The Exchange, taken over from the American Telephone and Telegraph Company, was run by a joint committee of the UGT, the union arm of the Socialist party, and the CNT, but it was dominated by the latter. The Anarchist operators tended to harass members of the PSUC making telephone calls. On the second, when a high official of the Republic, in Valencia, telephoned the government of Catalonia, the Generalidad, in Barcelona, he was told by the operator that "there was no such thing as a government in Barcelona, only a 'defence committee.'" Later on the same day, a conversation between Azaña, the president of the Republic, and Companys, president of the Generalidad, was interrupted by the Anarchist operator, remarking that the lines were needed for more important purposes than a talk between the two presidents! This was to take Anarchy past the point of anarchy, and the central governments in both Valencia and Barcelona decided to assert their authority. On the third of May, Rodriguez Salas, the chief of police in Barcelona, arrived at the Telephone Exchange, and established himself in the Censor's Department on the first floor, with the declared intent of taking over the building. But the Anarchists, legally there, refused to be dislodged and took up their rifles. From the second floor, they began firing down the great staircase in the general direction of the Censor's office. Rodriguez was not to be drawn; he remained out of sight and out of reach behind closed doors, and summoned help. Within minutes a truckload of civil guards, armed and ready to follow his orders, arrived at the building; and in their wake came two of the Anarchist leaders (themselves highly placed in the police) who persuaded their comrades to put down their arms and return to their switchboards. But in a final burst of high spirits the indignant telephonists fired their remaining ammunition out the windows, into the crowded square. Whether anyone was hit is not known; what is certain is that the unmistakable sound of gunfire racketing through the square (and the shouting that followed upon it) was misunderstood. It was taken to signal the beginning of something—whether unplanned violence, a deliberate *coup*, or a long-smoldering rivalry bursting into flame. Within hours, in their separate headquarters the various political parties had mobilized their followers, brought stored-up weapons out of hiding, and begun building barricades, in anticipation of a siege, guerrilla stratagems, the random fatalities that are inseparable from fighting in the streets. (Actually, by the eighth of May, when the riots were over and "peace" was restored to the streets of Barcelona, more than four hundred people had been killed, more than a thousand wounded.)

Orwell's firsthand experience of the events of May (the

uprising, the troubles, the riots?—one has difficulty in choosing the term most appropriate to what actually occurred in that week in Barcelona) was oddly unsatisfactory: a mix of tension, uncertainty, excitement, fatigue, and anticlimax. And oddly similar in those respects to his experience at the Aragon front. He devotes a chapter to it in *Homage to Catalonia*, "marvellously"—as Hugh Thomas says—and also so clearly written that for anyone interested in following Orwell through the week, not simply on the page but (as the present authors have done) in Barcelona itself, step by step as it were, it proves as efficient as a guidebook.

There, on the left-hand side of the Ramblas, a short walk down from the Plaza de Cataluña, is the Hotel Continental, where Eileen had been living since coming out in February; there, on the same side, further along, is the Hotel Falcon, which had been taken over by the POUM as a combination of dormitory and offices; and a few doors further, the Café Moka, where a group of Civil Guards had holed up, the only visible "enemy" but singularly peaceful and unthreatening. From the sidewalk in front of the Moka —continuing our "Orwell tour"—one crosses the three strips of the Ramblas: the road for cars; the broad, tree-lined central walkway, with its kiosks and stalls, each with its special items for sale (canaries in wicker cages; goat cheese and sausages; newspapers); and the parallel road for cars. Safely on the other side, one starts up the Ramblas towards the Plaza de Cataluña; midway, one arrives at the sometime Poliorama Cinema (still a cinema, but renamed), where for three nights Orwell was on the roof on sentry duty, waiting for action that never came: the predictable anticlimax.

It seems emblematic of the deflationary way in which he chooses to tell the tale—and which makes it all the more credible, therefore—that when, at midday on the third, a friend whom he encountered in the lounge of the Continental told him there had been trouble at the Telephone Exchange he shrugged the news aside. Perhaps he had only been half-listening. Later in the afternoon, however, as he was coming down the Ramblas, he heard gunfire behind him, turned, saw some Anarchist youths, carrying rifles, edging along a side street: they had been exchanging shots with a sniper high up in a neighboring church tower. Now the reaction that he might have had earlier in the day occurred: "It's started." But what had started he would not precisely know throughout the week it was happening: rumors, conjectures, guesses, and speculations figured importantly in the absence of concrete news. (And when he came to write of it, several months later, he followed the chapter of personal history with a chapter of political analysis, though even then he knew less than he would have liked, and apologized in advance for the mistakes he would almost certainly be making.)

He and an American friend hurried down to the Falcon: there, presumably, something was to be learned. But all was confusion, and he went out, and crossed the Ramblas to the Comité Local of the POUM, which had been set up in the dusty remains of an abandoned nightclub and theater. In one of the rooms weapons were being distributed, and Orwell was issued a rifle and a small supply of ammunition. What next? No news, of course; confusion, of course. Rumors and speculation: "a vague idea" that they would be attacked momentarily (by whom?); "a general impression that the Civil Guards were after the CNT and the working class generally," and if that was the case, there was no question as to which side he was on.

Time passed; and passed; and nothing seemed to be happening: no attack was made in the next moment (or any time during the week) on the Comité Local or the other POUM buildings. But out of sight and out of earshot, who could say? Barcelona is an immense city, and the bird's-eye view is not given to the ordinary participant in great events. One is reminded, as much by Orwell's predicament as his prose, of Stendhal's Fabrice looking for the battle of Waterloo. Outside in the streets there would be sporadic bursts of gunfire. In the Comité Local, the younger members of the POUM, boy soldiers, thought it all a kind of picnic; one of them even made off deftly with Orwell's rifle.

He had taken it for granted that the telephones would be out of service; in fact, the operators had long since gone back to their switchboards. Once he had tracked down the number of the Continental, he had no difficulty in reaching the hotel, but Eileen wasn't to be found. He had better luck with John McNair, who was standing close by in the lobby, and who took the message for Eileen that he would be spending the night at the Comité Local in case there should be an attack.

McNair asked him if he needed anything.

"Only cigarettes," Orwell replied jokingly.

But McNair was willing to oblige. He set out with two packs of Lucky Strikes, down the pitch-dark Ramblas, getting past two armed patrols, as he later recalled, by whistling alternately the Anarchist and Communist anthems.

THAT NIGHT, WRAPPED IN A CURTAIN HE'D CUT DOWN FROM the stage of the cabaret, Orwell slept fitfully until three a.m., when he was awakened by the man who seemed to be in charge, handed a rifle, and put on guard duty at a window. At dawn he was relieved of his post and his rifle—rifles were in much too short supply to be given out indiscriminately. Armed only with two primitive grenades, he went downstairs and outside. Barricades were being constructed of cobblestones, in front of the Comité Local, and across the Ramblas in front of the Hotel Falcon: for Orwell, a "strange and wonderful" sight. Surely today something was going to happen . . . where *he* was. (What he had no way of knowing was that attempts were already being made to end the fighting, both the PSUC and the CNT trying to contain their extremists as the party leaders got ready, not, as the innocent builders of the barricades might imagine, to battle, but to bargain.) He walked up the Ramblas, exposing himself in his great height to the stray sniper's bullet, paused for a cup of coffee and to buy a wedge of cheese at one of the few stalls opened for business, continued on to the Continental, where he had a brief reunion with Eileen, then back to the POUM Executive Building, in search of orders. From all over Barcelona came the din of street fighting, the roar of gunfire in a gathering crescendo: surely today something was going to happen . . . where *he* was. He was talking to Kopp in an office on the second floor, asking the usual question—what were they supposed to do?—when there was a terrific booming below, as though a field-gun were being fired.

Very calmly, as always, Kopp led the way downstairs to investigate what was going on.

POUM shock troopers, in the doorway of the building, were lobbing grenades along the pavement towards the Café Moka next door. There, some twenty or so Civil Guards had been barricaded since midafternoon of the day before. In the early morning they had emerged long enough for an exchange of gunfire—one POUMista badly wounded; one Civil Guard killed—then hastily drew back into the safety of the café. Now they had come out again to fire at an unarmed POUM militiaman dodging his way down the central walk; he had found temporary shelter behind a kiosk.

Kopp ordered the shock troopers to stop their game of skittles. In Spanish, French, German, Italian, and English, he repeated that there must not be bloodshed, no provocations. Then, in full view of the "enemy," he stepped forward and put his pistol down on the pavement. Accompanied by two Spanish militiamen, who also made a great show of taking off their weapons, he started slowly toward the entrance of the café, where the Guards, unnerved by the exploding grenades, huddled in terror. One of them came forward to negotiate with Kopp. The unarmed militiaman, crouching behind the kiosk, was no longer a worry to them; their concern was with two of the grenades that hadn't exploded and lay there on the pavement in front of the café, ready to go off at any moment . . .

Kopp returned to the group clustered around the POUM building and decreed that the grenades should be touched off. One of the troopers took up his rifle, aimed, fired, on target—the first grenade disposed of. But his next shot was a miss. Orwell asked for the rifle. He got down on one knee, aimed, fired, and missed.

A pity, really; for it was the only shot he fired during the eight days of the riots. As it turned out, no other opportunity was presented to him.

After the incident, Kopp resumed their interrupted conversation. Their role had been decided on by the POUM leaders; they were simply and exclusively to defend their buildings; unless it proved unavoidable, they were not to open fire. To Orwell's earlier question, "What are we supposed to do?" Kopp replied in a practical way by assigning him to guard duty on the roof of the building opposite. Above the Poliorama Cinema was the Science Club of Barcelona with a two-domed observatory on its roof. From the observatory one may well have had a splendid view of the stars above Barcelona; from the parapet, looking down, one had a wide-range, supervisory view of the Hotel Falcon and the POUM Executive Building, which would have to be defended if attacked, and the "enemy" stronghold, the Café Moka, in the ground floor of a building whose upper floors housed a hotel, and whose roof was now being used as a sentry point by Civil Guards from the café.

Orwell spent the next three days on duty at the observatory, but nothing happened to disturb the long hours of loafing: he grew used to the racket of gunfire rising up from different areas of the city, a kind of accompaniment to his reading (he'd brought a lot of Penguins with him), and he used to go across to the Continental for his meals. From his aerie he tried to puzzle out what was happening, but on the rooftop with all the city spread out before him, he found he was in no better position to answer the question than he had been on the ground. The newspapers, which continued to publish through the week, added to his confusion, since each adhered to its own party's line. Thus, on Tuesday the fourth, *Solidaridad Obrera,* the paper of the CNT, was outraged by the attack on the Telephone Exchange; on Wednesday the fifth (as the negotiations about which Orwell had no knowledge got under way) it was urging that the riots be ended and that people return to their jobs. *La Batalla,* the paper of the POUM, which managed to publish in spite of police harassment, took the contrary view: the riots must go on, the barricades be maintained. Orwell, summing up the mood of the first three days, tells us that, although people were still at the barricades, "everyone was sick of the meaningless fighting, which could obviously lead to no real decision, because no one wanted this to develop into a full-sized civil war which might mean losing the war against Franco."

But "meaningless fighting" can be made the pretext for real decisions, as Orwell himself was presently to discover; and even as he thought that "nothing was happening," accords were being reached, decisions arrived at, that allow historians to conclude, as Raymond Carr has done, that "As a consequence of the May events both the revolutionary forces in Barcelona and Catalan independence of the central government were destroyed."

On May 5 there had been a broadcast of an accord between the Government and the CNT leadership, but the barricades continued to be manned. Kopp warned Orwell that there might be more serious fighting, particularly if the POUM was outlawed. He had had "information" that that was going to happen; the Government might be moving against them that very evening. Feverishly they set to work to fortify the Executive Building, and drew up plans to seize the Civil Guards in the Café Moka as soon as word came that the news was definite. "Our only chance was to attack them first." There is an excitement at this point in Orwell's narrative that is unmistakable: at last something is going to happen, here, to him. Eileen, too, came over from the Continental, ready to act as a nurse should it be necessary, though there was a lamentable absence of supplies: not even iodine or bandages. Orwell lay down on a sofa for a half-hour nap before the start of the fighting in which he presumed he would be killed. Uncomfortable though he was with his pistol sticking into his back, he slept a long time. When he woke up in the morning, Eileen told him nothing had happened: the Government hadn't attacked, the POUM hadn't been outlawed. Evidently Kopp's information was false; in fact, it was merely premature.

The familiar sense of anticlimax—so much a part of his Spanish experience—added to the depression he felt going back to his post on the roof of the observatory. Nor did it lighten when news came in the afternoon that there had been some sort of truce arranged . . . short-lived in the event, but it was clear by now that the end was in sight . . . and clear, too, what at first he perceived only dimly, that when the disturbances were over, a scapegoat would have to be found, and who would be more likely than the POUM, the smallest, weakest, most uncompromising and revolutionary of the parties of the Left?

On the sixth of May, ships dispatched by the Government in Valencia—two destroyers and a battleship—arrived in the harbor. They brought four thousand Assault Guards, picked Government troops, impressive in their conventional uniforms and new, standardized equipment—a far cry from the ragtag "people's army" of the POUM. Soon they were everywhere in the streets, restoring "law and order," and the irony of their being there, rather than at the front, fighting against Franco, was not lost upon Orwell. On the seventh of May, the CNT asked for a return to "normality"; on the eighth, the last sporadic fighting ceased, and Barcelona was at peace again. The "May Days" entered into history, an extraordinary and tragic event to have taken place in the middle of a civil war. The consequences would be far-reaching: the suppression of a political party, the deposition and replacement of a prime minister, an end to the autonomy of Catalonia, an end to the hopes of a workers' revolution, the strengthening and bourgeoisification of the central government of the Republic. And among the minor consequences—but of crucial importance to the man himself, and to his work, and so ultimately to the millions of people who would become familiar with it and his name in succeeding generations—was the effect upon Orwell. His experience of the May Days completed the transformation that had begun in Wigan: henceforth he was a writer passionate in his political interests, sympathies, and convictions. For him it was no longer possible to separate art and politics; thanks to Spain, they had become inextricable.

On the ninth of May, as the semblance of peace and normality returned and the flags of the Republic were flying over Barcelona, the campaign of vilification began.

The POUM had been, all along, more provocative than Orwell may have recognized. It was disliked by the CNT and hated by the PSUC. Its continual exposures of the Moscow trials, its uncompromising denunciations of Stalinism as a betrayal of the Revolution had driven the Communists to a state of fury. It seems almost certain that the price of Russian military aid to the Republic would ultimately have included the suppression of the POUM; the May Days provided the necessary pretext. Hardly had the last gun been fired than the papers of the PSUC were describing the POUM as a Fascist party in disguise and demanding that it be outlawed. The widest possible circulation was given to a cartoon that depicted the POUM as "a figure slipping off a mask marked with the hammer and sickle and revealing a hideous, maniacal face marked with the swastika." For Orwell this was evidence enough that "the official version of the Barcelona fighting was already fixed upon: it was to be represented as a 'fifth column' Fascist rising engineered solely by the POUM."

He suffered a profound revulsion. At the heart of his Socialism, as we have seen, was a belief in honor and decency. And the ways in which the POUM was being misrepresented by its enemies seemed to him indecent and dishonorable: the politics of lying, the malignant distortions of language. (Here, surely, were the seeds of *Animal Farm* and *1984*.) He was not blind to the POUM's defects —only two weeks earlier he had come back to Barcelona intending to join the International Brigade. After the May Days, such a move was unthinkable. When his friend in Medical Aid, the English Communist to whom he'd originally broached the possibility, came to the Continental to ask if he was now ready to make the transfer, he replied, "Your papers are saying I'm a Fascist. Surely I should be politically suspect coming from the POUM." And he went on to say that he could never join any "Communist-controlled unit" for fear that it might be used against the Spanish working class.

The apparent peculiarity, not to say perversity, of his statement—especially for those who think of Communism and working-class revolution as synonymous—takes on a different aspect when set in context with the Spanish Communist party. For this, as Hugh Thomas writes,

> was no ordinary communist party. If its propaganda harked back to the Russian revolution, its practice suited, and reflected the desires of, the small shopkeepers, small farmers, taxi drivers, minor officials and junior officers who joined it between July 1936 and the end of the year, without reading much Marx or knowing much of Russia, in the hope of finding protection against anarchism and lawlessness. The communists stood for a disciplined, left-of-Centre, bourgeois régime, capable of

winning the war, with private industry limited by some nationalization, but not by collectivization, or workers' control.

This was a program that would not be likely to have offended a left-of-center Democrat in the United States or Labourite in Great Britain; certainly it would not have appealed to a militant Socialist such as Orwell had become. In any event, his commitment to the POUM had now become a matter of principle: it would have been dishonorable and indecent to desert it when it was so palpably the underdog in a struggle it could not possibly win. Before the end of June the Government would suppress this gadfly of a party, but in May it still had its enfeebled legal existence, as well as its militia on the Huesca front, to which on May 10 Orwell returned, as a lieutenant, commanding about thirty men, English and Spanish. It was, as before, a quiet front. Action, such as it was, consisted mainly of going out on patrols. There was a good deal of sniping on both sides, but nothing that could count as even a minor engagement. There was ample time accordingly for political discussions, and, as Harry Milton observed, the old naïve Orwell had been utterly transformed by his experience in Barcelona. Such discussions would go on for hours, and it was at five A.M. one morning, some ten days after his return to the front, while talking about politics, that Orwell was found out and brought down by a sniper's bullet. Georges Kopp, in a letter to Orwell's brother-in-law, Laurence O'Shaughnessy, described the wound so precisely that one can safely assume he was transcribing a medical report: "The bullet entered the neck just under the larynx, slightly at the left side of its vertical axis, and went out at the dorsal right side of the neck's base. It was a normal 7 mm. bore, copper-plated Spanish mauser bullet, shot from a distance of some 175 yards. At this gauge, it still had the velocity of some 600 feet per second and a cauterising temperature. . . . The hemorrhaging was insignificant."

For Orwell it was as though he had been "*at the centre of an explosion.*" Lying on the ground, dazed, he knew that he had been wounded, but did not yet realize where. When he heard someone remark he had been shot through the neck, he assumed he would die, for a minute or two wondered if he might already have been killed: he did not feel any pain, only resentment that his life should end so pointlessly. He thought first of Eileen, and then, in logical sequence, of this world he had come to value and which he was leaving, not heroically in battle, but stupidly, picked off by a sniper. On the stretcher, he began to feel pain, so strong as to convince him that he was alive, and his thoughts now were of the four men who were carrying the stretcher, no easy burden, a mile and a half over slippery terrain to the ambulance. Then he was moved down the line, pausing for rudimentary care at a succession of primitive military hospitals that were little more than first-aid stations, in a slow, eight-day progress towards professional diagnosis and treatment: five miles to Siétamo, a further twenty-seven miles to Barbastro, then to Lérida, where Eileen and Kopp came to see him. (The doctor took Kopp aside and told him that no essential organ had been damaged, already Orwell was stronger, he would survive, in a day or two he would be able to get out of bed and walk about—but when he attempted to talk, the best he could manage was a whisper; his voice was gone.) He spent five or six days at Lérida; then he was sent on to the hospital at Tarragona, where there were sufficient doctors and nurses and equipment to care for the wounded as they deserved.

There, eight days after leaving the front, he was given a careful examination, and it was determined that one of his vocal chords was paralyzed. This meant, the doctor told him cheerfully, he would never recover the use of his voice. (In fact, he would speak in a whisper for the next two months; then his voice did begin to come back; after another four months he spoke quite normally, though with an occasional squeak.)

On May 27, Kopp and Eileen drove the sixty-one miles to Tarragona to pick him up and bring him back to Barcelona. He was being released from the hospital with the recommendation that he report for further treatment at the POUM's Sanitorium Maurin, on the outskirts of the city. It seemed to Kopp that he was not quite as "voiceless" as he had been at Lérida. In his letter to Laurence O'Shaughnessy, he writes that "Eric was able to utter any articulate sound but feebly and with the characteristic grinding noise of the brakes of a Model T, very antiquated Ford. His speech was inaudible outside a range of two yards."

He spent the next three days with Eileen at the Continental, and on May 31, the day before he was to enter the Sanitorium Maurin, they had cocktails and lunch with Kopp in a restaurant near the hotel, an event so agreeable (and proof of Eric's progress) that Kopp mentioned it in his letters to Laurence O'Shaughnessy.

On June 1, he entered the sanitorium, and would spend much of the next two weeks there, receiving treatment, not for the "incomplete semi-paralysis of the larynx" which was apparently untreatable, but for the extreme pain he was suffering in his arm and shoulder. There was a good deal of time, however, when he was free to come and go as he pleased, and then he and Eileen would start out from the Continental to wander about the city, sightseeing, adding up all the obvious, sensible reasons why they should leave as soon as it was feasible. Obviously the sooner he was at home, the sooner he would regain his health. Obviously he could be of no further use as a soldier. Obviously there was nothing left for him to do for the POUM, *here:* its story would have to be told, and he had already made up his mind to tell it in his next book. But above all—however many sensible and obvious reasons he could call upon to justify leaving now—he was prey to an immense despair and revulsion: "I had an overwhelming desire to get away from it all; away from the horrible atmosphere of political suspicion and hatred, from streets thronged by armed men, from air-raids, trenches, machine-guns, screaming trams, milkless tea, oil cookery and shortage of cigarettes—from almost everything I had learnt to associate with Spain."

They would leave as soon as it was feasible—and honorable. It was the latter condition that led to the melodrama of Orwell's last days in Barcelona. If he had wanted, he might have been able to leave Spain on his British passport and as a journalist—it would have been entirely legal. But to do so would have been at odds with his concept of honor. He had served as a soldier, he would leave as a soldier, honorably discharged. When he had come out to Spain six months before, he had joined a voluntary group, formed in the first fervor of revolutionary action, and he had had great faith in the power of its enthusiasm. But the army was now being formally organized and unified, gathering in the militias, and depended on conscripts. Weapons would be needed to replace enthusiasm, and he was very doubtful whether they would arrive in sufficient numbers to bring about an ultimate, convincing victory. (Events were to justify his skepticism. Russian military aid to the Republic—the principal military aid from abroad—was generous up to a point, but was never allowed past the point where it might have outweighed the generosity of Hitler and Mussolini to Franco.) The change in the character of the army made his own position equivocal: one could no longer resign; and could one, having served with the POUM militia (now so open to question), count on being honorably discharged? Mightn't one just as likely be tossed into prison as a Fascist sympathizer? One heard such stories in Barcelona, but Orwell had also heard that he might be able to receive a proper discharge at the front: it would be worth the journey to find out, he thought, even though each day's delay added to the difficulty of getting safely out.

The doctors in the hospital in Tarragona had already determined that he was medically unfit. Regulations required that the diagnosis be confirmed by a hospital at the front. It was also necessary to have his papers stamped at the POUM militia headquarters. (No matter that he had been warned not to show his party card at the numerous paper checks that were taking place in Barcelona.) On June 15, he set out for Siétamo, just a few miles from Huesca, arriving there at midnight, in a truck bringing up troops for the new attack about to be launched against the city. Before he could explain why he was there, he was issued a rifle and ammunition, and ordered to stand by. That night he slept on the ground, fearing the worst but unwilling to be treated differently from the other soldiers with whom he'd come up to the front. Still, he was in a rather different situation from theirs, and he might, without apology, have pointed this out. In the morning, when it became evident that the attack would not be getting under way for some time—the inevitable anticlimax—he did show his hospital paper and set about to find the right place to be examined, going from Siétamo to Barbastro and Monzón and back to

280 ORWELL: THE TRANSFORMATION

Siétamo, which proved to be the right place after all: he was declared "useless," his papers were stamped, the discharge issued, and he started back to Barcelona. He arrived late on the night of the twentieth, and went straight to the Continental.

EARLIER THAT DAY EILEEN HAD WRITTEN TO HER BELOVED brother Laurence:

> Eric is I think much better, though he cannot be brought to admit any improvement. His voice certainly improves very *slowly*, but he uses his arm much more freely though it is still very painful at times. He eats as much as anyone else and can walk about and do ordinary things quite effectively for a short time. He is *violently* depressed, which I think encouraging. I have now agreed to spend two or three days on the Mediterranean (in France) on the way home—probably at Port-Vendres. In any case we shall probably have to wait somewhere for money. The discharge is not through but I think we can leave next week, wire you for money when we arrive at Port-Vendres or other resting place, go on to Paris and spend there the nights and the day between, and then get the morning train to England. I do not altogether like this protracted travel, but no urgent complication seems possible now and he has an overwhelming desire to follow this programme—anyway, it has overwhelmed me.

As he came into the lounge, Eileen hurried up to embrace him, smiled affectionately, and whispered "Get out," meanwhile moving with him to the door, whispering "You can't stay here, someone may call the police." Out on the pavement, she slipped her arm through his, and they strolled along the Ramblas, to the casual eye another pair of lovers —in fact, it was only now that she explained that the Government had finally taken the long-awaited action: the POUM had been suppressed on the fifteenth, the day he left for Siétamo. Since then there had been widespread arrests—more than a thousand, it was said, among them forty members of the central committee of the party. And Georges Kopp! The headquarters at the Hotel Falcon was closed: the hotel itself was "immediately turned into a prison."

For Orwell, out of Barcelona and on the move since the fifteenth, the news came less as a surprise than as a confirmation of his deepest fears: the suppression of the POUM put the seal on his Spanish experience.

He led her into a nearby café—you never could tell who might be following—and listened grimly as she related what she knew to be fact: that the police had burst into her room at the Continental in the early morning when she was still in bed, in search of "evidence." They had taken everything of his from the sanitorium, even his dirty laundry, and everything they could lay hands on in the way of papers. Only their passports and checkbooks, which were hidden under the mattress, went undiscovered: the police had apologized for disturbing her (the touch of Spanish gallantry) and did not ask her to get out of the bed. (John McNair was later to say that he preserved the notes and an early "manuscript version" of what became *Homage to Catalonia* by placing the folder in which they were contained on the sill outside the window when the police arrived to search the office of the ILP.)

The question was no longer, When would they leave? but, How could they avoid arrest while they waited to leave? They decided that Eileen would remain at the hotel, and he himself would go into hiding; his POUM card he tore up at her insistence.

There followed three days and nights of tension and a curious bravado. Although he slept "out"—in the crypt of a ruined church, on a park bench—he did not conduct himself as a "fugitive." By day he would meet with Eileen and McNair; he and Eileen would eat in "fancy" restaurants, as unlikely haunts for former members of POUM, and would revenge himself afterwards by scrawling the graffito "Visca POUM" in the hallways of the restaurant.

The scheme finally devised was that he, McNair, and Stafford Cottman, the very young English member of the group, would meet at the British consulate to enlist the consul's help in getting the three necessary stamps in their passports: from the French consul, so they could travel through France; from the Catalan immigration authorities; and from the chief of police. The last was the potential danger, for he might put Orwell under arrest if he recognized that the 29th Division, as indicated on Orwell's papers, was part of the POUM.

The consul proved helpful; telephone calls were made; late on the second day they would have the stamps they needed. But Orwell also was determined to do all he could to help Kopp. That afternoon he and Eileen visited him in prison. Kopp wanted them to retrieve a letter of his in the Ministry of War that might be a valuable credential; without it he was simply another Fascist-Trotskyist wrecker from POUM and, as he said with a lightheartedness that did not mask the seriousness of his situation, he might end up in front of a firing squad.

Going to visit the prison, going to the Ministry of War (which he did next), Orwell did not hesitate to put himself in a dangerous position—perhaps at such moments he subscribed to the traditional belief of the Englishman that somehow he was protected by a higher power when he was among foreigners, and that he couldn't be arrested unless he had broken a law. His confidence would seem to have been justified: not only did he secure the letter, but the officer who gave it to him shook hands with him when they parted—an action that Orwell would compare, in *Homage,* to an Englishman shaking hands with a German during the First World War. But the letter, duly delivered to Kopp, failed to serve its purpose; he would be held in that Spanish prison for another eighteen months, when he managed to escape and crossed into France to fight with the Resistance: he and Orwell would not meet again until the middle of the Second World War.

On the evening of the second day, with their passports and visas in order, they held back until the last possible moment before entering the railway station: their destination was Port Bou. But the train left forty minutes *early,* so they had to wait until the next morning. That night, their last in Spain, they spent in a cheap hotel run by a member of the CNT, who did not register them with the police.

For their second attempt, they decided to run the risk of interception by the police, and arrived in the station early. The train was already there, and they boarded separately: first Eileen, who had come from the Continental, then Orwell, then Cottman, then McNair, and they crossed the frontier without incident. Detectives did come through the train taking some names, but didn't bother with the four English, who were in the dining car and hence bourgeois and respectable. Looking bourgeois would have endangered them in Barcelona the previous December; now it was a passport to safety. At the frontier their names were checked against various lists, from which they were absent, and the police at the border seemed not to know that the 29th was the POUM division. Orwell felt they were lucky to get out alive.

At the border the quartet divided: McNair and Cottman would go straight on to England, Eileen and Orwell would spend a few days at Banyuls—not Port-Vendres—six miles into France, and the world at peace. Unexpectedly he felt a terrible urge to return to Spain: that was where real life was. He had experienced nobility and baseness, courage and betrayal, but his faith in the human, the crystal spirit, remained undimmed.

5

THERE IS A MEMORABLE SENTENCE BY V. S. PRITCHETT THAT portrays the legendary Orwell: "Tall and bony, the face lined with pain, eyes that stared out of their caves, he looked far away over one's head, as if seeking more discomfort and new indignations." But this is only a partial portrait, and like the legend itself somewhat misleading: in fact, he was looking (at and into and beyond) the subject about which he meant to write, and searching for the words that would allow him to bring it as precisely and powerfully alive as possible. His life was dedicated to his art as he understood it. He had his intense political and personal concerns: he was not abstracted, as the legend would have it, into a kind of saintliness. The difficulties and pleasures of ordinary life were important to him. But for the man who wrote—as a self-aware, protesting middle-class figure in twentieth-century England, heir to a great intellectual tradition of dissent—what he wrote was his overriding concern.

He had come to Spain with his politics untried and his ideals untested. As Harry Milton remarked of him after their first meeting: "He was a political innocent." Spain educated him in the complexities, ambiguities, compromises, and betrayals of politics. It cost him his innocence, but not, as might have seemed inevitable, his idealism.

Early in June, four weeks after the uprising in Barcelona —the decisive event in his political education—he wrote to Cyril Connolly from the sanitarium where he was slowly recovering from the wound in his throat: "I have seen wonderful things and at last really believe in Socialism, which I never did before." A decade later he would write: "Every line of serious work that I have written since 1936 has been written, directly or indirectly, *against* totalitarianism and *for* democratic Socialism, as I understand it." His seekings came to their resolution in Spain, and he was able to make peace with himself as a man, and find his way as an artist. And it was for this that he became George Orwell.

NOTES
INDEX

NOTES

Notes are given when it is not clear from the text where the sources are to be found, except in those few instances when the source of information did not wish to be identified. Letters from Orwell to Leonard Moore in the text which are not in *The Collected Essays, Journalism and Letters of George Orwell: An Age Like This, 1920–1940*, edited by Sonia Orwell and Ian Angus (New York, 1968), are in the Berg Collection, the New York Public Library.

p. 5   "In Communion with Reality," *The Times Literary Supplement* 21 December 1973, pp. 1153–5.

p. 15   Reviews the dates for which are not clear from the text: *Tatler* 11 January 1933, p. 52; *New Clarion* 21 January 1933, p. 139; *Adelphi* February 1933, pp. 381–2; *The Times Literary Supplement* 12 January 1933, p. 22; correspondence with Possenti and others in *The Times* 31 January, 11, 17, 21 February 1933.

p. 24   Details on printings and information on sales for *Down and Out* and other Orwell books are from the invaluable I. R. Willison, "George Orwell: Some Materials for a Bibliography," School of Librarianship, London University, 1953. Copies available in the British Library and the Stanford University Library.

p. 30   *New York Times Book Review* 6 August 1933, p. 4.

p. 40   Evelyn's and Frays: correspondence with John Bennett and C. A. Pratt, Chief Education Office, London Borough of Hillingdon; and interviews, Mr. and Mrs. H. S. K. Stapley and Graham Bennett.

p. 46 Rayner Heppenstall, *Four Absentees* (London, 1960), p. 58; T. R. Fyvel, "A Case for George Orwell," *Twentieth Century* September 1956.

p. 47 Avril Dunn, "My Brother, George Orwell," *Twentieth Century* March 1961, p. 257.

p. 53 American reviews of *Burmese Days*: *Herald Tribune Books* 28 October 1934, p. 3; *New York Times Book Review* 28 October 1934, p. 7; *Boston Evening Transcript* 1 December 1934, p. 3.

p. 86 Reviews of *A Clergyman's Daughter*: Compton Mackenzie, *Daily Mail* 21 March 1935, p. 4; Bonamy Dobrée, *Morning Post* 12 March 1935, p. 14; V. S. Pritchett, *Spectator* 22 March 1935, p. 504; Peter Quennell, *New Statesman and Nation* 23 March 1935, pp. 421–2; L. P. Hartley, *Sketch* 27 March 1935, p. xviii.

p. 89 Vincent McHugh, *Herald Tribune Books* 16 August 1936, p. 8.

p. 98 Heppenstall, p. 51.

p. 105 Frederick L. Gwynn, *Sturge Moore and the Life of the Arts* (London, 1952), p. 66.

p. 109 See Elizaveta Fen, "George Orwell's First Wife," *Twentieth Century* August 1960, pp. 115–26. Also interview.

p. 125 Isaac Rosenfeld, *Commentary* July 1955.

p. 128 Reviews of *Burmese Days*: *The Times Literary Supplement* 19 July 1935, p. 462; Sean O'Faolain, *Spectator* 28 June 1935, p. 1118; Compton Mackenzie, *Daily Mail*; Cyril Connolly, *New Statesman and Nation* 6 July 1935, p. 18.

p. 174 Reviews of *Keep the Aspidistra Flying*: Douglas West, *Daily Mail*; *The Times Literary Supplement* 3 May 1936, p. 376; Richard Church, *John O'London's Weekly* 2 May 1936, p. 164.

p. 188 Quoted in John Lehmann, *A Nest of Tigers* (Boston, 1968), p. 188.

p. 204 Fen, p. 117.

p. 206 Anthony Powell, *Infants of the Spring* (London, 1976), p. 136.

p. 213	We are particularly grateful to Mary Deiner, Richard Middletown Murry, Rayner Heppenstall, and Lawrence Bradshaw for talking to us about the Centre and other aspects of Orwell.
p. 236	Robert E. Dowse, *Left in the Centre* (London, 1966), p. 200.
p. 239	*Twentieth Century* September 1956, p. 256.
p. 241	Interview. See also John McNair, *James Maxton* (London, 1955), pp. 255–6.
p. 246	Bob Edwards, Introduction to *Homage to Catalonia* (London, 1970), pp. 7–11, for all quotations from Edwards. Also interview with him.
p. 246	Sybil Wingate to authors, 13 November 1967.
p. 250	*Daily Worker* 14 September 1937, p. 2.
p. 253	Peter Blackstein to authors, 8 January 1968.
p. 255	Franz Borkenau, *The Spanish Cockpit* (Ann Arbor, 1963), p. 183 (first edition, 1937).
p. 256	Dan MacArthur, *We Carry On: Our Tribute to Bob Smillie* (London, n.d.), p. 4.
p. 258	Raymond Carr, *Spain 1808–1939* (Oxford, 1966), p. 657.
p. 263	Hugh Thomas, *The Spanish Civil War*, 3rd ed., rev. and enl. (Harmondsworth, 1977), p. 653.
p. 271	Raymond Carr, *The Spanish Tragedy* (London, 1977), p. 174.
p. 274	Thomas, p. 646.
p. 275	British Library 49, 384 Georges Kopp to Laurence O'Shaughnessy, 10 June 1937, f. 5. Copy of lost 31 May–1 June letter.
p. 280	British Library 49, 384 Eileen Blair to Laurence O'Shaughnessy, 20 June 1937, ff. 14–15.
p. 284	V. S. Pritchett, *New York Review of Books* 15 December 1966, p. 6.
p. 284	8 June 1937, *Collected* I, p. 269.
p. 284	"Why I Write" (1946), *Collected* I, p. 5.

INDEX

Adam, (Aunt) Nellie, 8, 11, 49
Adelphi Centre summer school, 158, 213–14, 217
Adelphi magazine, 5, 8, 71–3, 75, 100, 103, 124, 138, 154, 158, 164, 166; Blair/Orwell contributions to, 5, 8, 17, 49, 68, 122, 124, 143–5, 218; reviews of Orwell books in, 18–19, 131–2
Anarchists, Orwell's sympathy with, 236; *see also* CNT
Anarcho-Syndicalists (CNT), *see* CNT
Animal Farm, 8 n., 14, 19, 60, 63, 225, 226, 235, 274; American publication of, 89; Ukrainian edition of, 153, 216–17
Anzaña (president of Spanish Republic), 263
Auden, W. H., 19, 181, 202, 221
"Auden & Co.," 181, 182

Balzac, Honoré de, 230
Barcelona: Eileen Orwell in, 247–8, 260–1; George Orwell in, 238–43, 258–61; May 1937 troubles in, 263–75
Batalla, La, newspaper, 270
Bates, H. E., 18
Bates, Ralph, 202
Beadon, Roger, 44, 50; *see also* Indian Imperial Police
Bedales School, 95
Belloc, Hilaire, 19
Bennet-Coles (Doctor), 47, 49
Bennett, John, and family, 40, 42, 45–7; *see also* Frays College
Berg Collection, New York, 247
Bertorelli's restaurant, 75
Best Poems of 1934, The, 138
Blair, Avril, 9, 11, 41, 47, 49, 71, 178
Blair, Eileen O'Shaughnessy, 37, 38, 79, 99–100, 107–11, 114–15, 117–18, 171–2, 176–80; death of, 110, 204; descriptions of, 117, 134, 140, 205, 206; educational background of, 113, 116–18, 127, 177; influence of, on husband, 110, 184; social status of family of, 112–13; in Spain, 247–9, 253,

Blair, Eileen O'Shaughnessy
  (*continued*)
  256, 260, 261, 265, 268, 276,
  277, 280–3; see also marriage, Orwell's
Blair, Eric: birthplace and
  deathplace, 92; illness, 47–8,
  50; lifestyle of, 43–4, 78, 79,
  94–8, 138, 172–4, 203–8;
  personality of, 100–2, 125–6,
  141–2, 198; physical appearance of, 45–6, 284; published works under name of,
  4, 8, 9, 17; schooling of, 4;
  as teacher, 25–6, 42–4; will
  of, 110; wounding of, in
  Spain, 275–7; writing habits
  of, 26, 32–3; see also Orwell,
  George, as pseudonym
Blair, Marjorie, 46; see also
  Dakin, Humphrey and Marjorie
Blair, (Lady) Mary, 198
Blairs, the, parents of Eric, 7–8,
  11–12, 41, 47–9, 67, 68, 71,
  106, 178, 208
Booklover's Corner bookshop,
  73–6, 78, 93, 94, 99, 100,
  102, 118–20, 130, 136, 142,
  154
"Bookshop Memories," 75, 119
Borkenau, Frank, 254
Boston Evening Transcript, 54
Bowen, Elizabeth, 18
Brailsford, H. N., 237, 240
British Weekly, 86
Brockway, Fenner, 240
Brown, William, 166

Burmese Days, 4–5, 13, 24–6,
  32–7, 41–3, 48, 50, 51, 60,
  80, 88, 103, 142, 202; American publication of, 50–4, 59;
  British publication of, 55–8,
  118, 127; Elizabeth Lackersteen in, 35, 36, 62, 76; Flory
  in, 35, 36, 51, 52, 60, 128;
  "libelous" material in, 50–8
  passim, 149, 150; Ma Hla
  May in, 76; reviews of, 53–4,
  128–32; sales of, 127–8, 132;
  setting of, 35; U Po Kyin in,
  76; Veraswami in, 36, 53, 58;
  Verrall in, 35
Burt, Cyril, 117
Butler, Samuel, 137

Cadbury, (Dame) Elizabeth,
  115
Caliban Shrieks (Hilton),
  144
Canterbury Tales, Orwell work
  on contemporary version of,
  102
Cape, Jonathan, publisher, 8,
  55, 122
Carr, Raymond, 258, 271
Carzorla, José, 259
Chamson, André, 202
Chapman, Guy, 17
Chatto & Windus, publisher, 49
Christy & Moore, 27; see also
  Moore, Leonard
Church, Richard, 175
Civil War, Spanish, see Spanish
  Civil War

class attitudes, Orwell's, 77,
111–12, 195–9, 201, 238
Clergyman's Daughter, A, 5,
25, 48, 53, 60, 80, 83–6, 97,
102, 103, 128, 132, 143, 230;
American publication of, 88–
9; British publication of, 55,
81–5, 118; Dorothy Hare in,
60–7, 76, 84, 86, 89–90, 128;
reviews of, 86–91, 131; setting of, 62; themes and plot
of, 62–6; Warburton in, 63,
64, 66
CNT (Anarcho-Syndicalist
Party), 239, 242, 254–60
passim, 262–4, 266, 268,
270–3, 283
Cohen, John, 117
Coleridge, Samuel, 214
*Collected Essays, Journalism
and Letters, The*, 38 *n.*, 124
n., 156, 217
College Days, 209, 211
Collings, Dennis, 10, 14, 38, 41,
68
Collings, Eleanor, *see* Jaques,
Eleanor
Collins, Norman, 56–8, 149,
154
colonialist themes and influences
in Orwell fiction, 34, 36, 37,
53–6, 128, 131–2, 157; see
also *Burmese Days*
Coming Up for Air, 60
Commentary magazine, 125
Common, Jack, 16, 150, 165,
195, 202, 203, 218, 246–7

Communism and Communists:
in Great Britain, 20, 160–1,
166, 226–7, 235–7; in Spanish Civil War, 239, 242, 250,
254–5, 257–60; *see also*
Spanish Civil War: Leftist
factionalism in
Companys (president of Spanish Generalidad), 263
Connolly, Cyril, 7, 23, 101, 129–
31, 173, 174, 181, 182, 204,
209, 285
Conrad, Joseph, 36, 100
Cooper, Lettice, 178
Copely, John, 105
copyrights, English and American, 29; for *Burmese Days*,
53
Cornford, John, 216
Cortada, Roldán, 259
Cottman, Stafford, 246, 251,
256
Coward, Noel, 61
Craig, Gordon, Jr., *see* Garrick,
Edward
Cruse, Amy, 144–5

Daily Mail, 17, 86, 128, 175
Daily Worker, 191, 227, 250
Dakin, Humphrey and Marjorie,
158, 167–8
Davies, W. H., 18–19
Deiner, John and Mary, 158,
163, 164
Dobrée, Bonamy, 86
Donohue, Patricia, 204–5, 207

Donovan, Paddy, 256
Down and Out in Paris and London, 3-4, 7-10, 13-22, 33, 34, 51, 56, 59, 60, 65, 80, 84, 88, 237; American edition of, 28-31; reviews of, 15-21, 29-30, 86; sales of, 24, 31

Edwards, Bob, 207, 245-6, 249, 251-2
Election Times, 209
Eliot, T. S., 8, 54, 144
Engels, Friedrich, 188
Etonian connections, Orwell's, 4, 10, 14, 23, 29, 34, 35, 57, 58, 72, 91, 102, 112, 129, 181, 182, 209, 211, 235
Evelyn's School, 13, 23, 25, 31, 39, 40, 66, 82
Evening News, 115
Evening Standard, 17

Faber & Faber, publisher, 8, 122
Facts of English Fiction, The, 56
Fairfield, Cicily (Rebecca West), 5
Farrell, James T., 29
Farrimond, John, 163, 188, 190
Fascist intervention in Spanish Civil War, 252
Fen, Elizaveta, 107-11, 115, 117, 118, 120, 197, 204-6, 208

Fierz, Adrian, 106, 133
Fierz, Fay, 134
Fierz, Francis and Mabel, 10-12, 25, 27, 28, 32, 41, 51, 73-5, 78, 84, 93-4, 103, 104, 106, 122, 133-7, 208
Forster, E. M., 33, 36
Fortnightly, 75, 119, 207
Fox, Ralph, 202
Frankfort, Frank, 250, 256
Frays College, 40-3, 47, 82; *see also* Bennett, John
Fyvel, T. R., 46, 239

Garnett, David, 17, 18
Garrett, George, 163-5, 202
Garrick, Edward (Gordon Craig, Jr.), 105
Gawsworth, John, 105
Gibson, William, 105
Gide, André, 156
Gille, Paul, 49
Gimson, Ernest, 97, 138
Gimson, Janet, 94-8, 107
Gissing, George, 77, 89-90
Gollancz, Victor, Ltd., publisher, 4, 9, 15, 99, 150-2, 225-6; break of, with Orwell, 224-5; commission of *Road to Wigan Pier* by, 99, 150-3, 186; foreword of, to *Road to Wigan Pier*, 227-30; handling of *Burmese Days* by, 50, 55-58, 81, 85; political orientation of, 150-1, 226-7, 230-1; publication of *A Clergyman's*

INDEX   297

Gollancz, Victor, Ltd., publisher (*continued*)
Daughter by, 81–5, 88-9; publication of *Down and Out in Paris and London* by, 4, 9, 15, 24; publication of *Keep the Aspidistra Flying* by, 75, 122, 149, 174–5; publication of *Road to Wigan Pier* by, 223, 225–7
Gorer, Geoffrey, 174, 176, 178, 188, 204
Gorman, Herbert, 30
Grady, Paddy, 159, 162
Gwynn, Frederick L., 105

Hamilton, George Rostrever, 105
Hamilton, Hamish, 52
Hampstead residences, 72–3, 92; Parliament Hill Road, 92–98, 101, 104, 106, 108, 120, 121, 132, 135, 138; Warwick Mansions, 73–5, 81, 92–4, 97
"Hanging, A," 184
Hannington, Wal, 160
Harcourt, (Sir) William, 45
Harpers', publisher, 28, 51–4
Harper's Bazaar magazine, 87, 150
Harris, Muriel, 16
Hartley, L. P., 87
Hassall, Christopher, 105
Hawthorns, The (rooming house), 25, 28, 32, 43
Heinemann's, publisher, 50, 51
Hemingway, Ernest, 191, 241

Henschel, (Sir) George, 93
Henty, G. A., 256
Heppenstall, Rayner, 46, 71, 75, 98, 104, 121, 132, 134–42, 152, 208, 215–16, 249
Herald Tribune Books, 29, 53, 89–91
Hillingdon Hospital, 40
Hilton, Jack, 144
Hilton, James, 37
Hitler, Adolf, 32, 121
Hodges, Sheila, 223
Hodgson, Ralph, 19
Hogarth Press, 183
Holdaway, N. A., 218
Holden, Inez, 207
Homage to Catalonia, 5, 225, 235, 240, 256; Edwards introduction to, 249–50; Spanish journal-letters as draft of, 248–9
Hound and Horn, 105
Hubbard, Margaret Carson, 53, 54
Hughes, Thomas, 145
Huxley, Aldous, 29, 72, 106
Hynes, Samuel, 5

Indian Imperial Police, 7, 53, 114, 212; *see also* Beadon, Roger
International Brigade, 236, 245, 250, 253, 274
International Labour Party (ILP), 236, 237, 240–3, 245, 247, 252, 260–1, 281

International Militia, *see* POUM
Isherwood, Christopher, 30,
    181, 191 *n.*

James, Henry, 111
Jaques, Eleanor, 10, 14, 26, 37–38, 41
John o' London's Weekly, 175
Jonathan Cape, publisher, 8, 55, 122
Joyce, James, 11, 30, 51, 61, 84, 87

Kay (Blair woman friend), 77–79, 99–102, 114, 115
Keep the Aspidistra Flying, 14, 60, 74, 83, 118–21, 126, 143, 145, 154, 161, 165, 230–1;
    Comstock in, 75, 78–9, 94, 103, 119, 122–5, 128, 130, 139, 143, 157, 164, 165;
    Creevey's School in, 81–2;
    Dorothy in, 81, 82; libel worries about, 149, 150; publication of, 122, 174–6; Ravelston in, 123, reviews of, 174–5;
    Rosemary in, 76–8, 102, 119, 125; themes and plotting of, 122–4; Wisbeach in, 95
Kennan, Joe, 159, 162, 167
Kentish Town residence, 136–40, 154
Kimche, Jon, 73, 74–5
King, Richard, 18

King-Farlow, Denys, 131 *n.*, 178, 204, 209–12
Kingsley, Charles, 145
Kipling, Rudyard, 154
Kopp, Georges, 245–6, 250, 256, 268–72, 275–7, 281–3

Labour Party, 236–7
Labour's Northern Voice, 158
Lanti, R., 49
Largo Caballero, 257, 259
Laski, Harold, 152, 224, 226, 227, 230–1
Lawrence, D. H., 33, 61, 106, 123, 214–15
Leavis, Q. D., 181
Left Book Club, 150, 152, 213, 223–32
Left News, 227, 230–1
Lehmann, John, 181–4, 202
Lewis, C. Day, 19–21, 181
Lewis, Owen, 105
libelous material in Orwell fiction, 50–3, 55–8, 81, 149, 150
literary Left, members of, 19–20
Low, Matt, *see* Garrett, George
Lynd, Sylvia, 87

Mackenzie, Compton, 17, 80–1, 86, 128
MacNeice, Louis, 181
Mairet, Philip, 144, 153
Malraux, André, 241

Manchester Guardian, 16
Mandarinism in literature, 30
Mansfield, Katherine, 61
marriage, Orwell's, 107, 176–80, 203–4
Marsh, Fred T., 30, 54
Marxism: of English Left, 19–20, 214, 237; in factionalism of Spanish Civil War, 239, 254
Maugham, Somerset, 30, 33, 36
Maxton, James, 240
McCarthy, Mary, 30
McHugh, Vincent, 89–91
McNair, John, 237, 240–1, 243, 247–8, 253, 255, 267, 281–4
Meade, Frank, 158
Melling, Carlton, 163
Mew, Charlotte, 19
Miller, Henry, 30, 35, 56, 137, 145, 237–8
Milton, Harry, 251–2, 255, 284
miners, Orwell report on, *see Road to Wigan Pier, The*
Mitford, Nancy, 196
money as theme in Orwell fiction, 122–4, 143; *see also* poverty as theme in Orwell fiction
Moore, Leonard, 3, 8, 10, 23–4, 26, 27, 41, 43, 46, 48, 51, 59, 80–1, 83, 149, 223, 225
Moore, Risette, 104
Moore, T. Sturge, and family, 75, 101, 104–5
Morning Post, 16, 86
Morrell, (Lady) Ottoline, 106

Morris, William, 79
Moult, Thomas, 138
Muir, Edwin, 101
Muir, Willa, 101
Murry, John Middleton, 134, 142, 144, 158, 214–15, 217–18
Murry, Richard Middleton, 134

National Unemployed Workers Movement (NUWM), 159–61, 165, 189
New Clarion, 18
New English Weekly, 8, 135, 143–5, 153, 154, 174, 207
New Leader, 236–7, 250, 256
New Republic, 29
News Chronicle, 56
New Statesman and Nation, 8, 9, 18, 87, 128–9, 197, 225, 252
New Writing, 182–4, 201–2
New York Times Book Review, 30, 53, 54
Niebuhr, Reinhold, 214
Nin, Andrés, 254–5
1984, 121, 184, 235, 274

Obermeyer, Rosalind Henschel, 93–7, 107–10, 118, 132–5
O'Casey, Sean, 85 *n*.
O'Faolain, Sean, 128
Orage, A. R., 144

Orwell, George, as pseudonym, 3–6, 8–12, 23, 72, 104, 198–199, 285; *see also* Blair, Eric
Osborne, E. B., 16–17
O'Shaughnessy, Eileen Maude, *see* Blair, Eileen O'Shaughnessy
O'Shaughnessy, Gwen, 116, 120, 178, 246
O'Shaughnessy, Laurence, Jr., 113–16, 120–1, 178, 206, 222–3, 248, 275, 277, 280
O'Shaughnessy, Laurence, Sr., Mr. and Mrs., 116, 178

fication), 239, 242–3, 245, 247, 250–5, 260–2, 265–75, 277–9, 281–2, 284
Pound, Ezra, 144
poverty as theme in Orwell fiction, 16–17, 20–1, 66, 90–1, 123; see also *Road to Wigan Pier*
Powell, Anthony, 56, 206, 207
Powell, (Lady) Violet, 207
Priestley, J. B., 17, 102
Pritchett, V. S., 86, 202, 284
Proust, Marcel, 111
PSUC (Spanish Socialist Party), 239, 242, 254–5, 260, 262–3, 268, 273

Pacifist movement in England, 217, 218
Pantisocracy, 214
Parliament Hill Road residence, 92–8, 101, 104, 106, 108, 120, 121, 132, 135, 138
PEN organization of writers, 100–1
Pitter, Ruth, 16, 78, 103, 105
Plowman, Max, 73, 218
poetry, Orwell's, 55, 122, 124 *n.*, 138
political views, Orwell's, 20–1, 106, 143–5, 181–2, 193; *see also* Socialist influences on Orwell
Pollitt, Harry, 191, 227, 235–6, 250, 252
Possenti, Humbert, 21–2, 27
POUM (Party of Marxist Uni-

Quennell, Peter, 87

Read, Herbert, 61
Rees, Richard, 10, 71, 73, 75, 80, 100, 103, 107, 108, 121, 124, 137, 144, 145, 149, 163, 164, 166, 193, 194, 215–17, 235
religion, Orwell's attitude toward, 26, 72, 75, 86, 87, 100, 101
Rilke, Rainer Maria, 110
Road to Wigan Pier, The, 34, 83, 99, 105, 139, 153, 180, 196, 221; Brookers' house in, 187–90; gathering of material for, 151–68; Gollancz foreword to, 227–30; invocation

Road to Wigan Pier, The (continued)
of Socialism in, 194–201; publication of, 223, 225–7; reviews of, 230; writing of, 185–92, 203, 218–19
Robinson, Captain, 36
Rodriguez Salas, 264
Rosenfeld, Isaac, 125

"St. Andrew's Day, 1935," 122, 124
St. Cyprian's School, 4, 14, 77, 82, 101, 129, 173, 181, 199; relation of, to Orwell's fiction, 66, 91, 125
Salkeld, Brenda, 10, 16, 26, 33, 38, 41, 63, 68, 72, 86, 92, 97
Sally (Blair woman friend), 77–79, 99, 102, 114
Saxton, Eugene, 5
Sayers, Michael, 98, 104, 121, 131–2, 135–8, 142
schools, in Orwell fiction, 81–2
Scots, Orwell's aversion to, 101
Searle family, 166
Secker & Warburg, publisher, 14, 225
Seyuan Shu, 105
Shahani, Ranjee, 105
"Shooting an Elephant," 83, 157, 180, 183–6, 189, 190, 202
shooting stick incident, 139–41, 216
Silone, Ignazio, 202
Sitwell, Edith, 188, 191

Sketch, 87
Smillie, Bob, 246, 256
Socialist influences on Orwell, 34, 45, 79, 99, 121, 123–4, 143–5, 151, 153, 181–2, 187, 193–201, 215–16, 218–20, 229–30, 239, 240, 285
Solidaridad Obrera, 259, 270
Soviet intervention in Spanish Civil War, 240, 252, 254, 258, 278
Spanish Civil War, 213, 216–17, 232; Aragon front, 243, 245, 248, 254, 256–7; Catalan government in, 254, 255, 263, 271; Fascist intervention in, 252; Huesca front, 275; Leftist factionalism in, 239, 242, 250, 254–5, 257–75; Orwell associates in, 245–6; Orwell journal-letters on, 248–9, 281; as "political education" for Orwell, 250–1, 261–3, 273–5, 285; Soviet intervention in, 240, 252, 254, 258, 278
Spectator, 128
Spender, Stephen, 19, 181, 182, 235
Stapleys, the, 44–6
Stores, The, *see* Wallington residence
Strachey, John, 152, 214, 224, 226–7, 235
Strachey, Lytton, 106, 144
Sunday Express, 24
Sunday Times, 86
Synge, J. M., 19

Tatler, 18
Thaelmann, Ernst, 161
Thomas, Dylan, 71, 75, 104
Thomas, Hugh, 219, 263, 265, 274
Thomson, (Sir) St. Clair, 22
Time and Tide, 207
Times Literary Supplement, 18, 21, 27, 87, 128, 174
Trilling, Lionel, 119

UGT (Socialist party union), 263
Upward, Edward, 181
Uxbridge High School, *see* Frays College

vegetarians, Orwell's dislike of, 199

Wallington residence (The Stores), 169–73, 198, 204–12, 247
Walpole, Hugh, 24, 102
Warburg, Frederic, 225
Warner, Rex, 181, 202

Warwick Mansions, 73–5, 81, 92–4, 97
Wells, H. G., 173, 199
Well Walk "aesthetical salon," 101, 104–6
West, Douglas, 175
West, Rebecca, 5
Westrope, Francis G., 73, 92–3, 120
Whittome, Maurice, 129
Wigan, Orwell's stay in, 157–65
Wilkes, Mr. and Mrs. Vaughan, 77, 101, 125, 126, 224
Williams, Bob, 245
Wilson, Mona, 105
Wingate, Sybil, 246
Winters, Yvor, 105
women, Orwell's relations with, 37–8, 76–80, 98–9, 120, 127; literary depictions of, 37–8, 60–2, 76–7
Woolf, Virginia and Leonard, 106, 133, 182

Yeats, William Butler, 105, 108
Young, G. M., 37

Zola, Émile, 230